D|03

Europe at Home

EUROPE AT HOME
FAMILY AND MATERIAL CULTURE
1500–1800

RAFFAELLA SARTI

Translated by Allan Cameron

Yale University Press
New Haven and London

Designed by Adam Freudenheim
Set by SNP Best-set Typesetter Ltd., Hong Kong
Printed in Italy
Library of Congress Cataloging-in-Publication Data

Sarti, Raffaella, 1963
    [Vita di casa. English]
    Europe at home : family and material culture, 1500–1800 / by Raffaella Sarti; translated by Allan Cameron.
        p. cm.
Translation of: Vita di casa.
Includes bibliographical references.
    ISBN 0-300-08542-7 (hardback : alk. paper)
    1. Europe—Social life and customs.   I. Title.
    GT129 .S2713 2002
    306'.094—dc21

                    2002002604

A catalogue record for this book is availabe from the British Library
10 9 8 7 6 5 4 3 2 1

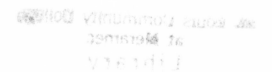

To the memory of my grandmother Sandrina,
who as a child ate barley soup every day,
and never tired of making clothes for the family.

To my mother, who for years shared her bed with her sister
and taught in mountain villages
where soup was eaten without plates
but rather with a ladle
from a pot in the middle of the table.

To my father, born on a farm from which not less than twenty
boys left for school every morning and at which
every now and then a tailor would stay just
long enough to make a new suit or dress for everyone.

Contents

Contents

Contents

Preface to the First English Edition

A crowded room: on the right, you can make out a fireplace around which three women are busy working. Next to them and lying on a floor carelessly covered with eggshells, there are various domestic objects, including a plate with a bread roll. On the left, you can see a bed in which a woman is lying; she is undoubtedly the woman who has just given birth, and is surrounded by more women, one of whom is spoon-feeding her. Close by, there is an empty cradle. The baby is more or less in the centre of the painting, being held in a man's arms. He is wrapped in a small sheet with lace decoration and a very bright red blanket. The man, no longer young, is standing close to a table around which there are other people, including a girl who is moving a beautiful padded chair, possibly for the man with the baby to sit on. They would appear to be father and child. One of those present is making the sign of the cuckold behind the supposed father's back, suggesting that the baby is not actually his. In any case they are celebrating the birth of the baby, and the picture represents a crucial moment in family reproduction. The party also involves consumption and expense: the man with the baby – clearly the head of the family – is putting his hand in the purse that hangs from his belt, next to large keys, as though about to give money to one of the women. The choice of this cover picture – *Celebrating the birth* by Jan Steen – proclaims all the main themes of this book: the organization of living space, furnishings, diet, clothing, consumption, family reproduction, kinship relationships and relationships within the home.

It was not however the cover of the original Italian edition of 1999. The painting by Steen was chosen for a new forthcoming Italian edition and has been adopted for the English version. It is not however only the cover that differentiates this edition from previous ones. The content has also changed.

This restless book underwent small changes for the second Italian edition (2000), while it was markedly updated for the Portuguese one (2001). On that occasion, I inserted passages to make it easier to understand that certain houses and possessions, often passed down over many generations, came to embody family values. Moreover, I attempted to clarify the role of clothes, particularly in defining social identities. I have made further additions to the present edition to make the book more fully European, to give a better account of the specificity of certain groups such as Jews, and to illustrate more clearly the changes that occurred over the three centuries that it covers. The final chapter, in particular, is now considerably enlarged, in part thanks to some recent publications.

As far as is possible, I have updated the bibliography for this new edition. References are generally to Italian editions. Replacing them with references to the corresponding English editions was a task that neither I nor the translator could hope to accomplish. I hope, however, that the richness of the bibliography will nevertheless make it useful to scholars and general readers alike. I would like to make clear that the book does not take into account all the new and old research in the field. No single academic could master such a great mass of scholarship. When I look at the number of books and articles that clutter my bookshelves, many still unread (and some destined to remain so) and when I see the lists of new works that are published every day, my feelings are complex. The guilt I feel about the many authors I have not taken into account is mixed with a sense of uneasy dissatisfaction and a disagreeable sense of impotence. Feelings of this kind accompany the writing of all my works, and in this case they are all the stronger because the book represents a general overview.

The book's aim is primarily to make the themes that today are challenging historical research accessible to a public beyond professional specialists and especially to students. At the same time, it aspires to be a useful instrument for professional scholars, because of its extensive bibliography and the attempt to interconnect research fields that are often kept separate, although the explicit references to historiographical debate are limited and mainly confined to the notes. In fact, the book reconstructs the material life of European families from the end of the fifteenth century to the beginning of the nineteenth by interweaving the results of recent research into the history of the family, women, consumption, architecture, furnishings, diet and clothing.

Of course, I do not claim to have discussed every possible aspect of the material lives of families. I am well aware that I have treated very briefly subjects that are far from secondary (at least to me), and I have done this because of my own particular expertise, interests and choices, as well as the clear impossibility of discussing everything.

I hope, however, that I have thrown some light on the subject I chose to examine, and that I have helped to outline the wide range of functions attributed to objects and possessions in family life in an era in which material conditions differed so greatly from today (at least in the West). While attempting to avoid both the triumphant exaltation of consumerism and its categorical denunciation (although I would be inclined to the latter), I have tried to show how different ways of being were translated into different ways of having and different ways of having influenced in turn different ways of being.

Bologna-Urbino, May 2002

Introduction

In the absence of a time machine, it is difficult to imagine houses as they were in the past. We cannot enter their doors unseen, peer inside and wander around their interiors. We cannot examine their furnishings, look into their cooking pots and larders, and observe what their occupants are doing. Had we such a contraption, we would find, depending on the social context, smoky rooms with low ceilings crowded with both people and animals, or perhaps labyrinthine buildings with plush and spacious interiors, exquisite furniture and ornaments, and hordes of servants in elaborate liveries. To understand the material life of families in the past, we therefore need to look at both the objects that have survived across time (houses, furniture, etc.) and the information that can be gleaned from written and pictorial sources. Although these are quite extensive, we often have to content ourselves with objects worn by the passing years, buildings that have been renovated over various centuries, partial and indirect sources and fragmentary accounts.

It takes imagination to comprehend how houses and things would have appeared to people at the time. Inevitably, the picture we recreate will be partly obscured by shadows, and the images will often be little more than outlines. In other words, they will be less vivid than those produced by direct observation (which also has its limitations).

Occasionally, and quite unexpectedly, the tiniest and quite banal daily activities became enmeshed in the sources and trapped there for centuries even though they were generally soon forgotten by those who carried them out. It is difficult to know what Sabbatina Masini, a female farm servant from the countryside around Bologna, would have thought of the fact that in 1991 someone would print a book stating that on the night of 16 June 1626 she slept in her mother's house 'in the very same bed' (or so she claimed).[1] Very many details of this kind lie hidden in documents that will provide material for future research. Others have already been the object of careful analysis by historians, so we now possess innumerable studies whose results can be put together as in a jigsaw puzzle, and allow us to identify local realities and social groups, distinguish between urban and rural settings, draw comparisons and trace the outline of long-term transformations.

1

But we should not get carried away with optimism. Much information has been lost, and still more awaits the arrival of a researcher to interrupt its slumber on some dusty shelf. On occasions the results of these studies are contradictory. On the subject of this book, you could write not one but a thousand volumes. Of all the things that could be discussed, therefore, much has to be left unsaid or mentioned only in passing. Although extensive and up-to-date, the bibliography only contains some of the works relating to the field. Our journey into the past is an attempt to cover different themes that are rarely examined together – such as the history of the family, women, gender identity, the home, consumption, architecture, furnishings and clothing – and to do so in an intentionally accessible manner in a relatively short book. It cannot, therefore, provide exhaustive coverage of the various problems in each of the different fields of study or of the results achieved. The fact that this work cuts across various fields of study and attempts to make them interact with each other is, I believe, one of its more interesting features.

Having established the book's purpose and its areas of study, there remains the question of how the various arguments were selected and how I chose to approach them. In the following pages, descriptions of 'banal objects'[2] and commonplace events in the lives of women, men, adults, children, youths, the elderly, the married, unmarried, and separated, widows and widowers, rich and poor, peasants and townsfolk, the middle class and the aristocracy, Protestants and Catholics, and Muslims and Jews, are interwoven with data and information on the significance and characteristics of a particular object, type of food or custom, and its diffusion amongst different time periods, geographical areas and social groups. For instance, when were potatoes first eaten in Europe, in what areas, and how and when did their cultivation spread? Initially, were they eaten by rich or poor people? Did people find them an interesting curiosity or were they regarded with suspicion? Did placing them on the table mean that you were one of the privileged, or some unfortunate who had been forced by hunger into accepting makeshift solutions?

The fragments of individual 'histories' are not merely given as examples and their role is not restricted to making the arguments more lively and vivid. They are the starting point for posing questions on the spread of specific customs and lifestyles. Their purpose is to penetrate the experience of men and women of the past and to demonstrate the extremely complex range of situations that can hide behind generalizations. As far as possible, these episodes will be narrated through the words of those involved, whose words from beyond the grave have been captured, albeit in a somewhat stilted form, in the records of interrogations, letters, diaries and wills, as well as some early printed texts. I have attempted to present an overview of what has so far emerged from historical research and to reflect on their results in such a manner that both presentation and reflection can be introduced, enlivened and occasionally even defined by the narration of episodes taken from published texts and archival sources.[3]

The relationship with the past is therefore quite direct on some pages, while on others it has been more reworked. The book resembles a meal in which sophisticated main dishes alternate with plain and only slightly dressed salads. What has survived from past centuries has been cooked in various ways in order that we may be better able to savour its taste, and to produce the aroma of what has been lost forever. The information provided derives in some cases directly from observation of houses and objects constructed in past centuries and surviving into ours; in other cases it has been drawn from documents in which one of our ancestors described or depicted for various reasons his own property and life, or those of his contemporaries; in other cases it is the product of data that historians have processed after examining the mountains of papers collecting dust in various archives, or after recording hundreds of buildings or objects; and in still other cases it arises from putting together and comparing the results of other history books. The illustrations provide the reader with some stimulating, suggestive and colourful material to back up the text, and apart from the photographs of houses and antiques, some paintings and prints provide the opportunity to assess the themes under discussion as they were described and interpreted visually.

Regarding the iconography and continuing the metaphors, this book, as it strives to bring together the great and the small, the close-up and the distant panorama, could be seen as a picture in which the painter has here and there used his finest brush to depict the tiniest details and then sketched the larger views with heavier brushstrokes, switching the scale so that the information and knowledge channelled into the work does not appear to have been reduced to the same level and dimensions, but rather appears varied and in perspective.[4]

If the book is a painting, then what does it depict? And what does the frame exclude? The title provides the answer: *Europe at Home: Family and Material Culture 1500–1800*. Its spatial and chronological boundaries are those of Europe in the early modern era. As we know, the concept of Europe has shifted over the centuries: in the eighteenth century, for example, there was an argument over whether or not Russia should be included within the family of European nations.[5] We will not be considering such questions, as we will not be analysing what Europe was for the men and women who lived between the end of the fifteenth century and the beginning of the nineteenth. As, of course, any border is ultimately there because it was agreed and accepted,[6] it is quite justifiable to draw an imaginary line on the map of the world to enclose our field of study, and adopt the territory of modern Europe, which extends from North Cape, Norway to the island of Lampedusa, Italy, and from the Urals to Portugal.

Of course, we will occasionally make comparisons with the customs of populations living beyond these frontiers, particularly those of European emigrants to America. But these will be purely marginal considerations, while the main purpose of this book will be to establish the differences between the lifestyles of people living in different regions and different social groups within Europe's current borders. Those who are interested in clarifying whether or not such lifestyles shared particular features that distinguished them from other continents are referred to other studies.[7]

As far as the chronological framework is concerned, traditional history textbooks claim that the early modern era commenced with the 'discovery' of America by Europeans in 1492 and ended with the French Revolution and the Napoleonic period (1789–1815). Putting markers down in the continuous flow of time is a somewhat arbitrary task, and consequently periodization is often a controversial subject amongst historians, and depends on the area of historical study.[8] The question therefore arises of whether, in a book on the material life of families, there is any sense in adopting a time framework that goes more or less from the end of the fifteenth century to the early nineteenth century. More specifically, the question is whether the beginning and the end of the period under examination really represent cut-off points in the history of the family, living conditions, food and clothing. The answer is not at all simple. The discovery of America, for example, led to the introduction of a great number of new products into Europe – from maize to potatoes – which were destined to transform radically the diet of a large part of the population. But the changes did not occur immediately: rather, as we shall see, they often occurred very slowly.[9] What then should be done? We could either base the periodization on the arrival of new products or on their introduction into general use. In the latter case, we would have the problem of choosing the date, as penetration of new customs was not always rapid, and not all regions were affected by these innovations at the same time.

Similar problems arise on other fronts. When we examine the spread of new objects it is not always possible to identify the precise turning point. Although, some years ago, a few historians were arguing that the first 'consumer revolution' occurred in late-eighteenth-century England,[10] today most scholars are convinced that consumption and the availability of consumer goods grew in a gradual, albeit uneven, manner over a long period.[11] In spite of the wealth of academic studies that have been produced in the last few years, the history of consumption is still in its early stages. We will undoubtedly know more in a few years and then we might be able to establish a more meaningful periodization. Even if it were possible to establish precise turning points, it is unlikely that those that appear to be emerging in the history of clothing and furniture took place at exactly the same time as those in the fields of food, architecture and the laws and customs that govern access to enjoyment of particular consumers goods. In this book, therefore, the periodization has been chosen out of the need to define the area of investigation, and it does not reflect the development of all the phenomena under examination from the beginning to the end or from one cut-off point to another. However, I have not been rigid in applying these limits, both because breaking through them occasionally seemed to make it easier to understand the subject and because I felt that the reader might wonder when certain trends started to occur or how we arrived at our current situation, which is so distant for most of us from the shortages and straitened circumstances that dominated the lives of the majority of our ancestors.

Now that the geographical and chronological context of the argument has been clarified, it would be worth taking a closer look at the subject itself. This work analyses the history of living conditions, eating and clothing. Personally I became involved in these questions through my interest in the history of women, gender, the family, the home and domestic servants in the early modern era. This background is clearly reflected in the book, and it is no coincidence that the opening chapters analyse living conditions starting with the relationship between the home and the family and ending with reflections on changes in the domestic sphere and the role of women both inside and outside it.

If a label really has to be attached to it, this book could be defined as a history of the family from the point of view of its material culture and, at the same time, a history of material culture that takes on the viewpoint of the family. If we think of the history of the family and the history of material culture as two partially overlapping areas, like a coffee stain that intersects a wine stain on the same tablecloth, then this book concentrates on the common area in the conviction that such a choice will be fruitful to both spheres. This is precisely what the title is attempting to say by bringing the 'family' and 'material culture' together. I certainly do not wish to suggest that these activities only occurred in the domestic sphere or that family life was only a question of clothing oneself, eating and living together, even though living together is interpreted in its broadest sense.

During the period under examination, the average European household (i.e. a group of persons linked by kinship, marriage, affinity[12] or work who live under the same roof) continued to carry out a vast range of functions linked to production, reproduction and consumption. The majority of children were born, brought up and educated at home, at least during their early childhood. Property was passed down from one generation to another principally in accordance with kinship patterns. Those who lived together often worked and ate together. They also slept together, protected themselves from the cold and bad weather together, dressed together, dressed up for special occasions together and, in other words, consumed together. Because of the way this book has been structured, consumption will be one of the various activities in the family context that will be subject to particularly close examination. Reproduction will not be neglected, but production will only be referred to on an occasional basis. The reader should certainly not infer from this that I consider reproduction and consumption to be more important than production. It is simply that, faced with the need to restrict the area of study, I decided to give greater importance to the first two questions, partly because they have been less studied than production and are therefore in greater need of analysis. Nevertheless, I have attempted where possible to take proper account of the fact that the domestic sphere was often characterized by dense and complex interrelations between reproduction, production and consumption.

For vast sections of society, although certainly not all of them, home life in the early modern era embraced a much wider sphere of activities than it does today. This does not mean, however, that families were always capable of producing everything they needed and were unfailingly self-reliant from an economic point of view. This was not true of families in towns and cities, and during the period we are examining, the development of a market economy was increasingly eroding large areas of private consumption even in the countryside. In other words, it became increasingly common to purchase goods and foodstuffs rather than produce them oneself. In the Grand Duchy of Tuscany, one of the areas in western Europe where private consumption was rather high, it is estimated that in the 1760s 73 per cent of agricultural produce was produced and consumed privately, as was 53 per cent of the total domestic product.[13] This was partly due to the fact that an increasing number of families did not have enough land to feed themselves solely with the produce from the fields they cultivated. In central Europe during the eighteenth century, at least 60 per cent of peasant families found themselves in this situation.[14]

This is one of the reasons why the family cannot always be defined as a production unit, to use the jargon of social sciences, but it was not necessarily a consumption unit either. Some of its members could leave home for periods of varying length to work (and consume) far from home or in the vicinity but receiving, as part of their remuneration from the employer, meals and goods in kind that did not benefit the family as a whole. Moreover, outsiders could share board, lodging or both with the family, as in the case of paying guests or babies with their wet nurses.[15]

Nevertheless, most decisions concerning purchases and consumption continued to be taken within the family. Because most needs relating to accommodation, eating and clothing were satisfied through the family, the viewpoint of the family does not appear a particularly narrow field for the examination of consumption and material culture. Indeed, it enables us to give consideration to a significant part of the European population in the early modern era. It is also one of the ways to avoid reducing objects and goods merely to their physical dimension and running the risk of studying them with a 'materialistic approach'. In other words, things have many facets and carry out many functions. I will attempt to identify a few of these, but without claiming to produce an exhaustive list.

Obviously they have a value in the broad 'economic' sense, which can be measured in terms of money or exchange through barter. On the basis of value, those who own an abundance of assets that are much sought after in the society in which they live are considered rich, and those who go without are considered poor. The first set of problems therefore arises from the attempt to understand the value placed in the past on a bed, a pair of shoes or a kilogram of bread in relation to the total property of a Sicilian farm labourer or a Parisian servant, to assess the relationship between a labourer's wage and the cost of a shirt or to estimate the proportion of a sharecropper family's total expenses that went toward clothing. Such problems are less easy to resolve than might at first be thought, because private consumption and barter were widespread. We also need to understand how the value of things changed over time.

But that is not the end of it. 'Look at that, now; he's married me', said a certain Maddalena Piccinini in 1558 to an acquaintance to whom she showed the ring her suitor had put on her finger after having declared that he was taking her as his wife. The importance of that ring to her was not its economic value but its meaning. For reasons that there is no need to dwell on here, the validity of Maddalena's marriage was not upheld by the Church authorities. However, when speaking to her friend, the girl was referring to a gesture – the *subarratio anuli* – which, according to the custom and statutes of her city, constituted one of the elements that turned a union into a legitimate marriage.[16] A simple circular band of metal contributed legitimately to a radical change in status (the change from unmarried to married woman) and made it visible. Given that today rings still play a part in the marriage ceremony, Maddalena's behaviour probably does not appear that strange. However, if a young man were to turn up at his betrothed's house on his wedding day to say that he had lost the sleeve of his shirt and that he wanted to search for it in her house, we would think that he had taken leave of his senses. Yet for a population living on the banks of the Volga, such demands were not considered at all unusual.

Thus objects help to model and structure social relations, and equally social relations are expressed through objects. To understand how goods carried out this function, we need to discover the meaning that it had for the people who bought them, inherited them, owned them, consumed them, wasted them, flaunted them, hid them, saved them, desired them, despised them, exchanged them, sold them, gave them away, received them as gifts and even stole them. We need to unravel, on a case-by-case basis, the complex tangle of economic worth, personal but still socially conditioned tastes, and meanings that are to a greater or lesser extent shared and codified.

The family is a very good observation point when it comes to understanding how objects communicate something and are sometimes used to build bridges between people and other times to erect barriers.[17] The fact that the family in the early modern era was often a unit of production, reproduction and, above all for our purposes, consumption, does not at all imply that its members had equal access to family resources or had the same influence when it came to deciding how to use them. If anything, the opposite was true: wives and husbands, parents and children, boys and girls, first-born and younger sons, mothers-in-law and daughters-in-law did not generally have the same power or the same rights, although there were marked differences according to region, period and social group. Access by various members to the goods that the family owned, purchased and consumed therefore contributed to defining and reproducing the solidarity, the differences and the hierarchy that on the one hand binds them together and on the other divides them. To understand how this actually occurred, we will follow the material creation of new families, examine who financed their establishment, outline their subsequent development and decline, and analyse some aspects of daily life, from how parents and children would sit around the table to the allocation of rooms in the home. Examining the family from the starting point of material objects will thus be a way to avoid taking family relations out of the material context in which they were used and by which they were modelled. It also means that we can attempt to grasp the mix of interests and emotions on which they were based.[18]

The fact that this book concentrates its reflections on the family does not stop it from going beyond and occasionally even ignoring the boundaries of the home and family in order to examine, for instance, what it means to wear a certain garment or how widespread was the consumption of coffee in the eighteenth century. However, before we can discuss fireplaces, kitchens, bedrooms, furniture, food and clothing, we must first examine the meanings attached to these two notions of home and family because of their central importance and the way they interrelate and overlap. In this introduction, they have been used as if they were interchangeable, but we have yet to see if this is actually the case.

I

Home and Family: Things Fall Apart

1. Did the lack of a home mean the lack of a family?

When in the introduction I used the metaphor of opening the door of a house and peering inside to discover the material conditions of European families in the early modern era, I was in fact taking for granted that home and family were the same thing.

But where do we put those who had no home? The homeless are certainly not a modern invention: for centuries there has been a great mass of people 'of no fixed address', who have neither hearth nor home.[1] They included the 'thieves' and 'ruffians' who looked for shelter under the arches of San Marco and the Rialto in Venice, although they did not always succeed given that they were often found dead from cold and hunger.[2] They included the horde of Neapolitan beggars who sheltered as best they could in miserable lodgings, stables, ruined houses and caves.[3] The early modern era had a wide assortment of homeless people: vagabonds, beggars, layabouts and delinquents who managed to scrape a living from begging, deception, fraud, theft and violence.[4] The scourge of vagrancy and begging afflicted the whole of Europe, although it manifested itself in different ways in different places and historical periods (Figs. 1–4).[5]

There can be no doubt that the ragged army of those with no fixed address included many who had no father, no mother, no husband or wife, and no children, siblings or relations of any sort. 'The place is rife with people who have neither kith nor kin', said the Prince of Strongoli in 1783 in relation to the beggars of Naples. Generally lacking a home as well as a family, they numbered perhaps 100,000 at the end of the century, out of a population of 400,000.[6]

However, it is not easy to be sure of the size of the shifting and fluctuating mass of vagrants and homeless people, particularly in a society where the number of poor could rise steeply in periods of crisis. Indeed, poverty did not only affect those who could not earn their living because they were disabled, ill, too old or too young, or what has been called 'structural poverty', which fluctuated between 4 and 8 per cent in cities like Rome, Florence, Venice, Lyon, Toledo, Odense, Norwich, Salisbury and many others. They were flanked by a mass equal to about

9

a fifth of the urban population that was liable to slip under the subsistence level with the slightest shift in the price of bread. Then there were those who saw the spectre of poverty appear as a result of loss of work, a long illness or a family bereavement. In moments of particularly acute crises, the numbers of poor could be half or sometimes even 70 per cent of urban families.[7]

Clearly, in a world where so many people risked occasionally or permanently slipping below the tenuous threshold of poverty, vagrants and the homeless accounted for only a part of those at or below subsistence level. Yet when the mass of paupers increased in times of crisis, famine and war, the number of homeless tended to increase as well. Many were peasants who, desperate and devoured by hunger, would spill into the cities in search of aid. Thus they would swell the numbers of those who regularly went to the city in the hope of improving their lot, finding work and an income, or at least receiving a little assistance.[8]

People who wandered in search of food or to escape the horrors of war, had often lost or abandoned the other members of their families. The lack of a family was one of the signs of their marginalized status, and in many cases it was the cause, particularly with children, old people and women.[9] At the beginning of the seventeenth century, a female vagrant from the countryside around Modena who had been accused of prostitution, said that her husband 'had left because of hunger and had never been seen again'.[10] In 1601, another source confirmed the situation in the Modena area by stating that 'the poor go out into the world cursing so as not to see their children die of starvation'.[11] Poverty and destitution created similar situations elsewhere: at the end of the eighteenth century, the parish priest of Athis in France complained that there were men who, 'worn out by the hard work of maintaining a family on a wage that is barely sufficient for one person . . . , collect the few clothes they posses together in a bundle and leave never to show themselves to their families again'.[12] Apart from hunger, there were many other ways in which misfortune could strike its victims. In 1744, a young girl in Bologna called Giulia Taruffi 'wandered through the night, because she had no shelter', following her father's imprisonment.[13] A vagrant Englishwoman called Frances Palmer was arrested in 1603 and flogged for illegitimate motherhood. Both her children, who were 'conceived and born through prostitution', came into this world on the streets and died there as new-born babies. If they had survived without being abandoned, they would probably have increased the ranks of vagrants, as often occurred to the children of young women like her, who were exposed to sexual abuse and forced into prostitution to make a living.[14]

Although the breakdown of family ties was often the origin of a life out on the streets, and it was not uncommon for poverty and misfortune to wear down family relationships, there were occasionally entire families that wandered without a home or found shelter in makeshift refuges. Famine in the winter of 1527–8 drove a great mass of peasants to Venice from the countryside of the Venice estuary, Vicenza and Brescia. Many had to resort to begging with their children in their arms because they were dying of hunger and numb with cold.[15] Visitors to Amsterdam around the close of the sixteenth century would have found hundreds of families camped out under the archways that reinforced the city walls. This Babel of misery included not only the paupers to be found in any city, but also a crush of Jewish refugees from Spain and Portugal, and Walloon and Flemish protestants escaping religious persecution.[16] Being home-less, therefore, did not necessarily mean being without a family (Fig. 4).

2. Mobile homes, multiple homes and refuges

'We have no roof, no village and no lands' went the words of a gypsy song.[17] From the early fifteenth century, the gypsies had joined the ragged and complex world of those who lived on the road in Europe. They did not have a 'real' home, but nor were they homeless vagabonds obliged to find makeshift solutions. They took their home and family around with them.[18] There were other professional wanderers such as actors and jestors who behaved in much the same way. Further away from the towns and cities, there were shepherds and horse-breeders who followed their animals with shelters mounted on wheels. To the north, we find different groups of Lapps or Sámi, as they call themselves. During the winter, the group of Sámi who bred reindeer lived in the forest, where there was an abundance of firewood. They lived in a closed conical tent (called *loudekota* or *korvakota*) covered by reindeer skin and a Saami *raanu* (woven woolen cover), which they moved every two or three weeks because the reindeer, their prin-cipal resource, trampled the snow and hardened it to the point of making it impossible to continue grazing the lichen and so they had seek food elsewhere. In the late spring the families used to migrate north of the bush to their summer village of peat huts in a circular shape, while the herdsmen stayed with the reindeer in the field, where they lived in light tents called *laavers* and kept constantly on the move. At the other end of Europe in the Dore Mountains of France, herdsmen would sleep in mountain huts (*burons*) and during the summer nights they would gather their animals around their huts. In order to manure their meadows, they would therefore shift their huts around. In the Carpathian Mountains of Ruthenia, Vlach herdsmen built extremely light wooden huts (*salasi*), which they carried around when they moved to new grazing. Some herds-men of the Pyrenees similarly had portable huts in which to shelter for sleep, although to our eyes they would appear more like coffins than houses (Fig. 5).[19]

When discussing houses of the past, we have to accustom ourselves to the idea that they were not always solid constructions with doors and windows. As will become clearer from the following pages, there was a wide spectrum of intermediary situations between those who slept under the stars and those who lived in grand houses. It is difficult to know where the concept of a house started at the lower end of the scale. There were those who lived in flimsy huts made of vegetable matter. Fishermen in the Baltic and along the French coast of the English Channel lived in old upturned boats.[20] The boundary between those who had a roof over their heads and those who did not was a rather vague one. If, as has rightly been argued, the history of housing cannot ignore the homeless and the tramps, then it is equally true that it cannot ignore this vast range of dwellings and shelters.[21]

The existence of rudimentary forms of housing was partly due to the survival of ancient traditions and partly to poverty. Another cause was the need to be able to move about, as in the case of the previously mentioned herdsmen. Mobility was itself caused by poverty in many cases. To deal with their poverty, many peasants from highland areas in the Alps, the Apennines, the Pyrenees and the Massif central migrated every year on a seasonal basis to supplement the meagre earnings from their fields with a wide variety of trades.[22] Contrary to what has long been believed, much of Europe in the early modern era was constantly on the move for a wide variety of reasons, and the distances involved could be long as well as short.[23] When they moved, some left their house behind, others took it with them and still others created several, as in the case of some herdsmen. Some, like the Sámi, came up with more than one system. While at the other end of the social scale, nobility and the wealthy multiplied their residences: town houses, country villas and ancestral castles.[24]

In this confusion of different solutions, the relationship between the home and the family ended up manifesting itself in an extremely wide variety of ways, as has already been suggested. Sometimes whole families were on the move, and sometimes only a few members left for periods of varying length or for good. On occasion whole families lived in makeshift shelters or in mobile houses. Families scattered and came back together, while others divided up forever.

3. Insecure housing and insecure families

The expression 'insecure housing' could be used to define not only a category of housing, given the presence of such dwellings as insubstantial huts, tents and 'caravans', but also to define the relationship established with the house. At the bottom of the social scale, particularly in urban areas, insecurity seems to have been the norm amongst the swelling ranks of lodgers, paying guests, tenants and subtenants who struggled to put together the money to pay for their accommodation.[25]

Between 2 and 4 per cent of wage-earners in Paris in the eighteenth century owned their own house, and the figure dropped to 1 per cent for domestic servants, who at that time did not always live with their employers. Altogether, about 80 per cent of Parisians live in rented accommodation. During the century rents doubled in relation to total expenditure.[26] Hence the poorest struggled along constantly moving from one place to another. In the suburbs, according to Sébastien Mercier, 'there are about three or four thousand families who never pay their rent, but shift every three months from one hovel to another taking furniture that altogether isn't worth 24 livres. They remove their furniture one piece at a time without paying and they leave one piece behind by way of payment'.[27] Some of those who did not have enough money for their back payments slipped away without anyone noticing.[28] Of course, Paris was a particularly crowded city, but housing was a problem for the least well-off even in cities that were not so overcrowded.[29]

We have seen that being homeless did not always mean being without a family, but it has also become clear that there often was a relationship between being without a roof and being without a family. This is also confirmed by analysis of the shifting population that lived in the worst housing. In many ways, insecure housing and insecure families went hand in hand. Of those in rented accommodation, widows who did not manage to remarry quickly and women on their own or with small children were forced within a few months to gather up their household goods and move to a cheaper but more dismal home. Because they were excluded from many trades and forced to work for miserable salaries that were much lower than those of men,[30] 'women without men' – i.e. spinsters, widows and those who had married 'badly' – were the inevitable victims of poverty and in the cities represented the majority of the destitute.[31]

Many of these women attempted to deal with the difficulties by setting up networks of solidarity with others in similar conditions.[32] Caterina Monari, the vagabond in the Modena area who was mentioned at the beginning of this chapter, lived for a period in Ferrara 'in the company' of a respectable old woman called Maria, 'who carded wool' and 'who struggled day and night in order to keep alive'. Caterina explained that she paid her a small sum for somewhere to sleep. By spinning and occasionally going around begging, 'I earned myself a living' and so 'between us we were able to pay the rent'.[33]

It will be recalled that Caterina was accused of prostitution. Prostitutes also confirmed the relationship between insecure housing and the absence of solid or 'normal' family relationships. They were constantly moving house either because they were driven off by neighbours or because they were pursued by the public authorities. As accommodation was generally beyond the means of a woman on her own of middle to lower social class, many were sub-tenants, whether they were living in Bologna, Warsaw or Cracow.[34] Hence prostitutes often lived together with other women. They lived with other 'colleagues' with whom they shared their expenses, with a landlady who also acted as procuress or with very poor 'honest' women who gave them a little space in exchange for a few coins.[35] This tended to give a bad name to the poorer streets and areas of a city where there was a particularly high number of women living together and of families in which there was no adult man.[36] Poverty and dishonour constantly risked becoming a vicious circle.

Insecure housing and insecure families were intertwined in other ways. More or less unstable relationships outside marriage were mainly formed amongst those who lived in crowded and miserable rented rooms. For the most deprived and marginalized, marriage was in some places (such as England) either too expensive or entirely beyond their grasp.[37] When in Paris around 1770 a police report revealed the existence of 'a great number of poor families that have not been united in matrimony', the authorities forced churches to marry their poorest parishioners free of charge.[38] As we shall see, the attitude of authorities was not always so helpful.

4. Cohabitation and marriage

We have started to 'deconstruct' the relationship between home and family and the very idea of a home itself, in order to avoid using familiar concepts and words and projecting them onto the past in an anachronistic or preconceived manner with their *current* meanings or allusions. Similarly, we are now faced with the concepts of marriage and cohabitation. The difference between the two seems absolutely clear to us, but this was not always the case. First we must attempt to examine what was considered a marriage and what was not by the Churches, the secular authorities, and the popular traditions in early modern Europe, starting with the situation *before* the Reformation and the Counter or Catholic Reformation.

Marriage by degrees

'He came to me when he wanted, because no one stopped him from coming as he was my *sposo* [husband]', said Domenica Cinti di Battista Mazzoni in 1548.[39] But Domenica and Battista were not married in the current sense of the term. They had simply exchanged promises of marriage. But at the time, the Italian word *sposo* meant 'betrothed', as it derived from the Latin verb *spondeo*, 'to promise'. The difficulty in relation to the current situation was not, however, the different meaning of the term, but rather the fact that, as well as the mutual promise to become husband and wife, it could also mean that they had uttered their consent to marriage (what we would consider the fatal 'I do'). This uncertainty occurred above all when the betrothal had only recently occurred or when the couple had not yet 'finished getting married', as it was well expressed by a woman of the time.[40]

It is already clear that not only was the situation very different from today, but also rather complicated. Legitimate marriages were of central importance in property relations between members of a family. A father could voluntarily leave something to his 'bastard' child, but the 'legitimate' children (i.e. those born within the marriage) had a right to inherit their parents' property. Moreover there were restrictions on the legitimization of 'bastard' children.[41]

Their use of the terms 'to marry' and 'spouse', which appear so strange and ambiguous to us now, reflected the realities of the time. For the majority of the population, marriage was not a single event by which a couple became immediately and indissolubly husband and wife. It was a process that went through a series of stages, each accompanied by various rituals and ceremonies.[42] The rituals that marked out the formation of new couples varied widely according to the region and not infrequently according to the persons involved.[43] However, the stages were more or less the same everywhere, although occasionally some were missed out.

Once contacts between the families or the two people who were to get married had been initiated, and an agreement had been arrived at, a promise of marriage was made. This constituted a formal commitment. After a relatively short period, there came the exchange of consent. The two betrothed declared their mutual intention to become husband and wife, often sealing their union with a ring. In Augsburg and in western and north-western France, they generally did this outside the church door. In Florence they did it before a notary in the bride's house. We have records of the exchange of consent occurring in fields, taverns and other unlikely places. Then there was the wedding, which was in fact the festivity surrounding the transfer of the bride to the home where the newly formed couple was to live. This could go on for several days, but occasionally it was kept to a minimum or even dispensed with altogether, because of the couple's poverty, their extreme youth or some other reason. Before or after the wedding, the couple were blessed by a priest, but this was not done everywhere.[44]

This long procedure gave rise to assertions that would be incomprehensible today. 'He has taken a wife here . . . but they have not held the wedding yet', was said of a man in Augsburg in 1528. 'I will go to church and streets according to Christian custom, with my husband to whom I am now married', stated a woman of the same city.[45] The vast range of local traditions and individual behaviours was made even more complex by the variability of sexual behaviour and the timing of the consummation of the marriage. While in many areas, particularly Mediterranean Europe, girls of marriageable age were strictly controlled, in the Alpine areas, Germany, Holland, England and some parts of France and Scandinavia, young men and women of the same age could mix fairly freely, although in the sixteenth and seventeenth centuries they probably did not have full sexual relations.[46] Apart from the differences in premarital sex amongst young people, there were the differences in the timing of the consummation of the marriage. On the one hand, this could occur after the exchange of consent or after the wedding, and occasionally not even immediately afterwards.[47] On the other hand, there were areas where the young couple were authorized to have sexual relations once there had been a promise of marriage or even during the negotiations between the families. Occasionally things were even more extreme. In Corsica, it was traditional for the girl to go and live with her future husband as soon as the initial agreements had been established between the families. In England, northern France, Aquitaine and German regions, premarital cohabitation was not uncommon in order to demonstrate that the union was a fertile one or, occasionally, to see whether husband and wife to be were well matched.[48] This naturally created ambiguous situations that were half way between the unmarried status and the status of husband and wife in the fullest sense of the terms. In some cases, it created the problem of the status of children born from these unions.

The Church's view of marriage

The Church's perception of what it meant to be married was different and less ambiguous. It considered marriage a sacrament and not a worldly affair. According to the interpretation that it had been attempting to impose on the whole of Europe since the eleventh century,[49] marriage was very simply a union between a man and a woman by mutual consent. To get married, it was enough to be of marriageable age (12 years for girls and 14 for boys), not to have a prohibited degree of relationship and to take the other freely as husband or wife by uttering the so-called *verba de praesenti*. The Church wanted these declarations to be made in church in the presence of a priest and witnesses and with the parents' consent. However, it also recognized and considered binding those marriages that lacked any form of public declaration (which were called 'informal' or later 'clandestine'), although it did consider them illegitimate. In other words, it was not necessary in the eyes of the Church for a marriage to have the previous commitment of a promise (*verba de futuro*) and the parents' consent, nor was there any need of a priest, witnesses, a dowry, rings or festivities. Moreover, the *verba de praesenti* were considered implicit when a promise of marriage was followed by sexual intercourse or cohabitation ('presumption of marriage').[50] A woman who had sexual relations with a man following a promise to marry her could legitimately request the competent authorities to enforce the promise. Generally this principle remained in force even after the changes to matrimonial practice brought about by the Council of Trent on the one hand and the protestant reformers on the other, although differences remained between regions and there was often a less responsive attitude to claims made by women (the man might simply be forced to pay the girl's dowry and then only if she was a virgin when he seduced her).[51]

Unlike tradition and not infrequently the provisions of civil law, the Church perceived marriage as being centred on a single moment, the exchange of consent, and not as being protracted over a series of stages. Undoubtedly it made the distinction between marriage and cohabitation much clearer, but it also based the distinction between informal marriages and concubinage only on the absence of declared intentions to marry (although concubinage was condemned by the Church, it was partially accepted by the secular world[52]).

The Church also made the bride and groom the unchallenged protagonists of the marriage ceremony. It therefore took away some of the collective nature of the marriage event and reduced the role of social recognition in a valid and binding union, an element to which tradition and often the law attributed great importance. The statutes of Bologna in 1454, for example, established that the exchange of consent, the ring and public nature of the ceremony were the three requisites of a valid marriage.[53]

By allowing young people to marry without their parents' consent, the Church diminished family control over marriage, which had traditionally been a means for creating alliances and kinships based on family interests, often without taking account of the wishes of those who were to be married. Here again, the Church's concept of marriage clashed with that of civil legislation, at least in some cases. In France in 1556, marriages entered into against the parents' will by 'children of the family' who were under thirty years in the case of men and twenty-five in that of women, were declared unlawful and the transgressors were punished by disinheritance.[54]

In practice, then, different ways of perceiving marriage and weddings were superimposed and became entangled with each other. The situation was further complicated when Luther declared that marriage was not a sacrament. From then on, the different perceptions of the Catholic and Protestant worlds were added to the many differences that already existed in Europe in relation to how marriages were celebrated and interpreted. One of the reasons, perhaps the principle one, that drove the Church of Rome to establish precise regulations for marriage was precisely this reaction to the statements of Luther and other reformers, which were considered heretical. In the protestant world, the new ideas also led to reforms, although they were introduced in a less rapid and uniform manner (as will be seen particularly in the case of England, where there was to be considerable confusion for a long time).

The Counter-Reformation or Catholic Reformation

For its part, the Catholic Church reasserted the sacramental status of marriage and, as part of the tremendous drive towards reorganization and rationalization that was launched during the Council of Trent (1545–63), it established norms aimed at standardizing marriage ceremonies. Its attention initially turned to clandestine marriages and marriages entered into without the parents' consent. The Church restated its condemnation of those who 'erroneously maintain that marriages contracted between children of families without their parents' consent are void'. However, it imposed a new ceremony to eliminate the possibility of a couple marrying in a valid and binding manner by exchanging consent on their own in a kitchen or in the middle of a field. According to the new rules, before a marriage could be entered into, the curates of both the bride's and the groom's parishes of residence must announce their intentions 'three times publicly in church, during high Mass, on three consecutive feast days'. After the reading of the banns and if there was no legitimate objection, they could then proceeded with the celebration of the wedding before the priest with at least two witnesses. All marriages contracted without these formalities were declared void, although there was the possibility of marrying secretly as long as there were a priest and witnesses, in the manner of Manzoni's *The Betrothed*.[55]

The Catholic Church also reaffirmed that sexual relations could only exist legitimately within the confines of married life. The Church therefore renewed its persecution of prostitution and concubinage, the latter being assimilated into the former (there were both spiritual and legal punishments for those living in a relationship of concubinage, particularly the women).[56] Hence part of the marriages celebrated under the old system became concubinary unions, and concubinage, which had once been tolerated, was now considered prostitution.

Naturally the new rules took time to be enforced. In Siena 291 couples were reported for concubinage between 1604 and 1628, 78 between 1629 and 1653, and only 21 in the following 120 years, between 1654 and 1773.[57] Perhaps this trend partly reflects the initial zeal of those enforcing the new rules, as well as the existence, in the early stages, of unions that in the previous situation would have been considered genuine marriages. In any case, it is symptomatic of a profound change in the concept of marriage and in the way the various possible relations between men and women can be interpreted.

However, ancient traditions cannot be stamped out so easily. In the countryside of Friuli, the custom of considering the exchange of promises followed by consummation of sexual relations to be a matrimonial bond in the fullest sense was still alive in the eighteenth century.[58] In various regions, such as some parts of Austria, Bavaria and in the Alps, sexual relations between unmarried persons continued to be considered lawful or were at least tolerated.[59] The fight against concubinage was not pursued everywhere with the same vigour. In Spain, it appears there was a certain tolerance towards cohabitation, particularly in cases where, as in the past, they represented a solution for couples of very different social extraction, as marriage would have led to a clash with at least one of their original families.[60]

The Catholic Church attempted to impose a clear and unitary definition of marriage through the directives of the Council of Trent. Obviously this meant confronting people who had their own traditions and convictions, and it was not always easy to eradicate these either quickly or very thoroughly. Besides, the secular authorities also had an interest in maintaining a certain control over the situation. In particular, France did not implement the directives relating to minors, and it made the rules against marriages without the parents' consent more severe, actually introducing the death penalty for rebellious children.[61] In 1782, Emperor Joseph II instituted civil marriage. A few years later, the Revolution in France proclaimed that marriage was a contract and introduced divorce (1791–2).[62]

The Protestant world

Luther and the other reformers were convinced that marriage was a worldly matter and not a sacrament, and that it should therefore be administered by the secular authorities, albeit on the basis of regulations that were inspired by the Bible. The parts of Europe won over to the Reformation therefore tended to secularize marriage, although only in a few cases was it completely laicized.[63] We will therefore examine the situation in the Protestant world, starting with England. From 1563, the Anglican Church rejected the sacramental nature of marriage, but it did not take any action to reform it. Thus the situation was to remain confused for a long time. According to the ecclesiastical courts, all that was required for a valid marriage was the consent of the couple. From the beginning of the seventeenth century, however, marriages that did not observe certain formalities were considered valid but not legitimate, and those who officiated them were punished. Civil courts, on the other hand, only recognized marriages celebrated in public, generally in church or outside the main entrance to the church. In other words, confusion reigned supreme. People got married in accordance with different practices: probably less than half the population married in full compliance with the rule of canonical law, and therefore in a manner that was considered valid and legitimate by everyone. It should also be remembered that the civil courts, which ruled on all cases concerning property, only recognized marriages in church, a woman who wanted to be sure of her dower once she had been widowed could only marry in the presence of a priest.[64] The same was also true of the children's inheritance.

In 1753, in order to eliminate the uncertainty and the abuses caused by this situation, it was established that marriage had to be celebrated before a minister of the Anglican Church and registered with the signatures of the bride and groom. The consent of the parents also became obligatory for those under 21 years of age. Marriages celebrated in any other manner were declared void.

The implementation of the law was transferred from the ecclesiastical courts to the much more efficient temporal courts. Jews and Quakers were not however required to observe the new provisions and were able to continue to marry in accordance with their own rites. The *Marriage Act* was not introduced in Scotland, which began to receive couples who in other areas would have been unable to marry. At Gretna Green, close to the border, the celebration of marriages on the spot for payment and without any indiscrete questions became a veritable business. But resistance to the new law possibly also led to an increase in the marriages celebrated in accordance with custom and practice that the Church would not have approved.[65]

In other areas affected by the Protestant Reformation, measures were introduced more promptly. In Zurich, Ulrich Zwingli founded a tribunal in 1525 that was made up of four lay people and ministers (*Leutpriester*) who were competent in matrimonial matters, and this was to serve as a model to other Swiss cities, such as St. Gallen, Berne, Basle and Schaffhausen. In Calvin's Geneva, questions concerning matrimony were ruled on by the Consistory founded in 1541; half its members were ministers and half were lay elders. This formula also reminds us that in the Protestant world the religious authorities rarely left matrimonial matters in the control of lay people (although Augsburg was one example of this). This was consistent with the principle that marriage also had a religious significance and had to be governed by biblical norms. The transition occasionally gave rise to jurisdictional conflicts between the clergy and lay authorities (as occurred in Strasburg and Nuremberg). In continental Europe there was no shortage of areas, particularly rural ones, in which the disappearance of traditional Church tribunals led to a kind of institutional vacuum.[66]

Because different reformers did not share a common perception of marriage, for a while there was some uncertainty about the criteria for determining the validity of marriages and the correct way to celebrate them.[67] In Sweden, there was some confusion arising from the different perceptions of the religious and temporal authorities: the Church considered children born out of wedlock to be illegitimate, but according to the law, they had the same rights as children born after the marriage, if their parents had made a commitment to marry each other.[68] In the Protestant cantons of Switzerland, the new concept proposed by the reformers clashed with the people's long-held beliefs and sometimes even with the courts responsible for ruling on matrimonial matters. Many people continued to believe that the exchange of promises authorized sexual relations. Of course, Protestant reformers, unlike the Catholic Church, attributed great importance to the promise, given that they considered it a necessary part of marriage. But in their eyes, it was not enough to make a couple husband and wife; nor did it authorize sexual relations. For there to be a valid marriage, it had to be celebrated in church before a member of the clergy.[69]

In Protestant regions, the parents' consent and the public nature of the ceremony tended to become obligatory for minors, although the age at which children were authorized to marry freely varied enormously according to time and place (between 16 and 25 among the various Swiss cantons, but in Basle children who married against their parents' wishes could be disinherited, irrespective of age).[70] Apart from the reduction in the impediments based on consanguinity, one common feature in the attitude to marriage in the continental reformation was the campaign against marriages contracted on the basis of a couple's mutual consent in the absence of witnesses or without the prior authorization of the parents. The Protestants required bans to be read and parents to give their consent to minors.[71] One hundred and sixty-seven clandestine marriages that had been entered into without the parents' consent went to court in Basle between 1550 and 1592, and as many as 133 marriages were annulled.[72] The severity of the authorities in Basle was not ubiquitous. In German towns, for instance, parents were not entitled to challenge a clandestine marriage if it was followed by sexual relations and the interested parties wanted to continue living together.[73] Another unifying aspect of the Protestant position was that divorce was allowed, and this was perhaps the greatest difference between Protestants and Catholics.[74]

Separations, annulments and divorce

Once the sacramental nature of marriage had been denied, it became possible to allow divorce. Although it did not believe marriage to be a sacrament, the Anglican Church remained 'loyal' to the pre-Reformation tradition that did not allow divorce,[75] just like the Catholic Church, which only allowed an annulment in cases in which the marriage was invalidated by impediments such as a prohibited degree of consanguinity, and separation *quoad thorum et mensam* (without the possibility of remarriage) in the event of adultery, apostasy, heresy or serious physical violence.[76]

Some of the reformers dared to adopt extremely liberal positions. Martin Bucer even allowed divorce on the grounds of incompatibility. In practice, the work of the tribunals mainly conformed to the much more rigid positions of Luther and Calvin, so that divorce was usually only conceded for adultery and abandonment. Only the courts of Basle and Neuchâtel appear to have regularly granted divorces on various grounds, particularly illness and impotence. The number of divorces in the Protestant world was overall very limited (in Basle between 1525 and 1592 there was an average of 0.57 divorces recorded for every thousand inhabitants, while the figure for the United States in 1980 was 5.2).[77]

Although the actual number of divorces in Protestant areas was not high, the formal possibility of obtaining a divorce constituted a difference of considerable importance in relation to the Catholic and Anglican religions, in which wives and husbands could only hope for an annulment or a separation, or make use of informal or clearly illegal solutions, such as consensual separation, abandonment of one's spouse, the so-called 'wife-selling' (in England) or even murder.[78]

Thus the European geography of marriage looked rather complex. It was in fact further complicated by the Jews (who allowed divorce)[79] and the populations of eastern Europe and the Balkans, where the Orthodox Christianity was dominant and rivalled Islam in the vast regions under the Ottoman Empire.

The Islamic world allows polygamy, and marriage was considered a civil contract that involved the 'transfer' of a woman from her father or guardian to the husband. This transfer was ratified by a payment for the bride. Divorce was possible, but the actual practice in Ottoman Europe is a question that historians have not yet examined in depth.[80]

For Orthodox Christians, religious marriage consisted of two public ceremonies, both of which were strictly carried out in church, one for the betrothal and one for the wedding. They also allowed divorce. The list of grounds for divorce was fairly long and changed according to time and place. Men and women did not have the same rights, given that adultery was only acceptable grounds for divorce for men. For wives, it was only grounds for divorce if accompanied by aggravating circumstances. Both husbands and wives could divorce a spouse who attempted to kill them. High treason by the husband constituted a justifiable cause for the wife, and the fact that the wife knew of plans for high treason that were kept secret was grounds for the husband to divorce. Wives could obtain a divorce from men who had damaged their reputations or sexual chastity, if they were sold as slaves or (only in Russia) their financial situation had been seriously prejudiced. The desire to take vows was another good reason for ending a couple's life together, given that the monastic life was considered superior to matrimony. This offered many women the opportunity to escape unhappy marriages. Undoubtedly, there were many husbands who took advantage of these opportunities to get rid of unwanted wives. It appears that the case of Gavrilko Oleksandrov *syn* Putilov was not uncommon. He came from Nizhnyi Novgorod, and according to his wife Tatyanitsa and father-in-law, around 1640 he abused his wife and forced her to enter a convent (even though she was pregnant) and then he remarried. Tatyanitsa got what she wanted from the patriarch's tribunal and Gavrilko was required to return her dowry and maintain her in the convent. She could have also requested the annulment of the man's new marriage, but probably after all that had happened, the prospect of returning to the conjugal bed did not seem particularly attractive.[81]

The exclusion of the poor

Orthodox Christians required celibacy only of monks and bishops (not priests), while Catholics also required it of priests and considered celibacy for the clergy to be a superior state in relation to married life. Protestants, by contrast, rejected ecclesiastical celibacy and turned marriage into the most suitable state for living a truly Christian life. According to Protestant reformers, marriage had to take place early to avoid the risk of disorderly premarital sexual conduct. However, the secular authorities, of whom they had required jurisdiction in matrimonial affairs, often imposed measures that made economic security and sexual maturity the criterion for marriage. In Augsburg in the 1560s and 1570s, measures were taken to prevent marriages between servants and other immigrants who were incapable of supporting themselves and were a burden on the public welfare system. They started to demand guarantees. Representatives of the city council began to investigate whether couples that intended to marry had sufficient income and if the man had fulfilled the obligations required of his trade. If they did not come from the city and did not have the necessary means, they were forced to leave.[82]

Augsburg was not the only place where they introduced legal restrictions on marriages between poor people. Similar provisions, even harsher ones, were enacted by many other cities and communities that were collectively responsible for welfare, particularly in German regions, and they were not necessarily Protestant.[83] In Tyrol, priests were prohibited from marrying destitute people without the permission of the local authorities. Similar measures were taken in Bavaria in 1553. It was also ruled that servants who married without the permission of their employers and sought refuge in the *Winkelherbergen* (refuges for the poor and homeless) had to be arrested and taken back to the houses from which they had escaped. Later such measures were to become even harsher.[84] In England, communities were able to object to marriages between the very poor and deny newly-weds in a state of destitution the right reside in their parish.[85] There were also laws placing considerable restrictions on marriages between poor people in Nordic countries.

As in other areas, the guild system placed restrictions on the rights of apprentices and day labourers to marry.[86] For artisans, marriage and the establishment of one's own workshop were interlinked or were supposed to be, although as time went on this link became less entrenched because the number of those unable to set up as independent master artisans was on the rise.[87] In the modern era there were many categories of servant.[88] However, like apprentices they were often unmarried. Particularly in central Europe, they were subject to measures limiting their ability to marry or even completely banning it for as long as they remained in that condition.[89] Generally servants did not have their own home. If, for some reason, they found themselves without an employer and did not quickly find other service, both farm servants and domestic servants were soon obliged to go 'roaming ad scattered through the streets without any kind of succour', according to members of the confraternity of servants, which was founded in Bologna towards the end of the seventeenth century to provide mutual assistance.[90] Those without an employer, either because they lost their work or because they voluntarily left it, were considered vagrants without any distinctions in England, Poland and probably elsewhere.[91]

In the countryside, marriage was also influenced by the strategies of landowners in relation to optimising the ratio between land and mouths to be fed. For instance, in central Italy sharecroppers[92] had to obtain permission to marry from their landowner, while in Austria, Poland and other regions of central Europe, widows and widowers were obliged to remarry as soon as possible if they did not want to be thrown off the land they were working.[93]

Where they existed, these restrictions on marriage rights were certainly enforced. In 1779 Carl Ferdinand Fausel, a carpenter from Nürtingen, wanted to marry Dorothea Schach and move to nearby Neckarhausen (Württemberg), where the woman lived. He therefore asked the village council if he could become a member of their community (*Bürger*). Before ruling the council assessed the situation in depth, but the couple could not give guarantees and there was the risk that they would end up being a burden on the village. A similar request from a man who wanted to marry another young girl from Neckarhausen, who in this case was pregnant, was rejected on the same grounds that there were already too many poor people requiring assistance.[94] In the village of Jungingen (Zollernalbkreis), those who wanted to marry had to request authorization from the seigniorial chancellery. The authorization was granted on the basis of specific conditions: the future householder had to be at least 25 years old and he had to have fulfilled a series of obligations. If he was an artisan, he had to have completed a three-year apprenticeship. The couple also had to demonstrate that it had sufficient assets to maintain a family, so as not to be a burden on the public purse. In the seventeenth century, their minimum value was 50 florins and in the nineteenth century it was at least 700.[95] It is not surprising then that the rate of illegitimate births rapidly decreased in Switzerland after 1874, when nearly all economic and political restrictions on marriage were abolished, although these rules were not the only factor that historically influenced the number of illegitimate babies.[96]

Clearer and more severe rules

While the boundary between marriage and cohabitation was rather vague at the start of the early modern era, clearer and more severe rules were implemented later in both Catholic and Protestant areas. Both the Reformation and the Counter-Reformation enforced a rigorous control over sexual morality. However, the persistence of ancient traditions in some regions and the exclusion of part of the population from the possibility of marriage, either by law or de facto (as will become clearer in the next chapter), meant that sexual relationships between men and women, even stable ones, also occurred outside marriage. It therefore follows that not everyone had legally married parents.[97]

It would be a digression to follow up the innumerable forms of extramarital sex, which varied from cohabitation, ancient rites to seal a pact, prostitution and rape.[98] The important point for now is the awareness of plurality and diversity of ways in which marriage was conceived compared with today, and the manner in which family relations from their very foundation were conditioned by the presence and absence of objects and wealth. We have begun to form a picture in which young people were forced into marriages by their parents for reasons of family interest, and poor people were unable to regularize their affections because they lacked the means. Moreover, we have begun to clarify what we are talking about through the effort both to understand how the relationship between home and family was organized and to discover what the home, marriage and cohabitation really were like in the areas and periods we are considering.

5. Welfare and imprisonment

On this first part of our journey along the roads and pathways of Europe, we have already encountered a small crowd: young vagrants in rags who were reduced to poverty by the loss of their parents, single men who had abandoned the excessive number of mouths they had to feed, pitiful families of beggars, gypsy caravans, herdsmen with their animals, tenants who move house in secret, restless prostitutes and cheerful wedding processions. But we have also met poor lovers who were forced to leave cities that, in order to minimize the number of those requiring benefit, refused all responsibility for the children they were to bring into the world. Indeed, numerous welfare organizations developed in the early modern era to stem a problem that was assuming gigantic proportions. As a result of the economic transformation and the changing relation between population and resources, a mass of destitute people and vagrants developed on the back of the demographic growth that marked the fifteenth and sixteenth centuries. In the early stages of the period under examination, the problem had already reached worrying proportions.[99]

Together with other factors such as new perceptions of begging, property and tolerable levels of poverty,[100] this led to a change in attitudes towards poverty. At the end of the Middle Ages and during the very early years of the modern era, the poor were transformed from the image of Christ who had to be assisted into a threatening mass that still had to be helped but also kept under control and neutralized. For a better understanding, let's go to Lyons in the 1530s.

'I'm dying of hunger, I'm dying of hunger', came the shout of over 4,500 inhabitants reduced to a pitiful state by the terrible famine of 1531. They had been joined by 1,500 people from the countryside, driven there in the hope of finding a crust of bread. People tried to help: those who could afford it gave food to the hungry who knocked on their doors and wandered the streets. The starving swooped on the food like vultures and devoured it so voraciously as to die from suffocation. They attacked their benefactors, fought amongst each other and wasted the food they were given. Fear destroyed pity. However, a group of citizens came to the conclusion that, while they could not renounce their duty to help their fellow men, they had to find a more rational and efficient system for disbursing private charity. This led to the creation of the *Aumône-Générale*.

This was a government body that centralized welfare, to which it was determined that all the charity distributed by churches and monasteries should be handed over. It was prohibited to give anything to beggars in the streets or public places, and all donations had to be channelled through employees of the *Aumône-Générale*. A census of all the poor in the city was carried out, the sick were sent for free hospital treatment and the rest were provided with cards that entitled them to welfare. They founded two institutions to receive poor orphans and foundlings when at the age of 7 they had to leave the *Hôtel-Dieu* that looked after abandoned infants. The boys were placed in workshops so that they could learn a trade to maintain themselves in adulthood. The girls were put into service or given work in the city's textile industry, and when they married they received a dowry.

But there was another more repressive side to these reforms. All forms of begging were banned. Anyone asking for alms received a flogging and was thrown out of the city. Vagrants were faced with a clear choice: either work or leave Lyons. More specifically, the choice was between going or breaking one's back digging ditches for the city's new fortifications and collecting rubbish, often kept in chains and all for just a little food. It was not therefore a very enticing prospect, but those who disobeyed were shut up in a tower that was used in the seventeenth century as a permanent place of detention for healthy beggars and vagrants: 'part prison and part workhouse'.[101]

The case of Lyons epitomizes the kind of measures taken in modern Europe to fight poverty, begging and vagrancy, and the philosophy behind those measures. In the sixteenth and early seventeenth centuries, a new attitude developed that was broadly the same throughout Europe. Its aim was to create welfare institutions to assist the poor who were unable to provide for themselves and, at the same time, to stigmatize and fight vagrancy and begging amongst healthy men. The battle was fought on two fronts and involved imprisonment and repression.[102]

We cannot stop to provide an exhaustive list of all the initiatives, to distinguish between those implemented by secular authorities and those by religious and private institutions, nor to evaluate their successes and failures. The reason we have taken a glance at the squalor of workhouses, prisons, orphanages, workshops where orphans learn trades and crowded hospital wards where the sick moan as they lie heaped on beds and makeshift sleeping places, is to start to understand the wide range of institutions and forms of cohabitation that existed in the early modern era.

As has been suggested, the development of welfare institutions was not only linked to the impoverishment of large sections of the population due to demographic trends, the increasing gap between food supplies and mouths to be fed, but also to the economic changes that were taking place. If such measures were introduced, it was not simply a case of increasing numbers of poor and destitute people. Values were also changing. For instance, there was the more rigid sexual morality required by the Council of Trent. Let us look at the reasons for this increasing severity.

In 1635, Bernardino Biasini, an apothecary from Pisa, and Portia, his maid, were accused of concubinage. Bernardino denied it and explained that he could not do without the woman, as he was old and sick. The following year, however, the same accusation was made against him, and yet again he defended himself and his maid: 'I have always held her to be an honest woman', he said. It would not be 'honourable to drive her off like a prostitute'.[103] In rejecting the accusations, Bernardino shows himself to be perfectly aware of the way concubinage and prostitution had been put on the same level by those who wished to take Portia away from him, and he may even have shared that view. Generally, however, a concubine had a stable relationship with a man, while sexual promiscuity and venality typified a prostitute's life. As the Sienese 'public woman' Bettina clearly stated concerning her relations with the noble Marc'Antonio Martinozzi: 'I am not his concubine because I give it to everyone'.[104] But these distinctions tended to blur during the Counter-Reformation.

There were two sides to the fight against prostitution, like the measures taken against the poor. On the one hand, prostitution was condemned and transgressors dealt with harshly, while on the other, preventive action and rehabilitation of such women was at least attempted.[105] In some parts of the Catholic world, particularly in Italy, the fight against poverty and the fight against prostitution were interlinked: the 'conservatories' for 'spinsters' (i.e. institutions whose task it was to conserve the 'virtue' of young unmarried women), the institutions that paid the dowries of destitute girls and the homes for women of 'bad marriages' or the women 'at risk' were mainly motivated by the concern that poverty would induce honest or almost honest women to sacrifice their honour for survival. On the other hand, institutions for 'fallen women' offered to or imposed on those who had already sacrificed it the opportunity of 'salvation'.[106] The risk of falling into or returning to the female community of prostitution was thus dealt with by internment in institutions that were often modelled on convents.[107]

6. Religious life and family life

'I have understood for some time that our sister does not want to become a nun', wrote the Roman noblewoman Geronima Veralli on 5 February 1583 to her brother Giovanni Battista, concerning their younger sister Olimpia, who had been placed in a convent while awaiting a decision on her future, like most teenagers of noble family.[108] For her and many others, the choice was between life in a convent or marriage, between ‘murus aut maritus’ (wall or husband).[109] From this point of view, the situations were different in the Catholic and Protestant worlds following the Reformation. The abolition of celibacy for ministers of the faith and the different use of monastic institutions caused a division in Europe in terms of the incidence of home and family over other forms of cohabitation. The Reformation abolished the lay clergy and religious orders, and allowed ministers to marry. Recent research has discovered that this did not lead to the complete disappearance of convents. 'A number of convents and abbeys transformed themselves into

Protestant institutions,' while some Catholic convents survived in Protestant Germany into the nineteenth century.[110] It is not the case, as was previously argued, that the Reformation completely eliminated the convent as an alternative to family life, almost the only alternative for 'honest' women.[111] We therefore have to qualify the assertion that Protestantism took from women or those who decided their destinies the choice between *murus aut maritus*.[112] Nevertheless, the situation in Protestant countries was very different to that of Catholic Europe.

Indeed, monasteries and convents in Catholic Europe in the early modern era took not inconsiderable percentages of the male and female populations within their walls. For some social groups, such as the nobility, the need to avoid dividing up the family assets condemned a considerable number of their sons to celibacy, thus swelling the ranks of the religious orders.[113] Women only went into the regular clergy and men into both the secular and regular clergy. It has been estimated that between a quarter and a fifth of the sons of the lower nobility and propertied families in Catalonia undertook a career in the Church.[114] Of all the girls born to a group of noble families in Milan, whose fathers were born before 1650, about half took the veil or were forced to do so.[115]

Turning our attention to Protestant Europe, as many as 95 per cent of the daughters of the English aristocracy had the possibility of marriage following the abolition of the convents. Even when English aristocrats grew increasingly concerned about keeping their property intact to pass on to a male heir, the percentage of daughters who passed their fiftieth year without getting married never exceeded 25 per cent. In any case, these were women who mainly lived in family situations and not in institutions.[116] Taking Europe as a whole, the Catholic nobility was more likely than the Protestant one to force their children not to marry.[117]

Strategies for defending Property, differences in the organization of religious institutions and contrasting values all contributed to the greater or lesser dominance of family life. Catholicism and Protestantism attributed a different value to marriage. In spite of its greater recognition of marital life, the Council of Trent reasserted the superiority of virginity over marriage and confirmed the obligation of celibacy for the regular and secular clergy.[118] In the Protestant world, however, marital life was considered the best path to salvation.[119] Hence Catholic priests could not marry and set up a family under any circumstances, while the opposite was true of Protestant ministers. Family and religious life appeared to be more in competition with each other in the Catholic world than in the Protestant one.[120]

Although Catholic parents were invested with educative tasks and religious supervision of their children and anyone else in their charge,[121] it was principally in the Protestant world that the home became a 'genuine church' in which the father (and to a lesser extent, the mother) was, as Luther put it, 'governor, bishop, pope, doctor, priest, preacher, teacher, judge and lord'.[122] Reading the Bible together became one of the central moments in this domestic religion.[123]

This did not mean, however, that for Catholics religious life was completely separate from family life. If we consider the secular clergy, then priests certainly did not marry, but they often lived with their mothers. If not, they often formed a particularly type of 'couple' with their housekeepers, who were not infrequently relations. Of course, it was meant to be an asexual life, but in practice this was certainly not always the case.[124] The cohabitation of priests and housekeepers gave rise to domestic units that are defined as 'no family households' by demographers loyal to the precepts of the Cambridge Group for the History of Population and Social Structure (to whom we will return later).[125]

There is then the question of how far monastic life really was separate from the forms, sentiments and dramas of family life. Of course stricter seclusion was forced on nuns during the Counter-Reformation.[126] Convents also largely ceased to fulfil the role of substitute family that in the past they had had for widows, wives of bad marriages and any other women who for periods of varying length could not or would not live at home with their relations.[127] However, recent studies of convents, conservatories and other institutions for women,[128] have demonstrated the role and the significance of kinship links within such places. There were noble families for whom the choice of a particular convent or religious order was 'one of the many family traditions'.[129] Some convents were the 'fiefdoms' of this or that family. When women entered them, they found their sisters, aunts and cousins. No less than ten women from the Sfondrati family entered the Milanese convent of San Paolo between the mid-sixteenth century and the mid-seventeenth century, and they were related to innumerable other nuns in the convent.[130] In the convent of Santa Giulia in Brescia, where the doors and the walls of the cells occasionally even displayed the family coats of arms, there were as many as nine nuns and novices from the Martinengo family during the period 1650 to 1671.[131]

Moreover, it has been shown that there was a much greater flow of information and items between the inside and outside worlds than had been thought in the past. The same family strategies that sent a daughter to a convent to avoid the dispersion of property often continued to operate within the convents, contributing to the internal logic of such institutions. Far from being completely isolated from the world, convents were not infrequently the scenes of co-operation between cloistered women and family members living on the outside.[132] It therefore only appears paradoxical that, according to Geronima Veralli, her sister Olimpia's decision to get married mainly depended on her perception that her older brother had shown little concern for her. As the head of the family, he had not been sending her enough linen and money. In the light of this situation, the girl feared that if she became a nun, she would be 'abandoned by everyone' and would 'never again receive any tenderness nor be visited by living soul'. Then Geronima reproached her brother, because if he had looked after his sister as he could and should have done, and had made her feel part of the family even when within the convent walls, she would very probably have chosen to take the veil (to the advantage of the family funds, given that they would now have to provide her with a dowry to marry).[133] Thus life in a convent could also be part of family life, but it was not a family life in the home.

7. *Family and* familia

The concept of a family needs to be defined.[134] It is not as obvious as it may appear. According to most dictionaries, the family is the community of parents and children, as well as any other relations who live under the same roof. But it can also be a wider group of people linked by kinship, marriage or affinity, who are not necessarily under the same roof. Equally, it could be all the people who live together, including any domestic servants.[135] Even without venturing into further definitions (do homosexual couples constitute a family?), it is clear that today's concept of family is not clear-cut. We have to establish whether this was also the case in the past, and how our ancestors used the term.

In 1747, Marquis Luigi Albergati laid down in his will that, if his wife Eleonora Bentivoglio, once she became a widow, should decide not to remarry and not to take back her dowry, she was to have 'the free use of the apartments in the *palazzo* that she currently has the benefit of, for her own private use and for the use of her family both in summer and winter'.[136] Who were these family members to whom the marquis alludes? Were they perhaps his and his lady wife's children? Why then did he speak of 'her' family and not 'our' family? Were they perhaps her parents? To discover this and reply to the questions posed at the beginning of the paragraph, we must first analyse the etymology of the English word 'family', the Italian *famiglia*, the French *famille*, the German *Familie*, the Spanish and Portuguese *familia*, the Swedish *familj*, the Dutch *familie*, the Polish *familia*, the Czech *familie*, the Russian *familija*, the Romanian *familie*, the Albanian *familie* and so on.

'Familia' comes from 'famuli'
All these words derive directly or indirectly from the Latin *familia*.[137] Originally *familia* was used to refer to a group of servants (*famuli*) who worked for the same employer. As one of the principal ways by which Romans demonstrated their wealth was the number of slaves they had in their possession, the word also took on the meaning of 'estate'. Its semantic field began to grow in other

directions: it could mean all those who came under the head of the family (*pater-familias*), even if they were slaves or the children of others, or it could mean everyone who descended from the same progenitor and were therefore actually or potentially subject to the same *paterfamilias*, albeit one that was now extinct.[138] It was therefore dependency and not a shared roof that constituted the common theme to the various meanings the term had in Latin.[139] No surprise then that the concept of *paterfamilias* did not correspond exactly to biological fatherhood: the *paterfamilias* was the man who held authority within the domestic arena, and he might not have had any children of his own.[140]

The etymological meaning of the word *familia* returned to the fore in the Middle Ages, when it mainly meant everyone working for the same master.[141] This is the meaning with which the French term *famille*[142] was first recorded in the fourteenth century and again in the sixteenth. The English term 'family', which probably appeared just before the beginning of the fifteenth century, originally meant 'the servants of a house or establishment'.[143] As time passed, less unfamiliar meanings became dominant in both languages, and the meaning of a 'group of servants' declined until it finally disappeared. According to French dictionaries, the last records of *famille* as a group of servants date back to the seventeenth century, and in English the same sense for 'family' disappeared in the following century.[144] In Spanish, the term has retained this meaning to this day, at least according to authoritative dictionaries.[145]

In literary Italian, perhaps the last use of the term as a synonym for 'servants' was by the writer Giovanni Faldella, who lived from 1846 to 1928.[146] Today the expression *famiglia pontificia* still survives to describe the whole staff working for the pope.[147] But in the everyday spoken language, this use of the word appears to have become rare by the beginning of the nineteenth century, although one scholar found a few traces as late as the 1930s.[148] In the eighteenth century, it was still in common use, and this was what Marquis Albergati meant in the above quotation. In his final wishes, he was expressing his desire that his wife should have adequate accommodation for herself and her servants during her widowhood. The frequency of this usage is demonstrated by the fact that it appears with this meaning of 'domestic staff' in 65 per cent of the wills and codicils drawn up by members of his family between the end of the seventeenth and the middle of the eighteenth century.[149]

But even when they were not used in this sense, the various European words deriving from the Latin *familia* often had a different meaning to the current one. 'The family consists of the children, the wife, domestic servants, *famigli* and other servants', wrote Leon Battista Alberti in the fifteenth century.[150] Family means 'children who live or are kept under paternal authority and care, including also the wife, sisters, nephews and nieces of the father, if he has them staying in his house', states the Italian dictionary *Vocabolario degli Accademici della Crusca* in the four editions that appeared between 1612 and 1738.[151] Although these two definitions are different, they both perceive the family as a group of variable size that is dependent on the father, and not as a community that also includes the father.

In other cases, the element of a shared roof comes to the fore while the hierarchical element is diminished, thus creating an image of the family that is closer to our sensibilities, although still not restricted to just parents and children.[152] According to the author of *A Brief Tract on Keeping a Family* (*Breve Trattato del Governo Famigliare*) which appeared in 1609, 'by house we mean the physical house and the gathering of the persons who, living together, constitute and form a family',[153] while according to Giovan Battista Assandri the family is the 'bringing together of companies of people who are naturally united under the same roof, for mutual use and comfort in the necessary and daily chores'.[154]

Common to both past and present is the possibility of using the term 'family' in the sense of lineage. Thus 'family' could be used in more than one sense in the early modern era just as it can be today. But only a few of the possible meanings have remained more or less the same. This was not the only factor that separated the situation in the past from the current one.

The geography of the family

As we have already seen, the term began to be used fairly late in France and England, and for a long time it mainly referred to servants. In English, the first records of it being used for all the people living under one roof or under the same householder date back to the mid-sixteenth century, while its use for parents and children (irrespective of whether they live together or not) appeared a century later.[155] In French the use of *famille* for the people living under the same roof was still considered rare in 1762 by an important dictionary, although in other texts its use with this meaning was considered obvious.[156] It appears that, at least in some areas, it gained currency during the eighteenth century in the definition of bourgeois families as they resulted from a union between two 'private' individuals, and this differed from noble families – referred to by the term *maison* (house) – who lived in society and resulted from complex matrimonial alliances between aristocratic lineages.[157]

The spread of the term in German occurred even later than in English and French. Of course, jurists, philosophers and theologians (particularly those influenced by the concept of 'economy' attributed to Aristotle)[158] had already started by the end of the Middle Ages to consider groups of people living in the same house under the authority of a *paterfamilias* as clearly identifiable units distinct from the larger kinship group, and they had defined them in Latin texts with the term *familia*.[159] But those who wrote in German mainly indicated the same concept with the word *Haus* (house). This was the same term used by the authorities that entrusted the householder with the task of controlling and defending his subordinates. *Haus* was also used to identify specific units for tax purposes (in Italy, France and Spain in the late Middle Ages and the early modern era, they used for this purpose the terms *fuoco*, *feu* and *fuego*, which identified the house with the hearth).[160]

It was only in the seventeenth and eighteenth centuries that the word *Familie* finally started to spread in German, and it came not only from Latin but also as a borrowed word from French.[161] It is less clear whether the arrival of the new word involved the definition of a new concept. According to some scholars, in the societies from which the term was imported it already meant a family under the same roof made up of a married couple and their unmarried and dependent children, while still maintaining other meanings. This kind of family was widespread in western Europe, but was becoming an identifiable unit much more slowly in central Europe. Thus the term was introduced to describe this new entity, but as it was not yet well established, the word began to be used for many meanings.[162] The fact that *Familie* could indicate servants, a wider group subject to the head of the family, the group living under the same roof, or the kinship group, but initially was never used to define the nucleus made up of just the parents and the children, has led other scholars to claim that the spread of the term was not due to profound transformations in the way interpersonal relations were perceived. In their opinion, even when it was used to refer to the group living under the same roof, it was not the catchword for some new reality, but simply a term to replace *Haus*, which came to be used solely for noble families.[163]

What is agreed, however, is that Germans were late in starting to use the term *Familie*. Its penetration appears even later than suggested when you examine the situation in the countryside, in villages like Neckarhausen. It makes a tentative appearance in the community's records around the middle of the eighteenth century, and only really becomes used on any scale from the 1820s. It was used with many meanings, but principally it served to indicate the persons for whose maintenance a man worked and earned his living. In this sense, Salomon Hentzler and Salomon Bauer claimed that they could no longer provide for their families, while Ulrich Bauer emigrated in the hope of being able to feed his.[164]

The words, the relations and the powers
Naturally, women too could support a family, and they were undoubtedly able to do so at Neckarhausen. In this German village precisely at the time when the use of the term *Familie* began to spread, women became involved in agricultural work on a massive scale compared with the past, and were perfectly capable of

providing for themselves and their children if necessary. Even though it often did not refer to a clearly defined entity, when *Familie* was used in similar contexts to those just referred to, it alluded to a group of people who included wives, children and any relations and servants. It is not surprising then that the word was mainly used by the men of the village and by the local authorities in grave discourses about the management of the householder's affairs and his obligations to those subject to his authority. Women used the term in only 8 per cent of the recorded occurrences. They probably did not consider their economic activities to be separate from those of their men, nor would they have seen themselves as being maintained. Instead of *Familie*, which suggested a hierarchical structure in which women were subservient to their husbands, they preferred other terms, such as *hausen*, which suggested a dynamic group based on mutual dependence.[165]

The evidence that comes from Neckarhausen shows with remarkable clarity how the words that everyone uses (perhaps without being aware of it) are a means not only for expressing but also imposing one kind of relationship as 'normal' rather than another. Far from being 'neutral', words play a complete role in conflicts. They are the weapons used in struggles between people with different ideas and interests to gain control of particular areas and to shape the world according to their own interpretations and for their own gain. You only have to think of the campaign fought by the post-Tridentine Church to define as 'prostitutes' women who had previously been considered simply 'concubines' or even almost wives.[166] Labelling them one way or the other was not simply an innocent play with words. Those words were as heavy as stones, and referred to a conflictual situation in which the imposition of a certain 'label' – in this case that of 'prostitutes' for 'concubines' – resulted in a change to the meaning suggested by the word 'concubine'. In the war of words, every battle ends with some term being weakened and another strengthened; some words extend their dominion, others withdraw, some die and still others enter the fray.

The fact that definitions of words are neither altogether crystalline nor set in stone, but rather a confused mass that is constantly on the move, has perhaps been even more clearly demonstrated by the question of the family than by the distinction between marriage and cohabitation. First of all, we discovered that 'family' had more than one meaning during the period we are analysing. Some of those meanings were more or less the same as the ones we have today, but others were very different. We then ascertained that some meanings of the term were prevalent in a particular moment and then declined, while other asserted themselves. Furthermore, the chronology of the spread of the use of the word throughout Europe was not uniform. Lastly, the realities that most closely resemble the current prevailing definitions of a 'family' – namely a group of people linked by kinship, marriage and possibly employment who live together, or parents and their children – were to have different fortunes.

The first reality was defined in various ways: 'household', *casa, Haus, maison*, 'hearth', *fuoco, feu, ménage*, and so on,[167] but 'family' and its equivalents in other languages were also introduced at a certain stage.

For a long time the second reality was not defined at all, such was the difficulty in disentangling it from the family in the sense of kinship and from the family in the sense of a household that included the servants. For a long time, the etymological meaning of family as a group of servants extended its tentacles like an octopus to wives and children in the name of the dependency they shared with the servants, thus impeding unity between spouses or between parents and children. So 'family' often meant the wife, children and servants as a group distinct from the father, who was head of this group without being part of it. This hierarchical interpretation was also present in those cases in which wives and children managed to separate themselves from the domestic staff (as in the definition provided by the *Vocabolario della Crusca*). The existence of this or other interpretations naturally meant that there were people who supported it and considered it 'normal' and the right way to deal with interpersonal relations. Learned jurists explained, for instance, that the position within a family was one of the elements, together with nationality and whether one was free or a slave, that determined the status that people enjoy and their legal powers.[168]

The spread of the word 'family' and support for the idea that a hierarchically structured domestic community made up of a father, a mother, children and servants represented a fundamental building block in society received support from ideas influenced by Aristotelian thought,[169] and actual state policies that believed the subordination of the family to the father guaranteed the subordination of subjects to their sovereign or in any case attributed to the *paterfamilias* extensive powers over his wife, children and servants.[170] Support also came from religious directives that invested the householder with the tasks of supervising the moral and religious life of all those under his roof.[171] Such directives existed in the Catholic countries, but were even more significant in Protestant ones, where there was no longer the presence of the confessor and spiritual father to advise and instruct from outside the family. Laws and customs thus gave the father powers to reform those subject to him and they were required to obey him. They allowed him to control the lives of his children, they prevented children living with their father from selling, buying or making a will without his authorization, even if they were adults, and they laid down that wives were not free to use their own property as they wished, as we shall see more fully in the next chapter.[172]

In other words, the word 'family' was intentionally loaded with servile connotations for the entire period under examination, when referring to groups of varying sizes that were dependent on the father. It implied highly hierarchical relations even when (I would venture only very occasionally) it included the father himself. Understandably, there were those who preferred this term and those who preferred to use others.

Of course, in practice relations did not always follow rigid hierarchies. Emotions, a son's influence over his father, a wife's over her husband or the power that richer wives occasionally had over their spouses could mitigate against the inequalities created by custom, the law and religion. 'I went to refer this proposal to my wife', wrote the Parisian glass-maker Ménétra concerning a business proposition he had received, in his remarkable *Journal* written from 1764 to 1803. 'She absolutely wouldn't hear of it. It was pointless trying to explain to her that there was no need of any advance and I was not even being asked for a guarantor. I couldn't get anywhere and I clearly realized that I was not the only head of the household. . . . This was the cause of not a little affliction. . . . I was no longer the boss; my wife got involved in everything. To have a little peace, I let the matter rest'. Here was a wife who – at least if we are to believe her husband's grievances – had reversed the roles through her strength of character and, quite probably, her purse. She had, in fact, advanced the 300 francs for Ménétra to set up his workshop.[173]

The inequalities established by custom and law represented the framework in which everyone had to act, be they father, wife, child or servant. It was therefore very different to the situation in which equality (between husband and wife or brother and sister) is established as the general rule and any hierarchies arise from the aggression, weakness of character or wealth of one of the family members. From the eighteenth century it became increasingly common for people to base family relationships at least partly on a more egalitarian basis. It became increasingly common to criticize certain aspects of the family institution, which has, however, retained hierarchical features until recently (and in part still does).[174] But clearly cultural, economic, demographic and political factors all came together to produce the family predominantly based on the parent–child relationship that we know today.[175]

8. Houses with families

These changes, whose features we will return to later in the book, are in part linked to changes in the functions and the concept of the house itself. One writer has argued that the birth of the family, as we know it today, presupposed a notion of the house that has been reduced to its walls, roof, doors and windows, thus losing the idea of a domestic community invested with the thousands of tasks and responsibilities we referred to earlier.[176] It is an interesting observation. Of course, in Italian people still talk of *casa Savoia* (the 'House of Savoy'). The term is not restricted to the aristocracy, as when responding to a phone call people say *casa Rossi*, meaning 'this is the house of the Rossi family'. We are reminded of previous usages of the word in other languages too. *Grüße von Haus zu Haus* ('greeting from house to house') is an expression used in Austria.[177] The terms *household* and *Haushalt* are of course still used in English and German.[178] Nevertheless, the change has been profound.

While part of the population was homeless or had to make do with extremely unreliable forms of accommodation, there were also those who linked their whole identity to their house. One might say there were houses that had a family, rather than the other way around. Noble families often took their name from their estates and castles. In the Pyrenees, houses had names that identified and were applied to those who lived in them, and these names were handed down from one generation to another. In some areas, if the heir to a house was a woman and her husband moved into the house at the time of marriage, then people gave him the name of his wife's house. Children inherited the patronymic from their father and the name of the house from the mother, to the point that it was even used in contracts.[179] In such cases in Westphalia, the husband quite simply took on the wife's surname, and it was generally the same as the name of the house.[180] Dependency on the house was very marked in the whole of central Europe. Every farm (*Hof*) had a name that was transferred to the family that lived on it. When the family moved, people changed their name and not the house. In some areas, surnames only became fixed in the nineteenth century, about three or four hundred years later than in England. This innovation satisfied the requirements of the state bureaucracy, but not the peasantry. For the those who were used to the old system, the introduction of house numbers which further undermined the houses' 'identity', was a profound change and life at home took on a different flavour.[181]

We started by asking ourselves whether home and family could be considered interchangeable concepts, and we have discovered a considerable variety of meanings for both 'house' and 'family', and equally a considerable number of interrelations between the two, whether used with the current meanings or with those of the past.

On the one hand, the central importance of the notion of 'house' in the perceptions and social organization of the early modern era and the frequent tendency to superimpose the concept of 'family' onto that of 'house' justify our initial image of opening the door to a house in order to examine the material life of a family in the past. But on the other hand, during this first stretch of our journey into the past, we have discovered a series of situations in which 'house' and 'family' do not coincide with each other. It would be best then to bring the various threads of this initial survey together.

9. Transient distinctions

We have wandered across Europe in the early modern era in search of situations that would allow us to assess the extent to which the house and the family coincided with each other and to understand the extent of 'home life', in order to mark out the boundaries within which to carry out a more detailed analysis in the following pages. We have primarily discovered that the terms 'house' and 'family' do not coincide. Of course there were many people without a roof who also had no family, but there were also entire families that were homeless.

Our examination of Gypsies, Sámi, shepherds and fishermen has shown us how the concept of a house was a flexible one. In the early modern era, not all houses had roofs, doors and windows. As we will see later, there were many much less substantial houses. They did not always stay in the same place: there were some people who carried their house and sometimes even their family around with them. There were also those who had several houses in order to deal with a life that was constantly on the move. The distinction between those who had a house and those who did not was not always that clear.

This was partly due to the fact that part of the population lived in conditions of extreme insecurity, often moving house and for certain periods not having one at all. Although there were entire families without a roof, insecure housing and insecure families were not unrelated. We have seen that there was a great number of women amongst the poor living in broken homes. This partly depended on the fact that women were mainly expected to live in a family as daughters or wives. Together with other factors, this idea that their destiny lay in the family led to their exclusion from many trades and to poor pay in those they had access to. Once they lost a family (and more particularly an adult male) they quickly became destitute, unless they were very rich.[182]

While the loss of one's family could result in poverty (particularly for women, old people and children, but not only for them), a family's poverty could impede its formation. Before permission to marry would be granted, in various parts of Europe it was necessary to demonstrate that you had the means to maintain any children that might be born from the union.

As we shall see more fully in the next chapter on setting up home, it was by no means a simple or straightforward affair. The difficulty in setting up home was one of the various factors that contributed to explaining the presence of forms of cohabitation of varying degrees of stability alongside families made up of married couples. Although the law only defended the rights of wives and children in legitimate relationships, during the early part of the period under examination, the distinction between marriage and cohabitation was still fairly confused and only became clearer as time went on.

Particularly in Catholic areas, this meant distinguishing between wives and concubines. During the Counter-Reformation, the increased concern over female morality translated into the creation of several types of institution that aimed at saving 'fallen' women, and above all preventing young girls from ending up in prostitution. More generally, the attempt to resolve the problem of poverty was leading in the whole of Europe to the creation of various kinds of welfare institution, sometimes involving internment.

There was therefore an increase in the types of institution in which a non-family community life took place. To some extent, these institutions replaced the family, given that not infrequently those who ended up in them were poor precisely because some disaster had befallen their family history and the chances of recreating a family situation were slight without some form of assistance.

Even the women who filled the convents and the men who went into the priesthood often did so because they were forced by circumstance. Usually in their case the circumstances involved wealth rather than poverty, as it was in order to avoid the dispersion of property that wealthy families only allowed one of their sons and one of their daughters to marry. They would take most of the family's resources, and the others would be obliged to follow a religious career. In this sense, the Protestant policy of suppressing the monasteries and convents (although not all), and the abolition of the priesthood, meant that the house and family model had fewer alternatives in the Protestant world than in the Catholic one.

Further, it should be added that the possibility of going into the army had been opened up to men in the whole of Europe. Indeed a military career, next to the religious one, became one of the typical outlets for sons of noble families who had been excluded from the possibility of inheriting a sufficient sum of money to support a family at a level fitting to their rank in society. With the development of modern armies, military life was increasingly becoming an alternative to family life. As late as the eighteenth century, however, there were still women who took their children and followed their husbands to their barracks, where they lodged as best they could amongst the other soldiers. Some worked as sutlers or in other trades, but amongst so much promiscuity, others ended up as the regimental prostitutes.[183]

The forms of non-family community life were therefore not the same for men and women. For men, there were various educational institutions. If girls were not educated at home, they were often sent to a convent. Apart from the traditional forms of education for boys such as university life, seminaries were created for training priests in Catholic countries, and colleges for boys of good families who were now much less likely to be educated through domestic service as pages for some aristocratic house.[184]

Prisons were increasingly used during the early modern era for long periods of incarceration and therefore separation from the family.[185] Together with monasteries and other establishments, there were many buildings or, if you like, houses whose residents did not constitute families.

This does not mean that all these institutions were hermetically sealed off from family relations. We have seen in the case of convents that this was not necessarily so. Together with many other factors (to which we will return later), this demonstrates that belonging to the same family did not always mean living under the same roof. The family could extend beyond the walls of its house.[186] But the interrelation between house and family, and the meanings of the words themselves, changed according to the context. Seized by a kind of destructive frenzy, in this chapter we have demolished stereotypes and certainties. At the end of this deconstructive operation, we find before us a somewhat nebulous scene. We should therefore move on to the more constructive stage.

II

Home and Family: Bringing Things Together or Setting up Home

1. Getting married

Shouts and uproar in the street. A crowd of people surround a cart that is conveying the bride's possessions to the house where the married couple will live. Where would we encounter such a scene? We could be in Renaissance Florence, nineteenth-century Soule Valley or Sardinia. The transport of the bride's property to the newly-weds' living quarters was a more or less public and ritualized event and an important part of the wedding ceremony in most of Europe (Figs. 6–7).[1]

If we were to join the wedding party and follow the cart, would we be directed towards a new and separate home? Not necessarily. Marriage did not automatically mean the formation of an independent family and a new unit of cohabitation. In other words, getting married did not always mean setting up home on one's own. In Carinthia, there were farm-servants who did not even live together after the wedding.[2] In Switzerland, there were cases of men who, having been forced to marry women with whom they had had sexual relations on the basis of a promise of marriage, refused to cohabit with their wives.[3] Conversely, the formation of a new domestic grouping did not necessarily require a wedding. There were regions and social groups where all men who married brought their wives to the parental home, thus creating families made up of various couples and their children (what scholars of family structures call 'multiple families'). Examples were Russian serfs and the peasant families of central Italy that worked the sharecropping system called *mezzadria*. Communities in Auvergne, Bauges, Bourbonnais, Nivernais and Morvan even went so far as to create families of up to fifty people, and the great Balkan families called *zadruga* could reach around eighty members (Figs. 11–12).[4] However, the domestic grouping cannot grow endlessly. There comes a point when it has to be divided and some of its members transfered to another house, thus creating a new family without the immediate involvement of a wedding.[5]

Does this mean that newly-weds in the early modern era never went off to live on their own? If this had been the case, the title of this chapter would have been generally misleading. However, in England, Iceland, Denmark, Norway, northern France, Holland, some parts of Germany, the south and south-east of the Iberian peninsula, southern Italy and Sardinia, the great majority of couples set up home on their own after marriage. Their families were made up of parents, children and any domestic servants. In academic terminology, they followed the 'neolocal' residence pattern and formed 'nuclear (or simple) family households'. In northern Spain and Portugal, the Pyrenees, southern France, central Italy, parts of northern Italy, the Alps, Austria, a large part of Germany, Sweden, Finland, eastern Europe and the Balkans, it was common for a newly-married couple to go and live with the bridegroom's family ('virilocal' residence). Although there were considerable differences from one area to another and from one period to another, this meant that these regions had a greater number of 'complex family households'. Such families either have more than one couple with children ('multiple family households') or have one or more relations living with the couple and their children ('extended family households').[6]

Each area had very much it own customs and practices. The differences did not, however, derive solely from local traditions. The type of settlement, the demographic trend, the type of socio-economic organization in the area, the law and, in rural areas, the decisions made by landowners all played an important part in differentiating one area from another and in the same area between one period and another and between social groups. The kinds of economic activity families were engaged in and their income levels were also significant. So if, instead of looking at Europe from afar, we were to zoom in like astronauts on re-entry in a spacecraft, we would suddenly find that apparently uniform areas were teeming with a thousand differences.

Studies into cities in regions in which complex families were widespread, like Lyons, Mâcon, Oporto and various others in northern and central Italy, have shown that in the city there were more nuclear families than in the surrounding countryside. Very probably this can be explained by features of urban life, such as the lack of room, the shortage of housing, the presence of immigrants without family, a higher mortality rate than in the country, and other economic and cultural factors. Not everyone lived in the same way: artisans and the middle to lower ranks of society in particular lived in nuclear families, while nobles and the propertied classes had a more marked tendency to live in complex families. This latter tendency was to be found in towns situated in areas where the nuclear family was also prevalent in the countryside, as in the case of Turi, a town in Apulia.[7]

Differences between social groups were also noticeable in the country. In rural Galicia in the mid-eighteenth century, for example, noble families and *hidálgos* were complex in 30.5 per cent of cases, while in other social groups the percentage was much lower (fluctuating between 10 and 25.5 per cent). But differences, and occasionally very marked ones, could be encountered just amongst those who worked the fields. Landless farm servants and more generally agricultural workers who did not have their own holdings to work living as far apart as northern Portugal, many Italian regions, Hungary, the German village of Belm or the Spanish community of Melina, near Valencia were all more likely to live in nuclear families than if they were working their own holding either as a tenant or an owner.[8] Unsurprisingly, then, the high number of farm labourers in the rural population is considered to be one of the reasons for the prevalence of nuclear families in southern Italy and many parts of the Iberian Peninsula.[9] Nor should it be any surprise that peasants with smallholdings often lived in complex families. They needed more hands to help them work the land, and therefore having a large family was a good solution, although not necessarily the only one. When they were short of hands, they could take on labourers or farm servants, who were a more flexible solution than relations (and the preferred one in much of north-western Europe).[10] As we shall see later, there were other reasons that could favour the presence of complex families amongst peasants working a farm.

Hence, there were couples who went off to live on their own, men who took their brides back to their own house, and husbands who transferred to their wives' houses on getting married, although the latter case was undoubtedly the least common and not so much linked to local customs as to particular demographic and social conditions. 'I lost the most wonderful opportunity in the world', said Ménétra in relation to a 'delightful' widow with a flourishing business which he had worked for. He had a relationship with the woman but being a restless *tombeur de femmes*, he left her to enjoy a little bit longer his freedom without a wife to cramp his style. However, young artisans who had completed their apprenticeships were finding it increasingly difficult in the early modern era to open their own workshops, and one of the best solutions was to marry the widow of a master artisan and set up in his house.[11]

The same was true in the countryside for young men without property who managed to marry girls who, not having any brothers, were to inherit a farm (the absence of male heirs apparently affected 20 per cent of families, while the actual percentage of heiresses was often about 30 per cent).[12] While such a match could be financially advantageous for the bridegroom,[13] in many communities or at least in the French countryside, he was exposed to being called disparaging nicknames and suffering pranks of varying cruelty when it came to the wedding. Significantly, such nicknames were not used in Brittany or Bas-Léonnais, where 'uxorilocal' marriages (i.e. ones where the husband went to live in the wife's house) were frequent.[14] Although each was geographically small, there were areas where such marriages were widespread, such as Apulia, Alto Minho (Portugal) and the small islands in the Aegean Sea.[15]

In France and possibly elsewhere, the husband occasionally brought the trousseau himself in this type of marriage (*mariage en gendre*), and was transported in a cart to the bride's house. This reversal of roles risked undermining the traditional hierarchy between men and women, and it appears that where they were not common, they were subject to tension and conflict.[16]

2. Trousseaus, bottom drawers and 'complete beds'

We then arrive at the question of what the brides brought with them in their carts to the new home where the couple were to live. Upper-class women in Renaissance Florence had chests, which were replaced with large baskets called *zane* after 1450. These contained devotional works, shirts 'produced in the custom of the newly-wed woman', handkerchiefs, scarves 'for the head', 'for the shoulder' and 'for the neck', pinafores, socks, clogs, slippers, occasionally sheets for childbirth, swaddling, clothes for home and for feast days, belts, ornaments, combs, mirror, perfumes, ribbons, sewing equipment, distaff and spindles.[17]

Spindles and distaffs were also to be found in the trousseaus of women in the middle and lower classes. In Florence and elsewhere, these much more modest trousseaus, unlike those for women of the upper class, did not restrict themselves to items that concerned the bride's body and soul or her *toilette* and pastimes. Of course, they too included a chest (which towards the end of the early modern era was increasingly replaced by a wardrobe). However, it contained linen for the entire family, sheets and various kinds of cloths. Trousseaus could also contain a few kitchen utensils, tools and foodstuffs.

Unlike the customs of the daughters of affluent Florentine families in the Renaissance and probably most of the European aristocracy in the following centuries,[18] there was one item taken to the marital home in most parts of Europe in the early modern era that was of particular importance given that a new couple was being created with the wedding – and that was a bed.[19]

It took on a special importance in relation to the bride's property. In sixteenth-century Augsburg, families that were too poor to give their daughters a real dowry, attempted at least to give them a bed. The city's dowry fund, which had been established to help the poorer citizens to marry, paid out sums of 10 florins, an amount that at the time could buy a good quality bed and have some change left over.[20] Similarly a bed was often the most precious item in a peasant woman's dowry in the countryside around Pisa, where however it was only in the eighteenth century that beds became a regular feature in it. In the seventeenth century, there were brides who did not provide one; we do not know whether the husbands provided one, as with the Florentine elite, but it is more likely that these were simply too poor to buy one at all. As we shall see, there were still people in the early modern era who could not afford the pleasure of sleeping on a bed.[21] When we assess the value of these beds that brides brought to their marriages, it should be remembered that they were generally equipped with all the accessories and ready for use. In some Italian regions, they were referred to as *letti compìti* (complete beds), which meant complete with mattress, sheets, pillows and blankets.

The value and significance of a bed to marital life was not only practical but also symbolic. In many areas during the Middle Ages, the priest, accompanied by the wedding guests' bawdy songs, went to the house of the bride and bridegroom to bless the nuptial bed to propitiate the couple's fertility and to keep away evil and malign spirits.[22]

Sometimes handed down from mother to daughter in matrilineal fashion, beds were a genuinely female territory. The first night of the wedding, entering the bed was dangerous particularly for the man, as he had to be capable of 'taking possession' of his wife in the carnal sense. From 1434 in Florence, the consummation of the marriage was even a condition for payment of the dowry or at least those dowries deposited in the dowry bank (*Monte delle doti*).[23] In sixteenth-century Augsburg, it was necessary for husband and wife to form a hereditary bond. Impotence was grounds for the annulment of a marriage for both the Protestant and Catholic Churches.[24]

With such attitudes, it was not surprising that the elimination of these superstitions proved difficult both for the Protestants who prohibited them and for the Catholics who allowed them to continue but at the same time attempted to make them the vehicle of expressing the religious concept of marriage. Following the Council of Trent, the Catholic Church tried to impose a version of the rite that was imbued with entirely different values, which became obligatory in France: these values were the sanctity of marriage and the discipline of married life. However, the bed continued to be associated with particular connotations that made it the symbol of the couple's whole life, and the clergy found it far from easy to erase the underlying popular beliefs (Fig. 10).[25]

However central the importance of the bed in the married couple's life and in the wife's dowry, the dowry was not limited to this important 'piece of furniture' and some domestic items. Apart from 'a bed provided with feather pillows, linen and woollen sheets, a bedcover, a chest with lock and two or three items of clothing', girls in the region between Garonne and Ariège in the sixteenth century received a sum of money of between 50 and 150 livres and occasionally a small piece of land.[26] When the peasant woman Catharina Haiß, who we will also be meeting again later, married Matheis Größer in 1671, her parents gave her a few meadows, a field, a cow, a chest, a bed and some linen. Matheis also received fields and meadows from his family. Apart from that, he contributed to the family's material wealth with a horse and cart. In this manner, the couple had the bare essentials: a bed and chest as furniture, a cow in the barn to provide milk daily, a horse and cart for agricultural tasks and fields to cultivate.

In the light of these cases, like so many others, there can be no doubt that most of the wife's contribution concerned the domestic sphere.[27] In Apulia and some parts of Sicily and England, the bride not only provided furnishings but also contributed to the house where the new couple were going to live.[28] However, to claim that the wife's contribution was limited to the strictly domestic would be misleading. Although women had less access to land ownership than men, there was no shortage of peasant women who contributed fields and meadows to the family economy. This was particularly true of arable land in the Piedmontese community of Felizzano, where it circulated primarily through dowries, while the market was the principal means for exchanging meadows, woodland and houses.[29] In Apulia and Sicily, where the property and the work of the peasantry were organized in completely different ways, women offered their husbands, who were generally landless labourers, not only the opportunity of a house but also a small plot, which in itself was often not sufficient to support the family but was generally indispensable for its survival.

In sixteenth-century Lucca and Florence, the dowry for weavers' daughters included, along with the trousseau and money, the loom that the new family needed to earn its living. In cities, it was not at all uncommon for women like Ménétra's wife to make it possible for the husband to set up shop with the financial side of their dowries. This is not to mention noble families for whom dowries could reach staggering sums and contribute to saving fortunes facing ruin. An extreme case of this typical strategy, was the marriage between the noble from Bologna Carlo Filippo Aldrovandi Marescotti, heir to an illustrious but heavily indebted family, and the beautiful Teresa Gnudi. In 1784, Aldrovandi agreed to marry the girl, who came from a much lower social rank, because her father, the banker Antonio, intended to consolidate his recent ennoblement through this marriage, and in order to do so, he undertook to settle his future son-in-law's debts and pay a substantial dowry of 60,000 lire for his daughter.[30]

This leads us to the important question of who paid the dowries, and who ultimately had to provide the 'material basis' for the new couple. We have looked in the chests brides brought to the marital home and we have provided a brief description of their contribution and that of the grooms. But where did these shirts, money, beds, fields, cows, looms and other items come from? There is the matter of whether these were provided by the newly-weds themselves or by others, such as their family, kinship group, friends or welfare institutions. It is by now easily understood that the situation was complex and changed according to the social, economic, legal and religious context. However, we will attempt to categorize the differences in accordance with the principal variables.

3. The rich and the poor

The first variable to be considered is undoubtedly that of the degree of wealth. Generally speaking, the poorer the couple the less they could take from the family resources when they got married. In Sardinia, a traveller noted in the eighteenth century, 'custom has established that there is no marriage until the man has been provided with oxen and various tools required for agriculture and the woman has been provided with a bed, other furniture and household utensils. As the poor have no one to assist them, they have no choice but to acquire the necessary capital to provide the previously mentioned items by offering their labour in service for wages'. But it took years to accumulate the necessary capital, partly because it was the tradition that the newly-weds would go and live on their own, and it was the husband's task to build or buy the house and the wife's to furnish it. For these reasons, the traveller observed that the age of marriage was rather high in Sardinia.[31] This was true of women as well as men, as the local traditions required them to obtain their dowries by themselves.[32]

The situation was similar north-western Europe and for the middle and lower orders in cities pretty much everywhere. This was partly due to the fact that the tendency for artisans to pass down their workshops from father to son was probably not as marked as previously thought, and this in turn was partly due to the implications of second marriages by the widows of master artisans.[33] To get married you had to scrape together enough money to set up home on your own, and to do that, you had to work hard and be patient. With a bit of luck, a man could hope to marry around age 27–28 and a women around 24–25.[34] But it was not unusual to have to wait longer, nor did everyone succeed in their intent. There were those who never managed to save the absolute minimum required and therefore remained unmarried all their lives. In north-western Europe, the percentage of those who never married was rather high, although it varied according to the social group, the area and the period.[35] In England from the mid-sixteenth to the mid-nineteenth century, the figure fluctuated between 4 and 24 per cent. Significantly it was lower when wages were higher, while it grew when they were lower. Real-wage trends also influenced age at first marriage. In other words, when people earned less, the number of those who could not manage to marry increased. In the eighteenth century there was a shift to earlier and more universal marriage, while in other parts of Europe people were generally getting married less often and later.[36]

Before getting married many young people would find employment as domestic servants, agricultural labourers or assistant artisans in the hope of being able to run a workshop, a farm or some other business and start a family, not being able to settle down meant a life without marriage and never escaping from the status of servant.[37] As we saw in the previous chapter, that condition was occasionally an obstacle to marriage in itself. There were areas in which attempts were made to block off the route to marriage to all those who did not have the means to support a family.[38] Not being able to start a family because of poverty did not therefore solely depend on an individual assessment of one's own abilities to manage: in some contexts, the ability to marry was subject to specific forms of control by the authorities. Not infrequently such forms of control, as in the case of Augsburg, distinguished between locals and immigrants, and offered the former some kind of assistance, occasionally with the dowry.

For the very poor who lived in areas where there were legal obstacles to marriage between poor people, and for those who managed to get round the laws where they existed, the good thing about poverty was that it allowed them to choose their partner independently, although poverty does not tend to make people attractive to members of the other sex. The same was true of those who used their own resources to scrape together the necessary assets to get married, whether or not they lived in areas where this was common practice.

In his autobiography, the French writer Nicolas Restif de la Bretonne, son of a rich peasant, tells how he revealed to a friend his love for a peasant girl from a poor peasant family, and his companion brutally brought him back to earth by reminding him that his parents would never allow such a marriage. 'I am happy to be the son of Blaise Guerreau rather than the son of *Monsieur* Réti, as I am master of my own decisions. You are *Monsieur* Nicolas and you will pay for your high rank', his friend declared rather sententiously. 'Those with greater standing, have more to suffer.'[39]

In terms of the transference of property, marriage in rich families involved not only the bride and groom as individuals, but also their families. In general, this involvement increased as you went up the social scale, just as the part of material wealth require to set up the new couple that derived from family resources increased in relation to that provided by individual work.[40] In such cases there was little room for taking into account individual choices and preferences. As has already been suggested, the interests and strategic alliances of a family group often took precedence over the feelings of the young men and women involved, who not only did not have a choice over whether they married or followed a life of celibacy in the Church, but were also parcelled off with partners of their parents' choice.

4. The transfer of property

As has probably already been understood, the possibility of using the family resources did not only depend on whether you came from a rich or poor family. In cases in which the family of provenance had some property, this opportunity also depended on the manner in which property was handed down to the children. If it passed on to the next generation on the death of the parents, anyone who wanted to start a family had to either find their own resources or resign themselves to waiting for the parents to die. The situation was different where some form of assistance was expected of the parents when the children left home or married, even if it was only allowing them to live in the parental home after the marriage.[41] In particular geographical and social contexts, the transfer of property was governed by specific rules and customs, although behaviour patterns were often fairly flexible and actual practices diverged from expected customs and the law.[42] Moreover, the law was not infrequently confused by the juridical pluralism that typified much of Europe the early modern era.[43]

Assistance or managing on your own

Young Sardinian women, for example, were not inevitably poorer than their cousins in Sicily and southern Italy, who like them usually went to live with their husbands in a separate home once they were married. If their parents had something to leave them, they did so when they died. As we have seen, they had to manage the business of getting a dowry on their own. They therefore married later, rarely before the age of 25. Sicilian and southern Italian women, on the other hand, usually received dowries from their parents and married very young: between the ages of 15 and 20, or even 13 and 14, as claimed by an English traveller of the eighteenth century.[44] It will be no surprise then that servant women (and men) were much more numerous in Sardinia than in southern Italy and Sicily.[45]

In areas where newly married young men simply took their wives home to their parents' houses without necessarily becoming heads of their own families, the problem of scraping money together in expectation of marriage did not exist or at least was not so dramatic as in the case of those who had to provide for themselves or wait for an inheritance. According to some scholars, this condition favoured a low age at marriage for both men and women, and led to a small number of servants and people likely to remain unmarried all their lives, and to a large number of complex families. Although data are difficult to come by and regional differences were great, this situation apparently existed to the east of an imaginary line between Trieste and St. Petersburg, if exceptions are made for residence rules and family forms (but not for the age at marriage) of parts of Greece and Hungary, Romania and Bulgaria. West of this line there were some areas where the marital age was low (eastern Finland, Ireland, the southern part of the Iberian Peninsula, Sicily and some parts of southern Italy). However, it was generally high, while family forms and residence patterns were highly differentiated. In fact it is impossible to identify an almost mathematical relationship between post-marital domestic customs, the number of servants and unmarried people, the average age at first marriage, and whether or not there are nuclear or complex families, as some scholars suggested a few years ago. These are not the only factors that have to be taken into account: there are many variables and the possible interactions are innumerable.[46]

Thus the *mezzadri* or sharecroppers in Tuscany in the late Middle Ages and the sixteenth century, who used to bring their wives home to the parental home after the wedding, nearly all married and they did so rather young. In many ways, their behaviour was fairly similar to that found in eastern Europe. When the population began to grow, farmland began to get scarce, and for many there was the danger of becoming penniless labourers continually in search of work that was not always available. The *mezzadri* started to restrict access to marriage, partly by their own initiative and partly because of pressure from landowners who were attempting to optimize their use of holdings by controlling the marriage rate amongst the peasantry. Perhaps from around the last few decades of the seventeenth century, the age of marriage started to increase, as did the percentage of those who never married at all. If there were many adults (particularly men) and few children on a farm, the ratio between hands to work the land and mouths to feed improved. In the long term, this also partially kept down the population increase in the future generations that would have to live on the same farms. At the same time, at least in the Prato area, there was an increase in the number of women who moved from the country to the cities and towns to work as servants, basket-workers and in other sectors, so the ratio between men and women in *mezzadro* families became profoundly imbalanced. As time went on, the shortage of land led to the expulsion of part of the population and the restriction of marriage opportunities and the possibility of having children for those who stayed behind. Conversely, in the Russian village of Mishino, like many others in eastern Europe, the fact that the village community redistributed land regularly between families on the basis of their size meant that the problem that so affected the lives of the Tuscan *mezzadri* was practically non-existent. Everyone married and everyone married young.[47]

Just and unjust shares

As they did not own their own land, the *mezzadri* did have the possibility of transferring to another farm when the size of the one previously worked proved to small.[48] This option was not open to peasants who owned their own land or those who had the right to pass on their tenancy to their sons. The problem of finding the right balance between available land and the composition of the family was for them a much more serious one. As dividing the land between all the sons would have led to each one being given a plot that would have been insufficient to maintain a family, many peasants chose just one to take over the running of the farm. His brothers were then supposed to continue living with him in the parental house without marrying and in a more or less servile position or to go with the pay-off for their inheritance.

As a result of the question of creating the material basis to establish a new couple, it is now clear that the position of the preferred son who took over the house and the land was very different to that of his brothers who had to choose between staying unmarried in the family home or leaving if they wanted to marry. But it would be simplistic to distinguish solely between the privileged and the excluded: the manner, the timing and the severity with which one lot were preferred and the other rejected had important repercussions in everybody's life, as can be shown by the cases of Jean Chailan and Johann Pichler.

Jean was the eldest son of a peasant with a small property in Castelot-de-la-Robine, a village in Upper Provence. On 22 September 1687 he married Catherine Béraud, a girl from a town not far from there. Catherine went to live with her husband's family, as was expected by local custom and in accordance with the agreements between Jean and his father, who had chosen him to inherit the farm. On the basis of these agreements, Jean was to have lived together with Catherine under the authority of his father. On the latter's death, he was to become head of the family, but up to that moment he was to be completely subservient to his father economically, socially and legally, just as though he were still a child. Without his authorization he was not able to buy, sell, make a will or carry out any other transaction. If this settlement did not work out, then Jean was free to go: he would lose all his rights to the inheritance, but would have received a legacy of 300 livres, which was normal in those parts when sons who had been excluded from inheritance of the farm preferred to leave with a little money in their pockets rather than remain in their father's house in a state of total subservience and without the hope of ever being a householder themselves. Sons who left in this manner were generally emancipated with a ceremony of Roman origin: the father would say 'go, my son, I make you a free man', with his open hands above the son who was kneeling bareheaded in front of him in the presence of two representatives of the local authorities.[49]

We now move from late seventeenth-century upper Provence with its stone houses and only slightly inclined tiled roofs, and shift forward in time by almost a century to Lower Austria in the Waldviertel, on the border between Bohemia and Moravia. This is where Johann Pichler lived. In 1784, at the time of his marriage, he and his wife Gertraud entered into a contract with his parents, Joseph and Anna Maria: the old people sold them the house and the fields for 100 florins. They then deducted 20 florins from this sum, as their wedding gift to their son. The remaining 80 had to be paid in four instalments on 29 September of each year. The parents reserved the right to live for the rest of their lives in a room in the house (*Stübl*) free of charge and to have the use of part of a meadow and a vegetable garden to grow cabbage and potatoes. Johann was also required to provide them every year with 7 bushels of corn, 32 bales of hay and 2 stacks of firewood.[50]

Let us now consider the similarities and differences of these two cases. Both in Upper Provence and in Waldviertel (as in a large part of Austria), the farm, house and fields were passed on undivided to a single heir, although in Austria the central nucleus of the farm was indivisible by law,[51] while in Upper Provence properties had to be equally divided amongst the sons if the father left no instructions.[52] There is, however, a remarkable difference between these two Johns: Jean and Johann! After his marriage, Jean had to remain obedient and respectful for a long time if he really wanted to become head of the family in the house of his birth. Johann, on the other hand, took on the position of authority from the moment he married.

Contracts of the kind agreed in the Pichler home, by which the parents transferred the farm to the son while guaranteeing themselves a kind of pension, were very common in central and northern Europe.[53] Of course, not all parents with a farm settled their affairs with their sons in this manner, but those who did allowed the chosen heir to have access to property and therefore have a solid base for starting a family, without having to wait to inherit it on their death.

Conflicts obviously arose between impatient sons and parents who did not want to let go of the reins of power: 'father, when will you give me the farm, father, when will you give it away? My girl is growing by the day and no longer wants to be on her own', are the words to a song sung in Waldviertel at the beginning of the twentieth century, but it probably expressed centuries-old disputes.[54] The tension must have been slightly lessened by the fact that the customs of Lower Austria required that the heir to the farm should be the last-born son, the one most likely to reach marriageable age when the parents were already old.[55] However, poor Matthias Küpfel ended up marrying at the age of 40 because for a long time his father did not want 'to retire'.[56] He certainly was not the only one: it must have been a bitter experience for the old men to retire, as we are reminded by many proverbs or the habit in several parts of Austria of using the term *ableben*, 'to die', to mean 'retirement'.[57] Only a small part of most farms actually ended up being passed down to the last-born son (or the first-born in areas where primogeniture was the custom). Even when there were sons, a not inconsiderable percentage ended up for one reason or another in the hands of people who occasionally were not even relations.[58]

In Upper Provence, tension between father and son as occurred in Austria was not even on the cards. As the father remained the householder, the chosen heir did not have to wait forever before marrying. But this did not mean that everything was sweetness and light. Men in the prime of life did not always passively accept that they should be obedient lap dogs to failing patriarchs consumed by old age. On the whole, a breakdown in the relationship was relatively rare. But less than two years after getting married, Jean preferred to take his 300 livres and fend for himself. His father then made a similar agreement with his second-born, Joseph. Upper Provence was an area of primogeniture, but life's many unforeseen events meant that customs were not always observed, as in this case.

The stories of Jean and Johann demonstrate how, even within the systems that privileged a single heir who was destined to marry and live with his parents, the timing and the manner in which the transfer took place could not only differentiate the life of the son chosen to succeed the father in running the farm from his brothers, but also change the destiny of young men who, in various situations, rose to the rank of chosen heir. The fact that the actual transfer of land and the role of householder occurred at the time of marriage or when the father fell ill, retired or died, gave rise to a vast range of possibilities, as did the similarly different ways in which the settlements for the other brothers could be arranged. The various family situations typified by the choice of a single main heir to the house and the land, who was destined to live with his parents after marriage, are often defined by scholars as stem families, though not all consider as such households with retired parents.[59] Where they were most widespread, you often found houses whose names embodied the family's identity in the very walls of the building.[60] In the early modern era, stem families were common in the north-western and northern Iberian Peninsula, southern France, the Alps, the entire German-speaking area, England, western Scotland, and some parts of Ireland and Scandinavia.[61]

These forms of family organization were to encounter a crisis when systems of inheritance based on equality for heirs were introduced, however much people might have found ways of getting around the law. These systems were introduced throughout France during the Revolution and with the Civil Code of 1804, and in Italy definitively with the Pisanelli Code of 1865–6.[62] In Germany, the possibility of leaving a farm to a single heir continued through the Nazi era, and the Nazis actually strengthened the custom by making all medium-sized farms indivisible and the rules on inheritance from father to son even stricter.[63] In Italy, the custom still survives for a certain type of farmstead in south Tyrol (*geschlossener Hof / maso chuso*), in the name of the constitutional principle of regional autonomy, even though it contravenes the principles of equality between men and women and between siblings, also established by the Constitution. Only 2001 were local laws passed which did away with discrimination against women in the inheritance of such farmsteads.[64]

The description so far has only presented a very rough and purely suggestive map of the different customs. In the Alps, where different cultures have always co-existed, the situation was particularly complex and erratic. There were areas in which the system of indivisible succession prevailed, and others, particularly in Switzerland and Italy, in which the family property was divided amongst all the male heirs or, sometimes, both male and female heirs.[65] It was possible to find profoundly different situations in valleys only a few kilometres apart. At Saint-Véran in Queyras, an area of Occitan culture, the stem family prevailed, but slightly to the east in the Varaita Valley, also of Occitan culture but in the territory of the House of Savoy, all sons had an equal inheritance, while the women had to make do with the legal minimum which was generally paid out through the dowry. To avoid dividing the land, the married brothers often lived together on the undivided property. They also tended to stay together after the death of their parents, thus forming what social scientists call *frérèches*, that is families made up of married brothers living under the same roof. Thus in the same environment, different solutions were found to similar problems. In these two cases, both solutions involved the creation of complex families (both stem families and *frérèches* are complex), given that in the Varaita Valley, the system of equal succession did not translate into the creation of nuclear families, in which each son took his own piece of land and settled his family on it.[66]

Aristocratic exclusions

Situations similar to the one in the Varaita Valley were widespread in the late Middle Ages and the sixteenth century amongst Italian noble families. The sons inherited equal shares from the parents, but they rarely divided them. This gave rise to large family groups linked by agnatic kinship,[67] who either lived together or very close to each other.[68] From around the beginning of the sixteenth century, however, the Italian nobility, as in most of Europe, started to hand down property to a single heir, generally the first-born, in order not to divide their estates. Moreover, they entailed the property so that the heir also had to pass it on to a single heir as a whole without selling it.[69] 'An estate may be as great and splendid as you like, but if it is divided between the sons, it will become small and miserable', wrote the author of the short anonymous tract *An uxor sit ducenda* (*Whether One Should Take a Wife*), which summarized the philosophy behind such inheritance policies.[70]

This policy meant that many cadets[71] ended up in the clergy or the army without taking a wife, and many young girls remained in convents. As they had been excluded from the greater part of the inheritance, it would have been impossible for them to have found a match suitable to their rank and they would not have been able to maintain a lifestyle 'in keeping' with people of their social standing.[72] In some situations, the percentages of those excluded from marriage were startling. In the previous chapter, it was stated that about half of the daughters of noble Milanese families whose fathers were born before 1650 became nuns. But overall there were many more who did not marry. The noblewomen who reached the age of 50 without marrying made up around three quarters of the total; 50 per cent of their brothers did not marry.[73] Later, the percentage for women fell dramatically (13 per cent between 1750 and 1799), but much less so for men (36.5 per cent remained unmarried in the second half of the eighteenth century).

Elsewhere the trend was in the opposite direction. In Manduria in the Kingdom of Naples, in the sixteenth century about 80 per cent of sons and all the daughters of the local nobility, the so-called *nobili viventi*, married, but by the end of the eighteenth century, the number of unmarried men and women, having increased consistently for two centuries, reached 60 and 66 per cent respectively.[74] Not all the nobility followed this pattern.

We have already noted that failure to marry was less common amongst the Protestant nobility than the Catholic one. About half the children of dukes and lords did not marry in France and Florence before 1700, in Milan before 1750, and in Toulouse before 1760, but only a quarter or less of the children of the Protestant aristocracy of Geneva or the English aristocracy of the seventeenth and eighteenth centuries did not marry.[75] But the religious denominations, with their different values, do not explain everything, as can be seen from the comparison between Milan and Manduria, both Catholic areas. Then there was the situation of the daughters of the lower nobility in Catalonia, amongst whom less than a fifth of the daughters remained unmarried in the seventeenth century (for their brothers the percentage was much higher and similar to other Catholic areas, a little under 50 per cent).[76] In the case of German noblewomen, they married more than their co-religionists in other countries, whether Catholic or Protestant, probably because, like the Catalan women, they married men of a lower social rank.[77]

In other words, the world of the nobility was varied and many-sided in its matrimonial behaviour, as in so many other ways. We cannot analyse in further detail the causes of these different types of behaviour. It will be sufficient to emphasize that, although behaviour varied, bachelorhood and spinsterhood overall were high amongst the nobility, and in general higher than amongst the rest of the population. In some cases, it was so high that it transformed tireless self-defence of one's own privileges into a suicidal practice that provoked the actual demographic extinction of the nobility.[78]

The other side of the coin

'I implore each of my sons to believe that I love them all as tenderly as the oldest, even though I have not been able to make them heirs along with him, but have resolved to appoint a single heir for the good of the family', wrote the Savoyard noble the marquis of Yerre in 1721.[79] He was clearly well aware that the unequal division of property could engender resentment towards him and the chosen heir amongst the excluded sons. There can be no doubt that systems of undivided inheritance could give rise to conflicts and tensions.[80] As one scholar has written of England, where until 1660 the father maintained an extraordinary power over his sons, heirs were forced, whether they liked it or not, into the situation of waiting for the death of their fathers, just as younger brothers might hope for the death of that elder brother, who they could replace if he went off into the next world without children.[81] In southern France in the eighteenth century, undesirable members of the family were sometimes poisoned or crushed between a door and a wall. These were no accidents and the practice, which was called a 'locking' in Gévaudan, was principally used to eliminate old people who were in the way. Those who have studied these and other forms of domestic crime believe them to be a product of the very way in which relations between family members were structured in the stem family, particularly in a situation where the average lifespan was increasing the population and the presence of older patriarchs. Given the lack of alternative openings, this meant an increase in the number of the excluded who were forced against their will to stay in the family home and not marry.[82] But the destinies of the excluded amongst the nobility and the peasantry were not always marked by feelings of frustration.

In the first place, succession to the position of head of the family and inheritance of property did not entirely coincide. Even land was not always reserved solely for the chosen heir. In Austria, to quote one example, apart from the land attached to the house to form the indivisible farm unit (called *Hausgrund* in Lower Austria), there was other land, referred to as *Überlandgründe* or *walzende Gründe*, which could be freely bought, sold and handed down to heirs.[83]

The exclusion could be of varying degrees according to different local traditions. In Upper Provence in the eighteenth century, the advantage of the preferred heir was never more than a quarter. It therefore appeared to be somewhat limited. Perhaps this was why, apart from those who went into the priesthood, everyone married, whether or not they were first-borns.[84] The degree of exclusion could vary according to how far some parents were willing to go to make their children's lives less wretched. In the village of Orwell in Cambridgeshire, the surviving wills written between 1543 and 1640 show that the peasants were split in equal parts between those who thought it best to leave the land to a single heir and those who divided it between all their children.[85] As with the Austrian cases previously described, there was a degree of choice and flexibility,[86] so that on occasion the difference between egalitarian and non-egalitarian succession began to fade.[87]

Of course, this flexibility could prove to be entirely to the detriment of those who had been excluded. The available data on the Italian nobility appears to show that as time went on, younger sons were paid off with smaller and smaller amounts.[88] In eighteenth-century England, the aristocracy and the gentry introduced innovations to their hereditary system that reduced the power of the father over his sons and the discrimination against younger sons and women.[89] Apart from the overall tendencies in one direction or the other, those who were not resigned to their fate were able to make use of the flexibility in customs. They could negotiate better treatment with their privileged brother, not always with success of course, but occasionally with such success as to undermine the strategy that had led to the unequal division in the first place. The logic of prestige could backfire when the assets made over to the cadets to guarantee their standard of living ended up burdening the first-born's estate with fixed payments and mortgages, as he usually had to settle the hereditary rights of the excluded brothers.[90]

If we are to believe the frequent complaints of the preferred heirs in Esparros in the Pyrenees, the younger sons' shares were far too high and were bleeding them dry.[91] Undoubtedly such arguments would have been heard from preferred heirs in other parts of Europe. They would not always have been groundless complaints, when the resources to be divided were often limited, even when split in unequal parts. In some parts of England, for example, it appears that the concerns of parents over not being too harsh in the exclusion of some of their sons from land ownership were the cause of considerable fragmentation of peasant land and led to the disappearance of many medium-sized farms, with a polarization between small and large landownership.[92]

Although the complaints of the 'privileged' heirs could occasionally be justified,[93] their condition did offer them advantages not shared by the other sons, who had to count on their own individual abilities if they were to find a reasonable position in life.[94] 'Study!', wrote the noble Orazio Spada to one of his sons. 'You're not in the position of Bernardino, who being the first-born will have the means to have a good position in the world.'[95] Land and ready money were not in fact the only ways to settle children's rights and provide them with a future. Giving them an opportunity to carry out and finish an apprenticeship or obtain an academic qualification were methods used particularly by the middle-class and some of the nobility, while in the middle and upper classes one of the most frequent solutions was to set them off on a career in the Church, not infrequently establishing benefices[96] and other sources of income for them.[97] 'He should be happy with his lot and not ask for any other inheritance, given that, more than the other children, he was given the opportunity to learn to read and write, and to obtain a post as a hatter which cost a great deal of money', Pierre Coulet, a minor official in Hyères (Provence) wrote of one of his sons in his will drawn up in 1661, the same year as Orazio Spada's warning to his son.[98] It is not surprising then that some argue that younger sons were generally better educated than the eldest brother.[99]

Those who had internalized the family culture that underscored their exclusion from earliest childhood, may not have found anything strange in the fact that they were to inherit a smaller share. Even if in their heart of hearts it caused them bitterness and frustration, they could understand the logic of the family line that required a single heir to be preferred. As we saw with the marquis of Yerre, his discrimination was justified by an appeal to the family interests: evidently he thought that the excluded sons would consider this a good reason. It was only in the second half of the eighteenth century that criticisms of these systems of inheritance increased. The Italian Enlightenment figure Alessandro Verri complained of the endless arguments that they caused, and another such figure, Gaetano Filangieri, became a mouthpiece for the widespread concern over the issue and launched a desperate appeal for far-reaching reforms. 'First of all, remove primogeniture, and remove fideicommissa', he passionately argued. 'These are the causes of the excessive wealth of the few and the poverty of the great majority. Primogeniture sacrifices many cadets to the first-born in the family, and the fideicommissa sacrifice many families for the sake of just one. Both radically reduce the number of landowners in the nations of Europe, and both are today the ruin of the population'. During the eighteenth century, the criticisms eventually led to profound changes and the limitation or abolition of fideicommissa and, during the French Revolution, parity between all heirs was introduced.[100] Before these changes, there was no shortage of younger sons who engaged with other family members in a kind of team sport aimed at improving the family's standing. In such cases, group solidarity prevailed over possible personal frustrations.[101]

Some nobles who pursued a career in the Church were able to establish important connections and amass genuine fortunes. This could be personally rewarding, but it could also be to the advantage of the whole family, which often actively supported its sons' careers. '[Work hard] for your own good, and in the service of your brothers and our family', wrote Orazio Spada to his son Fabrizio, who five years later became a cardinal and on his death left to his heirs a fortune of 92,251 *scudi*.[102] In a kind of reversal of roles, the 'victims of the family line', the younger brothers, could become the 'architects of its greatness'.[103]

Other cadets could not resign themselves to their fate of honourable celibacy, as their family intended. Francesco, another member of the Spada family, secretly married in 1609. He managed by deception to force the family to accept his marriage and therefore the formation of a second line alongside that of Giacomo Filippo, his oldest brother.[104] In general, however, most younger sons of noble families were excluded from the possibility of starting a family.

What happened in the peasantry to those who were excluded from succession to house and land? The situation in Upper Provence, where they all married,[105] was probably an extreme case. But even in other areas where the peasantry predominantly accepted the preferential transfer of house and land, the excluded sons were not necessarily completely cut out of the marriage market. They were if they did not abandon their father's house, as were for the most part those who became independent from their married brother but took on work as farm servants. Significantly in Austria, where impartible transfer of the farm (*Anerbenrecht*) was prevalent, the rate of illegitimate births was particularly high. (In Styria it was 11.2 per cent at the beginning of the nineteenth century, twice that of England during the same period at 5.5 per cent).[106] In spite of this, it was not entirely unthinkable to settle down with the fruits of one's own labour and one's own share of the inheritance which, although meagre, was generally paid out at the time of leaving the paternal home or at the time of marriage. However important it was to have land, cultivating one's own plot was not the only way to earn a living.[107] There was work as a farm servant, labourer or in some craft or proto-industrial activity. Alternatively, one type of work could supplement the other.[108] Thus in Esparros in the Tireneiuna, a considerable number of younger brothers married, albeit at an average age of about 31–2 years, while the heirs usually settled down at around 27–8 years. There was no denying it: having a house and land was an advantage for anyone who wanted to marry.[109] The situation was not the same everywhere. In some areas where there was a development of proto-industrial activity (but not in all), those without land or with only a little could marry and have many children. This was not only possible; it was even advantageous, because the children could be speedily employed in the manufacturing process.[110]

In the case of younger brothers, those who could not survive at home, could choose the path of emigration. Younger brothers contributed massively to the intense mobility that typified Europe (or at least western Europe) in the early modern era. Perhaps this is why they were so often heroes in the literary reflections of this reality.[111] The system that led to their exclusion was undoubtedly unjust, particularly by our standards, but for enterprising young men in search of adventure or simply disinclined to obedience, it could prove desirable. In the end, Jean preferred the state of *enfant doté* to that of the heir forced into a condition of subservience.

Brothers and sisters

Enfants dotés was the expression used in France for children who received their endowment or share of the inheritance on leaving home. Their situation differed from region to region. In the Paris basin, the son could put back his endowment into the family assets on the death of his parents in order to take part in the share-out of the inheritance.[112] In western and north-western France, this practice was obligatory and therefore transfers to sons during the life of the parents were of a temporary nature. On the parents' death, all the children (male and female in many areas, only males in Normandy) were supposed to take part in the division of the property. In southern France, on the other hand, the *enfants dotés* were permanently excluded from the inheritance. The endowment was the final settlement of their rights.[113]

We know that customs were flexible. But in as much as traditions were observed, the various system for handing down property expressed and reinforced different ways of perceiving the relationships between parents and children, elder and younger brothers, husbands and wives, and men and women.[114] As far as relations between brothers and sisters were concerned, in some areas they were treated as equals and in others the sons had the advantage. In systems with a preferred heir receiving an advantage (called *préciput* in French), the age distinction was added to the one between male and female. To assess what this meant, we will return to Upper Provence, which we already know.

Enfants dotés, men and women, shared the same experience, both in the way they were defined and in the kind of relationship with the parental property, although there were important differences between them. The male dowries or endowments were larger than the dowries for women. When fathers wrote a will, they often left something to their sons, who had renounced their hereditary rights by accepting the endowment, while the daughters who had received dowries were generally only left 5 *sous*, and then only to avoid having the will annulled.[115]

But apart from these differences, with a single heir both women and younger brothers were 'excluded', and the principal line of demarcation did not run between men and women, as was the case with systems where all male heirs inherited equally (this was the situation in Normandy, for instance). In preferential regimes, some of the men found themselves in similar conditions to those in which women normally found themselves. Where there were systems of indivisible succession, the ideal succession was from father to son. Usually women only inherited the farm in the absence of brothers. But usually does not mean always.

In some valleys of the Pyrenees, the tradition was for the farm to go to the first-born, irrespective of the child's sex.[116] In 13 per cent of the wills in the German village of Belm between 1650 and 1860, the house and land went to a daughter, and in one case out of four, these were women who had brothers, but for some reason they were preferred to the men.

In Belm, as in the rest of Westphalia,[117] the men who married these heiresses, adopted their surnames, which were generally the names of the farms. The same happened to those who married the widow of a male heir, and if the widow and her previous husband had had children, one of them would have been the next heir. If they had not had any children, then the man who married the widow acquired full property rights over the farm, which would then be passed down to one of his own children. In such areas, people with the same surname could live in a house for centuries. This did not imply that the property was passed from father to son with each generation, in accordance with a direct and uninterrupted line (patrilineage). It might, in fact, have been passed down from a father to a daughter, from man to his widow, and from the widow, if she did not have any children and remarried, to her child by second marriage. In other words, the property[118] could be handed down to persons who were not relations. In such cases, it was as though the stability of the house was projected onto the residents and created a sense of continuity between them. The house gave its name to those who lived in it and who could inherit it, whether they were men or women, relations or in-laws.[119]

Dowries, separation of property and joint estates

In Westphalia, the continuity of the house appears to have been ultimately more important than the patrilineal line. During the Middle Ages, the strengthening of patrilineage had led to weaker property rights for women in southern Europe. The return of the dowry from the tenth and eleventh centuries was one of the ways in which this weaker position manifested itself.[120] The return of the dowry was related to the return of Roman Law. However, there were profound differences between the situation that emerged in the Middle Ages and the early modern era and the situation for which Roman Law had been devised.

In ancient Rome, brides presented their husbands with a dowry, but the husbands also gave them a wedding gift (*donatio propter nuptias*). This exchange was nothing more than a symbolic manifestation of what was happening in the marriage. Receipt of a dowry did not exclude women from their inheritance. Of course, the role of *paterfamilias* was handed down the male line, but the daughters who at the time of his death were still under his authority (*patria potestas*), inherited together with their brothers in the same condition.[121]

In the Middle Ages and the early modern era, the dowry increasingly became a cost that fell entirely on the bride's family, as the size of husband's gifts to the wife were drastically reduced, both in the form of *donatio propter nuptias* and in the form of wedding gifts in accordance with Lombard Law, which in the early Middle Ages had great significance. At the same time, the dowry came to represent a final settlement of a woman's hereditary rights (*exclusio propter dotem*).[122] Scholars are still divided over whether it represented a kind of inheritance in advance or a means for settling a smaller share of the inheritance on the daughters, precisely because they were women.[123] There were, however, women willing to fight with their families to avoid receiving inadequate dowries.

'Your lordship knows that Olimpia was given the same dowry by our late departed Lady mother that I received myself,' wrote Geronima Veralli to her brother Giovanni Battista concerning the dowry of her sister who wanted to marry and not take the veil in the convent where she was a boarder. 'The poor girl', she added, had to have at least 'as much as I had'. Otherwise, she would be entitled 'to complain about everyone'. In other words, she was not to be given some miserable dowry. The sister warned that the dowry had to be a rich one, partly out of 'respect for our family'. She told her brother not to be 'overcome by avarice', 'especially as by not giving her too little, your Lordship's interests and honour will be favoured.[124] By giving his sister a good dowry, Giovanni Battista was supposed to have improved his own chances of achieving a good marriage to a bride with a rich dowry.

Dowries were, in fact, an integral part of a complex game of deals and alliances between families. Their level was determined above all by the husband's social status. Geronima Veralli went on to point out that with a dowry like the one she had had, currently it would no longer have been possible to find 'a private gentleman who was one of our Romans'.[125] So while receipt of a dowry restricted or even permanently settled any rights a woman might have over the family assets, this did not mean that families were not willing to pay out considerable sums to marry their daughters as part of the alliances they formed with other families. Indeed these sums became ever more substantial with the extraordinary increase in the average dowry to which Geronima refers.[126]

It also follows that, as girls could expect nothing or almost nothing else from their family apart from the dowry, it came to represent their inalienable right and consequently an absolute duty for their fathers and brothers. In southern Europe, a marriage without a dowry was almost inconceivable. A dowry was even necessary for entering a convent, although it was generally smaller than the one required for marriage.[127]

For this reason, the question of how to give a dowry to spinsters ceased to be a family problem and became a social one.[128] In a society with death rates far higher than today and very low incomes, many young women had no family or were too poor to afford a dowry. They risked prostitution as well as not being able to marry or enter a convent. Thus there was an increase in initiatives aimed at ensuring or facilitating dowries for young women.

In 1425, the *Monte delle doti* (Dowry Bank) was established in Florence. It was an institution into which parents with a young daughter could pay a sum of money that could be withdrawn with interest many years later at the time of marriage. Later, similar institutions were founded in other cities, like Bologna.[129] More specifically welfare initiatives were also developed. Corporations and confraternities generally made dowry contributions available to daughters of their members. Dowry funds for young girls without means were established thanks to charitable legacies, and in Tuscany one was set up in the seventeenth century by the Grand Duke himself.[130] It has been calculated that around 30–40 per cent of the women who married in Rome between 1637 and 1755 benefited from the dowry subsidy provided by the *Confraternita dell'Annunziata*, the principal institution in Rome that provided dowries for young women in need, but not the only one.[131] For very rich families, paying dowries for poor girls was a means of exercising patronage, which was not infrequently based more or less explicitly on a broad concept of the family. A noblewoman from Bologna who died at the end of the seventeenth century left dowries in her will for the daughters of all her servants. Girls who worked as servants could hope that their employer would leave them a dowry or, at least, a 'complete' bed. For female domestic servants, the creation of a dowry could also be remuneration for years of work, as negotiated with the employer.[132]

The dowry was important because it represented the woman's contribution to the formation of the new family. As far as property relations between husband and wife were concerned, the dowry system provided for separation of the spouses' assets. This did not mean that women had control over their own dowries, which were in fact administered by their husbands who used the profits.[133] But in the case of his death, the dowry had to be returned to the wife. Only in widowhood, then, were women finally free to use their dowries as they liked.[134]

If a wife died without having any children, the husband had to return the dowry to the wife's family. As time went on, there was a tendency for widowers to keep part of the dowry or even all of it, as occurred in some cities of Lombardy.[135] Although the history of women's property rights has not been a linear development,[136] there was an increase during the early modern era in the number of strategies to incorporate dowries into the property of the husband's family, to get round the rules on their inalienability often to the detriment of a woman's interests and freedoms, and to restrict a woman's right to use her dowry (a right that was already limited to widowhood) and any other property (*beni stradotali*).[137]

Wills appear to have been issues in which the more or less latent marital tensions found expression through the disposal of property. While there were women who showed a stubborn desire to write a will and decide themselves who was to benefit from their property,[138] there were in some areas increasing numbers of husbands who wrote wills aimed at incorporating their wives' property into the assets of their own families.[139] Such provisions were left by Marquis Luigi Albergati in 1747, as we have already seen.[140] It will be recalled that he established in his codicils that his wife Eleonora Bentivoglio, once she was a widow, could continue to enjoy 'free use both of the summer and winter apartments', where she was already living, only in the event of her not remarrying and not requesting the return of her dowry.[141]

The tendency to incorporate dowries permanently and to avoid their return probably expressed and reinforced the formation of the husband, wife and children as the identifiable unit, marking the eclipse of the medieval situation by which – at least in some areas and classes – men and women belonged each to their own lineage rather than the conjugal family created by marriage.[142] After all, the latter unit was only an ephemeral one. If the wealthy Florentine women we encountered at the beginning of the chapter were widowed young, they might have been forced by their fathers and brothers to abandon their dead husband's family and their own children, thus becoming 'cruel mothers', and to return to their original family with their dowries to await a second marriage and departure to another house, where again they would be partly outsiders.[143]

Although the continued presence of widows and their dowries in the husband's family was linked to the formation of the conjugal family, it has to be said that consolidation of this kind of family came about by subsuming the woman and her property into the property of the husband's family. A new communion was created, but at the same time the identity of one of the participants was, at least in part, negated.

Consequently, the fact that women could not be heirs of their children and could not therefore draw any material advantage from their children's deaths meant that widows were more reliable guardians than uncles, aunts or other relations who could inherit, according to magistrates who had to rule on who would be the guardian of children who had lost their fathers in Tuscany during the early modern era. By entrusting children to their mothers, magistrates encouraged the consolidation of mother–child relations and gave credence to the idea of disinterested maternal love.[144] Yet again, property, wealth and the way they were distributed and handed down contributed to the structure of interpersonal relations and emotional attachments.

Returning to the question of property relations between spouses, we will now examine areas where joint estates prevailed. While the dowry system was most widespread in Mediterranean Europe, there was a prevalence of joint estates between spouses north of the Loire and in the whole of north-western Europe. In these areas, the dowry, although desirable, was neither an obligation for the father nor indispensable for marriage. There were of course exceptions. South of the Loire, joint estates were practised in Istria, Sardinia and some part of Sicily,[145] to mention only those in Italy, while to the north, the dowry system was used in Normandy.[146]

Although a dowry was not necessary in the joint-estate system, many girls worked outside the home as marriage still required a certain capital, even a minimal one. Precisely because of the purpose for which they worked, this custom does not appear to have been stigmatized, as sometimes occurred in the Mediterranean world, although many women worked there too. In Italy, those who established charitable legacies to provide dowries sometimes actually excluded servant girls from the possibility of applying, because the very fact that they had worked in the house of a master who could easily have taken advantage of them meant they were suspected of indecent behaviour.[147]

In the joint-estate system, the wife's contribution to the creation of the family was merged into the husband's, and he took control of the family property, whether this contribution came from the wife's labour or from her family.[148] Here again, women were officially excluded from management of property, even though reality could, as usual, be more flexible. It was particularly for widows that the situation was different to that of women living under the dowry system. In the joint-estate system, women were due part of the family assets (half or a third, according to the area). In England, a widow's situation was settled by an agreement at the time of marriage. The husband usually made over to the wife a 'dower' equal to about a third of the value of the family assets she would have enjoyed if she had had at least one child. In any case, the widow had the right to remain in the marital home.[149]

5. Who paid?

In 1563, a woman from Venice called Marina Locatelli made a will. She was probably pregnant and feared that she might die during childbirth. Amongst other provisions, there was the establishment of a legacy of 200 ducats 'as funds for getting married' to the daughter of one of the brothers of the Scuola di

San Giovanni Evangelista, a Venetian brotherhood. Marina's fears (assuming they existed) fortunately proved to be unfounded. We find her again in 1588 as a widow who promises her daughter Lucrezia in marriage to a lawyer, Antonio Rizzo. Lucrezia's dowry consisted of 600 ducats in cash, property worth 200 ducats, and a building that Marina had had as payment for her dowry.[150] Marina was therefore financing her daughter's dowry with her own assets and handing down part of her dowry. Her actions both inside and outside the family encapsulate the vast network of relations that could be involved in the funding of a new couple.

As we have seen, it could involve the entire community to which the future couple belonged. This was not only true in Mediterranean Europe. In England, as in other areas, all the friends and relations made a collection to assist a new couple.[151] In many French communities, no one found anything amiss if poor girls who were going to be married went through their villages door-to-door begging for a little hemp and flax to weave their trousseaus.[152]

To summarize this rapid survey, we can conclude that both bride and groom contributed financially to the foundation of the new family. Amongst the peasantry and even more so amongst the nobility, land was mainly provided by the husband, although women might have had the odd field or meadow as part of the dowry. Not infrequently, a preference was given to moveable assets and money when making up the dowry. Amongst the lower classes in many parts of Europe, the marital bed was traditionally part of the wife's contribution.

The ways in which men and women obtained these assets differed according to the economic, social and cultural context. In general, it has emerged that, when it comes to examining the funding of new couples,[153] it would be a simplification to concentrate one's attention only on the couple: families, employers, trade groups, communities, welfare institutions and others all made their contribution to the material basis of the new union. With the possible exception of secret weddings and marriages in the very bottom layers of society, weddings triggered a considerable inflow of assets. The methods by which the necessary funds were found for marriage influenced the age the couple married and affected whether or not they set up home on their own, even though, as always occurs with human behaviour, they were capable of finding different solutions to the same problem. The search for absolute and inevitable causal links between one element and another is always going to end in failure.

6. The meaning of things

As we have seen, Geronima Veralli implored her brother to provide Olimpia with a rich dowry, and stressed that this would also bring honour to him and to the family.[154] Consequently, a man could measure his social position by the size of the dowry that the family of his future bride was willing to pay up to bring about the marriage.[155] All this reminds us that the function of the man and the woman's contribution to the marriage was not exclusively economic. The house in which the new couple was to live, the clothes and jewels that they were to wear, the food that they were to eat, and the gifts that they were to make were all indicators of their status.[156]

Hence, during the Renaissance, when husbands of the Florentine elite got married they gave expensive jewellery to their wives and occasionally even rented it so as to show off their wives and assert their status.[157] Occasionally the weddings were so magnificent and ostentatious that the authorities were eventually obliged to bring in laws to restrict them, as occurred later in other cities.[158] In some areas of Italy, the carts that bore the trousseau had supports for attaching the bride's dress, so that everyone could see it.[159] In Florence the contents of the chests were put on display during the wedding procession and then later at the husband's home during the banquet.[160] The linen and other items provided by the wife were displayed in public in many other places. In Lutheran Germany, the bride sat on a cart that went around the city loaded with wedding gifts and the trousseau, so that everyone could admire them.[161] In some parts of France, there was still the custom in the twentieth century for the linen in the trousseau to be displayed so that everyone could see it after it had been taken into the couple's bedroom.[162] Even people who were fairly poor wanted to make an impression and they did not scrimp when it came to a wedding. 'I would rather be a cuckold than have her go without stuff for her trousseau', said a poor peasant women of her daughter in the eighteenth century.[163]

Sumptuous wedding banquets played a similar role, and were organized more or less everywhere and by practically all social classes (Fig. 9). 'Except at the time of wedding feasts, the peasants eat like pigs', claimed Girolamo Cirelli at the end of the seventeenth century.[164] Inviting friends and relations to banquets, like the exchange of gifts, was not only for the purpose of feasting and ostentatious display. Weddings caused the circulation and exchange of goods that also had a symbolic function.

The ring had a long tradition. Amongst the ancient Romans it constituted a guarantee of the promise of marriage and in the early Middle Ages amongst German peoples it was used in the *desponsatio*, which committed the parties to the marriage contract. But from the eleventh century, the Church started to turn the ring, which up till then had mainly been an engagement ring, into the principal symbol of legitimate marriage. It will be recalled that the Church's conception of marriage was mainly centred on the exchange of consent between the bride and groom.[165] Not surprisingly then, the handing over of the ring shifted from the moment of the agreement between the families to the reciprocal declaration by the couple of their becoming married.[166]

The handing over of the ring thus came to embody the Church's idea of a 'real' marriage. This challenged both the German and Lombard traditions, in which the central moment of the wedding ceremony was the procession that took the bride to the husband's house,[167] and the more popular conceptions that attributed the almost magical transformation of man and woman into husband and wife to the exchange of any object, as long as it was done in the name of marriage. The latter was possibly a folk interpretation of the Church doctrine of consensual marriage. On this basis, Guillaume Foucher offered Marguerite Gueux a pear, that she ate; Jean Bertrand gave Jacquette Gaudouart a tin mug in 1506; Jean Simon gave Jeanne Lepage a belt in 1530, while two years later Pierre Pellart took Marguerite widow of Jacomart and, according to her, said, 'Marguerite, so that you have no fear that I will abuse you, I put my tongue in your mouth, in the name of marriage'. These cases would have been somewhat unusual at the time they occurred, given that records have been preserved amongst the papers of the court before which one of each pair dragged the other who denied having really been married. However, they testify to a popular belief that the exchange of virtually any object or even erotic outpourings was binding, as long as it was done in the name of marriage. In parts of France at least, the Church was only to eradicate these beliefs completely in the seventeenth to eighteenth century. These popular beliefs were much less out of the ordinary than might at first be supposed. A late medieval legal tradition considered the offer of any small gift as an element from which to infer the complete validity of a marriage, when it followed a betrothal. Like the *toccamano* (the bridegroom taking the bride by the hand) and the placing of a ring on the finger, the kiss was a symbol of consent to be married.[168]

What in Florence had been called the 'day of the ring' (*il dì dell'anello*) came to be the wedding day. In general, this demonstrated the increasing control of Church institutions over matrimonial practices. But in Florence, the fact that in the fifteenth century marriage, increasingly was consummated on this day was probably due to the regulations of the Dowry Bank (*Monte delle doti*), which only paid out dowries after the consummation of the marriage.[169] It should also be noted that in most of Europe the ring, which was supposed to be the symbol of consensual union between two people who were, at least in relation to the marriage ceremony, on an equal level, proved the limits of such a concept in practice. There was, in fact, generally only one ring, and the husband placed it on the wife's finger, thus showing that she was his. He was symbolically assured of her faithfulness, without providing a corresponding pledge of his own.[170]

In any case, the ring became 'the only object universally legitimized in the context of the religious ceremony' for marriage.[171] This does not mean that other objects loaded with symbolic meaning completely disappeared from the matrimonial scene. The spindle and the distaff, which so often took pride of place amongst the items the bride took to her new home, were not just tools for work (Fig. 6). They were often decorated and tied up with ribbons, and symbolized the honest and hardworking woman, to the point of representing a kind of augury that she would turn out to be a good wife and a good mother. In Yorkshire, the bride was carried around the town on a cart ('brideswain') while she was intent on spinning, and her friends and relations threw money and loaded furniture and utensils onto the cart. Similarly, in some areas of Sardinia, the bride was taken to the new home seated on a cart with spindle and distaff in her hand.[172]

Because they were the starting point for a new entity, weddings were full of gestures designed to bring good luck or avert evil. The plethora of symbolic meanings also involved the materials goods in which the new union was embodied or which constituted the material landscape the marriage was to experience, as we are reminded by the propitiatory and religious rites to which the marital bed was subject (Fig. 10).[173]

7. Rites of passage

The particularly high number of rituals, taboos and actions that could either bring good luck or ward off evil, with which marriage was associated, depended on the fact that marriage represented an important moment of passage both for men and women. Unlike other cultures, European civilization during the period under examination did not have any initiation rites by which adolescents passed into adulthood. Consequently, marriage took over this role for a large part of the population.[174] This is demonstrated by the fact that in the early modern era, the terms used to indicate teenage girls often refer to whether or not they are married, rather than their age, so that they can be used in relation to elderly women who never married.

An example is the Italian word *zitella* or *citella*, which means 'spinster'. Etymologically it derives from *zita* or *cita*, an abbreviated form of *piccitta*, meaning 'little girl'.[175] It apparently referred to an age band, and very often simply meant 'teenage girl'. But it could also be used to mean elderly women who had never married, and it is in this sense that it has survived (it now also has a pejorative sense). Implicitly, then, the definition *zitella* refers to a cycle in a woman's life that is defined socially and not biologically. Those who do not go through the established stages, remain *zitelle* or spinsters, and therefore girls, irrespective of their actual age and the physical appearance of their bodies. This is only one of the many examples we could cite to demonstrate what a complete break marriage represented in a woman's life (as was entry to a convent, but then this too was, so to speak, a marriage because every nun was a bride of Christ).

The wedding procession and the carriage of the chest or wardrobe with the trousseau were therefore the visible and material expression of the passage that was occurring in the woman's life.[176] In Renaissance Florence, where the unity of the marital couple was still very weak, there was an echo of this ritual in reverse, when the chest was returned to the paternal home on the husband's death, always supposing the wife chose to return to her original family or was forced to do so.[177]

On foot, on a cart or riding a horse, and accompanied, preceded or followed by her possessions, a woman passed with the wedding procession and marriage ceremony from the house of her original family to the one where she would live with her husband, and at the same time from the status of unmarried girl to the status of married woman, and from supposed virginity to a sexually active life. Marriage was also important in the life of men: in many cases, it was not only the starting point for his own family but also involved changes in his status in the world of work. As we have seen, for many (although not all), it coincided with taking on the running of a farm or a workshop, and marked his release from a situation of subservience. For artisans it could be a condition for becoming member of the guild.[178] The passage was not, however, exactly the same for men and women: while for the former it coincided with the achievement of financial independence, women only achieved such independence with widowhood, if at all.[179]

Weddings did not only represent an important passage for those who were getting married; they were also important in the lives of their families and the communities in which they lived. It is no surprise, then, that complex rites of passage accompanied the promise of marriage that endorsed the start of the intermediate period between the unmarried status and the married one. These rites could in fact be as complex as those for the wedding, and they can be categorized as rites of separation, rites of 'margin' and rites of admission.

The following are some of the rituals that marked the break with adolescent life as they were gathered and categorized by ethnologists and anthropologists: they would empty containers, cut or throw away an object associated with childhood or not being married, beat up childhood friends or be beaten up by childhood friends, they would wash themselves, or have themselves washed by someone else, they would put on particular kinds of clothes, change hairstyle or the style of their beard, they would break an object that symbolized virginity (for example a necklace), remove a particular kind of belt, change their diet or introduce taboos on certain kinds of food, or change their name.

A similar list of wedding rites in Europe during the early modern era would lead us off on a tangent. However, the available sources show that there was a wide range of behaviour patterns that could be defined as rites of separation. Before having a bath became a taboo, as we shall see later, girls who were going to get married in some German cities were in the habit of going to the public baths with their girlfriends and having themselves washed by these friends.[180] In some areas, young women put up resistance and cried when it came to having to leave their mother, their family or their companions of the same age. In some cases, they would hide from the groom, run away on his arrival, have themselves followed and even abducted, giving rise to scenes in which real feelings were mixed with ritualized actions that often led to material and symbolic compensations for the group that lost one of its members through marriage (gifts, banquets, etc.).

Once separation had been sanctioned, admission to the new family had its ritual expressions. Some rites of admission emphasized the union between husband and wife. The gift or exchange of rings, belts, bracelets, or garlands, and the customs of tying themselves together, offering each other food or drink, eating together or from the same plate, drinking the same drink or using the same glass, and entering the new house together, were both material and symbolic rituals that created, sanctioned and publicized the new relationship, the marriage union between a man and a woman. As we have seen, the Church in the Middle Ages and the early modern era considered the handing over of the wedding ring to play this role, while in the folk perception many objects could fulfil the same purpose. In spite of the Church's efforts to simplify the ceremony, it continued to be loaded with a wide variety of symbols. For example, German brides wore a garland, generally made of flowers, on their heads as they paraded through the city in the wedding procession, and this symbolized their virginity which was to be 'gifted' to the husband. It was then removed as the girl entered the bedroom. Custom then required that she started to cry out of shame. Girls who were no longer virgins at the time of marriage could even be forced to wear a crown of straw or a broken garland. Garlands were also worn by brides in Renaissance Florence.[181]

Also in Florence, the gift of rings to the bride by the husband's relations consolidated her membership of the new family and indicated her position amongst the women of the house.[182] Rites were, in fact, often associated with introducing either the bride or the groom to the new family, new house or new village, while others concerned the bringing together of two groups (two families or kinships). Examples are the exchange of gifts or visits, the participation in processions, religious ceremonies, banquets and dances.[183] 'We arrived just in time to sit down at the table,' wrote Ménétra of a wedding at which he was a guest. 'At the end of the meal, the toasts,' and then dances and jokes. 'The wedding feast lasted three days.'[184]

In relation to the passage accomplished through marriage, the thresholds of the bride's original home, the house to which the couple will go and live, and occasionally even the church, were particularly significant places and often the setting for particularly complex ritual practices.[185] Amongst the Mari, an Ugro-Finnic people (formerly called the Cheremis) living in Russia along the middle course of the Volga, the wedding procession that went to pick up the bride stopped before the entrance to the courtyard of the *isba* where she lived. Only the *sabus*, the master of ceremonies, was allowed to enter the house where he was offered food and drink. He asked the girl's father if the procession could enter, explaining in response to a standard question that the purpose of the visit was to look for the missing sleeve from an item of clothing belonging to the girl's betrothed. The answer was no and the *sabus* left. He had to return two more times to make the same demand before he could obtain permission, which then gave rise to another series of rituals, which could be classified as rites of admission. Records of these ritual practices amongst the Mari date back to the late-nineteenth century, but they probably relate to much more ancient traditions.

There are records of similar rites in most areas of Europe (and elsewhere). In the Asturias, at the opposite end of the continent to the Mari, when the groom's procession went to the home of the girl he was to marry, a lively ritual took place at the threshold. In several parts of Scandinavia, when the groom went to collect his wife, she would hide in the barn underneath a pile of hay, and she would be discovered after he had searched in several other places. In Austria, the young man found the door closed and had to pay to enter. Similarly, after the wedding ceremony, the bride would find the door to the husband's house closed and had to obtain permission to enter from two young gatekeepers, one of whom then offered her a loaf of bread and the other a wooden knife. In many parts of Italy, the bride would cry in a more or less ritualized manner and hide or cling on to the furniture, to demonstrate that she did not want to leave her parents' home. When she reached the groom's home, she had a ritual conversation with her mother-in-law, who interrogated her about her abilities. The mother-in-law then embraced her, gave her a ladle, and invited her in. Occasionally, the young bride had to undergo a series of tests on her housekeeping abilities in order to be fully accepted. In some areas, a broom was laid across the threshold. Similar customs occurred in various parts of France.[186] Other rites were more explicitly concerned with the couple taking possession of the new home, further enriching the stunning range of ritual practices that our folklore has produced.

In the past, therefore, there were, according to the area and social group, differences in the material environment in which newly-created couples and later their children lived. Although in some cases it is possible to detect common features, the methods by which they took ownership of particular items of property during the wedding feast and the days that followed, and the significance they attributed to their possession, use and loss were often different, as were the meanings that the objects could express.

8. So much hard work!

Having left the wedding scene, we have returned to our starting point, thus completing our journey in search of all the different ways of setting up home and their consequences and implications. Leaving aside all the many differences, the birth of the new couple in modern Europe, particularly western Europe, now appears something far from obvious, banal or inevitable. Of course, there were plenty of marriages carried out on the spot for various reasons: undoubtedly such unions were not uncommon in England's squalid wedding halls before the 1753 reform.[187] Usually however, the creation of a new couple was the result of a protracted and laborious process for the bride, groom and their families, relations, friends and neighbours. It turned out generally to be anything but individual and 'private', particularly for the landed classes. Types of residence, inheritance customs and property relations between husband and wife were interwoven so as to create many permutations. Access to marriage and ways of experiencing marriage differed dramatically, but they marked out the lines along which family relationship could run either to solidarity or conflict. We will now consider types of family, solidarity and conflict more directly in relation to the physical space that made up the home.

III

Configurations of the House
and the Family

1. The functions of the house

While inquisitively wandering around the continent of Europe, we have come across couples who behaved in different manners after their marriage: in some areas and amongst some social classes we noted that the majority went to live in a house on their own, following what social scientists define as the neolocal residence pattern or rule. In other cases, we discovered that the wife went to live with the husband's family (patrivirilocal rule), but we also came across husbands who moved to the wife's house, occasionally even adopting her name (uxorilocal rule).

We can infer that the families made up of couples who went off to live on their own, giving rise to a nuclear family household, were generally smaller than those in which the couple resided with the husband's or the wife's original family (complex family households that could be either extended or multiple). We must now ask ourselves whether there was a link between the size and complexity of the family household on the one hand and the configuration of the house on the other. Was it the case that the more numerous and complex the families were, the larger the house and the greater the number of rooms? In other words, did the family mould the house according to its needs, or was it the availability of houses of a certain kind that influenced the form the family took?

We have already seen that the majority of families in Sicily were neolocal. The houses were in fact often small and cramped, with only one or two rooms.[1] The same could be said of many cities, where there was usually a preponderance of nuclear families. In the eighteenth century, four-fifths of Parisians lived in one or two rooms.[2] In the countryside of central Italy, dominated by sharecropping (*mezzadria*), complex families were numerous and we find that there were large and complex farm houses. Upper class families, who more often followed the patrilocal rule, had spacious houses. According to one historian, in the early modern era one-room hovels were generally home to 'families that were small in number and simple in structure', while the crude shacks that often surrounded

75

villages mainly housed 'broken families', whose survival mainly depended on the charity of their neighbours.[3] Another historian, referring to the case of the Balkan *zadruga* and the community buildings of Alvernia and Bauges,[4] argued that when it came to analysing housing, the 'first fundamental distinction' was between the ' "individual" house of the nuclear family' and the house of an extended family.[5] It would, however, be simplistic to assert a more or less automatic link between complex family and large house.

If we return to the higher social classes, the power and the success of a family were partly measured by their ability to attract and offer protection to relations (and also their servants), and this meant they had to be able to provide them with accommodation.[6] To some extent, there was a connection between high social rank, complex family and large house. But the size of the house not only reflected the need to offer a shelter to a co-resident group. In the early modern era, a house could also be a place of work. Its size and complexity responded to a wide range of functions, and not just the size and complexity of the family itself.[7] For instance, the farm houses of central Italy often had areas used for keeping and processing corn, oil, wine and other products.[8] We can therefore conclude that the organization of work in the peasant world tended to create a chain of interconnections between the non-nuclear family, the plurality of functions carried out in the domestic context and the structure of the house.

For instance, agricultural workers who only sell their labour individually to employers in exchange for wages without being tied to the land they work in any way (farm servants, day labourers, etc.) often lived in small and confined houses. In Italy, they lived in houses 'of very few rooms, mainly insalubrious and badly kept', whether they worked on the large farms run as early capitalist enterprises in the Po Valley or on the large estates in the south of Italy.[9] On the other hand, at least from the eighteenth century and in many cases from the seventeenth, the houses of peasants working on small or medium-sized farms either as owners or sharecroppers were larger and more spacious. They were constructed on two or three floors, and had a considerable number of rooms used as living spaces, as well as others for work and storage.[10]

But, yet again, there was no shortage of exceptions. The poorer kind of housing continued to be used by peasants working their own land and the tenants tied to their land in the 'depressed areas of mainland southern Italy'.[11] It should not be forgotten that entire rural families of all sizes were still living in one- or two-room houses as late as the twentieth century, albeit increasingly in the poorer regions and among the most impoverished levels of society. Such houses were, for instance, the norm in nineteenth-century Poland.[12] In the Russian village of Mishino, where in the early nineteenth century the average family consisted of 8–10 people, houses were usually a single room measuring between 15 and 34 square metres, but about half that area was occupied by the stove (Fig. 12).[13] Small dwellings were not only to be found in the East: there were peasants in Germany that squeezed themselves into a few square metres around a fireplace, and even in wealthy Holland there were hovels that hid innumerable residents.[14]

We can summarize the situation as follows: a house was primarily a shelter and therefore those who could afford to do so adapted it to the size of their own family, but many could not. As we shall see in the next chapter, the concept of what was the right size of house in relation to the number and composition of the residents was not the same for everyone. It varied according to social group, historical period and probably also geographical region. The house for many was a workplace as well as a shelter. Its structure was therefore primarily affected by such functions, and the matter of organizing domestic space came second. A weaver's loom might be placed in the only available room. Those who had sizeable flocks of sheep or a certain number of cattle generally needed the appropriate facilities, from a simple enclosure to a large barn.

Rural houses were not the only ones with more than one function. This was also true of the houses of artisans and shopkeepers. For a time, Ménétra had to sleep in a room in his employer's warehouse: an excellent example of the overlap between productive and residential functions in an urban environment, and certainly not an isolated one.[15] However, the various functions of rural housing were perhaps more akin to what aristocratic houses had once been like, as they were based on the processing and preservation of agricultural produce.[16]

There was a specific literary genre that for centuries explained to fathers and mothers of aristocratic families how to run their houses and families and how to behave in relation to their spouses, children and servants. This genre on housekeeping, or *Hausväterliteratur* (i.e. literature for the head of the family), tended to depict the aristocratic home as an almost completely self-sufficient unit, thanks to the agricultural produce supplied by peasants working on the lands of the *paterfamilias*.[17] In reality, it was a highly ideological interpretation, at least as far as western Europe was concerned, given that aristocratic families were part of the market and the network of business relations.[18] It is true, however, that noble families did make use of the commodities and products provided by their landed interests. Their estate buildings included warehouses to store them and in some cases equipment for processing them. They had coach-houses and stables, as well as cellars and warehouses. They normally had accommodation for servants covering a wide variety of duties, and sometimes for artisans and craftsmen as well. This abundance and variety of rooms was also a status symbol, and this undoubtedly tended to loosen the link between the size of the house and the size of the family: a grand stately home could in fact be home to a married couple, a solitary aristocrat or a widow, although they would generally be surrounded by servants.

A stately home was not only a symbol of wealth, power and social prominence. It had a particularly significant role in embodying the continuity of the patrilineal family. In the case of medieval Italian nobility, members of a kinship group usually lived in adjacent houses that took over part of a city, and that area was occasionally fortified. The nuclei were often made up of several brothers who lived together in order not to split their inheritance, which was handed down equally to all the sons. From around the beginning of the sixteenth century, the nobility adopted the indivisible *fideicommissum* to avoid the fragmentation associated with partible inheritance: increasingly the family's assets were handed down to a single heir, usually the first-born son, who was then entailed to hand them down to his first-born. The idea was clearly to ensure that the wealth remained intact as it passed from one generation to another. The stately home, embellished with coats of arms, came to embody the continuity of an orderly lineage, as it was passed down from father to son. It was home to the heir, his parents (if alive), his wife and children and possibly some brothers who were forced by the logic of inheritance to remain unmarried. More distant relations lived elsewhere. A family's authority, which had once been linked to the size of the kinship group that lived together in physical proximity, was now increasingly expressed through the wealth and honour of the patrilineal line, of which the stately home was the embodiment.[19]

2. Flexible families

In 1792, the family of Marquis Alamanno Isolani, a nobleman from Bologna, was made up of 18 people. Another visit in 1796 would have found the marquis's beautiful *palazzo* in Piazza Santo Stefano to be much emptier: the family members reduced to just 13. By 1799, it was again more crowded, with as many as 19 people, including 7 servants. Changes in the number of servants contributed only very slightly to these fluctuations. In all three years there were 5 female servants and there were 3 male servants in 1796 and 2 after that. It was the numbers of the rest of the family that changed: 10 in 1792, 6 in 1796, and 12 in 1799.[20]

A cursory examination of the composition of families over different periods soon reminds us of the degree of complexity and mutability in a domestic group. A young couple could go and live in a house on their own and then take in a parent who had ended up alone or, indeed, some other relation.[21] On the other hand, they might have gone to live with one or the other's parents immediately after the wedding, while waiting for a more independent situation, perhaps when the arrival of children led to a lack of space.[22]

Families were not therefore something stable and static. They were constantly growing and shrinking. In some periods they could be made up of just parents and children (nuclear or simple families), in others of a couple, their children and some other relations (extended families), and in still others of more than one couple living together (multiple families). Family members are born, others die and others are acquired through marriage. Occasionally relations who have encountered hard times are taken into the family. The young leave home to find work elsewhere or to marry and move with their spouse. Complex groupings break up into smaller units.[23]

Obviously this dynamism was not entirely suited to the rigidity of a structure made of walls and partitions, although houses in the past were generally more adaptable than modern ones, because of the kinds of building materials used. This was not always the case: in 1769 a young member of a large sharecropper family in the countryside around Prato wanted to marry, but he did not know where to put the marriage bed. The house in which he lived was so short of space that some of the family slept on the kitchen floor.[24] This poses the question of how families adapted their houses to the changing requirements of family life, and how much the houses in which they lived influenced their possibilities of expansion and contraction.

Of course, there is no single answer to these questions. However, analysis of some examples will allow us at least to sketch out a general overview. We have discussed Italy in great detail, so let us shift to Norway at the other end of Europe, where the nuclear family was dominant and yet towards the end of the period under examination there were other relations living with a third of the families, quite often parents or in-laws of the householder.[25]

Since the fifteenth and sixteenth centuries, joint estate or common ownership of property had spread throughout Norway, while in the Middle Ages property had been kept separate. According to laws passed in 1604 (*Norske Lovbog*), a widow would retain half of the joint property, which from 1687 also included allodial property (not subject to a feudal superior).[26] The death of the head of the family did not however automatically lead to the division of the land and the cohabiting group, as the widow was not obliged to divide the half of the property that was not hers amongst her children until they were 25. In any event, she was entitled to stay in the farmhouse until her death, irrespective of her children's ages. By promising to provide her with meat, milk, bread and wool, they could propose alternative accommodation to the farmhouse. Whether or not this possibility was exploited probably depended on relations between the mother, the sons and any daughters-in-law, and the availability of space for everyone, even if that meant makeshift solutions.

English common law clearly demonstrates the kind of constraints that this type of house imposed. According to this law, the widow was entitled to a dower,[27] which had to be made over to her within forty days of her husband's death, and during that period she could remain in the latter's home at the expense of the undivided estate. She was also entitled to an alternative house to the main residence, as well as a third of the land. If, however, the husband only had a house in town, she was entitled to a third or a half of it, according to the provisions concerning her right to remain in the marital home ('free bench').

These provisions demonstrate how decisions concerning cohabitation when a continuity of family life has been broken were influenced by the physical structure of the house and the various degrees of flexibility that different situations provided. The fact that a more or less substantial group of relations lived under the same roof depended therefore on a wide range of influences that circumscribed the areas of choice and created various degrees of restriction. Such influences included local and social traditions concerning the manner in which families should be constituted and the relations with whom one would live at different periods of one's life, individual preferences and idiosyncrasies, the financial and practical implications of living together and separating, and the possibilities of settling old people and spinsters in public or collective facilities, such as hospices, hospitals, 'conservatories' and poor houses.[28]

3. Getting along and arguing

The question of whether or not people got on was important for those who could afford to follow their own inclinations. For example, in 1789 the famous playwright and son of the previously mentioned Marquis Luigi ed Eleonora Bentivoglio,[29] Francesco Albergati Capacelli, was preparing to marry for the third time, on this occasion to Teresa Checchi Zampieri. Their agreement established that should she become a widow without children of her own and not wish to live together with Luigi's son by his first marriage, she was to receive a cheque for 800 *scudi* every year 'as well as a respectably furnished flat with use of kitchen, granary and cellar, entirely equipped in his *palazzo* in Bologna, and also three beds, one for her own use and two for family use.[30] Twelve years later in 1801, when drawing up his last will, Francesco returned to the question of Teresa's treatment in the event of widowhood. He wrote that if she and my son Luigi '*do not want to live together as one family at one and the same table*, I then order and require that my said spouse receive . . . five thousand lira annually . . . , that she has the simple use and enjoyment of the aforementioned apartments in the city, which should be furnished as befits, . . . two carriages, . . . two horses'. He went on to demand that his heir allocate 'a cellar, a washroom, a granary, a wood-shed, and linen, . . . sufficient wardrobe and accommodation for the servants'.[31]

Exactly ten years before Marquis Albergati was drawing up his first will, Michael and Maria Redl, a peasant couple from Taures in Austria, were giving serious thought to the question of how to deal with tensions in their family. Their worries did not however concern what would happen after their death, but what they could expect in their own future. They were in fact drawing up a contract of sale of their farm to their son and daughter-in-law that was similar to the one for Joseph and Anna Maria Pichler examined in the previous chapter. They reserved the right to continue to live in the house, but also established that if they were unable to get on with their son and daughter-in-law 'a separate room will be built inside the house'.[32] Clauses of this kind were not uncommon in contracts by which parents handed down house and land to one of their sons, particularly in central Europe. Occasionally, there was a requirement for the chil-dren to pay the parents' rent in another house.[33] In some areas, farms had a shack on its own to which parents were supposed to withdraw, although there were those who preferred to rent these to landless peasants (*Heuerlinge*) and keep their parents in the main house.[34]

Not everyone, however, had the choice of freely choosing whether or not to live with their own relations and in-laws according to their feelings towards them. The cost of such decisions could be extremely high. In the Franche Comté, serfs could only inherit from each other if they lived under the same roof, warmed themselves at the same fire and ate at the same table. Obviously this created intolerable situations: when the French Revolution broke out, they sent a *cahier de doléances* to the States General in which they complained that every house appeared 'a mere prison' in which the prisoners were forced to live together in order not to lose their share of the land that they 'had watered with the sweat of their brow'. In other words, the sons had to remain in the paternal home, even if they were continually arguing, and they had to continue to do this when they married and their wives did not fit in peacefully into the family. Apart from the enforced cohabitation, the tension was aggravated by the fact that, if one of the members of the family left, the inheritance of the remaining members increased. Exasperating other family members and putting their patience to the test in order to get them to leave was an effective strategy and one that was put into practice.[35]

Such situations were to be found in other regions. Towards the end of the eighteenth century, it became common practice for Russian feudal lords to obstruct or restrict the division of their peasant families. This explains why the *isbe* in Mishino were so crowded.[36] A similar practice was introduced after 1754 along the eastern border of the Habsburg Empire where families provided soldiers for the army. Given that it was easier to recruit soldiers from larger families rather than small ones, it was decided to prohibit their division. *Zadrugas*, the large family groups typical of the region, probably reflected the needs of the empire more than those of the peasants themselves.[37]

Conversely, in Poland feudal lords tried to stop peasant sons from staying with their parents when they married. It was not in the landowner's interest for several men to live under the same roof, as the money paid to the lord was proportional to the size of the farm and not the number of people who worked it. Feudal lords therefore attempted to settle peasants on as many plots as possible. Moreover, as the presence of a married couple was essential for guaranteeing the productivity of a farm, they forced widows and widowers to remarry quickly or face the loss of their land. Similarly, if an unmarried son inherited from his father, they forced him to get married in a hurry. In the case of large holdings with pack animals, however, they did all they could to avoid fragmentation through the system of partible inheritance observed by the peasants, but not always with success. A few new farms without pack animals would not have guaranteed the same productivity as a large farm with such animals.[38] In Courland, feudal lords also forced widows to remarry and they attempted to force peasants to leave their land to a single son. They had to request authorisation from their lord in order to split farms.[39] In eastern Europe, lords generally prevented their peasants from marrying outside their lands in order not to lose their workforce, and in Italy sharecroppers had to ask the landowner for permission to marry.[40] In other words, you could not always choose freely the person whose daily life you were to share.[41]

4. Cohabitation and kinship

This complex patchwork of restrictions and opportunities, which existed on various levels, forces us to weigh up the determining factors or the relative freedom of choice of family members on a case-by-case basis. It is particularly important to remember that very similar systems of inheritance transmission and family formation can lead to different family forms. For example, I have referred extensively in the previous chapter to inheritance systems with a priviledged heir of land and buildings. In the Provence model, where the father retained the role of *paterfamilias* until his death, it was very probable that a stem family would be formed when the heir married. In the Austrian and German cases we examined who was supposed to live in the parental house, if the parents withdrew, and contracts of sale of the farm to the son often dealt with the problem of guarantee-

ing *separate* accommodation for his parents. There were therefore different out-
comes in different cases at different times, even for the same family: everyone
could live under the same roof, possibly eat at the same table, or, as we have seen,
parents could set up independent accommodation within the house or close-by.[42]

All this means that we must not overestimate the importance of forms of
cohabitation as the distinctive element when we analyse the characteristics
and changes in the family. In Corsica, for example, it has proved difficult to distinguish different households because, according to activity and season, nuclear
family units agglomerated or separated from each other. Some Hungarian
villages were characterized by the presence of many different types of accommodation. An anthropological survey of Átány in the Great Plain region showed
that peasants did not consider living under one roof important in defining their
families. Moreover, in Átány, as in other Hungarian villages, mean lived together,
separate from their women.[43] The size and features of the kinship group have to
be taken into account as well as the composition of the cohabiting group.[44]

In this context, it is interesting to analyse the ways in which recognition of
membership of a kinship group or family structure influenced the establishment
of networks of individual relationships and determined each person's rights and
duties, irrespective of whether or not they lived together.[45] For example, sons
who were lax in looking after their ageing and no longer self-sufficient parents
were much more likely to be forced to do their duty in a city like Rome than
in England. Indeed, in England consanguinity does not appear to have created
such binding obligations, although recent studies have softened images of the
English-speaking world as a place where family-formation rules led to the severe
isolation of old people.[46]

Concerning the question of the relationship between house and family, it
should be emphasized that in Rome the obligation to maintain a relation did
not mean that the provider of maintenance and the beneficiary had to live
together.[47] Indeed, one scholar has recently argued that it is now possible to
distinguish between a Europe in which family links were weak (central and
northern Europe) and a Europe in which they were strong (Mediterranean
Europe), regardless of whether the most common form of cohabitation in the
past was the nuclear family or the complex family. An important factor in the
establishment of this demarcation line is supposed to have been the fact that it
was much more common in northern Europe than in southern Europe to send
children into service during adolescence, so they became accustomed to living
away from their parents.[48]

Returning to the case of Rome, it has already been established that the elderly
could be maintained by their relations without sharing the same domestic space
as their benefactors. Conversely, cohabitation did not imply the same financial

condition for all members of the group that lived together, as will have become clear in the preceding pages. Living together did not necessarily involve shared finances in which all incomes were pooled, and this was true of both rich and poor families. Many poor families lived under the same roof, which could not in any case be relied upon, and it was every man for himself.[49] It should not surprise us then that in a census carried out in Bologna in 1796 to establish the conditions of the poor, some members of the same family could be defined as destitute and others as poor.[50]

In the Salerno area, property was divided equally amongst the sons, and after they married they lived with their families in separate areas of the same house or in adjacent houses. These were nuclear families, but there were also 'kinship neighbourhoods' made up of buildings with relations with the same surname living alongside one another. Agnatic kinship (i.e. relations along the paternal line) established networks of social cohesion and solidarity that were expressed through their form of accommodation.[51] Interestingly, one scholar has suggested that kinship networks were particularly important in societies characterized by partible inheritance and transmission of land to all or many children, while in those characterized by impartible inheritance and transmission of the farm to a privileged heir the house and coresidence played a central role.

Leaving aside the family structure, examination of cohabiting units without due consideration of kinship would also be misleading in the case of the Piedmontese community of Santena. Families that did not live together established 'kinship fronts' and individual 'hearths' did not act independently of each other. They acted within much larger alliances that were generally held together by consanguinity along the male line. Principally because of the diversification in their economic activities, they pursued 'a collective interest that went beyond the different vicissitudes and characteristics of each individual nucleus in the kinship group and each individual person within the nucleus'.[52]

Having examined a case from the south of Italy and one from the north, we should now look at the situation of sharecropping families in central Italy. As I have already suggested, families were often complex because of the need to maintain a balance between the hands available to work the land and mouths that had to be fed (not surprisingly women were more often expelled from villages than men).[53] When the balance between the land and the family was upset, there was a choice: either slip into the ranks of destitute farm labourers who had no rights in relation to the land or transfer to a farm that was more suitable to the family's needs.[54] There was therefore a very different relationship between residence and kinship from the one we have identified in the Salerno area. In the latter, there were nuclear families firmly rooted in neighbourhoods inhabited by relations with the same surname, while in central Italy complex sharecropper families could shift from one farm to another relatively often, and they generally had few links with relations who did not live under the same roof.[55]

5. Shifting patterns

As we have seen, there were isolated families in the middle of the countryside and others surrounded by relations, and thus the relationship between house and family was structured in different ways according to the context. As with a kaleidoscope whose pieces of glass form changing images, different patterns are formed not only by these two elements, but all the others we have examined, such as the methods of transferring property at the age of marriage, forms of cohabitation, duties to other relations, type of settlement, wealth and so on. We have attempted to perceive the variety and richness of the alternatives and to discover their implications. In doing this, we have constantly concentrated our attention on the house and the family, and the way they interact, overlap and occasionally become disjointed. We have assessed the significance of bricks and mortar on the free development of family relations, but our image of the house itself remains very vague. The *isbe* of Mishino were small and crowded, but we have yet to see whether this was also true of the house of an Italian *mezzadro* or a German *Bauer*.

IV

The Home

1. Peasants and towns people

During the period we are studying, the majority of the population lived in the countryside, although the cities were growing. If you include Russia, the population that lived in towns and cities with more than 5,000 inhabitants grew from 10.3 per cent in 1500 to about 12 per cent between 1600 and 1800. If you exclude Russia, it was around 11 per cent in the sixteenth century, 13 per cent in the seventeenth and 14 per cent in the eighteenth. The situation in Europe varied greatly: in the sixteenth century there were levels of urbanization of over 30 per cent in the regions surrounding Venice, Seville, Ghent and Antwerp. At that time, slightly under a third of the population of the Netherlands lived in cities. During the seventeenth century, the country's 'golden age', the rate of urbanization reached unprecedented levels. By 1675 it had reached 43 per cent. At the opposite extreme, the rate of urbanization in European Russia was (according to the different estimates) between six and eight times lower than that of the Netherlands, and during the early modern era it tended to fall because the rural population was growing more rapidly than the urban one.[1]

Hence the majority of the European population between the sixteenth and the eighteenth century lived in the countryside, although there were significant differences between regions and between one period and another. One important distinction was between the rural populations of western and eastern Europe. In western Europe, the gradual decline of serfdom, which had already commenced in the Middle Ages, was continuing. The number of peasants who were deprived of personal freedom and bound to their landlord's land was falling all the time, and the labour they provided was increasingly paid in cash. The trend in eastern Europe was exactly the opposite, and in the sixteenth and seventeenth centuries the number of free peasants was considerably reduced (serfdom was not abolished in Russia until 1861).[2]

This was not the only difference that divided the rural world of Europe. There were differences in social position in the countryside just as in the city. For peasants, this was often associated with the relationship they had to the land. There were peasants who owned their own land, peasants who rented their land, farm servants, day labourers and, particularly in eastern Europe, serfs. Within each particular context, the social structure could be either uniform or hierarchical. Taken as a whole, the trend in the early modern era was towards differentiation between peasants, and in many areas there was a growth in the number of those who were not securely settled on the land they cultivated.[3]

These rural proletarians who often did not manage to work on a continuous basis were particularly inclined to eke out their meagre earnings from agricultural work by weaving for merchants who provided them with the raw materials. Weaving, either for the market or for private consumption, was also practised by peasants who owned their land, if they did not have very much or if their farming involved long periods in which the work was not very demanding. The term 'proto-industry' has been coined to describe these non-agricultural activities for the inter-regional and international markets. They represent the start of industrialization, even though the areas in which they were highly developed did not always turn into industrialized areas. Indeed, flourishing proto-industrial development could on occasions lead to a process of de-industrialization.[4]

Even in places where there was very little or no proto-industrial development, it was still not uncommon for peasants to diversify their activities. In many mountain areas, seasonal migration was used to supplement earnings from agriculture with those from a wide variety of trades, which sometimes constituted the greatest source of income.[5] Lastly, not everyone who lived in a village was a peasant and not everyone obtained their principal source of subsistence from agriculture. There were millers, blacksmiths, other artisans, priests and more. In other words, working the fields was not the only activity carried out in the countryside.[6]

2. Villages and scattered houses

'[They] live isolated from one another, alone with their families and their animals; they live in terrible hovels made of mud and wood and are roofed with straw. They eat a kind of black rye bread, porridge oats or pea and lentil soup. They drink almost exclusively water and milk. Their clothing is limited to a few smocks made of ticking, a pair of laced boots and a felt hat. These people never rest, and work from morning to night. They take their livestock and produce to town to be sold, and with the proceeds they buy what they need. [They] have to work for the lords several times a year: they work their fields, pick their fruit, fill their barns, cut their firewood, build their houses and dig their ditches. There is no limit to what these poor people are forced to do for their lords; there is nothing, if so ordered, that they can refuse to do without putting themselves at risk.'

These were the words the German scholar Sebastian Münster wrote about peasants in 1544 in his *Cosmographia universa*. He summed it up briefly: 'Their life is unpleasant and poverty-stricken.'[7] The peasants of whom he spoke were obviously the ones he knew, but as I have mentioned, they did not all live in the same conditions and their lives were not to remain unaffected in the coming centuries. In the following pages, we will verify whether everyone really did live in hovels, and whether they were clothed in rags and ate rye bread. For the moment, however, we will concentrate on the types of settlement.

According to Münster, they lived on their own. In reality, the majority of the population lived in villages surrounded by fields. The scattered settlement did however spread to vast areas during the early modern era (but not southern Italy and the Spanish Meseta), and in some cases the phenomenon had started to appear in the Middle Ages. The change was due to the reduction in the threat of external aggression, which during the previous era had encouraged the concentration of populations. Other reasons were the passing or at least weakening of feudal relations (in western Europe) whereby access to the land was exchanged for the provision of labour as a community, the increase in cultivated land, the decline in village solidarity resulting from the reduction in the open field system and community rights, and the spread of forms of land management based on compact farm units worked by tenants or sharecroppers.[8]

Naturally, not all villages were the same. Some had only a few houses, while others could have a hundred or more households. In some, generally the more ancient ones, the houses were scattered in a haphazard manner. The roads were simply established by continuous transit, but once this had happened they influenced the possible development of new houses. In other villages, generally the newer ones, houses and roads were planned and laid out in a more orderly fashion. Some settlements, particularly in eastern Germany, Poland and the lower reaches of the Danube, but also to some extent in Great Britain and western Europe, were made up of two lines of houses along a road with fields that stretched out behind the houses parallel with each other. Some villages, particularly in Slav areas, had houses built around a central empty space where animals could graze. There was often a pond or a well, and at the centre or to one side of the space there might be a church and occasionally a cemetery or other communal facilities. If a market was held in the village, its stills would be set up there. In the eighteenth century Hungarian plain, following the expulsion of the Turks, they developed a rectangular or grid plan. Highly compact settlements were to be found in the belt that runs from the Paris basin to the Russian steppes and various parts of Mediterranean Europe, while in southern regions subject to Ottoman rule, the *čiflik* was an area of land subject to a *bey* (the Turkish landowner) and the settlement within it was made up of a courtyard dominated by the house belonging to the *bey* and his factor and surrounded by barrack-like quarters occupied by the Christians who worked the farms (*rayas*).[9]

Although villages could be very different, life within them had some common features that distinguished them from life in scattered houses, in which the cohabiting unit was often an extended or multiple family. The latter lacked the bitter conflicts between groups but also the mutual assistance typical of village life. In the village, ploughing, harvesting and building were collective activities rather than individual or family ones.[10] This could often constitute a handicap for isolated farms which, according to some historians, were less likely to use heavy ploughs and had simpler and less decorated buildings.[11] Obviously there were exceptions: in the Po Valley, there was a precocious development of large capitalist agricultural businesses with isolated farmhouses lived in by salaried staff who were not related and worked their employer's lands using advanced methods. In central Italy throughout the early modern era (but particularly in the eighteenth century), rural architecture underwent development and innovation as a result of the investment of urban capital in the countryside and the commitment of architects paid by city-based landowners to the construction of well-organised and functional houses designed for a more rational exploitation of the land.[12]

Of course, community control and the influence of social hierarchies might have been less of a factor for isolated houses, but in the case of tenant farmers the contractual power in dealing with the landowner would also have been lower and subjugation greater.[13] For those who lived far from the village, it was more difficult to get to market, to church and to school, if one existed. In other words, families that lived in scattered houses had to be more self-sufficient than those who lived in villages.[14]

3. Country dwellings

What were the peasants' houses like? Tacitus, in his *Germania*, described dwellings dug out of the ground and covered with branches: more like lairs than houses. Yet such forms of shelter remained in use for centuries. Even in the nineteenth century, when travelling along the Hungarian *puszta* or the Bulgarian and Romanian plains, it was possible to see on the horizon the strange profile of a straw roof resting on the ground, with a brick chimney and an entrance that led into an underground house (Fig. 13).[15] Even in the Netherlands, there were houses partially set into the ground, while in southern Italy and in Morvan in France, there were houses carved out of the rock.[16]

A very similar kind of house to prehistoric models was very common in the countryside up until the end of the Middle Ages. It was rectangular in shape and had an earth floor, sometimes covered with sand or straw. It consisted of one or two rooms, and there were often no windows. It was not uncommon for the central fireplace to be little more than a hole in the ground. The house itself was built of wood and organic material mixed with mud or clay, with a roof of straw or reeds. During the early modern era, these buildings were gradually abandoned or used for non-residential purposes (byres, barns, storerooms). The process was slow and uneven: it initially involved the more affluent sections of rural communities in wealthier areas, and then the less affluent and the poorer regions.[17]

To have an idea of the social difference, we can recall that in north-west Germany, the landless *Heuerlinge* lived in cottages next to the farmhouse of the *Altbauern* who granted them lands in exchange for their labour (*corvées*).[18] Around 1770, in a farm in Altopascio (Tuscany), the workers lived in straw shacks and slept with the livestock.[19] In Tierra de Campos in the Castilian valley of Duero, during the eighteenth century, the houses of the wealthier inhabitants had several floors and spacious rooms divided by brick walls or curtains, while those of the less well-off had one or two floors and small windows to keep in the warmth, and were built from a wooden frame filled with mud and straw (*tapial*). Only in the nineteenth century was there to be a widespread adoption of stone and brick in house-building.[20] In France (but also elsewhere),[21] woods-men and charcoal-burners lived up until recent times in extremely rudimentary shacks made of organic material, and were often looked on as almost savages by townspeople and country folk alike.[22]

Interestingly the architect Sebastiano Serlio (1475–1554/55), who was born in Italy and lived for a long time in France, claimed in Book Six of his treatise *De Architectura* that there was a wide variety of housing in the countryside, which differed on the basis of the social position of those who were to live in them and according to whether the builder had intended to follow the Italian fashion or the French tradition. Serlio was interested in everyone: poor, mid-dling and rich peasants, artisans, townspeople, merchants of varying degrees of wealth, gentlemen, princes, tyrants and even kings. He only ignored the 'poor beggar', whose shack was not worthy of mention. He proposed a different kind of house for everyone, one that had been thought out and planned precisely for their needs, from the poor peasant's 'hovel' with just one living room and a barn to the sumptuous country house of a king (Fig. 15–16).[23] These were of course plans, but in a way they still reflected the variety of the architectural land-scape of the countryside.

From the Renaissance, one of the trends that contributed to this increasing complexity and change in rural buildings was the fashion for a 'villa', which spread from Italy to the rest of Europe.[24] The nobility in most of western Europe shifted its principle residence to the city during the late Middle Ages and the early modern era, and hence the country villa, although grandiose, was generally a secondary residence. This was not the case in England, where 'ownership of a country residence was an essential condition for belonging to the local elites, from whose ranks the ruling class originated'. The importance of these residences was such that families were defined by both their surname and the name of the house, which 'became on the one hand, the embodiment of ancestral patrimony and the outward symbol of the dignity and authority of [its] owner, and on the other the machine for living the life of an English country gentleman'.[25]

The development of English country houses started in the sixteenth century, at the time when the countryside ceased to be such a dangerous place and it was possible to abandon the medieval fortified home. In the following centuries, new residences were built and old ones modernized, leading to a profound change in the landscape. 'Picturesque' panoramas were built to satisfy the tastes of their owners. The spread of the fashion for the isolated villa built on top of a hill with a garden and surrounded by an enormous park led to restructured, rationalized and hidden coach-houses and other outbuildings and to the destruction of peasant houses in the shadow of the landowner's home. The farm was kept at a distance. In some cases, entire villages were razed to the ground and rebuilt elsewhere to provide space for a park suitable for foxhunting and capable of providing the country house with appropriate level of privacy.[26]

In the early modern era, the European countryside contained a variety of housing that ranged from sumptuous palaces to shelters similar to an animal's lair. This architecture was enriched not only by the construction of villas for the elites, but also by the enlargement and modernization of rural housing which, as has already been suggested and will be demonstrated further in the following pages, was a typical feature of many parts of Europe during this period. Although to some extent there were differences everywhere between the houses of rich peasants and those of poor ones, there were plenty of areas where their differences were more limited. In Poland, to take one of the many examples, the most common rural house even in the nineteenth century was made of wood, with a stone foundation and a clay floor. The cottage roof with thatch or shingles. They had no more than two rooms, one for sleeping and the other, which had a central fireplace without a chimney, for cooking. Not surprisingly, the bedroom was called the white room (*biala izba*) and the other the black room (*czarna izba*), as it was blackened from the smoke that could not escape.[27] When a serf's *isbe* in Russia had the luxury of a second room, the rooms were also called the black and white rooms, but during the harsh Russian winters, the white room could only be used for storage. It was only a living space during the summer.[28]

4. Keeping warm

Fireplaces and stoves

It was not only the strength of tradition that caused houses with central fireplaces and no chimney to survive so long in some areas and social classes. Nonflammable materials of stone or brick are required to construct a fireplace in the wall, whether you live in the countryside or in town, and metal would be required as well if you wanted a stove. These were expensive innovations that required relatively extensive changes to the structure of a house.[29] In some areas they built external ovens or small kitchens, thus avoiding the risk of fire and the considerable costs involved in modernization, but on the other hand they were not exploiting the heat source to its full.[30] In order to have a fireplace in a side wall, one solution was to build just one of the walls of brick and the other three of organic material, as in the case of the *bourrines* in the marshes of the Vendée.[31]

The fireplace in a side wall, which appears to have been an Italian invention, was probably introduced in Venice between the twelfth and thirteenth centuries. The first one of whose existence we can be certain was built in 1227.[32] Since then, stove repairers, chimneysweeps and great architects have been vying with each other in the study of the correct angle for cowls and chimneys to improve the draught and the extraction of smoke. Over the centuries, the cowl was lowered and the flue bent. In the meantime, the fireplace spread from Italy to the rest of Europe.[33] It made it possible to have rooms that were less smoky, but much of the heat was lost.

A more rational exploitation of a heat source became possible with the introduction of stoves. It started with the development of simple stone, brick or clay ovens, possibly in the southern Alps.[34] A brick version that was occasionally covered with majolica tiles (*Kachelofen*) spread throughout Switzerland, Austria, Germany, Hungary, Poland and Russia. Sometimes they were positioned between two rooms, which they then managed to heat at the same time. Benches were positioned around them for sitting and sleeping in the warmth. Until very recent times, old people in Tyrolese farmsteads slept on top of or next to the stove (Fig. 17).[35]

We have the account of an Italian traveller at the end of the sixteenth century. Francesco da Pavia was on several occasions a guest in Polish houses in which the entire family slept on benches covered with cushions and furs, and positioned around the stove. Guests were given a place to sleep along with members of the family. Francesco took advantage of such situations to find a place close to one of the women in the house. Sometimes his advances were well accepted, but on others he only received scratches (without anyone being woken).[36]

But let us leave the slightly risqué story of Francesco da Pavia and return to that of the stoves. As has already been suggested, those our traveller observed were most common in central, northern and eastern Europe, while the open fireplace continued to prevail in the southern Slav areas.[37] The stove did not have great success in Italy, southern France and Portugal, where sidewall fireplaces were common. Stoves were also to be found in the north, particularly in Norway and England. They were often modified to burn coal in England, where they started to spread in the sixteenth century, but remained a luxury for a long time.[38] In Spain they used braziers, in spite of the fact that houses were built of stone, and they did this partly because of the availability of firewood that did not produce a lot of smoke and flames. In these areas, the fire was a portable piece of furniture, a kind of heater.[39] In Tierra de Campos and Tierra de Pan in Castille, where there was a shortage of firewood, they kept warm by burning straw in underground pipes.[40] From the seventeenth and eighteenth centuries, iron and cast iron stoves were developed and initially used in the Netherlands.[41] In 1740 the Franklin stove was invented and it was to become very popular.[42]

Window glass

Better heating of the home was also achieved from the spread of glass windows, as well as fireplaces and stoves. The poorest of English cottages (like much of the worst housing) had not only no glass but also no windows throughout our period[43], and even in the nineteenth century there were peasant houses whose windows could only be closed with solid wood shutters, so that when it was cold there was a choice between light and warmth. In other words, windows were a luxury that not everyone could afford. They were also considered a luxury by the authorities, at least in some countries like England and revolutionary France, where they were one of the commodities subject to a tax on wealth.[44] They began to be used in houses of cities like Genoa and Florence as far back as the fourteenth century. During the early modern era, glass windows ceased to be found exclusively in churches and the grand houses of the rich, and began to be more commonplace. They were used along with wooden shutters but replaced oilpaper and cloth covers (*impannate*), where they had been in use. The latter were made by putting cloth on a frame and generally soaking it in turpentine to make it semi-transparent.[45] A traveller in Tuscany in the mid-eighteenth century observed that there was glass in the windows of all the houses, and he dated their introduction to about eighty years before.[46] As time went on, the glass became clearer and more transparent, providing extra light. The small panes and circles held together with lead were replaced by increasingly large panes of clear glass.[47]

Windows in rural houses, where they existed, remained small for a long time. Gradually, however, staying warm in winter ceased to mean having the entire family huddled together around a smoky fire in the half light, covered with as many clothes as possible, with the livestock close-by to make use of their heat (until recent times it was common in many areas to pass the evening in the warmth of the barn, Fig. 79).[48] There was a slow and limited reduction in the dependence of human activity on daytime and night-time, and on summer and winter.

Lighting a fire and fuel for warmth

Lighting a fire started to be a slightly less difficult and laborious operation with the invention around 1530 of the first rudimentary matches. These were not yet matches that could ignite by themselves when rubbed against a surface, which were not introduced until the beginning of the nineteenth century. They were simply little pieces of wood, cane, hemp, rolled paper or cotton which had been coated with wax and were easy to light. To light them, a piece of steel and a flint shard were struck together hard in the hope of producing a spark that would be hot enough and last long enough to light a piece of cloth, the tinder. This was then used for lighting the match, which in turn lit the actual fuel.[49] This long and tiring operation, which had to be done in the dark and, during winter, with hands numb from the cold, was generally entrusted to servants, if there were any, or to women (Figs. 19–20). A seventeenth-century English ballad tells of the tasks a woman had to do: '. . . when that I rise early in the morn, / Before that I my head with dressing adorn, I sweep and cleane the house as need doth require, / Or, if that it be cold, I make a fire'.[50] Not surprisingly then, those who had plenty of fuel kept their fire constantly alight, and it was not unusual to ask a neighbour for an ember from their fire.[51]

These problems could be very serious in some areas. The range of fuels was extremely varied according to local availability and individual possibilities. Hence the advantages and disadvantages of each fuel were equally varied.[52] There was straw, hay, coal, peat, animal excrement and various mixtures of each. Edward Daniel Clarke recounts that while he and his company were travelling through Cornwall and Devon in 1791, his heart was touched by seeing 'an old woman hobbling after our horses in hopes of a little fuel from their excrement', and this provides an excellent example of how onerous the business of collecting fuel could be.[53] The reason dung was almost exclusively used by poor people was due to its smell and not because it was a bad fuel. Its calorific value (4.0) is in fact higher than the average for firewood (3.5), identical to that of peat and more than half that of bituminous coal (6.9).[54] The problem of supply appears to have been particularly bad in England. In 1696, 15 per cent of its land surface was woodland, but by the 1920s it was only 5 per cent, making it the European country with the least woodland after Portugal. After 1840 coal, which had been used for some time, largely replaced firewood. Previously, however, particularly in the late eighteenth century, firewood had become increasingly scarce and costly. In his study into the conditions of the poor (*The State of the Poor*, 1797), Sir Frederick Morton Eden complained that the poverty of agricultural labourers in the south of the country was such that preparation of food was limited to boiling water twice a day for tea. The bread they ate every day and the roast that enriched their Sunday meals were cooked by the baker. Many of them had never tasted a hot meal.[55]

The symbolic value of fire

Apart from the problems of fuel supply and its cost, a live fire had a tremendous symbolic and almost sacred significance. It embodied the family, hospitality and life itself. It should not surprise us that in Sardinia, where central fireplaces were prevalent, the fire was only put out in the event of bereavement. In many areas, women, who in the absence of servants appear to have been mainly responsible for the maintenance of the fire, devoted particular care to cleaning and maintaining the appearance of the fire, which was surrounded by many beliefs and superstitions.[56] In various languages it was a metonym for the family, given that a household was referred to as a hearth (*feu* in French and *fuoco* in Italian). The neo-Latin versions derive from the Latin *focus*, which means 'hearth' or 'home'. [57]

The practical and symbolic centrality of the fire in relation to family life emerges very clearly from Serlio's description of the house for wealthy peasants. 'Firstly,' he wrote, 'I propose that there be a room common to all in the middle, and at its centre there shall be a fire, so that more people can get round it and everyone can see the others' faces when engaging in their amusements and storytelling.'[58] We can almost see this family sitting around the fire as they interweave their face-to-face relations and express their unity through their entertainment and discussion (Fig. 16).

Shifting the fire from the centre of the room to the wall, the introduction of more than one fireplace and hiding the live flame in a stove were not just ways of modifying the means of heating a home and at least in part the preparation of food. They also meant giving life to environments that allowed different ways of socializing for family members. They made it possible to transform and diversify the world of the imagination. They tended to alter the symbolic harmony of the home not only in relation to its internal space but also in its cosmic dimension. One author has claimed: 'the dark and smoky chimney with its blackened cowl was a kind of celestial conduit that put the house interior in contact with the remote vastness of the sky'.[59]

'What a difference between a stove and a fireplace,' Sébastien Mercier is supposed to have commented in 1788. 'The sight of a stove extinguishes my imagination, saddens me and makes me melancholic: I prefer the biting cold to this invisible, tepid and lifeless heat. I love to watch the flames, which stir my imagination.'[60] Indeed the stove and the fireplace referred to two different cultures and to two different ways of relating to fire, heat and light (the fire in a stove gives off no light). Perhaps this is why in areas where there was a solid tradition of fireplaces, such as France and in particular Italy, the struggle against the cold led to their increased number rather than the adoption of the stove, which did however make it possible to save fuel and exploit it better (about two-thirds of the heat from a fireplace is lost up the chimney).[61]

In houses with only a single room, the fire was the focal point of the interior. The same was true of houses that had only one room with a fire and those which had a communal room with a fire that, although not the only one, fulfilled several functions, such as providing light, heat, flame, embers and hot cinders for cooking. In houses of those of higher rank, the family coat of arms was sometimes displayed over the cowl. The increased number of fires and their differentiation (fires for cooking, fires for heating and fires for ostentation) therefore represented 'a profound change in the very blueprint of the living space', both in function and in symbolic terms.[62]

5. Innovations

It is not altogether surprising that progress in lighting and heating was often interlinked with other changes. The newly built houses tended to be larger, they developed upwards and had more differentiation of the interior spaces. In the countryside, the simple single or double room house of prehistoric origin was developed into the so-called *longhouse*, a lengthened structure on one or two floors that had rooms for livestock and tools next to the living quarters. In the Alpine region, there was the spread of the *Blockhaus* or *maison-bloc*, which had more than one floor. The ground floor was made of stone and the others were made of wood.[63]

Important architects in several areas undertook to redesign rural housing. Peasant houses, according to Leon Battista Alberti back in the fifteenth century, had to provide 'useful' space to the family, livestock and agricultural produce. 'There must therefore be a large kitchen that is not dark ... with an oven, fireplace, well and sink. Next to the kitchen, there will be a room for the head of the family, with a chest for bread, salted meat and the indispensable things for daily needs. The other members of the family shall be organized in such a manner that each is close to their own things and ready to use them.'[64]

'It is essential,' argued Francesco Milizia in 1781, 'that rustic houses for farm workers and country matters be distinguished in their simplicity by a salubrious position and convenient layout. On the one hand, the house shall have a spacious kitchen with a fire in the middle and bedrooms around it, and on the other, it shall have rooms and storerooms for keeping agricultural tools and agricultural produce. On the floor above, there could be some rooms for the use of the owner or his factor.'[65] The house was only supposed to be complete when it had a courtyard, colonnade, cellars, barns, cowsheds and dovecotes, all planned for the mixed agriculture of the Italian peninsula.[66] A French historian has noted that in the sixteenth century, a new architectural genre appeared, albeit one with distant antecedents. The humanist Charles Estienne, who provided the ideal description, defined it as the 'rustic house' (*maison rustique*). The precepts determined by Estienne in 1564 were to remain in force and exercise a considerable influence on house construction until the end of the eighteenth century.[67]

Larger houses on more than one floor, equipped with stoves or fireplaces, required relatively solid building materials. During the early modern era, particularly in the eighteenth century, there was a tendency to replace more perishable building materials with stone or bricks, and straw or thatch roofs were replaced with tiles, slates and other materials. In villages, brick and stone construction was generally adopted for more important buildings, such as the church and the houses of the better-off and the priest or minister. Only later (if at all) did it spread to the lower ranks of the population. Brick or stone construction had many advantages: it was more lasting, it reduced the risk of fire, and it offered less protection to insects, cockroaches, mice and rats, which could carry diseases such as the plague. Where stone was not particularly abundant, it cost a great deal more than organic materials. One French scholer has calculated that a house made of brick or stone could cost between ten and fifteen times more than one built with lighter materials.[68]

Once we have identified this trend, we must not exaggerate and apply schematic concepts too rigidly. House-building was influenced by the availability of one material in relation to another in each particular area. The use of a specific material did not necessarily imply that a house was of good or bad quality. In Mediterranean regions, stone had always been the principal building material, mainly because of its abundance. Even miserable hovels lacking all comforts were therefore made of stone. Similarly in other areas, as one historian has noted, houses in Brittany and Cornwall were 'of granite, in Burgundy they were of limestone, and in Ile-de-France they were of stones'. On the other hand, the so-called *Fachwerkhäuser*, which were to be found all over central and northern Europe, particularly where stone was scarce, were built from wooden structures filled with a clay and straw mix and could be almost luxurious (Figs. 21

and 40). In other words, the local availability of a material constituted an important limitation, particularly for the worse-off.[69] For example, it was precisely the abundance of trees with long straight trunks, such as pines and firs, that encouraged the development of the *Blockhaus* (*maison-bloc*) in Alpine regions. However, cultural factors interacted with the local availability of materials. It was mainly in areas colonized by Germany that houses of this kind were found,[70] as though a particular culture provided a filter that made it easier to perceive the usefulness of one material rather than another.[71]

Therefore, we must not exaggerate the environmental limitations: populations could move, taking with them their building traditions and techniques to environments where they might not have been rational.[72] The same could be said of the spread of some fashions and architectural customs to regions where they lacked any usefulness or were indeed quite unsuitable, such as the tiled roofs in vast areas of eastern France that were not very suitable to the local climate.[73] According to one historian, the spread of stone buildings was itself due to the example set by Roman civilization first and Renaissance Italy later. In other words, it was Rome that spread 'the stone disease beyond the Narbonne region', even to areas where stone was hard to get. However, 'the victory of stone over wood', argues the same author, 'took two thousand years', and 'was more complete in France, the Po Valley in Italy, Europe of the Rhine basin, rather than in Germany around the Danube and square-shaped Bohemia, and more complete in Great Britain than northern Europe in the strict sense of the term. Stone never prevailed in the Baltic, Poland, Russia and Scandinavia, except in residential districts.'[74]

The influence of the local availability of materials was also weakened by the production of and trade in brick, tiles and other building materials and by the allocation of available resources to other fields. 'England is a country made of bricks,' observed a foreign traveller in 1790. The vast increase in the use of bricks in England from the middle of the seventeenth century and the contemporary disappearance of timber frame buildings was due to the fact that oak was being employed on a massive scale in the shipbuilding industry.[75]

Ultimately, by the seventeenth century and certainly by the eighteenth century, peasant houses were no longer small, smoky and gloomy hovels overcrowded with people and animals, with floors covered with puddles and home to rats, insects and cockroaches. Such miserable housing was now relegated to the very poor or the poorest regions. The miners of Alvernia or Sicilian farm labourers lived in one-room houses called *barriades*. But if you moved up 'the social scale to the peasants of the plains of the Ile-de-France, Flanders and Loraine, and then to the peasant farmers who owned and tilled their own land in the Languedoc and Provence, and finally the rural master tradesmen or the vine-dressers of Burgundy and the Loire Valley', you would find spacious houses with several living rooms and then barns, byres and cellars.[76] During the early modern era, even the houses of Italian *mezzadri* or sharecroppers became large and spacious, as did those of the German *Bauern*, and many others around Europe.

6. Excuse me, can I come in?

Let's take a closer look at houses belonging to an affluent peasant. Let's enter the house of Jacob Größer and Agatha Deuggerin, who were husband and wife, and the grandparents of Matheis whom we came across earlier.[77] They lived in the German village of Jungingen (Zollernalbkreis) around 1625. The house was a large *Fachwerkhaus* in the middle of the village with the typical black and white motif that contrasted the timber frame from the material used to fill the gaps (Fig. 21). There were no rooms for human habitation on the ground floor. The main entrance opened on to a courtyard. Inside, an extensive corridor cut the house in two and led to another door, which opened onto the nearby stream. Agricultural tools leant against or were hung on the walls this corridor. The rooms on the left were used as storerooms for provisions. There was possibly also a laundry room. On the right, there was a byre with a small window and a double door that led into the yard. Under the stairs that led to the first floor, it appears there was a block of wood for butchering animals, and perhaps a chicken coop and a cage for pigs.

The presence of entirely distinct areas for humans and animals was the sign of a rather sophisticated form of accommodation. At the time, it was not uncommon for small animals to be kept in the *Stube* or main living room.[78] Even the barn where the larger animals were kept was often immediately next to the rooms for human habitation in order to make use of their warmth and to make it easier to look after them and milk them without leaving the house. In this case, the only precaution was generally to build the barn in a slightly lower position to the area for people so that the effluent did not run into it.[79] Forms of cohabitation between people and animals were to be found in many areas, from the Apennine Mountains near Bologna to Courmayeur, and from northern Italy to Holland, particularly amongst the poorer people.[80] Until recent times, there were primitive types of *longères* ('longhouses') in Brittany, which had a central fireplace. Humans and animals lived inside under the same roof, people squeezed into one end and animals into the other, and they were only separated by a few pieces of furniture (wardrobes, chests, etc.) or a wooden partition with openings (see Fig. 14).[81] 'If the poor man has a few animals and at the very most some oxen, he will have to have a small byre attached to the house; . . . there will be a window in the wall facing the fire, so that the oxen see the fire by night and do not take fright during the day', wrote Serlio in the sixteenth century on the subject of the poor peasant's 'hovel' in which 'he lived with his family by his hard labour' (Fig. 15).[82] However, the cohabitation between people and animals could be even more extreme. The missionary John Lanne Buchanan, who visited the Hebrides in the 1780s, reported that the peasants lived in simple shacks along with cows, goats, sheep, geese, ducks and dogs. They were very concerned with keeping their houses dry by collecting cows' urine in large basins and then throwing it away. But they only removed the accumulated excrement once a year and nothing could be said to convince them of the appropriateness of removing it every day.[83]

You would have breathed a very different air in the house of our German peasants. The main living room, the *Stube*, was on the first floor and entirely separate from the area where the animals were kept. It was a well-lit room with two rows of windows (almost certainly fitted with glass) that looked onto the street and met at one corner. On the opposite wall, there was a green majolica stove, which was stoked from the kitchen: hence the *Stube* was a warm but completely smoke-free environment. There were benches next to the stove, and the smallest child's cot was kept close by. There was a recess in the stove to keep a receptacle filled with water, so the house always had a supply of hot water. The furniture was rather simple: there was a large table in the corner diametrically opposite the stove. Benches fixed to the wall and the chest containing clothes, cloth and sheets were used as seating (and if necessary for sleeping). There would be shelves with the family Bible, earthenware jugs and bowls, while clothes and utensils would hang from the walls. There must have also been a candlestick somewhere, or at least a torch-holder. Agatha Deuggerin's wool-winder would have been kept in a corner. Of course, this room was not restricted to eating, sitting and receiving guests; it was used for work such as spinning, sewing, darning and mending tools. However, the *Stube* would not have been used for the preparation of food, so there was a certain degree of specialization in the use of rooms.

In the kitchen, there would have been a cupboard, a few iron and copper pans hanging from the wall, earthenware and wooden dishes, baskets, a large water container, a butter-churn, a cider cask, a knife and chopping board, and a pile of firewood. There was the opening for stoking the stove, which would probably have also been used for cooking. Tongs (*Ofengabel*) would undoubtedly have made it possible to put pans and bowls on the hot embers.[84] There would have been a lot of smoke as chimneys were not introduced until the eighteenth century. Smoke passed through some openings into the loft and out through the straw roof with two slopes. We would consider this type of kitchen to be unpleasant for anyone who was in it. However, it did have a few advantages: the smoke protected the beams from woodworm and insects. Similarly, Lapp reindeer herdsmen smoked their summer huts made of peat, in order to kill all the insects.[85] As it rose through Agatha's and Jacob's house, the smoke dried the corn and fruit stored in the loft along with flax and hemp. There was a narrow stair leading to the loft. In the Jura, on the other hand, smoking was done in purpose-built rooms.[86]

In our peasants' house, the other rooms (probably three) were bedrooms; they were not heated and were cold in winter. In the main bedroom there was a linen chest, which Agatha had brought at the time of her marriage, and she was still working on the linen. The Größer family was made up of five members and two servants. There were only three beds in the house. This was not surprising as a bed with mattress, sheets and blankets was worth a fortune. For day labourers in Sologne during the eighteenth century, its value was never less than 40 per cent of all the property they owned and often represented a similar percentage in the poorer circles of the French village of Genainville (Vexin).[87] It has been calculated that in eighteenth-century Tuscany, a sharecropper family capable of spending 10 lira a year on textile products, representing 12 per cent total income, took between three and six years to purchase a bed with all its accessories in the 'peasant' style. While the sharecroppers or *mezzadri* were on average probably capable of paying out such figures, most farm labourers were undoubtedly incapable of doing so. Unsurprisingly then, it was unusual in the early modern era to have a bed all to oneself. The shepherd at Genainville, Antoine Poutrel, only had one bed in a state of disrepair and a simple bed-frame for his five children to sleep on. In the village's more modest families, there was often just one bed for everyone (there was an average of 1.2 beds per family amongst labourers, 1.4 amongst artisans and 1.7 amongst peasants). In Tuscany, almost all beds were of a large size. *Lettucci* (i.e. single beds) were very rare, and this demonstrates that not only husband and wife slept together, but also other members of the family.[88] Even in the nineteenth century, it was still uncommon for *mezzadri* to have single beds.[89]

Returning to the house of Jacob Größer and Agatha Deuggerin, it was so spacious that it did not mix people and animals. It had two warm rooms, the kitchen and the *Stube*, and the latter was completely smoke-free. It had separate bedrooms for parents and children. Of course, the *Stube* was a relatively mixed area and the kitchen was full of smoke. Moreoover, there were no sanitary facilities of any kind and the situation was to get worse, as the village's public baths were to close in the eighteenth century. Overall, however, the house had many comforts, and it has to be asked how common such houses were at the time.

At the beginning of the seventeenth century such conditions were undoubtedly relatively rare. However, the situation was changing, although the future did not always bring progress: for example, the Thirty Years War (1618–48) was to bring misery and destruction to the village of Jungingen, as it did to many parts of Europe, particularly Germany. While at the beginning of the conflict, the village had about 75 families, in 1640 there were only 29 householders and 4 widows.[90] But demographic growth also brought its problems: particularly in the eighteenth century, it meant for part of the population an increase in overcrowding and a reduction in available space. The house that the family of Jacob and Agatha had lived in was to be occupied by more than one family.[91] In England, the enclosures led to the abandonment and possible destruction of many rural houses, and part of the population cleared from the countryside ended up crowding into the worst urban housing.[92]

Generally, however, there was a tendency for housing, furniture and comfort to improve from the sixteenth to the eighteenth century (and not only in the countryside). On average, houses became larger, more solid and healthier to live in. Their interior furnishings became more lavish and the number of objects multiplied. According to some historians, these changes did not come about through a sudden revolution but through gradual development over a long time, even during periods in which there was economic decline.[93] This was the case, for example, in eighteenth-century Venice.[94] But, as I have mentioned before, this development was not uniform across different regions and social groups.

As far as housing in England was concerned, an intense activity of rebuilding housing got under way in the last quarter of the sixteenth century, particularly in central and southern parts of the country. This development reached its peak in the seventeenth century, but continued afterwards.[95] As a result, one- and two-room cottages became more rare. In the village of Wigston Magna in Leicestershire, the inventories in the fifteenth century described the houses (but not the houses of the poor, which it did not cover)[96] as made of wood and earth walls with thatch roofs. They had one or two rooms, a multi-use room and a spence (a room that acted as a pantry and kitchen). Only two houses had a real kitchen. The kitchen became more common during the sixteenth and seventeenth centuries. By then, houses generally had a kitchen, a hall and parlour,[97] and occasionally they had another room. The houses of the rich were larger, but the tendency to increase the surface area used as living space occured across the board, and involved changes in the ways houses were planned. Rectangular houses were replaced by L-shaped houses, with a kitchen at right-angles to the rest of the house. At the beginning of the eighteenth century, probably the most widespread house had three rooms. Brick houses became much more common during the century, although traditional houses made of wood, earth and thatch continued to exist.[98]

7. 'The luxury of the peasantry'[99]

I will attempt to follow the principle lines of development in the greater comfort and availability of goods. To do this, I will first reveal the situation in two English regions, the Berkeley Valley in Gloucestershire and eastern Kent, one of the richest parts of Great Britain, typified by agriculture and considerable development in trade and crafts in the small towns and villages.[100] In these areas during the second half of the seventeenth century, between 80 and 90 per cent of the poorest householders whose estates were valued on their deaths at between 10 and 50 pounds[101] owned a bed with a frame and they all had at least one mattress to lay on the ground, as had been common in the sixteenth century and continued to be common amongst emigrants to America (Chesapeake). The latter had, it is true, acquired greater freedom and availability of land and food by crossing the ocean,[102] but they often lived in extremely straitened circumstances as far as their material conditions were concerned. They had almost no furniture and not infrequently sat and slept on the floor. In Maryland (St. Mary County) and Virginia, between 55 and 70 per cent of the poor did not have anything to sit on, and the percentage was still about 50 per cent in lower-middle-class families, 70–80 per cent of whom also did not own a bed.[103]

In the areas of England mentioned above,[104] on the other hand, even amongst the poorest the majority owned a table, although only half of them had chairs, benches and stools for sitting on. Tables, beds and something to sit on were to be found in the houses of all those whose property was worth more than 50 pounds, and their houses generally had at least five rooms.[105] Only a few decades later, however, the owners of tables and chairs had considerably increased. Taking the whole of England as the basis for our observations, they consisted of between 70 and 90 per cent of those whose property was not worth 50 pounds at the end of the seventeenth century and at the beginning of the eighteenth.[106] At Genainville (Vexin), the shepherd Poutrel, whom we have already met, only had a small table and a straw chair, both in a state of disrepair, when it came to meals for his numerous family. In the Duero valley in Spain, the least well-off in the eighteenth century only rarely owned chairs, which were still a luxury item, and the only objects in the houses of the poorest people that could appear a concession to superfluity, if valued in purely material terms, were religious prints hanging on the wall, whose miserable value was 2 or 3 *reales* each. Of course, they were far from superfluous in the world of beliefs and religious practices in which those who had bought them moved.[107] But let's leave sunny Spain to go back to peek into the English houses which, as I have already said, were undergoing profound change during this period.

In the English regions under consideration between a third and a half of the poor owned a wardrobe in the second half of the seventeenth century. It was generally of little value and probably small, old and rather crude. Only a few owned a sideboard or linen cupboard. However, a few pots and some earthenware was to be found in their houses.[108]

According to post-mortem inventories in the English countryside taken as a whole between 1675 and 1725, there were references to cooking pots in 69 per cent of them, pewter dishes in 43 per cent and earthenware in 35 per cent. Probably many people were still using wooden bowls of very little value. Everything we associate with a table that has been set for a meal was relatively rare. Tablecloths were to be found in 35 per cent of these cases, and knives and forks in 2 per cent, but as we have seen, often there were no chairs and no table. Many other objects considered indicators of a comfortable environment were in short supply: curtains were mentioned in 6 per cent of the cases and pictures on the wall in 5 per cent. Other elements that demonstrated a certain sophistication and 'modernity' were not entirely absent. In 16 per cent of the inventories there was a reference to a silver object, which was a luxury item but probably also a way of hoarding wealth. There were a few books in 17 per cent of the houses and spectacles were even more widespread than printed paper (21%). Between 1675 and 1725 the families that had a clock almost quadrupled from 8 per cent to 31 per cent, a sign that it was becoming less the case that the relationship with time was governed exclusively by the alternation between night and day.[109] However, books and pictures were extremely rare amongst the very poor, as were objects that might appear even more indispensable, such as chamber pots and some form of lighting.[110]

Inventories from other regions, such as Brittany, Brie, Ile-de-France and Normandy, also provide information confirming the scarcity of means of lighting. In the Caen Plain between 1700 and 1715, only 57 per cent of families possessed at least one source of light. Lighting was becoming more common, and the figure rose to 88 per cent for the period between 1770 and 1789. However, for a large part of the period under examination, very few lights challenged the supremacy of darkness when sun went down over the villages. The only light was the glow of the fire, the trembling flame of a few foul-smelling tallow candles, a few small torches, some oil lamps or sticks of resinous wood that had been set alight – not without a certain risk.[111] Rush pith candles were used in many areas in the interior of England, Wales and Ireland. Old people, women and children had the task of cutting green rushes, soaking them in water, pealing them, squeezing them, drying the pith and covering them with any greasy substance that could be found. Some people made tallow candles at home, but from 1709 to 1831 this constituted a clandestine activity because they were subject to taxation and had to be bought through an authorized retailer. The taxation was even higher on wax candles, which do not smell, stay alight far longer than tallow ones and are less likely to go out. But wax candles were a luxury all over Europe and not everyone could afford them, so in England rush pith candles were often used even in the servants' quarters of aristocratic homes.[112]

There was a joke widely told in England to demonstrate the traditional meanness of the Scots, and it reveals a world in which lighting represented a problem and a not inconsiderable cost. It also illustrates again how people and animals were all mixed together. A tailor called Leper, so the story goes, passed the night in the farmhouse of a poor Scotswoman, who laid out straw on the ground and put his bedclothes on top of the straw, all in the dark. Very soon, Leper realized that his bed was moving. In the darkness the peasant woman had unwittingly prepared the bed on top of a sleeping calf! The tailor, who was sitting by the fire, decided to take his revenge and called the 'bed' over. It actually moved and the woman was terrified. Her meanness was thus punished and her poverty ridiculed.[113]

While Leper was happy to sleep on the floor and risked ending up in the embrace of some animal, a bed was universally to be found in the houses of Norman peasants from the beginning of the eighteenth century, in a similar situation to the English areas we have just examined. Tables, on the other hand, came into general use towards the middle of the century and chairs at the end. From this point of view, it would appear that Norman houses were taking longer to acquire the new commodities than their counterparts on the other side of the English Channel. The available data clearly shows the changes in these domestic environments. As far as furniture is concerned, every family had at least one chest by the eighteenth century. At the beginning of the nineteenth century, chests were replaced by wardrobes or linen cupboards (which already existed in the eighteenth century) and by chests of drawers. Concerning utensils and other objects for food preparation, practically everyone (98%) owned a pot or pan for boiling food by the beginning of the eighteenth century. This was not the case with other items. Between the periods 1700–15 and 1770–89, those with utensils for types of cooking that did not involve boiling increased from 85 to 88 per cent, those with plates from 92 to 100 per cent, and those who had at least one tablecloth from 61 to 76 per cent. Judging from this data, the kitchen appears to have become slightly more elaborate, and the table mainly appears to have been affected by good manners. Like tablecloths and plates, glasses and cutlery became much more common. Glasses, which were initially only to be found in

28 per cent of families, spread to about half the households. Table knives, which no one had in the earlier period, made their appearance on 10 per cent of tables between 1770 and 1789. Forks had a sudden success during this period and jumped from 4 to 60 per cent.[114] In the Swabian village of Kirchentellinsfurt am Neckar, the arrival of cutlery dates back to the eighteenth century, but until the end of the nineteenth century its use was only amongst the elite. The majority of peasants ate with a wooden spoon or with their hands.[115]

Change did not therefore occur in a uniform manner. Eastern England was an area where new products spread more quickly than in other parts of the country.[116] It would also appear from the available and still somewhat limited data that it was at the forefront compared with many other parts of Europe as well. Although the pace of change and the manner in which it took place differed, similar trends still affected many areas of Europe. To demonstrate this, we will return from the north to the south and take one last trip, this time through the beautiful countryside around Pisa and Prato. Here we discover that the great majority of peasants had a bed, although in some cases it was just a couple of benches with a straw mattress on top or 'a small bed of two trestles used for benches with an ancient and broken straw mattress, a dirty piece of torn-off sheet and a ripped counterpane'. Some people must certainly have been putting up with similar conditions to those offered for a night to Leper the tailor. For example, Agnolo Ciatti from Tobbiana in the countryside around Prato. 'In the hovel that was his home,' there were no 'pieces of furniture, no household goods of any kind except a little straw with a ragged blanket of no value on which they slept and a rotten old chest covered with woodworm and only good for burning.'[117] But, the case of Agnolo was an isolated one and increasingly rare. Utensils such as the andiron and chain for the cooking pot had already been introduced back in the late Middle Ages, but during the eighteenth century wooden or earthenware plates and mugs came into general use, glasses made a first appearance and cutlery was no longer a rarity. Tablecloths were not more widely used, but on average every family had two of them in Tuscany which had become 'civilized' very early in the late Middle Ages. There was, however, an increase in the number of napkins, dish towels and towels, both in the kitchen and for personal hygiene. Sheets became more common and, taken as a whole, household linen owned by an eighteenth-century family was about twice that which would have been found in a peasant house during the sixteenth century.[118] It is no surprise then that in the eighteenth century people started to talk about the 'luxury of the peasantry'. We would not consider it any kind of luxury, given that rural interiors were not exactly overflowing with mirrors, lacquered corner-cupboards, armchairs or porcelain, all of which could be found in the homes of the rich. Yet the debate reflected a perception that living conditions had changed in parts of the rural world.[119]

8. Adoption or adaptation?

We have to ask ourselves to what extent these innovations affecting the countryside originated in the cities and gradually radiated out to increasingly remote areas. It is a complex question and the available data that could provide an answer is still rather difficult to come by. Perhaps the most complete information, which concerns England, demonstrates that urban interiors, and particularly those in London, were on average better equipped with tables, pans, pottery, pewter plates, porcelain, cups, teapots, silverware, cutlery, curtains, books, clocks and paintings, when compared with rural dwellings.

However, the differences were not equally pronounced in all areas. In some English regions, the degree of assimilation appears to have been greater than in others. Are we then to conclude that cities were islands of high consumption surrounded by countryside that was always and exclusively imbued with 'traditional' values and strongly resistant to change?[120]

Undoubtedly the differences between the town and the countryside were not the same everywhere because of the ways the production and distribution of individual commodities were organized, as well as other factors. Let's consider the case of porcelain, which started to arrive in Europe in not insignificant quantities from the fifteenth century.[121] The reason it was practically unknown in villages during the seventeenth and eighteenth century and was more common in London than in other cities was probably that it was still all imported from China and entered England through the East India Company auctions that took place in the capital. There it was bought by so-called 'chinamen' who retailed it, sold it to other businesses in London and, to a lesser extent, distributed it to other large cities.[122] Porcelain constituted an extreme example that shows how not all towns and cities were equally part of the distribution network. On the whole, it was easier to find goods in the city, given that shops and retail outlets were usually more concentrated there, but it was also easier to learn about innovations, to appreciate them and want them, both because of the presence of retail outlets and because of the concentration of people and a more complex social structure.

Concerning the distribution of particular lifestyles, social composition obviously played an important role. It is not just a question of verifying where the greater wealth was concentrated, because rich people are not always the most innovative, as the English case demonstrates. The gentry rarely had more books and porcelain than rich merchants, professionals and the clergy, but they clearly had a higher social rank and their average assets were worth more. They were even 'beaten' when it came to paintings and tablecloths, although not by much.[123] In England, therefore, the urban middle class did not ape the gentry, at least not in relation to these commodities. The spread of these consumer goods did not trickle down the rungs of the social ladder. Various social groups had different lifestyles, which probably made some innovations more attractive to one group than another. Thus the objects and innovations that each person bought or ignored, according to his or her tastes and purchasing power, contributed to defining and redefining the group identity.[124] On this point, it has been suggested that between the end of the sixteenth and the end of the eighteenth century, European elites were prey to an increasing interest, not to say obsession, with consumer items.[125]

Financial limitations were not the same for everyone. However much European aristocracies differed one from the other, their members were generally required to maintain a lifestyle that involved a whole range of expenses aimed at displaying consumption and maintaining status: large houses, carriages, liveries, horses, dogs, jewels and so on. To some extent, these expenses and not the revenues were the independent variable. In other words, nobles had to spend money to remain nobles, and in order to ensure they had certain assets and consumer goods, even if it meant getting seriously into debt.[126] There were even institutions whose purpose was secretly to assist impoverished nobles so that they could maintain a certain decorum. There was a great deal of debate in the eighteenth century as to whether conspicuous consumption by the nobility stimulated the economy or depressed it.[127]

The question of the role of consumption and consumer goods in the definition of group identity brings us back to the relationship between town and countryside. The urban environment could make some items more attractive in the city than in the country, as with curtains. They were one of the goods for which the difference between town and countryside was most accentuated: 43 per cent of London houses referred to in inventories had them in the period between 1675 and 1725, while they were to found in only 6 per cent of houses in the countryside. They were one of the items that spread most slowly in the countryside, as the percentage of those who owned them only increased by two and a half times over this period, while owners of clocks quadrupled and owners of pictures quintupled. Naturally, there is the suspicion that the low population density in the countryside made curtains less interesting to those who lived in villages or scattered houses, and overcrowding in the capital made them desirable to Londoners, 62 per cent of whom owned them in 1725.[128]

In this case then, adoption appears selective. Making use of objects first thought of in the city may well have involved large and small changes to their functions. As one historian has noted, consumers 'were adapters not mere adopters'. They did not restrict themselves to adopting certain goods; they adapted them to their own needs and sensitivities.[129] In this sense, it would not perhaps be too far off the mark to argue that the different activities pursued in the countryside and the different objects that were used could have led to changes relatively independent from the influence of towns and cities. As the city and the countryside had different lifestyles, we need to examine the particular characteristics of the city during this period and the changes that were taking place.

9. The growth of cities

At the beginning of this chapter, I provided information on population levels in towns or cities with more than 5,000 inhabitants during different historical periods and in different regions. However, it was absolutely not the case that a population of 5,000 was the dividing line between a village and a town or city. Many centres that were quite clearly cities had fewer citizens. Even if we were to agree that the number of inhabitants should be the basis for distinguishing between urban and rural settlements, the number of medium-to-large centres was growing during the period we are studying, so the lower limit of what constitutes a city would have to change over time. In any case, quantity is insufficient as a criterion. Division of labour, presence of a market and representatives of the power structure are other elements that generally contribute to the definition of an urban reality. As historians of urban development know only too well, it is more or less impossible to find uniform and consistently valid criteria for what does and does not constitute a city. 'A city is always a city', wrote the great scholar Fernand Braudel.[130] So we will have to be happy with this tautological definition and limit ourselves to asserting that the number of large cities increased during the early modern era and the geography of distribution changed.

The number of cities and towns with more than 10,000 inhabitants doubled (from 309 to 618). Those with more than 100,000 inhabitants quintupled.[131] Around 1500, excluding Constantinople (which had 250,000 inhabitants and was geographically in Europe), this category based on size included only Paris (225,000), Naples (125,000), Milan (100,000) and Venice (100,000). A century later, it included London, Seville, Lisbon, Palermo, Rome and Prague. At the beginning of the eighteenth century, Amsterdam, Madrid, Moscow and Vienna could also be included. In 1750 London had 675,000 inhabitants, and fifty years later an incredible 950,000.[132] During the three centuries we are considering, the concentration of great cities shifted from the Mediterranean region to northern Europe.[133]

Cities did not just grow; their appearance changed. In some cases, the change was due to the establishment of a court. The French court was in Paris from

1528. In 1561 Philip II chose Madrid as his capital, although he later built the Escorial outside the city. The Dukes of Savoy established themselves in Turin in 1563. The first Russian tsar, Ivan IV (1533–84), rebuilt Moscow. The Habsburgs established themselves in Vienna following the defeat of the Turks at Kahlenberg in 1683. For practical and symbolic reasons, cities that became capitals took on a new importance. Being a centre of power changed them. The development of fortifications, the modernization of ports, technological progress, demographic growth, the development of a money-based economy, bureaucratization, and the 'need to represent the new public and private interests in some external form' all led to measures affecting the fabric and architectural heritage of a city, even if it wasn't a capital or had been one for a long time. In 1530 Florence was adapted to its function as the capital of the Grand-Duchy ruled by the Medici family. In the second half of the sixteenth century, Spanish viceroys rebuilt Palermo and Naples. In London the court was organized at Westminster (the city was rebuilt after the fire of 1666). The kings of Sweden and Denmark expanded their capitals in the sixteenth and seventeenth century. In the Netherlands, the maritime cities grew during their 'golden century'.[134]

10. The urban environment

Houses crammed together and strong smells

Most European cities, with the exception of the majority of English ones, were surrounded by a wall during the early modern era. From the sixteenth century, these were often replaced by expensive bastions and ramparts capable of with-standing artillery.[135] This change meant that it was practically impossible to change the city boundaries without knocking down the walls and building ones over a wider area, as had occurred in the past when demographic growth caused overcrowding.

As we have seen, the population was growing in many cities during the early modern era. To overcome the problem of the lack of space, they had to exploit space within the walls to the full. Houses (with the exception of those of the rich) were stretched inwards, presenting their shortest side to the road. 'The houses of the poorest in the cities . . . are narrow and long,' wrote Serlio.[136] Then buildings with flats were developed. At the beginning of the sixteenth century they were rare in Italian cities, but during the century they increased in number in Naples, Genoa and Venice. Buildings with flats for different social ranks appeared in Rome after 1650. Families of high social rank lived on the *piano nobile* or 'noble floor', and families of lower social rank on the other floors. This type of building spread from Rome to other cities, particularly Turin and

Naples.[137] The number of floors also increased. Although it was built over canals, Amsterdam saw four-storey buildings become more common during the seventeenth century. In Paris, a law of 1667 prohibited buildings higher than 15.6 metres and from 1783 a ratio between the height of the building and the width of the street had to be observed. Towards the middle of the eighteenth century, four-storey buildings became predominant, but the tendency to build higher and higher continued in later years and there were six- and seven-storey or even higher buildings.[138] In some city districts, there were about 500 people to a hectare, and in some parts of London the figure was actually 800.[139] Chaotic and squalid suburbs grew outside many city walls, and in some cases they blurred the boundary between rural and city worlds.

At the same time, however, the cityscape was increasingly differentiating itself from the rural landscape, even though the cities contained parks and market gardens, and the countryside continued, particularly in the case of smaller cities, to permeate the city's rhythms, needs, colours, smells and life in general, while the city in turn projected its requirements, money and power onto the surrounding countryside.[140]

The larger a city was, the more difficult it was to smell the open fields. As in the case of many peasant houses, the urban environment provided many strong and unpleasant sensations for the nostrils, at least in terms of our modern sensitivities.[141] Before the Great Fire of 1666, which destroyed a large part of London, the city was growing westwards to escape the unwholesome stench of the buildings crowded together in the East End, as the prevailing wind was from the west. It appears then that there was a certain sensitivity to the smell even at the time.[142]

Refuse and rubbish

Towns and cities with high population densities generally made the disposal of refuse more difficult and complicated. In Europe, it appears that the only clean cities were in the Netherlands, judging from the stunned admiration they produced in foreigners. 'The beauty and cleanliness of the streets are so extraordinary', wrote an English traveller on this point, 'that Persons of all ranks do not scruple, but even seem to take pleasure in walking them'. They were 'paved with brick and . . . [as] clean as any chamber floor'.[143]

In the Netherlands, where cleanliness came to symbolize freedom, the upright citizens considered it their civic duty to clean the paving in front of their house,[144] but elsewhere the situation was entirely different. The streets were filthy with excrement from the animals used to pull carts and carriages and from the pigs and other animals reared in the courtyards and streets. As late as 1746, it was prohibited to keep pigs in Venice, a sign that there were still people in the city who did so.[145] Not infrequently, chamber pots were emptied into the public thoroughfare, occasionally without bothering to check whether it could land on a passer-by. On 30 August 1740, a certain Falgherij, 'servant of Senator Vizzani', sued a man who 'mended spectacles in the street of the central market' in Bologna, 'because he had soaked his trousers and waistcoat when carelessly emptying a pot of piss'.[146] Even in the cleanly Netherlands, there must have been some people who disposed of their waste in this manner, as the regulations laid down that anyone who was dirtied by filth thrown from the window into the main streets was entitled to demand compensation. But the simple shout of 'mind the water!' was protection enough for householders against such demands, if they emptied their chamber pots and basins into the side streets.[147]

A man, whose words have remained enshrined in the court proceedings of Bologna, claimed that he was looking for something to eat in the 'shit', because he 'was dying of hunger'. His statement not only demonstrates the gravity of the famine in 1590, but also reveals the fact that there were piles of excrement in the city.[148] This was in spite of the fact that even as late as the beginning of the nineteenth century quite a few people were making their living from collecting dung and selling it to peasants.[149] Clearly their work was not sufficient to clean up the city. The same could be said of the hard work carried out by 'able-bodied' vagrants who were forced off the streets and into work which often involved the collection of excrement.[150] Although effort was put into the collection of dung and its use as manure, occasionally fuel and even, in some cases, detergent,[151] cities were still usually covered with it.

In western Europe, there were practically none of the public baths so widely used in the East. A Syrian who visited Paris at the end of the seventeenth century experienced considerable discomfort, as he explained to Guilliame-Joseph Grelot. During a hot Parisian summer, the man, who came from Damascus, 'decided to eat a large plate of water melon and curdled milk to cool himself down, and then go to the suburb of St. Marchel [sic] where he had business'. Grelot then goes on to tell us

> When returning from this walk, the agitation caused by his slog and the freshness of the water-melons with milk that he had eaten, together with the hot weather, started to turn his stomach, and when he was close to Place Maubert, he suddenly needed to go to the lavatory. . . . Given that his complaint was getting worse with every step, he started to look around everywhere for one of those *Adelpkanas*, which in his country are so clean and comfortable, but all he could see on all sides were a great crowd of people, open shops and streets unsuited for him to offload his heavy burden. He felt he was the most

embarrassed person in Paris, as he had no idea what he should do in such circumstances. This situation, so serious for a Muslim, made him yearn for the *Geroun* in Damascus, which is a large square surrounded by thirty of these useful public places. . . . But in the centre of Paris, where there are more people than stones in the paving, what was he to do in order not to be seen and noticed in a position hardly consistent with modesty? All these considerations could not prevent the poor Syrian from giving in to the violence of such a pressing need before the reached the Pont au Change. He was thus obliged to let go. . . . He desired more ardently than anything he had wanted in the past that instead of being at the great Châtelet he was at the warm and health-giving baths on the Isle of Milo, which are a little distance from the city, so that he could immediately withdraw and clean himself inside, while waiting for someone to wash his clothes or bring him other ones.[152]

But, unlike Muslims who were used to baths and washing as required by their religious rituals, Westerners at this time looked on water with great suspicion. The situation that so upset the Syrian traveller was of little concern to Parisians who, like most Europeans, were used to cities without public lavatories.[153]

Human and animal excrement was not, however, the only waste matter that dirtied the streets. There were also pollutants that were occasionally very powerful, and derived from various production processes and treatments, such as slaughterhouses and tanneries. Not surprisingly, many cities and towns attempted to concentrate such activities in a peripheral area.

The cleanliness of the Dutch streets partly depended on the fact that they were 'paved with brick',[154] and conversely the lack of hygiene in many other cities depended on the fact that generally they were not paved at all or only covered with sand and cobblestones. Rainwater mixed with wastewater and refuse to form puddles, mud and sludge. The problems created by the lack of paving were not restricted to covering shoes and skirt hems with mud. They also included the ease with which refuse entered the subsoil and polluted the water-bearing strata, which were also often exposed to leakage from cesspools.

In the early modern era, cesspools became increasingly common in courtyards or any other available space. In the sixteenth century, Serlio proposed popular housing provided with the 'necessary', namely a latrine that could be located at the end of the vegetable patch, in the courtyard, in a corner near the bed or in the kitchen.[155] In seventeenth-century London, houses often surrounded a courtyard that contained a latrine, a pump and other facilities used by the inhabitants of the buildings facing onto the courtyard.[156] Towards the end of the period we are examining, there was usually at least one lavatory for each building. It was generally located in a courtyard or communal area. In houses for the well-to-do, lavatories could be relatively numerous and some would be conveniently located close to bedrooms.[157] As sewers were rare, the wastewater from lavatories and latrines usually ended up in a cesspit or septic tank.[158] The most hygienic lavatory, using running water, had been invented by Sir John Harington as far back as 1596, but did not start to be widely used until the end of our period.[159] The use of latrines went alongside the use of chamber pots and, amongst the rich, commodes, which were chairs containing a chamber pot.[160] Chamber pots were also emptied into cesspits or directly into the street, as we have seen.

Overcrowding, the absence of paving and the dangerous proximity between wells and latrines meant that there was a serious problem of seepage into the water supply. 'A well must be at least three outstretched arms [equal to 5.84 metres] from any cesspits', wrote Augustin-Charles D'Aviler in his *Cours d'Architecture* (1691), reflecting a concern amongst architects to keep the problem to a minimum. 'If the well cannot be kept away from the cesspit because of a lack of space, it is necessary to build, apart from the construction wall against which it is set . . . , a reinforcement wall . . . with a thickness of eighteen inches.' The floor of the cesspit had to be inclined to safeguard the well as much as possible.[161] It has to be asked whether these minimum safety requirements were observed, given that the water in wells was often polluted.[162]

The water supply

The pollution of wells, which represented one of the main sources of water, made the problem of obtaining the necessary water much more serious, and the problems were very different in the town from those in the countryside. In the countryside, the difficulties arose from the distance people had to go. Not every house had a well, fountain, river or stream nearby. In England at least, almost everyone had a container to collect rainwater, but this was not normally sufficient. The women in the house had to arm themselves with buckets, pitchers or other receptacles, and sometimes walk long distances to get the quantities of water they needed. While water-sellers (who mainly worked in towns or cities) were generally men, the task of collecting water from the well or fountain for domestic use was the responsibility of women, as well as children and servants. A tough and tiring job because of the weight of the water, it became a particularly thankless task in the event of a drought that imposed longer distances to obtain the absolute minimum for cooking a little soup or making tea. A survey carried out in England at the beginning of the twentieth century into a sample of farm-labourers' houses showed that the nearest well was often 400 metres away and a subsequent inquiry in Scotland showed that over half the houses were without running water and distance from the water source varied from about 20 metres to over 1.5 kilometres.[163] Very probably the living conditions of the families in these homes were similar to those that were the norm in the early modern era as far as water supply was concerned.

Distance was less of a problem in the city and the sources were more numerous and varied. Even where there had been Roman sewers and aqueducts, these had often fallen into disuse during the Middle Ages and very rarely were they restored or expanded by similar water works. There were a few exceptional cases. In Rome, Pope Nicholas V reintroduced the so-called Vergine aqueduct which dated back to 22 BC, Sixtus V reintroduced the Felice aqueduct and Paul V restored the Traiana aqueduct in 1609, which was renamed Paola. In Paris, the Belleville aqueduct was restored in 1457, and therefore worked alongside the Pré-Saint-Gervais aqueduct, one of the few medieval works in this field. In 1613 Maria de' Medici had the aqueduct rebuilt at Arcueil and over half a century later Louis XIV undertook the works to bring the water of the Eure to the capital. In 1481 the imposing aqueduct in Segovia was operating again. In seventeenth-century Portugal, an exceptional case, aqueducts were working in Coimbra, Tomar, Vila do Conde and Elvas. A new one, the *Das Águas Livres* (the Free Waters) was built for Lisbon between 1729 and 1748. In the eighteenth century Charles III of Bourbon had one built to a design by Vanvitelli to bring water to his royal palace in Caserta. From the sixteenth century, fountains became more common in cities, and wells were also quite numerous.[164]

In towns and cities then, a water supply was generally quite close, but the water itself was more easily polluted. Anyone who went to a well or fountain was often forced to queue because of the overcrowding. Of course, the wait could provide an opportunity to chat with the neighbours, but if it went on for three or four hours, as it appears was not uncommon in Exeter during the 1820s, then it became a truly enervating task. If it was also cold or blazing sunshine, then the tedium could also become an affliction. It seems that the quantity of water transported by an adult woman varied between 5 and 30 litres each time, and that the average was around 15 litres. Those who had to drag the water up to the fifth or sixth floor possibly suffered a greater exertion than those who walked a kilometre with a pitcher on their heads or buckets in their hands.[165] A more simple solution was to buy water from the itinerant sellers who were found in many different places. But this was expensive and not everyone could afford it.[166]

Apart from some monasteries and particular situations, pumps and pipes were only very slowly used to bring water to the houses of a few privileged people. The Renaissance palace of the Duke of Urbino had an enviable system for providing drinking water and for removing wastewater. In 1530, Pope Clement VII had a bath with hot and cold taps constructed at Castel Sant'Angelo. In 1596 Sir

John Harington invented a water closet, and architects attempted to provide the kitchens of the rich with plenty of running water (Fig. 68). In spite of this, for a long time only a very few people could enjoy such comforts.[167] London, which was advanced even by European standards, was the only city in the whole of Great Britain to have a degree of variety in its plumbing systems. Around 1660, part of the population had water from specially built water mains, while others used a pump driven by horses or a water-wheel on the Thames. From 1582 there was a machine operating on London Bridge that raised water from the river.[168]

In the seventeenth century, the rich showed an interest in the uses of water. This partly arose from the fashion for fountains and water displays in gardens. In France, in particular, they spent staggering sums on construction works that would have put the pharaohs to shame. But interest, particularly in England, was also of a scientific and technical nature. This resulted in various innovations, but ones that spread only very slowly. Most people living in cities like Paris continued for a long time to rely on wells for their water supply, in spite of the existence of aqueducts and the gradual adoption of pumps from the seventeenth century. In the French capital they also made considerable use of the polluted waters of the Seine, which appears to have inevitably produced diarrhoea and other disorders amongst visiting foreigners. The city therefore created work for thousands of water carriers and sellers. Their jobs were threatened by the introduction of the Perrier brothers' pumps for bringing water into the home in 1782, but the company became involved in a financial scandal (1788) and so it was some time before they completely disappeared from the city's streets.[169]

The per-capita availability of water in Paris at the beginning of the eighteenth century was probably less than 5 litres a day, which was less than the amount the World Health Organization declared in 1970 to be the absolute minimum for the maintenance of life. By 1789 it had perhaps increased to 10 litres, while in 1976 it was estimated that the daily per-capita requirement in towns and cities with more than 10,000 was over 400 litres, and even 1,500–2,000 litres in the large American, Canadian and Australian conurbations of the 1980s.[170] According to most calculations, the majority of the urban population without running water in eighteenth-century English cities only consumed more than 25 litres per day in exceptional cases and on average were happy with about 15 litres.[171] Bologna had an extensive network of canals that used a complex system of ducts to take water into the cellars of most houses, but in the summer they washed their clothes in slimy polluted water because the canals had almost dried up.[172]

Not surprisingly, death rates throughout the entire early modern era were higher in urban areas than in the countryside. The urban environment was in fact unhealthy and favoured the spread of disease.[173] Cities only grew because of the massive influx of people from the countryside.[174] The problem of combating the foul odours of urban environments became particularly pressing only in the eighteenth century, and that they started to address the question of cleaning the streets, and that changes in hygiene, health and cleanliness made realities that had been tolerated for centuries appear intolerable.[175]

11. City lights

One of the imperatives of the eighteenth century was to open cities to better air and light.[176] Cities were not only dirty and smelly, but also dark. Houses, which had become increasingly crammed together, took light away from each other. As they climbed higher, they often had floors that protruded over the street, thus transforming the public thoroughfare into a kind of dark tunnel. It is true that from the sixteenth century, streets started to be widened to allow carriages to travel along them, and new architectural and town-planning concepts were put into practice in an attempt to impose rectilinear systems that exploited views with a vanishing point on to the incoherence of the medieval urban structure.[177] The century of the Enlightenment therefore espoused light not only in the metaphorical sense, but also involved a challenge to the night. There were 2,736 public streetlights in the French capital in 1697, 6,400 in 1740, and at least 7,000 in 1766 (1817 saw the arrival of gas lighting, which had been introduced in London in 1813).[178] Even the glazier Ménétra contributed to this change, as he often recorded in his *Journal* that he had cut glass to make lamps to improve the city's lighting.[179]

For centuries the use of light on a large scale had only been justified by the need to worship the divine or celebrate some extraordinary event. 'Illuminations' were often an important element in collective manifestations of joy. This was transposed into literary terms by Teofilo Folengo's *Baldus* in the tale about a priest who used oil for the holy lamps to fry up a nice bit of fish. The story very clearly depicts a society in which light entailed consumption of costly materials beyond the means of most people. With the development of street lighting, however, night began to appear less imposing.

Light became a little more democratic, and started to take on the features of a public good. It lost some its connotations as a luxury item that only the rich could have in any abundance as a form of ostentation.[180] Lights became more common within houses as well as outside in the street. During the eighteenth century in the French capital, even the lower-middle class built up a stock of lanterns, candelabras and other types of lighting that was not inconsiderable, to say the very least. On average there were five light sources in every flat, both at the upper and lower ends of the social scale. Candelabras constituted 63 per cent of these light sources, and this figure tended to rise after the period 1750–60.[181] The city lights contrasted with the darkness that still dominated the countryside.

The poor were not so successful in capturing daylight as the rich who installed large windows in their houses (which were truly impressive in Dutch houses). From around 1720–30, new buildings were fitted with larger and more numerous windows, which became more luminous through the replacement of oiled paper and cloth with glass and the replacement of small glass panes with larger and more transparent ones.[182] The presence of glass windows instead of oiled paper, cloth covers or simple wooden shutters also reduced the draughts and made it less difficult to keep candles alight. In other words, it also facilitated lighting during the night.[183]

12. Fires

The main problem was clearly to reconcile the need for light with the need to protect oneself from the cold, which was not exclusively a problem for the poor. In February 1695, water and wine froze in the glasses on the king's table at his palace in Versailles.[184] As houses of poor people were small and crowded, they were sometimes better heated. In eighteenth-century Bologna, the minimum space for renting was called a *camino* ('fireplace'), which was made up of a room with a fireplace with the possible addition of a storeroom and a *luogo comodo* ('comfortable place'), namely a lavatory.[185] In late seventeenth and eighteenth-century Paris, there was an average of two fireplaces in each house, and one fireplace for every two rooms. While single-room flats nearly always had one, at the beginning of the eighteenth century there was no shortage of houses with over twenty rooms that only had four.[186] If anything, it was within each individual family that access to heat created hierarchies and inequalities. Sébastien Mercier wrote that in his times the maid, the tutor and the butler each had their own fireplace. In reality, however, a study into 3,000 Parisian houses showed that servants' rooms nearly always lacked a fireplace.[187]

Thanks to technical progress that improved thermal efficiency, the struggle against the cold and perhaps also people's indifference to it appears to have intensified from 1720. Increasingly, new houses had a fireplace in each room. The post-mortem inventories in Paris from the middle of the century produce a figure of two fireplaces for every three rooms. Around 1740–50 and then to an even greater degree between 1760 and 1770, stoves finally became widely used.

There was now a considerable range of methods of heating. In spite of this, a German who visited Paris in 1787–8 and was used to rooms uniformly heated by stoves, complained that in Parisian houses you either burnt yourself close to the fire or froze if you shifted slightly further away.[188] Leaving aside Herr Volkman's comments, which would be true of all rooms heated with an open fire,[189] Paris was better heated than many provincial towns and cities, and indeed the countryside in France. This was in spite of the fact that heating was more difficult in the city than in the countryside in terms of supply and storage (the use of coal was banned in Paris to avoid pollution as far back as the seventeenth century).[190] In cities, moreover, overcrowding sometimes led to the renting of rooms and cellars that had neither fire nor stove, and could only be heated by dangerous and cumbersome braziers.

The tendency to build higher in urban situations to make better use of the available space made less flammable building materials such as stone, bricks and tiled roofs more favourable. German cities often imposed the use of brick and stone by law in order to reduce the risk of fire.[191] The risk could never be entirely averted, however: the Great Fire of London in 1666 destroyed at least 13,000 houses mainly built of wood, yet they were rebuilt with the same materials.[192]

13. Beds

The fight against the cold possibly explains the central importance of the bed amongst household furniture. While the fireplace represented one pole of the domestic arena and family relations, the bed undoubtedly represented the other. In wealthier Dutch houses, it dominated the centre of the room.[193] In middle-class homes it was undoubtedly the most costly item. A simple bed to put against the wall was worth between 15 and 25 guilders, whereas a decorated four-poster bed, to be put in the middle of the room, could cost more than 100 (a worker earned 5 guilders a week, and an affluent shopkeeper could buy a house worthy of his status with 1,000 guilders).[194] In Paris it was usually the first piece of furniture listed in post-mortem inventories, and it was described with a precision that reflected its value. Beds represented 15 per cent of the property left by poor people during the eighteenth century. For labourers the figure was 25 per cent, and for domestic servants 39 per cent. Beds, which were to be found in practically every household in the town or city, had a wide variety of styles and shapes, from a mattress alone (which, however, it appears was never laid directly on the ground) to a four-poster bed. In the eighteenth century, at least the main bed in the house was nearly always fitted with bed curtains to keep out draughts and create a protected environment, a genuine 'house within the house'. Of a sample of over 3,000 Parisian beds during the period 1690–1789, 72.5 per cent were fitted with curtains. Occasionally the bed was positioned in an alcove, particularly north of the Alps. This recess in the wall was closed off at the front by a curtain or door.[195]

The differentiation of beds into a wide variety of types dated back to around the fifteenth century. Previously, the great majority of the population slept on straw or straw mattresses placed on wooden boards, platforms or chests. As we have already seen, these kinds of solutions survived for a long time. Towards the end of our period, simpler beds were made of a few boards on top of low trestles with a mattress possibly made of straw (Figs. 30–31).[196] During the fifteenth century, bedsteads became imposing pieces of furniture in wealthy households. They were fitted with a headboard and surrounded on the other three sides by chests that were used for storage and as a platform, a seat and, as it were, a bedside table. Other developments were beds on casters that could be easily moved and kept under the bedstead, single beds and folding beds. The fashion for 'chest' beds went into decline towards the end of the century, at the same time as the changes in the curtains that insulated beds. Originally they had rings that ran along wooden or metal poles attached to the ceiling. Later, four-poster or canopy beds were developed with curtains falling exactly alongside their perimeters, probably to make it easier to open and close the curtains without getting out of bed. This made it inconvenient to have the chests, which were in any case facing competition from other pieces of furniture, particularly wardrobes. The four posts, the canopy and the curtains, which were either attached to the ceiling or held up by the posts, gave the bed an almost architectural appearance for both aesthetic and functional reasons. Thanks to these elements it became a space that could be completely isolated from all sides.[197] It is significant that the space enclosed by the curtains was called a 'room' in Tuscany.[198]

It seems reasonable to suppose that the sense of protection, warmth and comfort derived not only from the fact that it was 'closed', but also from the presence of mattresses, blankets and other bedclothes, which were as varied at the structure of the bed, given that they ranged from straw alone and miserable straw mattresses to an abundance of mattresses and expensive bedspreads. Even in households that were not wealthy, the complexity of the kit used for the bed was quite surprising and confirmed the practical and symbolic importance of this piece of furniture. In Renaissance Italy, for instance, a bed made up as it should have been had a canvas straw mattress over the boards, and over that a mattress, or rather mattresses, given that those who could afford it had more than one and often as many as three or four. Mattresses were usually stuffed with tufts of wool or feathers of low quality. The upper mattress, on the other hand, was filled with softer feathers. Then came the sheets, generally made of linen, but of coarse canvas in the case of servants and the less well-off. The bedcover was a quilt and a woollen blanket or both. *Sargie* and *celoni* were types of bedding that were also used as bedspreads. The bedspread, bolster and pillows were the final touches, which could occasionally be so lavish that governments imposed wealth taxes on them.[199] A few centuries later, the bedding used on the beds of Tuscan *mezzadri* was similar: straw mattress, mattress filled with wool (or flax and hemp waste from cardings in the case of the poorest *mezzadri*), feather mattress (or cotton mattress from the eighteenth century onwards), bolster of the same width as the bed and a short pillow, both stuffed with feathers, a woollen blanket, a quilt stuffed with raw cotton or cotton waste, possibly a *sargia*, and lastly the sheets, whose number was a good indicator of a family's wealth (in the seventeenth century, peasant families on average owned about four or five).[200]

Using the case of Tuscan peasants and their large beds, it has been demonstrated that sleeping alone was fairly rare in rural areas. But what was the situation in the city like? How many people slept in each bed? In Norwich, which at the time was the second largest city in England, from the beginning of the eighteenth century, 'parlour chambers' were increasingly used as bedrooms, and these rooms, which were located above the parlour, were by definition on the first floor. However, truckle or trundle beds, which ran on castors and had previously been common, were no longer to be found. This probably meant that servants and children had stopped sleeping in the same room as their masters and parents. It is not however possible to ascertain whether this change was in some way interlinked with the greater use of individual beds.[201] In Paris, it appears that in the seventeenth century it was common for children to sleep two and more rarely three to a bed, even in relatively affluent families. In the eighteenth century, on the other hand, single beds became much more common, and were often folding beds. Couples continued to keep very small children in their beds, in spite of warnings by those who remembered cases of new-born babies smothered by the body of a parent.[202]

Although the trend was towards single beds, there were many even in the cities who still could not afford such a luxury. In wealthy Paris between 1695 and 1715, the average was 1.9 persons per bed amongst domestic servants and 2.3 amongst labourers. Around 1780, the figures were still 1.8 and 1.9. In the overcrowded rooms of the lower classes, there were plenty of cases of entire families crammed into the same bed: sometimes five, six or even seven people all sleeping together.[203] If we give credence to the words of Ménétra in the late eighteenth century, the lower classes in Paris did not consider sleeping to be an entirely private activity: a couple with whom the glazier was friends let him sleep in their bed one night when he was locked out of his home, without raising too many objections. He often slept in inns in which strangers shared, if not his own bed, then at least the same room – a promiscuity that could prove dangerous, particularly for women. One morning, for example, Ménétra, without so much as a by-your-leave, slipped into the bed of a young woman sharing the room after her mother had got up leaving the girl on her own: 'the sun was just starting to rise, the object was quite adorable, and I took full advantage', he tells us in his *Journal*. 'Ah! What a pleasure when something like this comes out of the blue! I asked a Burgundian in the next bed whether he would like to take his chance. He responded that I had overexcited him. I left the way open to him and went off to have a sleep.' The following morning, Ménétra wanted to repeat the experience, but discovered that this time the girl had got up and not the mother, who started to scream and create a scene when she felt the intruder coming into her bed. This was not the only occasion on which the enterprising and shameless glazier took advantage of mixed sleeping arrangements. Some time before, he had discovered that a cutler was bringing his betrothed 'dressed up as a tailor' into the workmen's lodgings where they were both living, and when the young man left her on her own, Ménétra did not let the opportunity slip in spite of the young girl's protests and resistance.[204]

Whereas there was a distinct lack of beds and a certain degree of promiscuity in lower-class homes, there was a profusion of beds in the vast houses of the more fortunate. Even husband and wife often had separate bedrooms, although often adjacent or connected by secret passages. In the eighteenth century, high-ranking married couples in England used to sleep together, while in France the lord and lady had separate beds and separate bedrooms.[205] It would be incorrect to deduce from the number of beds that beds were exclusively part of private activities. In France, in particular, a bed was a luxury item that had to be put on display. Early on, it became the centre of royal life. It could be said that the sovereign ruled from a magnificent bed.[206] Ladies received guests in their beds: the space between the bed and the bedroom wall, which was called the *ruelle* in French and *corsello* in Italian, was the stage on which intense social activity took place.[207] These expensive beds from which guests were received were not the same as the ones used for sleeping. Since the Renaissance, there had been the custom in wealthier households to have private beds on which one actually lay down and then the bedrooms and beds 'for show', which were to become much more widespread from the second half of the seventeenth century (Fig. 29).[208] 'The following bedroom is more for show than for use,' wrote Augustin-Charles D'Aviler in 1691, when explaining one of the plans in his *Cours d'Architecture*.[209] Giovanni Biagio Amico reflected the same views in his *Architetto pratico* (1726 and 1750),

> After two or three antechambers . . . you enter a larger room . . . which is used for feasts, evening receptions and other receptions, and from there you enter the room for sleeping. However, when after the two or three antechambers you want immediately to enter the room for sleeping, then this room will be the large one, and the bed in the middle will be used purely for show, so the room will be called the show bedroom. It will have the same functions

that were just mentioned, and behind it there will be another small room . . . in which you will actually sleep.[210]

The variety of beds and their functions was much greater in the early modern era than today. They ranged from miserable straw mattresses that hardly fulfilled their role of providing warm shelter for sleeping at night to monumental beds in which no one slept. The latter were used for receiving important guests or displaying one's wealth and power to inferiors. Today beds are something intimate and private, but this was not necessarily the case in the past. There were private beds and there were beds for show, built for being displayed in public. There were also beds that, although conceived for ostentation, could be closed off to prying eyes by closing the curtain with which they were often fitted. Overall, beds were a more crowded and promiscuous affair than they are today, and much of the population did not have one entirely to themselves.

14. Tables, chairs and socializing together

Five paintings, three tables, a child's cot and chair, some books, Delft pottery and tiles, pewter mug and plates, a wool winder, seven lace curtains, two beds and bench with a mattress on it, a chest, a linen cupboard, various cushions, two mirrors, about twenty chairs, six complete sets of bed linen, forty-one napkins and birdcage; according to an inventory, these were the possessions belonging to the moderately well-off Dutch tailor, ter Hoeven, when his house was sold in 1717. For Holland, ter Hoeven has been considered a 'reasonably typical' example of 'his social group'.[211] Judging from the inventory of his possessions, his family's home appears to have been reasonably comfortable.

Compared with peasant interiors, urban interiors, particularly those in large cities like Paris and London, generally appeared rich in furniture and objects that were often new and sophisticated. We have examined the spread of tables and chairs in rural and semi-rural environments; in the eighteenth century a not inconsiderable percentage were still without them although the figure was falling. As in the Dutch interiors, we would have found a great number of them in Paris during the seventeenth and eighteenth century: three or four tables per household on average (even the unskilled labourers called *gagne-denzers* usually had at least two). Not infrequently these were folding tables, which were suited to the lack of space in urban life. Each house also had an average of a dozen pieces of furniture that provided seating. The great majority were chairs, but there were also stools, footstools, armchairs and settees.[212]

Benches and stools, which had once been much more common than chairs, dropped in number during the eighteenth century. The century of the

Enlightenment also saw the spread of armchairs and sofas, which had been introduced at the beginning and end of the seventeenth century respectively. Whereas the sofa reflected an eastern influence ('sofa' derives from the Arabic *suffa*, meaning cushion), the armchair, which came earlier, evolved from and enlarged upon the large chair with armrests that was often used in patrician homes during the Renaissance by the head of the household, almost as a symbol of his power within the domestic context. These large symbolic chairs, which could occasionally be granted to particularly important guests, were larger than the wife's chair and the chairs used by other family members who, although important, came after the head of the household. The way chairs were made and the right to use them could therefore reflect specific familial and social hierarchies. The inequalities between men and women were also translated into chairs; there were in fact chairs *pro muliere* (for women). These chairs were much smaller than the average, either to emphasize the subordinate position of women or to provide them with a more suitable chair, given that they spent more time at home.[213]

Access to chairs when there were too few to go round continued for a long time to reflect and express inequalities and hierarchies.[214] In this period, there were still poor people's houses in the countryside that had no chairs at all. The only places to sit were on the floor or on a chest or bed, if there were any. In a capital like Paris, there were plenty of chairs even in flats where families of low social rank lived.[215] Not all cities, however, were so well provided. In Venice, for example, it was not always possible to find a *careghin* (small chair). Here again it was a matter of using a chest (still widely used) and a bed, which was by now in general use, whereas in the sixteenth century it was not uncommon for families only to own mattresses, in some cases straw mattresses. The fact that beds were used as seats perhaps helps to explain why they became places for social encounters.[216]

Similarly, the abundance of chairs in Parisian homes cannot only be explained by the large number of inhabitants that every house concealed, as claimed by an astonished man of letters from Hainaut. The inhabitants of each household were generally much less numerous than the seating places, of which there were a dozen on average. Households with a single room, which constituted 31 per cent of the total, were usually home to two or three people. Those with two or three rooms (42%) had three or four people living in them. Those with between three and seven rooms (20%) were home to a similar number of people. Only households that were larger than these (7%) were home to many people, who were mainly domestic servants.[217]

The high number of seating places and the presence of folding tables suggests there was a great deal of socializing. We can imagine parties in elegant aristocratic salons alive with learned conversations, furnished with sofas and armchairs made of expensive woods, velvet and damask, and organized by sophisticated women who cultivated cultural activities. But we can also conjure up images of working-class homes crowded with friends, neighbours and relations seated on simple straw chairs in front of the fire or around the table, while some of the women held spindles and distaffs and others were intent on playing cards, chattering or listening to one of the company who read a book out loud.

Of course, during the early modern era it became increasingly common for people to read to themselves, and spaces designed for this solitary activity rapidly increased in wealthier homes.[218] But reading aloud constituted an important social activity and form of communication, partly required by the illiteracy levels (which varied according to geography, social group and sex) and the relative scarcity of books.[219] Although not numerous, books were to be found in the cities, even amongst the middle and lower classes. In 1700, there was at least one book in 13 per cent of post-mortem inventories for labourers in Paris and in 30 per cent of those for domestic servants. Eighty years later, these percentages rose to about 35 per cent and 40 per cent. As far as the totality of families was concerned, about 23 per cent owned a few volumes in 1750, and in the second half of the century it was higher, but still probably lower than 50 per cent. In London, 31 per cent of the inventories listed books as far back as the period between 1675 and 1725, while in other English cities the percentage fluctuated between 21 and 23 per cent, and in the countryside it was 17 per cent.[220]

The lists contained in dusty centuries-old inventories, however dreary they might appear, do allow us to envisage other forms of relaxation, amusement and social activity. In late sixteenth-century Venice, which was an important publishing centre, books were still fairly rare and the notaries who drew up inventories do not appear to have been very well acquainted with them, as they seldom indicated the author and title, preferring to use vague expressions like 'large and small books', 'Greek and Latin books' or 'books on humanities'. There were obviously exceptions; when someone found a copy of *Orlando furioso* in the house, they usually referred to it as 'an Ariosto' and occasionally they provided fairly detailed lists of books. Thus we know, for example, that the engraver Andrea Fosco, who was fairly well-known in his own times, had a book collection that contained 'a large book on architecture in folio, a book by Sebastian Serlio in folio, a book by Leon Battista Alberti on architecture in quarto and a book said to be on the five orders of architecture by Giacomo Barotio da Vignola'. Andrea also owned a 'lute with its box'. Whereas his library appeared fairly atypical, ownership of an instrument was not. In that period, the notaries of Venice recorded the presence of an instrument even in modest households, while for the aristocracy and the merchant class, 90 per cent of inventories included harpsichords, cithers, lyres, harps and other instruments. The streets and small squares of Venice must have resounded to their playing. The massive presence of musical instruments implies that there was a lively musical scene, very different from the situation that still existed two centuries later in small rural centres such as the French village of Genainville, where they appear to have been completely absent. The situation was also very different in a capital city like Paris, where in the eighteenth century it seems musical instruments were not widely found outside the circles of professional musicians.[221]

15. Pots, dishes and porcelain

Tables and chairs suggest not only evenings passed in chatting, games, playing instruments and reading out loud to others, but also other forms of social behaviour, such as eating in company. Pots, dishes, tablecloths and cutlery were amongst the items that during the early modern era increased most in number and underwent the highest degree of change. New materials were introduced for making both new objects and those that had always existed. Stoneware, glass, majolica and earthenware replaced wood, tin and to some extent copper. In some cases, the enrichment of domestic interiors was due to the increased number of sophisticated goods and the introduction of items linked to new forms of consumption, such as expensive silver tea and coffee sets, chocolate pots and sugar bowls.[222] In other cases, it was due to the spread of cheap articles that everyone or nearly everyone could afford.

It is significant from this point of view that the value of kitchen utensils owned by Parisian labourers and domestic servants almost halved between the periods 1689–1715 and 1775–90 in absolute terms. It fell by even more when assessed as a percentage of total assets, from 20 to 7 per cent in the case of labourers and from 5 to 2 per cent in the case of domestic servants. These changes were mostly due to the appearance of new materials and products. As they were cheaper, they existed alongside or replaced traditional articles, particularly metal ones, which therefore became more rare. Whereas at the beginning of the eighteenth century, notaries listed an average of ten metal utensils per family, at the end of the same century the figure had fallen to six.[223] In the seventeenth and eighteenth century, imitations of luxury items like porcelain began to circulate. This created twin markets. Those who could afford it bought the original and looked askance upon imitations, and those who had fewer financial resources, bought and often appreciated articles that were not the real McCoy.[224]

Studies have demonstrated the change in and spread of consumer goods in England. In 1675, for example, only 9 per cent of families had pewter plates. Fifty years later, they were owned by 45 per cent. During the same period, households that owned earthenware, which was to replace pewter pots and dishes over the long term, rose from 27 to 57 per cent. Cups and other utensils for hot drinks, which initially nobody owned, were to be found in 15 per cent of families by 1725, while the households with knives and forks increased from 1 to 10 per cent.[225]

The spread of these items contributed at least in part to the redesign of furniture and to the changing distinctions between urban and rural life. The owners of earthenware increased more than fivefold in London during the fifty-year period in question from 14 to 75 per cent. The percentage increased in the countryside as well, but much less markedly. In fact, it rose from 26 per cent to 51 per cent. The differences were even more pronounced if you look at the spread of porcelain. Initially it was unknown. By 1725 it could be found in about a third of London homes (35%) and in less than a twentieth of homes in the country-side (4%). Owners of utensils related to the consumption of hot drinks were ten times more numerous in the capital than in rural areas (60 per cent and 6 per cent respectively).[226]

These changes were part of the trend towards an increasing number of articles found in households, which reflected new uses, customs, forms of consumption (the drinking of tea or coffee), the spread of a taste for varying degrees of luxury according to social rank, and a degree of comfort that extended to ornaments, porcelain, clocks, mirrors, pictures, upholstery and curtains to brighten up rooms and keep the cold out, comfortable armchairs, card tables and new furniture for a more rational organisation of the increasing number of domestic articles.

The value of these goods was not merely financial. In the fifteenth century Leon Battista Alberti, in the third of his books on the family, spoke of house-hold goods in terms that were not purely material. While the word he used to define them, *masserizia*, originally meant 'savings' (in money), Alberti attributed a new value to it that was full of moral implications. In the pages of his book, *masserizia* was the sum of the goods owned by a family to be carefully conserved almost as though they were 'the heart of the [family's] identity and its existence, the foundation of its reputation'. This position expressed and justified the new consumer customs that were appearing in Renaissance Italy where the urban elites were increasingly less inclined to be suspicious, diffident and even hostile towards wealth in the way that an important part of the medieval culture and religious tradition had been in the past. Since the fourteenth century, secular lit-erature in Tuscany had been attacking poverty and describing it as a potential source of corruption, while in the fifteenth century Florentine humanists were developing 'a new philosophy that stressed the potential of wealth and the splen-did opportunities it offered to encourage the virtues of liberality and generosity, which are denied to the poor'. This does not of course mean that wealth was no longer stigmatized or that there was no unease in relation to it. Stigmatization did not disappear in the following centuries, as family chattels were to prove full of meaning that went beyond their financial and material value in various situations.

Hence domestic interiors, particularly those of the better-off, often displayed brand-new goods alongside others that had been handed down over many generations. The latter heirlooms with their ancient patina testified to the family's antiquity and this accounted for at least part of their value. This was demonstrated by the care Venetian notaries took to specify that silverware was 'ancient' or even 'very ancient'. The same epithets were often used for the paintings that started to adorn Venetian houses at a very early date. Many of these were family portraits and for those who commissioned, bought and carefully preserved them in order to hand them down to their heirs, their value was not limited to their financial worth or artistic merit, but appears also to have included their ability to memorize a visual image of the family history. The elegant wardrobes handed down from one generation to the next by Dutch families in the seventeenth and eighteenth centuries seem to have had a similar value. They were often displayed in a prominent position in the principal room in their houses. Their solid material presence embodied the family's continuity and prosperity, while protecting the carefully folded linen, clothing and occasionally jewellery, as well as the family's memories.[227]

16. Everything has its place and everything in its place

A Dutch poet used the above expression to extol the virtues of a wardrobe, which could hold great piles of linen, costly ribbons, various types of shiny satin and other marvels. Just as the wardrobe made it possible to keep items in an orderly manner, it became increasingly rare for pots, dishes and utensils not to be tidily kept above or around the fireplace in the room used for cooking. There was an increasing number of sideboards and other types of furniture. In kitchens as in other rooms, old trunks and chests tended to disappear, as they were generally used for keeping more or less everything thrown in together. The thieves who broke into the chest belonging to Matteo Lazzaretti da Budrio one April evening in 1630, in the flatlands surrounding Bologna, found linen and cheese being kept together. In wealthier homes, the decline of the chest started as far back as the sixteenth century, perhaps because of the more sedentary lifestyle adopted by elites during the fifteenth century and the decline in their custom of travelling around taking much of their furniture with them. Then wardrobes spread to priests' homes and later still to private homes (Figs. 45–6). The replacement of the ancient, easily transported and multi-functional chest also encouraged the introduction of the chest of drawers and tallboy in the seventeenth century. While in the period 1695–1715 Parisian labourers had practically never heard of a chest of drawers and only a few owned a sideboard, by the end of the eighteenth century 37 per cent had a sideboard and as many as 57 per cent had a chest of drawers. At the same time, those who owned a chest fell from 62 per cent to 18 per cent.[228] During our period then, wardrobes, chests of drawers, tallboys, corner cupboards, bookshelves and linen cupboards became increasingly widespread, and they made it possible to arrange items in precise categories and separate them according to their function and use.[229]

17. Bedrooms and corridors

Public elegance and private comfort

The tendency towards specialization did not only involve furniture. The house itself was reorganized in order to create separate spaces for different functions. The upper classes had specialized areas even during the Middle Ages, and often there were genuine kitchens. Occasionally, particularly in large complexes such as monasteries and abbeys, kitchens were in separate buildings to avoid the fire hazard.[230] In other cases, they were located on the top floor, which was inconvenient for the supply of water and firewood, but sensible in terms of reducing the risk of seeing the entire building going up in flames, particularly when houses were largely made of wood.[231] In spite of this, it was very common to have a single room with a fireplace for both cooking and eating, even amongst social ranks towards the upper end of the scale.[232]

From the fifteenth century, the house was subject to increasing attempts at rationalization, especially in the context of Italian Renaissance culture, which later became a model for the whole of Europe. The 'fortress' home was abandoned at the top of the social scale, and a new type of house, the urban *palazzo*, was born, particularly in Florence. The change related to the development of the urban economy, the Church's lessening moral disapproval of wealth, the increasing conviction that expenditure on building, far from reprehensible, was advantageous both to the owner and the city that the building adorned, and the desire of the newly rich and powerful to assert their status symbolically through their own homes.[233] The words *Elegantiae publicae et commoditati privatae* ('for public elegance and private comfort') appear over the entrance to the fifteenth-century Palazzo Castani in Milan.[234] Italian Renaissance *palazzi* were inspired not only by magnificence, symmetry and order,[235] but also by comfort and convenience. According to the gentleman and architect Alvise Cornaro, 'a dignified and charming building' is preferable to one that is 'exquisitely beautiful and uncomfortable'.[236] Architects were therefore interested in the 'layout of the rooms'.[237] Domestic space started to be divided into service areas, entertainment areas and private areas.[238] From the fifteenth century, those who could afford it started to reserve a few rooms for their personal use.[239]

Bedrooms, antechambers, lavatories and small studies

The owner of the house received his guests in the room with his bed, which was perhaps the most important space in the building. But some people started to be irritated by this coming and going in a room where they kept their most precious possessions and where they rested. The solution that evolved to the problem was the antechamber. As the word implies, another room started to be built in front of the bedroom in which to transfer some of the activities normally carried out there. An antechamber also offered other advantages; you could eat in it and keep some of your possessions there. Moreover, it was possible to have a servant sleep there during the night in case he was needed, but without having him on top of you. You could also have a servant stay there during the day to check who was coming. The number of antechambers was increased to achieve a greater degree of privacy in the bedroom and to monitor access more carefully. It seems that they were originally called 'guard-chambers', possibly because of this role.[240]

In the sixteenth century, the custom of building a second room with a bed separate to the one used for receiving guests (leaving aside the closest relationships), was introduced so as to create a relatively private personal space.[241] In some cases the distinction between private bedroom and the bedroom 'for show' was the same as the distinction between the summer bedroom and the winter one.[242] In their search for comfort and decorum, the more fortunate had a summer bedroom built. Sometimes this would be on the ground floor, where it was cooler. The winter bedroom would be smaller and cosier, so that it could be more easily heated. It was usually on the 'noble floor' (i.e. the first floor).[243]

The search for greater comfort did not stop there. Other smaller associated rooms started to be built behind or next to the bedroom, and these were called *destri, studi e camerini* ('lavatories, studies and closets') by the architect Francesco di Giorgio Martini around 1480.[244] There is no denying that having a lavatory near at hand was a not inconsiderable comfort. During this century, however, the rich shifted their preference from the lavatory, which was generally a hole connected to a cesspit, to the commode, which was kept in a corner of the bedroom or in one of the small rooms adjacent to it.[245] As can be easily imagined, the study was the personal space where one could withdraw to read and write undisturbed, and also keep books, letters, important documents and other objects of value. According to some historians, this space, which was mainly but not exclusively enjoyed by men, was the first expression of a new need for privacy and personal comfort which was to develop in the coming centuries.

The Italian *studio* or study was in a way the antecedent of the elegantly furnished French *cabinets* and English 'closets' that were to become so important in the seventeenth and eighteenth centuries.[246] Following the Renaissance, the tendency to create small adjacent rooms around the bedroom was to become more firmly established. 'The main bedrooms must be accompanied by a reasonably sized *cabinet*, *arrière-cabinet* [rear closet] and two boxrooms. A third small *cabinet* could be added with a bed for resting on, and it would be given the name of *boudoir*. Many hallways with different uses should also be created', wrote Charles-Etienne Briseux in 1743, thus demonstrating the degree to which this trend that started in Renaissance Italy had become established.[247]

The apartment

This increase in the number of rooms around the bedroom in the Italian Renaissance *palazzo* gave rise to the apartment, a kind of house within a house for the private use of the owners. This arrangement was to prove a lasting success. An apartment, in order to be complete, had to have at least four rooms, 'namely an antechamber, a room with a bed, a lavatory and a linen room, which must always be provided with a stair', D'Aviler argued in the seventeenth century.[248] In fact the presence of a stairway or 'secret' exit was a practically indispensable feature of an apartment. In its ideal form, it was a series of consecutive rooms along which you increasingly distanced yourself from the public areas as you penetrated further into the private area. At the end of this sequence, there was an exit or secret stairway that allowed the owner of the room and his or her servants, spouse and clandestine lovers to come and go without passing through the more public and visible parts of the house.[249]

'Husband and wife should both have their own bedrooms', Leon Battista Alberti stated authoritatively in the fifteenth century.[250] It was a short step from the single bedroom to the apartment in which the bedroom was surrounded by antechambers and closets. During the Renaissance and the early modern era, husband and wife in the upper classes often had an apartment each, and sometimes they had two, one for summer and one for winter. Even children had one, once they had grown up, as did any other adult relations who lived in the house.[251] As far as I know, the sexual division of the interior space of affluent homes has not been the subject of detailed study. It appears that in Renaissance Italy the wife had a room behind the husband's, when she did not have her own personal apartment. In seventeenth-century France on the other hand, it seems the ladies lived on the 'noble floor', alongside the ceremonial rooms and the rooms 'for show', and that the lady of the house had a larger apartment than her husband's.[252]

Furniture and rooms

In Renaissance *palazzi*, which were often built with a central courtyard, the reception hall, drawing room or another type of hall that could be used as a dining room, some antechambers and the chapel were generally found on the side that corresponded to the facade. The opposite side was increasingly used for works of art and books (the gallery and the library). Another side was used for the more private rooms and the last side was used for the main staircase, a few antechambers and service rooms.[253]

In these *palazzi*, entertainment areas, service areas and private areas were generally kept fairly distinct, although there were grey areas where functions overlapped. Some rooms took on a specifically functional role, clearly stated by the types of furnishing that were being developed. The study, for example, was furnished very simply in the fifteenth century, but it usually contained a table with a writing surface, shelves for placing objects and one or more bookstands.[254] This piece of furniture was eventually destined to evolve towards forms that we would more easily recognize as a writing desk, and at a subsequent stage to the one described it was defined in Venice as a *scrittor*. In Florence it was more often referred to as a *studiolo*, and *scrittoio* was the room in which it was kept, which in turn was called a *studio* in Venice. But in both cities the terms were sometimes inverted. The furniture characterized the room and the room ended up being identified with the furniture. In other words, the furniture made such a significant contribution to the definition of the functional purpose of the space in which it was kept that the words for each became interchangeable.[255]

Eating, receiving guests and sleeping

Nevertheless, many rooms remained multi-purpose in a Renaissance *palazzo*. Even in rooms that had a more precise identity, activities were often interlinked that we now usually keep separate. There were often two bedrooms for the owners of the house – one for show, in which important guests were received but only very rarely slept, and the other private, which was not, however, only used for sleeping. Women used the latter rooms for embroidery and often received those with whom they were particularly close. These rooms were also sometimes used for reading and not infrequently for eating.

Indeed, there wasn't a room specifically for eating. If there were many guests or a feast, then tables were put up in the reception hall. When there were no guests, the householder's family could eat in the cosier environment of a small room. However, they might also have eaten in an antechamber, while others chose to eat their meal in their own apartment either in company or on their own.[256] Not surprisingly, tables in the fifteenth century were often made up of boards over trestles that could be quickly folded away. It was mainly in the sixteenth century that tables with fixed legs and even elegant tables for grand occasions spread.[257]

'The dining room C 7 can be used as the antechamber to the bedroom with alcove C 4. . . . The antechamber H 7 can be used as a dining room', wrote D'Aviler at the end of the seventeenth century when explaining one of his projects.[258] A bedroom 'will be used purely for show', argued Giovanni Biagio Amico a few decades later.[259] By the turn of the eighteenth century, a room specifically designed for meals still had not appeared in the houses of the rich and even by the mid-eighteenth century there were still people who used a bedroom, albeit one for show, for receiving guests. This does not mean, however, that for centuries the whole situation remained unchanged. Although antechambers could be used for eating, 'it is very much the custom to allocate a particular room as a dining room', asserted D'Aviler.[260] Available data demonstrates that at the very top of society dining rooms were starting to catch on.

In country houses of the English upper classes, the ancient 'hall', was a communal room where everyone ate, people lingered and chatted, and some servants actually slept, but it lost these traditional features in the seventeenth century. The owner preferred to eat in a purpose-built dining room, and the hall became the refectory for the servants. As time went on, another room was created for the servants' meals, and was often located in the basement. Once the focal point of the house, the hall declined in importance and became a simple entrance area.[261]

In France, 'citizens . . . and merchants have a place to eat', wrote Pier Jacopo Martello in 1718, thirty years after the publication of D'Aviler's work.[262] However the spread of the dining room in Paris outside the circles of the very rich appears to have been a phenomenon of the second half of the eighteenth century.[263]

The Ca' Zenobio ai Carmini was built in Venice between 1682 and 1690, and is considered 'the most complete prototype' of the new home that was to spread through eighteenth-century cities. It had a small dining room for the owners positioned directly above the one for the servants.[264] In fact the dining room was to become practically universal in the homes of the richest Venetian families during the following century.[265]

The dining room also took on a new importance in Scotland. It became the place for arranging the more precious and prestigious objects in the house, and was mainly used for male get-togethers based on the conspicuous consumption of alcohol and meals involving large amounts of meat. In middle-class houses, the dining room continued to contain a bed, which was however kept very isolated from the rest of the room by a curtain.[266]

In other words, dining rooms were becoming increasingly common in the whole of Europe. On the other hand, if we are to go by Parisian inventories, they were not very widespread once you start to examine classes beyond the wealthier ones. In Paris in the second half of the eighteenth century, they were referred to only for 14 per cent of the houses.[267] Overall in eighteenth-century Paris, dining rooms only accounted for 12 per cent of all main rooms referred to in the inventories. Kitchens accounted for 17 per cent. All other rooms were simply *chambres*.[268]

What was meant by a *chambre*? A *chambre* 'is generally a place where you sleep and receive guests', explains an important seventeenth-century dictionary.[269] 'On the whole, they receive people in the same place that they sleep', confirmed Pier Jacopo Martello, a writer from Bologna, with reference to French citizens and merchants.[270] Not surprisingly, a great number of chairs and seats were generally to be found in a *chambre*.[271] This multi-purpose nature of rooms did not just arise from the lack of space in many buildings, as we have seen. Of course, the poor were obliged to make do with a single room for eating, sleeping, receiving company and not infrequently working. For example the Parisian inventories preserve the memory of a master tradesman who lived with his wife in accommodation that consisted of one room which also contained desks for schoolchildren and of a producer of soft drinks who prepared and sold his lemonades in the kitchen of the house, which was also the bedroom.[272] Yet the *chambre* was the place for sleeping and receiving guests for those people who could afford separate rooms for carrying out their professional activities and for the preparation of food, as Martello observed. This kind of set-up was also found in the homes of the nobility where there was plenty of space. As we have seen, the more fortunate had private bedrooms alongside the bedroom for show. Nevertheless, Madame de Maintenon slept in the room where the king received his ministers. While the king discussed affairs of state with them, the chambermaids undressed her and helped her to bed, while the only privacy was provided by curtains.[273]

It was during the reign of Louis XIV that we start to see the first signs in France of the tendency amongst the wealthier sections of society towards a greater specialization of rooms, and this trend was to become more firmly established in the second half of the eighteenth century, as can be demonstrated by the chronology of the spread of such terms as 'bedroom', 'dining room' and 'salon' (the fashion for *salons* had originated in Italy).[274] During the seventeenth century, the balance between ostentation and comfort, which we have already noted in the Renaissance, tipped in favour of the former.[275] The 'architecture of magnificence, promoted by Louis XIV to exalt the state' ended up influencing private individuals in the final decades of the century. But in the early decades of the eighteenth century, the balance shifted in the other direction away from pomp and magnificence and towards comfort and luxury in housing.[276]

Some themes that had already existed in the Italian Renaissance and which were to develop further, particularly in England, were taken up and elaborated upon by French architects, whose influence often extended beyond the borders of their own country. 'Houses are built to live in, and not to look on; therefore let use be preferred before uniformity,' wrote Francis Bacon in his essay *Of Building*.[277] 'Decoration ... is undoubtedly most interesting in architecture, but however much it might appear essential, it is insufficient without comfort', argued the French architect and essayist Jacques François Blondel in 1752.[278] The question of how rooms were distributed and considerations on how to make them comfortable and functional came to the forefront of architectural thinking. Pierre Patte, who continued Blondel's *Cours d'Architecture civile* was to write somewhat immodestly, 'Nothing brings more honour than the invention of the art of organizing apartments. Before us, . . . houses were only made for the life of society, and not for private comfort'.[279]

The separation and specialization of rooms took on a particular importance in this context of the renewed search for comfortable, 'delightful and charming' homes in which it is possible to escape 'troublesome visitors'.[280] The bedroom was devoted to sleep and private activities. 'It is only in the event of illness that the bedroom can receive a more numerous company,' explains the article in the *Encyclopédie* to cover the subject.[281] But in the eighteenth century, only one Parisian out of ten had a genuinely separate bedroom. Kitchens solely used for the preparation of food were equally rare, both at the beginning and the end of the century. By the end of the period we are examining, dining rooms, sitting rooms and reception halls (*salons*) were still unknown to the middle classes (*couches moyennes*).[282] New requirements were coming into force even in this environment dominated by the lack of space: the understairs cupboards and closets used for keeping old junk, firewood and other bits and pieces were converted into lavatories, anterooms, linen cupboards and other minuscule rooms that provided a minimum of privacy. These little *dépendances* multiplied and tended to lose their original connotations of intermediate spaces between inside and out. They were in fact integrated into the domestic realm.[283]

In the French capital, these changes were accompanied by others: household units (obviously excluding those consisting of a single room with no *dépendances*) were structured vertically, with rooms and closets spread over two, three or four floors. In other words, the horizontal organization of space and the flat as we know it today were still rare before the period 1720–30, and they were only to become prevalent in the second half of the century.[284] To the extent that this involved a more compact use of space by a single family, this change also contributed to the clearer and sharper definition of the boundaries between outside and inside, and the creation of a household unit more closed in on itself and less open to the collective life of the building in which it was contained.

In the Ghetto

On the evening of 29 May 1782, a Jewish woman called Anna Tedeschi was lighting a fire 'to cook a little soup' after having returned from the funeral of a grandchild who was born to her daughter-in-law the previous day and only survived a few hours. She had not finished this operation when Giuseppe Tedeschi and his son Serve, tenants in the 'adjoining attic', burst into the room where Anna was in the company of her husband and her daughter-in-law. The two men picked up a pan of water and put the fire out, claiming 'the smoke was causing them great vexation'. Serve asserted 'it was not the time for lighting fires'. Anna replied that she could not have lit it earlier, as she had had to attend to a new-born baby who was dying and then she had to deal with the burial. This did not calm people down: indeed they became even more worked up and insults and blows were exchanged. Poor Anna ended up with a cut on her head. For her the day had started badly and finished worse. We do not know exactly why her grandson died, but it was the sad destiny of many babies to leave the world barely twenty minutes after entering it. We can however assert with some certitude that overcrowding in the Turin ghetto was one of the reasons for the violent argument and possibly the only one.

In the Turin ghetto, as with others like the Roman one, Jews were not permitted to enlarge the accommodation assigned to them. Conversion was deliberately made the only way to escape the overcrowding. There were considerable restrictions even in those cities where some expansion was possible. Even outside the Jewish ghettos (which were introduced in the sixteenth century), demographic growth occasionally caused an increase in the promiscuity of housing, while inside them it translated into a sharp reduction in the space available to each inhabitant. This was very far from the trend towards the specialization of rooms or the creation of private areas. Jews living in the ghettos (who were generally unable to own real estate) were faced with the prospect of living in a single room. The most they could hope for was two rooms with the addition of a workshop.

Living space was sometimes so restricted that, beyond a certain point, it made no sense to accumulate possessions. The fact that they could not invest in many material goods probably contributed, along with other factors, to the tradition in Jewish communities of investing in culture and enrichment of the mind.

We will now leave the suffocating atmosphere of the ghetto and examine the living conditions of those who were not forced to live in such restricted accommodation.[285]

Country folk and townsfolk

In Paris, different social groups expressed similar needs, albeit in different ways and in accordance with their own possibilities. Compared with the pomp of this great city, rural living conditions were not always distinguished by 'backwardness' in terms of the availability and organization of space. The difference was not necessarily one of the 'savage' compared with the 'civilized', although the more frequent proximity between humans and animals that characterized the rural world might easily have led one to brand all its inhabitants as 'bestial'. From this point of view, it is significant that Serlio – the first architect to attempt to deal with the housing needs of all social classes, as we have seen – put forward in the sixth book of his treatise a progression of available space and its organization that proceeded more or less in parallel in the city and the countryside. In both contexts, he planned a one-room dwelling for the poorest and then enlarged and enriched the proposed houses as he climbed the social hierarchy (for the peasant houses designed by Serlio, see Figs. 15–16).[286]

This parallelism claimed by Serlio does not appear entirely out of place in the social reality of the early modern era. There were, in fact, areas in which the development of rural housing led to the creation of large dwellings in which the functional diversification of rooms affected not only activities relating to the production and treatment of agricultural produce (byres, cellars, dovecotes, barns, oil mills, etc.), but also domestic life itself. Hence, the plans of architects who wanted to improve the countryside of central Italy included, from as far back as the fifteenth century, at least the distinction between the kitchen and the householder's room and, later on, the distinction between kitchen and bedroom.[287] In eighteenth-century rural Tuscany, the bed was nearly always in a bedroom and only rarely in a kitchen or a communal room.[288] In the seventeenth century, Jacob and Agatha, like other affluent peasants, had a separate *Stube*, kitchen and bedroom.[289]

It might appear then that the countryside was ahead of the city, although this probably wasn't the case. On the other hand, we cannot be too certain about this. To some extent, the rural and urban worlds developed independently of each other, but only to some extent. For instance, many of the architects that influenced the rural landscape came from the city and represented urban interests. The interdependence that existed was linked to the specific realities of their respective environments. In the countryside, the need for functional diversification could be particularly marked and the problem of space less pressing. Not surprisingly, the villas that the rich had built in the countryside represented a freer environment for experimentation, given that they no longer had to take account of all the restrictions imposed by the presence of streets and other houses in the urban environment.[290] 'Many gentlemen's houses prove to be more beautiful and better proportioned outside the city than in, and this occurs because in the city you rarely find a rectangular site on its own, while in the countryside you can build a house in any shape you wish,' Serlio noted on this point.[291] At the opposite extreme, peasant houses could exploit the same advantage, even though the diversification of rooms, as we have seen, was very far from involving all rural social groups. It may be (but the question requires further research) that the availability of space and the sense of privacy and intimacy were structured differently in the countryside compared with the city: ultimately, as we have seen, the houses of *mezzadri* had highly specialized rooms, but as late as the nineteenth century several people were still sharing the same bed.[292]

Towards specialization

Studies carried out so far appear to indicate definitively that there was a widespread trend towards specialization of individual rooms within houses. New rooms were created alongside what has been the termed 'the primordial dwelling space', namely the French *salle*, the German *Stube*, the English 'hall' and so on, and these were named *chambre*, *Zimmer*, 'chamber', 'parlour', 'inner room' and 'borning room'. These rooms then underwent further specialization (bedrooms, dining rooms, etc.).[293]

The available data, which is still deficient for many social realities, suggests that the timing and phases of these changes varied according to the situation, but the second half of the eighteenth century appears to have been the time of greatest change in many areas. For instance, it appears that the show bedroom appeared later in England than it did in Italy and France, but it also disappeared earlier. Spouses of high social rank appear to have slept together more often than on the continent.[294] The trend towards specialization of rooms appears to have been somewhat earlier in London compared with other parts of Europe, and markedly so when compared with other parts of Britain. It is certainly the case that beds could be found in practically every kind of room in seventeenth-century London homes: in workshops, kitchens and halls. They were placed alongside tables, benches, chairs, kitchenware and a great variety of objects. This indicates a degree of promiscuity and a limited level of room specialization. In spite of this, rooms on the upper floors in the seventeenth century were mainly used for bedrooms and the preparation of food usually occurred in the kitchen.[295]

Overall, specialized rooms were on the increase more or less everywhere, even though the bedroom understood as a private place for resting, the dining room, the study, and the sitting room as a place for social encounters and contact with guests, were slow to become disentangled from each other. Obviously the change established new boundaries between social groups: many families continued to live in rooms in which they slept, ate, received guests and even worked because of custom or lack of space, while others introduced a few innovations into the organization of their domestic space, but would never have had a dining room, a study or a library. In general, however, the process led to a distinction within the home between the more private rooms and the rooms more open to the outside world. This implied a profound change in the perception of the way rooms were used and the relations between the people who used them.[296]

The enfilade *and the corridor*

Rooms were not only multi-purpose during the Renaissance and the early modern era. They were generally linked in such a manner that it was impossible to move from one to another without going through those rooms between the room you were leaving and the room you wished to get to. Facilitating movement primarily meant increasing the number of doors, and in many Renaissance *palazzi* there were up to four doors in each room. Leon Battista Alberti had written that it made sense to locate doors so as to make it possible to reach the greatest number of areas within the building. Living space organized in such a manner meant that domestic life involved all activities being interrupted at any time by people passing through and that there were continuous chance encounters between family members and guests simply because of the need to move around.

As we have seen, the way to find a little peace and quiet in the houses of the rich was to shut oneself up in the inner parts of the building behind a barrier of antechambers and create a personal apartment equipped with secrets exits and stairs. Although this solution did make it possible to monitor access by guests to the personal rooms and to escape disagreeable and importunate ones without them knowing, it did not allow you to completely cut yourself off from other members of the household, particularly the servants. The introduction of the corridor was to change profoundly this organization of space and the very relations between people living under the same roof.

It is not easy to establish exactly when this transformation took place. There had been architectural elements similar to corridors since ancient times. In 1558 Maddalena Piccinini, the girl we encountered earlier when she was showing off her wedding ring, claimed that she had carried out the matrimonial rite in the kitchen of a couple of friends located 'beyond the corridor'.[297] According to the learned authors of the Italian *Vocabolario degli Accademici della Crusca*, a *corridoio* ('corridor') was a 'passageway over buildings for going from one part to another, called by some in Latin, *pergula*',[298] a definition that referred to an idea of a corridor that was not only different to the current one but also not very useful. It appears from what Maddalena said that the term 'corridor' indicated a passage that led from the outside door or the main room of the building to the internal courtyard, which was often to be found in urban architecture.[299] There was also something similar to a corridor in country homes. As we have seen, the ground floor of the house belonging to Agatha and Jacob was divided across its width by a passageway onto which cellars, byres and other rooms opened.[300]

Since the Renaissance, as has already been suggested, the homes of the moneyed contained secret and hidden passageways that led to stairs or communicated with other rooms whose principle entrance was definitely not the one used by those who entered by such narrow and tortuous passages, be they chambermaids or secret lovers. They were often equipped with small doors hidden in a corner.[301] Alberti said that both the husband's and the wife's room 'should have a separate door, beyond which there should be a corridor to connect them, so that they can go to the other's room without anyone seeing them'.[302] The Duke of Urbino had a passageway through the garden by which he could go to his wife's apartment.[303] In this case, the corridor was an architectural feature outside the house. Similarly the term *corridoio* was used to describe the covered passageway which allowed the pope to go from the Vatican Palace to Castel Sant'Angelo.[304]

The concept of a corridor did therefore exist. However, in all these cases, they were not corridors in the modern sense of the term, namely long and narrow spaces with doors entering directly into each room. If anything, architectural trends during the Renaissance initially led to a reduction in those features that resembled the modern corridor. Indeed the attempt to achieve privacy by monitoring entrance through antechambers was diametrically opposed to the concept of a corridor. It has been argued that 'once the fully-fledged apartment had been devised, where the intention was to channel visitors *through* a sequence of rooms, a true corridor would have nullified such an arrangement'.[305] On the other hand, the arrangement of rooms *en enfilade*, so that each one led into the next, was preferred for aesthetic and symbolic reasons. By positioning a door in each room at the same height in the wall, it was possible to play with perspective and impress visitors with the vastness of the building (Fig. 37). 'From the hall you enter the antechambers, of which there should be many with the doors in a row to enhance the magnificence of the house, i.e. one opposite the other, so that when they are all open you can see the last room from the first', explained Amico in the first half of the eighteenth century, taking up a theme dear to many architects and owners of large houses.[306] With this room layout, the entire length of two sides of the building could be seen from the rooms on one of its corners.[307]

However, the inconvenience of this arrangement was apparent to one person. 'What, by God, is the purpose of those endless successions of rooms, one leading into the other, as they are not suitable for placing a bed, except perhaps in the last one?' Martello asked himself in 1718. Anyone who was 'condemned' to sleep in one of the others would have had to resign themselves to watching 'everyone bouncing along in front of them, when they want to run the whole length of the rooms either for some urgent need or for the amusement of enjoying the paintings, tapestries, chinaware and statues'.[308] It was the corridor that provided a satisfactory solution to this kind of problem.

The first 'modern' corridor was possibly the one built for a residence designed by John Thorpe in Chelsea, England in 1597.[309] The planning innovation, which attracted a great deal of curiosity, was described as 'a long entrance running through the entire house'.[310] Paradoxically, given the Italian styles of the time, the central corridor became more widely used at the same time that English architecture fell under Italian influence. Coleshill House, in Berkshire, which was planned between 1650 and 1667 by the amateur architect Sir Roger Pratt for a cousin, possibly represents the most radical and systematic application of the new layout of rooms. Each floor had a corridor that ran the length of the house and had backstairs at each end. There was a two-storey hall at the centre of the building with a main staircase. Each room had a door that opened either onto the corridor or onto the hall (Fig. 38).

Pratt explained in his notebooks that the passageway that ran the length of the house responded to the need to avoid having the work in the service rooms constantly in view. In other words, Pratt wanted to overcome the kind of layout that obliged the owners to go through service areas as they moved about the building, whether they like it or not. At the same time, the corridor meant that domestic servants were no longer forced to go through rooms used by the owners, in order to carry out their work.[311]

However, the idea of the room with a single door opening onto a corridor did not immediately catch on. 'The word corridor, madam, is foreign, and sig-nifies in plain English no more than a passage; it is now, however, generally used as an English word', the architect and playwright John Vanbrugh explained to the Duchess of Marlborough at the beginning of the eighteenth century.[312] When, in 1728–32, the architect James Gibbs designed a country house at

Kelmash, in Northamptonshire, and put in a corridor that connected all the rooms, there were still those who considered this to be a complete innovation. It took time, but eventually all the rich were persuaded to adopt it.[313] During what might be called an intermediate phase, rooms often had doors that communicated with one after the other, mainly for the aesthetic reason of creating a sense of perspective, with other doors that opened onto the corridor, for functional rather than aesthetic reasons. The functional reasons were to win through in the end, and they transformed each room into an isolated unit. The activities carried out in each were removed from view and there was no longer the possibility of other members of the household casually passing through. The corridor facilitated communication between rooms for specific purposes, while it reduced the number of chance encounters.[314]

This change probably expressed, and at the same time reinforced, a new sense of modesty, a growing need to conceal certain activities from other people, a more pronounced need to select the people with whom one engaged in certain practices and a more profound desire to spend time on one's own.[315] But outside elite circles, particularly English elite circles, the success of the corridor was primarily a nineteenth- and twentieth-century phenomenon.

18. Privacy

Rooms for the 'family' and linen rooms

If we are to believe the arguments of Roger Pratt, the need for privacy mainly developed in relation to servants. Pratt may well have been right. In the early modern era they were undoubtedly aware of the problem of finding a proper balance between comforts provided by servants and the desire to avoid the noise and smell of the stables and kitchens, and perhaps also the inconvenience of having too many people underfoot. As we have seen, service areas and rooms for domestic servants started to appear in Renaissance *palazzi*. Serlio called them 'rooms for the family'.[316] In the following centuries, these became standard features of all large houses, but this did not mean that a genuine spatial segregation existed between master and servant.

There was, in fact, a vast range of domestic servants in a large stately home: butlers, accountants, secretaries, chaplains, tutors, waiters, escorts, footmen, cooks, stewards, cellar-men, scullery-boys, grooms, stable-boys, governesses, chambermaids, maids-in-waiting, wet nurses and so on.[317] Although there were specific areas for some of the activities carried out by servants, such as kitchens and stables, the majority of the functions and the way the rooms were laid out meant that their presence was more or less pervasive. The hierarchical separation between servants and their masters was expressed through food and clothing as well as, and perhaps even more than, spatial segregation.

We get a very good idea of how every corner of these buildings was teeming with servants from the places where they were expected to sleep. Giuseppe Leoncini wrote in his *Instruttioni architettoniche pratiche* in 1679 that 'linen rooms or cupboards, armouries, sleeping quarters for servants and other features relating to them will be located [in] the upper apartments and under the roof'. But not all servants were banished to the loft during the night. He added, 'Particularly in that place where the sideboard is kept, there will be a sleeping place for the person responsible for guarding the silver'. There was to be a place 'for sleeping for the errand boys who look after these animals'.[318] A few years later, D'Aviler located the servants' rooms in the stable-yard (*basse-cour*),[319] above the coach-house. He also argued that the steward had to sleep next to the place where the silverware and other valuable items were kept and that the grooms had to have accommodation close to the stables. He decided there should be a small room close to the entrance for the doorkeeper. Lastly, one of the dressing rooms next to the owners' bedroom was for valets and chamber-maids to sleep in, so that they could be easily reached, should they be required.[320] Practically all the sources, including the *Dictionnaire de Furetiere*, the *Dictionnaire de Trévoux*,[321] D'Aviler, Briseaux, Milizia and Gambardella,[322] confirm that in seventeenth- and eighteenth-century France and Italy the dressing room or one of the dressing rooms was used during the night for 'those servants that one wants to have sleeping nearby',[323] namely 'those persons among the servants who must be close to their masters, so that they can be found ready when they are needed'.[324]

Therefore it was not only in the countryside and in the homes of the middle and lower-middle classes that servants and their masters were living elbow to elbow. In the latter social classes, a maid might sleep under the stairs, in the kitchen, together with the mistress of the house[325] or even with more than one member of the owner's family, as in the case of Marie Alexandre who in 1725 told the police that she had always slept in the same bed as her mistress and her mistress's oldest son.[326] Even in the houses of the rich, which contained rooms and dormitories for servants, at least one servant was close to the master or mistress during the night, not because of the lack of space but to deal with their every need. Sometimes they even shared the same bed. Towards the end of the fifteenth century, Anna Sforza slept not with her teddy bear but her black slave-girl.[327] Two centuries later, Madame de Liancourt still felt that she had to tell her niece not to share her bed with her chambermaids because this ran contrary to the respect they had to show her and to the norms of cleanliness and decency. However, she advised the young woman to have one or two women in her bedroom.[328] During this period, Louis XIV had a servant spend the night in his room.[329]

Early morning erections

Servants taking personal care of their masters and mistresses, when they were not sleeping with them, shared their daily lives and were at their sides when they engaged in activities that we would consider private. An affair that involved Francesco Albergati Capacelli (whom we have encountered before) gives us an insight into the matter. In 1751, when his first wife asked for an annulment of their marriage on the basis that he was impotent, his valets were able to testify to his virility because they had happened to notice his early morning erections when they were dressing him. 'I declare', said one of them, that 'having served in the capacity of manservant to his excellency Marquis Francesco Albergati for the period of about eleven years, that I can say and give account that on three or four occasions I saw the said marquis getting out of bed with a perfect erection of the male organ'. 'And this I saw and observed', he added, 'with complete certainty and without being deceived, because I was in a position to observe it and see it at my ease because of my employment'. Another servant declared that he had had occasion to observe the marquis 'with a hard and perfect erection', while he was putting on his shirt. According to the evidence of the servants, Albergati and other knights had no scruples about kicking up a 'rumpus' one evening and chasing after each other practically in the nude in the presence of their servants, who then commented on how well-endowed the marquis was. One noted that he had 'excellent assets' and another that he had a 'fine thing'.[330]

Does this mean that the marquis had absolutely no sense of propriety and neither had his peers? We know, for instance, that Monsieur de Vendôme received the Bishop of Parma while sitting on the commode and that once Madame du Châtelet happily had a bath in the presence of Longchamp, a valet whom she asked to pour hot water into the bathtub while she widened her legs to avoid being scalded.[331] But we should not use these examples to come to any hasty conclusions.

In the early modern era, the modesty about one's person was different to that of today. When dealing with people of lower rank, a kind of immodesty was permissible, and in some cases it was used to underscore the social division and one's own superiority.[332] Thus Louis XIV transformed a humble task such as putting on his shirt into an honour for the person that did it. This daily ritual, whose every detail was governed by protocol, was a theatrical representation of his power. Those who helped him to dress were representatives of the aristocracy for whom access to the sovereign's private life constituted a privilege.[333] To assert that modesty was manifested in a different manner compared with today does not imply that it was altogether absent.[334]

The behaviour of Marquis Albergati, as described above by the first servant, was evidence of this. One morning, the marquis's erection lasted even when 'I was putting on his ankle socks'. The marquis was 'not wearing pants, and I could easily see that with one hand he was trying to push down his erection. I remember that for this precise reason I said, "Marquis, the air is very bracing this morning'. And he replied, 'Indeed, it is too much so".'[335] In Albergati's emotional make-up, the convenience or the habit of having servants in attendance had got the better of his modesty, but only to a certain degree.

Barriers

The need to have servants nearby in order to be attended to promptly and in all circumstances (thus even being assisted in activities that to our eyes are extremely personal and should be carried out with no one else present or, at the very most, in the company of people with whom we are very intimate) slowly lost ground to the increasing desire for separation and privacy. According to one historian, this led in England to four innovations: the obsolescence of the old-style hall through the creation of separate dining rooms for masters and servants; the tendency to confine the servants to the basement or a separate wing connected to the main body of the residence by a passage that could be closed off; the introduction of corridors and backstairs; and the development in the second half of the eighteenth century of systems of ropes and bells that made it possible to call servants quickly when they were needed without being obliged to have them constantly close at hand. By the beginning of the nineteenth century, the last innovation had become so sophisticated that there were bells in the servants quarters for each room in the house. Each bell had a label to indicate the room it was being rung from, so the servants knew exactly where to go and to go there quickly.[336] In other words, all the servants could now sleep in the servants' quarters. It was no longer necessary for any of them to settle down on a camp bed in the dressing room so as to be ready to bring their master or mistress a glass of water in the middle of the night. When thirsty, the employers could easily call their servants without having to put up with their constant presence.

On the other side of the Channel, there undoubtedly was interest during the early modern era in finding ways of reducing the inconvenience of servants, without however being quite so obsessed with the problem as in England. D'Aviler argued that linen rooms should have access and exits so that 'the servants are not continuously obliged to pass through their masters' apartment' and that servants' communal areas should not be located in the principal courtyard.[337] Alessandro Galilei wrote that 'the kitchen must be placed as far away as possible from the apartments because of the constant noise made by those who work in it'. He added that to solve the problem, 'Italians have started to put them in the basement and with the convenience of secret stairs that conveniently lead to all the apartments'.[338] Briseux suggested that in order to avoid the smell and noise, kitchens should be located in a separate building. He then discussed the various pros and cons of corridors, which in his opinion are not such a great solution as they take up a great deal of room and do not insulate the owners sufficiently from the noise they produce. He preferred an increase in the number of backstairs to avoid the owners being disturbed 'either during their sleep or during their pursuits'.[339] According to Francesco Milizia, it is important that the personal apartments of the master and mistress 'be far from the courtyards and from the sight of the servants, in order to avoid the noise they inevitably make'. The various rooms and closets that make up an apartment also had to be kept 'free by passageways, so that the servants can do their chores without disturbing their masters'.[340]

In other words, servants were a problem and architects were racking their brains to find a way round it. Various historians have observed that the problem appeared to get more and more serious as the early modern era progressed, and it took on a significance that had been previously unknown. A comparison between building projects in different periods can be very revealing about this aspect. The plans published in France by Charles-Antoine Jombert in 1764 provided for the traditional side wings or detached quarters for servants, but also reflected the need to have servants nearby. In the plans produced by Johann Karl Krafft and Pierre Nicolas Ransonette at the end of the eighteenth century, the physical distance between masters and servants was further increased and the layout was organized in such a manner that domestic work disappeared from view. The scullery boys and kitchen maids were confined to the basements and the valets and personal servants to upper floors.[341]

The end of the 'family' in its original sense

In practice, not very many people were involved in these changes. Less wealthy families certainly could not afford to have separate areas for servants. Many people obviously did not have servants to worry about. The changes that have just been examined did however express a change in attitude. Those who could afford it distanced their servants and the servants' chores from their private life. Servants had always been looked on with a degree of suspicion, and in the Middle Ages they had been called enemies in the home (*domestici hostes*), but now they were increasingly considered useful but disruptive intruders.[342]

On the other hand, the servants themselves appeared increasingly to want their own private sphere and greater autonomy. From at least the late seventeenth century, there was an increase in the number of male servants who did not live permanently with their employers. Some rented rooms to which they could occasionally retire, while others lived with their families and went to work during the day. Still others obtained authorization from their employer to spend a few nights with their wives during the week (female servants continued to live under the same roof as their employers for much longer).[343]

These changes perhaps had a linguistic outcome: after having survived for centuries, the etymological meaning of the term 'family' – namely a group of servants dependent on the same master – disappeared from the European languages that had inherited it from Latin. In French, it appears to have fallen into disuse in the eighteenth century. In English, the last recorded uses go back to the end of the eighteenth century. Traces of the original use remained in Italian until the 1930s, but it was already outdated in the nineteenth century.[344] The time when a lady could hardly object to eating at the same table as her female servant because they both shared the same bed was becoming a very distant one.[345]

19. Living and eating

The lady's possible objections shift our attention to eating habits. We have now examined accommodation varying from subterranean homes to luxurious palaces and how they developed through the early modern era. We have considered how they were heated, how they were supplied with water and how they were lit. We have observed the increasing number of domestic items, the types of furnishings and the layouts of interiors. The time has now come to shift our attention to other themes, even though there is still much that could be said about housing.

We have already caught a glimpse of the pots boiling as they hang from a chain over the fireplace in the houses of the poor. The debates between architects have made us aware of the smells coming from the kitchens of the rich. We have noted the way chairs tended to replace stools and benches. We have studied the increasing number of plates, pots and cutlery. We have envisaged the genesis of the dining room in middle-class homes. Now we have to ask what was boiling in those pots, what it meant to eat when seated on an individual chair rather than a bench or on the ground, and what were the implications of eating in a room intended solely for the business of eating and not in a room with a bed. What were the new boundaries of shared mealtimes? To answer these questions, we must look at how families ate in the past and observe what and how they ate. We have to consider the hierarchies that were expressed through food and the way it was prepared, served and eaten.

V

Food

1. Good table manners

The 'civilized' and the 'uncivilized'

During his travels around Europe, an account of which he published in 1672, the French gentleman Jouvin de Rochefort supped one evening in an Alpine hut in South Tyrol. The cowherds, who were desperately embarrassed to have such a noble and well-regarded visitor, settled their guest down on 'the very best of their chairs, namely an upturned basin', and set the table 'on which there were no table cloth, no napkins, no knives, no forks and no spoons'. Turnips cooked 'in a pot with flour, salt, butter and milk' were served up in one wooden bowl, and six eggs, half a cheese and a few pieces of bread in another. For the occasion, they produced a little 'tasteless wine' (cowherds usually only drank milk). The family sat down on the floor around the table. The father handed the plate with the eggs to the guest, and he took one and gave out the rest to his fellow diners. Then the father handed him the plate with the turnips. 'I immediately put my hand in,' relates the gentleman, 'and the rest of the family did the same. No one dared take another until I took one'. He was brought a wooden cup in which they served the wine: 'I drank to the good health of my companions, who daren't follow suit'. Some of them stood up to drink milk, and then they brought him a little cheese and a plate 'of small fruits, very similar to grapes in appearance and taste, that grow in the woods and mountains' (bilberries?).[1]

The interior of this home to South Tyrolean cowherds was wretched, but it was similar to other rural dwellings of the time. Those described in 1694 by Girolamo Cirelli, a citizen of Rimini, had a few more comforts: a kind of tablecloth, presumably some chairs, and perhaps a greater amount of food. Cirelli wrote that the peasants

> do not use a tablecloth, but only a coarse cloth, which is really only a piece of canvas with a hem coloured dark blue that does not even cover the table. They have no napkins, and wipe their mouths with the sleeve of their jackets or shirts. They eat with neither fork nor spoon, in place of which they use a slice of bread taken from the table where they eat, which is covered with pots

still filthy with ashes, and even the cauldron. They keep the bread in a pile in the middle of the table. . . . They put meat in the plate used for their soup, and they break it up with their hands. . . . Similarly, they put the wine in the middle of the table and they all indiscriminately drink from the same jug.[2]

A century earlier an anonymous writer had written a kind of verse analysis of the living conditions of the highland peasants of Frignano, in the Appenines of Emilia: 'Do not expect mats or a tablecloth / for here they don't go in for such fripperies / . . . / Don't bother to ask for a drink; / there's a jug or bowl in the middle of the table: / both the cleric and the master of the house use this for drinking / Don't even talk about glasses'.[3]

In the ancient world, it had been thought necessary to use tablecloths to avoid pots leaving a mark on the table. This advice arose from a magical perception of reality, as it was believed that as in other similar cases there was a bond of *sympathy* between the pot and its mark, and that one was part of the other. Anything done to one was also done to the other, and it was therefore possible to cast magic spells on the pot by acting on the traces of ash left behind. The tablecloth was therefore required to avoid the risk of someone exploiting this to cast a spell.[4]

Although the use of a tablecloth reflected these ancient beliefs, its use was not universal in the early modern era. We have already seen in the previous chapter that the use of tables, chairs, pots and kitchen utensils was taken for granted. If we stop to examine the social and cultural significance of this uneven distribution of household goods, it emerges, particularly from Cirelli's description, that the poverty of the peasant diet and the lack of crockery and cutlery were not simply a sign of material want. Given that they were inextricably linked to the peasant's lack of education, they appeared to the majority of townspeople and the middle and upper classes to be a sign of a savage and animal nature. Their ignorance of good manners was evidence of the profound value of social distinctions concerning the ability to sit at table 'in the proper manner'. Being a peasant had negative connotations that contrasted with the urbanity of bourgeois citizens and the courtesy of aristocrats.[5] A proverb recorded in Calabria, a region where extreme poverty left its mark on peasant interiors well into the twentieth century, states that 'a townsman can be recognized from [his behaviour] at the table' ('A tavula e tavulinu, si canusci u' cittadinu'). An old woman interviewed in the early 1970s said, 'At that time we didn't have a table and we put everything on a trivet, with all of us around it in a circle. We put the trivet in the middle, we reset the fire and that is where we had to eat'. Her words were largely reiterated by the other interviewees.[6]

Of course, the terminology of good manners was not the same everywhere and it did not always express the same social point of view. Good manners, including table manners, played an important role in defining the process of civilization, where by civilization we mean the creation of a coherent set of characteristics and behaviour patterns that are valued. This process involved the whole of Europe, although the way it manifested itself differed from place to place.[7]

Around the mid-sixteenth century, the Frenchman Calviac wrote that 'Germans eat with their mouth shut, and think anyone disgusting who does anything different. On the other hand, the French open their mouths, and consider inelegant the manner used by the Germans. The Italians chew less vigorously and the French more robustly, and so they find the manner of the Italians to be too finicky and affected'. Moreover, 'the Italians generally prefer each person to have their own knife. The Germans consider this so important that it is a cause of considerable irritation if someone else takes or asks for it. The French, on the contrary, use only two or three knives for an entire table surrounded by people, and it is not a problem to take or ask for one, and neither is it a problem to pass one, when asked'. The author also examines the different use of the spoon and fork in the three nations. In his opinion, the Germans tended to prefer a spoon, the Italians a fork, and the French used both according to whichever they found easier.[8]

The history of cutlery is an important element in the changes to the relationship between westerners and their food, and therefore also the changes in the ability to control one's physical instincts and drives, and in the ways of expressing oneself through gestures.[9] 'Hunger is hunger, but hunger assuaged by eating cooked meat with a knife and fork is different to hunger assuaged by gobbling raw meat with the help of hands, nails and teeth.'[10] Of course, someone who eats with his hands is not necessarily devoid of self-control, either generally or in relation to eating. Yet anyone who eats with cutlery cannot fall greedily on their food like an animal. That person must learn to handle the knife, fork or spoon, and co-ordinate the hand with the mouth. He has to wait for a mouthful to be prepared before putting it in his mouth. At least as far as eating is concerned, he has to acquire a minimal degree of self-control that someone who eats with his hands may or may not have.

Cutlery, tablecloths, napkins, plates and glasses

Spoons were used in ancient Egypt, and there were two types in Rome, which were made of bone, bronze or silver. This first type, called a *cochlear* or *cochleare*, from *cochlea* meaning shell, was mainly used for eating shellfish and eggs, or for taking medicines. The other type, called *ligula*, was flat and shaped like a bay leaf. It was possibly used for piercing food, and has recently been considered a forerunner of the fork rather than the spoon. It appears that during the Middle Ages the spoon was generally made of wood and more rarely of gold or silver, and in any case it was little used. Towards the end of the Middle Ages, it did begin to spread and was made of expensive and precious materials (ivory, crystal, gold and silver). The styles diversified, particularly in England, where great families engraved their coats of arms on their spoons.[11]

The knife also has a long history. Rudimentary blades obviously go back to the dawn of time. The small knife for 'domestic' use in the broad sense, as opposed to knives for other uses, appears to have been brought in by invading 'barbarians'. As society became less warlike, the use of knives became restricted as the sight of them could arouse fear and recall violent situations. Things in Europe did not go as far as they did in China where knives were banned from the table. During the Renaissance, increasingly refined manners led to the creation of the table knife with a rounded end. It spread along with the custom of cutting meat on the plate. Its success was partly due to the decline in the habit of stabbing food with the point of the knife and lifting it directly to the mouth. This decline was largely the result of the wider use of forks.[12]

The ancient Romans used carving forks and possibly ordinary forks mainly for handling food in the kitchen. The genuine fork, which was possibly invented in Byzantium, was used for bringing food to the mouth, and already existed in the Byzantine Empire and Italy in the tenth and eleventh centuries. The banquet for the wedding of the Greek princess Argillo to the son of the Doge of Venice, which took place in 955, is perhaps the first occasion on which the fork appeared on a table in western Europe. The sophisticated princess used a fork while everyone else ate with their hands. Associated with the Byzantine world during the period of tension created by schism between the Orthodox Church and the Church of Rome (1054), forks were perceived by the Catholic clergy as a symbol of Satan and their use was considered a sin. This stigma continued to have influence for centuries. Even in the seventeenth century, when their use was widespread in Italy, Monteverdi had three masses said every time he was obliged to use one out of politeness, so as to expiate the sin he had committed.[13]

In Italy, forks did not start to appear in any significant manner until the fourteenth or fifteenth century.[14] In Naples at the time of Robert of Anjou (1309–43), some thought that to eat hot and slippery pasta you should pierce it with a kind of wooden spike, the forerunner of the metal fork. Of course pasta was an expensive food at the time, and the use of this utensil would have been restricted to the court. Before becoming a popular food, pasta and the fork to eat it with needed to gain success among the middle classes.[15]

The fork spread from Italy to other European countries during the early modern era, but this occurred rather slowly. It was already in France by the sixteenth century, as Calviac himself reported. It was possibly introduced to the court by Catherine de' Medici, who married the King of France in 1533. Her son Henry III attempted to make its use obligatory by dint of orders and regulations. These also had the effect of provoking widespread ridicule in relation to the Italianized sophisticates who wouldn't touch their food with their hands. The French nobility's aversion to the fork was only finally overcome in the second half of the seventeenth century. Even as late as 1730 it was not in common use at the very top of society and even in the court there were some people who put their hands on the food on their plates.[16] In England, James I used a fork but on his death in 1625, hardly anyone had followed his lead. A century later (1725), only 10 per cent of English families owned table knives and forks.[17] In Germany they spread even more slowly, although this hardly seems possible. Forks started timidly to appear on the tables of the more sophisticated only in the late seventeenth century. A century later, however, their use was well established in the upper and middle classes of the whole of Europe. Subsequently their use spread to other social classes.[18] But by the time the fork was found on every table, practically a thousand years had passed since the wedding feast at which the cultivated Argillo made such a great display of one, possibly for the first time in western Europe.

The spread of the use of plates amongst the upper classes was much more rapid, and from the sixteenth century they replaced the wooden chopping boards that had been used in the Middle Ages. Although they had been known in medieval times, it was from this time that simple wooden plates were challenged by an increasing number of pewter, tin and silver ones. The display of wealth occasioned by the use of plates at banquets was sometimes discouraged by taxes on luxuries. Thus Pius V imposed the replacement of silver plates by ones made of majolica, whose production had started to develop in Spain and Italy during the Middle Ages.[19]

'Once we ate our soup from a single plate for everyone without a whole lot of fuss' and 'we used to put our fingers and bread into the stew', went the words to a seventeenth-century French song. 'Today everyone eats soup in a plate and you have to take your food with a spoon and fork'.[20] From the beginning of the sixteenth century, it became increasingly common in good society to provide each guest with a plate, a glass, a spoon and a knife, while forks were introduced more slowly. One or more napkins would be provided, and were not infrequently changed during the banquet, as was the tablecloth. The practice of passing this or that utensil to one's neighbour was abandoned. Only serving spoons and forks remained for communal use, but it became a sign of bad manners to put one of these in one's mouth.[21] Individual plates, glasses and cutlery, as well as chairs, isolated each person from his fellow diners, and therefore contributed to the end of what one historian has called 'convivial promiscuity'.[22]

Changes were not, however, linear and unambiguous everywhere. While the Italian word *posate* came from *posare*, 'to place', and therefore refers to the fact that objects are placed on the table,[23] in German-speaking areas, the corresponding term, *Besteck*, originally meant the sheath that held the knife. Later this sheath was used for keeping spoons and forks as well, and it therefore consisted of a predominantly male accoutrement. It was also something strictly individual (we should recall Calviac's observation that Germans do not like to lend their knives). Only later did they move on to a table laid out with cutlery that was for individual use but did not belong personally to each person eating.[24]

But even then the situation was not entirely similar to what we know today. In German villages during the early modern era, everyone had at least one wooden spoon, but even the families that enjoyed the luxury of cutlery often only had one table knife and one fork. This was cutlery that consisted of one of each utensil, and their use was restricted to the head of the household, the father or the mother. In the Swabian village of Kirchentellinsfurt, it only became customary for the better-off to own more than one of each type of cutlery in the 1860s.[25] In Italy the use of a fork even in recent times could express a hierarchical situation: 'we women ate everything with our hands. Only the men had a fork', reported Genoveffa, a bricklayer's daughter and the wife of a peasant who owned his own land, was born in the Treviso area in 1906.[26]

In other words, tablecloths and individual napkins, plates and cutlery only recently entered into universal use in the western world.[27] 'When we ate soup, we were all together, but there were only three or four glasses and so we would say "empty your glass because I want to drink now"', recalled a women called Teresa who was born in 1898 in Mercatale, in the province of Arezzo.[28] Even a few decades ago, there were houses in Calabria in which everyone drank from the same glass or, more often, from the same jug, and they wiped themselves with the same napkin.[29] Accounts from the 1950s from the same areas in which Jouvin de Rochefort had travelled tell of families gathered around their table to eat a gruel made of milk, butter and flour, from a single bowl placed in the middle of the table. Each person had just a personal spoon (this was in a German-speaking area) that after the meal was to be cleaned perfunctorily, possibly on the hem of an apron or the inside of trousers or a skirt, and hung from the wall.[30]

2. Solidarity and hierarchy at the table

Eating together

The reverence the poor cowherds showed to Jouvin de Rochefort reminds us that a meal can express both solidarity and difference. On the one hand, eating together is a sign of trust and fraternity or, at least, similar status, and on the other, 'the principal social relations are expressed at table'.[31]

We have already referred to ritual gatherings for wedding feasts. Other social occasions of a convivial nature or generally relating to food could have similar significance. In Denmark, anyone who joined a village community had to offer drinks to the entire neighbourhood in order to validate the newly acquired membership. In other regions, the fee for joining gatherings was extended to cover the expenses of paying for wine or beer for the whole community: it was called 'entrance beer' in the Baltic island of Fehmarn.[32] A sacral element was often attributed to the actual meal as a result of saying grace before starting to eat.

Naturally, it was not necessarily the case that all family members would eat together. Those who worked in the fields could take something along and eat it under a tree. In the poorest families, members had to look after themselves by earning, begging or stealing something to fill their stomachs. In wealthy families, the lord or lady could elect to eat alone in their bedrooms when there were no guests. There were endless reasons why members of a family might eat their meals separately. However, eating together was considered a moment in which family unity was expressed and achieved before the eyes of God and men alike, thanks to the recital of grace before meals and the benediction of food.

This has already been demonstrated by various sources such as Albergati Capacelli's will and the complaints from servants in the Franche-Comté.[33] We could add further evidence. In Tuscany, living 'with one bread and one wine' (*a uno pane e a uno vino*) was used to indicate membership of a family.[34] The large family communities of the Nivernais, which united several couples on an undivided holding often under the same roof, expressed their unity as living with the same 'pot, fire and salt' (*pot, feu et sel*).[35] In parts of Hungary, it was common for the married sons of peasants to live in detached houses close to the main building where their parents lived. They would work the same holding. Hence it was decided to consider a *familia* to be the persons who cooked together, even if they lived in different houses, for the purposes of the census for 1784–7 and for people not of noble birth in the censuses of 1804 and 1847.[36]

The association between eating together and belonging to the same family was so established that the fact that a man and a woman ate at the same table could give rise to suspicions of concubinage. In Siena in 1590, it was believed that such a relationship existed between Andrea of Milan, who 'ran a school for music and embroidery', and Virginia, a woman with whom he rented some rooms to German students. The rector of the parish church of San Pietro in Banchi admitted that they 'live and eat at the same table', but 'they sleep separately from what I have heard'.[37] A priest was needed to fend off the suspicions aroused by eating at the same table.

Similarly, the break-up of a family unit could find expression in the separation of eating habits. Catholicism did not allow divorce, but there were provisions for the separation of spouses 'of the bed, the table and the home' (*tori, mensae et habitationis*).[38] In 1769, tensions between Apollonia, a woman from Brusino Arsizio on Lake Lugano, and the in-laws with whom she lived were expressed through their eating habits: 'we make a single fire for all of us', said her mother-in-law, 'but each cooks his own pot'.[39]

Eating first and eating last, eating well and eating badly

Apart from convivial gatherings and clear separations, eating habits can also express sophisticated distinctions. The table is one of the places where social, gender and generational hierarchies are expressed and reasserted. While the highland peasants of South Tyrol kept the one seat and only available wine for their honoured guest, the ancient traditions of the Basque Country required women not to sit at the householder's table.[40] In various parts of Europe there are records that the custom was for men to eat sitting down and women and possibly children to eat their food standing up, often before the fire and sometimes only after the men had finished or had been served.[41] This practice continued into recent times, although it did become increasingly rare. 'The men were around the table and the women and children outside or in the barn', recalled Maria, who was born in 1898 in the countryside around Vicenza.[42] This custom was occasionally justified by the lack of chairs or seats, which were then reserved for the more important members of the family.[43] But in other cases, meals were an opportunity for segregation that reflected the family hierarchy and had nothing to do with the availability of seating. 'We were never seated at the table. Never. Only the men sat at the table, and the women on chairs, in a corner of the kitchen', recalled another woman from the Veneto region, whose home was clearly not short of chairs.[44] Hierarchies could also be expressed even when everyone was seated at the table. For example, a book published in England in 1724 claimed that in Germany wives were 'not allowed at the upper end of the table'.[45]

A study into northern Germany allows us to examine the subject in greater detail. It demonstrates the range of behaviour at mealtime in different areas. One custom, probably the more ancient, had women and children eating while standing up. Another involved the presence of all family members at the table (including servants), arrayed in hierarchical order with the head of the table assigned to the householder and men and women on opposite sides. Both would be seated in accordance with a pecking order: more senior servants and older children closer to the father. A third custom, undoubtedly the most recent, involved the separation of the owners' direct family from the servants, who would now sit at a different table that sometimes had benches and stools rather than the modern chairs found at the owners' table. Occasionally, their table would even be in a separate room.[46]

This study focused on a mainly rural situation in which the increasing separation between the owners' family and the servants was probably the result of nineteenth-century legislation that tended to deepen the social division between peasants and their employees. According to a scholar in the mid-nineteenth century,

> In many peasant villages, a single circumstance – whether or not the family group including servants eats at the same table – is sufficient to establish whether the relationship between the peasant farmer and his servants is a purely legal one or whether it is still to some extent patriarchal; in other words to establish whether the old traditions have disappeared or have been kept and developed.[47]

He was probably right. In families in which there were relatively few servants, their presence at the same table as their employers was a tangible expression of the fact that they were considered an integral part of the family community.[48] However, the existence of a pecking order around the table and differences in the manner and timing of their access to food meant that the family group, far from being something idyllic and egalitarian, was a rigidly hierarchical structure. In aristocratic families, hierarchy was even more structured, and a potent expression of this was precisely the number of tables.

The multiplication of tables
As became clear in the previous chapter, it was customary in aristocratic families during the early modern era to have separate tables for masters and servants, or in the houses of more important families, separate tables for servants of different ranks.[49] In 1563, there were as many as thirteen different tables at the court in Parma.[50] The spatial position of separate tables in relation to the employer was used to mark the greater or lesser importance of a servant. The trial in 1786 following the mysterious death (suicide or homicide?) of the second wife of Francesco Albergati Capacelli provides us with a particularly clear idea of the link between different tables and family hierarchies. The woman's death occurred shortly after lunch. While being questioned by the investigators, family members and servants explained what and where they ate.

We thus discover the presence of four different tables in this sumptuous country house that was the scene of the possible crime. The marquis, his wife, their two children, the children's tutor and the household violinist at the first table. After having served at his master's table, the valet ate at the second table with the personal servant woman. This table was in the servants' room, directly under the mistress's bedroom, to which it was connected by a bell and a back stairway. In his independent apartment, the factor dined with his wife, who was wet-nursing a baby. The kitchens in the basement were where sooner or later all the other male servants got to eat: footmen, stable-boys, cook, assistant cook and scullery-boys.[51]

The hierarchy in the Albergatis' summer residence, which informed the lives of the household members and the relations between them, was mirrored with almost mathematical precision in the 'stratigraphy' of tables and their positions in the far from neutral space within the stately home.[52] The women tended to form a group: Maria Pifaretti, Marianna Boscani, Maddalena Zambonelli and Lucia Franzoni undoubtedly had a different position within the servants' hierarchy, given that they were employed respectively as governess, maidservant, the embroidery teacher for the marquis's daughter Eleonora and the woman responsible for the heavy chores. They all ate together in an area close to the mistress's, almost as though the female identity was more powerful than rank as a servant. They were often referred to without distinction as the 'women of the house' and not infrequently they also referred to themselves as such.[53] For men, on the other hand, the relationship was much starker and almost completely unambiguous, with the exception of the cook who, although of a certain importance, was obliged to remain in the kitchen. For the others, the higher or lower position of the table coincided with the rank of the domestic staff.

3. Men and women and the preparation of food

Cooks and cook books

If we look more closely at the people who frequented and ate in the basement kitchen at the Albergati villa, we find the stable-boys Gaetano Barselli and Andrea Bontà, the cook Antonio Ungarelli, the assistant cook Gesualdo Pasudetti and the manservant Antonio Ercolin. There was also Giacomo Merli, the farm labourer who rented one of the senator's houses and worked in his service during the summer when he came to the countryside.[54] These are all men's names and so only men were found in the kitchen. The cook and the assistant cook, in particular, were men.

Another gentleman of Bologna, Francesco Tanara, wrote in his *The City-Dweller's Organization of a Villa* (*Economia del cittadino in villa*) in the mid-seventeenth century, 'I would be so bold as to argue in matters of good household management that it is more profitable to have a man as a cook than a woman'.[55] There is no denying that his advice was followed: in the early modern era, the kitchens of wealthy families were almost an exclusively male domain.[56] Men were preferred because food preparation required staff that could be trusted without reservation,[57] and therefore a predominantly male staff in a society organized on the basis of rigid sexual hierarchies. Whoever works in the kitchen must be 'clean, loyal and knowledgeable. Everyone knows that generally the dirtiest man is cleaner than the cleanest woman', Tanara explained. Women, who were thieving and wasteful, were also occasionally 'overly partial to wine, backbiting or given to witchcraft'. What about their intelligence? 'Any comparison between the average intelligence of a man and that of a woman would be a great insult to our sex', the author declared, before going on to pour out a vast catalogue of misogynous arguments to support his preference for male cooks.[58]

Apart from having to be men, staff dealing with food often had to be of high social rank, particularly in the case of those serving at royal tables in the sixteenth century. 'There are three honourable offices that great princes are in the habit of appointing for the care of what they eat and drink. These are the steward, the cupbearer and the carver. Each of these offices is not generally given to people who are not extremely noble, very trustworthy and on considerably familiar terms', wrote an author towards the end of the sixteenth century.[59] Indeed the master's life depended on the skill and trustworthiness of the kitchen and dining-room staff, as there was a great fear of poisoning. This is also demonstrated by numerous European fairy-tales in which the cook is a murderer in the employ of an evil man-eating master.[60] It is significant that in Italian both the furniture on which cold foods and plates rested and the manner of serving food without touching it with one's hands, by holding it between two napkins, two pieces of bread or two plates, were given the name of *credenza*, which derives from the Latin verb *credo*, 'to put faith in'.[61]

The honour of the household also depended on the skill and reliability of the staff responsible for food preparation. Banquets were privileged events which displayed the pomp and ostentatious wealth so closely linked to power-brokering under the *Ancien Régime*. An ordinary meal for Russian tsars involved the serving of about 150 different dishes, 50 types of strong drink and a dozen varieties of beer and *kvas*.[62] Banquets consisted of sideboards and plate racks loaded with silverware, dozens of courses, hundreds of marvellous and ingenious dishes, spectacular fountains of wine, magnificent statues made of butter, 'seven-headed hydras made of short pastry', peacocks and pheasants with their plumage restored and 'adorned with pearls, corals and gold and silver ribbon', roast horses, bulls and other animals out of which came live birds, hares and rabbits, 'cherubs made of sugar', and castles and ships made of pastry. All these created the theatre in which the powerful played out their high-ranking status and thus consolidated it. During the sixteenth century, there were even spectators.[63] It is no surprise then that governments, particularly those run on more egalitarian and democratic principles such as the Venetian Republic, attempted to restrict banquets through taxation.[64]

Given their immense responsibility for ensuring the success of important and meaningful events, cooks and catering staff appear to have been often subjected to intense psychological pressure, which occasionally produced devastating results. One particularly significant case involved Fritz Karl Watel, a Swiss known as Vatel, who was responsible for provisioning and preparing the food for the table of the Prince of Condé. In 1670, when the prince invited Louis XIV to visit him at his palace in Chantilly, Watel became mistakenly convinced that the fish that had to be cooked would not arrive in time. Such was his desperation that he committed suicide, unable to face up to such dishonour (his own and clearly also his prince's).[65]

The tracts that explained the tasks of the swarm of servants involved in food preparation and serving in the houses of the rich and noble referred exclusively to men: stewards, carvers, cellar-men, wine stewards, sommeliers, waiters, cooks, assistant cooks, scullions, and purchasers.[66] Only in the eighteenth century (and to a much greater extent in the nineteenth century) did female cooks and women in general become a presence in the kitchens of the upper classes. In Toulouse, for example, a source tell us there were 68 male cooks and 2 female cooks in 1695, while there were 52 male cooks and 173 female cooks in 1789. (Even today the chefs in the most acclaimed restaurants are nearly always men, though women's skills in the kitchen are finally being acknowledged at the highest levels.[67]

In the eighteenth century, the French, whose cuisine was a model for the whole of Europe, developed a taste for natural and simple food, which meant that less complicated dishes were served even at banquets. There was also an increased appreciation of 'bourgeois cuisine' which was traditionally prepared by the mistress of the house and her female servants. The first cook book for women in France appeared in 1746. *La Cuisinière bourgeoise*, written by a man, Menon, was to become a veritable best-seller of the eighteenth century. In little more than fifty years, it went through 62 editions and 93,000 copies were printed.[68]

Unlike the houses of the upper class, cooking was entrusted to women in middle- and lower-class families. Precisely because it required skill, and the material well-being of the family depended on it, it was delegated to servants less frequently than washing and cleaning.[69] In European fairy-tales, 'cooking is shown to be an important operation in the *ménage*, clearly marked out by a degree of ritual' and carried out by the mistress of the house, while conversely, 'it is significant that sweeping, washing, etc. were assigned to the scullery-maid – to

Cinderella'.[70] The desire to be different from the middle- and lower-class homes could also have contributed to the aristocratic preference for male cooks.[71]

The development of the sexual division of labour over time varied from one region and class to another. In England, it related not only to the split between upper-class cooking and that of the rest of the population, but also the choice between French and English cooking. Only in the very highest echelons of society did they eat in the French manner and have male cooks in accordance with traditions across the Channel. The rest of the population ate in the English manner and the cooks were women, either servants or the mistress of the house. In the eighteenth century, however, only a few aristocratic families followed the Gallic fashion.[72] Hence, it appears that a degree of competence in the preparation of food was even required of women of the middle- and upper-middle classes.[73]

The subject merits further study, but it appears that in Italy and France cooking was perceived as a refined and valued activity, but nevertheless a menial one. Ladies and maids of honour did not therefore have anything to do with it. 'The mother of good family should not be above occasionally working with her hands', an author explained. But 'not in kitchens or other sordid things that could sully the body'.[74] At the current stage of research we can only speculate about the causes of this supposed difference. It may be, for example, that ancient traditions of Roman origin had continued in neo-Latin Europe. According to Livy and Plutarch, the peace treaty between the Romans and the Sabines following the rape of the Sabine women stipulated that the women were not to carry out menial tasks such as grinding corn and cooking. This work was entrusted to slaves. Later, food preparation became more highly prized, particularly following the Asian war against Antioch (186 BC) banquets became increasingly sumptuous. Then, said Livy, 'cooks, who for our ancestors were the lowliest and most useless of slaves, started to be held very dear, and a lowly trade was considered an art'.[75] Whether it was valued or despised by the Roman elite, work in the kitchen appears to have been considered a male and slave activity.

We do not perhaps have to look so far back in history. The differences arose from the fact that cooking in England was considerably more 'domestic' than in France. In England, particularly after the seventeenth-century revolutions, the court did not have the same power as the court in France (or the Italian Renaissance courts),[76] nor did it have a similar role as the arbiter of fashion. In the French and Italian courts, banquets had a clear public function in displaying and consolidating the king's or the prince's power. The nobility was therefore encouraged to vie with each other in the use of roast meats, statues of butter and fountains of wine. Partly because of the lesser appeal of the court, the English nobility continued to live in country homes for a few months of the year. This, together with the fact that the presence of the gentry in England meant that it was difficult to define the lower boundaries of the nobility, probably helps to explain why British cooking had such feminine and domestic characteristics.[77]

From this point of view, it is significant that sixteenth- and seventeenth-century England saw the publication of books belonging to the literary genre of 'confidential anthologies' written by (or attributed to) noblewomen with the intention of instructing others in the necessary arts for best fulfilling the duties of their rank, and these books contained recipes. Similar texts in Italian and French provided at the very most 'recipes for marmalades, conserves and syrups', or other sugary specialities, which at the time were associated with therapies and not considered culinary recipes.[78]

Books like Thomas Dawson's *The Good Huswife's Jewell* (1585) and Gervase Markham's *The English Hus-Wife* (1615) contained arguments of a medical nature, instructions for the treatment of the more common diseases, chapters on processing milk, making beer and conserving foods. Markham described his book as 'Contayning the inward and outward vertues which ought to be in a compleat woman: As, her skill in Physicke, Cookery, Banquetting-stuffe, Distillation, Perfumes, Wool, Hemp, Flax, Dayries, Brewery, Baking and other things belonging to an Household'.[79]

Such books continued to be published in the late seventeenth and eighteenth century. At this time translations of recipe books from across the Channel appeared in England, as well as English texts that were more similar to French and Italian cook books, namely books written by professional cooks and aimed at their colleagues, with an emphasis on the preparation and presentation of food. But it was a limited phenomenon that only lasted until the early decades of the eighteenth century. Handbooks for the mistress of a country house were much more numerous and dominated the market at least from the 1730s. The authors were not always women. One of the most successful and the first to be written by a woman was *The Queen-Like Closet* by Hannah Wolley, which appeared in 1670. In the eighteenth century, however, there was a deluge of books written by women for women, generally for the mistress of the house or servant women who cooked in the homes of the middle class and the gentry.[80] In France, on the other hand, the first book of recipes aimed at women did not appear until 1746 and was written by a man, as we have seen. In Italy, the first book supposedly written by a woman (but it may not have been) was *La Cuciniera piemontese* (*The Piedmontese Female Cook*) which was published in 1771. The frontispiece shows a woman close to a cooking stove who is intent on carrying a plate to four people sitting round a table.[81]

To my knowledge, the only Italian data currently available on the feminization of kitchen staff concerns Bologna, and shows that the phenomenon occurred much later than in France. There is not even one reference to a female cook in the nine surviving files of the census carried out in 1796, covering about a tenth of the population of Bologna. In the *status animarum*[82] of the city parish of San Giovanni in Monte, where many nobles lived, there was a reference to a female cook in 1810, but there were none in either 1820 or 1830. Only later did their number start to increase. Women made up 2 per cent of those working with food and wine in 1850, 10 per cent in 1857 and 48 per cent in 1899. At that time, they were also 48 per cent in the nearby parish of San Bartolomeo, whose social composition was a little more bourgeois. Given this different social composition, feminization in this parish was more advanced. By 1840 female cooks made up 11 per cent of those employed in the sector. But here again there was no reference to them in 1810, 1820 or 1830.[83]

The fact that female cooks were not referred to explicitly does not however mean that there were no servant women who did the cooking. In the houses in which there was no cook, the majority of servant women on general duties would undoubtedly have been engaged in food preparation. 'I make bread that everyone enjoys' and 'tasty and appetizing cooking', declared a 'woman who was telling of her virtues in her search for work'. Her adventures were narrated in *La fantesca*, a poetic composition apparently written in the sixteenth or seventeenth century, and full of sexual allusions embroidered over the real activities of servant women.[84] But it was one thing to deal with the cooking along with a thousand other chores, and quite another to devote oneself solely to culinary activities. This specialization of female servants with the subsequent replacement of male cooks by them appears to have occurred rather late in Bologna compared with other parts of Europe. It has to be asked to what extent the city was representative of the situation in Italy as a whole.

Whatever the speed of these changes in the composition of domestic staff and the stages they went through, they only affected a minority of the population. On the whole, women in the middle and lower classes did the cooking for their families much more often than women of higher social extraction. Of course those who had no home, lived in squalid rooms with no fire or were too poor to buy fuel, had to make do by begging for a little food or by buying food that was ready-made or did not have to be cooked – primarily bread. In cities, after all, there were not only charitable persons and institutions that looked after the poor, but also taverns, sellers of foodstuffs and lower-class women who supplemented their family incomes by selling cooked foods in the streets and to neighbours and prisoners.[85] In 'normal' times when there was no a shortage of food, even those who could not cook could therefore buy or obtain food one way or another. In some areas, a diet of cold foods prevailed, as it did not require cooking. The diet of peasants in southern Italy mainly consisted of bread, cheese and wine, occasionally supplemented by a little soup.[86]

All other women usually cooked for themselves and their families. It is easy to imagine them boiling food in the ubiquitous pot hanging from a chain over the fire. Boiling was, in fact, the most popular form of cooking amongst the lower classes, as evidenced by the abundance of large pots in that period, while frying pans were less widely known.[87] However frying pans were becoming more widely used, although not everywhere. Thus we can also picture women sitting on low stools holding a pan over the flames and surrounded by containers and jugs on the floor. This activity at floor level only started to be raised a little in the eighteenth century particularly in the cities (Figs. 60, 61 and 69). They started to use trivets with a surface heated by hot coals, on which pots could be placed to cook and heat food. Brick stoves, which were heated by wood or coal and had been known about for some time, started to be more widely used. Kitchen ranges made of metal made their appearance around 1750 and spread slowly.[88]

Breastfeeding

The distance or indeed extraneousness of upper-class women, at least in Italy, involved not only cooking but also other forms of 'nourishment', most particularly the task often presented as quintessentially female and an extension of preparing meals for all the family, namely breastfeeding. Upper-class women and their husbands followed the custom of giving their children to wet-nurses for payment. The wet-nurses were either kept in the home or paid for breastfeeding and looking after the new-born babies at the wet-nurses' homes.[89] As having a wet-nurse in one's own home was very expensive, few families could afford such a luxury. Some only did so for their first-born son. The order of birth and sex of babies could affect the treatment they would receive. We know that in Renaissance Florence, boys were wet-nursed in their family home more than girls, and the same was true of first-born boys in relation to cadets. We also know that baby girls were weaned earlier than their baby brothers.[90] However, little girls were not always treated worse than little boys. Studies into some aristocratic families in seventeenth-century Latium show that here the order of birth influenced treatment of babies more that their sex, while research in Great Britain has shown that the time of weaning depended only very slightly on whether the baby was a boy or a girl.[91] In any case, it was reality itself, in a kind of nemesis, that turned practices considered a privilege into a handicap. The mortality of babies given to wet-nurses was higher than that of babies breastfed by their mothers. In Renaissance Florence at least, it affected boys more than girls.[92]

Doctors and scientists were agreed on the need to encourage breastfeeding by the mother, which they mainly did by emphasizing the negative effects a wet-nurse could have on a baby, although they did not start to criticize wet-nursing until the eighteenth century and then did so more and more forcefully.[93] What were the reasons for entrusting the children of upper-class families to wet-nurses?

> You need to look after yourself . . . so that your husband does not tire of you. Breastfeeding makes you lose weight, it spoils your colour and makes flabby that which should be firm. And then it is such a commitment. How can you enjoy any entertainment, go to a play, opera, or dance, engage in conversation or stay out of the house until sunrise?[94]

According to a polemical supporter of maternal breastfeeding, these were the 'pretexts' used by ladies to justify wet-nursing. Indeed, fashion and social conventions required noblewomen to maintain a certain figure that was not very compatible with breasts swollen with milk or sagging from repeated breastfeeding. They also needed to engage in an intense social life whose pace left little room for letting a baby suckle on the breast. The tight and rigid corsets that the need for elegance imposed upon ladies of higher social rank could create problems for their breasts.[95] While the practices used by noblewomen to dry up their milk after childbirth often caused inflammations or even tumours, it was also undeniably the case that women who breastfed often had breasts that had been ruined by being bitten by babies who were often weaned after their teeth had come through. Breastfeeding made the mother lose weight, which at the time was certainly not considered an advantage. In situations where the diet was not balanced in terms of mineral salts and calcium, breastfeeding could lead to the loss of teeth and hair, or even to more serious symptoms. In other words, the belief that breastfeeding made women ugly, wasted them and caused them to become prematurely old was not entirely without foundation. As it was believed that lower-class women, particularly peasant women, were more robust than ladies and had milk of higher quality and more of it, breastfeeding appeared more suited to them than to noblewomen. Some people therefore thought that babies of the upper classes were better off with a wet-nurse from the country than being breastfed by their own mothers.[96]

These were not the only reasons for wet-nursing. In the sixteenth and seventeenth centuries there was a widespread belief, originally based on Galen's theories, that a woman who was breastfeeding had to avoid sexual relations. It was believed that sex had a bad effect on the quality of the milk and therefore the health of the baby, and that a pregnancy would have an even worse effect. The convictions about sexual relations were completely overturned in the eighteenth

Fig. 1. Bartolomeo Schedoni, *Charity* (1611), Naples, Galleria di
Capodimonte.

Fig. 2. Giacomo Ceruti (il Pitocchetto), *The Two Lice* (*c.* 1730), Pinacoteca Tosio-Martinengo, Brescia.

Any history of the home and family cannot ignore the mass of poor people and vagrants who had no stable dwelling and often no family. They carried all their miserable belongings around with them, and lived off begging and other expedients (Figs. 1–3). Sometimes, however, entire families were homeless and wandered around the country. Mitelli's print blames the impoverishment of a family on the reversal of roles between the husband and wife, and the desperate desire for a good time (Fig. 4). But for many, poverty was the result of external circumstances and not the failure to observe the rules of socially acceptable behaviour. 'Poverty is not a vice' is justifiably stated on Lagnier's engraving (Fig. 3).

Fig. 3. Jacques Lagnier, "The person who wears all his clothes must be very warm indeed", engraving from Jacques Lagnier, *Recueil des proverbs*, Paris 1657–63.

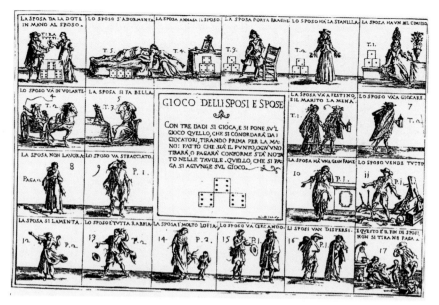

Fig. 4. Giuseppe Maria Mitelli, *The Game Husbands and Wives Play* [*Gioco delli Sposi e Spose*] (1691), Art Collection of the Cassa di Risparmio di Bologna, Bologna.

When it comes to analysing dwellings of the early modern era, we need to free ourselves from the stereotype of the house as a stable building with a roof, doors and windows. Many groups of herdsmen, for example, had 'houses' or mobile shelters that provided them with protection from the elements while they followed their herds (Fig. 5).

Fig. 5. Portable shack of the Pyrenean shepherds, Musée Pyrénéen, Lourdes (reproduction by Pierre Deffontaines).

Fig. 6. *The Dowry of the Peasant from Lucerne* (*c.* 1830),
Schweizerisches Landesmuseum, Zurich.

*Marriage constituted an important rite of passage for the bride, bridegroom, their
families and often the communities to which they belonged. Wedding ceremonies were,
therefore, full of ritual gestures that expressed the separation of the young couple from the
pool of unmarried youngsters and, particularly in the case of the bride, their original
families, as well as the possible inclusion of one of them in the other's family and the
creation of new kinship ties. As it was rare for a couple to live in the bride's home,
transport of the bride's belongings to the house where she was to live with her husband
(belongings often contained in a chest, which was gradually replaced by a wardrobe)
symbolized the passage from one life to another (Figs, 6, 7, 8 and 44). By bringing
friends and relations together to eat, wedding feasts (Fig. 9) signified the birth of a
new couple and the creation of a new kinship that joined the two groups.*

Fig. 7. Gustave Brion, *The Bride's Wedding Procession* (1873), Musée des Beaux-Arts,
Strasbourg.

Fig. 8. Painted chest (fifteenth century).

Funding the creation of a new couple involved not only the couple themselves but also their families and their communities. The contributions made by men and women to the material basis for the new family varied. In many areas, it was up to the woman to provide the marital bed, which was subject to particular rituals during the wedding ceremonies. Since ancient times, the benediction took place before the wedding night and was supposed to favour the fertility of the new couple. The guests often accompanied them with songs and quips full of sexual allusions. After the Tridentine Council, the Catholic Church imposed a new ritual that aimed to celebrate the sanctity of the marital bed and the discipline that governed relations between husband and wife (Fig. 10).

Fig. 9. Pieter Bruegel the Elder, *Peasant Wedding* (*c.* 1565–9), Kunsthistorisches Museum, Vienna.

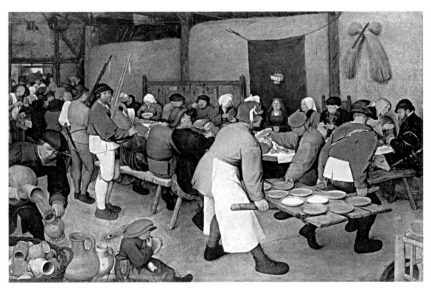

Fig. 10. Bernard Picart, *Benediction of the Wedding Bed* (1724), Musée des Arts et Traditions Populaires, Paris. © Photo RMN.

Not all couples went to live in a new house when they got married. In many parts of Europe, the bride moved in with the husband's family. In some cases, only one of the sons brought his wife to his parents' home. In others, there were residential groups made up of many couples with their children, as with the zadruga of the Balkans (Fig. 11). Composite families, made up of several couples and their children often lived in Russian isbe. This posed the problem of the ratio between the available space and the number of family members. In the Russian village of Mishino, for example, there were 8–10 people in each family at the beginning of the nineteenth century, and they lived in houses consisting of a single room whose area varied between 15 and 34 metres. The serfs' owner tended to obstruct the division of co-resident groups. The print by Le Bas (Fig. 12), which shows eleven people crowded into an isba, cannot be far from the truth.

There was a great variety of dwellings in the early modern era, some of which were based on prehistoric building methods, such as the subterranean houses of the Hungarian and Romanian plains (Fig. 13).

Fig. 11. Arthur Evans, *Zadruga*, in Arthur Evans, *Through Bosnia and Herzogovina on Foot*, London 1877.

Fig. 12. Jacques-Philippe Le Bas, *Russian Supper* (eighteenth century). Engraving from a work by J.-B. Le Prince, Bibliothèque Nationale de France, Paris.

People and animals lived together under the same roof in various parts of Europe until recent times. This was partly justified by the need to exploit the animals' body heat to keep the house warm (Fig. 14).

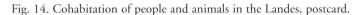

Fig. 13. 'Grubenhäuser', in John Paget, *Hungary and Transylvania*, London 1839.

Fig. 14. Cohabitation of people and animals in the Landes, postcard.

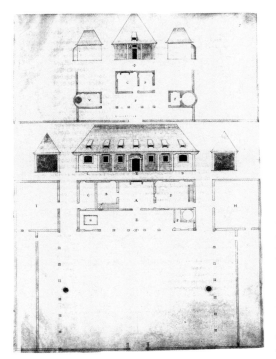

Fig. 15. Sebastiano Serlio, 'The house of the poor peasant with four degrees of poverty' (above) and 'The house of the mediocre peasant with three degrees of mediocrity' (below), from Book Six of *Architettura civile*, Iconographic codex 189, Fig. 1, Fol. 2r, examples 1 and 2, Bayerische Staatsbibliothek, Munich.

Several countries, such as Italy, France and England, underwent a profound renewal of rural architecture in the sixteenth and seventeenth centuries. Important architects, such as Sebastiano Serlio (1475–1554/5), contributed to this change. Serlio proposed various types of dwelling for poor peasants, according to their degree of poverty (Fig. 15, above). For the less well-off, he suggested a hut consisting of a single room (C). Those who owned a few animals, particularly oxen, needed a little more space. Serlio planned a house for them that, apart from the living-room for people, had a byre (S) with a window opening onto the living-room. Those who were a little wealthier could add a veranda (P) to this simple structure. If the peasant was 'considerably better-off in terms of family and possessions', he would need an oven (F) and a cellar (V). The house for the 'mediocre' or average peasant was much more complex. It had a hall (A) with fireplace, a bedroom (B), a cellar (C) above which there was a closet and a byre (D), also with windows opening into the hall. In front of the house there was a veranda (E), at the two extremes of which there were an oven (F) and a press (G). Above the oven there was a hen house and a pigsty beneath it. If the peasant was 'considerably better-off in terms of family and possessions', it was possible to build two side wings, one for a larger cowshed and the other for a massive cellar and ample space for making wine (I). A further step along the road to affluence would have produced two verandas along the wings, where the harvest could be kept under cover. The central courtyard was to be used 'for threshing' (at the bottom of Fig. 15).

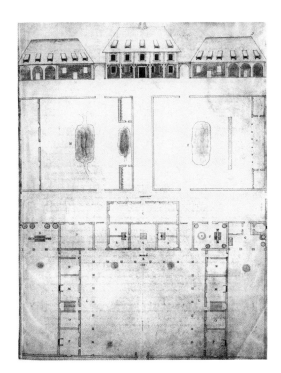

Fig. 16. Sebastiano Serlio, 'The house of a rich peasant with three degrees of wealth', from Book Six of *Architettura civile*, Bayerische Staatsbibliothek, Munich.

Serlio planned a house with the elements A–K for the rich peasant. For those who had an even greater 'abundance of family and assets', he suggested the addition of the verandas (L). For the peasant with the third of the three degrees of wealth, he suggested the addition of the apartments M, N, O and P (Fig. 16).

'Legend: A = communal hall, with a fire in the middle, so that ... everyone can look the others in the face when engaging in amusements or sharing things out, and the paterfamilias will sleep in the hall keeping the keys to everything throughout the night; B = room; C = byre; D = cellar; E = place for making wine with press and vats; F = oil press for olives and nuts, according to the area; G = oven with room for making bread and place for washing clothes ... with use of courtyard with well; H = large courtyard ... which will be used for all kinds of livestock, having on one side a large byre and on the other two pigsties, between which there will be a muddy ditch ... and in the middle of the yard there will be a ditch for water for the animals; I = yard for hens, ducks and other birds. The ditch in the middle I shall be for the animals, the other smaller ditch will be for the hens, which need to be in a higher and drier place, where there are two hen houses to be joined by a veranda so that the hens can shelter when there is rain and wind; K = veranda; L = verandas ... under which crops can be kept and the yard can be used for threshing; M, N, O and P = apartments joined at the back by a veranda. Given that in our times, armed men occupy all the villages ..., it would be a good thing if the places OP were for soldiers, so as to keep them away from the peasants' living quarters.*

Fig. 17. South Tyrolese *Stube* with painted decorations (1770), Südtiroler Volkskunde Museum, Dietenheim/Teodone (Bolzano/Bozen).

In relation to the central fireplace (Fig. 41), the wall fireplace, which was introduced in the twelfth century, is a recent invention that changed the layout of houses and made it possible to have less smoky environments, but it did mean a considerable loss of heat. A more rational exploitation of heat came with the stove, which spread in central, northern and eastern Europe. They were often surrounded by benches on which it was possible to sleep in warmth (Fig. 17). There were also other methods of heating, such as braziers (Fig. 48). Open fireplaces without chimneys survived until recently (Fig. 18). In addition to fireplaces, stoves and braziers, there were more specific means of heating, for instance hand- and foot-warmers. Beds were heated by placing warming pans, which were containers filled with embers, between the sheets (Fig. 42, in the lower left-hand corner).

Fig. 18. A kitchen with an open fire and no chimney (opposite a hencoop), Südtiroler Volkskunde Museum, Dietenheim/Teodone (Bolzano/Bozen).

Fig. 19. Flint, steel and box with tinder and matches, from William Smith, *Morley: Ancient and Modern,* London 1886.

Lighting a fire was a long and complicated operation. People usually used steel that was struck forcefully against flint splinters in the hope of producing a strong spark lasting long enough to set alight a piece of cloth or tinder which was then used for lighting matches, which were in turn used for lighting the actual fuel (Fig. 19). This long and exhausting operation had to be carried out in the morning while it was dark, and in the winter with hands numb from the cold. Usually it was the job of servants, where they were employed; otherwise, it appears that women were generally responsible for the fire (Fig. 20).

Fig. 20. *Fire* (1799), Williamsburg, Rockefeller Library, Colonial Williamsburg Foundation.

Fig. 21. The house in the middle of the village of Jungingen, which was the home of Jacob Größer and Agatha Deuggerrin in the seventeenth century, as it was around 1910, Heimatmuseum, Jungingen.

During the early modern era, there was a tendency to replace more perishable building materials with bricks and stone. Straw and thatch roofs were replaced with tiles and slates. Brick and stone buildings were more lasting, reduced the risk of fire and gave less shelter to rats, cockroaches and insects in general. As the construction of buildings depended on the local availability of raw materials, the use of a certain material did not necessarily mean that a house was of greater or lesser quality. In the Mediterranean area, stone was abundant and had always been prevalent. Even the houses of the very poor were made of stone. Conversely, the so-called Fachwerkhäuser *of northern and central Europe could be almost luxurious dwellings, in spite of being built out of a wooden structure filled with clay and straw or other similar mixtures (Figs. 21 and 40).*

Fig. 22. Sketch by Albrecht Dürer for a statue to commemorate the failed Peasants' Revolt of 1525 in Germany, from Albrecht Dürer, *Vnderweysung der messung mit dem zirkel vnd richtscheyt*, Nuremberg 1525.

Fig. 23. Chest thought to come from Innichberg, Südtiroler Volkskunde Museum, Dietenheim/Teodone (Bolzano/Bozen).

Fig. 24. Chest from Val Badia (1698), Südtiroler Volkskunde Museum, Dietenheim/Teodone (Bolzano/Bozen).

Chests were probably the most widely used pieces of furniture in peasant homes of the early modern era (Figs. 23–4). Unsurprisingly then, it was the only piece of furniture included in the monument Dürer planned to commemorate the failed peasant rebellion of 1525. The monument incorporated some typical elements of peasant life, one on top of the other (Fig. 22). In the countryside and, to an even greater extent, the towns and cities, chests were gradually replaced by furniture that allowed objects to be stored in a more orderly fashion, particularly the wardrobe (Figs. 45, 46 and 76). While houses of the better-off filled to the brim with furniture, ornaments and decorations (Figs. 10, 28, 29, 32–7, 43–7 and 64), it could not be taken for granted that peasant homes would contain such commonplace items as tables and chairs until the eighteenth century. Many pictures show people seated on the ground or at makeshift tables (Figs. 12, 31, 51–53, 55 and 63). However, the countryside too was affected by the increasing richness of furniture and belongings during the early modern era.

Fig. 25. A professional water-seller with halter and buckets, from Marcellus Laroon, with additions by Henry Overton, *The Cryes of the City of London Drawne After the Life*, London, Pierce Tempest, 1711 (first edn 1687).

The supply of water created different problems in towns and cities from those in the countryside. In the country, the problems mainly arose from the distances involved. Not all houses had a well, a fountain, a river or a stream in the vicinity. Women had to equip themselves with buckets or jugs, and on occasion, go very far to collect water. Water-sellers were generally men working in town and cities (Fig. 25), while collecting water for the home was the job of women, children and servants. Distance was less of a problem in towns and cities: fountains were more common. However, the water was more likely to be polluted. Overcrowding often meant that there was a queue at the fountain or well. The water-dsipenser depicted in the painting by Chardin was one of the means used for obtaining a store of water, for those who could afford it (Fig. 26).

Fig. 26. Jean-Siméon Chardin, *Woman at the Urn* (1733), National Museum of Fine Art, Stockholm.

Lighting was rare in the country-side and more common in the city. In eighteenth-century Paris at least, even the middle-to-lower classes kept a considerable stock of lanterns, candelabras and other types of lighting. On average there were five sources of light in each flat. 63% were candelabras, and the figure rose after 1750–60 (Figs. 27–8). There are chandeliers in Figs. 28 and 37. There is an oil lamp in Fig. 56.

Fig. 27. *The Night* (*c.* 1660), Bibliothèque Nationale de France, Paris.

Fig. 28. *Woman of Good Standing Dressing up to go Dancing* (*c.* 1685), Bibliothèque Nationale de France, Paris.

Fig. 29. Daniel Marot, 'Design for a 'show' bedroom' (1702).

The struggle to keep the cold at bay helps to explain the importance of the bed. While the fireplace is certainly one pole of the domestic space, the other is unquestionably the bed. The simplest beds consisted of a mattress on boards supported by trestles (Figs. 30 and 49). A widely used type of bed had curtains to keep out the draughts, creating a kind of 'house within a house' (Figs. 10, 27, 37–8, 42 and 62). Sometimes the bed was placed in an alcove or recess in the wall, which was closed off with a curtain or a panel door. Beds could be a kind of wooden 'box' (Fig. 63). For the rich it was a luxury item that had to be shown off. Some of the wealthy had two beds, an ostentatious one for show and a simpler one for actually sleeping in (Figs. 29 and 43).

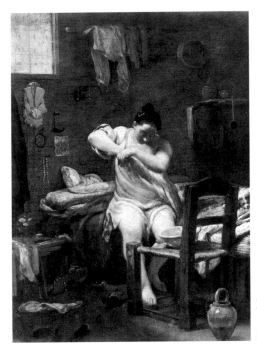

Fig. 30. Giuseppe Maria Crespi, *The Flea* (c. 1709), Uffizi Gallery, Florence.

Fig. 31. Gerrit Dou, *Reading the Bible* (*c*. 1650), Musée du Louvre, Paris.

Fig. 32. Anicet Charles Gabriel Lemonnier, *The Frst Reading of Voltaire's 'Orphan of China' in the Parisian Salon of Madame Marie Thérèse Geoffrin in 1755* (1812), Musée des Beaux-Arts, Rouen.

Chairs were in short supply in peasant homes for a long time, and people were obliged to sit on the floor, beds, stools, benches and makeshift seating. On the other hand, chairs were widely used in cities. In a capital city like Paris, in the eighteenth century there were plenty of chairs even in working-class homes. The high number of chairs, stools, armchairs and sofas are signs of an intense social life. At the top of society, many people met up to debate, develop ideas and read in the salons of sophisticated women who promoted cultural events (Fig. 32). However, reading aloud was an opportunity to bring together members of a family or a close group (Fig. 33). The emphasis that Protestants placed on reading the Bible (which the masses were banned from doing in the Catholic world) favoured the development of literacy even amongst women (Fig. 31).

Fig. 33. Jean-François de Troy, *Reading from Molière* (1728), private collection of the Marchioness of Cholmondeley.

Fig. 34. Michel Van Loo, *The Cup of Chocolate* (eighteenth century), Château de Versailles.

The spread of new forms of consumption, such as the drinking of tea, coffee and chocolate, created new opportunities for meeting and socializing, even within the family. It also marked out new geographical and social boundaries. Tea established itself in England, and in a relatively short time, it conquered all social groups. In many regions, coffee became a symbol of bourgeois efficiency that contrasted with chocolate, the preferred beverage of the aristocracy. These new drinks also led to the creation of new products: teapots, coffeepots and chocolate pots (Figs. 34–6).

Fig. 35. Richard Collins, *Tea in the Family* (eighteenth century), V & A Picture Library, London.

Fig. 36. William Hogarth, *The Strode Family* (*c.* 1738), Tate Gallery, London.

The value of goods was not only financial. Domestic interiors, particularly those of the better-off, often displayed brand-new goods alongside others that had been handed down over many generations. The latter heirlooms with their ancient patina testified to the family's antiquity and this accounted for at least part of their value. This was demonstrated by the care Venetian notaries took to specify that silverware was 'ancient' or even 'very ancient'. The same epithets were often used for the paintings that started to adorn Venetian houses at a very early date. Many of these were family portraits. The elegant wardrobes handed down from one generation to the next by Dutch families in the seventeenth and eighteenth centuries seem to have had a similar value. They were often displayed in a prominent position in the principal room in their houses. Their solid material presence embodied the family's continuity and prosperity, while protecting the carefully folded linen, clothing and occasionally jewellery, as well as the family's memories (Fig. 46).

Fig. 37. Emanuel De Witte, *Interior with Woman Playing at Virginals* (*c.* 1665), Museum Boymans van Beuningen, Rotterdam.

In Renaissance and early modern-European buildings, rooms were generally laid out in such a manner that it was impossible to move from one to another without going through those in-between. Movement within a building was primarily assisted by increasing the number of doors. The layout of rooms *en enfilade, whereby every room led into the next with doors all in a line, made it possible to play with perspective and display the vastness of a house to any visitors (Fig. 37). It could also be used to create privacy by filtering guests through a series of antechambers. Given that living space organized on the basis of this kind of layout meant that any kind of activity could be interrupted by someone passing through, the owners would locate their rooms as far away as possible from the public ones in order to obtain a little peace. They isolated themselves by having a barrier of antechambers in front of their rooms and closets (each group of antechambers, bedroom and closets constituted an 'apartment'). Their apartments also had 'secret' exits and stairways. Corridors created a very different layout to the enfilade. The first 'modern' corridor was possibly built by John Thorpe in a house in Chelsea, England in 1597. Coleshill House in Berkshire, which was designed by Sir Roger Pratt between 1650 and 1667, possibly represents the example in which the new technique for laying out rooms was adopted in the most radical and systematic manner. Every floor had a corridor running the full length of the house, with a back staircase at each end. At the centre of the building there was an entrance hall with landing above, and a double staircase. Every room had a door that opened onto a corridor or onto the hall or landing (Fig. 38). However, corridors took time to be widely adopted. It made every room an isolated unit and the activities pursued within it were removed from sight and the possibility of being interrupted by someone casually wandering through. This made it easier to meet up for specific purposes, while limiting the number of chance encounters.*

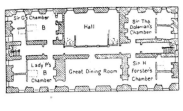

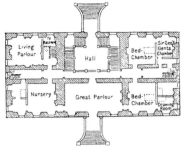

Fig. 38. Sir Roger Pratt, Plans for Coleshill House in Berkshire (1650–67).

During the early modern era, rooms started to be used for increasingly specific purposes, but it was common to receive guests in the same room one slept in or to sleep in the same room one ate in (Fig. 63). This even occurred in affluent families, such as the one depicted by Boissart to portray harmony (Fig. 39).

Fig. 39. Robert Boissart, *Harmony* (late sixteenth or early seventeenth century), Bibliothèque nationale de France, Paris.

Fig. 40. Albrecht Dürer, *The Wire-drawing Mill* (*c.* 1489), Kupferstichkabinett, Berlin.

Fig. 41. Jan Bruegel the Elder, *Visit to a Farm* (*c.* 1597), Kunsthistorisches Museum, Vienna.

Fig. 42. Jan Steen, *Celebrating the Birth* (1664), The Wallace Collection, London.

Fig. 43. Recently reconstructed furnishings of a room at the Hôtel de Sully in Paris.

Fig. 44. Chest with painted tondos by Bartolommeo Montagna (end of the fifteenth or beginning of the sixteenth century), Museo Poldi Pezzoli, Milan.

Fig. 45. Titian, *The Venus of Urbino* (1583), Uffizi Gallery, Florence.

Fig. 46. Pieter de Hooch, *At the Linen Closet* (1663), Rijksmuseum, Amsterdam.

Fig. 47. Interior of the Hôtel Lauzum, built by Louis Le Vau on the Ile Saint-Louis in Paris between 1650 and 1658.

Fig. 48. Giuseppe Gambarini, *Winter* (*c.* 1721–7), Pinacoteca Nazionale, Bologna.

Fig. 49. Maurice Quentin de Latour, *The Marquise Pompadour* (eighteenth century), Musée du Louvre, Paris.

Fig. 50. Agnolo Bronzino, *Portrait of Eleonora of Toledo and Her Son Giovanni de' Medici* (*c.* 1545), Uffizi Gallery, Florence.

Fig. 51. Giuseppe Maria Crespi, *Searcher for Fleas* (*c.* 1730), Museo Nazionale Civico San Matteo, Pisa.

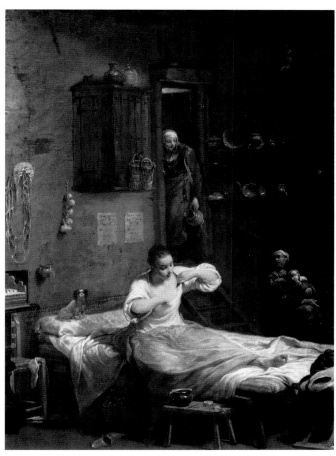

Fig. 52. Adrien van Ostade, detail from *The Weaver's Repose* (*c.* 1650).

For the poor, a meal might only consist of a little bread (Fig. 52). Families did not always eat together. Those who worked outside would take their food with them. In the poorest families, each person would fend for themselves by earning, begging or stealing something to eat. In the richest families, husband and wife might decide to eat in their rooms. In other words, members of the same family did not always eat together. However, eating together was considered a moment in which family unity was achieved and expressed both before others and before God through prayer and saying grace (Figs. 53 and 56–7). Eating around a table was a way to express both a family's unity and the hierarchies that existed within it. Tables and chairs spread slowly. Sitting down was a privilege given to men before women and especially children, who unsurprisingly are depicted standing or crouched on the ground in the illustrations (Figs. 39, 53–7, 60 and 63).

Fig. 53. Adrien van Ostade, *Saying Grace* (1653), Bibliothèque Nationale de France, Paris

Fig. 54. Louis Le Nain, *The Peasant Meal* (1642), Musée du Louvre, Paris.

Fig. 55. Louis Le Nain, *Peasant Family* (first half of the seventeenth century), Musée du Louvre, Paris.

Fig. 56. Claude Duflos, *Saying Grace* (second half of the seventeenth century), engraving from a painting by Charles Le Brun.

It took time for tablecloths and individual napkins, plates, glasses and cutlery to be widely adopted. When this did occur, it brought an end to the ancient promiscuity in eating habits. The development of table manners and the spread of cutlery and crockery led to the isolation of each diner from his or her fellow-diners. Once, everyone had used a single bowl (Figs. 53 and 55–6) and even where plates, cutlery and glasses had been used, they had been used communally. The last type of cutlery to be widely used was the fork. It originated in Byzantium, and started to spread in Italy in the late Middle Ages, and from there to other parts of Europe. But it spread rather slowly. The artists whose works have been selected for this book, depict knives (Figs. 39 and 67) and spoons (Figs. 53, 63 and 67). It appears that a fork can only be seen on the sumptuous banqueting table at a feast to celebrate the birth of the Prince of the Asturias, where however some diners are eating with their hands (Fig. 64).

Fig. 57. Abraham Bosse, *Grace at the Table* (seventeenth century), Bibliothèque Nationale de France, Paris.

Fig. 58. Jan Vermeer, *A Maidservant Pouring Milk* or *The Milkmaid* (*c.* 1658–61), Rijksmuseum, Amsterdam.

Women prepared the food in middle and lower-class families. Cooking was the activity that the mistress of the house was least likely to delegate to servants (particularly in northern European countries), while the most likely were cleaning, sweeping, washing dishes and washing clothes (Figs. 42, 58–61, 65, 69, 70–3 and 76–7). However, cooks were predominantly men in the kitchens of the nobility (Figs. 68 and 75).

Fig. 59. Bernardo Strozzi, *The Female Cook* (*c.* 1625), Galleria di Palazzo Rosso, Genoa.

Fig. 60. *The Peaceful Household* (second half of the eighteenth century),
Bibliothèque Nationale de France, Paris.

Fig. 61. Wolfgang Heimbach, *A Kitchen* (1648), Germanisches
Nationalmuseum, Nuremberg.

Fig. 62. George Morland, *Visiting the Baby at the Wet-nurse's* (1788), Drake Collection, Academy of Medicine, Toronto.

In families of the upper and middle classes, women usually had their children breastfed by wet-nurses (Fig. 62). The majority of women in the lower classes breastfed their own children (Fig. 79). Some apparently realistic paintings and drawings show men intent on feeding and cradling babies, thus challenging the stereotype whereby only women were busy with looking after the young (Figs. 48 and 63).

Fig. 63. Adrien van Ostade, *The Paterfamilias* (1648), Wellcome Institute Library, London.

Fig. 64. M. Desmaretz, The Duke of Alba's banquet in Paris for the birth of the Prince of the Asturias (1707), Bibliothèque Nationale de France, Paris.

At the top of the social ladder, banquets were an opportunity for displaying wealth and power through the abundance and quality of the food and drinks provided, their preparation and the sumptuousness of the 'spread' (Fig. 64). The theatrical side of such occasions was demonstrated by the crowd which, particularly in the sixteenth century, was often present.

Fig. 65. Pietro Longhi, *Maize Porridge* (*c.* 1735–40), Ca' Rezzonico, Musei Civici Veneziani, Venice.

Fig. 66. Bartolomé Esteban Murillo, detail from *Diego di Alcalà Distributes Bread and Potatoes to the Poor* (1645–6), Real Academia de Bellas Artes de San Fernando, Madrid.

Fig. 67. Annibale Carracci, *The Bean-eater* (*c.* 1580–90), Galleria Colonna, Rome.

Many types of food were imported from the Americas, and over the long term they were
to change the European diet profoundly. The most important were undoubtedly potatoes
and maize (Figs. 65 and 66). A diet of maize, which is short of vitamin PP, caused
widespread suffering from pellagra. Beans also came from America. The only
type of bean known in Europe before Columbus's discovery was what we now call the
black-eye bean (Fig. 67).

Fig. 68. Kitchen interior. Engraving from Bartolomeo Scappi, *Opera dell'arte del cucinare*, Venice 1570.

Fig. 69. Pieter Gerritsz van Roestraten, *Woman Preparing Pancakes* (*c.* 1670), Collectie Museum Bredius, The Hague.

Fig. 70. Jéan Siméon Chardin, *Scouring Maid* (1738), Glasgow, Hunterian Art Gallery, University of Glasgow.

Fig. 71. Giuseppe Maria Crespi, *The Scullery Maid* (*c*. 1710–15),
the Contini Bonacossi Collection, Florence.

*A woman's life consisted of a massive diversity of tasks, even when she was not working
outside the home (Figs. 48, 69, 70–4, 78–9 and 82–4). But in the early modern era,
the border between domestic and non-domestic work was different from today. Generally
female tasks, such as collecting water, were performed outside the home, as was washing
clothes, which often took place at a river or fountain (Fig. 73). There were also people
who carried out this task professionally. In some regions, men were employed. Many
female tasks had nothing to do with the cleaning now associated with domestic work.
Milking cows and feeding the hens were a woman's responsibility in most of Europe.*

Fig. 72. Jean-Siméon Chardin, *The Laundress* (1733), Photo:
The National Museum of Fine Arts, Stockholm.

Fig. 73. Giacomo Ceruti (il Pitocchetto), *The Laundress* (1736), Pinacoteca Tosio
Martinengo, Brescia.

Fig. 74. Sign from Roemer Visscher, *Sinnepoppen*, Amsterdam 1614.

Fig. 75. The treatment of milk as depicted in an engraving from Bartolomeo Scappi, *Opera dell'arte del cucinare*, Venice 1570.

In many regions, women were expected to make butter and cheese (Fig. 74). But in other areas, the treatment of milk was considered a specifically male task, which was occasionally even fundamental to a definition of virility. Amongst the Basques of Sainte-Engrâce, for example, cheese-making was the reserve of sexually mature men. Those who produced dairy products either professionally or for upper-class families were often men (Fig. 75). Sexual division of labour in the home therefore differed according to social class. In the houses of the very rich, male servants often carried out tasks which would have been the responsibility of women in middle and lower-class homes. The domestic spaces crowded with men making pastry and crushing herbs in a mortar disprove the tiresome prejudices that perceive the sexual division of labour as something based on the supposed natural inclinations of men and women (Fig. 68).

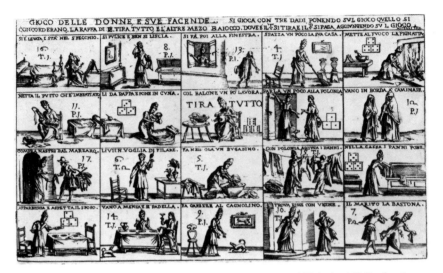

Fig. 76. Giuseppe Maria Mitelli, *Women's Amusements and Tasks* (c. 1695), the Art Collection of the Cassa di Risparmio di Bologna, Bologna.

Women were generally charged with looking after domestic objects and linen (Figs. 45–6 and 76), and they could be responsible for purchasing items of daily use. Moreover, they were mainly destined to leave their original families when they married taking only a few objects with them (Figs. 6–7). It was much more difficult for them to own property. They were excluded from the professions. Women therefore appear to have developed a different relationship with objects, which was more individual and more emotional compared with men. They seem to have invested great importance in objects because they had few alternative resources to construct their identity, establish social relations and leave a memory of themselves.

Fig. 77. Jean-Siméon Chardin, *The Hard-working Mother* (1738–9), Musée du Louvre, Paris.

Fig. 78. *Social Gathering* (seventeenth century), Bibliothèque
Nationale de France, Paris.

*In the early modern era, women were continuously spinning (Figs. 31, 48, 76 and
78–9). In many areas, the spindle and distaff were the symbol of the honest and
hard-working woman, particularly in the context of a marriage. In Fig. 6, it can be seen
how the distaff dominates the whole of the cart. This tool was probably attributed with
such significance precisely because it was possible to spin in intervals between other tasks
or even while carrying out other tasks. Thus during the evenings passed in the warmth of
the byre, women would spin while men courted them (Figs. 78–9). The disappearance of
hand-spinning undoubtedly constituted a profound change in women's lives and
probably also in their gender identity.*

Fig. 79. *Rural Social Gathering* (nineteenth century), Musée des Arts et Traditions
Populaires, Paris.

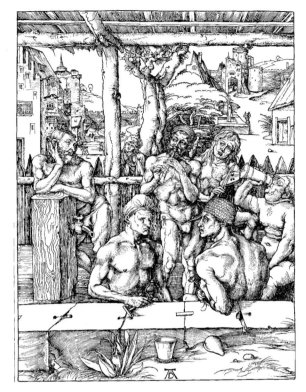

Fig. 80. Albrecht Dürer, *Men's Bath* (1496), Kunsthalle, Bremen.

The Roman tradition of public baths survived until the sixteenth century (Figs. 80–1). Then new beliefs about the body led people to consider baths dangerous to their health. Thus the seventeenth and early eighteenth centuries were probably the period in which people washed least. It was believed that cleanliness could be achieved not by washing but by frequent changes of underwear. Babies were generally wrapped in swaddling that was changed only rarely, and this probably contributed to the high level of infant mortality (Figs. 48, 76 and 84). Fleas and lice took over the human body (Figs. 30, 51 and 82–3).

Fig. 81. Albrecht Dürer, *Women's Bath* (1496), Kunsthalle, Bremen.

Fig. 82. Gerard Ter Borch, *A Mother Fine-combing the Hair of Her Child* (*c.*1652–3), Mauritshuis, The Hague.

Fig. 83. Georges de la Tour, *Woman Catching a Flea* (*c.* 1638), Musée Historique Lorrain, Nancy.

Fig. 84. Georges de la Tour, *The New-born Baby* (first half of the seventeenth century), Musée des Beaux-Arts, Rennes.

Fig. 85. Nicolaus Guérard, *The Wicked Couple and a Dispute Over a Pair of Breeches. The Reconciled Couple and the Breeches Surrendered to the Husband* (c. 1690–1700), Bibliothèque Nationale de France, Paris.

Clothes classified the wearer. Thus the demand by women for a position of authority could be represented by the struggle to take possession of a pair of breeches, the symbol of male power (Fig. 85). The image of a woman attempting to wear trousers prompted misogynous satires on the absurdity of the world turned upside down (Fig. 4). But it was not only sex that was identified by clothes. Under the Ancien Régime, *the prevailing idea was that there should be a correspondence between the clothing and the wearer's identity. This affected peasants as well as the rich, priests as well as Jews, who were branded with a distinguishing yellow mark. Legislation on luxury goods attempted to restrict luxury or prevent the splendour of upper-class clothing being copied, although not always with great success (Figs. 49–50). Even the family to which one belonged could be indicated by clothing. A servant's livery could distinguish which family he belonged to (Fig. 86). The French Revolution declared the right of everyone to choose their clothing freely.*

Fig. 86. Bernardo Bellotto, detail from *Warsaw – Miodawa Street from South-east to North-west* (1777), Royal Castle Collection, Narodowe Museum, Warsaw.

century, but up until then many men clearly believed that handing their children over to wet-nurses was the way to have their cake and eat it, as it ensured that children had supposedly good milk while they did not have go without sex with their wives.[97]

The decision to use a wet-nurse was generally taken by the father, although the woman's voice might be heard to some extent.[98] Once the decision had been taken, it was a matter of finding the most suitable person for such a delicate task. For many centuries people stubbornly believed that babies suckled the dispositons of their wet-nurses along with the milk.[99] In seventeenth-century Rome the choice of wet-nurse was a female concern,[100] but in other situations it was the *pater familias* who dealt with the problem. He was always the one who negotiated the wet-nurse's working conditions, often not with her but with her husband.[101]

The awareness, already widespread in the early modern era, that breast-feeding delays fertility after childbirth may have influenced decisions as to whether a baby should be given to a wet-nurse.[102] Male anxiety over ensuring the longed-for heir and a few other sons as back-up in the event of the designated heir dying or proving unfit put a heavy responsibility on wives to produce a large number of children, so that the family name and property could continue.[103] (Paradoxically, as has been shown, the mortality of children breast-fed by a wet-nurse was higher than for children breastfed by their own mothers.)

The frequency of pregnancies was in all probability an incentive to use a wet-nurse for those who could afford it.[104] It helped to lighten the load, although it did have undesirable effects for the mother, such as the previously mentioned inflammation in the breast which could be both painful and dangerous.[105] If we are to believe some polemical writings, breastfeeding and childcare were seen as the kind of irritating and exhausting tasks that rich people delegated to others and which, precisely for this reason, was considered too contemptible to be carried out by women of higher social rank. 'Breastfeeding is a peasant woman's job, and not for an educated woman', was, according to Giuseppe Antonio Costantini, the kind of thing ladies said when they did not want to breastfeed their own children.[106]

Whether or not they were capable of doing so, noblewomen and to some extent women of the urban bourgeoisie did not breastfeed their children, but this does not mean that they and their husbands did not care about their children. They simply lived in a context in which life, death, interests and emotions developed, intertwined and expressed themselves in manners very different to today.[107] According to some estimates, it appears that overall no more than 4 per cent of children were entrusted to a wet-nurse, although the figures fluctuated from one area to another. In mid-eighteenth-century Paris, the figure appears to have been somewhere around 10 per cent, but mainly because of the high number of foundlings that were coming in from the countryside. Amongst the lower social classes, almost the only children who were wet-nursed were those taken in by institutions that looked after abandoned children. In the country-side, peasant women usually wet-nursed both their own children and those of others. In the city, the use of wet-nurses was more widespread, but often only in the case of women who worked in particularly dangerous and unhealthy envi-ronments or whose working hours were incompatible with breastfeeding, such as the women who worked in the silk industry in Lyons.[108] In the great majority of cases, children were breastfed by their own mothers. Once they had been weaned, it appears that they were occasionally looked after by men. An engraving by Adrien van Ostade in 1648 provides a rather realistic picture of a peasant interior in which a man seated in a chair holds a child in his arms and feeds him with a spoon. A painting by Giuseppe Maria Crespi depicts an old man cradling a baby in his arms (Figs. 51 and 63).

Some of the first changes to the practice of wet-nursing were introduced in the seventeenth century. Many middle-class women in the Netherlands decided that breastfeeding was one of the duties of a good mother and English puritan women actually believed it to be a religious duty.[109] But only in the eighteenth century, particularly in the second half of the century, did the decline in the use of wet-nurses commence amongst the upper classes of Europe, at a varying pace in different countries.[110]

The abandonment of this practice was probably linked to the spread of birth control, which meant it was possible to devote more attention to each child. Another factor was the renewed emphasis on the advantages of maternal breast-feeding for both mother and baby, and one of the advantages was precisely its power to reduce fertility. The wider availability and increased reliability of arti-ficial food for babies also contributed to change. The increasing awareness of the upper classes to the question of hygiene must have made them more suspicious about the peasants' homes in which wet-nurses lived and, if they decided on wet-nursing, it must have encouraged them to hire a wet-nurse willing to trans-fer to the baby's home. The spread of maternal breastfeeding in the families of the rich was therefore part of a wide range of changes in the family, which involved an increasing emphasis on love in the choice of a spouse and women's maternal role, a reduction in the number of children for each couple and an increase in the life expectancy of those children.[111]

In some areas, opposing trends in social development occurred at the top and bottom of the social scale. With the development of industrialization and female factory work, the use of wet-nurses became more common among lower-class women than it had been in the past.[112]

Wet-nurses

In the early modern era, difference of class and culture meant therefore that the relationship between women and cooking and caring for children was not uniform. Generally women in the lower-middle and lower classes everywhere breastfed their children and did the cooking. At the top of the social scale, cooks were men and ladies did not breastfeed. In England, however, it appears that middle – and upper-class women were more likely to do the cooking than in France and Italy. Moreover, wet-nursing was never as widespread in England as it was in many other areas of the continent, and its decline came earlier.[113] 'Even the women of good family breastfeed their children', noted a foreign traveller in 1784.[114] This poses the question of whether these two things could be connected in some way.

By around the beginning of the eighteenth century the various tasks relating to childcare appear to have become more similar than in the past for women of all social classes and from every part of Europe. This was so much the case that they became a central element in defining female identity.[115] Even for noble and rich women, becoming a mother increasingly meant breastfeeding one's own children. The changes in cook books and handbooks on household management increasingly demonstrated that women were expected to know how to cook, whether they actually did it themselves or delegated it to their servants. In the latter case, they were required to be able to supervise and instruct.[116] At the same time, men tended to disappear from the kitchen, which increasingly became the domain of female cooks.

Of course, there is the objection that with industrialization many working-class women were obliged to use wet-nurses and as they worked in factories they could not always manage to prepare the food. It is probably the case that while upper-class women came closer to the realities of cooking, women workers to some extent distanced themselves from it. With the upper classes now accepting the idea that women should breastfeed, the fact that working-class women were less involved in feeding their own children and families was considered one of the many aberrations brought about by factory work. Yet for centuries it had been considered absolutely normal that noblewomen left the preparation of dinner to male cooks and that they did not breastfeed their own children despite much criticism.[117]

4. Who you are depends on when you eat and what you eat

Dinner is served

Again it is not possible to find a single answer to the question of when people ate. The poorest probably ate when they found something to put in their mouths. Even those who were not destitute were not obliged to eat at the same time every day.[118] A document relating to the court of Mantua, probably dating from the seventeenth century, appears to imply that all the 'commoners' did not have 'any rule' when it came to mealtimes. It argued for this reason that the table for the most lowly of the servants – the coachmen, litter-bearers and stable boys – 'should always have cheese, salami, ham and salad'. The Jesuit Giulio Cordara confirmed in 1783 that 'They care not whether it is midday or midnight. They toil by day and sleep by night. Still less are they concerned with the time of lunch and supper. They eat when they are hungry.' The thinly veiled contempt of the lower classes that emerges from these quotations means that we must not take them too literally.[119] Besides, even in higher social classes the eating routine could be interrupted by a snack when hunger required. The number of meals and their frequency were not always the same. Those who worked the fields knew that during the heavy work of harvesting they were entitled to a nutritional surplus, which could stretch to seven meals a day. During some festivities, people could stay at the table for hours or indeed days.[120]

Since ancient times, regular mealtimes had represented an ideal that was both dietary and moral. The consumption of food at regular intervals was considered an expression of civilized behaviour that contrasted with savage and disorderly conduct. At the beginning of the early modern era, its social usefulness was also sometimes emphasized. 'At one time, many nations did not prescribe precise mealtimes', claimed one author. 'It would be difficult to reconcile such practice with the kind of business carried out in civilized countries'.[121]

Even if we ignore factors that altered or undermined regular mealtimes, it is clear that not everyone in the early modern era ate the same number of times and at the same hour. The situation also shifted with the seasons and developed over the centuries. We will therefore have to examine the question in the proper order.

Towards the end of the Middle Ages in France, which is perhaps the country about which we are best informed, the commoners ate four or five times a day (in the summer, when the days are longer, there may have been an extra meal). Adult members of the upper classes only had two meals, *dîner* and *souper*. These meals were the main ones for everyone. It is difficult to generalize, but it appears that those who did not have breakfast (*dejouner*) ate lunch at around ten o'clock, while those who did, lunched between midday and one o'clock. Supper was eaten before dark, but those who had lunch at ten had a snack (*gouter*) before supper. By the sixteenth century, upper-class Italians were already having lunch at two o'clock and having supper at nine in the evening, after the theatre.

As time went on, the difference between upper- and lower-class mealtimes grew larger. Whereas mealtimes for commoners remained relatively unchanged, those of the upper classes gradually became later. Between the mid-sixteenth century and the late eighteenth century, the time of *dîner* in Paris was put back by about eight hours. While they ate it at about ten in the morning in the first half of the sixteenth century, by the beginning of the nineteenth they ate it at six in the evening. Supper was now at eleven and had been delayed by six hours. Change in the provinces was slower, so the already complex map of mealtime habits was further complicated by another variable.

France was not the only country affected by later mealtimes for the upper classes. Lunch in England shifted from eleven in the morning in the seventeenth century to two in the afternoon in the mid-eighteenth century. But the upper classes ate lunch as late as five and then had supper at midnight. Of course these were extreme cases. In the eighteenth century, however, the whole of upper-class Europe passed the evening at parties, balls or the theatre. They therefore slept late in the morning and inevitably lunched and supped much later, ending up with very different mealtimes from the rest of the population.[122]

Quality food for people of quality

There were innumerable differences concerning food in the early modern era. However, the distinctions between men and women, adults and children, masters and servants, persons of varying prestige, and city-dwellers and peasants were not only indicated through inclusion or exclusion from the dining table, one's place at table, the knowledge good manners or the lack of it, the ownership of plates, glasses and cutlery, the organization of the kitchen, serving at table, the actual preparation of food, mealtimes and whether one was breastfed by a wet-nurse or one's own mother. These distinctions were also expressed and signalled by the food itself. It was long believed that everyone should eat in accordance with their own 'quality', by which it was meant in accordance with not so much one's own constitution, health and age, but rather with one's social rank. 'He died in terrible pain because he was no longer able to eat turnips and beans', said Giulio Cesare Croce of the peasant Bertoldo, who had been forced by his unexpected rise up the social ladder to the court of King Alboino to eat only extremely refined dishes.[123] The literary work reflected a widely held and stubborn belief of a clearly classist nature.

This strongly held idea that each social group had its appropriate food was, at least in the sixteenth century, part of a series of beliefs that considered high to mean good and low to mean bad. God was supposed to have given a hierarchical structure to human society as well as to nature. The 'chain of existence' put the four elements (earth, water, air and fire) in ascending order between two poles represented at the bottom by material objects and at the top by God. Every plant or animal was associated with one of these elements and then classified in accordance with its assumed degree of nobility. For example, it was believed that both trees and bulbs belonged to the realm of the earth, but the former were more noble than the latter, because they reached up to the skies. Thus birds were considered the food of kings and princes, and they ate many that today would be unthinkable as food: cormorants, storks, swans, cranes, herons and peacocks. Brutish peasants were supposed to be suited to pork, because pigs grub around in the mud, and turnips, because they grow underground.[124]

Although it was believed that everyone should eat the food suited to their natures, it was also believed that the principle foods helped to forge those characteristics that were associated with a particular social group. One author of the sixteenth century claimed that '[we nobles] eat more partridges and other delicate meats, and this gives us a more acute intelligence and sensitivity than those who eat beef and pork'.[125] At the beginning of the early modern era, food was actually used for signalling the social divisions between people eating at the same table: the best dishes and pieces were given to the more important persons.[126] While French service, which spread throughout the period from the sixteenth to the eighteenth century, involved each diner helping himself freely from the plates placed on the table, in many other countries the stewards and carvers divided the food and the servants served the food to the diners starting with the most important and then the others in order of rank.[127] Given this outlook and the fact that different tables could be assigned to particular ranks, they not only ate in a different manner, they ate different dishes.

When in 1592 the Florentine authorities gave a dinner for two Bavarian princes who visited the city with their retinues, five different types of bird were served at their table (as we have seen, birds were considered the noblest food). There were only four types at the table of the most important people amongst the staff of the two princes. The thirty diners at the table of the most lowly servants, which was in another room, had to content themselves with sharing five dishes, each containing a single bird. The guests' horses and mules were included in the list for the organization of the banquet, given that they too had to be provided for. The 140 or so servants that carried out the most lowly duties and were lodged in the city's taverns, were listed after these animals, which was of course intentional.[128]

Masters and servants, and occasionally the various ranks of servant, usually ate different dishes and drank different drinks. The Italian expression, *confezione-famiglia* ('family pack'), used to indicate a large pack of cheap consumers goods (generally foodstuffs) that are not always of the best quality, derives from the expression *vino da famiglia*, which significantly was widely used in the early modern era for the wine used by domestic staff. 'Family' was being used in its etymological sense.[129] The expression *pane da famiglia* was used, at least in the Po Valley, to mean low-quality bread.[130]

Just as root vegetables that grow underground and the meat of pigs that root amongst the refuse were at the bottom of the hierarchy of foods, so the peasants who worked the land were in the lowest position in the human hierarchy. It was not just an abstract conviction that everyone had their rightful place in the world; the diet of city-dwellers really was different from what was eaten in rural areas. Urban domination of the countryside had been gradually imposed from the end of the first millennium, particularly in regions like Italy and Flanders. This translated into the fact that the middle and lower classes in the cities ate white bread, which was therefore made from wheat. With a few exceptions, such as in Sicily, peasants ate brown bread or used bread made from other types of corn, such as rye, barley, oats, millet, foxtail millet, chestnut flour, lupin, maize, and various mixtures according to local availability.[131] Landowners demanded that rent be paid in wheat, and city-dwellers could buy bread or flour at a market whose supply was controlled by the food-rationing authorities. Peasants were practically obliged to go without.[132] In Giulio Cesare Croce's *Dispute between Wheat Bread and Bean Bread Over Which is the Better* (*Contrasto del pane di formenti e quello di fava per la precedenza*), one side argues, 'Oh bread made of beans, what are you doing in this place [i.e. the city] where you are neither wanted nor valued? Why don't you go amongst the peasants where you are loved and revered?'[133]

The distinctions and social hierarchies relating to types of bread were not restricted to the difference between white bread and brown bread. In the city bread became whiter (i.e. more carefully sieved) as you went up the social scale. Only the middle and upper classes ate fresh bread every day, either produced by bakers or made at home (there were some people who made the dough at home and then took it to the baker's to be cooked).[134] Everyone else ate hard bread and therefore ate less. While it was not uncommon amongst the lower classes in the city to buy small amounts of bread every day,[135] peasants widely used the 'strategy of stale bread' to save time and fuel (a proverb reminds us that 'A good home has stale bread and dry firewood'). In some parts of the Alps they made bread only twice a year. Soup and drinks were then used to soften this hard food.[136]

However hard and brown it was, bread was sought-after, and was certainly not placed at the bottom of the hierarchy of foods. It was not easy to turn the inferior grains left to peasants into bread and so they were often eaten in other forms. They were used for gruels, porridges and mashes, which were not very tasty but had the advantage of either wholly or partially avoiding charges by the landowner on mills and ovens. Examples were millet mash in Sologne, Champagne and Gascony until 1700, millet, buckwheat and maize mash in northern Italy, buckwheat and milk or water *grou* in Brittany, porridge oats in Scotland

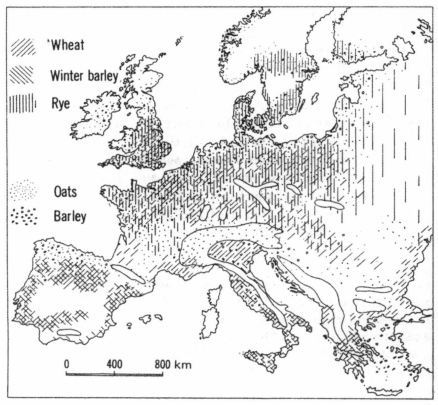

Cereal crop associations in Europe, seventeenth and eighteenth centuries (Norman J. Pounds, *An Historical Geography of Europe, 1500–1840*, Cambridge University Press, 1979).

and England, and *kasza* made of crushed, toasted and boiled rye, barley, millet or buckwheat in Poland, Lithuania and Russia.[137]

5. Eating bread and eating meat

Romans, Christians and 'barbarians'

The significance of bread in the European diet was the result of the fusion of two different traditions. There was the Roman tradition which, although it did not scorn the consumption of milk, cheese, vegetables and meat, concentrated on the triad of bread, wine and oil. Then there was the tradition of the 'barbarian' peoples who preferred meat, dairy products, beer and cider, although these were supplemented by oat porridges and flat bread made of barley. The bringing together of these traditions had two significant results: the prestige of eating meat was established and bread came to be widely used. The dietary value of meat was imposed by the victories of the Germanic tribes, who became the ruling class in early medieval Europe. From then on, those who could afford it, ate as much meat as they possibly could. The Romans had prized frugality, whereas the barbarians spread the conviction that the ability to swallow large quantities of food and drink was a sign of strength.[138]

From the twelfth and thirteenth centuries, new culinary fashions perceived a sign of distinction in the sophistication of food rather than the quantities consumed.[139] In spite of this, the elites continued to be overfed. It has been calculated that an average of 6,500 calories per day were consumed at the court of King Eric of Sweden in the sixteenth century and the retinue of Cardinal Mazarin managed to consume 7–8,000.[140] Food consumption of this kind could only have a bad effect on their health. Not surprisingly, gout, which is in part due to the excessive consumption of meat, was for centuries the disease of the European upper classes (compared with northern countries, the diet in the Mediterranean world continued however to involve less animal protein).[141] Paradoxically, the prestige attached to meat led to the preparation of foods for weaning babies of the upper classes based on broths and meat that provided less nutrition than mother's milk, paps or bread soups which were used by the lower classes.[142]

While the prestige of meat was imposed by the victories of the Germanic tribes, the significance of bread (and also wine and oil) spread with Christianity, a Mediterranean religion that had made these foods central to its worship.[143]

Protestants and Catholics

Unsurprisingly, the religious split in Europe caused by the Reformation had dietary repercussions as well. In Zurich, it was precisely the failure to observe Lent and the eating of sausages that started the Reformation in 1522.[144] Protestants rejected the dietary regulations of the Roman Church, which imposed numerous fast days throughout the year (primarily Lent), with their diet based on fish, vegetable oils and greens. This rekindled the ancient differences between a glutinous and carnivorous north and a frugal and vegetarian south, differences that had never entirely disappeared. Thus two Europes were created and they clashed not only in the religious field but also in the dietary one.[145]

Now there was a Protestant Europe hungry for meat and animal fats, in which the consumption of fish, at least in some areas like England, had diminished and oil was more or less banned and replaced from the seventeenth century by butter, even in salads. A fashion was introduced for creamy sauces, a veritable 'sea change in taste'. The fashion spread through the upper and middle classes of a large part of the continent and replaced the lean and acidic sauces based on wine, vinegar, citrus juice and spices. The passion for spices, which had dominated the Middle Ages was to decline just at the time when pepper, cinnamon and cloves were flooding in from recently discovered lands (partly as a result of journeys undertaken to facilitate their supply). Now that so many people could afford them, the rich started to spurn these spices, which were left to the palates of lower social classes and the cuisines of more peripheral areas.[146]

Then there was the more sober Catholic Europe with its preference for the products of the land. Its religious calendar prohibited the consumption of meat and animal fats on 140–160 days of the year.[147] The Italian-inspired fashion for vegetables amongst the French sixteenth – and seventeenth-century upper classes appears to have been favoured by the Counter-Reformation.[148]

A rigid application of this distinction, like any other, would risk oversimplifying the reality. The border between northern and southern dietary customs did not coincide exactly with either national ones or religious and confessional ones. In some Catholic areas where oil was difficult to get hold of, the Church allowed the use of butter on fast days. The countries that preferred oil were obviously not all Catholic.[149]

This reminds us that Europe was not only Protestant and Catholic; there was also eastern Europe and the Balkans. Concerning the relationship between religion and diet in the Balkans, the glorification of frugality by Greek Christians meant defending the Church against the risk of Islamization.[150] The Orthodox Churches imposed even more fast days than the Catholic Church. In Russia there were about 200 days on which the consumption of meat was banned and consumption of dairy products and fish was restricted.[151]

Dietary practices and group identities

Dietary practices were in fact an important element in group identity.[152] One of the experiences and perhaps difficulties of travelling, at least in the past, was the need to eat unusual foods, and occasionally those foods were actually prohibited for the traveller. The lack of Muslim travellers in Europe has been linked to the problems of observing their religion's rules on diet and hygiene.

On the other hand, the absence of impure foods in Christian dietary regulations, which were limited to a dietary calendar (and then only for Catholics and Orthodox Christians, but not Protestants) is supposed to have favoured European expansionism in the world. This absence is also supposed to have facilitated conversion from Christianity to Islam. The difficulty for Muslims in abandoning internalized dietary revulsions might be one of the causes in the limited number of those who have rejected this faith.[153]

Of course the battle between Islam and Christianity was also fought on a dietary level. The Poles, for example, attributed particular importance to the consumption of pork because it marked out their religious identity in relation to neighbouring Islamic communities. In Spain, a person's diet was used to reveal false conversions. The converts themselves attributed great importance to diet in defining religious identity.[154] When questioned by the inquisition about 'whether he had followed and observed the Turkish sect [i.e. the Islamic religion] and in what manner', the Greek convert Giovanni Mangiali interestingly replied that for thirteen years he had 'followed and observed the law of the Turks as did the Turks, by eating meat on Fridays, Saturdays, fast days, the four Ember days and Lent'. He then said that he did not eat meat in the presence of Muslims and he had 'observed Lent in the Turkish manner' (in other words, he had observed Ramadan).[155] Similarly Rosa Paleotti, a former 'Turkish' slave who had converted to Christianity and lived in Bologna around 1700, ended up before the inquisitor for having eaten meat on a fast day.[156]

Dietary and culinary customs were also one of the identifying elements of the Jewish community. The traditions of the 'Jewish way of eating', as recognized by both Jews and Christians, were developed on the basis of the many proscriptions contained in the Bible, although they varied from one community to another, partly because of contaminations and interchanges with surrounding communities.[157] In the event of conversion, 'dietary resocialization' therefore played an important role. We know, for example, that Jews in the House of Catechumens in Bologna, who were about to become Christians, were forced to eat foods proscribed by their religion, such as salami, other types of pork, fish without scales and snails.[158]

The longed-for pleasures of the flesh

Thus diet marked out precise cultural borders and different cultures expressed and defined themselves in terms of their diet. The spread of bread consumption amongst Germanic peoples coincided with the spread of Christianity. From a practical point of view, its production was obviously linked to the abandonment of a nomadic lifestyle by barbarian tribes and the adoption of arable land fit for cultivation. In the early Middle Ages, even the lower classes were continuously supplementing their diet of bread, porridge and mashes with meat from domestic or wild animals.

From the ninth century, the increased population and the subsequent expansion in cultivated land had led to a reduction in woodland. Moreover, from the tenth or eleventh century, secular lords, particularly in the less peripheral areas, appropriated the rights to use the uncultivated land and created reserves in which peasants were unable to hunt. They also restricted the peasants' rights to gleaning, herbage and keeping pigs in the woods (*ghiandatico*),[159] and this made it difficult to breed sheep and pigs. Some cities had reserved the right to exploit large areas of woodland exclusively for their citizens (*cives*). Lastly the landowners, whether they were secular lords, monasteries or, especially in Italy or Flanders, cities, seized the new surpluses for themselves. The peasant's diet was thus profoundly altered. Meat, particularly fresh meat and game, became increasingly rare, whereas up until that time it had been present, albeit in smaller quantities than for the dominant classes. The peasant diet had become largely vegetarian (cereals and vegetables).

It was not just the difference between the quality of the diet of rich and poor that was becoming greater. Between the twelfth and the thirteenth century, the distinction between the peasant diet and the urban diet had also been accentuated by very specific food-rationing policies.[160] Initially, the expansion of cultivated land and European economic growth had made it possible to keep a good balance between population and resources. From 1270, however, this balance proved no longer possible and famine returned. Eighty years later, a European population weakened by malnutrition was drastically cut down by the plague (1347–51).[161] The survivors and their children were then able to return to a richer and more balanced diet.

Up until the mid-sixteenth century, Europe was once again carnivorous, but the differences that had been appearing were not cancelled out. They took on another form. The upper classes continued to have a preference for fresh game, but they were more interested in pheasants and partridges than deer and wild boar. The better-off city-dwellers developed a taste for beef, thanks to developments in trade. Not surprisingly, beef became the most costly meat in urban markets. Where choice existed, the urban poor preferred mutton, in order to distinguish themselves from the peasants who ate salted pork. There were, however, differences between one type of pork and another. In Bologna during the early modern era, *mortadella* (Bologna sausage) and salamis, both made of pork, were costly luxury products mainly for export.[162] Naturally there was no shortage of geographical and cultural differences. During our period, the consumption of pork was particularly widespread in central and northern Europe, while the consumption of mutton was high in the Balkans and in Jewish communities.[163]

Returning to a chronological viewpoint, the mid-sixteenth century encountered the limitation imposed by the fact that production could not keep up with demographic growth, in spite of the cultivation of land that had been left to become scrub, the extension of fields and the reduction of areas used for pasture. The expansion of cultivated land was not enough; productivity had to be increased. Some important technical innovations had been introduced in the late Middle Ages and there was a sharp improvement in the science of agronomy. They realized that the insertion of a fallow year in the rotation of crops enriched the land and made it possible to keep a larger number of livestock, thus increasing the production of meat and milk, as well as manure for fertilizing the fields. But the new agricultural techniques were only applied in limited areas of the Netherlands and the Po Valley. Only in the eighteenth century did the continent witness an agricultural revolution, which, if it had been carried out two centuries earlier, would have made it possible to meet the dietary needs of the growing European population.[164]

In the sixteenth century, the European population probably returned to a level (84 million) similar to the one on the eve of the plague in the fourteenth century (90 million). During the early modern era, it increased further: by 1600 there were 111 million Europeans, a century later there were 125 million, by 1750 there were 140–5 million, and by the end of the eighteenth century there were 187 or 195 million, depending on which estimate you use.[165]

Thus dietary conditions deteriorated. The consumption of meat again diminished.[166] In Sicily, for example, the average consumption was 16–26 kilos per year for each inhabitant of the Jewish quarter of Palermo in the mid-fifteenth century and 20–2 kilos in Castrogiovanni. By the 1530s or 1540s, meat had disappeared from the normal diet of peasants and agricultural labourers (meat consumption held up in the city and increased amongst the upper classes).[167] Of course, the decrease was not as dramatic for everyone as it was for Sicilian peasants, nor was the trend always negative, particularly in areas that had always had profound differences in meat consumption. It is estimated that the per-capita consumption in Parma in 1580 was about 20 kilos; in 'plump' Bologna it was 46 kilos in 1593; and in Rome it was 38 kilos in 1600–05 (but only 21.5–24.7 in 1785–9).[168] Overall, however, there was a clear trend towards diminution. Agricultural labourers in the countryside around Narbonne in the Languedoc ate about 40 kilos every year between 1480 and 1534. Thereafter, the ration started to decrease, reaching 20 kilos by 1583. In nineteenth-century Berlin, they ate a quarter of a pound of meat per day, while in the late fourteenth century they had been eating three quarters of a pound.[169] In Naples in 1770, 21,800 head of cattle were slaughtered for about 400,000 inhabitants, whereas two centuries earlier they had been slaughtering 30,000 for about half that population.[170]

In other words, soup was for many people increasingly 'widowed', as they said in Tuscany when it contained no meat.[171] While meat consumption fell, the consumption of bread increased, but it was bread of poorer quality. Even in the cities, where they had been eating white bread since the thirteenth century, bread was becoming darker, particularly for the poorer sections of society. Varying quantities of inferior grain or even vegetables were being added to the wheat, not without protests from those who had to eat the resulting bread. Occasionally there was no wheat at all. While in the fourteenth century daily bread consumption appears to have been between 550 and 700 grams in Italian cities, the data for later periods appears to show continuously larger rations everywhere. In seventeenth-century Siena, the figure appears to fluctuate between 700 and 1,200 grams. In Geneva, rations of 1,100 grams were considered acceptable. In Beauvais the administrators of charitable institutes estimated that 1,300 grams of bread or 850 grams of bread and a plate of soup were the minimum daily fare. In eighteenth-century Paris the poor ate up to 1,500 grams of bread a day.[172] Apart from Norway and Iceland, where fish was the basic food,[173] the diet became increasingly monotonous and based on bread or at least cereals. It has been estimated that in Italy it accounted for between 15 per cent and 19 per cent of the calories in the diet of the rich and over 50 per cent in the diet of Sicilian agricultural labourers. Generally the lower classes did not fall below this threshold, but for a large part of the European population cereals provided between 75 and 90 per cent of their daily calories.[174]

Diet was therefore once again becoming heavily dependent not only on the seasonality of the agricultural world, but also and more seriously upon annual cereal production. Bad harvests were now having a heavy impact on mortality. This is what occurred in the thousands of small local food crises and in the great food crises of the early modern era (such as the one that affected the whole of Europe in 1556–7 and 1590–3, France in 1662, 1693–4, 1709–10 and 1739–41, Finland in 1696–7, Germany in 1739–40, England in 1741–3, Spain and Italy in 1764–7, and the Nordic countries in 1771–4).[175] But increases in cereal prices did not affect mortality uniformly. In areas where there were monocultures, the effects were more dramatic than in areas where there was a wider range of agricultural produce. Hence, the effects were more serious in northern France, which concentrated on cereal crops, than in the south. The effects were less devastating in England than on the continent for a variety of reasons. In the eighteenth century, the link between the increase in the price of cereals and growth in the death rate became slightly less marked, partly because of the development of trade in cereals.[176]

The fight against famine
The dependence on cereal production was partially offset by local and international trade in grain. Exports increased from such countries and regions as eastern Germany, Poland, Livonia, Estonia, Scania, Muscovy, Bohemia and Hungary, as a result of the harsh subjugation of the peasantry, which was obliged to produce wheat and eat cereals like barley and oats. From the end of the seventeenth century, exports also increased from the Turkish Empire, Sicily and the Barbary states. From the seventeenth century, England and her American colonies also became exporters. It was, however, only in the eighteenth century that they started to resolve a range of problems concerning the transport of

grain over long distances, thus allowing trade to reach hitherto unthinkable levels.[177]

6. Dietary innovations

Rice, buckwheat, tomatoes, peppers and kidney beans

The intensification of trade was certainly not the only weapon used in the fight against famine. Dependency was partially offset by the introduction and development of crops that were either new or had not been fully exploited in the past.[178] Rice was an example. It originated in southern Asia, and was known thanks to Arabs in Spain, from where it spread to the Low Countries in the sixteenth century. It had been cultivated in Lombardy with modern capitalist methods since the fifteenth century. Buckwheat, another example, could not be made into bread, but it was suited to very poor or mountainous land. Although known about for a long time, it was only cultivated on a larger scale in western Europe from the sixteenth century, particularly in the Low Countries, Germany, France and northern Italy.[179]

Then there were the plants that had come from the New World. Peppers and chillis became part of the Iberian diet fairly quickly, from where they spread to northern Italy, southern Slav countries and Hungary. They became a cheap substitute for pepper, which was very much in demand. Tomatoes, which were known in Italy, Spain, Provence and the Languedoc as early as the sixteenth century, only spread to the rest of Europe in the eighteenth century. Just as turkeys were assimilated without difficulty into European poultry, so kidney beans had little trouble in being accepted alongside traditional European staples such as chickpeas, lentils, peas and broad beans. They almost supplanted and in many languages took the name of the beans that already existed in Europe, which were similar to those we now call black-eyed beans. The latter are botanically another species (*dolichos*) from the beans that came from America (*phaseolus*). They provided a rich source of protein to the lower classes.[180]

Maize

Maize was brought back from Columbus's first trip to the Americas in 1493 and spread rapidly. In the early part of the sixteenth century, it was cultivated in many regions of Spain. Around 1520, it was to be found in Portugal and south-western France. Ten years later, it was in the area around Venice from where it spread to the Balkans and Hungary. The new plant needed a name and it was given several, which in some languages made it difficult to identify. In Italy it was called coarse millet (*miglio grosso*), sorghum (*sorgo*), coarse corn (*grano grosso*) and *melega* by association or confusion with known cereals. In south-western France, it was known as millet (*meillet*) of Spain with reference to the area from which it was introduced. In Portugal, northern Italy and Germany, it was referred to as Turkish corn, but the use of the term 'Turkish' was perhaps as a synonym for 'foreign' rather than to identify a particular region. Imaginations ran riot on its possible places of origin, producing corn of Rhodes, corn of India, Arab corn and corn of Egypt. In spite of its early spread, its cultivation remained marginal for a long time. It was used as fodder or relegated to vegetable gardens, where it had the advantage of not being subject to tithes or rents. Hence it was necessary 'to make *polenta* eight to ten times a year' the agronomist Giovanni Battarra had one of his protagonists say in his dialogue *Pratica agraria* [*Agrarian Practice*] (1778).[181] Interestingly maize was cooked in the same way as cereals that had long been used in Europe, and not in the American manner. The plant had been imported, but not the gastronomic technique used in its place of origin.

As with the other 'new' crops, the increase in the use of maize was limited in the seventeenth century. Expansion returned in the eighteenth century, and this time the scale and pace of change was far greater. It was now the landowners themselves who were encouraging its spread beyond the clandestine confines of the vegetable garden, given its high yield. They favoured maize as a replacement of the traditional low-quality cereals. Once it had become part of agricultural agreements, the cultivation of maize no longer escaped land rents, and because of its high yields, it increased the landowner's income. Its high yield also made it possible to devote more land to cultivation for the market and less land for the subsistence of peasant families. Not infrequently, peasants attempted to oppose these changes, but without great success, particularly as the famines of the mid-eighteenth century left them with little choice.[182] In the Balkans, for example, maize started to be cultivated in fields following the food shortages in 1740–1. First it was used alongside and later it replaced the barley and millet traditionally used for oven-dried biscuits and porridge. The same thing occurred in various parts of northern Italy, where maize porridge (*polenta*) ended up becoming the staple in peasant diet. 'Maize porridge and ditch water': this was their diet according to a protest song from Galeata in Romagna. The Jacini Inquiry (1877–84) confirmed that the diet in many parts of Italy was based on maize and that, in the case of agricultural labourers, it really was restricted to *polenta* and water.[183]

The consequences of such a monotonous diet were not only boredom and a frustrated palate. It was in fact the cause of pellagra amongst the peasantry due to a shortage of vitamin PP. As this disease runs its course, it produces suppurating lesions, madness and death. First recorded in the Asturias in 1730, it was for a long time the scourge of the populations of southern France, the Po Valley and the Balkans.[184]

Potatoes

Given its greater similarity to known cereals, particularly millet, which had always been used for making porridges and other foods, maize provoked much less resistance and mistrust than the potato. Although initially grown in vegetable gardens and other types of gardens as an exotic and extravagant plant, this root vegetable from the Americas was regarded with suspicion for a long time, perhaps partly because of a continuing belief in a dietary hierarchy that associated things of an animal nature with plants that grew underground. Paradoxically, even those who promoted the potato sometimes ended up associating it with animal feed. Battarra wrote, 'Bread can be made from these roots, they can be cooked in various ways, and they are eaten voraciously by cattle, sheep, pigs, poultry, pigeons, etc., which therefore fatten greatly'.[185]

In this climate of suspicion, there were inevitably those who argued that 'white truffles', as they were sometimes initially referred to in Italy, caused flatulence. Some even claimed that they carried leprosy. In reality, badly selected potatoes of the early generations were occasionally a little toxic. It is no surprise then that potatoes, which had been discovered in Peru 1539, still provoked such an aversion in townships on the Elbe in 1781 that it was impossible to find servants willing to eat them. They would rather change their master than eat potatoes.[186]

Only when necessity drove them, particularly during the famine of 1770–2, did people increase the cultivation of this root crop to their considerable advantage. It almost guaranteed a harvest, even in fields that had been occupied for months by an army. Its yield was about twice that of wheat. In some areas it was not subject to tithes.

Potatoes were apparently imported into England in 1588. Given the role of famine in the expansion of the cultivation of potatoes, they unsurprisingly did not spread on English soil, but in Ireland which was poorer. In the eighteenth century, when they were staple for the population of the island, it has been calculated that the daily diet of an adult man was 5 kilos of potatoes and a pint of milk (providing about 3,850 calories), with the addition of a little oats and some peas.[187] It has to be asked whether people who were used to swallowing such substantial quantities of food had a different perception of hunger from us. Whatever the perception, many were to experience it in a dramatic fashion in the mid-nineteenth century, when a couple of bad harvests were sufficient to cause one of the most terrible demographic disasters in European history: the Irish potato famine.

Military conflicts also favoured the spread of the potato. In Alsace, which had suffered greatly from warfare, they started to grow potatoes in 1660. There is evidence of them being grown in Lorraine, where they became a staple in the peasant diet over the following century. They had a degree of success in Switzerland, Sweden and Flanders, where their spread was 'encouraged' by the War of the League of Augsburg (1688–97), the War of the Spanish Succession (1701–14) and the War of the Austrian Succession (1740–8), which coincided with the famine of 1740. In Germany, the potato was already grown in vegetable gardens in the early seventeenth century, but it mainly spread because of the Seven Years War (1756–63), the famine of 1770–2 and the War of the Bavarian Succession (1778–79). Frederick William I (1713–40) and Frederick the Great (1740–86) encouraged the spread of potato cultivation in Prussia through legislation. It was there that Parmentier 'discovered' the potato while a prisoner during the Seven Years War. He was to become one of its greatest advocates.

The central importance of bread in the popular diet meant that the American root was not used in the same way as by the American Indians, who dried it. It was thought of in terms of bread, and initially people attempted to make loaves and roles from it (Parmentier was also convinced that potatoes could be made into bread).[188] This is not in fact the case, and at the very most it can be mixed with flour. This was the way it was used in Alsace. According to one account from 1773, they made bread 'by mixing potato with oats and vetch'. It is difficult to imagine what it must have tasted like. 'It is tastier if it contains a third of wheat', is the writer's comment.[189]

Changes in the geography of food and the deteriorating diet

By the end of the eighteenth century, the geography of vegetable produce had been considerably changed from what it had been two or three centuries earlier. Of the many slightly contrived divisions that could be perceived in Europe, there was now one between the 'potato-eaters' of central and northern Europe and the '*polenta*-eaters' of southern and south-eastern Europe. Obviously there were borders areas, such as northern Italy, in which both products were used, while marked local and regional differences remained.[190]

The anonymous traveller in the Appenines of Emilia (whom we encountered before) describes Frignano as an area where 'meat is not eaten' and 'bread is made of chestnut [flour]'.[191] In mountainous parts of Mediterranean Europe, chestnuts were dried, boiled, ground into flour and used for making loaves, *ciacci* and porridge. They continued to be an important part of the diet, and were actually quite rich from a nutritional point of view.[192]

In Italy, Neapolitans, as well as other southerners, were ceasing to be eaters of bread, cabbage and meat, and were becoming pasta-eaters or *mangia-*

maccheroni, to use an epithet first applied to Sicilians, who had been producing dried pasta since the twelfth century (fresh pasta, on the other hand, had been known since antiquity). Pasta became an important part of the popular diet in the seventeenth century. This was not yet pasta with tomato sauce, as the sauce was not to appear until 1830. It was made in various shapes, generally with wheat flour and was eaten with grated cheese. It was therefore a rich and nutritional food compared with dishes prepared with produce originating from the other side of the Atlantic.[193]

Ultimately, the diet of the European populations deteriorated overall between the sixteenth and the eighteenth century. This was obviously not true of everyone, and the extent of the deterioration differed from one area to another. The trend, however, appears to be fairly clear and to unite the Venetian peasant obliged to follow a diet almost exclusively of maize and the early English factory workers whose diet of bread and sugared tea was to become common at the beginning of the nineteenth century.[194] Tea and sugar were two products whose consumption grew during the early modern era.

Sugar, tea, coffee, chocolate, and spirits

Sugar, which originated in India, had been known in the Middle Ages. Initially it had been used in making medicines, but from the sixteenth century it found its way to the dinner table as a luxury flavouring for any dish. The passion for sweet and sour declined during the seventeenth and eighteenth centuries.[195] During the early modern era the consumption of sugar increased as a result of the development of cane plantations worked by slaves, first in Sicily, the Balearics, Crete and Cyprus, and then in the New World.[196]

Tea, which originated in China, was introduced from India at the beginning of the seventeenth century. The first crates were offloaded in Amsterdam at the very beginning of the century. Consumption spread mainly in England, where it found favour first with the upper classes and then with the population at large. The fashion for coffee had arrived from Asia, and in the late seventeenth century it created new places and forms of social encounter (called cafés, appropriately enough). The vogue for cafés in London must have been a primarily male affair, given that women petitioned against them in 1674. But a century later in Germany, where men remained loyal to beer, it appears to have been a typically female drink.[197] In Italy, it became a drink accessible to everyone in the eighteenth and nineteenth centuries: 'even the most lowly workers want it in the morning', wrote Giuseppe Maria Galanti. 'They believe that it helps digestion. Thankfully for their nerves, the coffee sold in cheap stores has only one thing in common with coffee and that is its colour'.[198] Precisely because it was a stimulant, coffee became the symbol of bourgeois rationality and efficiency. In this it contrasted with chocolate (cocoa had been imported from America), which was mainly used by aristocrats, a little paradoxically to our eyes, as a drink to keep one's spirits up when fasting. As occurred with other new products, tea, cocoa and coffee were initially used for medicinal purposes and only later for gastronomic ones.[199]

It should however be pointed out that the distinction between a medicine and a food in the early modern era was different from today. There were at the time none of the chemical methods of modern pharmaceuticals. Diet therefore played a central role, and it was believed that food acted upon the person who ate it. Thus the choice and dosage of foods were considered crucial and capable of curing certain diseases or maintaining good health. The fact that tea, coffee and cocoa were initially used in a medical context during the early modern therefore means that their consumption was initially attributed with therapeutic properties that were later diminished or even forgotten. One of the characteristics of this period is the gradual severing of the links between gastronomy and dietetics.[200]

Before this process was completed, extraordinary therapeutic properties were initially attributed to aqua vitae, as implied by the name itself which means 'water of life'. This prototype for all spirits had a similar fate to that of sugar, tea, coffee and chocolate. From the eighteenth century, it slowly started to move from the alchemist's laboratory and the apothecary's workshop to the tavern and inn. It multiplied into rum, grappa, kornbrand, whisky, vodka, gin and distilled cider. It made it possible to produce liqueurs and rosolio. Initially these drinks were for the upper classes, but their spread contributed to an increase in the problem of alcoholism.[201]

7. Beer and wine

'Now to tell the truth we were such poor women', said Margarita De Magni in 1578, and she went on to assert that her niece Francesca De Caranti no longer 'drinks water'. She was responsible for her niece and was explaining under interrogation why she had allowed the girl to have an unlawful relationship with a man, from which she had drawn some material advantage. 'Did you want her to go stealing?' she asked, given that the need to avoid the complete destitution that involves drinking water was justification for her niece's behaviour and therefore for her agreement.[202] Sebastian Münster and Jouvin de Rochefort also looked on the fact that peasants drank only milk and water as a sign of complete penury.[203] Drinking ditch water was presented by the peasants of Galeata as a sign of their poverty, and a couple of centuries earlier the author of the

Itenerario wrote that the wine of Frignano was 'of the clear spring', or in other words, water.[204] Yet again social hierarchies were reflected in food and drink. The hierarchies of wealth corresponded to the hierarchies of drink.

The distinction was not only between alcoholic and non-alcoholic drinks. It also reflected the level of alcohol, or rather the wateriness, given that there was no way of measuring alcohol content at the time. The *mezzadri* of Tuscany, which was and still is an important wine-producing area, only drank wine on feast days or during periods of intense agricultural labour. The rest of the time, they made do with *acquerello* or *acquato*, a drink with a revealing name. It was made by putting the crushed grape residue from winemaking in a container with water, where it fermented. The operation was repeated two or even three times, until the water was only slightly coloured.[205] In cities, it is worth remembering that the rich kept *vino da famiglia* for their servants and this was of an inferior quality to the one they drank.[206]

Apart from the wateriness of the wine, other factors were at play in the evaluation of wines, such as their acidity and colour, and in some cases these rendered the association between lower social class and watery wine inapplicable. Upper-class tastes were not always and everywhere the same, and, indeed, until the seventeenth century red wine was considered a coarse drink suited to the lower classes.[207] 'The meat of cows, bulls and pigs, bread made from red corn, beans, cheese, olives, red wine and other coarse foods make the seed coarse and of bad temperament: the son that is generated [after having consumed these foods and drinks] will be very strong. But he will be wild and will have the wits of an animal', an author claimed by way of that circular logic between food and the quality of people that we have already noted.[208]

Whereas the poorest city-dwellers drank only water and mountain peasants opted for milk and water from the stream, the majority of the population drank alcoholic drinks of varying strengths. The most widespread alcoholic drinks were wine and beer. Wine was widely used in Mediterranean Europe, but was prized by the upper classes of the entire continent. Beer was the principal drink in northern and eastern Europe, but it was also drunk in the Iberian Peninsula. In France, it was considered a poor man's drink, and not unsurprisingly its consumption increased in periods of crisis. However, the geography of drink that has just been described was not static, and over a period of time there was probably a reduction in vine cultivation and wine consumption in the northern European countries, whereas beer became increasingly accepted, thanks in part to the increased use of hops, which preserved it for longer and made it more marketable. In eighteenth-century Paris, England and Holland (but not Germany), consumption fell because of competition from spirits.[209]

Although the data is not always consistent, many scholars agree that consumption was on average very high. Consumption of wine was rarely under a litre a day, and the figures for beer were even higher. It appears that every member of an English family in the seventeenth century, both adults and children, drank at least 3 litres of it a day. Even recipes for mashes to wean babies could have beer as an ingredient.[210] Such heavy consumption was justified by the need to supplement the calories in the diet. Wine provided more than a third of daily calories in the diet of Sicilian agricultural labourers in the late seventeenth century.[211] However, it was also linked to the difficulty in obtaining drinking water and the widely held view that water was bad for one's health.[212] There was also the need to make it easier to chew and swallow hard bread, and to eat particularly salty food. Ménétra recalled, 'the salted pork had produced its effect, and we had to wash it down. This was done in abundance'.[213]

Salt was used for preserving meat and fish, as well as for seasoning cereals and beans, which are in themselves rather tasteless. It is estimated that people consumed between 3.4 and 8.8 kilos per head per year, according to the region. Today the average is 2.2 kilos.[214] (There were however quite a few areas, particularly in the Alps, the Carpathians and the Pyrenees, where difficulties in finding a supply of salt led to deficiencies that cause illnesses like goitre).[215]

Beer and wine were not only drunk because of the thirst brought on by salted meat or because well water caused diarrhoea. People drank to obtain a state of euphoria and excitement necessary – like the waste on feast days – to fight off the insecurities, the fears and the trials of daily life. It kept away the spectre of hunger or hunger-induced stomach cramps. It helped one fantasize about the land of Cockaigne. For this purpose, there appears also to have been wide use during the early modern era of the seeds of the opium poppy and other hallucinogenic plants, often involuntarily eaten amongst ground cereals or vegetables in soup.[216]

8. The variety and monotony of food

Everyday food and food for feast days

Around 1250 someone might, a little optimistically, have thought that the problem of hunger had been overcome. Yet during the entire period of the early modern, it represented a central question in the life of the great majority of the people, whether they experienced it or lived in fear of it. Paradoxically, the greater variety of foods corresponded to greater monotony and less nutrition in the diet of the lower classes. Because of their high yields, maize and potatoes prevented many people from literally starving to death,[217] but they contributed to an overall deterioration in diet. Several studies seem to confirm that the average height of the population decreased between the sixteenth and the eighteenth century.[218]

It would be wrong to think that the popular and peasant diet in the early modern era was one of complete deprivation. In his *Journal*, Ménétra, who cared greatly for the pleasures of life, often recalled meals that were anything but contemptible or inferior. Indeed he even managed to arrange a pleasant one when he ended up in jail. Lovers and women friends 'often come and bring me delicious little meals, which we eat together', he commented.[219] Even those who were less fortunate or of a less pleasure-loving nature could encounter some enjoyments in their diet. There were feasts and moments of plenty: wedding banquets, religious holidays and harvest-time feasts. For example, Goethe informs us that Naples at Christmas was a veritable orgy of culinary delights.[220] Around 1640 in Yorkshire some note:

> It is usual, in most places, after they get all the pease pulled or the last grain down, to invite all the workfolks and their wives (that helped them that harvest) to supper, and then they have puddings, bacon, or boiled beef, flesh or apple pies, and the cream brought in platters, and every one a spoon; then after they all have hot cakes and ale; for they bake cakes and send for ale against that time: some will cut their cake and put it into the cream, and this feast is called cream-pot, or cream-kit.[221]

Even the daily diet was not necessarily marked by complete disregard for the palate. People knew of and used herbs and aromatic plants like garlic, onion, marjoram, mint, parsley, sage, rosemary, fennel, aniseed, coriander and juniper, which made even the poorest foods agreeable.[222] 'I did not find them at all bad, nor poorly cooked', said Jouvin de Rochefort of turnips offered to him by Tyrolean cowherds, almost marvelling that he had eaten them with such relish. Although lower-class women whose task it was to cook could do so with considerable skill, they obviously could not produce miracles when they had nothing to put in the pot or when the available food was not only in short supply but also unchanging with inherent risk of deficiencies and diseases. We cannot know how many of them tried and tried again to make bread from potatoes, experimenting with different mixtures and applying a great deal more brainpower to the problem than Monsieur Parmentier! However, the kitchen gardens in which new plants were initially tested were widespread in the countryside and, to a more limited extent, the city. They contained fruit, vegetables and herbs which made an important contribution to people's diet.

Soups (with the addition of a little butter, lard, dripping or oil, and possibly a little meat) were very common. They could be made with onions, beans, cabbage, potatoes, turnips and other vegetables, often mixed with cereals or hard bread. Turnips and cabbages were found throughout Europe. In central and northern Europe, where it was difficult to have fresh vegetables in winter, sauerkraut was indispensable. In Poland, however, the importation of vegetables for soup appears to be due to Bona Sforza d'Aragona (1494–1557), the wife of King Sigismund I Jagiello. In fact, the word used for such vegetables was *włoszczyzna*, from the Polish *Włochy* for Italy (since the nineteenth century the word has been used for vegetables in general). Cabbage, turnip, beetroot, peas and cauliflower were all imported from Italy. Known in Poland since the fourteenth century, these vegetables had names that partly derived from Italian, as did leeks, onions, asparagus, courgettes and salad (the latter was also probably introduced by Bona Sforza). Their increasing importance in the Polish diet was a gradual process. In the nineteenth century, the very poor only ate cabbage, peas, carrots and turnips.[223] While at the beginning of our period vegetables we would consider poor and dull were a rarity in Poland, there was no shortage of them in southern Europe. Salads, in particular, were ubiquitous and occasionally all there was to eat. According to one account, the diet of Tuscan peasants at the end of our period consisted of three meals: one was *bullie de blé de Turquie* and salad, another was bread and kidney beans or other boiled beans with a little oil, and the last one was soup. Only on Sundays did they get to eat a little meat.[224]

In Mediterranean Europe, olives, dried figs and fruit were also important. It seems that some Calabrian peasants lived through the winter on bread and figs.[225] In central and northern Europe, apples, pears and cherries were widely eaten. Not infrequently and particularly in Germany, they were dried in the oven to ensure they would keep. In winter they might even become a substitute for bread. It is significant that in some cases the spread of potatoes and maize led to a reduction in their consumption. Instead they were used in more sophisticated foods. They were turned into jams, especially in Poland, and in Germany they were cooked with lard or together with meat. General Luigi Ferdinando Marsili, who was captured by the Ottomans in 1683 and ended up the slave of two poor Bosnians, recorded that the 'greatest delicacy' in his masters' house was a dish 'called *ozaff* in Turkish', which was prepared by boiling plums, apples and peaches in water (the only other foods eaten by the family of four brothers with wives and numerous offspring, who lived in a wooden shack blackened by smoke, were 'just flat bread made from flour of millet or oats' and, during the entire winter Marsili spent in their house, a single smoked bullock 'mixed with cabbage' to go with the bread). Apart from fresh fuit, there were oily nuts, which in some areas were of considerable importance, because of their oils and calories: almonds, pistachio nuts, pine-seeds, hazelnuts and walnuts (from which oil was extracted).[226]

Apart from hunting and fishing, which were not infrequently unlawful activities, other important sources of nutrition originated in the byre and the yard. As with the kitchen garden, management of the yard was usually a female task. Peasants ate chickens and rabbits quite rarely, as these were generally kept for the landowner or sold. They made greater use of the eggs, although some of these would have gone to the market.[227] In many areas of mixed agriculture, the preparation of butter and cheese was also a female task. In England, for example, young women hoping to get married were expected to be skilled in these activities.[228] In other areas, the treatment of milk was considered a completely male task, even central in defining virility. The occupation of cheese-making was reserved for sexually mature men among the Basques of Sainte-Engrâce. Cheese-making and procreation were associated with each other symbolically and linguistically. It was believed that the male seed made the menses coagulate in the womb, thus creating the foetus, just as rennet coagulates milk to make cheese. Old men, who were no longer capable of having children, were not therefore allowed to go to the huts in the mountains to make cheese. They stayed at home with the women and children, with whom they became associated.[229]

9. Spinning by the fire as the bread cooks

Men at home

Treating milk was a woman's job in some areas and a man's job in others, but in houses of the rich, it was one of the many duties of the male kitchen staff. We have seen how the sexual division of domestic labour in relation to food differed according to social class. In the houses of the very rich, male servants often carried out the tasks that in a middle-class homes would be carried out by female servants and maids. We can therefore discard those tiresome prejudices that linked the sexual division of labour to supposed natural inclinations in men and women not only by 'searching for women' in public arenas, but also by looking into the domestic sphere and discovering the multitudes of men who made pastry and crushed spices in a mortar (Fig. 68).

Leaving aside the upper classes, how was the division of labour in the home organized? The example of Sainte-Engrâce shows that the division of labour altered according to the context. Within a particular area, it was fairly rigid, but not necessarily totally fixed. 'Let's make an agreement', said a Welsh woman to her husband at the end of the eighteenth century following a bad harvest that promised months of difficulties and hunger. 'I'll make a bargain with thee; I'll see to food for us both and the children all winter if thou, in addition to looking after the horse, the cattle and the pigs, wilt do the churning, wash up, make the beds and clean the house. I'll make the butter myself'. 'How wilt thou manage?' asked the husband and she replied, 'I will knit. We have wool. If thou wilt card it, I'll spin'. The man accepted the proposal and the family managed to survive until the following harvest.[230]

Domestic chores and woman's work

These words remind us how many and how hard a woman's jobs could be. There were many tasks relating just to the preparation of food. Of course, it was not time-consuming for those who could afford little other than bread bought from the baker's. But the situation was different for those women who had to cultivate their kitchen garden, feed the animals, look after the beehive, milk the cows, beat the cream in the churn to make butter in areas where it was used, collect firewood and water, keep the fire burning, make dough for bread, dry fruit, pickle vegetables, brew beer (in England),[231] make jams and, in northern, central and eastern Europe, ferment cabbage to make sauerkraut. At the same time, they not infrequently had to breastfeed or wean a baby and look after the older children. A painting by Pieter Gerritsz, which is probably fairly realistic, depicts a woman seated on a low stool in front of the fire busy preparing pancakes. There is a small child on her right and a small wicker basket on her left, from which a baby is peering (Fig. 69).

One historian has calculated how women divided their time, using the information contained in diaries and other similar sources. It is, of course, only a rough indication given that women did not do exactly the same things, depending on whether they lived in the city or the countryside, whether they were rich or poor, whether they were unmarried, married or widows, and whether they were young or old. In spite of this, the results are interesting and they give us a vivid picture of tireless women constantly at work. The study showed that in Great Britain the preparation of food required 3 or 4 hours a day, fetching water and firewood about an hour, and lighting the fire and feeding small children another hour, making a total of 6 or 7 hours. On top of that, there was the time employed in the kitchen garden (1 hour) and milking and looking after the animals (2–3 hours), making bread and beer (3 hours a week for each activity) and from time to time the making of preserves and similar foods.[232] But these activites relating to the preparation of food were obviously not all women had to do. Childcare took 3 hours a day, cleaning the house 2 hours, making clothes 2 hours, other activities concerning clothing 2 hours and washing clothes 4 hours.[233]

A woman's life consisted of a thousand tasks. In peasant families, a considerable part of female chores had nothing to do with the cleaning we now associate so strongly with domestic work, given the endless hours spent on milking cows, growing vegetables and giving food to the hens. Moreover, the boundary between housework and work outside the home was different to what it is today. The task of fetching water, which was usually left to women, involved going outside the house. The same could be said of washing clothes, although it is true that there were people who did this work professionally, and in this case men could be employed in some areas.[234] The search for fuel, which was not necessarily a female task, was also done outside the house. In this sense, the development of water and gas pipes has made a 'woman's work' more domestic than it was in the past.

Naturally, many women in the early modern era carried out work outside the home in the modern sense of the term,[235] but even those who did not were coping with hundreds of other activities. According to Vincenzo Tanara in 1644, a male cook was to be preferred to a female cook partly because the woman 'having placed the loaf on the fire, . . . would spin while the food was cooking'.[236] It is not hard to believe that this really was the case for many women. 'A woman's work is never done', went a seventeenth century English ballad.[237]

Having analysed what people ate and who prepared the food, we will now follow, like Ariadne's thread, the infinite fibres that women of the early modern era spun in order to make cloth and clothes for themselves, their families and the market.

VI

Clothing

1. Spinning, weaving, sewing and buying

Spinning and weaving

Women of the early modern era spun and spun and spun, as we are reminded by so many fairy tales, such as Rumpelstiltskin and Sleeping Beauty. In many regions the spindle and distaff were symbols of an honest and hardworking woman. Occasionally this was so much the case that they retained their symbolic value even amongst the opulence of aristocratic marriages and far from the pressures of everyday life.[1] Such significance was probably attributed to spinning because it could be done during the short intervals between one activity and another or even at the same time as other activities. The abandonment of this practice undoubtedly marked a profound change in the way women lived and was probably a significant moment in the creation of an awareness amongst women of their sexual identity.

In the early modern era, girls spun thread to produce their trousseaus, and once they were married, for the needs of their family. However they also produced yarn for the market during this period. Whereas men and women worked on the mechanized spinning of silk which developed very early in Bologna,[2] domestic spinning was an almost exclusively female activity,[3] and to a much greater extent than weaving. Weaving was also organized by merchants who provided workers with the necessary raw material at their homes, and both men and women were involved.[4] The traditional domestic production of yarn and cloth for private consumption must however be seen as the context in which proto-industrial production centred on the home developed.[5]

Production, recycling and purchase

Spinning and weaving were accompanied in the production of clothes and bed linen by the sewing of new items and the alteration of used ones. Old clothes were endlessly recycled, purchased at second-hand markets, received as presents, given as charity, inherited from employers, and occasionally stolen. Clothes were constantly circulating from one person to another, undergoing alteration all the time.[6] This activity affected the majority of society. In France one of the privileges of the noblewomen who served the queen was to get her cast-offs.[7] It was common practice at all levels of society for servants to be given their master's and mistress's old clothes. It was one of their perks to be able to wear them after alterations or to sell them on. The trade in second-hand clothes played an important role in a situation in which the mass production of items of clothing had not yet been achieved. Stalls, street-markets and other outlets selling cast-off clothes were to be found in central areas of many cities, for instance the streets around Piazza Navona in Rome.[8]

'The deceased's clothes and linen have partly been disposed by being made available to the sons and partly by being sold for the purpose of having prayers to God on behalf of the deceased', declared the widow of Pierre Richandeau, a ribbon manufacturer in eighteenth-century Paris.[9] Like her, many would sell the clothes of a departed relation, not uncommonly to pay for expenses arising from the final illness or for the funeral rites. The costs incurred by a sick relation could be enough to force a family to sell or pawn their clothes.[10] An item of clothing, like any other object, could be used as a store of wealth to be made use of in difficult times. 'People pawn their short cape, cloak, sheet or wife's ring, and others sell their bedstead, coat, socks, benches, boxes, chairs and sideboard. Rent is a terrible thing', wrote Giulio Cesare Croce in *Il lamento de' poveretti i quali stanno a casa a pigione, e la convengono pagare* (*The Lament of the Poor People who Pay Rent for their Home, and they Better had Pay it*).[11]

Thus second-hand dealers received a constant flow of clothing left by dead people, sold to pay debts, stolen or discarded by the rich. The fact that employers often gave their clothes to their servants did not mean that clothes were not altered and recycled in families of higher rank, if we are to go by what happened in the Odescalchi household in Como in 1570s or in the home of Baron and Baroness Schomberg in late eighteenth-century Paris.[12]

Naturally people made use of cloth sellers and tailors in both the city and the countryside. As far as the rural world was concerned, studies in England have shown the increasing number of pedlars from as far back as the seventeenth century. They took small books, ribbons, cheap tobacco and cloth for making sheets, curtains, shirts and underwear to the remotest parts of the country. The people of picturesque but poor and far-off Penrith could buy Holland cloth, percale, calico, Indian muslin, silk cloth, linen, tartan, gloves, muffs, ribbons and other decorative elements from Roland Johnson, who died in 1683.[13] Apart from pedlars, there were itinerant tailors in more or less the whole of Europe who went from one house to another and stayed there until they had made up clothes for all the family.[14]

In other words, domestic production of both cloth and clothing for private consumption remained an important feature throughout the period we are examining, although its hegemony was being increasingly challenged by the development of the textile industry, professional tailoring and the retail of cloth and garments. These phenomena are distinct, each with it own chronology, but they were not unrelated.

'A network of monetary transactions was interwoven around textiles', one historian has noted. As this implied the sale of part of the agricultural produce in order to obtain the cash for such transactions, 'a breach was opened up within the subsistence economy through which monetary relations were able to penetrate', partly and perhaps mainly because of textile products.[15]

Falling prices and increasing supply

Unsurprisingly then, both consumption and transactions by peasants were on the increase in Tuscany. The stock of clothes and linen in the trunks and wardrobes of each home tended to expand. As has already been mentioned, the number of sheets owned by each family in the eighteenth century doubled in relation to two centuries earlier, and even shirts and clothes were probably more numerous. It should not be forgotten that the increasing population and the relative stability in agricultural technology up until the end of the eighteenth century led to a sharp increase in the price of corn, and the innovations that caused greater productivity in the manufacturing sector during the seventeenth and eighteenth centuries led to a fall in the relative price of textile products. If the price of corn and the price of textiles in 1565–74 are both set at 100, then for 1774–83 the figures are 223 and 75. Over two centuries the cost of textiles had been constantly falling. Thus peasants could afford to sell corn, whose price was rising over the long period, to buy cloth, whose relative price was falling.[16]

The available data suggests that similar trends were occurring elsewhere in Europe. In England, the prices of textile products remained stable or even fell in spite of the very high inflation from the second half of the sixteenth century. In other words, costs were already falling before industrialization began. It was a considerable fall, which was comparable in relative size with the price drop during the first half of the nineteenth century. Historians believe the price fell because of the adoption of the spinning wheel, the use of smaller quantities of thread or thread of poorer quality, the development of proto-industrial processes, increased competition from lighter and cheaper fabrics produced elsewhere in Europe or in Asia, the greater use of textile workers, poor relief paid out by communities which made it possible to offer very low wages and better distribution. However, historical opinion differs on how much emphasis should be attributed to each element.[17] Whatever their relative importance, the fact is that during the eighteenth century important innovations in technology and the organization of labour led to rapid industrialization.[18] In light of the falling price of textiles, at least in relative terms, in various Europeans regions, such as Tuscany, England and eighteenth-century Poland, it will be no surprise that research has shown that people owned much larger quantities of clothes and linen. It became possible to buy more items without spending more. This was very important in a society in which the lower classes spent between 60 and 80 per cent of their income on food (today the figure for western countries is between 20 and 33 per cent, a percentage not dissimilar to the one that has been calculated for the aristocracy in the *Ancien Régime*).[19]

Yet the lower relative cost of clothes and fabrics does not on its own explain the larger wardrobes. Studies of the situation in Paris show that the value of clothing in the average family during the eighteenth century grew, even if measured in terms of corn. By selling a dead man's clothes at the beginning of the century, it was possible on average to buy 128.3 *setiers* of corn, while around 1789 it would have been possible to buy 324.[20] The value of clothes as a percentage of moveable goods owned by wage-earners increased from 5 to 10 per cent, and from 10 to 25 per cent in the case of domestic servants.[21] Apart from the skirts and *culottes* in their wardrobes,[22] there were increasing quantities of underwear, handkerchiefs and other secondary items, which increased fourfold in the case of men and fivefold in the case of women.[23]

2. Underwear and hygiene

The war against baths

The greater use of underwear was a result of concepts of hygiene that started to appear in the sixteenth century. Up until then, the ancient system of Roman baths had continued to exist. Baths were associated with cleanliness and pleasure. Bathhouses were frequented by both men and women, 'without anyone committing dishonest acts',[24] until the fourteenth century, after which there was an increasingly rigid segregation between the sexes or women used the baths on certain days of the week and men on others. There were also baths in which the habitués found not only steam, hot water, tubs and baths, but also food, drink, beds and young women of easy virtues. It seems that this second type of bathhouse had become increasingly successful during the Middle Ages.

After the plague of 1348, people started to believe that public baths were places that could assist the spread of disease, and they were discouraged from visiting them during epidemics. However, the advice does not appear to have been followed very much. The spread of syphilis, which infected an enormous number of people after the discovery of America, appears initially to have led to the sick being kept away from the baths, rather than bathhouses being closed. In the sixteenth century, the determination to fight disease and the fear of contagion meant that attitudes to baths became more hostile, and the sex phobia of the Reformation and the Counter-Reformation reinforced this trend. The time was up for these ancient institutions, the great majority of which were closed in western Europe. Water was banned.[25]

It began to be thought that a bath was dangerous. Pores dilate when in contact with steam or water, particularly hot water. It thus became easier for pathogens to penetrate the body and humours to leave, provoking a dangerous debilitation. Only hands and the mouth continued to be washed with water, which was often mixed with vinegar, alcohol or wine. A bath eventually came to be considered possible only as a therapy for certain pathologies, and even then only with a mass of precautions.[26] It seems that Louis XIV only had one bath in the period between 1647 and 1711, and then only for therapeutic reasons.[27] Baths for newborn babies were also advised for therapeutic reasons, in the wider sense of the term. But after that water was banned for babies. At least until the eighteenth century, infants were wrapped in swaddling two or three times a day. Doctors advised that the swaddling should be greased with rose or bilberry oil or that the child should be sprinkled with various kinds of powder used for blocking the pores of the skin. This was supposed to make the body less permeable and therefore more resistant to disease.[28]

Thus a 'dry' concept of hygiene developed, which was to last at least until the 1760s, when the enlightened upper classes were affected by a mania for bathing and more especially for cold baths, which were supposed to invigorate and strengthen the body (rather than clean it). These were the circumstances in which bathrooms and baths began to become more common. However, they spread slowly. By 1750 only 6 per cent of private buildings were equipped with a bathroom. Although a bathroom became more common in houses built between 1770 and 1800, it was still fairly rare, given that two thirds of them still lacked one.[29] It was certainly true that baths and tubs were more common, but practical difficulties as well as traditional perceptions stood in the way of change.

Absorbent underwear

The traditional perception was in fact based on a kind of dry cleaning. The disappearance of the bath in the sixteenth and seventeenth centuries did not mean that people were less concerned with cleanliness. It was simply that cleanliness was no longer associated with immersing the body in water and ablutions, but rather with wiping off sweat, rubbing the skin with clean and perfumed cloths, and sprinkling it with sweet-smelling powders.

Underwear played a fundamental role in this system. It was believed that it absorbed dirt and the impurities of the skin. To remove dirt from the body, it was thought that you had to change your clothes often. Thus it would be possible to avoid or at least reduce the probability of it attracting fleas and lice as it degenerated. This in turn was based on the belief that parasites were created out of the decomposition of bodily secretions, so it was also possible to restrict them by modifying the composition of sweat through a proper diet.[30] Hence it was argued that the cells of Carthusian monks were not teeming with bugs like those of their servants, because the monks did not eat meat.[31] In reality, however, people were afflicted by parasites during the early modern era, as in reports of children delousing themselves like swarms of locusts on every street corner in Bristol towards the end of the seventeenth century.[32] Delousing children and removing their fleas was therefore one of every good mother's chores.[33] Though in an era in which bleeding and the application of leeches were widely used therapies, there were plenty of people who considered parasites useful for one's health.[34]

The important role attributed to underwear as opposed to baths clearly emerges from the words of Savot in his 1626 treatise on the construction of castles and great houses: 'The use of underwear . . . today allows us to keep our bodies clean much more conveniently than the ancients did with baths'. In those times, underwear was unknown, and they had to wash themselves to keep clean. But by [his more enlightened times] it was 'more convenient' to do without.[35] Given the role attributed to underwear in keeping the body clean, it inevitably became much more widely used.

Concerning the origins of underwear, the Roman world had an 'inner tunic' (i.e. a tunic that was worn under other clothes) and the Lombards probably wore one too.[36] It was, however, in the thirteenth century that a clear distinction started to be made between the lighter garments next to the skin and the heavier garments that covered them.[37] Originally underwear was hidden under other clothes, but in the fifteenth and sixteenth centuries it started to peep out around the collar and the cuffs with strips of cloth (called *lattughe* in Italy). It was puffed up at the fastenings between the shoulder and the sleeves (often detachable in that period). Its whiteness was displayed in the vents that appeared in clothes to let the undergarments be seen. Its whiteness was thus a *visible* indicator of the cleanliness of the person who wore it. Not surprisingly then, collars and cuffs became very elaborate during the sixteenth and seventeenth centuries, and changed out of all recognition into a kind of showcase of the wearer's cleanliness, but inevitably also of wealth and sophistication, given the lace, needlepoint and frills. 'They want it to be known that they have a most elegant linen shirt', Arcangela Tarabotti, who had become a nun against her will, acutely remarked of those who let their undergarments protrude.[38]

Once the connection had been established between personal cleanliness and the whiteness of underwear that could be seen by others, it became possible to manipulate appearances. Collars and cuffs became detachable, and could therefore be washed separately from other undergarments that were hidden by clothes. In other words, they said very little about the 'inner' cleanliness of the person who wore them.[39] Although our ancestors' concepts of hygiene in relation to the use of underwear were closely linked to health concerns, cleanliness was for a long time a primarily social question, a matter of good upbringing and decency.[40]

For this reason, it was barred to the lower classes. To the extent that cleanliness was equated with white underwear, being clean became a privilege of those who could afford a certain number of items to change into or, at least, to clean often what little they had. But not everyone was able to do this. First of all, underwear was expensive, particularly the whitest kind, which was made of high-quality linen and prohibitively priced. In France in 1610, Isabeau de Tournon's shirts were worth 8 francs each. A labourer had to work for about two weeks to earn such a sum. If he managed to put a little money aside, he would therefore have to be happy with a canvas shirt, which would often be yellowish and cost about 2 francs in the mid-seventeenth century, the equivalent of about three or four days' work.[41] Judging from post-mortem inventories not everyone in a city like Paris owned one at the beginning of the eighteenth century.[42] For many people it was not easy to whiten their yellowish underwear, as constant washing ruined it.[43] Those who had only one shirt could hardly go without when it was cold, in order to wash and dry it.

Washing clothes

In a society in which cleaning primarily consisted of changing one's underwear, washing clothes was an important part of hygiene. Washing clothes, as has already been mentioned, was the task of either the women in the home or professional washerwomen and washermen. In any event, it was hard and tiring work that required time and energy. It was often done outside the home, at a fountain or along a watercourse. There were various techniques for washing and removing stains. The latter was done with ammonia, oils and bran. Lemon juice, alum and Troyes stone were used for removing ink stains. Stains on white military uniforms were eliminated by covering them with white lead.[44]

As far as the method of washing was concerned, soap was a costly product right up until the end of our period. In England, it was used on a large scale only in the second half of the eighteenth century. Instead of soap, they used lye which is made of chimney soot (if wood is burnt in the fire) or urine which, in spite of its repellence to us, was capable of removing grease because of the ammonia it contained. They even used dung dissolved in water or urine (obviously it was removed through considerable rinsing, once it had been used).

Apart from being soaked in such mixtures, washing was also freed from dirt by being rubbed and above all beaten. In Ireland, however, women used to climb into a tub in bare feet and stamp on the clothes as though they were treading grapes in a vat. The frequency of washing was subject to many variables, such as the availability of time, the availability of water and the number of spare clothes.[45]

Changing underpants and changing shirts

In 1777, a priest wrote charitably 'you could not overstate the discomfort of the filth, smell, deprivation and squalor when the poor people are obliged to wear the same underpants for month after month'.[46] The inability to change underwear appeared to him to be one of the distinguishing features of poverty. This is further confirmation of the socially determined nature of cleanliness in the early modern era, even at this late stage. There were those who could afford clean and perfumed underwear and there were those who were condemned to filth and stench. Even the rich, however, did not change their underpants very often, unlike their shirts. Before his marriage the Baron of Schomberg changed his shirt and collar every day, his handkerchief every two days, and his underpants every four weeks (after his marriage he started to change them every week). His behaviour does not appear to have been particularly eccentric, given that he was following the instructions of handbooks on etiquette.[47]

Even towards the end of the eighteenth century, many people did not own a pair of underpants,[48] in spite of the fact that it was an ancient garment, known to the Lombards and the Franks.[49] In Italy, the first record of the term, which in Latin refers to the fact they were to be changed, is to be found in a will of 1268, in which they are listed as *mutandas de lino*.[50]

Medieval documentation shows that underpants were mainly a male prerogative, perhaps partly because they were confused with breeches.[51] Women wore them in Italy, at least, from the fourteenth century.[52] From the sixteenth century, their use was encouraged by the increasing use of systems to puff clothes out, including garments to keep a skirt away from the legs or what we would now call an underskirt or rigid petticoat.[53] In France, it appears that women's underpants were introduced by Catherine de' Medici, who put them on to be able to ride without offending against the rules of decorum. Many people approved of them because they protected private parts from indiscreet glances in the event of women falling and also 'from dissolute young men who push their hands under a woman's clothes'. But others condemned them, because they considered them an encroachment of male clothing and a breach of the Church laws against wearing clothes of the other sex.[54] On the whole, they had difficulty in catching on amongst women. As many as sixteen pairs of linen underpants and one pair of woollen ones were to be found in the inventory of the wealthy Venetian courtesan Giulia Leoncini and her sister Angelica, which was drawn up in 1569. But lower-class women during the early modern era rarely used them: when describing the actions of their attackers in trials for sexual violence, women who had been raped would generally say 'he lifted my clothes' (and not 'he pulled down my underpants'). 'I have seen it; it is as red as a rose; hers is black and white as snow', shouted Domenico Righi, according to many witnesses, in relation to the genitalia of Laura Fabbri, the girl for whom he felt a perverse passion that was not reciprocated. On the evening of 30 April 1630, he hid under the wooden stairway in the girl's home in the mountain township of Villa d'Aiano so that he could see Laura's 'shameful parts' under her skirt. Evidently he knew that they were not protected by underpants. In the German village of Neckarhausen in 1769, Andreas Köpple went further: he came home drunk and found Barbara Häfner sitting on the stairs and intent upon working on her linen. She lived in the same house with her husband, and Andreas lived with his wife. He pushed his hand under her skirt and his finger into her vagina. Barbara, who reacted to this brutal and violent approach by screaming that he should leave her alone, was also clearly not wearing underpants.

Higher up the social scale, the situation appears to have been contradictory. One study shows that this item of clothing was widely used by middle and upper-class women in the city of Split during the second half of the eighteenth century. A female historian has argued that trousseaus in Italy in the second quarter of the eighteenth century almost always included underpants. However, a massive study of the French capital has revealed a different reality.[55] At the beginning of the eighteenth century, they were to be found in only 3.5 per cent of the inventories of Parisian noblewomen, in 1.6 per cent of those of the city's female domestic servants and wives and daughters of officials, and in none of those of female wage-earners. Only artisans and shopkeepers had more (12%). They were in fact considered a garment for men chasers, actresses and prostitutes.[56] By the end of the century, they were more widespread, but still fairly rare (they were to be found in 7.2 per cent of the inventories of aristocratic women, 6.6 per cent of those of the wives and daughters of officials, and 2.6 per cent of those of female domestic servants, but were completely absent in the rest of the population).[57]

The main form of underwear at the time was the shirt rather than pants, as will have already been guessed. This ancient garment only became widely used in the Italian countryside in the fifteenth century, although it had been used since the thirteenth century and had occasionally been the only item of clothing that people owned. By the sixteenth century, according to Benedetto Varchi, Tuscan peasants changed it once a week on Sundays. However, it was not always worn under other garments. Especially in the summer, peasants wore only a hat and a shirt, which was more of a long smock with slits on the back and both sides up to the middle thigh and no collar.[58]

At this time, shirts were still very rare in the French countryside.[59] At court, however, they were very widely used and appear to have been changed nearly every day.[60] In other circles, they were not changed so often, but there was a tendency to do so quite frequently. By the end of the sixteenth century, educational institutions were advising that shirts should be changed every month, and a century later many colleges had fortnightly changes.[61] It should come as no surprise then that there were plenty of shirts in the wardrobes of Parisian domestic servants, whose life style was influenced by the life style of their employers. Inventories show that between 1700 and 1715, at least 88 per cent of female servants owned one and many had several dozen. Male servants had an average of 10 each, and as many as 25 during the period 1775 to 1790. But not everyone was so well provided for. In Paris itself, considered the European city with the greatest amount of underwear, many wage-earners went down to the Seine to wash their only shirt on a Sunday. By the end of the century of Enlightenment, it appears to have become the habit to change one's shirt every week or fortnight, at least in the warmer months, even if you only possessed a single shirt.[62]

In the Sardinian countryside, not changing your shirt for a year was a sign of mourning. One historian argues that this demonstrates that shirts were used and not changing it was a sacrifice.[63] But it also demonstrates that wearing the same garment for a year was nevertheless an acceptable practice, both for the mourner and for anyone who had to come close and put up with the smell. During the same period in England, it was even the custom to cover children with grease and sew their clothes onto them, so that they would always be covered and would not catch cold.

3. Protection and making oneself attractive

Cold and the plague

Protection from the cold is one of the functions of clothing. There are generally thought to be three functions: protection from the elements, concealment of parts of the body considered to be shameful, and decoration. This triad is referred to in German by the alliteration *Schutz, Scham* and *Schmuck*, which mean precisely protection, modesty and ornament, and we could add to these the functions of sending out messages and stressing identity and difference, as we shall see in the following pages. As clothes had to protect against the rigours of the climate, it will come as no surprise that in the badly heated Europe of the early modern era which suffered the cold winters of a small ice age that lasted from the late sixteenth century to the nineteenth century,[65] our ancestors' clothes were often made from heavy fabrics and occasionally lined with fur, particularly in the colder regions. Garments could also be worn one on top of the other, in a series of insulating layers.[66]

But in a time when the body was increasingly perceived as a threatened place and victim of external aggressions and horrible diseases that infected it by penetrating its pores and orifices, clothing was engaged in another form of defensive action: it constituted a body armour against plague and disease. The ruffs and crimped collars that dominated the second half of the sixteenth century and much of the seventeenth were used to lock up the body in a kind of protective shell.[67] When the plague was raging, there was even a specific garment that protected against contagion by forcing the pestiferous exhalations to slip away without causing damage. An author advised that during epidemics 'you must wear clothes made of satin, taffeta, moiré's silk and suchlike, which do not have hairs and are so smooth and tightly-woven that only with great difficulty could unwholesome air or any other infection penetrate or attach themselves to them, particularly if they are changed often'.[68]

The types of clothing and the ideas that surrounded them suggest an anxious society that felt itself under attack from mysterious agents carrying disease and that had to defend itself as best it could. It is perhaps no coincidence that the introduction of lighter clothes and the resumption of taking baths occurred after the disappearance of the plague from the European continent. The plague was still raging in 1709–12 in the Balkans, Austria, Bohemia, eastern Europe and the Baltic, and it struck Provence in 1720–22 and Messina and Reggio Calabria in 1743. It continued to ravage eastern Europe and the Balkans into the nineteenth century. But most of western Europe had been freed of it by 1670.[69]

Changes in clothing

Clothes became lighter, airy and colourful during the eighteenth century. Obviously the development of the textile industry and entrepreneurial speculations played a primary role in these changes. Perhaps improvements in the methods of heating also played a part. Whatever the case, studies into eighteenth-century Paris show that men's clothing, in which heavy fabrics continued to predominate, light woollen cloth, like flannel, or cotton fabric like nankeen, were becoming popular for jackets and waistcoats. Dark colours continued to be widely used, but their supremacy started to be challenged by blues, yellows, greens, pinks, stripes and checks. 'The man of the people was breathing the air of fashion', one historian has commented.

Of course the cuts were changing as well as the fabrics and colours. Apart from underwear, the main garments for wage-earners and domestic servants in the seventeenth and eighteenth centuries were the jacket, the *culotte* (breeches or knee-length trousers) and the jerkin (a long surcoat). These garments were found in 65 per cent, 80 per cent and 95 per cent of inventories respectively. The more fortunate also owned a cloak, which was listed by notaries in 27 per cent of cases. Some people had a coat, and many had a hat.

The situation was very different by the period 1775 to 1790. There were suits, with matching jackets and breeches, in 84 per cent of the inventories. The waistcoat replaced the jerkin. The *redingote*, a tight-fitting overcoat with an accentuated waist which nobles had adopted at the beginning of the century, was now found in lower-class wardrobes and competed with cloaks and coats. Judging from inventories, trousers were uncommon and during the Revolution they gave their name to the *sans-culottes*, which literally means without breeches. In other words, they wore long trousers rather than the knee-length breeches that during the years of revolution came to be seen as a symbol of the hated *Ancien Régime*.

By this stage, almost everyone had a hat on their head and shoes on their feet. While at the turn of the eighteenth century, shoes were only listed in 37 per cent of inventories, the figure was now 75 per cent. There were probably more people with shoes, particularly in the earlier period, as the dead may well have been buried with their shoes on, and so those who had just one pair of shoes took them to their grave. It cannot be ruled out that such a costly item disappeared before the notary registered them in the inventory. Inventories are a fertile source, but should be treated with due caution, especially in relation to items of clothing. They make it possible to identify changes in fabrics, styles and colours with some precision, but they are not as reliable when it comes to changes in quantities. Nevertheless, the increase in available items recorded by inventories is unarguable and quite significant: 'in cases where the notary recorded two in 1700, there were [now] three or four'.[70]

As far as footwear is concerned, Parisians appear to have been considerably better off than Tuscan peasants. A study into the property of sixty families in the Pisan countryside in the sixteenth century shows that together they only had fourteen pairs of shoes, which means they were owned by 4 per cent of the population. In eighteenth-century Tuscany, there were generally twenty pairs for every fifty families, and these were large and complex families. The great majority of people wore clogs or went barefoot.

In this period, Tuscan peasants, whose clothing had not undergone substantial changes between the sixteenth and the eighteenth century, wore woollen or occasionally linen or fustian trousers, as well as their shirt and hat. The trousers were rather baggy and generally *ammezzati* or just below the knee. (Having worn them full length in the sixteenth century, when loose leggings replaced tights, Tuscan peasants resumed this style in the early nineteenth century.) They wore socks to protect their calves. Over their shirt they wore a short waistcoat called a *camiciola, camiciotto* or *corpetto* and, in winter, a short jacket (*giubbone*), which was occasionally padded with raw cotton, or a cassock, which was longer and had tails. A hat made of straw or felt was almost universal, and for the coldest months the more fortunate covered themselves with heavy cloaks (*tabarri*) with hoods, short cloaks (*ferraioli*), long cloaks (*zimarre*) sometimes lined with fur, another kind of long cloak (*palandrana*), and yet other types of cloak.[71]

In the sixteenth century, Montaigne had found Tuscan peasant women 'very beautiful'. In the eighteenth century, another French traveller, Lalande, judged them to be very pretty. 'They wear', he said, 'simple skirts, which are short, light and usually blue or scarlet, and bodices without sleeves, so that all you see of their shirts is their sleeves. Around the shoulders of the bodice there are a great number of different-coloured ribbons that they let drop and flap in the wind'. Apart from the skirt, shirt and bodice, they also wore an apron that from the eighteenth century was increasingly made of Indian linen. On their heads they wore straw hats, bonnets or *sciugatoi*, which were shawls that could be worn on the head, around the neck or on the shoulders. As well as the traditional garments, the eighteenth century witnessed the spread of *andrienne*, which were low-necked dresses tight-fitting around the bust, *fisciù*, which were lace shawls for wearing around the neck, and silk garments which had once been the reserve of upper and middle-class city-dwellers. Analysis of contemporary inventories and legal judgements demonstrates that there was no lack of concern for external appearance, in spite of poverty. Women, in particular, not infrequently had some more sought-after garment to be worn on Sundays or at weddings.[72] Recent studies clearly show the importance – even among the lower-middle sections of the *Ancien Régime* and the eighteenth century in particular – of 'appearance' in maintaining one's respectability,[73] almost as though the growth in the availability of goods made it more necessary than in the past to exploit their potential in social relations. We should recall here the previously mentioned old peasant women who said she would prefer to be cuckolded than fail to provide her daughter with a proper trousseau.[74]

Whereas the clothing of Tuscan peasant women during the eighteenth century involved a few innovations and embellishments, the Parisian women's way of dressing appears to have undergone a veritable revolution. At the turn of the eighteenth century, it was made up of a skirt, occasionally accompanied by one or more petticoats, a shirt, an apron, a cloak and a bonnet or some other protection for the head. Like the peasant women's, it was divided in two at the waist, according to a custom that had established itself in the sixteenth century.[75] At the beginning of the eighteenth century, less than half the inventories for lower-class women recorded bodices or corsets. Their bodies were therefore fairly loose, unlike the rich women who were squeezed into their corsets.[76] Although they all had tights, the inventories suggest that those who owned a pair of shoes were in the minority. Clothes were mainly of wool, and underwear and aprons of linen or canvas. Cotton was still rare and, among the lower classes, silk was also rare, although it was worn by both men and women in the more affluent sections of society. Colours were dark: black, grey and brown. Black was also the most widely used colour amongst noblewomen, gentlemen and, to an even greater degree, the bourgeoisie. In Paris at the turn of the eighteenth century, the rich made themselves distinctive principally through their many white garments.

During the eighteenth century, dresses became more popular and corsets more widely used. Blouses, small jackets and short cloaks made an appearance. Lace shawls and other decorative garments replaced the old neckerchief. Wool gave ground to cotton, and silk became more common. All women were wearing shoes. They started to wear colours such as blue, yellow, green, white and a whole range of lighter shades. While bourgeois men and women continued to prefer the black and white contrast, the lower classes, like the nobility, were wearing clothing that was more cheerful and lively.[77]

4. The monopoly of colours

The country, being more traditionalist, was generally more closely tied to dark and lifeless colours. But during the eighteenth century, even peasants adopted more colourful garments than in the past. Blue became particularly popular in rural areas. For a long time, however, colours, or at least *some* colours, were restricted to a privileged few, or at least that was the law. In Württemberg, for example, green was the prerogative of the court and ducal hunters, and was therefore prohibited for all other men. They conformed with the letter of the law, in as much as they did not wear clothes of that colour, as stated in the legislation. But they broke the spirit of the law by demonstrating their independence and wearing green berets.[78]

In Bologna, only nobles could dress their servants in liveries of more than one colour or with silver braid and ribbons.[79] A servant who was found dead in December of 1740 was 'dressed in a heavy cloak of an iron-grey colour with yellow edging, jerkin of green cloth, matching shirt, barracan trousers of a grey colour, socks of yellow *cavadino*, undersocks of white thread, waistcoat of red wool, belt with leather fringes . . . calf leather shoes with brass buckle . . . black felt hat with black cord, ribbon of yellow tape in aforementioned jerkin above the right shoulder'.[80] This veritable walking rainbow was probably not wearing the colours of his master's coat of arms, as was often the case.

Colours were not alone in being subject to the legislation on luxuries in many European countries (but not the Netherlands, while in Switzerland, Germany, France and Italy they remained in force for a long time; the last edict on clothing in Rome was as late as 1824).[81] Styles, fabrics, materials and decorations were also subject to regulation. In Württemberg the clothing ordinances were renewed from 1549 to 1712.[82] In 1712 the lower strata of society were prevented from wearing clothes made from imported cloth. The ban was more rigid for peasants and somewhat less so for the urban working class, which was however prohibited from wearing Indian cloth. Only the upper classes could wear clothes in the French style.[83] Whereas 'typical' regional dress was a mainly nineteenth-century phenomenon, belonging to a national community was expressed through styles of clothing that the dominant powers tended to export over wide areas, at least amongst the upper classes. In the sixteenth century, the Italian fashion for crimson velvets and gold decorations gave way to the darker and more austere Spanish style. From the seventeenth century, French fashion was dominant and this was a little more colourful. By the end of the century it had started to change much more rapidly than in the past.[84]

The laws on luxury goods in Württemberg were concerned with both protecting local industries from competition and establishing barriers between one class and another in their dress. This was a typical element in this kind of legislation during the early modern era. The laws on luxury goods, which had been created in the Italian medieval communes as weapons in the city's struggle against aristocratic privilege, ended up in the early modern era as a means for maintaining barriers between social groups, paralysing society and preventing social mobility. As with food or perhaps even to a greater extent, the laws regulating clothing were aimed at protecting the privileged from imitation by other classes. In other words, this was an attempt to impose an idiom made up of fabrics, styles and colour to identify the elites with the backing of legislation. While they were not always heeded, the laws on luxury goods demonstrate that clothing was perceived in terms of expressing and displaying social distinctions.[85] In Bologna, for example (but there were innumerable other cases), it was established in 1749 that those who were not aristocrats could not 'own coaches or other carriages with gold, whether real or false; nor [could] they have servants in livery or use bags, and the women cannot use women's umbrellas' and could not use 'either gold or silver, whether real or false, in their clothing and garments'.[86]

5. Clothes that categorized people

Jews, prostitutes beggars and lepers

Recalling his stay in Carpentras, the glazier Ménétra wrote in his autobiography, 'one day, three or four of us were in the country, and we met a Jew without his yellow hat who was carrying two nice plump hens. We took the hens off him and ate them. He reported us to the magistrates . . . but he lost his case because he was not wearing his yellow hat'. In the Comtat Venaissin (Carpentras) 'poor Jews cannot go out without a yellow hat and their wives without a yellow ribbon on their bonnets'. A distinguishing mark was first imposed on Jews during the Fourth Latern Council (1215), although it did not specify what it was to be. In 1227 Pope Honorius III established that it had to be a circular or wheel symbol made of cloth and the Councils of Ravenna in 1311 and 1317 specified that it had to be yellow. In 1360, however, Innocent VI made it obligatory to wear a red beret, and then in 1425 Benedict XIII reintroduced the wheel symbol but this time coloured yellow and red. Later they reverted to yellow (1458). From the thirteenth century, however, city authorities started to introduce distinguishing marks and to run riot with the imposition of circles, wheels, veils, ribbons, earrings and stars, so there was no longer a standard symbol that was used everywhere. There was, however, a vast range of identifying elements that all had the purpose of making the 'diversity' of the Jews visible. The imposition of distinguishing marks on Jews was at least in part a reaction to the tendency since the early Middle Ages for some Jews to assimilate the customs and practices of the society in which they lived. Traditionally, Jews were easily distinguishable from their religious customs, such as wearing a beard and keeping their heads covered. In some cases, an original element in Jewish culture was transformed into a distinguishing mark that was imposed from outside. This was the case of the pointed hat that Jews were forced to wear in many German cities and which was adopted in the Italian cities of Venezia, Verona and Asolo.[87]

Jews were not alone in having to wear a badge to reveal the stigmatization to which they were subjected. Prostitutes underwent similar treatment, and in some cases were distinguished by yellow accessories, which then created confusion between prostitutes and Jewish women, as occurred in Bologna following the measures taken in 1525. The marks that distinguished prostitutes were even more varied than those for Jews: black cloaks, particular kinds of clogs and red hoods were just a few of them. In some areas a red cloak had to be worn by beggars. Both they and lepers were groups that had to wear distinguishing marks.[87] Prostitutes in many Italian cities had to wear yellow or scarlet. Beggars had to wear a red cap.[88] There was an attempt to identify through dress the groups that the majority considered to be marginal, such as Jews, prostitutes and beggars. Hence clothing was subject to rigid codification, as occurred with the laws on luxury goods, but for different purposes.

Meanings

Colours, cuts and fabrics could express precise meanings without being codified by the law. For example, the 'triumphal march of blue' started in the German village of Laichingen, as the preferred colour for men on festive occasions. Up until the middle of the century, peasants and farm labourers observed the regulations and chose grey for their Sunday dress, as did the weavers with brown. After that, however, they increasingly opted for blue, a colour that was introduced by outsiders who did not belong to the core population of peasants and craftsmen in the village. Although, at the time, blue was not a purely local phenomenon, in Laichingen it took on the characteristics of 'social movement and a historical turning-point'. The peasants, in particular, were quick to adopt it and demonstrate the strength of their desire to free themselves from the colour grey, which condemned them to be categorized as members of an inferior class. Moreover, this demonstrates that the criticisms of the absolutist pretensions in Württemberg at the time were not restricted to a small circle of officials and leading figures of the bourgeoisie. In other words, the choice of the colour blue was nothing less than a visible sign of the social emancipation of the peasantry.[89]

On the other hand, black was traditionally the colour of mourning, although other colours in fourteenth and fifteenth-century Italy were dark blue, green and mixtures of red and black such as roan and *morello*, a particularly dark red. In many parts of Italy, red was used for garments and accessories worn on wedding days. In the early modern era, white had not yet established itself as the colour of the bride's clothes, and it seems that only in Venice was there an ancient tradition of the bride wearing white.[90] Clothes, accessories, hairstyle and the way clothes were worn also distinguished unmarried girls, betrothed girls, married women and widows, as well as married and unmarried men. In Renaissance Florence, young women were only allowed to wear jewels received from their husbands at their weddings for a certain period after the wedding. In France, the inclination of the hat distinguished the unmarried from the married man.[91]

The main events in family life, such as the death of a relation or a marriage, were not infrequently expressed through dress. Some garments or accessories could take on particular ritual meanings. In Renaissance Florence, the bridegroom 'dressed' the bride for the wedding, in the sense that he bought clothes and jewels for her. He made her his, by dressing her in clothes that he had bought for her.[92] Men also 'dressed' their wives in Augsburg, while the wives made shirts for their future husbands.[93] In the Asturias, the bride was given a wristband, which the bridegroom had to redeem in order to make her his wife.[94]

Clothing for men and women

From the later Middle Ages, the identity most clearly expressed by clothes was that of sex. From the fourteenth and fifteenth centuries, male and female dress became highly differentiated. Men abandoned long, loose and flowing garments, which continued to be used only by particular categories, such as the clergy, old people and children, although specific clothing for children did not develop until the eighteenth century.[95] In other words, skirts and long garments became exclusively female items.

Male dress divided at the waist: men wore breeches and a doublet. Breeches tended to merge with stockings at that time, because they were tight-fitting and sometimes extended to the foot and had a sole. They were made up of two tubes of cloth that reached the groin and were attached to the doublet with pins, ribbons and loops. The doublet was a short padded garment. Women, on the other hand, mainly wore whole garments. For them, the division of clothing at the waist was to occur in the sixteenth century, as we have seen.[96] The shirt was virtually the only garment that was still common to both men and women, but in the fifteenth century the distinction between men's shirts and women's shirts started to appear, followed by the distinction between day shirts and nightshirts (the latter were to remain for a long time a privilege of the few: the majority of people continued to sleep naked or in the shirt they wore during the day).[97]

Even before this sharper distinction between male and female dress, breeches had become a symbol of male 'superiority'. Records of this interpretation date back to the thirteenth century. The question of who wears the pants became a classic theme for misogyny. By depicting a woman as attempting to wear the trousers, she could be stigmatized for attempting to subvert the natural order of things, and became the embodiment of a diabolic world turned upside down (Figs. 4 and 89). A recent author of a book on this theme acutely notes that the absolute division between women in skirts and men in trousers survives only on the small signs that distinguish male and female lavatories.[98]

Historically then, clothing emphasizes or attenuates the differences between the sexes. Even after the divergence of male and female dress in the late Middle Ages, there were phases and groups in which these distinctions became less clear. Sixteenth-century Venetian courtesans wore *braghesse* (breeches) and jackets with a male cut, and in the second half of the century women's clothing was in any case affected by a degree of masculinization.

On the whole, clothing during our period generally emphasized male and female attributes, even by using prostheses and rigid structures, particularly in the case of the upper classes. As far as men were concerned, the Renaissance codpieces, which were used to cover and protect the genitals where the breeches were attached, had padding which was sometimes explicitly phallic, and many women professed to be shocked. In 1533 the women of Ascoli, who had been prohibited from wearing skirts that were too short, retorted that the real scandal was not their skirts which revealed their slippers and a little bit of their ankle socks, but the men's codpieces, whose style was so shameless 'that we can no longer bear to look at it'.[99] Later, trousers were to become baggier, and in the seventeenth century they were so voluminous as to compete with skirts. In the eighteenth century, tight trousers were to return, at least amongst the upper and middle classes. This time, however, they were short and made of a single piece of cloth (i.e. they had become the celebrated *culottes*).[100]

A narrow waist and wide thighs were the feminine attributes that were most emphasized during the early modern era. Particularly in the upper and middle classes, women started from the fifteenth century to wear corselets reinforced with strips of wood or metal, which were forerunners of the genuine corset that appeared shortly afterwards. This was made up of a wooden or metal framework covered with linen or silk. The woman's body was thus moulded, stiffened and imprisoned in a garment that was so tight that it could damage her health. In the eighteenth century, Muslim women at the baths in Sofia, who were used to loose and comfortable clothes, asked Lady Montagu to undress and take a bath with them. When they saw her corset, they thought it was a kind of chastity belt forced on her by her husband.[101] But under the *Ancien Régime*, the upper classes often forced male children to wear a corset in order to accustom them to a stiff and austere bearing.[102]

Wearing clothes that made it impossible to move freely was also a way of underscoring one's remoteness from the need to work.[103] Nevertheless, upper-class women of the early modern era were literally encaged in a garment which, to our eyes, resembles an instrument of torture. At the beginning of the six-teenth century, various types of crinoline were introduced to accompany the corset. They came from Spain and spread to the rest of Europe. An initial type, the *vertugada*, was a pad around the abdomen that puffed out the skirt. This was followed by the *guardainfante*, which was made up of hoops of wood or iron to fulfil the same purpose. Originally created to protect women from knocks during pregnancy, it soon lost this function and only retained the aesthetic one. Indeed it was so exaggerated that it became impossible for women to move or sit down without being assisted.[104] In the sixteenth century, there was a fashion for soles and heels that could be as high as sixty centimetres. This meant that two servants would be needed even to walk a few steps.[105] From the Renaissance until the seventeenth century, it appears that women's makeup was so heavy as to create a kind of mask, which meant they could neither laugh nor turn their heads.[106] The increasing rigidity of society seems to have been reflected in how people dressed.

Apart from protecting their wearers from the cold, clothes also categorize people, or attempt to do so, in a rigid manner in more static societies, or in a continuous search for boundaries that are inevitably violated and then recreated in more dynamic societies. Clothes categorized the clergy, the laity, the nobility, the bourgeoisie and the military (whose uniforms developed during our period).[107] Perhaps more than any type of goods, clothes were subject to strategies of appropriation and distinction, symbolic struggles that led to things being redefined, new symbolisms and new meanings. They always communicated something, although the language changed according to time and place.[108]

This was the case when the custom of special clothes for Sundays and feast days, which went back to the Middle Ages, started to spread. In the eighteenth century in the German village of Laichinger, not even the poor labourers, shepherds and weavers were willing to forego this tradition.[109] Thus the religious calendar had its own garments, just like the seasonal one of hot and cold weather. At a more profound level, given that in this case the manner of dress was specific to the individual identity, the same can be said of virtue, as preachers and books of etiquette constantly reminded people of the importance of modesty and moderation in their clothing.[110]

Having tried to classify and clarify the many-sided world of clothing – skirts, petticoats, shirts, aprons, corsets, dresses, socks, clogs, shoes, *redingotes*, cloaks and so forth – and having dwelt in some detail on clothes that express the identity of sex, marital status, the principal in family life, and membership of a national community, we now turn our attention to clothes that express membership of a family.

6. Livery

There is evidence that in the Middle Ages there were clothes that used decorative motifs to communicate membership of a family or even kinship. In 1343, for example, several women married to men of the Florentine Albizzi family, some of whom lived in different parts of the city, had capes made of white cloth embroidered with vines and bunches of blood-red grapes.[111] During the early modern era, this custom, whose widespread existence has yet to be completely proven, appears to have fallen into disuse. At least in one case, however, family membership continued to be expressed through clothing. Throughout the early modern era, the nobility 'branded its men', although not with hot irons but clothes. The livery told the outside world that the person who wore it was in service, and indicated the identity of his masters to those who understood the code. The livery also provided other information: the quality of the material and accessories indicated the employer's wealth. Moreover, specific events in family life – baptisms, marriages and funerals – were communicated by the livery.[112] Liveries constituted a means for publicizing events, and they turned servants into a kind of media. The liveries 'sent out' at the time of a marriage often publicized the union between bride and bridegroom. The trousseaus of upper-class Florentine women during the Renaissance contained presents for the bridegroom's servants, including stockings with the colours of the bride's father on them. During the wedding the servants' legs proclaimed the matrimonial alliance between the two families.[113] After the marriage, the servants' clothing could continue to be an indicator of the relations between man and wife. One particular case helps us to understand how this happened.

In Bologna at the end of the seventeenth century, the senator Barbazza's wife left him because of his relationship with another noblewoman. Barbazza contacted his mother-in-law to get his wife to return to the marital bed, but she replied that not only did his wife not intend to return home, but was also 'making preparations to set up on her own in her own house, and to bring out a new livery that would be completely different from her husband's'. Barbazza was outraged at his wife's intention to ratify the separation and create her own public identity through her servants' clothing. He threatened that if he saw her in the streets accompanied by servants 'with another livery, she will live to regret it'.[114]

Several studies have demonstrated how changes that date back to the seventeenth century (the growth of the urban economy, the spread of fashions that blurred social distinctions, etc.) mean that the idea we have of clothing under the *Ancien Régime* (typified by inertia, immobility, a rigid correlation between dress and social position, a desire to control the situation through laws on luxury garments and other regulations concerning dress) is not wholly applicable. In France on the eve of the Revolution, people followed the fashion in choosing their clothes and attempted within the limits of their financial resources to reflect their own taste. 'They were greatly astonished to see me dressed in such new and fine clothes, with a pinchbeck watch that they thought was pure gold, silver buckles on my shoes and garters, and ribbons in my hat which I had done in Lyons', wrote the predictable Ménétra, who was proud of the impression his purchases produced on his father and his father's friends.[115]

However, the livery did indeed represent an aspect of the *Ancien Régime* that was still widely used in dress customs. The revolutionaries, who wished to sweep away all the last vestiges of the *Ancien Régime*, were well aware of this. On 19 June 1790, hereditary nobility, titles, coats of arms and liveries were abolished, and by grouping these things together, they showed an understanding of the intrinsic connections that meant for centuries the power of aristocratic families had been made visible to the outside world through the servants who belonged to their house. During the debate, Abbot Maury argued that by making liveries illegal they were striking at the very heart of the nobility.[116] The desire to create free and independent citizens led to the elimination of the means that had traditionally been used to sanction family membership. The next step was formally to proclaim the liberty to dress as one liked. This fundamental right was established on 8 Brumaire of Year II, or 29 October 1793.[117]

VII

Inside and Outside the Home:*
A Few Final Considerations

1. Production and consumption

Men, women and their possessions

At more or less the time when the idea of freedom of dress was beginning to be seen as everyone's right, clothes themselves were becoming freer, particularly for upper-class women. They abandoned the corsets, crinolines, high-heels, wigs and other artificialities that had been all the rage in preceding decades. At the beginning of the nineteenth century, there was a new style of neoclassical inspiration, which consisted of very light garments with low necklines, bright colours and high waists that let the material flow freely. Shoes had no heels and hair was loosely held up at the back without being powdered or covered with a wig. During the Restoration and particularly during the 1820s, corsets and crinolines returned to torment women's bodies.[1]

The changes in fashion and their spread from exclusive court and aristocratic circles to wider sections of the public had helped to undermine the foundations of the *Ancien Régime*, which was rigidly organized into distinct classes partly on the basis of dress. Women had undeniably played an important role in this transformation: as producers of yarn and cloth, as seamstresses, lace-makers, embroiderers, retailers and consumers of clothing, authors of the new fashion magazines and readers of this new literary genre.[2]

Turning our attention to the changes in personal wardrobes, we have already seen that during our period and particularly in the eighteenth century, the amount of clothing in each family tended to grow in most areas, although not everywhere.[3] In eighteenth-century Paris, this growth was quite spectacular, but the phenomenon did not affect men and women to the same extent, especially amongst wage-earners. At the beginning of the century, the average value of men's and women's clothing among the general population was more or less the

---

* I am borrowing the title of a seminar organized by the Società Italiana della Storiche [Italian Society of Women Historians] held in Florence on the 18 June 1994 (*Dentro e fuori la casa. Famiglie e «convivenze» nella storia delle donne, secoli XVI–XIX*).

same (17 and 15 *livres* respectively). But by the time of the Revolution, men's clothing had doubled in value and women's had actually increased sixfold (to 36 and 92 *livres* respectively). Thus the division between the sexes in dress habits that had already existed among nobles, bourgeois and servants was extended to the rest of society. Indeed, this division had slightly diminished by the end of the eighteenth century in the case of aristocrats and higher-ranking servants.[4]

If textiles were leading the way in the expansion of consumption, what are we to conclude from these statistics? Were women the main beneficiaries of the greater availability of clothes, at least in Paris? Was it principally their demand that sustained the import of fabrics and the development of the textile industry? Were women becoming consumers *par excellence*?

Before analysing these questions, we should try to understand if and in what ways men and women had a different relationship with clothes and consumer goods. Only recently has this subject begun to be examined, but there is some evidence to suggest that there was a difference in male and female consumption. In the context of the same economic activities or farms of the same size, women owned more new and decorative goods than men in England during the half century that straddled the end of the seventeenth century and the beginning of the eighteenth.[5] Even their perception of things appears to have differed. Recent studies on men's and women's wills in England, France, Italy and the United States between the late Middle Ages and the nineteenth century show that women had an emotional relationship with domestic furnishings and personal effects, whereas men spoke of them in a detached manner without referring to them individually.

While a man might have left all his linen to his servants in a generic manner or 'a ring worth thirty *scudi*' to a friend, women not infrequently gave detailed descriptions of each of the items they left to heirs in their wills. They spoke of them as their own possessions, which helped to mould their lives, expressed their individuality and could therefore pass on shared memories and their own history. They often left objects 'in the singular' – a jewel, a fork, a plate or a skirt – which related either to their bodies or their private daily life.[6] One woman left 'her chair with cushions in which she had herself been carried around the city', 'two small paintings close to her bed, one of our Lord carrying the cross and the other of our Lady of Sorrows', '[her] grey cape trimmed with fur'.[7]

Women were mainly destined to leave their original families when they got married taking only a few objects with them. It was much more difficult for them to own property. They were excluded from the professions. They were generally charged with looking after domestic objects and linen, and they could be responsible for purchasing items of daily use.[8] Women therefore appear to have developed a different relationship with objects, which was more individual and more absorbing than that of men. They seem to have invested great importance in objects because they had few alternative resources to construct their identity, establish social relations and leave a memory of themselves. It is significant that the items *explicitly mentioned* in women's wills in Turin became more numerous from the middle of the seventeenth century, a period in which women's property rights were under attack. One historian has speculated as to whether the lack of a permanent family identity and an identity linked to goods and chattels led women to develop an individual rather than a family identity. As this historian argues herself, though, it would be a mistake to attribute a purely compensatory role to women's attachment to their possessions. Possessions were something they could rely on and use creatively in their daily lives and in their network of relationships.[9]

This is also demonstrated by the fact that even middle-class women who owned property and were active in the business world often had a more emotional bond with their possessions than men. In Birmingham, which had already begun to industrialize, Sarah Skidmore, an affluent tradeswoman and widow who owned a house and a coach house, specified in her will that she was leaving her granddaughter 'her two best silk gowns and petticoats and one light cotton gown' (14 October, 1800). Almost a century earlier, Prudence Bryan, a middle-class widow who own a meadow amongst other things, left her 'best long scarf' to her loving friend Mrs. Tylor, and a 'pair of sheets marked with P.B. in Spannish stitch' to a granddaughter (7 June, 1703). It was probably Prudence herself who initialled the sheets. The items to which these women were so attached were, in fact, partly their own creations. Even when the domestic production of clothing and linen was replaced by purchased items, women's hands continued to leave their mark through decorations, embroidery, darning and recycling. Besides, even purchased fabric and clothing had at least in part been produced by women.[10]

While the role of women in domestic and factory production of consumer goods and then in their maintenance contributed to their special relationship with those goods, there remains the question of the role of women in their purchase. It could be argued that if women had an emotional bond with these things, it was because they had been responsible for choosing and buying them with care, attention to detail and good taste. But this argument ignores the fact that the objects to which they were so attached were often gifts or heirlooms. For example, the 'fine shift' that Hannah Owen, a poor widow of Birmingham, left to her granddaughter in 1778, had belonged to her mother. Moreover, it would be anachronistic to project into the past the stereotype of the housewife who regularly goes shopping or the mother and wife who shops for herself and the rest of the family, as we will see below.[11]

In light of the intense relationship that women had with household objects, can we then conclude that they were predestined to become the quintessential consumers when the number of available goods began to grow? It is a suggestive theory, but we still know too little about the mechanism of consumption in the past and how it developed over a period of time to be able to answer this question. We do not know whether overall women really were bigger spenders than men in proportion to their wealth. It would be wrong then to assume automatically that their more intense relationship with their possessions meant they had a greater propensity to consume than men.

The fact that women had more clothes, jewels and silver does not necessarily mean that they had a greater propensity for consumption. In Renaissance Florence, men 'dressed' their wives at the time of their wedding. A woman's rich clothing was not therefore an expression of a free decision on the woman's part. It reflected the man's choices, and in many cases, he remained the owner of the clothes.[12] Ultimately, a woman's body could act as the man's 'display case', to show off his wealth, power and success.

If we consider items other than clothing, we find that men owned more than women, as in the case of clocks and more particularly watches. One wonders what the results would be of any examination of the ownership of coaches and horses, which were the equivalent of the motor-car today. Finally, it should be added that, even if women were more emotionally attached to their possessions, this obviously does not mean that men were unconcerned about material objects. The diaries kept by the Sussex shopkeeper Thomas Turner (1754–65), the Reverend James Woodforde of Norfolk (1758–1802), the Somerset parson William Holland (1799–1819) and the East Yorkshire schoolmaster Robert Sharp (1812–37) demonstrate that these men were very much involved in petty domestic transactions and neighbourly gift relations, and were fully aware of the social value and 'desirability' accrued from the possession of particular items.[13]

Ultimately, we need much more information about how consumption was organized in families during the *Ancien Régime*, if we are to understand better the relative positions of men and women in relation to consumption. We need to know who actually decided which goods to buy and based on what criteria. It had long been argued that 'women have the task of preserving and men of purchasing': in other words it was the job of the husband and father 'to work hard in order to purchase the things that maintain a family' and for the mother 'to take care of . . . the family possessions within the house with diligence and reverence'. The concept of 'purchasing' obviously referred above all to the procurement of the means of supporting a family, but it also meant the purchase – in the commercial sense of the term – of the goods that were required. Within this tradition, only a few writers acknowledged the possibility of delegating this

task to women. This was, of course, a theoretical model and a highly ideological one at that, but one that demonstrates that 'shopping' was not considered a predominantly female activity.[14] It is worth remembering that as late as
1838 an Italian female writer complained that 'Italian husbands are so defensive
about their authority that they fear that by granting their wives a part of that
authority in the form of the internal running of the home, they would no
longer be able to exercise their control, so they keep their wives as outsiders in
their own home.' According to this writer, many women had no control or
authority over the housekeeping expenses.[15] In relatively recent times, the actual
behaviour of the families of 800 women born in northern Italy between 1890
and 1910 does not appear to have reflected the idea that decisions concerning
the purchase of clothing were exclusively the domain of the mother and wife,
although there were marked differences between social groups. While 30 per cent
of the wives of white-collar workers declared that during the first two years
of marriage they had taken such decisions on their own and 59 per cent had
discussed the matter with their husband, the balance was very different in the
families of agricultural workers. Only 6 per cent of the wives of sharecroppers
had made these decisions on their own; in 22 per cent of the cases, the decisions
were taken together by husband and wife and in 50 per cent of them by one
or both of the parents-in-law (those interviewed lived in areas of patrilocal
marriage). Unfortunately the available data does not tell us in how many cases
the mother-in-law took the decisions on her own. There is considerable evidence
that the mother-in-law often consulted her husband.[16]

In England, on the other hand, the diaries of a middle-class woman like
Elizabeth Shackleton of Alkincoats (1726–81) demonstrate that she dealt with the
shopping, and it has been argued that her writings provide 'powerful evidence to
support the widespread historical assumption that outside the households of peers
and plutocrats the daily *management* of consumption fell to the mistress and with
it control of routine decision-making'. The examination of men's diaries in the
eighteenth and nineteenth centuries has, however, demonstrated that men were
heavily involved in decisions and in the actual business of shopping. Moreover,
it has been shown that advertising in eighteenth-century England was directed
at men, leading to the conclusion that 'tradesmen viewed male consumers as
prime sectors of the purchasing market'.[17]

In other words, the situation was far from clear cut. Moreover, we need to know
the answers to other questions in order to understand the positions of men and
women in relation to consumption in various historical contexts. How were assets
distributed within the family? Were there people who benefited more than others
from new products and their increasing availability? Did the presence of new

objects create imbalances? In this book, I have attempted, as far as possible, to provide the current available information on these questions, on which historians of both sexes are still working.[18] There is a long way to go before we will have enough data to provide a clear picture. One of the reasons why the history of consumption has long attracted little scholarly attention is that, rightly or wrongly, women and consumption have been associated with each other.

Male production and female consumption?

In 1974, a historian argued that, during the period of industrialization, the massive use of female and child labour, which was badly paid but nevertheless paid something, threatened the authority of the paterfamilias, because of the importance of the women's and children's wage to the survival of the family. At the same time it made new forms of consumption possible. Indeed, the argument was made that it created demand for goods of central importance to the very development of industry. Precisely because work by women and children outside the home for wages threatened the delicate balance within the traditional family, its economic function was not recognized and its negative aspects (which certainly existed) were overemphasized by a chorus of voices denouncing terrible exploitation, the removal of women from the family and maternal role, the undermining of the householder's authority and the new opportunity for women to have their own money with which to indulge their vanity. As a reaction against contemporary reality, some people even rewrote the past. In spite of the fact that women and children had worked in pre-industrial society, it was argued that their labour constituted an iniquitous and unprecedented situation.[19]

The historian Neil McKendrick's impassioned arguments drawing attention to the role of women and children triggered a wide-ranging debate on the importance of female and child labour in the growth of production and the wider demand for consumer products. At the same time, it helped the development of studies into the reasons for the previous lack of interest in consumption amongst academics. It has been suggested that the principal reason was the establishment of theoretical positions that tended to contrast production, which in its 'proper' form was supposed to be a male activity not for women and children, and consumption, which was seen predominantly as a fatuous female activity. Thus consumption was stigmatized by moralists and underrated by many important economists. While the idea that women have a particular predisposition to consumption is at least as old as the story of Eve eating the forbidden fruit, there have been particular situations in which production and consumption have been characterized as male or female.[20]

2. *New boundaries and new hierarchies*

What kind of liberty?

> Never let it be said that according to the dictates of nature, we women must look after the home, limit ourselves to bringing up children while they are small and overseeing the servants' work, and that we do not have enough sharpness of mind or strength to manage the affairs of state, make peace or war, administrate justice or cross the boundless seas. Reason and experience fully demonstrate that we are quite capable of doing all these things. The unequal division of talents, by which everything is given to men and we women are reduced to the most inane leisure, demonstrates nothing other than the ambition of one sex, the male one, which is envious of the other.

Female (and indeed male) readers of the April 1764 issue of *Bibliothèque des dames* would have come across this explicit demand for greater equality between the sexes. Incipient female journalism, which mainly consisted of fashion magazines, offered women a new opportunity to intervene in the public sphere and a new platform from which to express their ideas.[21] Their voices increased in number throughout the eighteenth century, in places ranging from salons to theatres.[22]

At the other end of the social scale, women, far from being 'reduced to the most inane leisure', were actively engaged at many levels of the manufacturing and service sectors, and were in fact becoming important protagonists in the first sector to industrialize, namely textiles. In the eyes of their contemporaries, as we have seen, this involvement heralded the subversion of traditional hierarchies within the family and between the sexes. This was certainly not because previously women did not work; indeed, they laboured hard in the home, in the fields and in workshops. The causes were features of factory work: a sharper distinction between the domestic world and the world of work, more rigid working hours, the greater importance of women's and children's wages in the family budget and the increasing possibility of individual wages.[23]

Apparently, people could begin to think that there was no reason why women's enjoyment of an increasing freedom of dress, which even the law ratified at the end of the century, should not lead them to assert all the other liberties from which they had previously been excluded. And yet this is not what happened. Of course, the Revolution in France did bring important reforms in civil law: the introduction of equality between all male and female heirs, the introduction of divorce, and the introduction of the age of majority which allowed unmarried adult women to manage their own assets, enter into public contracts and exercise other rights. These reforms were then carried through to the Napoleonic

Code which, although on the whole less favourable to women than the preceding revolutionary legislation, was exported to many parts of Europe by French armies and influenced nineteenth-century legislation of many countries.[24]

During the Revolution, however, women were excluded from the possibility of participating in the public sphere by electing their own representatives or being elected.[25] The principle of universal suffrage was asserted for men, but not extended to 'the other half of the firmament'.[26] As is well known, women had to wait until the end of the Second World War before gaining the right to vote in France[27] and in Italy.[28] In much of Europe, women gained access to full political rights later than men. In some cases, such as France and Italy, the period between universal male suffrage and genuine universal suffrage was longer, and in others, such as Great Britain, it was shorter.[29]

According to one historian, the increasing centrality of women in relation to everything concerning appearance was the product of an explicit decision by men to forego all *parure* or ornamentation, 'a kind of conversion to an outward austerity'. This was a consequence of a break with the ancient social order; this academic argued that the simplification of male attire had 'clear egalitarian spin-offs'. Men gain 'in terms of real power what they lost in terms of appearance'.[30] In the light of all this, it has to be asked whether, following the Revolution, female predominance in this sector ultimately resulted from their exclusion from full rights of citizenship, however much women's fashion magazines might have been instruments through which they could publicly demand the rights they had been denied.

Something of the familia *remained*

Women (and minors) were not the only ones not to obtain recognition of their rights as citizens during the French Revolution. Servants were systematically excluded: only the Constitution of 1793 gave them the vote, but it was never applied. Albeit with a few interruptions, this exclusion remained in force in France until 1848. But even then they did not become citizens like everyone else. The last forms of discrimination against them did not disappear until 1930.[31]

In spite of the introduction of the age of majority, which strictly speaking was supposed to put adult unmarried women on a par with men, family membership remained a central feature in defining social identity for women and minors, just as it did for servants. They continued to be dependent on their paterfamilias and therefore were excluded from political activity. Precisely because they were still seen as subordinate to a superior within a unified organism, as the family was then thought of, they found themselves without liberty or independence. The family understood as a group of dependent persons was again demonstrating its staying power.[32]

The history of citizens' rights in Europe is a complex one. Because of the fervour with which the French Revolution asserted the concept of citizenship and the influence of this concept beyond France's borders, it is quite justifiable to devote greater attention to it, but it would clearly be wrong simplistically to apply interpretations arising from the French case to other situations. Broadly speaking, however, the period following the one we have examined in this book was characterized by the spread of the values and concepts of the liberal–bourgeois state which slowly led to broader sections of the European population being awarded the rights of citizenship, although this process obviously did not develop in a linear manner, as we have seen. Within this process, servants and, to an even greater extent, women were more or less everywhere at the 'tail-end'. As has recently been observed, 'male suffrage in the nineteenth century, whether partial or unlimited, was not really the individual ownership of political rights, but rather a citizenship principally restricted to male householders'.[33]

Home life as the supposed natural condition of women

One of the reasons for the exclusion of women was that many people considered them destined 'by nature' to work within the domestic sphere. The emphasis on the 'naturalness' of this role probably increased during the eighteenth century, but the idea that women were destined for 'home life' was ancient and had deep roots. 'Nature . . . made [women] of a weak constitution, so that they could attend to domestic matters and be mindful and diligent concerning family possessions', wrote one typical sixteenth-century author. Of course, there was no shortage of women who had no home or worked outside it, as we have already seen.[34]

Exactly what 'domesticity' meant was not set in stone. While the domestic space was being redefined as we have seen in this book, parallel changes of a profound nature were also affecting the position of the family within society. It would take another book to produce a detailed analysis of the problem, but it might be useful to compare the positions of various writers. Giacomo Lanteri from Brescia, who wrote *Della economia* in 1560, considered it to be a highly commendable aspect of the ancient republics that 'no one was admitted to public government or administration before he had demonstrated [along with other qualities] that he knew how to manage his family and home properly. Thence it could be argued that (as he knew how to govern his small province or native city) he was ready for government of the commonweal'.[35] In other words, Lanteri perceived the house and family as the basic unit in political society, a kind of microcosm that reproduced similar relationships to those within the city or state, but on a small scale. It was an idea that went back to Aristotle, who claimed that the father – the undisputed head of the family unit – exercised aristocratic power over his wife, monarchical power over his children and tyrannical power over his servants. Power was exerted within the confines of the home in ways that paralleled the world of politics. These opinions were widely shared by the authors of the many sixteenth- and seventeenth-century tracts on 'husbandry' as the science of domestic management, which aimed to teach householders the difficult art of 'ruling' their homes.[36]

When we look at a much later book, such as Caterina Franceschi Ferrucci's work on the 'moral education of Italian women' (*Educazione morale della donna italiana* 1848), we find the following passage:

> [Women] deserve to be called wise for the diligence and good judgement with which they manage their homes so as to render living there agreeable to their husbands and children, because of the calm, pleasures and comforts that they experience. Women should therefore provide this not inconsiderable part of private happiness; *she should arrange and order things with good sense within her little kingdom,* so that everything within it prospers and turns out well.[37]

This contrasts with Lanteri. For the gentleman from Brescia, the home was a kingdom where the head of the household could exercise (as in a gymnasium) virtues and abilities that could then be transferred to the world of politics. For the educated woman, the home is a place of private happiness (although not without important public responsibilities, given the mother's educative role that emerges in other parts of the book), the little kingdom in which the woman (and not the paterfamilias) rules, gives orders and makes arrangements. In this case, however, the exercise of domestic rule is neither similar to nor preparatory for the exercise of political rule as, according to Caterina, 'a woman's authority is restricted to management of the family', while management 'of the city or nation' is the reserve of men. In her opinion, the division of tasks between men and women is very clear: 'She rules the heart; he rules intelligence. She has the gift of persuasion, and he the gift of strength. Just as a woman's duty is to do the best for her family, so a man's is to do what is best for his country with justice and faith, and to contribute, as far as he can, to universal happiness'.[38]

Of course, libraries are full of books expressing different opinions, and we could easily find other texts with different ideas to these two writers. However, the quotations from Giacomo Lanteri and Caterina Franceschi Ferrucci express opinions that, in many respects, were widely shared within the periods in which they lived.[39] In other words, women were considered for centuries to be principally destined to work in the family and domestic sphere, but on the other hand, perceptions of the family and the domestic sphere differed. Different characteristics and functions were attributed to them according to the author, the context and, above all, the historical period.

The rigidity of women's domestic destiny was not the same everywhere. This was not only because a varying percentage of women did not marry because of poverty, lack of appropriate partners, work that excluded the possibility of marriage (in some areas this included domestic service) or, more rarely, a desire to live on one's own. There were, in fact, alternative behavioural models outside marriage, which also varied in significance. Christianity, in particular, had for many centuries attributed greater value to religious life than to family life. As time passed, however, Catholics increasingly valued marriage and family life, which were so important to Protestants. Nevertheless, religious celibacy and monastic life for Catholic women continued to be a legitimate and socially accepted alternative to the family. This was perhaps even more the case for Orthodox Christian women, given the supreme importance their Church attributed to monasticism. Of course, convents were used against women, but this does not mean that they could not also be an escape for those wishing to avoid the fate that awaited them as wives and mothers.[40]

Love and sentiment

Giacomo Lanteri argued that 'running a home is essential to human happiness in the same way that the helm of a ship is essential to its steering and safety'.[41] Nearly three centuries later, Caterina Franceschi Ferrucci also argued in terms of happiness, but unlike Lanteri she clearly distinguished between private and 'universal' happiness. The former was nurtured by women in the peaceful haven delineated by the walls of the family home, whereas the latter was supposed to be subject to the best efforts of men. This did not mean that she believed private happiness to be without consequences outside the family. She argued, in fact, that 'loving relationships within the family', a source of 'great consolation' for men, gave rise to 'many wonderful benefits to the behaviour of individuals and to the proper organization of civil society'.[42] She spoke of the family in sentimental terms that were entirely absent in the writings of Lanteri. Although she was a fervent patriot who was convinced that the upbringing provided by mothers in the home could help to improve 'the thoughts and costumes of Italians', her vocabulary was full of such expressions as 'sacred love', 'the holy joys of the loving family', and 'the sweetness and benefits of family affections'.[43]

Why was Caterina's language so different from Lanteri's? Was it because Lanteri intended to write a book principally providing practical instructions on how to run the domestic sphere properly or was it because the family had changed profoundly over the three centuries that divided the two works? The leading scholars who examined the nature of family relations in the 1960s and 1970s opted for the second hypothesis. They believed that over that period there had been a shift from a family in which there was coldness and a lack of affection between spouses and between parents and children to a family in which love, affection and intimacy played a central role.[44] While these historians had different opinions on how, why and where the 'modern family' came into existence, they agreed that it was linked to a profound change in the sensitivity of men and women, and more specifically to an increase in lovingness, as Lawrence Stone put it.[45]

But what then are we to make of the feelings of the bricklayer from Bologna who in 1462 wrote despairingly of the death of his wife Caterina in childbirth in his extraordinary diary: 'I did everything I could to save her, because I loved her with all the love that is possible, as I believe that there never was and never will be a woman that could be her equal'?[46] Then there was Giovan Tomaso, a Muslim slave in the Jesuit college in Palermo who converted to Christianity. Although 'loyal and diligent in his work', he was tempted to escape, as he admitted around 1550, so that he could 'work and earn money to pay the sum required to free his wife and son', who were captured at the same time as he was and were also slaves. In 1556, when he was still a slave, he had reached such a state of desperation that he was no longer 'certain whether he should live or die'?[47] What are we to make of the fears of Elisabeth de Boullion, who in the early seventeenth century, confessed that she suffered 'the maddening passion of a mother who is always afraid, too weak to believe in God's promise to turn all to the good', when her children were ill?[48] These are fragments of a distant past that give the impression of powerful feelings, relationships and love within the family. In recent years, research has uncovered a great quantity of documents of a similar tone, and today, quite a few historians are emphasizing the importance of love in family relationships under the *Ancien Régime*.[49] Are we then to conclude that – contrary to what was believed a few years ago – nothing changed in the relationship between husband and wife, or parent and child, over a period of centuries? This would be a rather hasty conclusion.

Stability and instability in family relations
Demographic trends alone would suggest some changes must have taken place. Family relationships must have been affected by the end of the 'age of the plague' in the second half of the seventeenth century, which since the Black Death of 1348 had meant that recurrent epidemics had claimed the lives of countless victims and left in their wake shattered families, people without family, orphans, widows and widowers. Those who were left with no family often went to stay with some distant relation or even people who were not blood relations, in order

to deal with the problems of everyday life. Men and women remarried and created composite families in which the children of different marriages lived together. Paradoxically, the disappearance of the plague did not necessarily mean a reduction in the death rate, but its greater evenness must have made life seem less precarious and strategic planning more possible for families.[50]

The vertiginous peaks in the death rate during plague years were not the only causes of the precarious and volatile nature of family relationships and the manner in which families frequently disintegrated and then reformed in a cruel kaleidoscopic game. Although situations varied widely, death rates in early modern Europe were always very high, particularly for children. Babies breastfed by their mothers had greater chances of survival than those who were wet-nursed and even greater chances than those who were not breastfed or were weaned very early. Thus, the decline in the use of wet-nurses that typified family life of the upper classes from the end of the seventeenth century helped make a baby's life less hazardous and the relationship with his or her parents more stable. It probably also meant that the baby's relationship with the mother was more intense. Given that breastfeeding reduces fertility, its greater popularity amongst women stabilized family life in other ways. In an era in which women risked their lives in childbirth, a reduction in the number of pregnancies increased their chances of survival. The spread of contraceptive practices from the seventeenth century initially in France and then elsewhere, also strengthened this trend towards greater stability in the family.[51]

However, we should not get carried away by the greater sense of security that this trend implies. Although it can be disturbing, we need to analyse the reasons for the considerable uncertainty that for centuries typified family life. The fact that in many areas one or both parents married at a fairly advanced age made it very likely that one of them would die while still young, and that children would lose one or both parents.[52] Changes to marital customs, as well as the death rate, had effects on family relationships.

According to a short Italian treatise published in the early seventeenth century, the paterfamilias should choose a bride 'of tender age, in order that she can easily be instructed in the behaviour that the husband requires . . . and this youthfulness will also be useful because, as the man is so much older, she will always be respectful and reverent.' However, the husband was not to be so old as to appear the father of his bride. At the time of the wedding, the wife was to be 'about eighteen years old and the husband a little over thirty'.[53] Such opinions were widely held in that period.[54] Amongst the upper classes of the Italian Renaissance and seventeenth-century cities, the age difference between spouses was very high: about ten to twelve years in Genoa and Milan, and as high as fifteen in Florence. This meant that women were often widowed while relatively young and either chose or were forced to remarry.[55] Where the patrilinear traditions were particularly strong, as in Florence, women might be forced to act as 'cruel mothers', as one contemporary complained, and abandon their own children in the home of the dead husband.[56] Only during the seventeenth century (as we saw earlier) did Tuscan magistrates start to appoint widowed mothers as guardians of their children, because they could not inherit from the children precisely as a result of this strictly patrilinear succession, and therefore had no financial interest in neglecting the children or even assisting their deaths with various degrees of actual intent. The decisions of these magistrates were eventually to reinforce the idea that a mother's love was unqualified and disinterested.[57]

Over time, the large age difference between husbands and wives of the Italian nobility gradually declined. In some cases, such as Turin, this started in the second half of the seventeenth century, while in others like Milan, it started around 1750. The period that man and wife could reasonably expect to live together therefore started to increase. Women tended to be widowed at a later age and therefore more rarely remarried. Their persons and their property were more securely incorporated into the husband's family.[58]

From 'My illustrious lord' to 'Delight of my soul'

How did relations between husbands and wives change over this period? Some of the large amount of correspondence in the archives might provide an idea of the feelings that existed between men and women in the past. 'My most illustrious lord' and 'Most esteemed lord' were the expressions used by Aurelia Pallavicini, an Italian noblewoman, to head her letters to her husband in the period around 1630–40. 'My dear and most beloved lord and husband' was the formula used a century later by another noblewoman (Teresa Margherita Del Vernaccia) who married into the same family, the Gozzadini of Bologna. As we move on in time, we find 'My dearest' and 'Delight of my soul'. This was the more passionate language used by Maria Teresa Serego Alighieri in the mid-eighteenth century, when writing to her husband who was also one of the Gozzadini. The words and formulas used by these women reflect wider trends. Italian Nobles born in the sixteenth and seventeenth centuries addressed their spouses with a cold but respectful *Vostra Signoria* ['Your Lordship' or 'Your Ladyship'], and applied the third person singular to verbs when speaking to each other. The formalities decreased somewhat for the generations born between 1700 and 1780. *Vostra Signoria* was abolished and women started to address their husband with the *voi* form (second person plural), which was a little less remote. Husbands and wives of the Italian nobility born after 1780 then started to call each other by their names and use the confidential *tu* form.[59]

In England, the question of how to address one's spouse (and more particularly how wives should address their husband) was publicly debated at the turn of the eighteenth century. 'Call him your lord', 'and do not rudely too familiar grow', was the advice given by a conservative who opposed the new custom of middle- and upper-class women calling their husbands 'John or Geoffrey, William, George or James', like peasant women. However, during the eighteenth century this habit became increasingly established.[60]

How do we explain this change? Was the spread of a more familiar language between husband and wife in the upper classes due to the smaller age difference between them? In the case of Italy, this reduction in the age difference probably did contribute to the change, but more generally, it does not appear to have been the principal reason. In England, the age of marriage for the principal heir of a squire in the sixteenth century was very low (around 21–22 years), unlike the rest of the English population. Their wives also married very young – at around 20 years of age. Couples were therefore almost of the same age. Later, the age of marriage (first marriage) started to increase. By the late eighteenth century, when the more informal language was well established, men married between 27 and 29 years of age, while for women it was 22–23. Amongst the landed gentry in England, the age difference between married couples therefore increased, exactly the opposite of what occurred amongst the Italian nobility.[61]

Who chose the spouse?

According to one historian, one of the reasons for the increase in the age of marriage was the greater willingness on the part of parents to allow their children a certain freedom in choosing a partner. Choice obviously needed a little more time. Parents' interest and ability to decide their children's fate and influence their decisions were the greater where the living conditions of the children were more dependent on family assets. From this point of view, the lower classes, who owned neither land nor workshops, enjoyed greater freedom, as has already been explained. The fact that many young people married after having spent many years in service away from home also undermined parental authority. On the other hand, the fact that in England the majority of the population married late meant that they married when their parents were already dead. Whatever the case, it appears that after 1660 only parents from the very highest levels of the aristocracy did not systematically grant their sons and daughters at least the right to veto any potential partner they might suggest.[62] But from the second half of the seventeenth century and, to an even greater extent, in the eighteenth century, many of the parents who could have heavily influenced their children's decisions went even further: they accepted that the young people should make the choice and they limited themselves to exercising a kind of veto over socially or financially unacceptable candidates. Patriarchal power in the landowning classes was effectively diminished. The adoption of a legal instrument, the so-called 'strict settlement', which aimed to prevent the alienation of family wealth and to determine the shares due to descendents had paradoxically produced the effect of weakening the ability of parents to impose their preferences. The 'strict settlement' laid down that the father had to hand a large part of his property to his first-born son at the time of his marriage and establish how this son would subdivide it amongst his children who were yet to be born. Thus, in each generation, the father could no longer threaten his children by shouting that he would disinherit them.[63]

The problem, however, is not simply a matter of who chose the spouse, but also a matter of understanding the motivations for these decisions and the way they changed over time. It would be naïve to believe that in choosing a partner, parents were only motivated by material interests and the young people were only concerned with love. In the 1740s, a certain Grosvenor, who was deep in debt, was ready to marry a rich heiress even without seeing her, although in the end he behaved differently. On the other hand, many parents were genuinely concerned about their children's happiness when it came to looking for a prospective partner.[64]

The idea that love and affection should be a premise for marriage and not simply a consequence was gaining currency during our period. Daniel Defoe argued, 'where there is no pre-engagement of the affection before marriage, what can we expected after it? . . . There is not one in ten of those kinds of marriages that succeed'. In the late eighteenth century, not only was sober and temperate fondness gaining legitimacy as a reason for marriage, but also sexual attraction and 'romantic' passion, in spite of the endless criticisms they still provoked. Previously the latter had been generally seen as emotions that could not be trusted, as they were too unstable and fickle to form a solid basis for marriage.[65]

Following the period between the mid-sixteenth and the mid-seventeenth century in which patriarchal power was strengthened,[66] an increasing number of English people were of the opinion that their children should choose their spouses on their own on the basis of their own feelings of love and affection. In the sixteenth and seventeenth centuries in countries like France and many of the Protestant countries, the power of the paterfamilias over his children increased, as we saw at the very beginning of this book.[67] After that, eighteenth-century European culture featured criticisms of the tyrannical power of fathers and pronouncements in favour of the right to individual choice. Arranged marriages were stigmatized. Particularly in the latter half of the century, there was a flood of novels and plays telling stories of passionate love to a public eager for emotional excitement. The nature of this change, its speed and its various stages varied from one region to another.[68] Obviously it would take several books to do justice to this subject, but in order to have at least an idea of the variety of situations in Europe, it might be useful – in summarizing some of the long-term changes – to concentrate our attention on a relatively limited case which was rather different from the English one.

'In Italy they scout [flout] every idea of decency and morality'

We shall follow in the footsteps of an English woman, Hester Lynch Salisbury. In her youth, Hester married the brewer Henry Thrale. Her mother arranged the marriage on the basis of propriety. As an obedient daughter, Hester did not object, although she did not feel any particular attraction to Henry (nor he to her). For almost twenty years she experienced a loveless marriage. She was widowed in 1781, and following a year of mourning and uncertainty, she married the man she loved, the Italian singer and composer, Gabriel Mario Piozzi. She abandoned her four daughters and Dr. Johnson (the famous writer who lived in her house) and left with her new husband for Italy, a country whose con-jugal relations at the time were a source of immense wonder and surprise to the English and other foreign travellers, although recent historical research has sug-gested that the situation was not so different as previously thought. Women of the upper classes all had a *cicisbeo* or *cavalier servente* ('serving knight') who accompanied them to church, the theatre and other public occasions, and kept them company, occasionally becoming their lovers. Many French travellers were shocked by such free behaviour, although according to some Italians the *cicisbeo* was an imitation of the libertinism that was rampant in France. The custom was so firmly established that even Hester Piozzi was reluctantly obliged to engage one (to ridicule a fashion she did not approve of, she opted for an octogenarian priest).[69] Let us take a closer look at the situation in Italy.

The Tridentine Council, it will be remembered, had confirmed that the parents' consent was not necessary for the validity of a marriage. In the following decades, the Church often attempted to force families to respect the wishes of their chil-dren.[70] This was particularly advantageous to women, who traditionally were often treated by propertied families as little more than pawns to be deployed in the creation of family alliances. In cases that came before Church courts, they were not infrequently encouraged to analyse their own inclinations and desires, irrespective of those of their parents. In Florence in 1578, vicar Sebastiano Medici – adopting words of the kind often used by colleagues in similar circumstances – explained to Francesca di Niccolò Gerbini, who had promised to marry Stefano di Pietro Pieri, but did not want 'to upset' her father who disapproved of such a union, that 'her father was not the master of her will, and she alone was free in this case to make of herself what she wanted, either to become a nun or to take a husband'.[71] According to a well-established tradition, there were only two alternatives (marriage or a convent), but the idea that the choice could and should be made independently was beyond question.[72] Nevertheless, there was no shortage of women who knew how to exploit this freedom to choose between two men, and not just between the walls of a convent and the walls of a home, and no shortage of ecclesiastical judges who gave a looser interpretation to this right to choose.[73]

When, during the seventeenth century, patrilinear culture and rigid hierarchical society – which was obsessed with defending family honour and keeping the distance between social classes – was reinforced, many clergymen and jurists became more willing to accept the logic of family interests. There was an increasing tendency to give greater weight to parental consent and to discourage *mesalliances*. Young women seduced by the promise of marriage were the ones who suffered. They were increasingly depicted not as victims to be protected but as cunning social-climbers ready to concede their charms to naïve young men of good family in order to force them into marriage or, at the very least, to obtain payment of a dowry (the tendency to accuse women of this became even stronger in the following century).[74]

The affirmation of patrilineal succession also created greater inequalities between first-born sons and cadets, and subjected the choice of spouse for the principal heir to rigid rules. This led to an increase in family conflicts, as can be seen from the worrying explosion in law suits between brothers, sisters, cousins, uncles, aunts and other relations.[75] Clearly, not everyone accepted the logic of the 'team spirit' that fought to preserve or improve the position of the family as a whole while sacrificing the happiness of individual members at the altar of the family name. It was not, however, simply a question of personal decisions. Legal instruments such as entailment could create real confusion and ambiguity, in spite of the manic and obsessive efforts of those who left property to programme the future by providing a long list of substitutes in the event of the chosen heirs or descendents (generally male descendents) dying without issue.[76]

It could be argued that this increasing inflexibility in the logic of family succession, which prevented an increasing number of younger sons from marrying and forced narrowly calculated marriages on first-born sons, not only increased family conflicts but also created the need for some kind of compensation. This need can perhaps explain the custom of *cicisbei*, which spread throughout Italy in the seventeenth century and was to continue for about a century, much to the horror of foreign visitors. A *cicisbeo* was not necessarily a lover, but he could be. In any case, the opportunity to be or have a *cicisbeo* was important to nobles who married in order to protect family assets rather than out of personal feelings. It meant the possibility of having a relationship with someone other than the spouse. For women the advantage was clear, as they, unlike their husbands, were not free to have fun with those of a lower social class. But there were not inconsiderable benefits for men as well, particularly unmarried younger sons, who could thus have a publicly acknowledged relationship with a woman of their own class.[77]

The clearly dysfunctional system of entailment was the object of increasing criticism. The main complaints were the tyranny of the home, the unhappiness of those who were subjugated to implacable family interests, and the impediment to 'free trade' it caused. Criticism of entailment became so intense during the eighteenth century that various Italian states were amongst the first in Europe to introduce legislation to prohibit or limit its use. This process was then completed by the arrival of the French under Napoleon, who abolished primogeniture and entailment, and introduced equality between heirs, both male and female. It can be no coincidence then, that this was the time that custom of *cicisbei* came to an end.[78]

Obviously, the entire system became increasingly unbearable as much of Europe began to be affected by a culture that emphasized individual freedom, free emotions and 'romantic love'. Parents of the middle and upper classes needed to allow their children considerable independence if they were to apply such values to their choice of spouse. Respect for one's children's desires was increasingly presented as one of the possible demonstrations of parental love, which was also becoming more important with the greater awareness and sensitivity towards family sentiments. Judging from the manner in which parents were addressed, relations between parents and children were also undergoing change, although the chronology was different to that of the changing relations between husband and wife. In the noble families of central and northern Italy in the seventeenth century and much of the eighteenth century, children addressed their parents as *Signor Padre* ('lord father') and *Signora Madre* ('lady mother') and they used *vossignoria* ['your lordship' or 'your ladyship'] in place of the pronoun, and *lei* in the eighteenth century, both requiring the verb in the third person singular. The parents called them 'son' or 'daughter', and used the second person plural *voi*, which in Italian at the time was less formal than *lei* but more formal than *tu*. Children were endlessly reminded that they had to 'honour their father and mother', in accordance with the fourth commandment. Good manners required not only the use of verb forms that expressed detachment and respect but also the use of deferential gestures. On presenting themselves to their parents, they had to bow or curtsy low and kiss their hands. In the generation born at the end of the eighteenth century and the beginning of the nineteenth, parents became much more relaxed in their relationship with their children: they called them by name and used the *tu* form. Only in a few cases, however, did children abandon their use of *Signor* and *Signora*, or start to use the *tu* form, which was to enter into general use in relations with parents in the generations born after 1820.[79]

Material interests and emotions

In the generations born towards the end of the period studied in this book, relations within the family ultimately appear to have been more informal and more intimate. But can we conclude that married couples loved each other more? Did parents and children love each other more? In reality, codes for expressing emotions vary from one society to another, and it is difficult or even impossible to know what feelings are hidden in a person's heart.[80] The deference to authority, which for so long was considered appropriate to family relationships, appears cold to our eyes, but this was not necessarily the case.[81] 'Your lordship must believe that I can only think of you, and time does not pass unless I regularly look at your portrait day and night', wrote the Florentine Lucrezia Brandi in 1615 to Giulio Marucelli for whom she felt an 'ardent love', as she put it herself. Lucrezia, the sole heir to a large fortune, was passionately in love and her love was reciprocated. However, her family did not want her to marry the object of her passions, and in the end, she married a man of higher social rank who was acceptable to the family. Did material interests always end up prevailing over emotions? The reality is more complex. When Lucrezia was called before a Church court by Giulio's family for having broken her promise of marriage, she forcefully defended her decision. It is true that she admitted that she discovered that Giulio was much poorer than she had ever imagined, but her feelings towards him changed because he had shown her passionate love letters to others.[82] It would appear a narrow and simplistic interpretation to say that in her case material interests got the better of love.

It was not, however, only in Lucrezia's case that the border between family interests and emotions appears to have been elusive. As a historian pointed out quite a few years ago, feelings can be not *less* but *more* intense, when relationships have economic consequences and are decisive for survival.[83] Property and material assets can be used to communicate affection and feeling, as though words of a material language. Most obviously, we are reminded of this by gifts or legacies in wills to friends and relations in the memory of common experiences and emotions, to mention just two possible examples.[84] Finally, it should be observed that an increased emphasis on love does not necessarily imply a reduction in the uneven distribution of power, as can be seen from nineteenth-century middle-class culture, which attached great importance to love and intimacy in family relations, but was also profoundly rooted in rigid hierarchies. This was so much the case that it has been argued not without good cause that the position of married women was not better in the nineteenth century than many situations in the *Ancien Régime* and may even have been worse.[85]

Following the implications of a few passages from the writings of Giacomo Lanteri and Caterina Franceschi Ferrucci, we started by asking ourselves how family relationships and feelings had changed. There can be no doubt that, while some demographic changes did contribute to greater stability in family relations, Europe witnessed the formation of a culture that exalted the role of love in the choice of a spouse and the role of love and its expression in relationships with children. But this certainly does not mean that previously families were loveless; it is just that these feelings and their expression were perceived differently. It was thought that husband and wife were supposed to love each other, but love was often considered the consequence of and not the premise for marriage. It was also believed that for the good of the children, it was more appropriate to be severe than tender and affectionate. For many parents, it must have been fairly difficult to follow these rules, judging from the frequency with which mothers and fathers were reported for being to indulgent with their children and from the content of many documents relating to their actual behaviour.[86] For many children, love and attraction undoubtedly did constitute the premise for and not the consequence of marriage, judging from the innumerable complaints about young love (particularly in social classes in which economic factors played a larger part) and from the way they often spoke of their feelings. 'What persuaded you to promise to take the Knight as your husband?' asked the judge of a certain Margherita Guardi in 1574. 'The love that I hold for him', replied the girl. Explain 'whether you say this out of fear or awe', urged the judge. 'No, my lord. I tell you it was love', she rebutted with conviction. She managed to convince him, and the following day she married the man she loved.[87]

In other words, it appears difficult or even impossible to establish a chronology for the changes in emotions. There are endless quantities of case studies in every period, and the evidence they provide is contradictory. What may appear an historically determined fact is perhaps only the explicit manifestation of the manner in which love was exalted as a driving force and central element in family relationships, and the family was perceived as the context for such sentiments.

This sentimental perception also included the home, given that it was where families lived. The officials who organized the English census of 1851 wrote, 'The possession of an entire house is strongly desired by every Englishman; for it throws a sharp well-defined circle around his family and hearth – the shrine of his sorrows, joys and meditations.'[88] The desire for a whole house was not so strong everywhere in Europe: elsewhere people were happy with a flat, but the idea of the home as a 'sanctuary' or 'temple' of warmth and affection to be jealously protected from external interference was gaining ground. Home sweet home . . .[89]

Public and private

Let us return to our reflections on the difference between the positions of Giacomo Lanteri and Caterina Franceschi Ferrucci. While for Caterina, the house was the kingdom of loving relationships over which the woman ruled with kindness and attentiveness, Lanteri thought that women should not live in the house as a whole. They needed to be kept 'separate . . . from all the rest of the family', and they had to have their rooms 'far away from the entrance', in the 'most secret part of the house'.[90] In other words, not all the house was the unchallenged 'kingdom' of the female sex. This difference was at least partly due to the fact that for the former, the family was both a public and a private environment, while for the latter it was strictly private.

Let us reflect more fully on these complex concepts of 'public' and 'private'. It should be said that the trend towards greater specialization of space within the home, with some areas increasingly designated as private and intimate, and others as more public, was more or less paralleled by a trend towards a similar division in society. Although there were profound differences from one area to another, and between one social group and another, a clear distinction was being imposed on two supposedly separate spheres, which in the modern usage of the terms are called the public and the private.[91] In the end, the family came to correspond to and become entirely incorporated into the latter sphere. Even though the house was sometimes open to 'penetration' from the outside and at other times it was more closed and shut within the intimate life of the family, it too tended to be classified as 'private', precisely because of its privileged position in family relations.[92]

To avoid confusion, this certainly does not mean that previously men and women did not feel the need for solitude, intimacy and confidentiality, as we have seen when we were examining the creation of the apartment. Equally it does not mean that they lacked a sense of modesty, as has already been said. Still less does it mean that they were unaware of the concepts of 'public' and 'private', as can be shown by the rather obvious fact that they used these two terms, which are of Latin origin.[93] Sometimes they displayed relatively modern sensitivities, as demonstrated by the words of the sixteenth-century author who wrote:

> There are very many things that the father of the family should do not openly but secretly under his own roof for reasons of modesty and honour, such as feeding, admonishing and instructing his children, training his wife and similar things, which can legitimately be carried out in the home and under cover, but not outside the home in public. This is one of the reasons for which houses have been built.[94]

In general, however, our ancestors had different ways of perceiving and experiencing these factors, which are always elusive and cannot be enclosed in watertight definitions.

To some extent, the change that we are attempting to understand was limited to a new way of looking at things and a new way of classifying a reality that in many ways had considerable continuity with the past. On the other hand, the new concepts and sensitivity were translated into decisions to build corridors and walls where there had once been open spaces, new laws that redefined social groups and the distribution of privileges and burdens between men and women, adults and minors, masters and servants, on the basis of new principles.

Separate and inextricably linked spheres
The contrast between the public and private spheres has been the subject of endless discussion. According to the ideology that advocated this distinction, the different spheres had several opposing features. One was private, the reserve of affections and the traditional area of dependence and subordination, whereas the other was public, the reserve of rational activity and the new area of freedom and equality.[95] Naturally this clarity between the two faded into uncertainty as soon as one went from the contemplation of ordered theoretical concepts to the consideration of what people said about the public and private in everyday life. For women in London, who undoubtedly constituted 'the public', which various journals and authors wrote for, going 'out in publick' could mean going to the theatre or the opera.[96] Establishing precise demarcation lines was very difficult even if you concentrated on the fact that the home, which was supposed to be private, contained areas that were more public than others. Where were you to draw the line between the two spheres? At the entrance to the house or in the sitting room?

The confusion becomes even greater when you turn your attention to the increasing number of working-class homes in which women got up early to go to work in a factory while their men were completely dependent on the salaries of women and children, or to the many peasant women who still worked on family farms where the distinction between inside the home and outside or between domestic and non-domestic work made little sense. Then there were the middle-class women engaged in a hundred different charitable activities that not only took them away from the home but also gave them a role that could quite reasonably be defined as public, and there were the elegant ladies who crowded the theatres and concert halls.[97]

The very women authors who wrote successful books exalting the role of women who angelically kept the hearth and home, to some extent contradicted the model they so enthusiastically promoted, given that thanks to the sales of their books, which they offered to the public, they became public figures (more or less consciously challenging a morality for which the only conceivable public woman was a prostitute). The learned and pedantic Caterina Franceschi Ferrucci went further. In her rhetorical and emphatic style, she called on women to prize the 'peaceful responsibilities and chaste joys of the family', to live in the family 'as though in their own kingdom', to take pleasure in the prosperity of the home and 'finding themselves respected and loved by husband and children' to turn their thoughts 'in thanks to God, who wanted them to find peace in their souls and happiness in their lives through fulfilment of such sweet and holy tasks'. Yet Caterina, an ardent patriot, committed herself fully to the achievement of national unity during the Italian *Risorgimento*: she wrote articles, appeals, patriotic songs and even a letter to Pope Pius IX. But that was not all: as a cultured woman of letters, she gave public lectures and speeches, although she was frightened of speaking to large crowds.[98]

For these and a thousand other reasons, the distinction between public and private was not always easy to identify. When you look at the reality, it becomes difficult to a make a clear distinction, always supposing that one can be made in the first place.

However, the new emphasis on the correspondence between home, family and the private, in opposition to the public sphere, was not without consequences, given that it guided the decisions of legislators, reformers, philanthropists and others. It had always been affirmed that wives and servants were part of the family and therefore had to obey the head of the family. But in the *Ancien Régime*, even householders were seen as people who were in some way kept in check by a network of dependences: they had to serve their king and all their superiors. The monarch himself was often represented as the servant of the Eternal Father and it was common to depict society as an uninterrupted chain of masters and servants.[99]

Although there were debates and clashes between reactionaries, conservatives, reformers and revolutionaries, a perception of society emerged in the nineteenth century that was based on the equality of citizens who act freely and independently. Those who, like servants, were considered incapable of acting freely and independently, in practice were stigmatized and suffered a worsening in their relative position, given that they had failed to acquire rights that others had. Along with many other factors, this relative deterioration in their position led to men abandoning domestic service, which became an almost exclusively female occupation during the nineteenth century. This caused the houses of the rich to become more feminine environments than they had been in the past.[100]

In many ways the destiny of women was similar to that of servants. Generally speaking, they too were considered dependent and incapable of making their own decisions. But while the dependence of domestic servants was simply a consequence of their work, many thought the dependence of women was intrinsic to their nature. Unlike servants, therefore, women had no hope of sooner or later escaping their position of dependency (male servants could always change jobs).[101] The reorganization of the ancient balance of power thus ended up marginalizing women more than in the past from legally recognized involvement in 'official' politics (of course this did not include the movements demanding their rights that had been denied or those social and philanthropic activities in which women were widely engaged and led to a presence, even a significant presence, in public life).

When family affairs and the affairs of state overlapped, women were not entirely excluded from the exercise of power. Thanks to the multifunctional nature of the family as an institution, which meant that a wide variety of responsibilities were carried out within the home, women could become queens precisely because of their family membership, or regents, where the law of Salian Franks was in force.[102] They continued to play this role where traditional forms of power were maintained.

Where, on the other hand, family and state were two totally separate entities, women were completely excluded on the basis of their membership of the family and domestic sphere. Towards the end of the nineteenth century, the development of the welfare state would in part bring the two spheres closer together, albeit in a totally different manner than in the past and without leading to an automatic recognition of women's political rights. During the second half of the eighteenth century and through most of the nineteenth, it is possible to identify a tendency to impose a sharper separation between the two spheres, even though it was resisted by the continuation of some forms of traditional life and some features of the innovations that were being introduced. To put it bluntly, there had been queens, empresses and tsarinas, but the new principles did not produce women senators, women ministers or women presidents. In situations where the principles of elected representation were applied, for a long time women were unable to elect their own representatives or be elected themselves.

The new values of liberty and equality, although denied (and in part precisely because they were denied), also created new incentives for women, new tensions among them and new demands from them. It would take lengthy struggles and profound changes before their involvement in public life would be acknowledged and accepted in law.

The past and present

During the period we have examined in this book, and particularly in the latter phase, profound changes started to take place in the organization of places and spheres of activity. New material and symbolic boundaries began to appear. These changes tended to reduce the role of the family as a form of social organization that engaged in a multiplicity of functions, from the exercise of power to economic production and from biological reproduction to consumption.

As we have seen, under the *Ancien Régime* the home was an area in which production, reproduction and consumption were interwoven. The development of the market economy, however, tended to erode the possibilities of private consumption. Whereas in the late Middle Ages there were works on an industrial scale which crowded together large numbers of workers (such as the silk mills in Bologna), it was in the latter phase of our period that factories spread on a massive scale, creating a sharper separation between places outside the home allocated to production and places within the home allocated to reproduction and consumption.

I have written at length on how consumption changed during the early modern era. We have followed the changes in the material conditions that family members in the early modern era had to deal with. We have seen that 'the world of goods'[103] was enriched with many objects, goods and foodstuffs, while others tended to become obsolete and fall into oblivion. We were able to ascertain that consumption and the material conditions of existence changed for the majority of Europeans. The variety of foods increased, although the diet deteriorated for many people. Houses generally became more solid, better heated and more specialized in the use of space, although in some cases overcrowding worsened as a result of population increases. Inside furniture and furnishings were often more plentiful and wardrobes contained more clothes.

There is still much to be done to understand how these changes relate to changes in the family's internal balance and the transformation in relations between husbands and wives, parents and children, brothers and sisters, first-born sons and their younger brothers, sons following one career versus sons following another, masters and servants, and members of the nuclear family and other relations. By patiently putting together the results of at least part of the studies that have so far been carried out, we have gained a general idea of the problem, even though we ventured into an area where economic interests and emotions meet and almost dissolve into each other.

The distinction between that which is emotion, love or sentiment and that which is self-interest or calculating reason is, I believe, inseparable from the cultural values of each individual. In the past these values were often very different from our own. The very manner in which men and women use objects and resources has proved to be a product of a complex culture that does not simply aim at the satisfaction of given and unchanging biological needs.[104] If it were a matter of such restricted needs, how would we explain the ritual squandering of resources in the event of marriages and feasts, which are typical of peasant societies constantly living on the very edge of survival?

We have demonstrated that objects cannot be assessed solely at face value, always supposing there was ever any need to do so. Their use and consumption cannot be separated from the significance they take on within a particular culture. If people believed, as they did in the late Middle Ages, that poultry led to sexual arousal, it comes as no surprise that widows, who were supposed to maintain their chastity, were advised not to eat it. The famous preacher Bernardino da Siena (1380–1444) thundered, 'Widow, I want to say to you . . . do not do as you did when you had your husband – when you ate the flesh of small birds'.[105] It goes without saying that ideas concerning the cosmos, the characteristics attributed to east and west, north and south, right and left, and back and front must have influenced the orientation and layout of houses, buildings connected to them, crops and places for keeping domestic animals. One historian has commented that buildings 'were made of spiritual acts and categories, just as much as earth, wood and straw'.[106] As far as is possible we have attempted in the pages of this book to throw some light on these complexities.

The examination of the characteristics and meaning of the objects in the past, the uses they were put to in social relations to build bridges or create barriers between people,[107] and the manner in which they spread, helps us to understand better our own world in which new forms of poverty have grown up alongside the more traditional ones, while objects allure us from shop windows, fill our houses, pollute our environment, take up every available space and permeate our lives.

Acknowledgements

I would like to thank those who have helped me to complete this work, while I obviously am the sole person responsible for what I have written.

The merit (or blame) for the existence of this book primarily goes to Marzio Barbagli. It was in fact his idea to transform the long article I had written on the subject into a book. But part of the merit (or blame) must go to the original Italian publisher Laterza, for having believed in the project.

The full text, with additions and corrections, was read by Giancarlo Angelozzi, Licia Berrera, Cesarina Casanova, Matilde Callari, Lucio Gambi, Alberto Guenzi, Lucia Ferrante, David Kertzer, Gianna Pomata, Silvia Salvatici, Simonetta Soldani and Vinicio Sarti. All or part of the more or less complete version was read by Renata Ago, Marzio Barbagli, Alberto Capatti (Chapter V), Paolo Cornaglia (Chapter IV), Silvia Evangelisti (Chapters I–II), Antoinette Fauve-Chamoux, Lucia Ferrante (Chapter I), Christiane Klapisch-Zuber, Aurelia Martín Casares (Chapter I), Manuela Martini, Massimo Montanari (Chapter V), Maura Palazzi, Ivan Tocci and Gabriella Zarri.

I was generously provided with bibliographical and archival information by Mauro Ambrosoli, Adanella Bianchi, Carlo Calderan, Franco Cazzola, Stefano Cavazza, Sabina Crippa, Allen Grieco, Hans Grassl, Luciano Guerci, Daniela Lombardi, Francesca Medioli, Ottavia Niccoli Paul-André Rosental and Fabio Viti. I asked Adelina Modesti to look at the initial version of the illustrations.

Given the impossibility of thanking everyone specifically, I extend my thanks to everyone who assisted in whatever form. Their criticisms and advice were much appreciated.

As is well known to anyone who has undertaken the task of writing a book, even a book of an introductory nature like this one, it is a considerable commitment. The support of those who are close to you is of great importance. Apart from assisting me in improving the text from a purely academic point of view, the great majority of the persons referred to have encouraged me and stimulated my ideas. To the other names I would also like to add those of Giovanna Sarti and Patrizia Delpiano. As well as reading and commenting upon the text, Roberto Brigati was close to me during the years in which I was engaged in this work.

It is impossible to mention all the people who helped me with suggestions and criticism over the last three years, though I am thankful to everyone who patiently read the text and gave me their impressions. Let me name at least some of those who helped me.

For the discussion of the book at the Department of History in Bologna I am grateful to the Director, Paolo Prodi, to the organizers, Cesarina Casanova and Lucia Ferrante, and to the discussants, Marzio Barbagli and Massimo Montanari. I am indebted to Luciano Allegra and Giuseppe Ricuperati for inviting me to the Department of History in Turin; to Daniela Lombardi and Anna Scattigno for the seminar organized at the University of Pisa, as well as to Maura Palazzi and Mario Neve for inviting me respectively in Bologna and Modena. Another instructive experience was the Summer School on women's history and culture "Annarita Buttafuoco" (Siena) on the theme *Interni* (interiors). Questions asked during conferences in small towns (Campagnola, Millan/Milland) allowed me to confront a larger public with my ideas, while the invitation to Aosta by Viviana Rosi permitted me to have contact with teenagers.

As concerns mass-media, let me thank at least Chiara Frugoni and Paolo Malanima for discussing the book on a radio program.

Besides those I have tried to thank specifically in the Notes I would like to thank for their help Giulia Calvi, Matteo Casini, Sheila Cooper, Angelo D'Ambrosio, Hester Dibbits, Isidro Dubert Garcia, Silvia Evangelisti, Antoinette Fauve-Chamoux, Angela Groppi, Olwen Hufton, Sara Matthews Grieco, Małgorzata Kamecka, Aurelia Martín Casases, Giovanna Giordano, Anne-Lise Head-König, Cesary Kuklo, Margareth Lanzinger, Andrea Lastri, Isabella Palumbo Fossati, Ofelia Rey Castelao, Lino Marini, Vittorio Monelli, Giovanni Sacchini, Sølvi Sogner and Matthew Wollard. My own students also have to be mentioned. I am grateful to Sandra Cavallo for commenting on the new version of chapter VII as well as to Isabel Santos, who translated the book into Portuguese, and Allan Cameron, who is responsible for this English translation.

A final thanks goes to Jacques Le Goff and David Kertzer who commented so positively on the book. Last, but not least, I would like to thank Yale University Press for trusting the book and particularly Adam Freudenheim.

No thank you would be sufficient to express my gratitude again to Roberto Brigati for his patience and support.

Notes

Introduction

1. Niccoli 1991, pp. xx–xxi (Bologna State Archive, *Tribunale criminale del Torrone* (Criminal Court), Court proceedings, vol. 5472, interrogation of 22 June 1626), and now more fully Niccoli 2000, pp. 43–64.

2. Roche 1997.

3. Given that much of my research has been at the Bologna Archive, the cases drawn directly from the sources, without reference to other scholars, are mainly related to the situation in Bologna.

4. On the cognitive implications of shifting the scale of observation, see Levi 1991a (Ital. trans. 1993), and 1996; Ginzburg 1994; Grendi 1994; Revel 1994.

5. On the different concepts of Europe and the creation of a European identity, see Chabod 1991; Europa 1984; Todd 1990; Malettke (ed.) 1998.

6. Febvre 1970 (Ital. trans. 1980); Zanini 1997.

7. This subject has obviously provoked a great deal of interest. As far as the history of the family is concerned, see purely by way of example the classic work by Hajnal 1965 (Ital. trans. 1977); the collection of essays by Ehmer, Hareven and Wall (1997); the research currently being carried out in the context of the EurAsian Project on Population and Family History, one of whose aims is a comparative analysis of Asian and European family systems (http://www.ec.lu.se/~ekhtbe/eapp/) and the arguments put forward by Jack Goody (2000, pp. 11–14), who challenges the distinctive nature of the European family, as maintained by other authors. As far as the history of material culture is concerned, a good deal of information of a comparative nature is contained in the book by Braudel (1979, Ital. trans. 1993), which is something of a milestone in this academic sphere, although more recent works have a comparative slant as well. For example, Shammas 1993 compares Great Britain and North America, whereas Burke 1993 and Adshead 1997 develop comparisons between Europe and China. There is, however, no shortage of those who denounce the European and North American ethnocentrism of some of the more important recent works; see Clunas 1999, pp. 1504–7.

8. For the classic work on this subject, see Kelly-Gadol 1977. For a recent contribution to the question of historical periodization, see Lanaro 1997.

9. See chapter V.

10. McKendrick, Brewer and Plumb 1982.

11. For example, Shammas 1989; Vries 1993, especially pp. 95, 99 and 107, who suggests the term 'consumer revolution' should be dispensed with; Styles 1993, pp. 535–42; Fairchilds 1993b, note 4, p. 852; Miller 1995, p. 167; Levi 1996, pp. 197–8. Growth was not restricted solely to England. According to Goldthwaite 1987a, p. 16, 'modern consumer society, with its insatiable consumption setting the pace for the production of more objects and changes in style, had its first stirrings, if not its birth, in the habits of spending that possessed the Italians in the Renaissance' (see also by the same author 1987b and 1993 [Ital. trans. 1995]). Other historians, such as Porter 1993, continue to use the interpretative key of English eighteenth-century origins to the consumer revolution, while admitting that the theory is open to debate (p. 65). The use of concepts that have not been rigorously defined has compounded

the difficulties in establishing a universally shared chronology, according to Shammas 1989 and Styles 1993. On the question of chronology, see also Stearns 1997 and the interesting observations by Clunas 1999. There has however been much lively and scholarly investigation into the history of consumption in recent years. Apart from the works already referred to, recent publications include Berg and Clifford (eds) 1999.

12. Affinity refers to relationships by marriage or godparentage.

13. See, for example, the case in Tuscany studied by Malanima 1990.

14. Sabean 1990, p. 97.

15. Sabean 1990. On the problem of defining the domestic unit on the basis of co-residence or consumption, see Wall 1983 (Ital. trans. 1984) and Laslett 1983 (Ital. trans. 1984).

16. Archive of the Archbishopric of Bologna, *Court of the Archbishopric, Sgabello II*, fol. 12, n. 20, quoted in Ferrante 1994b, p. 18 (p. 22 on the statutory provisions).

17. Douglas and Isherwood 1979 (Ital. trans. 1984), p. 14.

18. Medick and Sabean 1980 and Medick and Sabean (ed.) 1984.

I. Home and Family: Things Fall Apart

1. Roux 1976, p. 43. For an extensive analysis of the concept of 'home', see Mack (ed.) 1991.

2. Marin Sanudo, *Diarii* XLVI, coll. 323 and 326, quoted in Zorzi 1990, p. 168 (the quotation refers to November 1527).

3. Braudel 1979 (Ital. trans. 1993), p. 495.

4. On the various types of vagrants as they appeared to some contemporaries, see, for example, R. Frianoro [*alias* G. Nobili], *Il Vagabondo, overo Sferza de' bianti e vagabondi*, Viterbo 1621, in Camporesi (ed.) 1973, pp. 79–163; and the reflections of Giovanni Battista Scanaroli in Geremek 1974 (Ital. trans. 1992), p. 94; Zemon Davis 1975 (Ital. trans. 1980), p. 31.

5. Hufton 1974; Farge 1979; Geremek 1988 and 1992; Woolf 1988; Ricci 1996.

6. Francesco Pignatelli, Prince of Strongoli, *Ragionamenti economici, politici e militari riguardantino la pubblica felicità*, Naples, 1783, I, p. 51, quoted in Braudel 1979 (Ital. trans. 1993), p. 495, and in Dal Pane 1958, pp. 192–3. The population of Naples was 339,000 inhabitants in 1730 and 430,000 in 1800, see Bairoch 1987, p. 257, table 4 and Bairoch, Batou and Chèvre 1988, p. 45.

7. Pullan 1978, 988–90, Woolf 1988 (Ital. trans. 1988), pp. 8–9. It has proved much more difficult to make estimates of the incidence of poverty in the countryside.

8. Zemon Davis 1975 (Ital. trans. 1980), p. 55; Geremek 1988 and 1992; Woolf 1988 (Ital. trans. 1988), p. 11.

9. Reher 1998 seems to suggest that the link between the absence of family and poverty was stronger in Mediterranean countries than in those of central and northern Europe.

10. Bologna State Archive, *Ufficio delle Bollette*, Filza, 1604, quoted in Ferrante 1996b, p. 206. The woman was called Caterina Monari. Her family situation appears to have been disastrous before the disappearance of her husband. She told the judges who were interrogating her, 'I don't remember ever having known my father or my mother, and I have two brothers whose whereabouts I haven't known about for what must be four years'.

11. Quoted in Camporesi 1980, p. 51. *Malabiare* is an Italian word that has fallen into disuse. It derives from the Spanish *mal*, 'badly' and *loablar*, 'to speak', see Battaglia 1961 (under the entry for *malabiare*).

12. Arch. Dépt. Calvados, H. Suppl. 1308, quoted in Hufton 1971, p. 93. See also Hufton 1974.

13. Quoted in Palazzi 1986, p. 43.

14. Reference to the *Court Book* of Bridewell Hospital, taken from Stone 1977 (Ital. trans. 1983), p. 719.

15. Marin Sanudo, *Diarii* XLVI, coll. 612, quoted in Zorzi 1990, p. 179.

16. Cosenza 1974, p. 125. On the particular worries raised by vagrancy in Holland and

the efficacy of the measures taken to combat it, see Schama 1987, pp. 579–83; on Jews pp. 587–96.

17. Quoted in Camporesi 1978, p. 181.

18. Geremek 1982 (pub. 1992); Lucassen 1997.

19. Deffontaines 1972, pp. 125 and 133–4. On the history of the Lapps or Sámi, the internal diversification of this population and the development of reindeer breeding during the early modern era, see Meriot 1980; Pounds 1989, p. 27. I am grateful to Ludger Müller-Wille, Jukka Pennanen and Marjatta Rahikainen for information about Sámi material culture.

20. Deffontaines 1972, p. 137.

21. Roux 1976 (Ital. trans. 1982), p. 45.

22. Woolf 1988 (Ital. trans. 1988), p. 9, Merzario 1989, 1996a and 1996b.

23. Braudel 1982 (Ital. trans. 1986), vol. I, pp. 14–38; Lucassen and Lucassen (eds) 1997; Fontaine 1993; Hoerder, Page Moch (eds) 1996; Rosental 1999. But there were also areas in which a considerable part of the population was very stable, see for example the Russian village of Mishino, Czap Jr. 1983 (Ital. trans. 1984). On the abolition of the freedom of movement of the still semi-nomadic Russian peasants in the sixteenth century, from 1580, and the process that bound them to the land, see Rösener 1993, pp. 40 and 158–74 and chapter IV, section 1 of this book. The fixed settlement of serfs in eastern Europe (who were, however, occasionally moved around at the behest of their landowners) contrasted with the mobility of the so-called 'master-less men'; see Geremek 1977 (Ital. trans. 1992), Naser 2001.

24. For example, on England, Laslett 1971 (Ital. trans. 1979), pp. 80–2 and Stone 1977 (Ital. trans. 1983), p. 369.

25. Le Roy Ladurie and Couperie 1970; Giusberti 1982; Palazzi 1985, 1986 and 1988; Roche 1981 (Ital. trans. 1986), pp. 129–45 and 1997.

26. Roche 1981 (Ital. trans. 1986), p. 144; Pardailhé-Galabrun 1988, p. 199. On the types of residence of domestic servants, see also Sarti 1994a, pp. 239–40 and 253–4, 1995

and 1999a. The situation appears to have been different in a small city like Chartres: between 1700 and 1720, the percentage of those who owned the house in which they lived was 40% for agricultural labourers, 65% amongst master craftsmen, 44% amongst wage-earners and 25% amongst women living on their own. Only servants did not own property. In the following years, the situation tended to deteriorate, but the percentages still remained considerably higher than those for Paris (in the period 1780–90, the figures were 46% for agricultural labourers, the only group that recorded an increase in the number of home-owners, 45% amongst master craftsmen, 13% amongst wage-earners, 6% amongst women on their own and servants continued not to appear as home-owners). Overcrowding also appears to have been less of a problem in Chartres: at the end of the century, only 35% of wage-earners only had a single room, while the figure in Paris was 63%. See Garnot 1989, pp. 197 and 200.

27. Louis-Sébastien Mercier, Le Tableau de Paris, Amsterdam 1781–88, 12 vols, vol. X, pp. 353–8, quoted in Roche 1981 (Ital. trans. 1986), p. 143.

28. Roche 1981, (Ital. trans. 1986).

29. Although apparently lower than in Paris, the mobility of tenants was also rather high in Bologna, and lower-class tenants moved on average every three or four years. This was in spite of the fact that in eighteenth-century Bologna, unlike the French capital, the population was substantially stable and the increase in tenancies was less than the increase in foodstuffs; see Palazzi 1985, pp. 373–5 and 385–9, and 1997, pp. 187–246 and, for the beginning of the nineteenth century, Giusberti 1982.

30. Groppi 1996a, pp. 126–8 and more generally Groppi (ed.) 1996.

31. Fauve-Chamoux 1981; Wall 1981; Henderson and Wall (eds) 1994; Woolf 1988 (Ital. trans. 1988); Lombardi 1988; Palazzi 1986, 1988 and 1997; Ferrante 1996.

32. This emerges from the research carried out in Bologna by Mavra Palazzi (see Palazzi 1985, 1986, 1988 and 1997).

33. Bologna State Archive, *Ufficio delle Bollette*, Filza, 1604, quoted in Ferrante 1996, p. 206.

34. On Bologna, see the previously mentioned works by M. Palazzi; on Poland, see Kludo 1998.

35. Ferrante 1996, pp. 225–8.

36. Palazzi 1985, p. 383.

37. Hufton 1995 (Ital. trans. 1996), p. 123. A tax on marriage was introduced in England in the 1690s and it required the payment of the costly duty stamps on licences and marriage certificates, see Stone 1977 (Ital. trans. 1983), p. 37 and 1990, p. 52.

38. Quoted in Burguière 1986c (Ital. trans. 1988), p. 134.

39. Archive of the Archbishopric of Bologna, *Cancelleria Vecchia, Matrimoni* I, Domenica Cinti *vs* Battista Mazzoni, 1548, quoted in Ferrante 1994b, p. 6.

40. Archive of the Archbishopric of Bologna, *Foro Arcivescovile, Sgabello II*, fol. 12, n. 20, quoted in Ferrante 1994b, p. 23. The woman who used this expression was the mother of the Maddalena we encountered at the beginning of this book when she showed her ring to her friend. On the meaning of the term, see pp. 4, 8 and 18 in Ferrante, and under the entries for *sposo* and *fidanzato* in Cortelazzo and Zolli 1979–88.

41. See also Hughes 1996, pp. 46–7; Lombardi 2001, pp. 9 and 25.

42. Stone 1977 (Ital. trans. 1983), p. 34, and 1990; Roper 1985, pp. 63–7 and 1989, pp. 132–64; Gaudemet 1987; De Giorgio and Klapisch-Zuber (eds) 1996, p. x; Ferrante 1994b.

43. Burguière 1978; Gottlieb 1993, particularly pp. 68–71; Klapisch-Zuber 1979 (Ital. trans. 1988), and 1981 (Ital. trans. 1988).

44. Burguière 1978; Klapisch-Zuber 1979 (Ital. trans. 1988) (in Renaissance Florence, the clergy took no part in the wedding service for middle- and upper-middle-class families, while the poor slipped on a wedding ring in the presence of a notary, as the very rich did in church before a witness; see particularly pp. 115–19, 128–31 and 148); Roper 1985,

pp. 65–6; Bossy 1985 (Ital. trans. 1990), pp. 24–32; Gottlieb 1993, pp. 68–71; Ferrante 1994a and 1994b; Hughes 1996.

45. Stadtarchiv Augsburg, *Urgichten*, Michel Hurrenbain, 29 August 1528; *Handwerksakten*, Bader und Barbiere, 31 August 1563, quoted in Roper 1985, pp. 66–7.

46. Gillis 1974 (Ital. trans. 1981), pp. 42–3; Shorter 1975 (Ital. trans. 1978), pp. 98–107; Laslett 1977b; Stone 1977; Mitterauer and Sieder 1977 (Eng. trans. 1982), pp. 123–4; Flandrin 1981, pp. 279–321; Burguière 1986c; Matthews Grieco 1991b; Rogers 1993, p. 296; Schindler 1994, pp. 315–16; Savrer 1997.

47. Klapisch-Zuber 1979 (Ital. trans. 1988), pp. 122–3 (who noted the tendency in Renaissance Florence to consummate the marriage after the exchange of consent, but before the ceremony of the transfer of the bride to the bridegroom's house); Hughes 1996, pp. 29–31; Pelaja 1996, p. 391; Ferrante 1994b, pp. 12–16.

48. For a summary of the problem, see Burguière 1986c; Mitterauer and Sieder 1977 (Eng. trans. 1982), p. 124.

49. De Giorgio, Klapisch-Zuber 1996, p. viii. The Fourth Lateran Council (1215) reduced impediments from the seventh to the fourth degree of consanguinity or affinity. Marriage was also forbidden in case of spiritual affinity resulting from godparentage, see pp. 128–9; Lombardi 2001, p. 32.

50. Stone 1977 (Ital. trans. 1983), p. 35; Gaudemet 1987; Ferrante 1994b; Hughes 1996, pp. 22–6; Dear, Lowe (eds) 1998; Watt 2001; Lombudi 2001, p. 32.

51. On the situation in Italy, see Pelaja 1994; Lombardi 1996 and 2001; Zarri 1996; Bianchi 1997; in Switzerland and 2001, see Head-König 1993; in the Netherlands, see Schama 1987, pp. 440–3; in Protestant areas see Watt 2001, pp. 137–8.

52. Ferrante 1998. One the scale of concubinage, see Hughes 1996, pp. 47–9.

53. Ferrante 1994b, p. 22.

54. Flandrin 1975 (Ital. trans. 1980), pp. 43–4; Lebrun 1986b (Ital. trans. 1988), p. 107; Hanley 1989, p. 9.

55. Quotation from Lebrun 1986b (Ital. trans. 1988), pp. 98–9. For the original Latin, see Alberigo, Joannou, Leonardi and Prodi (eds) 1962, p. 731 (Session XXIV, 11 November 1563, *Canones super reformationes circa matrimonium*, Chapter I, *Tametsi*). On the directives of the Council of Trent, see Gaudemet 1987 (Ital. trans. 1989), pp. 278–95; Ferrante 1994a, 1994b and 1998; Zarri 1996 and 2000, pp. 203–50; Lombardi 1996 and 2001, pp. 99–126; Pelaja 1994 and 1996; Fazio 1996, pp. 160–4; Accal 1998.

56. Head-König 1993, pp. 443–4; Di Simplicio 1994b; Ferrante 1996a.

57. Di Simplicio 1994b, p. 188.

58. Cargnelutti 1994 and Sarti 1994c, p. 685.

59. Burguière 1986c (Ital. trans. 1988), pp. 128–9; Stone 1977 (Ital. trans. 1983), pp. 684–6. When it was carried into the urban situation, far from family control, this custom of having premarital sex with the fiancé increased the probability of girls who were new to the city falling into prostitution. Scott and Tilly 1975 (Ital. trans. 1979) and Tilly, Scott and Cohen 1976.

60. Casey 1989 (Ital. trans. 1991), p. 133.

61. Lebrun 1986b (Ital. trans. 1988), p. 107; Hanley 1989; Stone 1990, pp. 55–6; Fauve-Chamoux 2001; Watt 2001, pp. 140–1.

62. Gottlieb 1993, p. 70; Fazio 1996, p. 164. In France, civil marriage was introduced by the Constitution of 1791 and more particularly by the Law of 20 September 1792. In the Civil Code (1804), the family is no longer perceived as something that arises from a contractual union, but from a natural community; see Rosanvallon 1992 (Ital. trans. 1994).

63. Ozment 1983, pp. 30–2; Roper 1985, p. 64; Bonfield 2001, pp. 100–01. Watt 2001, p. 127. For a critical debate on Luther's position, see Johnson 1992.

64. A dower was an allocation that in some areas, such as England, the husband made to the wife to ensure her maintenance in the event of widowhood.

65. On the situation in England, see Stone 1977 (Ital. trans. 1983), pp. 34–41, and 1990, pp. 49–137; Lebrun 1986b (Ital. trans. 1988), pp. 108–9.

66. Ozment 1983, pp. 30–3; Watt 2001, pp. 126–7; Bonfield 2001, p. 102.

67. Van Dülmen 1990, vol. I, p. 161; Head-König 1993, pp. 444–5.

68. Rogers 1993, p. 296.

69. Head-König 1993, pp. 444. In Switzerland, the legislation on marriage differed greatly from one canton to another, and occasionally amongst the individual communities within a single canton.

70. Head-König 1993.

71. Ozment 1983; Gaudemet 1987; van Dülmen 1990, vol. I, pp. 157–86; Watt 2001; Bonfield 2001 etc. In Holland, the requirement for parental consent was introduced in 1580, see Schama 1987 (Ital. trans. 1988), p. 450.

72. Burguière 1986c (Ital. trans. 1988), p. 124.

73. Ozment 1983, p. 39.

74. Roper 1985, pp. 67–8 and 96–7; 1989, pp. 132–205; Zarri 1996, p. 440; Harrington 1995, pp. 85–92 and 145; Bonfield 2001, pp. 109–11; Watt 2001, pp. 130–7; Fauve-Chamoux 2001, pp. 252–4.

75. Stone 1990; Bonfield 2001, pp. 110–11. In England, however, it was possible to obtain a divorce through an act of parliament, although this was a long and tortuous process.

76. Phillips 1991, pp. 1–6; Seidel Menchi 2000, pp. 89–90.

77. Watt 2001, pp. 130–5.

78. Stone 1990, pp. 139–82; Phillips 1991, pp. 81–92; Seidel Menchi 2000, p. 29 etc.

79. Lieber, Schereschewsky 1971; Ainsztein, Kashain, Posner and Schereschewsky 1974; Schereschewsky 1972; Bonfield 2001, p. 108.

80. Bonfield 2001, pp. 107–8 and 112–13.

81. Levin 1989, pp. 89, 114–26. For information on the case of Tatyanitsa and Gavrilko, see Russkaja Istoričeskaja Biblioteka, vol. II, 946–9, no. 206, quoted in Levin 1989, p. 122.

82. Levin 1989, pp. 298–350 (Orthodox priests may marry, but if they are celibate before ordination they cannot marry afterwards); Roper 1985, pp. 85–7.

83. Amongst other works, see Kramer 1985; Burguière 1986c; Schwab 1979, p. 279; Head-König 1993. Ehmer 1991, pp. 45–61.

84. Later it was prohibited for married servants to enter the *Winkelherbergen*, but also to become day-labourers in order to avoid the ban. In 1616 the destitute were prohibited from seeking refuge in Bavarian cities; see Mitterauer and Sieder 1977 (English trans. 1982), p. 123. On Tyrol see also Lanzinger 2001.

85. Hufton 1995 (Ital. trans. 1996), pp. 58–9, 62 and 123; Stone 1977 (Ital. trans. 1983), pp. 718–19.

86. Rogers 1993, pp. 294–7.

87. Sewell Jr. 1980; Roper 1985; Wiesner 1989; Ehmer 1991 and 1992; Palazzi 1997, pp. 128–9.

88. Mitterauer 1990; Sarti 1997b.

89. Berkner 1972; Czap Jr. 1983 (Ital. trans. 1984), p. 154; Burguière 1986c (Ital. trans. 1988), pp. 126–9.

90. *Riforma* 1719, p. 3. Discussed in Sarti 1999a.

91. Berkner 1972 (Ital. trans. 1977); Geremek 1977 (Ital. trans. 1992).

92. Essentially, *mezzadri* were peasants who did not own the land they worked, and their farms were given to them in exchange for part of the harvest, usually one half (hence the name). In practice, however, *mezzadria* contracts varied according to the particular situation. In Italy this type of contract developed in the last centuries of the Middle Ages and over time it became more favourable to the landowner. After having been profoundly changed by Law no. 756 of 15 September 1964, it was completely abolished by Law no. 203 of 3 May 1982. See the next note and Bevilacqua (ed.) 1990; Della Pina 1990; Salvatici 1995, all with bibliographies.

93. On *mezzadri*, for example, Poni 1982; Biagioli 1986; Palazzi 1992–93 and 1997. On enforced marriages for widows, see Kula 1972; Kochanowicz 1983; Mitterauer and Sieder 1977, English translation 1982, p. 122; Burguière 1986a (Ital. trans. 1988), p. 57.

94. *Gerichts- und Gemeinderatprotokolle*, Neckarhausen, vol. III, fol. 201 (4/2/1779)

and fol. 15 (26/7/1780), in Sabean 1990, p. 106.

95. Hochstrasser 1993, pp. 100–1. The three obligations were the oath of serfdom (*Leibeigenschaftseid*), the profession of hereditary vassalage (*Erbhuldigung*) and the oath on obtaining citizenship (*Bürgereid*). The payment of a small sum would remedy the absence of the age requirement and the training journey.

96. Head-König 1993, p. 462.

97. In the eighteenth century, in particular, new factors combined with more traditional ones to produce a sharp increase in the number of illegitimate births in some areas; see Laslett 1977b; Laslett, Oosterveen and Smith (eds) 1980.

98. The bibliography on this subject is enormous. Apart from the works referred to in the previous note, see also Stone 1977 (Ital. trans. 1983); Pelaja 1994 and 1996; Di Simplicio 1994b; Ferrante 1996b.

99. On demographic trends in various areas of Europe, see Dupâquier 1987; Livi Bacci 1998 (particularly the summary on pp. 14–15, table 1.1).

100. Zemon Davis 1975 (Ital. trans. 1980), pp. 23–90.

101. Jean de Vauzelles, *Police subsidaire a celle quasi infinie multitude des povres survenus a Lyon l'an Mil cinq cens trente Ung*, fol. A III *r*. Quoted in Zemon Davis 1975, p. 33; see also p. 51.

102. On changing attitudes to the poor and the development of welfare institutions and places of confinement, see Vauchez 1975; Geremek 1988 and 1992; Scarabello 1987; Woolf 1988 (Ital. trans. 1988); Rosselli 1996; Pastore 2000; Zannetti (ed.) 2000.

103. Archive of the Archbishopric of Sienna, *Foro misto*, 5367 (1635), fol. 179 and 5368 (1636), fol. 21, quoted in Di Simplicio 1994b, pp. 190–1.

104. Archive of the Archbishopric of Sienna, *Cause criminali*, 5558 (1668), quoted in Di Simplicio 1994b, p. 192. On the perception of concubines as prostitutes and tradition of the concubine-housekeeper, see Ferrante 1996 and 1998.

105. Paradoxically, prostitutes in the Papal State, although prosecuted by the Church authorities, were required to pay a tax to exercise their profession 'legally'. Prostitutes were tolerated for a long time within the territory of the Papal State, as in other Italian states. The Reformation, on the other hand, closed public brothels and banned any form of prostitution, although the efficacy of the measures is uncertain (in England, even the brothels were not permanently closed). France and Spain prohibited prostitution in 1560 and 1632 respectively, see Ferrante 1996, p. 218; Hufton 1995 (Ital. trans. 1996), pp. 258–85; Roper 1989, pp. 102–31; Harrington 1995, pp. 217–22.

106. Amongst other texts, see Ferrante 1983, 1986 and 1996; Groppi 1994.

107. On the use of service as a method of reinserting prostitutes into society that was implemented relatively little in Italy, see Lombardi and Reggiani 1990; Groppi 1994, pp. 166–73.

108. Rome State Archive, *Archivio Spada Veralli*, b. 465, *Lettere al fratello Giovanni Battista della Signora Geronima*, letter dated 5/2/1583, in D'Amelia 1993, p. 392.

109. The expression *aut murus aut maritus*, used in *Ancien Régime* sources, was used in Ulrike Strasser's title, *Aut murus aut maritus. Women's Lives in Counter-Reformation Munich (1579–1651)*, Dissertation, University of Minnesota, 1997.

110. Roper 1989, pp. 242–3; Wiesner 1998, pp. 47–62. For bibliographical information on women and the Reformation, see also Wiesner 1987.

111. In the Middle Ages, there had been semi-religious lifestyles for women (Franciscan tertiaries and beguines) which, as time went by, were gradually integrated into the mendicant orders, see Benvenuti Papi 1983, pp. 113–17; Vauchez 1981; Scaraffia and Zarri (eds) 1994.

112. Zemon Davis 1975; Bossy 1985.

113. Zanetti 1972 (pub. 1983); Delille and Ciuffreda 1993; Ferrer i Alòs 1993; Medioli 1999.

114. Ferrer i Alòs 1993, pp. 545–6, tables 4–5.

115. Zanetti 1972 (pub. 1983), p. 242. The percentages fell to 30% amongst daughters of fathers born between 1650 and 1700, to 13% when the father was born in the first half of the eighteenth century and 3% when born in the second half of the century.

116. Stone 1977 (Ital. trans. 1983), pp. 50–1 and 782, fig. 3. At the most, 15% of the daughters of English lords born in the first half of the seventeenth century had never been married when they reached the age of 50. In the following half century, the figure reached a maximum of 25%, and in the eighteenth century it fluctuated around 20%.

117. Cooper 1976; Hurwich 1998.

118. Lebrun 1986b (Ital. trans. 1988), p. 98.

119. Van Dülmen 1990, vol. I, pp. 157–86; Roper 1985.

120. See above, notes 111 and 112.

121. Amongst other works, see Biondi 1981, pp. 260–8; Prosperi 1981; Bossy 1985 (Ital. trans. 1990), p. 137; Casali 1979 and 1982; Frigo 1985; Sarti 1991 and 1994d.

122. Luther, *Predigten über das 2. Buch Mose*, Weimarer Ausgabe, vol. XVI, p. 490, quoted in Schwab 1979, p. 264.

123. For a summary, see Lebrun 1986a (Ital. trans. 1987), pp. 68–75. On the Reformed world Roper 1989; Stone 1977 (Ital. trans. 1983), pp. 170–2.

124. Zemon Davis 1986, p. 54; Di Simplicio 1988 and 1994b.

125. Fauve-Chamoux 1993, p. 502.

126. For an overview of the changes in monasticism in the Catholic world, see Scaraffia and Zarri (ed.) 1994.

127. Baerenstein 1994.

128. Groppi 1994.

129. Zanetti 1972 (pub. 1983), p. 237.

130. Baerenstein 1994, p. 798. On families in monasteries, see Zarri 2000, pp. 82ff.

131. Evangelisti 1995, p. 100 and Evangelisti 2000, who talks of the 'dynasticization' of convents. See also the interesting example analysed in Cabibbo and Modica 1989.

132. Groppi 1994; Levi 1996; Evangelisti 1995.

133. Rome State Archive, *Archivio Spada Veralli*, b. 465, *Lettere al fratello Giovanni Battista della Signora Geronima*, letter dated 5/2/1583, in D'Amelia 1993, pp. 391–2.

134. On the importance of posing this kind of question, see, for example, Goody 1972; Mitterauer and Sieder 1977; Héritier 1979; Guerreau-Jalabert 1981; Casey 1989 (Ital. trans. 1991), pp. vii–x and 3–20.

135. Battaglia 1961–; Palazzi and Folena 1992, under the entry. Concerning the current meaning of the corresponding terms in French, English, German and Spanish, see the entries in Robert 1953–64 and Trésor 1980; Oxford 1989; Duden 1976–81 and Real Academia Española 1992.

136. Bologna State Archive, *Famiglia Albergati, Strumenti and scritture*, b. 215, fol. 16 (23/12/1747).

137. Both the Latin *familia* and the French *famille* contributed to the German word *Familie*.

138. See under the entry in Lexicon 1864–1940; Baudry 1896; Walde and Hofmann 1938–65; Ernout and Meillet 1959–60; Thesaurus 1900–; Darling Buck 1949. See also Radin 1914; Finley 1973 (Ital. trans. 1977), p. 5; Benveniste 1969; Herlihy 1991; Sarti 1994b.

139. See under the entry in Lexicon 1864–1940; Baudry 1896; Walde and Hofmann 1938–65; Ernout and Meillet 1959–60; Thesaurus 1900–; Darling Buck 1949. See also Radin 1914; Finley 1973 (Ital. trans. 1977), p. 5; Benveniste 1969; Herlihy 1991; Sarti 1994b.

140. Finley 1973 (Ital. trans. 1977), p. 5; Benveniste 1969 (Ital. trans. 1976), vol. I, pp. 161–3.

141. Under the entry in Glossarium 1883–87; Bloch and Wartburg 1960; Duby 1974, p. 52; Schwab 1979, pp. 256–7; Hammer 1983, p. 247; Duro 1986–94.

142. Under the entry in Tobler and Lommatzsch 1952 (26th edn); Huguet 1925–73; Robert 1953–64. The term did not however appear in Godefroy 1881–1902.

143. Oxford 1989. 'Family' did not appear in Borden 1982.

144. Robert 1953–64; Oxford 1989. On the use of the term in England, see Trumbach 1978 (Ital. trans. 1982); Tadmor 1996.

145. Real Academia Española 1992. Covarrubias 1987 (pub. 1611 and 1674) appears to have considered it an ancient interpretation back in the seventeenth century.

146. Giovanni Faldella used the term with this meaning in a short story published in *Racconti della Scapigliatura piemontese*, Gianfranco Contini (ed.), Milan, 1953 (p. 94: 'e tutta la famiglia dei donzelli mi dava la berta').

147. Moroni 1840–61; Duro 1986–94. For the *familia* of Italian princes in the early modern era, see Mozzarelli (ed.) 1988.

148. This was the result of an initial survey I carried out; see Sarti 1994b. For the survival of the term into the twentieth century, see Pasquali 1939.

149. Bologna State Archive, *Famiglia Albergati, Strumenti and Scritture*, b. 148, folder 21 (also in 22) and folder 23 (also in 24); b. 151, folder 17 (also in 18, 19 and 20); b. 170, folder 24 (also in 25) and folder 26 (also in 27, 28, 29 and 30); b. 179, folders 18 and 21 (also in 21 and 22); b. 215, folders 16 and 19.

150. Alberti pub. 1969, p. 226.

151. Vocabolario Crusca 1612; 1623, 1691, 1729–38. The other definitions were: 'servants'; 'sergeants or servants of the Court [. . .] beadles and a body of armed retainers'; 'company, [. . .] conversation'; ancestry, lineage.

152. The hierarchical element is, however, still present in one of the definitions provided by Battaglia 1961–, 'all of those who live under the same roof and are dependent on the same *paterfamilias* (wife, children, other blood relations, as well as persons in service)'.

153. Vizani 1609, p. 4. The attribution of this text to Pompeo Vizani, a noble from Bologna, was challenged by Fantuzzi 1781–94, vol. VIII, pp. 206–13, according to whom the work was written by 'Emanuele Tesauro, Piedmontese gentleman, and completed in the year 1581, on 20 July, as recorded in the manuscripts of Pompeo [Vizani]' (p. 211).

154. Assandri 1616, p. 27.

155. Oxford 1989. By 950, the word 'house' already had as one of its meanings, a co-resident group and by around 1000, a family consisting of ancestors and descendants. In the fourteenth century, the term 'household' for a group of co-resident persons began to spread.

156. This was the fourth edition of the *Dictionnaire of the Académie Française*, quoted in Schwab 1979, p. 268, which argued that the common term was only used in this sense in the expressions *chef de famille* and *avoir une grande famille à nourrir*. In French, a group of co-resident persons could be defined as a *ménage*, which derived from the Latin *mansio*, as did *maison* ('house').

157. Elias 1968 and 1975 (Ital. trans. 1980), pp. 44–67; Karnoouh 1979.

158. Aristotle and the author of the treatise on economics attributed to him perceived the house (in Greek *oikos*, and 'economics' derives from *oikonomiā*, which means 'house law' or the science of home management) as the natural unit in social organization. Relations between members of a domestic community reflected those that were typical of a state: a husband's power over his wife was 'aristocratic', his power over his children was 'monarchical' and his power over his slaves was 'despotic or tyrannical'. It is not possible to examine this argument further here, but for further analysis, see Brunner 1950; Schwab 1979; Sabean 1990, pp. 91–3. The revival of Aristotelianism also played an important role in France and Italy in creating the image of the home and the family as a clearly identifiable and possibly self-sufficient hierarchical unit. On the situation in Italy, see Frigo 1985; Casali 1979 and 1982 and the critical considerations of Ambrosoli 1987; on the situation in France, see Francia Schwab 1979, pp. 268–9.

159. The term *familia* in the domestic unit always included the servants and never referred to the parent and children group. Moreover, it was used more often to describe kinship, or the servants on their own, than it was used for the co-resident family unit, see Schwab 1979, pp. 266–8.

160. Sabean 1990, p. 93. For more general information, see Hochstrasser 1993, p. 96; van Dülmen 1990, Vol. I pp. 12–23. On the concept of *feu* and *fuoco*, see for France Guerreau-Jalabert 1981, p. 1030; Zeller 1983 on Italy see es Herlihy Klapisch-Zuber 1978.

161. Grimm 1854–1956; Brunner 1958 (Ital. trans. 1970), p. 143, Schwab 1979. Many of the results of Brunner's have been justifiably criticized, see particularly Opitz 1994; Derks 1996. As far as I know, no criticism has been made of the point I refer to here.

162. Mitterauer and Sieder 1984, pp. 18–21.

163. Schwab 1979, pp. 269–71. Only in the second half of the eighteenth century did the concept of *Familie* start to change in any significant manner (pp. 271–301).

164. *Gerichts- und Gemeinderatprotokolle*, Neckarhausen, vol. VIII, fol. 215 (31/12/1816) and *Nürtingen Oberamtsgerichtsprotokolle*, Staatsarchiv Ludwigsburg, F190II, Band 257, fol. 37 (14/4/1827), in Sabean 1990, pp. 117–18.

165. Sabean 1990, pp. 148–56, 171. In the sources examined by Sabean, the verb *hausen* is used in the sense of living together, being married, getting on with each other, doing well, being diligent and, more rarely, behaving (pp. xvii and 101–16). The analysis was based on the legal documents for the village in question.

166. Ferrante 1998.

167. On the centrality of the concept of 'house' in the Iberian world, see Martin Casares, forthcoming.

168. Ago 1995, p. 113.

169. See note 158 above.

170. See amongst other works Stone 1977 (Ital. trans. 1983), pp. 168–70; van Dülmen 1990, pp. 12–23.

171. See para. 6 above.

172. Schwarzenberg 1982; on wives, see Hufton 1995 (Ital. trans. 1996); Ago (ed.) 1995; Arru (ed.) 1998; Calvi and Chabot (eds) 1998; Groppi and Houbre (eds) 1998.

173. Ménétra pub. 1982 (Ital. trans. 1992), pp. 202 and 194.

174. It should be remembered that in Italy the father was officially the head of the family until the reform of the Family Code in 1975.

175. The bibliography on these changes is vast. For the situation in Italy, see Barbagli 1996, which has an extensive bibliography on the other European countries and comparative information.

176. Mitterauer and Sieder 1977 (Eng. trans. 1982), pp. 7–10.

177. Mitterauer and Sieder 1977 (Eng. trans. 1982), p. 8.

178. See the Introduction.

179. Fauve-Chamoux 1987 and Fauve-Chamoux and Ochiai 1998; Burguière 1986b (Ital. trans. 1988), p. 63. See also Deffontaines 1972, p. 122 (on the Netherlands).

180. Schlumbohm 1998.

181. Mitterauer and Sieder 1977 (Eng. trans. 1982), p. 9.

182. Further to the previously quoted Hufton 1995 (Ital. trans. 1996), p. 53.

183. Loriga 1990, pp. 281–93 and 1992.

184. Ariès 1960 (Ital. trans. 1989); Brizzi 1976; Julia 1996 etc.

185. Foucault 1975 (Ital. trans. 1976).

186. See among other works Hareven 1991.

II. Home and Family: Bringing Things Together or Setting up Home

1. For the transport of the bride's goods in Renaissance Florence, see Klapisch-Zuber 1982 (Ital. trans. 1988), especially p. 160 and 1984 (pub. 1988), p. 194; Witthoft 1996, pp. 136–42; Chabot 1994; pp. 421–32; Van Gennep 1980–82, vol. I, p. 352 on transporting the *trousseau*, p. 353 on the Soule Valley; Corso 1948, pp. 11–12 for the whole of the Basque Country; De Gubernatis 1878 for Sardinia. The bride's property was not always carried on a cart. Occasionally, it was carried by hand or on the shoulders, see, for example, Witthoft 1996, p. 138. In some cases, it arrived with the bride on the wedding day, and in others at a different

time: the day before (Fine 1984, p. 167) or the day after (Klapisch-Zuber 1979 [Ital. trans. 1988], p. 160). As has already been pointed out (see above, chapter I, para. 4), it is not possible to give a detailed analysis of wedding traditions and ceremonies here, given that they were so varied. It should be noted, for example, that in eighteenth-century England the aristocracy developed a tendency to avoid the traditional public features of wedding ceremonies, see Gottlieb 1993, p. 82.

2. Mitterauer 1981.

3. Head-König 1993.

4. Poni 1982; Biagioli 1986; Barbagli 1996; Czap Jr. 1983 (Ital. trans. 1984); Ralison 1977, p. 119 and pp. 121–2; Burguière 1986a (Ital. trans. 1988), pp. 51–2; Fauve-Chamoux 1993, pp. 490–1; Hammel 1972; Palazzi 1997, pp. 310–27.

5. Hajnal 1983 (Ital. trans. 1984); Laslett 1983 (Ital. trans. 1984); Kertzer 1995, p. 376. In the case of complex sharecropper families in Italy, there were rules governing the division of property in the event of separation, see Poni 1982; Palazzi 1992–93 and 1997.

6. Wall, Robin and Laslett (eds) 1983 (Ital. trans. 1984); Rowland 1987; Osswald 1990; Barbagli 1996 and 1987; Rogers 1993.

7. Barbagli 1996, *passim* (p. 488 on Turi) and 1987; Osswald 1990; Rogers 1993.

8. On the situation in Galitia, see Dubert-García 1992, pp. 119–20. On the labourers, see Barbagli 1996 and 1987; Osswald 1990; Andorka and Faragó 1983, pp. 294–6; Schlumbohm 1998, p. 58 (Belm is in Osnabrück, but in the early modern era it was part of Westphalia). Garriolo Arce 1998, p. 213. See also the case of the landless family in Courland in Plakans 1975, p. 652. According to Kaser 1998, p. 172, the spread of nuclear families in the Mediterranean societies was linked to the high level of urbanization in the area (such families were common in south-western Spain, southern Italy and in parts of Greece).

9. Rowland 1987; Barbagli 1996; Da Molin 1990 (Ital. trans. 1992); Delille 1985; García Gonzalez (ed.) 1998.

10. Hajnal 1983 (Ital. trans. 1984).

11. Ménétra pub. 1982 (Ital. trans. 1992), p. 70; Mitterauer and Sieder 1977 (Eng. trans. 1983), pp. 3–4. On the marriage of artisans' wives, which was discouraged in Italy but not always elsewhere (for example in London), see Laudani 1996 and Hanawalt 1994.

12. The 20% was recorded by Goody 1976, p. 10. I am grateful to Antoinette Fauve-Chamoux for information about the actual percentage of about 30% to be found in many areas.

13. See, for example, on this point, Ferrer i Alòs 1993, p. 540.

14. Van Gennep, tome I, vol. II, pp. 499–500.

15. Delille 1985; Hufton 1995 (Ital. trans. 1996), p. 124; Van Gennep, tome I, vol. II, pp. 499–500.

16. Segalen 1981, pp. 155–7; Fine 1984, p. 164. For conflicts, see the cases described by Collomp 1984. On the images and practices in the early modern era relating to 'women in command', see Zemon Davis 1975 (Ital. trans. 1980), pp. 175–209.

17. Klapisch-Zuber 1984 (pub. 1988), pp. 201–4. On the changes that led to the disappearance of the chests from the public view at weddings in Florence, see Klapisch-Zuber 1994 and 1998. For a description of them, see Thornton 1991 (Ital. trans. 1992), pp. 192–204; Callmann 1996.

18. According to the available data, it does not appear that beds were part of the dowries of German noblewomen or the Catalan gentry (the trousseaus of Catalan noblewomen were taken to the bridegroom's house in chests called 'brides' chests'), see Hurwich 1998, p. 183; Ferrer i Alòs 1993, p. 543. The presence of furniture in the dowry appears to have been rare in Turin as well, at least between 1650 and 1710, see Cavallo 1998, p. 197.

19. Roper 1985; Klapisch-Zuber 1984 (Ital. trans. 1988), pp. 205–6; Segalen 1981; Malanima 1990, pp. 11–12; Fine 1984; Hauser 1994, pp. 363–73; Fazio 1996; Muzzarelli 1999, pp. 69 and 110.

20. Roper 1985, p. 72.

21. Malanima 1990, p. 12.

22. Van Gennep, tome I, vol. II, pp. 370–3; Burguière 1978, pp. 645–6 and 1986c (Ital. trans. 1988), pp. 108–9; Roper 1985, pp. 89–91; van Dülmen 1990, pp. 155–6 and, more generally, on fears of the evil eye when weddings took place, Klapisch-Zuber 1979 (Ital. trans. 1988), p. 124.

23. Klapisch-Zuber 1979 (Ital. trans. 1988), pp. 124–5. For information on this institution, see para. 4 of this chapter.

24. Roper 1985, pp. 91–3; Gautenet 1987.

25. Burguière 1978; Lebrun 1986b (Ital. trans. 1988), pp. 108–9; Roper 1985, p. 92.

26. Zemon Davis 1982 (Ital. trans. 1984), p. 18. This is the region in which the family of Martin Guerre lived, and his story is well known thanks to the film (*The Return of Martin Guerre*, directed by Daniel Vigne and starring Gérard Depardieu).

27. Hochstrasser 1993, p. 102.

28. Fazio 1992 and 1996; Hufton 1995 (Ital. trans. 1996), pp. 80–1.

29. Levi 1976, p. 1103.

30. Casanova 1997, p. 217.

31. A. Bongino, *Relazione de' vari progetti sovra diverse materie che riflettono la Sardegna*, in *Il riformismo settecentesco in Sardegna*, Luigi Bulferetti (ed.), Cagliari, 1966, pp. 129–379 (p. 224), quoted in Barbagli 1990, p. 31 and 1996, p. 516.

32. Barbagli 1990 and 1996, pp. 513–20.

33. Ehmer 1998, pp. 70–3; Hanawalt 1994.

34. Hajnal 1983 (Ital. trans. 1984). It should be remembered that the average life span was very short. In the context of reigning families, it was 32.1 years for men and 36 for women in the sixteenth century, and 36.1 and 38.3 respectively in the eighteenth century. From 1750 to 1759 it was 36.9 years in England, 27.9 in France and 37.3 in Sweden. As far as the population as a whole was concerned, life expectancy at the time of birth varied between 25 and 35 years. Of course this was largely due to the very high infant mortality: those who reached the age of 20 could hope to live for a few decades more. Nevertheless, the demographic situation was very different to the current one, see

Dupâquier 1987, p. 5; Livi Bacci 1989, p. 113, and 1998, pp. 79–80 and 85–6; Viazzo 2001.

35. Hajnal 1965 (Ital. trans. 1977) and 1983 (Ital. trans. 1984); Laslett 1977a (Ital. trans. 1977) and 1988; Barbagli 1990 and 1996 which corrected some mistaken ideas about Italy propounded by the previous two writers; Sarti 1997a.

36. Wrigley and Schofield 1981, pp. 257–65 and 424–5; Livi Bacci 1998, pp. 127–50.

37. Sarti 1997b.

38. See above, chapter I, para. 4.

39. Restif de la Bretonne, *Monsieur Nicolas*, ed. J.-J. Pauvert, vol. I, 1959, quoted in Burguière 1986c (Ital. trans. 1988), p. 135 (the italics for the title *monssieur* are mine).

40. For some reflections on parental assistance at the time of marriage, see Wall 1983 (Ital. trans. 1984).

41. On the significance of parental assistance, Wall 1983 (Ital. trans. 1984), p. 53.

42. Sieder and Mitterauer 1983 (Ital. trans. 1984); Hoock and Jullien 1998; Fauve-Chamoux and Ochiai (eds) 1998, especially the essay by Schlumbohm.

43. For an example of juridical pluralism, i.e. the superimposition of different legal traditions within the same area, see Povolo 1994.

44. Barbagli 1990 and 1996, pp. 513–20.

45. Ortu 1988; Benigno 1989; Da Molin 1990 (Ital. trans. 1992).

46. Hajnal 1965 (Ital. trans. 1977) and 1983 (Ital. trans. 1984); Hammel 1972; Laslett 1977a (Ital. trans. 1977); Wall, Robin and Laslett (eds) 1983 (Ital. trans. 1984); Kaser 1998, pp. 172–5; Wall 1998, p. 261; Toderova 1998.

47. Biagioli 1986; Della Pina 1990; Barbagli 1987 and 1996; Pescarolo 1990; Torti 1989; Czap Jr. 1983 (Ital. trans. 1984).

48. Martini 1993.

49. Collomp 1984, pp. 150 and 154–5. For peasant reproduction strategies, see Augustins 1989.

50. Niederösterreichisches Landesarchiv, B.G. Litschau, *Herrschaft Heidenreichstein*,

n. 66, fol. 187, quoted in Berkner 1972 (Ital. trans. 1977), p. 120. Strictly speaking this was not a sale, but an inheritance.

51. Berkner 1972 (Ital. trans. 1977), p. 118; Sieder and Mitterauer 1983 (Ital. trans. 1984); Ehmer 1998.

52. Collomp 1984, p. 158.

53. For a history of such contracts, see Gaunt 1983 (Ital. trans. 1984).

54. Berkner 1972 (Ital. trans. 1977), p. 121.

55. Ehmer 1998, p. 61.

56. Niederösterreichisches Landesarchiv, B.G. Litschau, *Herrschaft Heidenreichstein*, n. 101, *Inventursprotokolle*, 1754–74, fol. 307, quoted in Berkner 1972 (Ital. trans. 1977), p. 122.

57. Mitterauer and Sieder 1977 (Eng. trans. 1982), p. 167. The use of *ableben* has been demonstrated in southern Burgenland and some districts of Syria.

58. Sieder, Mitterauer 1983 (Ital. trans. 1984); Ehmer 1998.

59. On the relationship between inheritance systems and family structures, see Goldschmidt and Kunkel 1971 (Ital. trans. 1977); Berkner and Mendels 1972 (Ital. trans. 1977) and now particularly in relation to stem families, Fauve-Chamoux and Ochiai (eds) 1998, which looks into the complex problems in defining the concept that have necessarily been ignored here. It should be remembered that the concept of a stem family (*famille-souche*) in French was introduced in the nineteenth century by Frédéric Le Play and later became the object of various interpretations, partly for ideological reasons, see Douglass 1993; Verdon 1996; Cerman 1997; Emmer 1998.

60. Fauve-Chamoux and Ochiai 1998.

61. See the maps produced in Todd 1990, which were based on data that was more recent than the data analysed here, and, for France, Yver 1966.

62. Fauve-Chamoux 1987 and 1994; Ungari 1974. For other cases of getting round egalitarian laws, see Derovet 1994, pp. 47–91. Palazzi 1997, pp. 67–77.

63. Schilumbohm 1998.

64. Consolidating Act no. 8 of 7 February 1962; Dozen by Provincial Consolidating Act (Province of Bolzano) no. 32 of 28 December 1978; Provincial Laws no. 10 of 26 March 1982, no. 5 of 24 February 1993 and no. 17 of 28 November 2001.

65. Viazzo 1989 (Ital. trans. 1990).

66. Albera 1994. The accounts on which this analysis is based refer to the situation in the nineteenth century. On the Alps, see Cole and Wolf 1974; Viazzo 1989 (Ital. trans. 1990).

67. The agnatic kinship consists of relations along the paternal line.

68. Hughes 1975 (Ital. trans. 1979); Barbagli 1996; Casanova 1997.

69. Primogeniture, fideicommissum, majorat, *droit d'aînesse*, entail, strict settlement, etc. were various legal instruments by which this strategy was carried out in different countries. The chronology of the changes in inheritance strategies was not the same everywhere.

70. Quoted in Zanetti 1972 (pub. 1983), pp. 238–9. The author of the short treatise is generally thought to be Giovanni Della Casa, who also wrote *Il galateo*.

71. Cadets are the male first-born's younger brothers and, in a wider screr, sisters. In systems based on primogeniture, they are excluded as a matter of principle, although in practice there were cases in which the first-born was not the heir, see Ago 1994a.

72. On the nobility's ideology and behaviour, see Zanetti 1972 (pub. 1983); Cooper 1976; Stone 1977 (Ital. trans. 1983); Stone and Fawtier Stone 1984 and 1986 (Ital. trans. 1989); Labatut 1978 (Ital. trans. 1982); Donati 1988; Visceglia 1988; Visceglia (ed.) 1992; Ferrer i Alòs 1993; Delille and Ciuffreda 1993; Bonfield 1995; Casanova 1997, pp. 85–109; Ago 1998b; Hurwich 1998; Sarti 1999c.

73. Zanetti 1972 (pub. 1983), p. 242.

74. Delille and Ciuffreda 1993.

75. Cooper 1976, p. 291; Hurswich 1998.

76. Ferrer i Alòs 1993.

77. Hurwich 1998; Ferrer i Alòs 1993.

78. Zanetti 1972 (pub. 1983); Delille 1986.

79. Quoted in Burguière 1986b (Ital. trans. 1988), p. 68.

80. See the reflections of Rudolph 1992, pp. 132–3.

81. Stone 1977 (Ital. trans. 1983), pp. 93–5. On the system adopted by the English upper class, see also Bonfield 1995. On the strategies for replacing first-born sons without issue in the Milanese aristocracy, see Zanetti 1972 (pub. 1983).

82. Burguière 1986b (Ital. trans. 1988), p. 60.

83. Ehmer 1998, pp. 60–1. On the distinction between succession and inheritance see Augustins 1982 and 1988. See also Bourdelais and Gourdon 2000, pp. 28–9; Rosental 2000, pp. 57–8.

84. Collomp 1984, p. 157

85. Spufford 1976, p. 158.

86. Apart from the previously mentioned reference, see Cavallo 1998.

87. Ravis-Giordani and Segalen 1994, p. 16.

88. Casanova 1997, p. 108.

89. Bonfield 1995.

90. Casanova 1997, pp. 85–109.

91. Fauve-Chamoux 1994, p. 182.

92. Spufford 1976.

93. Apart from the previously mentioned references, see Collomp 1984; Ferrer i Alòs 1993; Bonfield 1995.

94. Ravis-Giordani and Segalen 1994, p. 19.

95. Rome State Archive, *Famiglia Spada Veralli*, b. 611, 9 April 1661, quoted in Ago 1994a, p. 232.

96. A church benefice is the income used to maintain the holder of a church office, for example a parish priest. Under the *Ancien Régime*, it principally derived from the ownership of land.

97. Ferrer i Mòs 1993

98. Quoted in Burguière 1986b (Ital. trans. 1988), p. 68.

99. Ago 1994a.

100. A. Verri, *Il Caffè*, ed. Silvestri, 1818, vol. *discorsk vaxi*, p. 82; G. Filangieri, *Scienza*

della legislazione, Philadelphia (but probably Livorno), 1799, book II, vol. I, chapter IV, p. 282, both quoted in Mainoni 1900, p. 924. For the changes in Italy, see Ungari 1974, pp. 39–41; Barbagli 1996, pp., 176–88. *Fideicommissa* were reintroduced in the nineteenth century. See also chapter 7.

101. Ago 1992.

102. Rome State Archive, *Famiglia Spada Veralli*, b. 611, 27 October 1670, quoted in Ago 1990a, p. 163. For Fabrizio's career, see pp. 77–81; for his inheritance, see p. 166.

103. Ago 1994a, p. 236.

104. Ago 1994a, pp. 231–2.

105. Collomp 1984, p. 157.

106. Mitterauer and Sieder 1977 (Eng. trans. 1982); Stone 1977 (Ital. trans. 1983), p. 692 and graph 16. On illegitimacy in the Hapsburg Empire see Saurer 2000, who also considers the role of military service.

107. Sieder and Màterauer 1983 (Ital. trans. 1984), pp. 209–11.

108. Rudolph 1992 and Pfister 2001, which helpfully summarizes the terms used in the debate on the influence proto-industrialization had on families. By proto-industrialization, we mean the development, particularly in the textile sector, of work carried out in the home and organized by merchant-entrepreneurs. On this subject, see also chapter 4, para. 1 of this volume.

109. Fauve-Chamoux 1994, p. 190.

110. Mendels 1972; Kriedte, Medick and Schlumbohm 1977 (Ital. trans. 1984); Rudolph 1992; Pfister 2001.

111. Biet 1994.

112. A similar practice was discovered in the Porto area, see Osswald 1990.

113. Yver 1966; Le Roy Ladurie 1976. On the exclusion of *enfants dotés* in England and Germany, as well as France, from the fifteenth century, see Burguière 1986b (Ital. trans. 1988), pp. 68–9.

114. Le Roy Ladurie 1976.

115. Collomp 1984, pp. 158–9.

116. Fauve-Chanioux 1994, p. 181.

117. As has already been mentioned, Belm is today in Osnabrück, but was once in Westphalia.

118. There was a feudal lord in Belm, the peasants had rights of ownership over their land, see Schlumbohm 1998.

119. Schlumbohm 1998, pp. 53–4.

120. Hughes 1978 and 1996.

121. Thomas 1990; Pomata 1994b.

122. Hughes 1978 and 1996; Chabot 1994; De Giorgio, Klapisch-Zuber (ed.) 1996; Martini 1996; Scardozzi 1998. But see also the interesting and very different case examined by Turchi 1998. Moreover, in Apulie the Lombard tradition of a marital gift (*antefato*) survived until the eighteenth century, see Delille 1996b, p. 71.

123. Goody 1976 and 1983 (Ital. trans. 1984); Hughes 1978 and 1996

124. Rome State Archive, *Archivio Spada Veralli*, b. 465, *Lettere al fratello Giovanni Battista della Signora Geronima*, letter dated 10/10/1584, quoted in D'Amelia 1993, p. 394. The brother did not agree to Geronima's suggestions, partly because the family's assets were by that time in considerable disarray.

125. Ibid. For the use of dowries, see, for example, Molho, Barducci, Battista and Donnini 1994.

126. On the steep rise in the value of dowries, see Chabot 1994 and Chabot and Fornasari 1998.

127. Goody 1976 and 1983 (Ital. trans. 1984); Hughes 1978 and 1996; Ago, Palazzi and Pomata (eds) 1994; Lazio 1992 and 1996; De Giorgio and Klapisch-Zuber (eds) 1996; Alessi 1996; Martini 1996; Delille 1996a and 1996b.

128. Palumbo 1996; Klapisch-Zuber 1998.

129. Kirshner and Molho 1978; Carboni 1999.

130. Fubini Leuzzi 1994; Chabot and Fornasari 1998; Groppi 1994.

131. D'Amelia 1990; Pelaja 1994, p. 32; Groppi 1994.

132. Bologna State Archive, *Famiglia Marsili; Strumenti and Scritture*, b. 73, folder 8, *Tes-*

tamento della Signora Anna Maria Ranuzzi Marsigli Rossi (21 February 1685), quoted in Sarti 1994a, pp. 144–5.

133. For the question of the husband's varying control over 'valued' and 'non valued' goods listed in marriage contracts, see Martini 1996. Trousseaus could be seen as part of the dowry or part of the 'parapherna-lia', which originally meant the property that stayed under a married woman's control.

134. Palazzi 1997.

135. Klapisch-Zuber 1984 (Ital. trans. 1988), pp. 196 and 198 (which emphasizes the tendency for paraphernalia to be assimilated into dowries); Hughes 1996, p. 36; Martini 1996, p. 49.

136. Cavallo 1998, pp. 188–9.

137. Ago 1995; Fazio 1990; Delille 1996a, pp. 291–3 and 1996b, pp. 76–7; Cavallo 1998, especially p. 188. On the decreasing independence of wives in nineteenth-century Bologna, see Martini 1998b. Assets that were *stradotali parafernali* were those belonging to a married woman beyond her flowery. Sometimes the definition of *beni stridotali* referred only to those as sets obtained by women during the marriage through a legacy or substitution.

138. Ago 1995, p. 122. Not all wills by women can be read as expressions of those women's wishes, free from any pressure, if only because they were often read out in the presence of family members, relations and friends when they were ill and feared they were dying, Cavallo 1998, p. 194.

139. Cavallo 1998, pp. 198–9. But in Florence, provisions of this kind already existed during the Renaissance, see Klapisch-Zuber 1983 (Ital. trans. 1988), pp. 290–1.

140. See chapter I, para. 7.

141. Bologna State Archive, *Famiglia Albergati, Strumenti e scritture*, b. 215, f. 16 (23/12/1747).

142. The increase in the legal powers of parents over children, and particularly over their marriages, which some historians have detected in the seventeenth and eighteenth centuries, could be interpreted in this manner. Apart from the above reference

(chapter I, para. 4) on France and England, see Cooper 1976, p. 304.

143. Klapisch-Zuber 1983 (Ital. trans. 1988).

144. Calvi 1994a and 1994b.

145. Nicoloso Ciceri 1994 on Istria and for a comment on this, Sarti 1994c; Barbagli 1987 and 1996, pp. 513–20 on Sardinia; Martini 1996, p. 50.

146. Hoock and Jullien 1998.

147. Palumbo 1996; Chabot and Fornasari 1998.

148. A distinction was, however, made between two types of joint ownership: one related to all assets, and the other to assets accumulated during marriage.

149. On the situation in England, see Stone 1977 (Ital. trans. 1983); on the situation in Austria, see Ehmer 1998; on the situation in Norway, see Sogner and Sandvik 1990. On joint ownership of property, see also chapter III, para. 2 of this volume.

150. Venice State Archive, *Avogaria di Comun, Matrimoni*, register 157, fol. 68, 8/9/1588, quoted in Bellavitis 1998, p. 154.

151. Hufton 1995 (Ital. trans. 1996).

152. Van Gennep.

153. Levi 1996.

154. See above, para. 4.

155. See, for example, the reflections on this subject in Klapisch-Zuber 1982 (Ital. trans. 1988), p. 154.

156. Belmont 1978; Klapisch-Zuber 1984 (pub. 1988), pp. 193–4; Fine 1984; Roper 1985; Hufton 1995 (Ital. trans. 1996).

157. Klapisch-Zuber 1982 (Ital. trans. 1988), p. 170.

158. Klapisch-Zuber 1982 (Ital. trans. 1988), pp. 185–91.

159. Witthoft 1996, pp. 138–9.

160. Chabot 1994, p. 430.

161. Hufton 1995 (Ital. trans. 1996), p. 120.

162. Fine 1984, p. 167.

163. Malanima 1990, p. 143.

164. Montanari 1991, p. 250, see also n. 2, chapter V.

165. See above, chapter I, para. 4.

166. Klapisch-Zuber 1979 (Ital. trans. 1988), pp. 131–2; Hughes 1996, pp. 18–26.

167. Hughes 1996, pp. 17–18.

168. Burguière 1978, pp. 642–3. The author does not provide the sources of the cases referred to. The translation is taken from this text. On the medieval juridical tradition relating to the kiss and the gifts, see Niccoli 1995 and 2000, pp. 109–29. See also Watt 2001, p. 138.

169. Klapisch-Zuber 1979 (Ital. trans. 1988), pp. 124–7.

170. Klapisch-Zuber 1982 (Ital. trans. 1988), p. 132. For the spread of the custom of the ring in wedding ceremonies in various parts of Europe, see Burguière 1978; Ferrante 1994b; Stone 1990, pp. 74–5. In Augsburg, there were two rings and they were exchanged, see Roper 1985, p. 81.

171. Klapisch-Zuber 1979 (Ital. trans. 1988), p. 132.

172. Hufton 1995 (Ital. trans. 1996), p. 119; De Gubernatis 1878. For an overview of French wedding traditions relating to the spindle, see Van Gennep, tome I, vol. 1, pp. 357–9 and vol. II, pp. 465–7.

173. See above, para. 2.

174. Belmont 1978; Roper 1985, p. 83.

175. On the meaning of the term, see Vocabolario Crusca 1612; 1623; 1691; 1729–38, entries for *zita, zitella* and *zitello*; Tommaseo 1851–52, vol. I, n. 304; Tommaseo and Bellini 1865–79; Cortelazzo and Zolli 1979–88, under the entry. On the etymology, see especially Devoto 1967. According to Pianigiani 1907, the term derives from the medium-high German *Zitze*, meaning breast, unweaned baby girl or young girl.

176. Klapisch-Zuber 1994; Martini 1996. In Florence, there were often two chests, see Chabot 1994 and Witthoft 1996.

177. Chabot 1994

178. See above, chapter I, para. 4. As has already been mentioned, young people often worked as servants until they married. Not surprisingly then, the words for young man or woman and for servant were the same in many European languages; see Mitterauer 1990.

179. Roper 1985, p. 87.

180. Van Dülmen 1990, p. 148.

181. Roper 1985, pp. 87–8; Hufton 1995 (Ital. trans. 1996), p. 119; Klapisch-Zuber 1979 (Ital. trans. 1988), p. 119.

182. Klapisch-Zuber 1979 (Ital. trans. 1988), pp. 174–85.

183. Van Gennep 1909 (Ital. trans. 1981), pp. 100–24.

184. Ménétra pub. 1982 (Ital. trans. 1992), pp. 60–1.

185. Van Gennep 1909 (Ital. trans. 1981), pp. 116–17; De Gubernatis 1878; Van Gennep, tome I, vols I–II; Caprettini 1975 etc. An *isba* or *izba* is a typical rural house in Russia.

186. For rituals, see Van Gennep 1909 (Ital. trans. 1981), p. 117; on the Asturias, Scandinavia and Austria, see Corso 1948, pp. 8, 27 and 42; on Italy, see De Gubernatis 1878; Corso 1948; Barbagli 1996, pp. 389–92; on France, Van Gennep, tome I, vol. II, pp. 495–6.

187. See above, chapter I, para. 4.

III. Configurations of the House and the Family

1. Gambi 1976.

2. Roche 1997, p. 118.

3. Collomp 1986 (Ital. trans. 1987).

4. On these communities see Raison 1977; Burguiere 1986a (Ital. trans. 1988), pp. 51–2.

5. Raison 1977, p. 119 and pp. 121–2.

6. Burguière 1986a (Ital. trans. 1988), p. 37.

7. Roux 1976 (Ital. trans. 1982); Pounds 1989; Schwarz 1989.

8. Barbieri and Gambi (eds) 1970; Gambi 1976.

9. *Latifundia* are large landed estates that have not been divided up into small farms for tenants, and belong to a single landowner. They are used for extensive agriculture or grazing for livestock.

10. Gambi 1976, pp. 486–8.

11. Gambi 1976, p. 488. The wage-earners who worked and lived on farms in Lombardy generally had access to more common facilities than farm labourers in the south of Italy.

12. Pounds 1989. On the peasant family in Poland, see Kula 1972.

13. Czap Jr. 1983 (Ital. trans. 1984), pp. 150–2 and 161–6.

14. Cosenza 1974, p. 89 and p. 125.

15. Ménétra pub. 1982 (Ital. trans. 1992), pp. 182–3.

16. Gambi 1976, p. 480.

17. Brunner 1950 (Ital. trans. 1970); Casali 1979 and 1982; Frigo 1985. This kind of literature was strongly influenced by Aristotelian thought. See above, chapter I, para. 7.

18. Ambrosoli 1987; Opitz 1994; Derks 1996.

19. On financial pressures and the large houses as status symbols, see Roux 1976 (Ital. trans. 1982), pp. 9 and 25–6; Luttazzi-Gregori 1983, p. 143. Until the sixteenth century, different noble families in Italian cities were often brought together on a territorial basis, see Casanova 1997; on the situation in Genoa, see Hughes 1975 (Ital. trans. 1979). On the situation in Florence, see Herlihy and Klapisch-Zuber 1978 (Ital. trans. 1988); Bizzocchi 1982, pp. 15 and 40–1. On the role of the *palazzo*, see Goldthwaite 1980 (Ital. trans. 1984), and 1993 (Ital. trans 1996), pp. 202 and 227–8; Casanova 1997, pp. 63–4.

20. Archive of the Archbishopric of Bologna, *Parrocchia di Santo Stefano, Status animarum*, 1792, 1796 and 1799. See Sarti 1991, p. 255.

21. Kertzer 1995.

22. Kertzer 1995.

23. Goody 1972 (Ital. trans. 1977); Berliner 1972 (Ital. trans. 1977).

24. Malanima 1990, p. 13.

25. Rogers 1993.

26. Sogner and Sandvik 1990, p. 634. Allodial property was free from feudal restrictions and obligations.

27. See above, chapter I, para. 4.

28. Kertzer 1995; Groppi 1994 and 1996b; Reher 1998.

29. Sarti 1994a. On Francesco Albergati Capacelli, see Mattioda 1993.

30. Bologna State Archive, *Fondo Albergati, Strumenti and Scritture*, b. 223, folder 10, fols no number. The 'family' to which the marquis referred was obviously the domestic servants; see above, chapter I, para. 7. It was common practice for wills to make provisions for situations in which tensions existed between the heirs.

31. Bologna State Archive, *Fondo Albergati, Strumenti and Scritture*, b. 233, folder 6, fols n.n. (the italics are mine).

32. Niederösterreichisches Landesarchiv, B.G. Litschau, *Herrschaft Heidenreichstein*, n. 66, fol. 187, quoted in Berkner 1972 (Ital. trans. 1977), p. 120. On this kind of contract (*Ausgeding everträge*) see also Chapter I.

33. Ibid.

34. Schlumbohm 1998.

35. Quoted by Goody 1976, p. 33.

36. Czap Jr. 1983 (Ital. trans. 1984).

37. Kaser 1997, pp. 525–98 and 2001, p. 35.

38. Kula 1972; Kochanowicz 1983, pp. 161–3.

39. Plakans 1975 and 1983, pp. 200–1.

40. On eastern Europe, see Kula 1972, p. 950; Kochanowicz 1983, p. 162; Plakaus 1975, p. 654; Ehmer 1991, p. 46. Kaser 2001, who thinks 'that the owner's intervention in household composition is largely a west European phenomenon', p. 37; on sharecropping in Italy, see Poni 1982.

41. There are even those who argue that in the absence of impediments and restrictions, all western residential groups tended to become nuclear families, see Verdon 1996.

42. Goody 1976, p. 19.

43. On Corsica see Augustins 1982, pp. 63–4. On Hungary see . . . Wall 1983 (Ital. trans.

1984), pp. 40–1; Andorka and Faragó 1983. For the anthropological survey on Átány see Edit Fél, Tamás Hofer, *Proper Peasants*, Chicago 1969. I am grateful to Tamás Farago for information about Hungarian families.

44. Goody 1972 (Ital. trans. 1977); Levi 1990 (Ital. trans. 1992); Casanova 1997, pp. 33–8.

45. Levi 1990 (Ital. trans. 1992); Raggio 1990; Groppi 1996b.

46. Groppi 1996b.

47. Groppi 1996b; Laslett 1988; Kertzer 1995.

48. Relier 1998.

49. Groppi 1996a, p. 127; Lombardi 1988; Martini 1998b.

50. Giusberti 1990.

51. Delille 1985. See also Raggio 1990, pp. 81, 89–90 and *passim*; Comaschi 1983. For the situation in medieval England, see Razi 1993. On the different roles of house and kinship in different contexts see Augustins 1982 and 1989.

52. Levi 1985, p. 64.

53. Poni 1982; Biagioli 1986; Barbagli 1996 and 1990; Kertzer 1981 and 1984; Palazzi 1992–93; Torti 1989; Della Pina 1990; Salvatici 1995.

54. Martini 1993.

55. On this point, see the observations by Casanova 1997, pp. 73–8.

IV. The Home

1. Bairoch, Batou and Chèvre 1988, pp. 255–9, tables B1 and B2; Lepetit 1995, pp. 297 and 302–4. For other data on the degree of urbanization, see de Vries 1984 and Livi Bacci 1998, p. 51.

2. Rösener 1995, p. 41; Aymard 1995.

3. Aymard 1995, pp. 147–8, 182, 192–4 and especially 226–32.

4. Mendeli 1972; Kriedte, Medick and Schlumbohm 1984; Rudolph 1992 and Ogilvie (ed.) 1993, with bibliography.

5. Cazzola 1988, with bibliography.

6. Among other works, see Pounds 1979 and 1989, pp. 105 and 117–18.

7. Sebastian Münster, *Cosmographia universa* (1544), quoted in Rösener 1995, p. 223. 'Ticking' was a coarse cloth made of hemp, jute or flax for sacks, mattresses, etc.

8. Pounds 1989, pp. 100–4 and 114; Rösener 1995, pp. 192–3; Malanima 1997, pp. 150–61.

9. Pounds 1989, pp. 110–13.

10. Pounds 1989, p. 118; Rösener 1995, pp. 232–53.

11. Pounds 1989, p. 118.

12. Gambi 1976. On the nature of the heavy plough and its adoption in the Po Valley, see Malanima 1997, pp. 208–11.

13. Casanova 1997.

14. Pounds 1989, p. 118.

15. Pounds 1989, p. 121. Cuisenier 1991, p. 91, draws attention to the continued existence of underground house in Romania up until the present day and the use of underground buildings in central Europe for a long time. The latter had external kitchens or summer kitchens.

16. Cosenza 1974, pp. 125, 134 and 140.

17. Roux 1976 (Ital. trans. 1982), pp. 111–13; Schwarz 1989, p. 92; Pounds 1989, pp. 126 and 132.

18. Rösener 1995, p. 194.

19. Malanima 1990, p. 13.

20. Yun 1994, pp. 127 and 130.

21. Rosati 1995, p. 34 on the situation in Tuscany.

22. Cuisenier 1991, pp. 94–8.

23. Serlio pub. 1994, pp. 43–119.

24. For an introduction to the question, see Jestaz 1995 (Ital. trans. 1995), pp. 83–90.

25. Stone and Fawtier Stone 1984 and 1986 (Ital. trans. 1989), p. 243.

26. Stone and Fawtier Stone 1986 (Ital. trans. 1989), pp. 243–329; Barley 1985, pp. 600–19.

27. Pounds 1989, p. 126.

28. Czap Jr. 1983 (Ital. trans. 1984), pp. 150–2.

29. Roche 1997, p. 141. There were also fireplaces built almost entirely of wood, which

were obviously rather dangerous, see Pounds 1989, p. 283.

30. Pounds 1989, pp. 195–6 and 206.

31. Cuisenier 1991, p. 99.

32. Grassi, Pepe and Sestieri 1992, under the entry.

33. Braudel 1979 (Ital. trans. 1993), pp. 272–4; Thornton 1991 (Ital. trans. 1992), pp. 20–6; Montenegro 1996, pp. 43–4.

34. Gerola 1936.

35. See some of the splendid images produced in the 1970s in *Case contadine* 1979.

36. Braudel 1979 (Ital. trans. 1993), p. 275.

37. Pounds 1989, pp. 196–8.

38. On the situation in England, see Deffontaines 1972, pp. 110–11; Braudel 1979 (Ital. trans. 1993), p. 274. I am indebted to Paolo Cornaglia, who informed me of the existence of metal stoves in eighteenth-century Turin.

39. Braudel 1979 (Ital. trans. 1993); Deffontaines 1972, p. 125.

40. Deffontaines 1972, p. 131.

41. Pounds 1989, p. 196.

42. Gottlieb 1993, p. 29.

43. Davidson 1982, pp. 101–2.

44. Davidson 1982, p. 101; Esquirou De Parieu, n.d. (Ital. trans. 1865), pp. 301–13; Cieraad 1999 (on Holland under French rule).

45. Braudel 1979 (Ital. trans. 1993); Roux 1976 (Ital. trans. 1982); Stone and Fawtier Stone 1984 and 1986 (Ital. trans. 1989), pp. 280–1; Pounds 1989; Thornton 1991 (Ital. trans. 1992), pp. 27–30; Schuurman and Walsh 1994; Garnot 1994; Montenegro 1996, pp. 26, 32 and 42–3, who reminds us that in the fifteenth century glass production was concentrated in Venice, France and Flanders; Roche 1997, pp. 137–8.

46. Malanima 1994, p. 121. The traveller was J.J. Lalande (*Voyage en Italie*, Geneva, 1790, vol. II, p. 144).

47. See above, note 45.

48. For example, Zemon Davis 1975 (Ital. trans. 1980), p. 270, for the sixteenth century;

Burguière 1986c (Ital. trans. 1988), pp. 127–8.

49. Collina-Girard 1994, pp. 9–35; Davidson 1982, p. 96.

50. Quoted in Davidson 1982, p. 207. At the end of our period, bellows driven by a wheel had been invented, and they were often worked by the children of the house, Davidson 1982, pp. 96–7. For fire lighting as a task for women and servants, see pp. 188 and 195, and also Schama 1987 (Ital. trans. 1988), p. 458.

51. For example, Davidson 1982, p. 93.

52. Coal provides a high caloric yield, but is very dirty and emits particularly toxic fumes; peat has a lower caloric yield, but leaves very little residue, while wood ash can be used for washing and other tasks, see Davidson 1982, pp. 73–100.

53. Edward Daniel Clarke, *A Tour through the South of England, Wales, and part of Ireland, made during the summer of 1791*, London, 1793, p. 116, quoted in Davidson 1982, p. 76.

54. Davidson 1982, p. 77.

55. Davidson 1982, p. 77.

56. Davidson 1982, p. 73 and, on the situation in Sardinia, see Deffontaines 1972, p. 106.

57. On the use of this definition, see above, chapter I, para. 7; for its etymology, see Cortelazzo and Zolli 1979–88; Palazzi and Folena 1992. The actual word for 'fire' in Latin is *ignis*. On the symbolic value of a fire, see also Kykwert 1991.

58. Serlio pub. 1994, p. 48.

59. Camporesi 1989, p. 5. On the chimney as the vertical axis joined to the sky and the stars, see also Cuisenier 1991, p. 340.

60. Louis-Sébastien Mercier, *Tableau de Paris*, vol. X, p. 303, quoted in Roche 1997, p. 143.

61. Roche 1997, pp. 141–4.

62. Cuisenier 1991, p. 338; Thornton 1991 (Ital. trans. 1992), p. 20.

63. Roux 1976 (Ital. trans. 1982); Rapoport 1969; Pounds 1989; Cuisenier 1991; Barbieri

and Gambi (eds) 1970; Gambi 1976; Deffontaines 1972; Schwarz 1989.

64. *De re aedificatoria*, I, 5, quoted in Gambi 1976, p. 496.

65. *Principj di architettura civile*, part II, 1, 3, chapter VIII, para. 3, quoted in Gambi 1976, pp. 496–8.

66. Gambi 1976, pp. 496–502. But see also Cuisenier 1991 on France.

67. Cuisenier 1991, pp. 26 and 33.

68. Roux 1976 (Ital. trans. 1982), p. 159; for the particular situation in England, see Barley 1985, pp. 591–600.

69. Collomp 1986 (Ital. trans. 1987), p. 402; Goubert 1987.

70. Cosenza 1974, p. 91.

71. Barbieri and Gambi (eds) 1970.

72. Roux 1976 (Ital. trans. 1982), p. 157 (who quotes Vidal de la Blache).

73. Pounds 1989, p. 126.

74. P. Chaunu, *La Civilisation de l'Europe des Lumières*, Paris, 1971 (quoted in Roux 1976 [Ital. trans. 1982], p. 158).

75. Cosenza 1974, p. 129; Barley 1985, especially p. 591, from which the quotation was taken. Brick production in England commenced in the sixteenth century. Previously bricks had been imported from Holland, see Stone and Fawtier Stone 1984 and 1986 (Ital. trans. 1989), p. 245.

76. Collomp 1986 (Ital. trans. 1987), p. 402.

77. See above, chapter III, para. 2. The description of the house comes from Hochstrasser 1993.

78. Van Dulmen 1990, pp. 56–7.

79. Pounds 1989; Cuisenier 1991.

80. Cosenza 1974, pp. 125 and 137; Borghi and Pozzi 1990.

81. Cuisenier 1991, p. 104.

82. Serlio pub. 1994, pp. 45–6. Serlio was the first architect to concern himself with the houses of the lower social classes.

83. John Lanne Buchanan, *Travels in the Western Hebrides: From 1782 to 1790*, London, 1793, pp. 91–2, quoted in Davidson 1982, pp. 116–17.

84. Hochstrasser 1993 speculates that there might have been a fireplace on which food was cooked in pots placed on a trivet over the flames or an oven for cooking bread with the oven door on the balcony (p. 116).

85. On the Lapps, see Deffontaines 1972, p. 107.

86. On Jura, see Deffontaines 1972, pp. 107–9.

87. G. Bouchard, *Le Village immobile: Sennely-en-Sologne au XIIIe siècle*, Paris, 1972, p. 98, quoted in Collomp 1986 (Ital. trans. 1987), p. 404; Waro-Desjardins 1993, p. 5.

88. Waro-Desjardins 1993, p. 6; Malanima 1990, pp. 44 and 15.

89. In Florence, it appears that it was common amongst the lower classes for more than one person to share a bed, see Casalini 1997, p. 215.

90. Hochstrasser 1993, p. 130. On the depopulation caused by the Thirty Years War in Germany, see Livi Bacci 1998, p. 119, fig. 4.3.

91. Hochstrasser 1993, pp. 25–37.

92. Roux 1976 (Ital. trans. 1982), pp. 175–6. The term 'enclosures' referred to the process of fencing off and privatizing the common land of villages.

93. De Vries 1993, p. 100 and more generally the whole volume edited by Brewer and Porter 1993. For a review of historical studies into consumption (mainly based on English-language works), see Glennie 1995.

94. Palumbo Fossati 1995, p. 166.

95. Barley 1985, p. 653.

96. The so-called 'post-mortem inventories' were descriptions of the possessions left by a dead person at the time of inheritance. They also provided information on the rooms in which individual objects were usually kept, and have therefore proved very useful for the study of material cultures. As the criteria used by those who collected the information were not always the same, comparisons between one region and another should be treated with care.

97. For the definitions of 'hall' and 'parlour', see Barley 1985; Brown 1986; Watkin 1986 (Ital. trans. 1990), p 250. In a previous age, 'halls' had been the main room in a house, where people ate, drank and entertained. As time went on its role was diminished to that of an entrance room or passageway, and the role of reception room was taken over by the 'parlour'. On this point, see also para. 16 of this chapter.

98. W.G. Hoskins, *The Midlands Peasant: Economic and Social History of a Leicester Village*, London, 1957, quoted in Roux 1976 (Ital. trans. 1982), pp. 171–2. On the changes in housing in rural England, see Cosenza 1974, p. 129; Barley 1985; Horn 1994, pp. 78–9. For the situation in Wales, see Smith 1985.

99. This is the title of Malanima 1990.

100. Weatherill 1988, pp. 52–3 and p. 49, fig. 3.3.

101. As we are reminded by Horn 1994, p. 72, there are few sources for assessing the living conditions of the very poor, whose property was worth less than ten pounds sterling.

102. Green Carr 1994, p. 83.

103. Horn 1994, pp. 73–4.

104. On the differences between the different parts of Great Britain, see Weatherill 1988, pp. 43–69 and p. 76, fig. 4.1 for a categorization of the differences between the town and the countryside. On this subject, see also paras. 14 and 15 in this chapter.

105. Horn 1994, pp. 72–6.

106. Green Carr 1994, p. 88.

107. Waro-Desjardins 1993, p. 6; Yun 1994, p. 128.

108. Horn 1994, pp. 72–3.

109. Weatherill 1988, p. 76, fig. 4.1 and p. 88, fig. 4.4.

110. Horn 1994, pp. 72–3, 76 and 78.

111. Roche 1997, p. 136; Dessureault, Dickinson and Wien, 1994, p. 108. For the types of lighting, see Davidson 1982, pp. 101–14.

112. Davidson 1982, p. 103 and Thornton 1991 (Ital. trans. 1992), pp. 275–82.

113. Douglas Graham, *Fun upon fun; or, Leper, the tailor*, Glasgow, fol. 1840, quoted in Davidson 1982, p. 101.

114. Dessureault, Dickinson and Wien 1994, pp. 102–3 and pp. 108–9.

115. Hauser 1994, p. 265.

116. Weatherill 1993, p. 209.

117. Malanima 1990, p. 13.

118. Malanima 1990, pp. 20–2 and 161.

119. Malanima 1990 and 1994. For a more general look at the eighteenth-century debate on luxury, see Borghero (ed.) 1974; Magnusson 1995.

120. Weatherill 1988, pp. 70–90. See also Weatherill 1993, p. 209.

121. Thornton 1991 (Ital. trans. 1992), p. 110. Even at the end of the sixteenth century, Chinese porcelain was still a much-treasured rarity.

122. Weatherill 1988, pp. 87–8.

123. Weatherill 1988, pp. 166–89.

124. For the question of the social differentiation of the means of appropriation, see Bourdieu 1979 (Ital. trans. 1983); Weatherill 1988; Brewer and Porter (eds) 1993; Levi 1996; Roche 1997. For the restrictions placed on the freedom of choice by the law, see in particular chapter VI.

125. Burke 1993, p. 157.

126. For the concept of ostentatious consumption, see Veblen 1899 (Ital. trans. 1969). For aristocratic behaviour, Burke 1982 (Ital. trans. 1988) and 1993; Visceglia 1988 and 1992 (ed.); Ago 1992 and 1994; Martini 1998b; Sarti 1994a, especially pp. 106–69 and 1999c, all with bibliographies for further information.

127. Ricci 1996. As far as this debate is concerned, see Borghero (ed.) 1974; Roche 1989 (Ital. trans. 1991), pp. 452–5; Sarti 1994a, pp. 179–92; Magnusson 1995.

128. Weatherill 1988, p. 88, fig. 4.4.

129. Glennie 1995, p. 169.

130. Braudel 1979 (Ital. trans. 1993), p. 451. For the difficulty in defining a city, see amongst other texts Tocci 1988 and 1997; Weatherill 1988, pp. 72–3.

131. Bairoch, Batou and Chèvre 1988, p. 270, table B8; Aymard 1995, p. 536.

132. Bairocli, Batou and Chèvre 1988, p. 278, table B14 and, for the figures for London, p. 33; Roux 1976 (Ital. trans. 1982), p. 177; de Vries 1984.

133. Livi Bacci 1998, pp. 54–5. The differing structures of urban development from one region of Europe to another are one of the factors that help to explain why the circulation of goods and innovations between the city and the countryside was not the same everywhere.

134. Benevolo 1996, pp. 127–8.

135. Braudel 1979 (Ital. trans. 1993), pp. 461–2; Fara 1993.

136. Serlio pub. 1994, pp. 119–20.

137. Simoncini (ed.) 1995, pp. 10–13.

138. Cosenza 1974, p. 124; Pardailhé-Galabrun 1988, p. 212 and pp. 217–18 and 224 (a traveller reported that there were nine-storey houses as far back as the seventeenth century); Teuteberg (ed.) 1985. The situation was different in small cities like Chartres, where there was a prevalence of buildings on one or two floors; see Garnot 1989, p. 199.

139. Roux 1976 (Ital. trans. 1982), p. 183.

140. Braudel 1979 (Ital. trans. 1993); Lepetit 1995, p. 313.

141. For the history of smells, see Corbin 1982.

142. William Petty, *Traisé des taxes et contributions*, in *Oeuvres économiques de Sir William Petty*, 1905, I, pp. 39–40 quoted in Braudel 1979 (Ital.. trans. 1993), p. 514. On this expansion, see Stone and Fawtier Stone 1984 and 1986 (Ital. trans. 1989), p. 273, with bibliographical references.

143. *The Present State of Holland; or a Description of the United Provinces*, London, 1765, p. 211, quoted in Schama 1987, p. 375.

144. Schama 1987, p. 378 and more generally pp. 375–84.

145. Braudel 1979 (Ital. trans. 1993), p. 456. See also Pardallhé-Galabrun 1988, p. 244.

146. Bologna State Archive, *Tribunale Criminale del Torrone, Carceratorum*, 18/1/1740–26/8/1742, 30 August 1740.

147. Schama 1987, p. 378.

148. Bologna State Archive, *Tribunale Criminale del Torrone, Atti processuali*, 1590, vol. 2337, fols 256–9.

149. Ferrante 1978; *Status animarum* for the parish of Santa Maria della Carità in Bologna (Parish Archive).

150. Zemon Davis 1975 (Ital. trans. 1980), p. 50.

151. For its use as a combustible, see above, para. 4; on its use as a detergent, see chapter VI, para. 2.

152. G.J. Grelot, *Relation nouvelle d'un voyage de Costantinople*, Paris, 1681, pp. 299–301, quoted in Scaraffia 1993, pp. 89–90. On the closure of public baths, see chapter VI, para. 2.

153. Vigarello 1985 (Ital. trans. 1988) and 1993 (Ital. trans. 1996).

154. *The Present State of Holland*, London, 1765, p. 211, quoted in Schama 1987, p. 375.

155. Serlio pub. 1994, pp. 119–23.

156. Brown 1986, p. 571.

157. See the texts republished in Simoncini (ed.) 1995, vol. II, pp. 618–57.

158. On the lack of sewers, see Pounds 1989.

159. Davidson 1982, p. 26; Pounds 1989, pp. 247–8, 274 and 277–8; Vigarello 1985 (Ital. trans. 1988), p. 130 and *passim*; Montenegro 1996, p. 69; Sorcinelli 1998, pp. 38–42. In his book, *The Metamorphosis of Ajax* (1596), Harington described the water closet with a flush that he had installed at his home in Kelston, near Bath. On the slow pace of modernization at the court of Savoy, see Cornaglia 2000.

160. On commodes, see Thornton 1991 (Ital. trans. 1992), pp. 245–9; Montenegro 1996, pp. 31, 92 and 95; Sorcinelli 1998, pp. 38–9.

161. Augusrin-Charles D'Aviler, *Cours d'Architecture* (1691), part of which appears in Simoncini (ed.) 1995, vol. II, pp. 611–623, quotation on p. 612.

162. Pounds 1989, pp. 274–80; Roche 1997, pp. 156 and 161; Pardailhé-Galabrun 1988, pp. 348–54; Vigarello 1985 (Ital. trans. 1988) and 1993 (Ital. trans. 1996).

163. Davidson 1982, pp. 7–14.

164. Pellati 1929; Braudel 1979 (Ital. trans. 1993), pp. 203–4; Pounds 1989, pp. 274–80.

165. Davidson 1982, pp. 12–14 (the author also describes the various ways in which water was transported).

166. Davidson 1982, p. 16.

167. Montenegro 1996, pp. 48–9 and 69; Simoncini (ed.) 1995, vol. II, pp. 618–57.

168. Davidson 1982, p. 21.

169. Roche 1997, p. 172; Mukerji 1993; Davidson 1982, pp. 21–8; Braudel 1979 (Ital. trans. 1993), p. 205.

170. Roche 1981 (Ital. trans. 1986) and 1997, pp. 152 and 173; Davidson 1982, p. 19. The figures for the estimated average daily water requirement in contemporary cities are not limited to purely domestic uses. Thus, in 1946, for example, it was calculated that in towns and cities with more than 10,000 inhabitants there was an average requirement of 120 litres per head for domestic usage, which included the watering of gardens, between 25 and 50 litres for industry and agriculture and about 50 litres for street-cleaning and sewers, see Roche 1997, p. 152.

171. Davidson 1982, p. 18. It is reasonable to suppose that the consumption of agricultural labourers was 5–10 litres, partly because of the distance they had to go and partly because there was less stuff to clean in their houses than in those in the towns where pollution levels were higher.

172. Guenzi 1983, p. 176; Guenzi and Poni 1989.

173. See amongst other works Braudel 1979 (Ital. trans. 1993).

174. Davidson 1982, pp. 28–9; de Vries 1984, pp. 175–249

175. Vigarello 1985 (Ital. trans. 1988) and 1993 (Ital. trans. 1996).

176. Vigarello 1985 (Ital. trans. 1988), pp. 170–1.

177. Braudel 1979 (Ital. trans. 1993); Pounds 1989; Pardailhé-Galabrun 1988; Benevolo 1996, p. 130; Tocci 1988 and 1997.

178. Roche 1997, p. 135; Pounds 1989, p. 283.

179. Ménétra pub. 1982 (Ital. trans. 1992).

180. Thornton 1991 (Ital. trans. 1992), p. 275; Roche 1997, pp. 130–2. For the episode of the priest in Folengo, see *Baldus*, vol. XXV, pp. 269–73, quoted in Montanari 1997, p. 46.

181. Pardallhé-Galabrun 1988, pp. 342–8.

182. Pardallhé-Galabrun 1988, pp. 253–4 and 341; Cieraad 1999 (I would like to thank Kester Dibbits for having informed me of this article).

183. Thornton 1991 (Ital. trans. 1992), p. 282.

184. Braudel 1979 (Ital. trans. 1993), p. 272.

185. Palazzi 1986.

186. Pardailhé-Galabrun 1988, pp. 332–3.

187. Pardailhé-Galabrun 1988, p. 334.

188. Brewer and Porter 1993; Pardailhé-Galabrun 1988, pp. 331–41; Pounds 1989, p. 283.

189. For the situation in England, see Davidson 1982.

190. Pounds 1989, p. 283.

191. Cosenza 1974, p. 122; Deffontaines 1972, p. 114.

192. Roux 1976 (Ital. trans. 1982), pp. 178–9; Braudel 1979 (Ital. trans. 1993), pp. 511 and 514.

193. Cosenza 1974, p. 127. For the situation in Flanders, see Montenegro 1996, p. 51.

194. Schama 1987 (Ital. trans. 1988), pp. 320–1.

195. Hayward 1965 (Ital. trans. 1992); Roche 1981 (Ital. trans. 1986), pp. 174–80; Pardailhé-Galabrun 1988, pp. 275–89 (quotation on p. 275); Montenegro 1996; Taylor 1996.

196. Hayward 1965 (Ital. trans. 1992); Grassi, Pepe and Sestieri 1992, under the entry; Thornton 1991 (Ital. trans. 1992), pp. 111–14; Montenegro 1996, pp. 34–5.

197. Grassi, Pepe and Sestieri 1992, under the entry; Thornton 1991 (Ital. trans. 1992), pp. 114–49; Montenegro 1996, pp. 34–5, 51, 70, 94–5, 112 and 137. Canopy beds had curtains attached to a single point on the ceiling, which formed a kind of cone as they hung down to the bed.

198. Malanima 1990, p. 19.

199. Thornton 1991 (Ital. trans. 1992), pp. 162–7.

200. Malanima 1990, pp. 15–20. On the accessories that went with Parisian beds, see Pardailhé-Galdbrun 1988, pp. 280–1.

201. Priestley, Corfield and Sutermeister 1982. Between the mid-seventeenth century and 1730, the overall number of beds in each house decreased. This change was, however, mainly due to the reduction in mobile beds. In the absence of information on the average size of families, it is not possible to establish whether the number of persons per bed remained unchanged, decreased or even increased.

202. Pardailhé-Galabrun 1988, pp. 284–6. In order to avoid new-born babies being squashed by the bodies of the adults and particularly wet-nurses with whom they slept, a kind of protective cage made of wood and metal, called an *arcucciò*, was invented in Renaissance Florence. However, there was a widespread use of cots, often made of wicker (fig. 50), but for the rich they were usually more elaborate, see Fildes 1986, pp. 89–90 and 112; Thornton 1991 (Ital. trans. 1992), pp. 253–7.

203. Roche 1981 (Ital. trans. 1986), p. 175.

204. Ménétra pub. 1982 (Ital. trans. 1992), pp. 162, 129 and 90.

205. Montenegro 1996, pp. 30 and 156. But see also para. 16 of this chapter.

206. Grassi, Pepe and Sestieri 1992, under the entry.

207. Montenegro 1996, pp. 106 and 110; Ranum 1986 (Ital. trans. 1987), pp. 171–4.

208. Montenegro 1996, pp. 30, 106 and 110. In eighteenth-century France, it appears to have mainly been ladies who had two bedrooms, of which one was for show, see Montenegro 1996, p. 156. The *chambre du roi* in the castle of Ancy-Le-Franc, planned by Sebastiano Serlio, was dominated by a magnificent and ostentatious bed, see Frommel 1998, especially p. 173.

209. Augustin-Charles D'Aviler, *Cours d'Architecture*, partly republished in Simoncini (ed.) 1995, vol. II, p. 620.

210. Giovanni Biagio Amico, *L'architetto pratico, in cui con facilità si danno le regole per aprendere l'Architettura Civile, e Militare*, vols I–II, Palermo, 1726 and 1750, partly republished in Simoncini (ed.) 1995, vol. II, quotation on p. 636.

211. Schama 1987 (Ital. trans. 1988), pp. 320–1. On the Dutch lifestyle, see also Schama 1993 and Wijsenbeek-Olthuis 1994.

212. Pardailhé-Galabrun 1988, pp. 257, 303–5 and 309–13.

213. For the evolution of seating arrangements, see Elias 1969 (Ital. trans. 1982); Hayward 1965 (Ital. trans. 1992); Thornton 1991 (Ital. trans. 1992), pp. 168–91 (p. 168 on seating for women); Montenegro 1996, pp. 50, 94 and 137. On the presence of chairs for women in sixteenth-century Venice, see Palumbo-Fossati 1987, p. 141.

214. See chapter V, para. 2.

215. Pardailhé-Galabrun 1988, pp. 257 and 310–13.

216. Palumbo Fossati 1995, p. 170.

217. Pardailhé-Galabrun 1988, pp. 236–42. The level of crowding amongst wage-earners was 2.3 persons per room at the beginning of the eighteenth century and 2.7 at the end, see Roche 1981 (Ital. trans. 1986), p. 158.

218. See para. 16 of this chapter.

219. Chartier 1986 (Ital. trans. 1987) and 1987 (Ital. trans. 1988); Ranum 1986 (Ital. trans. 1987); Engelsing 1978; Schenda 1986 and 1987; Sarti 1991. On cultural consumption, see the essays in part IV of Brewer and Porter (eds) 1993.

220. Roche 1981 (Ital. trans. 1986), pp. 287–8; Pardailhé-Galabrun 1988, p. 403. On the situation in Great Britain, see Weatherill 1988, p. 77, fig. 4.1.

221. Palumbo-Fossati 1984, pp. 126 and 133–4; Pardailhé-Galabrun 1988, pp. 419ff.

222. Roche 1981 (Ital. trans. 1986), pp. 192–4; de Vries 1993.

223. Roche 1981 (Ital. trans. 1986), pp. 190–5.

224. Fairchilds 1993a.

225. Weatherill 1988, p. 26, fig. 2.1.

226. Weatherill 1988, p. 88, fig. 4.4.

227. On Alberti, the concept of *masserizia* and attitudes towards consumption in the Renaissance, see Goldthwaite 1993 (Ital. trans. 1995), particularly pp. 215–23; Pullan 1978, pp. 997–8 (from which I obtained this quotation on the humanist view of wealth). For the study of an example of unease with affluence, see Schama 1987 (Ital. trans. 1988). On the situation in Venice, see Palumbo-Fossati 1984, who takes up the concept of *patina* that appeared in Grant McCracken, *Culture and Consumption. New Approaches to the Symbolic Character of Consumer Goods and Activities*, Bloomington, 1988.

228. For the Lazzaretti affair, see Niccoli 2000, pp. 183 and 206; on the decline of the chest, see Thornton 1991 (Ital. trans. 1992), pp. 16 and 370, note 25. On the Dutch poet, see Dibbits 1995, pp. 125–6 (his name is not provided); on the situation in Paris, see Roche 1981 (Ital. trans. 1986), p. 198, fig. 4.

229. Hayward 1965 (Ital. trans. 1992); Braudel 1979 (Ital. trans. 1993); Roche 1981 (Ital. trans. 1986) and 1997; Pardailhé-Galabrun 1988; Weatherill 1988; Thornton 1991 (Ital. trans. 1992); Brewer and Porter 1993; Montenegro 1996.

230. Pounds 1989, p. 206.

231. Thornton 1991 (Ital. trans. 1992), p. 315.

232. Thornton 1991 (Ital. trans. 1992), p. 290. For English 'halls', see this same paragraph.

233. Goldthwaite 1980 (Ital. trans. 1984) and 1987a; Thornton 1991 (Ital. trans. 1992), p. 11; Montenegro 1996, p. 30.

234. Quoted in Thornton 1991 (Ital. trans. 1992), p. 369, note 17.

235. Watkin 1986 (Ital. trans. 1990), pp. 184–223; Thornton 1991 (Ital. trans. 1992), pp. 319–20; Montenegro 1996, p. 46.

236. Quoted in Thornton 1991 (Ital. trans. 1992), p. 284 and in Montenegro 1996, p. 30.

237. Francesco di Giorgio Martini, *Trattato di architettura* (1475–80 and 1484–87), ed. L. Maltese De Grassi, Milan, 1967, p. 72, quoted in Thornton 1991 (Ital. trans. 1992), p. 284.

238. On the subsequent developments of this division of space, Montenegro 1996, p. 91.

239. Montenegro 1996, pp. 47–8.

240. Thornton 1991 (Ital. trans. 1992), p. 294.

241. Thornton 1991 (Ital. trans. 1992), p. 288. See also para. 13 of this chapter.

242. 'The following bedroom was more for show than for use, although one could sleep there in the summer, because in winter one would withdraw to small and lower apartments, which are less airy and therefore easier to heat', D'Aviler wrote in *Cours d'Architecture*, in Simoncini (ed.) 1995, vol. II, p. 620. See also Mezzanotte 1995, pp. 41–2.

243. Thornton 1991 (Ital. trans. 1992), p. 288.

244. Francesco di Giorgio Martini, *Trattato di architettura*, p. 72, quoted in Thornton 1991 (Ital. trans. 1992), p. 298.

245. Thornton 1991 (Ital. trans. 1992), p. 298; Montenegro 1996, p. 32.

246. Thornton 1991 (Ital. trans. 1992), p. 13, fig. 4 and p. 296.

247. FOL.E. Briseux, *L'Art de bâtir des maisons de campagne, où l'on traite de leur distribution, de leur construction, et de leur décoration*, Paris, 1743, part I, partly republished in Simoncini (ed.) 1995, vol. II, pp. 629–34, quotation on p. 632.

248. Augustin-Charles D'Aviler, *Cours d'Architecture* in Simoncini (ed.) 1995, vol. II, p. 616.

249. Thornton 1991 (Ital. trans. 1992), p. 300.

250. *De re aedificatoria*, V, chapter XVII, quoted in Thornton 1991 (Ital. trans. 1992), p. 288.

251. Thornton 1991 (Ital. trans. 1992), p. 288; Elias 1975 (Ital. trans. 1980); Vigarello 1985 (Ital. trans. 1988), pp. 128–9; Montenegro 1996, pp. 30 and 156.

252. For the situation in Renaissance Italy, see Thornton 1991 (Ital. trans. 1992), p. 295 on; for the situation in seventeenth- and eighteenth-century France, see Augustin-Charles D'Aviler, *Cours d'Architecture* and

FOL.E. Briseux, *L'Art de bâtir*, both in Simoncini (ed.) 1995, vol. II, pp. 616 and 633 respectively.

253. Montenegro 1996, pp. 30–2 and 45–7.

254. Thornton 1991 (Ital. trans. 1992), pp. 222–9; Montenegro 1996, p. 35.

255. Thornton 1997 and *The Study Room in Renaissance Italy, with Particular Reference to Venice, circa 1560–1620* (doctoral thesis at the Warburg Institute, London University, 1990), quoted in Thornton 1991 (Ital. trans. 1992), p. 391, note 3. Initially studies were furnished simply, but later they were decorated with ancient and precious objects (sometimes defined as 'antiques'), and this was to give rise to what was called a *Wunderkammer* in German, i.e. a room where strange and wonderful things were preserved, Thornton 1991 (Ital. trans. 1992), pp. 296–8.

256. Elias 1969 (Ital. trans. 1982); Thornton 1991 (Ital. trans. 1992), pp. 290 and 295; Montenegro 1996, pp. 30–2, 45–8 and 66–9.

257. Thornton 1991 (Ital. trans. 1992), pp. 206–14; Montenegro 1996.

258. Augustin-Charles D'Aviler, *Cours d'Architecture*, in Simoncini (ed.) 1995, vol. II, p. 616.

259. Giovanni Biagio Amico, *L'architetto pratico* . . . , partly republished in Simoncini (ed.) 1995, vol. II, quotation on p. 636.

260. Augustin-Charles D'Aviler, *Cours d'Architecture*, in Simoncini (ed.) 1995, vol. II, p. 620.

261. Stone and Fawtier Stone 1984 and 1986 (Ital. trans. 1989), pp. 292–3. On the rooms used for the servants' meals, see para. 2 of chapter V. The question is extensively debated in the handbooks on the organization of the homes of cardinals, which are analysed by Fragnito 1991.

262. Pier Jacopo Martello, *Il vero parigino italiano*, in *Prose degli arcadi*, Rome, 1718, partly republished in Simoncini (ed.) 1995, vol. II, pp. 624–7 (quotation on p. 626).

263. Pardaiihé-Galabrun 1988, p. 260.

264. Fontana 1995, pp. 145 and 148.

265. Palumbo Fossati 1995, p. 169.

266. Nenadic 1994, pp. 148–9

267. Pardailhé-Galabrun 1988, p. 260.

268. Pardailhé-Galabrun 1988, p. 255.

269. This was the *Dictionnaire universel* by Antoine Furetière (1619–88), which was published posthumously in 1690, quoted in Pardailhé-Galabrun 1988, p. 256.

270. Pier Jacopo Martello, *Il vero parigino italiano*, in Simoncini (ed.) 1995, vol. II, p. 626.

271. Pardailhé-Galabrun 1988, pp. 255–67.

272. Pardailhé-Galabrun 1988, pp. 256 and 259.

273. Vigarello 1985 (Ital. trans. 1988), p. 128.

274. Pardailhé-Galabrun 1988, pp. 259–60.

275. See Montenegro 1996, p. 107.

276. Mezzanotte 1995, p. 25.

277. Francis Bacon, 'Of Building', in *Essays*, London, 1972, p. 133.

278. Jacques-François Blondel, *Architecture Françoise* . . . , Paris, 1752, vol. I, book I, p. 35, quoted in Mezzanotte 1995, p. 37.

279. Quoted in Montenegro 1996, p. 134.

280. Quoted in Montenegro 1996, p. 134.

281. Quoted in Pardailhé-Galabrun 1988, p. 256. The *Dictionnaire de l'Académie Française* (1694) had already suggested that *chambre* was primarily a place for sleeping.

282. Pardailhé-Galabrun 1988, pp. 255–67.

283. Roche 1981 (Ital. trans. 1986), pp. 158–9.

284. Roux 1976 (Ital. trans. 1982), pp. 184–6; Pardailhé-Galabrun 1988, pp. 250–1; Roche 1981 (Ital. trans. 1986), pp. 149–53 and 1997. In Genoa, the replacement of vertical houses with 'intermediate' to be rented out floor by floor was achieved through the reconstruction of the city following its bombardment by the French fleet in 1684, see Simoncini (ed.) 1995, p. 12.

285. Allegra 1996, pp. 255–7 (has taken the case of Anna Tedeschi from the Turin State Archive, *Sezzinoi Riunite, Vicariato di Torino*, vol. 1048, *Miscellanea* (1754–1800). In 1805, 414 families lived in the one building that

constituted Turin's ghetto. The first European ghetto was in Venice, dating back to 1516.

286. Serlio pub. 1994.

287. See para. 5 of this chapter.

288. Malanima 1990, p. 13.

289. Cosenza 1974, p. 95.

290. Thornton 1991 (Ital. trans. 1992), p. 15.

291. Serlio pub. 1994, p. 58.

292. See para. 6 of this chapter.

293. Ranum 1986 (Ital. trans. 1987), pp 168–9.

294. Barley 1985, pp. 611–12; Montenegro 1996, pp. 30, 135 and 156; Maza 1983, p. 186, note 71.

295. Brown 1986.

296. Blok 1995; Sarti 1995. For information on the *salon*, see Salvati 1995.

297. Archive of the Archbishopric of Bologna, *Foro Arcivescovile, Sgabello II*, fol. 12, n. 20, quoted in Ferrante 1994b, p. 17.

298. Vocabolario Crusca 1612, under the entry.

299. On this point, see the plans in Serlio pub. 1994, p. 121 and IV, fig. 45, Ex. VI.

300. See para. 6 of this chapter.

301. On secret stairs and exits, see above, in this paragraph.

302. Leon Battista Alberti, *De re aedificatoria*, V, chapter VII, quoted in Thornton 1991 (Ital. trans. 1992), p. 288.

303. Thornton 1991 (Ital. trans. 1992), p. 288.

304. Battaglia 1961–, under the entry.

305. Thornton 1991 (Ital. trans. 1992), p. 313 (Italics in the original), p. 314.

306. Giovanni Biagio Amico, *L'architetto pratico*, in Simoncini (ed.) 1995, vol. II, p. 634.

307. See, for example, Augustin-Charles D'Aviler, *Cours d'Architecture*, in Simoncini (ed.) 1995, vol. II, p. 616.

308. Pier Jacopo Martello, *Il vero parigino italiano*, in Simoncini (ed.) 1995, vol. II, p. 624.

309. Evans 1978. According to the available descriptions, Holland developed architectural elements similar to 'modern' corridors very early, see Cosenza 1974, p. 127.

310. *The Book of Architecture of John Thorpe*, ed. John Summerson, Glasgow 1966, quoted in Evans 1978 (German trans. 1996), p. 90.

311. Sir Roger Pratt, *Sir Roger Pratt on Architecture*, ed. R.T. Gunther, Oxford 1928, pp. 62 and 64, quoted in Evans 1978 (German trans. 1996), p. 90. As far as Italy was concerned, Paolo Cornaglia has kindly informed me that the ground-floor apartment at Palazzo Carignano in Turin, the seat of the collateral line of the House of Savoy and therefore a 'second royal palace', has rooms facing to the north and the south attached to a central corridor that ran the full length of each wing of the building. It was built by Guarino Guarini in 1679.

312. John Vaubrugli, *The Complete Works*, ed. B. Dobrée and G. Webb, London, 1927, vol. IV, p. 71, quoted in Stone and Fawtier Stone 1984 and 1986, pp. 345–6. According to quotations contained in Evans 1978, neither Thorpe nor Pratt appear to have ever used the term 'corridor'. The most ancient reference to the term was in 1591 according to the *Oxford English Dictionary*, but it referred to an element in the architecture of fortifications. All the occurrences of the term with the other listed meanings dated from the seventeenth century at the earliest.

313. Stone and Fawtier Stone 1984 and 1986 (Ital. trans. 1989), p. 294.

314. Evans 1978 (German trans. 1996), pp. 91–3.

315. On these changes, see Elias 1969 (Ital. trans. 1982); Ariès and Duby 1986 (Ital. trans. 1987); Blok 1993; Meldrum 1999.

316. Serlio pub. 1994, p. 71.

317. Sarti 1994a, 1997a and 1999a.

318. Giuseppe Leoncini, *Instruttioni architettoniche pratiche concernenti le parti principali degli edifici delle case . . .* , Rome, 1679, partly republished in Simoncini (ed.) 1995, vol. II, pp. 604–6, quotation on p. 605.

319. The *basse-cour* in large urban houses was the courtyard separated fom the main one. It

was surrounded by coach-houses, stables, kitchens, offices, etc.; see Elias 1975 (Ital. trans. 1980), p. 38, note 9.

320. Augustin-Charles D'Aviler, *Cours d'Architecture*, in Simoncini (ed.) 1995, vol. II, pp. 621–3.

321. Francesco Milizia, *Principj di architettura civile*, vols I–III, Finale, 1781, vol. II, *Libro terzo. Della distribuzione*, partly republished in Simoncini (ed.) 1995, vol. II, pp. 643–51, quotation on p. 648.

322. Apart from the sources already referred to, see FOL.E. Briseux, *L'Art de bâtir*, in Simoncini (ed.) 1995, vol. II, p. 633.

323. Roche 1981 (Ital. trans. 1986), p. 155; Maza 1983, pp. 184–5; Fairchilds 1984, pp. 38–9. In twentieth-century Germany, female servants were often still sleeping in a kind of raised recess in the kitchen (called a *Hängeboden*), see Müller 1985, p. 183.

324. Raffaello Gambardella, *Istruzioni di architettura composte secondo il metodo matematico*, Naples, 1798, partly republished in Simoncini (ed.) 1995, vol. II, pp. 654–7, quotation on p. 657.

325. Quoted in Pardailhé-Galabrun 1988, p. 263.

326. Archives Départementales du Calvados, Dépòt de Caen, 2B 883, March 1723, quoted in Maza 1983, pp. 184–5. On the presence of servants even in families of fairly low social rank, see Sarti 1994a, pp. 210–35, with references.

327. Luzio and Renier 1891, p. 143. Beds on casters, which often appeared in Renaissance inventories and were called *chariolles* in French and *cariole* in Italian, were often stored under the 'large' bed and were not infrequently used by servants, see Thornton 1991 (Ital. trans. 1992), p. 113.

328. Duchesse de Liancourt, *Règlement donné par une dame de qualité a' M** sa petite-fille pour sa conduite et celle de sa maison*, Paris, 1728 (1698 1st edn), quoted in Maza 1983, p. 185.

329. Vigarello 1985 (Ital. trans. 1988), p. 84.

330. Bologna State Archive, *Fondo Albergati, Strumenti and scritture*, b. 210, f. 4. Of course,

the possibility cannot be excluded that the servants were lying to defend their master. Even if this was the case, however, their statements are still of interest to us, as they had to be believable lies, i.e. versions of events that would appear acceptable or 'normal' to their contemporaries.

331. For information on these events, see Elias 1975 (Ital. trans. 1980), p. 41, note 14; Duerr 1988 (Ital. trans. 1991), pp. 143–4; Vigarello 1985 (Ital. trans. 1988), pp. 111–12.

332. Duerr 1988 (Ital. trans. 1991), pp. 143–9.

333. Elias 1975 (Ital. trans. 1980), pp. 94–7.

334. This is probably an intermediate position between that of Elias 1969 (Ital. trans. 1982), and that of Duerr 1988 (Ital. trans. 1991). In his polemic with Elias, Duerr argued that modesty was practically universal to the human species.

335. Bologna State Archive, *Fondo Albergati, Strumenti and scritture*, b. 210, f. 4.

336. Stone and Fawtier Stone 1984 and 1986 (Ital. trans. 1989), pp. 292–6. On changes in domestic service in eighteenth-century England, see also Hecht 1980.

337. Augustin-Charles D'Aviler, *Cours d'Architecture*, in Simoncini (ed.) 1995, vol. II, pp. 620 and 622.

338. Alessandro Galilei, *Della Architettura Civile and dell'uso e modo del fabbricare e dove ebbe origine* . . . (1731), Florence State Archive, *Fondo Galilei*, file O, no. 15, partly republished in Simoncini (ed.) 1995, vol. II, pp. 627–9, quotation on p. 628.

339. FOL.E. Briseux, *L'Art de bâtir*, in Simoncini (ed.) 1995, vol. II, pp. 630 and 634.

340. Francesco Milizia, *Principi di architettura civile*, in Simoncini (ed.) 1995, vol. II, p. 646.

341. Roche 1981 (Ital. trans. 1986), pp. 153–5. For a comparison between the two house plans, one from the early-eighteenth century and the other from the 1780s, which were taken from the Jombert and Krafft collection and the Ransonette collection respectively, see Fairchilds 1984, pp. 49–50.

342. Sarti 1995.

343. Sarti 1995 and 1999a; Arru 1995.

344. For the Italian, see Sarti 1994b. For the French and English, see the entries in Robert 1953–64 and Oxford 1989. See also para. 7 of chapter I.

345. Quoted in Montanari 1991.

V. Food

1. A. Jouvin de Rochefort, *Le Voyageur d'Europe*, Paris, 1672, partly republished in Montanari 1991, pp. 233–5.

2. Girolamo Cirelli, *Il villano smascherato*, ed. Gian Ludovico Masetti Zannini, in *Rivista di storia dell'agricoltura*, 1967, I, partly republished in Montanari 1991, pp. 250–1.

3. *Itenerario di uno peligrino incognito,* partly republished in Camporesi 1989, p. 8.

4. Deonna and Renard 1961 (Ital. trans. 1994), p. 54.

5. Montanari 1991, p. viii.

6. 'A tavola and al tavolino riconosci il cittadino', Teti 1978, p. 178 (as with other reference to our folk heritage, there is always the problem of exactly dating material collected in more recent times) and p. 310 (Caterina I., San Nicola da Crissa, illiterate peasant woman, 84 years at the time of the interview in 1972–3).

7. Febvre 1930 (Ital. trans. 1992); Elias 1969 (Ital. trans. 1982), especially pp. 197–255 on behaviour at the table; Bertelli and Calvi 1985; Revel 1986 (Ital. trans. 1987). After 1820, the term 'civilization' took on the more neutral meaning of *all* the features of *any* social group, while retaining the former meaning of the positive features and values typical of a group such as to make it superior to other groups.

8. Calviac, *Civilité* (1560), partly republished in Elias 1969 (Ital. trans. 1982), pp. 205–6 and in Montanari 1991, pp. 100–1.

9. Elias 1969 (Ital. trans. 1982); Grottanelli 1985 and the whole of Bertelli and Crifò (eds) 1985.

10. Karl Marx, *Grundrisse der Kritik der politischen Ökonomie* (1857–9), quoted in Spode 1994, p. 20.

11. Acanfora 1985; Marchese 1989, pp. 26–8; Grassi, Pepe and Sestieri 1992, under the entry.

12. Elias 1969 (Ital. trans. 1982), pp. 245–50; Marchese 1989; Grassi, Pepe and Sestieri 1992, under the entries for *Coltello* and *Posate*; Spode 1994, p. 27.

13. I refer to the version in Spode 1994, p. 22. Marchese 1989, pp. 42–7, argues that the princess was called Maria and was the sister of Romano Argiro, who was to become emperor.

14. Grassi, Pepe and Sestieri 1992, under the entry.

15. Anonymous fourteenth century writer at the Angevin court, in Faccioli (ed.) 1992, pp. 19–41, especially p. 34; Rebora 1998, p. 19. For information on the manner and the speed with which the use of pasta spread, see para. 6 of this chapter.

16. Elias 1969 (Ital. trans. 1982), pp. 167–9; Braudel 1979 (Ital. trans. 1993), p. 181; Spode 1994, p. 25; Flandrin 1996a, p. 444.

17. Spode 1994, p. 24; Weatherill 1988, fig. 2.1, p. 26 and p. 156; Weatherill 1993, pp. 215–16.

18. Spode 1991, pp. 237–43 and 1994, p. 30.

19. Grassi, Pepe and Sestieri 1992, under the entry; Pounds 1989; Goldthwaite 1989; Thornton 1991 (Ital. trans. 1992), pp. 105–11.

20. Song composed by the Marquis de Coulanger around 1660 and quoted in Elias 1969 (Ital. trans. 1982), p. 206; in Montanari 1991, pp. 225–6 and in Spode 1994, p. 25.

21. Elias 1969 (Ital. trans. 1982); Braudel 1979 (Ital. trans. 1993), p. 181; Flandrin 1996a, p. 444

22. Flandrin 1996a, p. 444. For tablecloths and napkins, see Garbero Zorzi 1985.

23. Cortelazzo and Zolli 1979–88, under the entry.

24. Spode 1994, p. 26 and p. 40, note 23; Ilauser 1994, pp. 307–8; Grassi, Pepe and Sestieri 1992, under the entry.

25. Hauser 1994, pp. 307–8.

26. Quoted in Barbagli 1996, p. 405.

27. Pounds 1989, p. 208, who dates the universalization of the use of tablecloths, napkins, forks and other cutlery on Western tables to the end of the nineteenth century. The accounts referred to lead us to shift this universalization to more recent times, but undoubtedly even today there are pockets of poverty and isolation, whether traditional or new, in which what Pounds defines as the 'niceties of eating' are not used. The question really is to identify the stages by which a certain manner of eating became the norm.

28. Quoted in Barbagli 1996, p. 439, note 80.

29. Teti 1978, p. 310.

30. The account of Licia Berrera, a teacher in a few mountain villages in South Tyrol at the end of the fifties.

31. Valeri 1977, p. 352.

32. Rösener 1995, p. 244.

33. See chapter III, para. 3.

34. Klapisch-Zuber and Demonet 1972 (Ital. trans. 1983) and Montanari 1994, p. 63.

35. Fauve-Chamoux 1993, p. 491.

36. Andorka and Faragó 1983, p. 285. For the question of whether to treat cohabitation or consumption as the distinctive elements in a family, see previously mentioned Wall 1983 (Ital. trans. 1984) and Laslett 1983 (Ital. trans. 1984).

37. Archive of the Archbishopric of Siena, *Denunce di concubini*, 5619 (1590), fol. 9, quoted in Di Simplicio 1994a, p. 186.

38. Di Simplicio 1994b; Sarti 1994c, p. 686.

39. Quoted in Merzario 1996a, p. 232.

40. Corso 1948, p. 11. By the term 'gender', we mean the male and female identities as social and cultural constructs specific to every culture and society.

41. For example, Stols 1997, p. 240.

42. The account of Maria, born in San Vito (Province of Vicenza) in 1898, the daughter and wife of a *mezzadro* or sharecropper, quoted in Barbagli 1996, p. 405.

43. Baumgarten 1965, p. 10; Valeri 1977, p. 352; Stone 1977 (Ital. trans. 1983), p. 217; Dülmen 1990, p. 73.

44. Account of Genoveffa, born in Lancenigo (Treviso) in 1906, daughter of a bricklayer and wife of peasant who owned his own land, quoted in Barbagli 1996, p. 405.

45. *A Critical Essay Concerning Marriage by a Gentleman*, London, 1724, in *Local Population Studies*, 12, 1974, pp. 46–9 (quoted in Stone 1977, p. 324 [Ital. trans. 1983, p. 356]).

46. Baumgarten 1965.

47. Wilhelin Riehl, *Die Familie*, Berlin, 1854, p. 150, quoted in Berkner 1972 (Ital. trans. 1977), p. 131.

48. In should be remembered that in many regions, particularly German ones, the servants (*Knechte*, if male, and *Magde*, if female) might have been brothers or sisters of the head of the family who had been excluded from the succession.

49. See above, chapter IV, paras 16 and 17.

50. Romani 1997, p. 734.

51. ASB, *Tribunale criminale del Torrone, Atti processuali*, 8374/5, folder 100. For a more detailed analysis of this event, see Sarti 1994a, pp. 91–101.

52. We would expect hierarchies to be even more rigid in a city residence, where social relations were less relaxed than in a country home.

53. ASB, *Tribunale criminale del Torrone, Atti processuali*, 8374/5, folder 100, initial interrogation of Eleonora Albergati, fol. 35r ('women's room'; these were the words used by, for example, the factor Giuseppe Donini, fol. 100v), fol. 38v ('I started to call and shout so that the women came running, and I went down to where they were'), fol. 40r ('shortly afterwards I told the women of what I had seen'), fol. 44r ('women's room'); interrogation of Maria Pifaretti, fol. 48r ('in the room where I and the other women stayed': for such expression as 'our room', etc., see also fol. 5r; interrogation of Maddalena Zambonelli, fol. 62r; interrogation of Lucia Franzoni, fol. 73v; interrogation of Marianna Boscani, fol. 85r), fol. 53r ('we women': such expressions were used by Maddalena Zambonelli, fols 63r–65r; Lucia Franzoni, fol. 76v; Marianna Boscani, fol. 94r and fol. 98r–v); interrogation of Giuseppe Donini, fol. 103r ('women of the house');

interrogation of Francesco Mazzoni, fol. 114v; interrogation of Gaetano Barselli, fol. 122r; interrogation of Andrea Bontà, fols 125v, 126v; interrogation of Giuseppe Vilz, fol. 129r–v; interrogation of Maria Pancaldi, fol. 142r; interrogation of Orsola Donini, fol. 144r; interrogation of Paolo Franzoni, fol. 167r; second interrogation of Francesco Albergati, fol. 212v.

54. ASB, *Tribunale criminale del Torrone, Atti processuali*, 8374/5, folder 100, *passim*.

55. Vincenzo Tanara, *L'economia del cittadino in villa*, Venezia, 1655 (1644 1st edn), partly republished in Montanari 1991, pp. 209–11 (quotation on p. 209).

56. Hom 1975, p. 6; Fairchilds 1984, pp. 15–16 and 51; Sarti 1997a; Capatti and Montanari 1999 (I would like to thank the authors for having allowed me to read part of their book on cooks before its publication). A. Martín Casares informs me however that in sixteenth-century Granada, the most demanding tasks in the kitchens of upper-class homes were entrusted to the female slaves.

57. Manciulli 1996; Nazarov 1997, p. 848.

58. Vincenzo Tanara, *L'economia . . .* , in Montanari 1991, pp. 209–10.

59. Cervio 1593 (pub. 1980), pp. 1–2. The author complained that these tasks and the staff responsible for them were falling into disuse. The steward had the task of co-ordinating the work of all those involved with providing food for the house and directing the serving at his lord's table. The cup-bearer served his lord with drink during the meal and the carver cut the food at banquets.

60. Milillo 1994, p. 54. On food in fairy-tales, see also Cusatelli 1994.

61. Manciulli 1996, p. 329. Originally, side-boards were simply tables on which people placed plates, pots and food. Given that the opulence and abundance of one's crockery was an indicator of one's *status* that everyone was supposed to see, people started to build surfaces to display them. The number of surfaces itself became an indication of the house-owner's rank; see Thornton 1991 (Ital. trans. 1992), pp. 207 and 220–1; Montenegro 1996, p. 68.

62. Nazarov 1997, p. 847. *Kvas* is a slightly alcoholic drink made from the fermentation of starchy or sugary substances.

63. Faccioli 1973; Bentini, Chiappini, Panatta and Visser Travagli 1988; Bertelli and Crifò (eds) 1985; Calvi and Bertelli 1983; Ricci 1994; Montanari 1994; Spode 1994; Manciulli 1996; Romani 1997. The quotations were taken from Vincenzo Cervio, *Il trinciante*, Rome, 1593 (1581 1st edn) and Bartolomeo Stefani, *L'arte di ben cucinare*, Mantova, 1662 and Venezia, 1666. Both texts were republished in Faccioli (ed.) 1992, pp. 528–37 and pp. 676–82 respectively.

64. Montanari 1994, pp. 104–5.

65. M. de Rabutin-Chantal, *Lettres*, ed. E. Gérerd-Gailly, Paris, 1953, I, pp. 232–6, in Montanari 1991, pp. 231–3; Fairchilds 1984, pp. 28–31. For further information on Watel, see Michel 1999.

66. Fragnito 1988 and 1991; Sarti 1994a, pp. 51–91 and 1997a; Manciulli 1996. The fact that this literature came into existence to illustrate and to propose the organizational model for the cardinals' courts probably contributed to explaining why such figures were all male.

67. Interview with Italy's premier female chef, Nadia Cavaliere Santini transmitted on 4 March 1998 by TG2 *Costume and Società*. On the breakdown between male and female cooks in Toulouse, see Fairchilds 1984, p. 51.

68. Hyman and Hyman 1996, p. 509.

69. See amongst other works, Weatherill 1988, p. 149.

70. Milillo 1994, p. 54.

71. Mennell 1985 (French trans. 1987), pp. 287–8.

72. Mennell 1985 (French trans. 1987), pp. 142, 185 and 287–305; Hecht 1980, pp. 43, 65 and 287–305. French cuisine was to experience greater success between the end of the Napoleonic Wars and the mid-eighteenth century.

73. Weatherill 1988, pp. 149–50.

74. Tasso 1969, p. 543.

75. Tito Livio, *Ab urbe condita*, XXXIX, 6, quoted in Deonna and Renard 1961 (Ital. trans. 1994), p. 62, note 52. See also p. 45.

76. See above, note 63.

77. Mennell 1985 (French trans. 1987), especially pp. 159–94.

78. Flandrin 1996a, pp. 441–2.

79. Quoted in Mennell 1985, p. 84.

80. Mennell 1985 (French trans. 1987), p. 95; see also pp. 95–8, 233–5 and 330; Davidson 1982, pp. 45–57; Weatherill 1988, pp. 145–50.

81. See Capatti and Montanari 1999, to whom I am indebted for the correct dating of this work, which is *La cuciniera piemontese che insegna con facil metodo le migliori maniere di acconciare le vivande . . .* , Vercelli, 1771. The text was republished at least 11 times between 1771 and 1863; see Bibliothèque Internationale de Gastronomie 1994, vol. I, p. 549, n. 608 (which even reprints the frontispiece). There is a facsimile print of the 1798 Turin edition (Bologna, 1980).

82. The *status animarum* were censuses of the population of each parish carried out every year by the parish priest to check that everyone took communion at Easter.

83. Bologna State Archive, *Legato, Censimento di famiglie distinto per parrocchie (ex notificazione 2 maggio 1796)*; Archive of the Parish of San Giovanni in Monte in Bologna, *Status animarum*, 1810, 1820, 1830, 1850, 1857 and 1899; Archive of the Parish of Santi Bartolomeo and Gaetano in Bologna, *Status animarum*, 1810, 1820, 1830, 1840, 1870 and 1902. See also Sarti 1992, tables 1a and 1b, p. 248.

84. *Fantesca* n.d., p. 480v.

85. Hufton 1995 (Ital. trans. 1996), p. 146; Stols 1997, pp. 239–41.

86. Visceglia 1991, p. 223.

87. See chapter IV, para. 7. For the different types of cooking, see Davidson 1982, pp. 44–60; Flandrin 1996c, pp. 519–20.

88. Roche 1981 (Ital. trans. 1986), p. 195; Pardailhé-Galabrun 1988, pp. 291–2; Davidson 1982, pp. 47–8.

89. Stone 1979 (Ital. trans. 1983), pp. 474–80; Klapisch-Zuber 1983a (Ital. trans. 1988); Barbagli 1996, pp. 336–63; Fildes 1986 and 1988 (Ital. trans. 1997); Matthews Grieco

1991a; Hufton 1995 (Ital. trans. 1996), especially pp. 168–73; D'Amelia 1997; Fiume 1997, pp. 90–7. On the social construct of the maternal role, see Fiume (ed.) 1995; D'Amelia (ed.) 1997.

90. Klapisch-Zuber 1983a (Ital. trans. 1988), pp. 221–2 and 239–45; Fildes 1988 (Ital. trans. 1997), pp. 107–8; Matthews Grieco 1991a, pp. 46–7.

91. D'Amelia 1997, pp. 36–7; Fildes 1986, p. 370.

92. Among the nobles in England, who were in the habit of using a wet-nurse for their children, one out of five died during early infancy, while the national average was one out of seven, see Hufton 1995 (Ital. trans. 1996), p. 171; Fildes 1986, p. 204. In Renaissance Florence, the death rate for babies given to a wet-nurse was 18% and was higher amongst boys than girls, see Fildes 1988 (Ital. trans. 1997), p. 113. It should also be remembered that up until the eighteenth century doctors believed colostrum, the first milk to be produced after childbirth which is thick and yellowish, to be unhealthy. Upper-class children, whose parents followed medical advice, did not therefore get any colostrums from either their mothers or their wet-nurses (while they were waiting for the milk to turn white, they were fed artificially or by a special wet-nurse). This deprived them of the important nutritional and protective elements in colostrums and exposed them to the risk of infections and disease while they were waiting for the 'clear' milk; see Fildes 1986 and Matthews Grieco 1991a, p. 22.

93. Barbagli 1996, pp. 337–9; Fildes 1988 (Ital. trans. 1997), pp. 118–19.

94. Giuseppe Antonio Costantini, *Lettere critiche, giocose, morali, scientzfrche, ed erudite alla moda, ed al gusto del secolo presente*, Naples, n.d., vol. VII, pp. 81–2, quoted in Fiume 1997, p. 91.

95. Fildes 1986, pp. 121–2 and 1988 (Ital. trans. 1997), pp. 141–2 and 149. See also above, the other texts referred to in note 89. Only after the mid-seventeenth century did it become widely believed that babies should be breastfed at regular times and not every time they cried.

96. Matthews Grieco 1991a, pp. 17–18.

97. Stone 1979 (Ital. trans. 1983), pp. 475–6; Klapisch-Zuber 1983a (Ital. trans. 1988), pp. 245–50; Barbagli 1996, p. 343; Pomata 1995. It is, however, reasonable to question whether wet-nurses, particularly those who continued to live with their husbands, really abstained from sex for many months in order to protect the quality of their milk; see Fildes 1986, p. 121 and 1988 (Ital. trans. 1997), p. 104.

98. KIapisch-Zuber 1983a (Ital. trans. 1988), pp. 226–8; Barbagli 1996, p. 349; Fildes 1988 (Ital. trans. 1997), pp. 97–8; D'Amelia 1997, pp. 12 and 30.

99. *Madre Cristiana* 1732, pp. 102 and 104. Because of this belief, there were considerable concerns over feeding babies with animal milk. It was used only in the absence of a wet-nurse or in the case of babies suffering from syphilis (this disease can be transmitted from the baby to the wet-nurse and vice versa). In this case, babies could be attached directly to an animal's teat; see in particular Fildes 1986 and 1988 (Ital. trans. 1997).

100. D'Amelia 1997, pp. 12 and 30.

101. See above, note 98.

102. Fildes 1986, p. 121.

103. See above, note 89.

104. Barbagli 1996, p. 350.

105. Stone 1979 (Ital. trans. 1983), p. 476; Fildes 1986, p. 91; D'Amelia 1997, p. 33.

106. Giuseppe Antonio Costantini, *Lettere critiche . . .*, pp. 81–2, quoted in Fiume 1997, p. 91. See also Stone 1979 (Ital. trans. 1983), p. 479 and Matthews Grieco 1991a, p. 20.

107. See above, note 89.

108. Hufton 1995 (Ital. trans. 1996), p. 168.

109. Stone 1979 (Ital. trans. 1983), pp. 476–7; Schama 1987 (Ital. trans. 1988); Fildes 1986, p. 121; Hufton 1995 (Ital. trans. 1996), pp. 168–70.

110. See in particular the chronological table in Fildes 1986, p. 400.

111. Stone 1979 (Ital. trans. 1983), pp. 477 and 480; Barbagli 1996, especially pp. 354–63; Fildes 1986, pp. 162–82, 398–401 and 1988

(Ital. trans. 1997), especially pp. 162–97 and 268–326; Hufton 1995 (Ital. trans. 1996, pp. 171–2; D'Amelia (ed.) 1997.

112. Tilly and Scott 1978 (Ital. trans. 1981). In Italy this phenomenon occurred in the second half of the nineteenth century, see Barbagli 1996, pp. 354–5; Fiume 1997, p. 91.

113. Stone 1979 (Ital. trans. 1983), pp. 479–80; Fildes 1988 (Ital. trans. 1997), pp. 135 and 192. Significantly, Pietro Verri, one of the first noblemen to abandon the custom of wet-nursing in Italy, was condemned by parents and relations, and accused of wanting 'to behave like an Englishman', see Barbagli 1996, p. 357.

114. Johann Wilhelin von Archenholtz, *Tableau de l'Angleterre*, Gotha, 1788, vol. II, p. 156, quoted in Stone 1979 (Ital. trans. 1983), p. 479.

115. In England, according to Weatherill 1988, upper-class women in the eighteenth century became less personally involved in the preparation of food for the family.

116. See also Sarti 1988, pp. 91–2 and 1994d.

117. Barbagli 1996; Pomata 1980; Fiume (ed.) 1995; D'Amelia (ed.) 1997.

118. Flandrin 1993 and 1996a, pp. 444–5; Montanari 1994; Stols 1997, pp. 233 and 240–1; Sanga 1994.

119. Mantua State Archive, *Archivio Gonzaga*, b. 394, *Ordini per le foresterie de principi*, quoted in Romani 1997, p. 735; Giulio Cordara, *De' vantaggi dell'orologio italiano sopra l'oltremontano*, Alessandria, 1783, quoted in Niccoli 2000, p. 6.

120. Camporesi 1989, p. 28. For eating patterns, see in particular Aymard, Grignon and Sabban (eds) 1993.

121. L. Lémery, *Traité des Aliments*, Paris, 1755 (3rd edn), vol. I, p. liv, quoted in Flandrin 1993, p. 198.

122. Flandrin 1993 and 1996a, pp. 444–5.

123. Giulio Cesare Croce, *Le sottilissime astuzie di Bertoldo* (1606), ed. Piero Camporesi, Turin, 1978, partly republished in Montanari 1991, p. 174.

124. Grieco 1996, especially pp. 375–80, emphasizes the difficulties with the inclusion

of quadrupeds in the chain of existence; Montanari 1994, pp. 104–15; Flandrin 1996c, p. 515; Romani 1997.

125. Florentin Thierriat, *Discours de la pre-férence de la noblesse*, quoted in Grieco 1996, p. 375.

126. Manciulli 1996.

127. Flandrin 1997a, pp. 446–7. At banquets served in the French manner, those who did not have a servant to go and get the food arranged on dishes far from the table had to be content with anything offered to them by their fellow-diners seated nearby. Given that drinks were laid out on a separate buffet, those who did not have a personal valet ran the risk of a parched throat. It was not easy to attract the attention of the waiters working for the house.

128. Grieco 1996, p. 375.

129. Pasquali 1939; Battaglia 1961–, vol. V, p. 623.

130 Guenzi 1982, p. 26, note 26; Romani 1997, pp. 730–2. Documents relating to the courts of the Po Valley distinguished between bread and wine 'for princes', 'for gentlemen' and 'for servants [*famiglia*]'. Occasionally there were even more complicated hierarchies.

131. See the map on p. 172.

132. On the different types of bread, see Braudel 1979 (Ital. trans. 1993), pp. 112–14; Aymard and Bresc 1975, p. 53; Camporesi 1989, pp. 17–23, 111–19 and 1989; Guenzi 1982; Davico 1987; Visceglia 1991, pp. 223–5; Kaplan 1996 (French trans. 1996); Montanari 1994, especially pp. 65–71; Flandrin and Montanari (eds) 1996.

133. Quoted in Camporesi 1989, p. 34.

134. Guenzi 1982.

135. Guenzi 1982, p. 28.

136. Visceglia 1991, pp. 223–5; Flandrin 1996b, pp. 471–2.

137. Bloch 1970, p. 233 and Montanari 1994, p. 134 on the charges imposed by land-owners; Flandrin 1996b, pp. 471–2.

138. Montanari 1994, pp. 1–36 and 1997.

139. Montanari 1994, pp. 71–6.

140. Livi Bacci 1998, pp. 66 and 79.

141. It appears that today, in every part of the globe, the higher social strata eat more meat than the lower ones, Harris 1985 (Ital. trans. 1990) and 1992, p. 15.

142. Fildes 1986, p. 393.

143. Montanari 1994, pp. 24–30 and 1997.

144. Simon-Muscheid 1997, p. 344.

145. Montanari 1994, pp. 137–45. The Lenten diet became the subject of disputes relating to the acceptability of fish, cheese and eggs, see Visceglia 1991, p. 220; Simon-Muscheid 1997, pp. 344–8.

146. Flandrin 1983, 1996a, pp. 447–8, 1996c and 1996d; Montanari 1994, pp. 141–50 and 1997.

147. Montanari 1994, pp. 99 and 141–3; Nigro 1997.

148. Flandrin 1996a, pp. 437–8 and 1996d.

149. Flandrin 1983, 1996a and 1996c; Montanari 1994, pp. 137–44 and 1997.

150. Matthaiou 1997, p. 321.

151. Nazarov 1997, p. 846.

152. Douglas 1975 and Douglas (ed.) 1984; Fischler 1985.

153. Scaraffia 1993, pp. 57–86 and 95.

154. Scaraffia 1993, pp. 60–2 and 75.

155. Scaraffia 1993; quoted on p. 57.

156. Sarti 1999b.

157. Soler 1997; Motis Dolander 1997; Toaff 2000.

158. Sarti 1999b.

159. Gleaning rights made it possible to gather ears of corn that fell during harvest-ing. Herbage was the right to make hay and graze animals on the common land; *ghian-datico* was the right to gather acorns.

160. On food-rationing institutions, see Guenzi 1995 and more generally *Archivi di storia dell'alimentazione* 1995.

161. On changes in diet between the ancient world and the late Middle Ages, see Montanari 1994, pp. 51–67 and 87–90.

162. Guenzi 1984 and 1986.

163. Braudel 1979 (Ital. trans. 1993), pp. 168–71; Montanari 1994, pp. 91–7; Flandrin 1997; Matthaiou 1997; Motis Dolander 1997.

164. Ambrosoli 1992.

165. Braudel 1979 (Ital. trans. 1993), p. 15; Montanari 1994, pp. 126 and 161; Dupaquier 1987; Livi Bacci 1998, pp. 14–15, fig. 1.1.

166. Braudel 1979 (Ital. trans. 1993), pp. 171–5.

167. Aymard and Bresc 1975, pp. 551–4. For a more comprehensive view of the Italian situation, see Visceglia 1991, pp. 218–20.

168. The figures were taken from Romani 1975, p. 186; Guenzi 1984, p. 63; Revel 1975, p. 474 respectively.

169. Flandrin 1996a, pp. 428–9.

170. Sereni 1981, p. 370; Galasso 1982, p. 157.

171. Clemente 1985, p. 226.

172. Montanari 1994, pp. 130–2.

173. Morineau 1996, p. 459.

174. Visceglia 1991, p. 221, table 1; Montanari 1994, p. 134; Flandrin 1996b, pp. 469–70.

175. Braudel 1979 (Ital. trans. 1993), pp. 45–9; Livi Bacci 1987, pp. 70–8; Montanari 1994, p. 127; Flandrin 1996a, p. 429.

176. Livi Bacci 1998, pp. 73–8.

177. Braudel 1979 (Ital. trans. 1993), pp. 99–104. For bibliographical information on the corn trade, see Guenzi 1995.

178. Istituto Internazionale di Storia Economica F. Datini, Prato 1998.

179. Braudel 1979 (Ital. trans. 1993), pp. 111–30; Montanari 1994, pp. 125–8; Flandrin 1996a, p. 432.

180. Flandrin 1996a, pp. 434–5.

181. Girolamo Battarra, *Pratica agraria* (1778), republished in Montanari 1991, p. 342.

182. Levi 1976 and 1991b.

183. The quotation was taken from Camporesi 1989, p. 48, which also includes various extracts from the Jacini Agricultural

Inquiry. For information on the diet in Italy following unification, see Somogyi 1973 and more recently Capatti, De Bernardi and Varni (eds) 1998.

184. On the introduction of maize into Europe, see Braudel 1979 (Ital. trans. 1993), pp. 130–2; Levi 1979 and 1991b; Montanari 1994, pp. 130 and 170–5; Visceglia 1991, pp. 226–8; Flandrin 1996a, pp. 432–3; Istituto Internazionale di Storia Economica F. Datini, Prato 1998; Wendt 1998. On pellagra, see Finzi 1976 and 1990.

185. Girolamo Battarra, *Pratica agraria* (1778), in Montanari 1991, p. 343.

186. Braudel 1979 (Ital. trans. 1993), p. 141; Montanari 1994, pp. 173–4.

187. Morineau 1996, pp. 455 and 463.

188. Salaman 1985 (Ital. trans. 1989); Braudel 1979 (Ital. trans. 1993), pp. 139–43; Montanari 1994, pp. 130 and 170–5; Istituto Internazionale di Storia Economica F. Datini, Prato 1998; Wendt 1998.

189. Quoted in Flandrin 1996b, p. 472.

190. Montanari 1994, p. 171. On maize in southern Italy, see Visceglia 1991, p. 227.

191. Quoted in Camporesi 1989, p. 9.

192. Dal Pane 1969; Camporesi 1989; Flandrin 1996a, p. 433 and 1996c, pp. 473–4.

193. Sereni 1981; Aymard and Bresc 1975; Marchese 1989, pp. 49–57; Montanari 1994, pp. 175–80; Rebora 1998.

194. Drummond and Wilbraliam 1958; Levi 1996, p. 200.

195. Flandrin 1996d; Montanari 1994, pp. 149–50.

196. Mintz 1985 (Ital. trans. 1990); Huetz de Lemps 1996; Sarti 1999b with bibliographical references.

197. Van Uytven 1997, pp. 76–7.

198. Giuseppe Maria Galanti, *Breve descrizione di Napoli and del suo contorno*, Naples, 1803, p. 271, quoted in Visceglia 1991, p. 222.

199. Huetz de Lemps 1996.

200. Jeanneret 1994, p. 16; for the ancient origins of this concept, see Pomata 1994a, pp.

271–7, Vigarello 1993 (Ital. trans. 1996), and Flandrin 1996d.

201. Braudel 1979 (Ital. trans. 1993), pp. 215–20; Montanari 1994, pp. 153–4; Flandrin 1996b, pp. 484–5; Van Uytven 1997.

202. Archive of the Archbishopric of Bologna, *Recuperi attuariali*, notary Marco Antonio Balzani, *Liber testium*, n. 262, evidence of 20 October 1578. I am indebted to Adanella Bianchi for this reference. For information on this trial, but not the point to which I have referred, see Bianchi 1997.

203. See above, chapter IV, para. 2 and chapter V, para. 1.

204. See above, para. 6 and Camporesi 1989, p. 9.

205. Clemente 1985, pp. 226–9. But see also Camporesi 1989.

206. See para. 4 of this chapter.

207. Flandrin 1996b, pp. 479–83.

208. G. Rosaccio, *Fabrica universale dell'huomo sotto titolo di microcosmo dichiarata* . . . , Venice, 1627, pp. 45–6, quoted in Camporesi 1980, pp. 95–6.

209. Braudel 1979 (Ital. trans. 1993), pp. 212–13; Van Uytven 1997; Spode 1991.

210. Fildes 1986, p. 393; Montanari 1994, p. 151; Van Uytven 1997, pp. 59, 66 and 72.

211. Visceglia 1991, p. 221, table 1.

212. Sorcinelli 1998, pp. 55–9

213. Ménétra pub. 1982 (Ital. trans. 1992), p. 196.

214. Flandrin 1996c, p. 526. See also Braudel 1979 (Ital. trans. 1993), pp. 183–4.

215. Livi Bacci 1998, p. 62.

216. Camporesi 1980.

217. Morineau 1996, p. 583.

218. Montanari 1994, p. 181; Komles 1988.

219. Ménétra pub. 1982 (Ital. trans. 1992), p. 139.

220. Johann Wolfgang Goethe, *Viaggio in Italia*, Novara, 1982, pp. 141–2, republished in Montanari 1991, pp. 357–8.

221. H. Best, *Rural economy in Yorkshire in 1641* . . . (1641), pub. 'Surtees Society Publications', 1857, ed. FOL.B. Robinson, vol. XXXIII, p. 93, quoted in Laslett 1971, p. 73.

222. Thirsk 1997; Teti 1978, p. 78 on the use of aromatic plants in southern Italy in the early nineteenth century; Flandrin 1996b.

223. Wyczanski 1986; Pospiech 1997, p. 225.

224. Sismonde de Sismondi, *Tableau de l'agriculture toscane*, Geneva, 1801, p. 99, quoted in Malanima 1994, p. 118.

225. Teti 1978.

226. Flandrin 1996b.

227. Flandrin 1996b.

228. Hufton 1995 (Ital. trans. 1996), pp. 133–5.

229. Sandra Ott, 'Aristotle among the Basques: the cheese analogy of conception', *Man*, n. 4, 1979, quoted in Pomata 1983, p. 1439.

230. Richard Jones, a Welshman born in 1789, gave this autobiographical account of his own parents; quoted in Davidson 1982, p. 185.

231. In England, the domestic production of ale, which was entrusted to women, survived the introduction of beer produced in breweries by men longer than elsewhere; see Bennett 1996; Van Uytven 1997.

232. Weatherill 1988, p. 143, table 7.1.

233. Weatherill 1988, p. 143, table 7.1.

234. Palazzi 1990a.

235. Groppi (ed.) 1996, with an extensive bibliography.

236. Vincenzo Tanara, *L'economia* . . . , republished in Montanari 1991, p. 209.

237. Davidson 1982, p. 207.

VI. Clothing

1. See chapter II, paras. 2 and 6, as well as Schama 1987 (Ital. trans. 1988), pp. 410 and 425.

2. Poni 1994.

3. We occasionally find some evidence of male involvement in spinning in the home.

See, for example, the print (n. 28) reproduced in FOL.D.M. Cossar, *The German Translations of the Pseudo-Bernardine Epistola de cura rei familiaris*, Göppingen, 1975, which shows a man holding a distaff in his left hand and a wool-winder in his right. See also Roche 1989 (Ital. trans. 1991), p. 375.

4. Laudani 1996; Guenzi 1990. On the part played by women in the production of clothing, see Wiesner 1986; Roche 1989 (Ital. trans. 1991), pp. 290–328.

5. On proto-industrial developments, see chapter IV, para. 1.

6. Ribeiro 1984; Roche 1989 (Ital. trans. 1991), pp. 328–61; Lemirce 1991; Hufton 1995 (Ital. trans. 1996), pp. 147–8; Vickery 1993b, p. 282; Dinges 1993; Malanima 1994, p. 37; Muzzarelli 1999, p. 12.

7. Ribeiro 1984, p. 61.

8. Ribeiro 1984, p. 61; Roche 1981 (Ital. trans. 1986), p. 251 and 1989 (Ital. trans. 1991), pp. 82, 101–2, 329–61 and 382; Simon-Muscheid 1993; Sarti 1988, pp. 152–3, and 1992. In many places, the trade in old clothes was one of the sectors open to the Jews; see Zorzi 1990, p. 195 and Groppi 1999.

9. Archives Nationales, Paris, *Minutier Central*, LXIX, 185, 1701, quoted in Roche 1989 (Ital. trans. 1991), pp. 86–7.

10. Roche 1989 (Ital. trans. 1991), p. 88.

11. *Il lamento de' poveretti . . .* , Bologna, 1617, reprinted in Camporesi 1980, pp. 72–3.

12. Mira 1940, p. 161; Visceglia 1991, pp. 213–14; Roche 1989 (Ital. trans. 1991), pp. 380–2, and also p. 82.

13. Spufford 1984, pp. 4 and 21. See also Lemire 1991.

14. Roche 1997, p. 216.

15. Malanima 1990, p. 8.

16. Malanima 1990, pp. 161 and 166–7. It should be noted, however, that farmers generally have surpluses in years in which the price of cereals is low because of the good harvests. On the other hand, when the harvests are bad and the price of corn is high, they have little or nothing to sell; Malanima 1990, pp. 44–5.

17. See Shammas 1994, who relates the phenomenon primarily to improvements in distribution and the increased exploitation of workers due to increasing competition. See also Fernandez Pinedo 1995, pp. 291–4.

18. Although the factory system spread on large scale during the eighteenth century, its origins were in the Middle Ages; see Dal Pane 1969, p. 81 and Poni 1976.

19. Malanima 1990, pp. 168–9 and 1997, pp. 529–49; Shammas 1983.

20. Roche 1989 (Ital. trans. 1991), p. 94, table 6. A *setier* was a measurement of volume.

21. Roche 1981 (Ital. trans. 1986), p. 221, table 1 (the percentages are slightly different in Roche 1989 [Ital. trans. 1991], p. 94, table 6).

22. *Culottes* were tight trousers that reached the knees, and were typical of the period.

23. Roche 1981 (Ital. trans. 1986), p. 223 and 1989 (Ital. trans. 1991), pp. 153–82; Matthews Grieco 1991b, p. 61.

24. P. de Bourdeilles (called Brantôme), *Les femmes galantes*, in *Oeuvres*, Paris, 1864, vol. IX, p. 290 (ms. 1585), quoted in Vigarello 1985 (Ital. trans. 1988), p. 40.

25. Braudel 1979 (Ital. trans. 1993), p. 298, who reminds us that the tradition of public baths continued in Eastern Europe; Vigarello 1985 (Ital. trans. 1988), pp. 31–46 and *passim*; Duerr 1988 (Ital. trans. 1991), pp. 24–68, who considers the fight against disease to be less important in the closure of baths and emphasizes the role of the Reformation and the Counter Reformation (p. 34 and pp. 219–20, note 62).

26. Vigarello 1985 (Ital. trans. 1988), pp. 17–25; Sorcinelli 1998, pp. 60–7.

27. Duerr 1988 (Ital. trans. 1991), p. 67; Vigarello 1985 (Ital. trans. 1988), p. 21.

28. Barbagli 1996, pp. 354–9; Vigarello 1985 (Ital. trans. 1988), p. 25; Hufton 1995 (Ital. trans. 1996), p. 173.

29. Vigarello 1985 (Ital. trans. 1988), pp. 114–15 and 182–3; Sorcinelli 1998, pp. 60–7.

30. Vigarello 1985 (Ital. trans. 1988), pp. 54–5 and 239–40.

31. J.-B. Thiers, *Traité des superstitions*, Paris, 1692, p. 35, quoted in Vigarello 1985 (Ital. trans. 1988), p. 57.

32. Cunningham 1995 (Ital. trans. 1997), p. 121.

33. Hufton 1995 (Ital. trans. 1996), p. 177.

34. Sorcinelli 1998, pp. 35 and 37–8.

35. Quoted in Vigarello 1985 (Ital. trans. 1988), p. 76.

36. Finzi and Cognasso 1930a; Levi Pisetzky 1995, pp. 107 and 117.

37. Braudel 1979 (Ital. trans. 1993), p. 286; Vigarello 1985 (Ital. trans. 1988), pp. 62 and 74; Matthews Grieco 1991.

38. Quoted in Levi Pisetzky 1995, p. 248. On Tarabotti, see Medioli 1990.

39. Levi Pisetzky 1995, pp. 191, 198, 215, 235, 250 and 254–5; Vigarello 1985 (Ital. trans. 1988), pp. 73–100 (especially pp. 77–9 and 86).

40. Vigarello 1985 (Ital. trans. 1988), pp. 79–80 and 88.

41. Vigarello 1985 (Ital. trans. 1988), p. 89.

42. Roche 1989 (Ital. trans. 1991), p. 160, table 16.

43. Roche 1981 (Ital. trans. 1986), p. 239.

44. Roche 1989 (Ital. trans. 1991), pp. 366–7.

45. Davidson 1982, pp. 136–63.

46. Giulio Cesare Luigi Canali, *La carità del prossimo celebrata, spiegata and promossa in più ragionamenti . . .* , Bologna, 1763, vol. II, p. 57, quoted in Camporesi 1980, p. 63.

47. Roche 1989 (Ital. trans. 1991), p. 382. The data refers to the period 1750–60.

48. Braudel 1979 (Ital. trans. 1993), p. 297; Roche 1981 (Ital. trans. 1986), pp. 231, 233 and 259 and 1989 (Ital. trans. 1991), pp. 163–4, tables 18–19.

49. Levi Pisetzky 1995, pp. 177–88 and 120.

50. Aruch Scaravaglio 1934.

51. Aruch Scaravaglio 1934; Metken 1996, pp. 15–23.

52. Aruch Scaravaglio 1934; Levi Pisetzky 1995, p. 170.

53. Levi Pisetzky 1995, p. 211.

54. Quoted in Matthews Grieco 1991b, pp. 62–3; Levi Pisetzky 1995, p. 211.

55. On the inventory of the Leoncini, see Muzzarelli 1999, pp. 55–6. For some cases of women who said, 'he lifted my clothes', see Niccoli 2000, pp. 126–7. I would like to thank Georgia Arrivo, whose doctoral thesis, *Il sesso in tribunale. Dottrine, prassi giudiziaria e pratiche sociali nei processi per stupro nella Toscana delle Riforme* (Turin University, examined on 26 January 2001), confirmed my belief in the absence of references to underpants in the trials that she examined. On the case of Domenico Righi and Laura Fabbri, see Niccoli 2000, p. 66, who obtained the information from the Bologna State Archive, *Tribunale criminale del Torrone, Atti processuali*, 5761. On the case of Andreas Köpple and Barbara Häfner, see Sabean 1990, pp. 106–7 (Gerichts- und Gemeinderatsprotocolle, Neckarhausen, vol. I, p. 204). On Split, see Božić-Bužančić 1986, p. 511; on eighteenth-century Italy, see Levi Pisetsky 1995, p. 267 (the author claims that nearly all trousseaus included under pants, but she did not carry out studies that were as quantitatively extensive as those of Roche in France.

56. Roche 1981 (Ital. trans. 1986), pp. 225, 227 and 231; Matthews Grieco 1991b, p. 62.

57. Roche 1989 (Ital. trans. 1991), p. 161, table 17 and p. 163, table 163.

58. Benedetto Varchi, *Storia fiorentina*, ed. L. Arbib, Florence, 1838–41, vol. II, p. 115, quoted in Malanima 1990, p. 36. See also Malanima 1990, pp. 25–6; Muzzarelli 1999, pp. 70, 75 and 78–9.

59. Malanima 1990, p. 26.

60. Vigarello 1985 (Ital. trans. 1988), p. 83.

61. Vigarello 1985 (Ital. trans. 1988), p. 93.

62. Roche 1981 (Ital. trans. 1986), pp. 223–40.

63. Braudel 1979 (Ital. trans. 1993), p. 286.

64. Hufton 1995 (Ital. trans. 1996), p. 177.

65. Le Roy Ladurie 1967 (Ital. trans. 1982), especially p. 245.

66. Jütte and Bulst (eds) 1993; Roche 1997, pp. 138–9; Muzzarelli 2000, p. 11.

67. Bailieux and Remaury 1995 (Ital. trans. 1996), pp. 17–19.

68. F. Citoys, *Avis sur la nature de la peste*, Paris, 1623, p. 20, quoted in Vigarello 1985 (Ital. trans. 1988), p. 18.

69. Dupàquier 1987, p. 10; Livi Bacci 1998, pp. 104–5.

70. Roche 1981 (Ital. trans. 1986), pp. 227–32 (quotation on pp. 232 and 229–30) and 1989 (Ital. trans. 1991), pp. 129–41.

71. Malanima 1990, pp. 27–30.

72. Malanima 1990, pp. 31–4. The author took Montaigne's comments from *Journal du voyage en Italie (1580–1)*, ed. A. d'Ancona, Città di Castello, 1895, pp. 386 and 434; and Lalande's from *Voyage en Italie*, Geneva, 1790, vol. II, p. 295.

73. Roche 1997; Medick 1995.

74. Malanima 1990, p. 143.

75. Levi Pisetzky 1995, p. 210.

76. For information on corselets, see para. 5 of this chapter.

77. Roche 1981 (Ital. trans. 1986), pp. 217–64, 1989 (Ital. trans. 1991) and 1997.

78. Medick 1995, pp. 524–6.

79. Frati 1923, p. 223. More specifically on the legislation in eighteenth-century Bologna, see Sarti 1999c.

80. Bologna State Archive, *Tribunale criminale del Torrone, Atti processuali*, 8036/2, folder 2, Città, 1740, fols 2v–3r. Barracan was a cloth made of goats' wool, see Palazzi and Folena 1992, p. 208. *Cavadino* was a cloth made from silk scraps, see Guenzi 1990, p. 249. See also Coppola 1992.

81. Wijsenbeek-Olthuis 1994, p. 43 on the situation in Holland; Roche 1989 (Ital. trans. 1991), pp. 50–2 and 1997, p. 219; Levi Pisetzky 1995, p. 34 on the situation in Rome.

82. Later, legislation on luxury consumption was to be introduced throughout the century with specific regulations for mourning, dress when attending church, dress for those in service and uniforms.

83. Medick 1995, pp. 522–4. For the ban on the importation of Indian cloth in France and England, see Malanima 1997, p. 548.

84. Braudel 1979 (Ital. trans. 1993), pp. 288–9; Roche 1997, p. 211. According to Levi Pisetsky 1995, p. 75, the possibility cannot be excluded that the success of the colour black was due to the influence of Venetian rather than Spanish fashion. However, its affirmation as a prestigious colour was also due to the fact that at the time it was a difficult dye to obtain; see Muzzarelli 1999, pp. 165 and 249.

85. Levi Pisetzky 1973 and 1995, pp. 30–6; Hughes 1983 (Ital. trans. 1984); Visceglia 1991; Muzzarelli 1996, pp. 99–154; Sarti 2002, forthcoming.

86. Benedetto XIV 1751, p. 416. For the situation in France, see Roche 1989 (Ital. trans. 1991), p. 100.

87. Ménétra pub. 1982 (Ital. trans. 1992), pp. 93–4 and 96.

88. Ricci 1996, pp. 88 and *passim*; Hufton 1995 (Ital. trans. 1996), p. 260. For the history of prostitution, see Mazzi 1991.

89. Medick 1995, p. 525.

90. Corso 1948, p. 55.

91. Klapisch-Zuber 1982 (Ital. trans. 1988), pp. 167–74; Roche 1997, pp. 211–12.

92. Klapisch-Zuber 1982 (Ital. trans. 1988), pp. 161–2, 167 and 186.

93. Roper 1985, pp. 82–3.

94. Corso 1948, p. 8.

95. On children's clothing, see Ariès 1960 (Ital. trans. 1989); Levi Pisetzky 1995, pp. 239–40 and 257; Roche 1989 (Ital. trans. 1991), p. 116.

96. Finzi and Cognasso 1930c; Levi Pisetzky 1995; Malanima 1990, p. 32; Matthews Grieco 1991b; Bailieux and Remaury 1995 (Ital. trans. 1996), p. 32.

97. Levi Pisetzky 1995, pp. 118, 191, 215 and 266; Roche 1981 (Ital. trans. 1986), p. 226; Malanima 1990, p. 36.

98. Metken 1996.

99. Quoted in Levi Pisetzky 1995, p. 228.

100. Levi Pisetzky 1995, p. 228; Giorgetti 1992; Mafai 1998.

101. Finzi and Cognasso 1930b; Montagu 1717 (pub. 1981), p. 134.

102. Barbagli 1996, p. 355.

103. Levi Pisetzky 1995.

104. Aruch Scaravaglio 1933.

105. Levi Pisetzky 1995, p. 27.

·106. Matthews Grieco 1991b.

107. Roche 1989 (Ital. trans. 1991), pp. 221–58.

108. Burgelin 1977.

109. Medick 1995, p. 521.

110. Levi Pisetzky 1973; Majorana 1996; Zarri (ed.) 1996.

111. Hughes 1983 (Ital. trans. 1984), pp. 94–5, and 1991.

112. See Sarti 1994a, pp. 154–9 and 2002 forthcoming.

113. Klapisch-Zuber 1984 (Ital. trans. 1988), p. 205, note 44.

114. Ricci 1891, p. 153.

115. Roche 1989, pp. 59–61 and 1997, p. 214. But this was not the case in Laichingen in the mid-eighteenth century; see Medick 1995, p. 522.

116. Maza 1983, pp. 312–14.

117. Fairchilds 1993b, p. 850.

VII. Inside and Outside the Home: A Few Final Considerations

1. Levi Pisetzky 1995, pp. 286 and 295; Gigli Marchetti 1995, pp. 34–51. There was the occasional use of false curls and plaits.

2. Roche 1989 (Ital. trans. 1997).

3. Malanima 1997, p. 548.

4. Roche 1989 (Ital. trans. 1991), pp. 95, 98–9, 103, 109–10 and 115.

5. Weatherill 1986. On the different relationship of men and women with objects and material culture, see Donald and Hurcombe (eds) 2000, and the notes below.

6. Zemon Davis 1986, p. 62; Vickery 1993b, pp. 291–4, with further bibliographical refer-

ences; Berg 1996; Cavallo 1998, pp. 202–4 and Cavallo 2000.

7. The quotations were taken from Cavallo 1998, p. 204 and Zemon Davis 1986, p. 62.

8. Frigo 1985; Vickery 1993b, pp. 280–1.

9. Cavallo 1998, pp. 205–6 and Cavallo 2000.

10. Berg 1996, pp. 421–2, 426–7 and 429; de Vries 1993, pp. 112–13 and 118–19.

11. Berg 1996, p. 422.

12. On female ownership of clothes, jewels and silver, see Weatherhill 1986; Roche 1989 (Ital. trans. 1991), pp. 95, 98–9, 103, 109–10 and 115; Berg 1996, pp. 418–20 and Berg 1999. On Renaissance Florence, see chapter VI, para. 5 and Klapisch–Zuher 1982 (Ital. trans. 1988), pp. 167–74.

13. On clocks and watches, see Donald 2000; on the content of the four diaries, see Finn 2000.

14. Quotations are taken respectively from Tommasi 1580, p. 54 and Gozze 1589, pp. 48–9.

15. Pepoli Sampieri 1838, p. 43. See also p. 54.

16. Barbagli 1996, pp. 389–402.

17. On Elizabeth Shackleton see Vickery 1993b (quotation on p. 279); on the male diaries see Finn 2000 (quotation on p. 135).

18. Weatherhill 1986 and 1988; Goubert (ed.) 1988; Brewer and Porter (eds) 1993; Fairchilds 1993b; Schuurman and Walsh (eds) 1994; Glennie 1995; Levi 1996; Roche 1997 etc.

19. McKendrick 1974.

20. Vickery 1993b, p. 274; Kowaleski-Wallace 1997, particularly p. 4; de Grazia, Furlough (ed.) 1996. On the underestimation of consumption, see Goldthwaite 1989, pp. 16–18; Levi 1996, pp. 190–2.

21. *Bibliothèque des dames*, April 1764, p. 211, quoted in Roche 1989 (Ital. trans. 1991), p. 488.

22. Craveri 2001 and Hufton 1995 (Ital. trans. 1996), pp. 362–94, with bibliographical references.

23. On women's labour, see Brown 1986; Tilly and Scott 1978, Ital. trans. 1981; Istituto Internazionale di Storia Economica F. Datini, Prato 1990; Nava (ed.) 1992; Groppi (ed.) 1994; Palazzi 1997, etc.

24. The bibliography on this subject is quite extensive. For further information, see Ungari 1974; Garaud and Sramkiewicz 1978; Buttafuoco 1988–89; Palazzi 1990 (Ital. trans. 1992); Burguière 1991; Sarti 1995; Hufton 1995 (Ital. trans. 1996), pp. 395–420; Fiorino 1999.

25. The royal directive of 24 January 1789 for convening the electoral assemblies did not completely exclude female participation, but it was applied restrictively and after that women were consistently excluded from the suffrage, see Buttafuoco 1988–89; Sarti 1995; Fiorino 1999.

26. Duhet 1971; Devance 1977; Buttafuoco 1988–89; Rosanvallon 1992 (Ital. trans. 1994); Fiorino 1993; Bonacchi, Groppi 1993; Scott 1993; Perrot 1998. The 1793 Constitution, which was never enacted, introduced universal manhood suffrage. The elections in the summer of 1792 only excluded a few categories of men.

27. Ordinance of 21 April 1944, which acknowledged the right of French women to vote and stand for elected office.

28. Vice-Regal Legislative Decree no. 23 of 1/2/1945, which introduced universal suffrage; Decree no. 74 of 10/3/1946 on the eligibility of women.

29. Women obtained unconditional voting rights at the same time as men only in Finland, Holland and Ireland. In other European states, the interval between the introduction of universal male suffrage and its extension to women varied from 10 years in Austria and Great Britain to 120 in Switzerland. In France, there was almost a century, in Germany about 50 years, and in Italy a little more than 30. The fact that, in Europe, the campaign for votes for women was fought alongside the campaign to dispense with the property qualification for men meant that the exclusion of women was less visible than in the United States, where property qualifications for white men were abolished in the 1820s and 1830s, see Bock 2001, pp. 248–9.

30. Roche 1989 (Ital. trans. 1991), p. 38. See also Kuchta 1996, who recalls the 'great masculine renunciation of clothing' which took place in England in the late eighteenth and the early nineteenth centuries.

31. Rosanvallon 1992 (Ital. trans. 1994), pp. 210 and 426–7; Sarti 2002.

32. Rosanvallon 1992 (Ital. trans. 1994); Costa 1999, pp. 558–60; Sarti 1997a and 2002.

33. Sarti 1997a and 2002; Bock 2001, p. 224.

34. Gozze 1589, p. 49; Outram 1995 (Ital. trans. 1997), pp. 105–13 and Sarti 1995, with bibliographical references. For the eighteenth century debates on women's 'appropriate' position, see for instance Guerci 1988a and b.

35. Lanteri 1560, p. 10.

36. Brunner 1950 (Ital. trans. 1970); Bianchini, Frigo and Mozzarelli 1985; Frigo 1985, particularly pp. 65–82 and 206–7; Costa 1999, pp. 36–42 and *passim*.

37. Franceschi Ferrucci 1848, pp. 178–9 (my italics).

38. Ibid., p. 173.

39. Concerning the degree to which Lanteri's ideas were representative of his time, see note 36; and for Franceschi Ferrucci, see below.

40. Apart from chapter I of this work, see Scaraffia and Zarri (eds), 1994.

41. Lanteri 1560 p. 11.

42. Franceschi Ferucci 1848, p. 159.

43. Franceschi Ferrucci 1848, pp. 282 and 156–7, respectively.

44. Philippe Ariès has argued that childhood has been identified as a specific stage in life only since the seventeenth century, and only then did small children start to be seen by parents as human beings for which they were responsible. Lawrence Stone argued that the 'child-oriented, affectionate and permissive mode' was established in the English upper-middle class and 'squirarchy' between 1660 and 1800. Edward Shorter believed that 'motherly love' was linked to the development of capitalism, which made it possible for mothers to devote more time to their children by increasing the standard of living of the middle classes. He also believed that the

development of capitalism was responsible for 'romantic love', which supposedly arose within the industrial working class. As workers were increasingly part of a market economy, they were supposedly the first to develop an individualistic mentality that aimed at the satisfaction of subjective desires rather than the observance of rigid traditional norms. According to Stone, on the other hand, the shift from arranged marriages to love matches occurred amongst the English middle classes commencing from around 1660. See Ariès 1960 (Ital. trans. 1989); Stone 1977 (Ital. trans. 1983), particularly part IV on the affirmation of what he calls 'affective individualism'; Shorter 1975 (Ital. trans. 1978).

45. Stone 1977 (Ital. trans. 1983), p. 296.

46. Nadi, ed. 1886, facsimile reprint 1981, p. 52.

47. Marrone 1972, pp. 246–7; Bono 1999, p. 384.

48. Quoted in Pollock 2001, p. 196.

49. Ozmet 2001; Pollock 2001 etc. Challenging the idea that Europe or capitalism invented the nuclear family, Goody 2000 (pp. 11–12) recently argued 'we know of virtually no society in the history of humanity where the elementary or nuclear family was not important' and drew attention to the fact that 'in no society are the ties between mother and child (and in the vast majority, between father and child) unimportant, sentimentally and jurally, even though in some ideological contexts those ties may be played down'.

50. See, for instance, Viazzo 2001, pp. 157–62, 182–7, with further references; Fauve-Chamoux 2001.

51. Viazzo 2001, particularly pp. 164–75; on wet-nursing, see chapter IV.

52. Viazzo 2001; pp. 182–7; Pollock 2001, pp. 214–15. In sixteenth-century England, by the age of 10 about 39% of children were orphans (and about 30% of marriages were remarriages). In the eighteenth century, 27% of 10-year-olds were orphans.

53. Vizani 1609, p. 10. For further information on this book, see chapter I, note 153.

54. Barbagli 1996, pp. 325–8.

55. Klapisch Zuber 1983b (Ital. trans. 1988); Barbagli 1996, pp. 325–8; Cavallo 2000.

56. Klapisch Zuber 1983b (Ital. trans. 1988).

57. Calvi 1994a and 1994b.

58. Barbagli 1996, pp. 329–30; Cavallo 1998 and 2000.

59. Barbagli 1996, pp. 302–13.

60. Stone 1977 (Ital. trans. 1983), pp. 364–5.

61. Stone 1977 (Ital. trans. 1983), p. 52.

62. Stone 1977 (Ital. trans. 1983), p. 52 and 301–359; Trumbach 1978 (Ital. trans. 1982). See also chapter I. Daniel Defoe maintained that 'persons of a lower station are, generally speaking, much more happy in their marriages than Princes and persons of distinction. So I take much of it, if not all, to consist in the advantage they have to choose and refuse' (*Complete English Tradesman*, London, 1725, p. 26, quoted in Stone 1977, p. 326).

63. Stone 1977 (Ital. trans. 1983), pp. 269–71; Bonfield 1995.

64. Stone 1977 (Ital. trans. 1983), p. 323.

65. Daniel Defoe, *Conjugal Lewdness, or Matrimonial Whoredom*, London, 1727, p. 199 quoted in Stone 1977, p. 276.

66. Stone 1977 (Ital. trans. 1983), pp. 167–225.

67. Hanley 1989 and chapter I of this book.

68. See for example Barbagli 1996; Shorter 1975 (Ital. trans. 1978); Trumbach 1978 (Ital. trans. 1982); Stone 1977 (Ital. trans. 1983); Anderson 1980 (Ital. trans. 1982) pp. 65–84; Bizzocchi 1999; Lombardi 2001, p. 13 etc.

69. The quotation in the heading was taken from *Henry, Elizabeth and George, 1734–80*, ed. Lord Herbert, London, 1939, p. 71, quoted in Stone 1977, p. 518. On Hester Lynch see *Thraliana. The Diary of Mrs. Hester Lynch Thrale, 1776–1809*, Oxford, 1951, quoted in Stone 1977 (Ital. trans. 1983), pp. 346–7, 407–9 and in Barbagli 1996, p. 334. On the 'cicisbei' see *ibid.*, pp. 331–6; Ungari 1974, pp. 61, 78–9 and 260; Guerci 1988a, pp. 80–121; De Giorgio 1996, pp. 320–3; Bizzocchi 1997 and 2001. Bizzocchi compares the Italian *cicisbeo* to the French *ami de maison* and *petit-*

maître, as well as the Spanish *cotejo*, and at the same time he demonstrates the analogy between noble *cicisbei* and popular traditions that accepted privileged relationships between men and women who were not married, such as the *comparatico di San Giovanni* and the French *valentinage*. Thus he diminishes both the social and the national particularity of the *cicisbeo*.

70. Lombardi 2001, particularly pp. 249–50.

71. Archive of the Archbishopric of Florence, *Cause Criminali Matrimoniali*, 6, 18 November 1604, quoted in Lombardi 2001, pp. 256–7. On the opening of new areas of freedom and independence from families, particularly for women, see Ferrante 1994a; Zarri 1996, pp. 468–70; Seidel Menchi 2000, p. 28.

72. On the choice *murus aut maritus*, see chapter I, para. VI.

73. Lombardi 2001, p. 249 and pp. 309–13.

74. Guerci 1988a, p. 106; Lombardi 2001, pp. 375–412; Pelaja 1994 and 1996; Alessi 1995 etc.

75. Mainoni 1900, pp. 922–4; Lombardi 2001, p. 375.

76. On the concept of a 'team game' applied to family strategies, see Ago 1992; on the problems created by fideicommissum, see Mainoni 1900, pp. 922–4.

77. Contemporaries generally considered the custom of *cicisbei* to be a reaction to arranged marriages; see Barbagli 1996, pp. 334–5, who asks however why it was a peculiarly Italian phenomenon. Marriages were also arranged in other countries. For an attempted explanation, see Bizzocchi 1997.

78. Mainoni 1900, pp. 924–6. In 1729, the Constitutions of Amedeo II of Savoy introduced considerable limitations on fideicommissum, which was banned altogether by Charles Emmanuel IV in 1794; in Tuscany, the first restrictions were introduced in 1747; in 1782 Leopold I ordered the abolition of divisible fideicommissum and in February of 1789 he abolished it almost entirely; considerable restrictions were also imposed by the code introduced in Modena in 1771. In France, fideicommissum was abolished on 4 August 1789, but effective suppression was achieved by two decrees in 1792. On the disappearance of *cicisbei* in relation to the suppression of fideicommissum, see De Giorgio 1996, p. 320 and Bizzocchi 1997, p. 89.

79. Barbagli 1996, pp. 292–302. There was also a certain degree of formality between brothers and sisters. In the generations born during the seventeenth century, it was common to use the *lei* form, and in the eighteenth century, they used the *voi* form. The *tu* form started to be more widely used in the generations born after 1780 and became general usage by those born after 1820.

80. See the reflections of Barbagli 1996, pp. 249–50; Di Simplicio 1994, pp. 305–11; Lombardi 2001, pp. 302–4.

81. Apart from sources already referred to, see Ferrante, Palazzi and Pomata (eds) 1988 on the possibility of relationships that are both loving and asymmetrical.

82. Lombardi 2001, pp. 301–13.

83. Thompson 1977.

84. Medick and Sabean 1984, particularly p. 13, proposed to analyse property as a 'relational idiom' which communicated the exchange of interests and emotions. In this book I have attempted to take this argument into account, and have extended it to other aspects of material culture, as well as property.

85. Sarti 1995 and Sarti 2002 with further references.

86. Pollock 2001, p. 191.

87. Archive of the Archbishopric of Florence, *Cause Civili Matrimoniali*, 22, n. 10, 1574, quoted in Lombardi 2001, pp. 251–2. On the stigmatization of 'flirting' and 'making love' (which some authors explicitly considered to be behaviour typical of low social extraction), see Guerci 1988a, p. 82 and 1988b, pp. 68–74; Lombardi 2001, pp. 359–75.

88. General Report to *Census of Great Britain, 1851* (1852), I, XXXVI. Quoted by Hall 1986, p. 74.

89. Hall 1986, Ital. trans. 1988; Bassanini 1995.

90. Lanteri 1560, pp. 17–18 and 37.

91. See particularly Elias 1969; Ariès and Duby (eds) 1986 (Ital. trans. 1987), vols. III and IV. The changing role of the state and methods of administration, increasing literacy and the emergence of new forms of religions are some of the phenomena used to explain this change. It is not possible to examine the debate relating to this problem here.

92. Sarti 1995, with further references.

93. Duby 1985 (Ital. trans. 1987); Pollock 1993; Bassanini 1995, pp. 16–18; Sarti 1995, pp. 19–22.

94. Gozze 1589, p. 10.

95. For instance Ariès and Duby (eds) 1986 (Ital. trans. 1987), vols. III and IV; Hall 1986 (Ital. trans. 1988); Davidoff and Hall 1987; Sarti 1995.

96. Vickery 1993a, p. 412.

97. Davidoff 1989; Vickery 1993a; Sarti 1995, all with further references. Vickery even argues that the development of the ideology of separate spheres could be a reaction to the expansion of the possibilities for women to engage in activities outside the home.

98 Franceschi Ferrucci 1848, p. 162; Soldani (ed.) 2002.

99. Rassem 1982 (actually published in 1984), pp. 40–8; Sarti 2001, pp. 1–3.

100. Sarti 1995 and 2002.

101. Sarti 2002.

102. The law of the Salian Franks excluded women from succession to the throne; see Cosandey 2000, pp. 19–54.

103. Douglas and Isherwood 1979 (Ital. trans. 1984).

104. Veblen 1899 (Ital. trans. 1969); Douglas and Isherwood 1979 (Ital. trans. 1984); Levi 1996; Roche 1997; Kowaleski-Wallace 1997.

105. Quoted in Grieco 1996, p. 374. In spite of these beliefs, poultry was eaten in monasteries, see Zarri 1986, p. 392 and D'Ambrosio and Sperticato 1997, pp. 18 and 56.

106. Cuisenier 1991, pp. 12 and 38–47.

107. Douglas and Isherwood 1979 (Ital. trans. 1984), p. 14.

Bibliography

Acanfora, Elisa, 1985, 'La tavola', in Bertelli and Crifò (eds) 1985, pp. 53–66.

Accati, Luisa, 1998, *Il mostro e la bella. Padre e madre nell'educazione cattolica dei sentimenti,* Milan.

Adshead, S.A.M., 1997, *Material Culture in Europe and China 1400–1800,* London and New York.

Agnew, Jean-Christophe, 1993, 'Coming up for air: consumer culture in historical perspective', in Brewer and Porter (eds) 1993, pp. 19–39.

Ago, Renata, 1990, *Carriere e clientele nella Roma barocca,* Rome-Bari.

Ago, Renata, 1992, 'Giochi di squadra: uomini e donne nelle famiglie nobili del XVII secolo', in Visceglia (ed.) 1992, pp. 256–64.

Ago, Renata, 1994a, 'Destin de cadets et carrière ecclésiastique dans la noblesse italienne du XVIIe siècle', in Ravis-Giordani and Segalen (eds) 1994, pp. 231–9.

Ago, Renata, 1994b, *Giovani nobili nell'età dell'assolutismo. Autoritarismo paterno e libertà,* in Levi and Schmitt (eds) 1994, pp. 375–426.

Ago, Renata (ed.), 1995, 'Diritti di proprietà', *Quaderni storici,* XXX, no. 88, pp. 3–154.

Ago, Renata, 1995, 'Ruoli familiari e statuto giuridico', *Quaderni storici,* XXX, no. 88, pp. 111–33.

Ago, Renata, 1998 (1994 1st edn), *La feu-dalità in età moderna,* Rome-Bari.

Ago, Renata, Maura Palazzi and Gianna Pomata (eds), 1994, 'Costruire la parentela', *Quaderni storici,* XXIX, no. 86, pp. 293–510.

Ainsztein, Reuben, Reuben Kashani, Raphael Posner, and Ben-Zion (Benno) Schereschewsky, 1971, 'Marriage', in *Encyclopaedia Judaica,* Jerusalem, vol. XI, cols 1025–51.

Albera, Dionigi, 1994, 'La Maison des frères', in Ravis-Giordani and Segalen (eds) 1994, pp. 169–80.

Alberigo, Giuseppe, Perikle-P. Joannou, Claudio Leonardi and Paolo Prodi (eds), 1962, *Conciliorum Oecumenicorum Decreta,* Freiburg.

Alberti, Leon Battista, pub. 1969, *I libri della famiglia,* ed. Ruggiero Romano and Alberto Tenenti, Turin.

Alessi, Giorgia, 1995, 'Le gravidanze illegittime e il disagio dei giuristi (secc. XVII–XIX)', in Fiume (ed.) 1995, pp. 221–45.

Alessi, Giorgia, 1996, 'Ordinamenti giuridici e differenze di genere nel sistema del diritto comune, in Donne e proprietà', 1996, pp. 5–19.

Allegra, Luciano, 1996, *Identità in bilico. Il ghetto ebraico di Torino nel Settecento,* Turin.

Ambrosoli, Mauro, 1987, 'Il padre di famiglia', *Quaderni storici,* XXII, no. 64, pp. 223–9.

Ambrosoli, Mauro, 1992, *Scienziati, contadini e proprietari. Botanica e agricoltura nell'Europa occidentale,* Turin.

Anderson, Michael, 1980, *Approaches to the History of the Western Family 1500–1914,* London (Ital. trans. *Interpretazioni storiche della famiglia. L'Europa occidentale,* Turin, 1982).

Andorka, Rudolph and Faragó Tamás, 1983, 'Pre-industrial household structure in Hungary', in Wall, Robin and Laslett (eds) 1983, pp. 281–307.

Appleby, Joyce, 1993, 'Consumption in early modern social thought', in Brewer and Porter (eds) 1993, pp. 162–73.

Archivi (Gli) per la storia dell'alimentazione, 1995, Ministero per i Beni Culturali e Ambientali, Ufficio Centrale per i Beni Archivistici.

Ariès, Philippe, 1960, *L'Enfant et la vie familiale sous l'Ancien Régime,* Paris (Ital. trans. *Padri e figli nell'Europa medievale e moderna,* Rome-Bari, 1989 [1968 1st edn]).

Ariès, Philippe and Georges Duby (series eds), 1985, *Histoire de la vie privée,* vol. II, *De l'-Europe féodale à la Renaissance* Georges Duby (ed.) (Ital. trans. *La vita privata dal feudalesimo al Rinascimento,* Rome-Bari, 1987).

Ariès, Philippe and Georges Duby (series eds), 1986, *Histoire de la vie privée*, vol. III, *De la Renaissance aux Lumières*, Philippe Ariès and Roger Chartier (eds), Paris (Ital. trans. *La vita privata. Dal Rinascimento all'Illuminismo*, Rome, 1987).

Ariès, Philippe and Georges Duby (series eds), 1986, *Histoire de la vie privée*, vol. IV, *De la Révolution à la Grande Guerre*, Michelle Perrot (ed.) Paris (Ital. trans. *La vita privata. L'Ottocento*, Rome-Bari, 1988).

Arru, Angiolina (ed.), 1998, 'Gestione dei patrimoni e diritti delle donne', *Quaderni storici*, XXXIII, no. 98, pp. 269–414.

Arru, Angiolina, 1995, *Il servo. Storia di una carriera nel Settecento*, Bologna.

Aruch, Scaravaglio, 1933, 'Guardinfante', in *Encldopedia Italiana*, vol. XXIV, Rome, pp. 23–4.

Aruch, Scaravaglio, 1934, 'Mutande', in *Enciclopedia Italiana*, vol. XVIII, Rome, pp. 164–5.

Ash, Douglas, 1965, 'Gotico', in Hayward 1965 (Ital. trans. 1992), pp. 25–34.

Assandri, Giovan Battista, 1616, *Della economica, overo disciplina domestica [. . .] libri quattro. Nei quali s'ha quello appartiene alla casa per renderla fornita dei beni d'animo, di corpo e di fortuna*, Cremona.

Augustins, George, 1989, 'Esquisse d'une comparisons des systèmes de perpétuation des groupe domestiques dan le sociétés paysannes européennes', *Archives européennes de sociologie*, 23, pp. 39–69.

Augustins, Georges, 1989, *Comment se perpétuer? Devenir des lignées et destins des patrimoines dans les paysanneries européennes*, Nanterre.

Aymard, Maurice (ed.), 1995, *Storia d'Europa*, IV, *L'Età moderna, secoli XVI–XVIII*, Turin.

Aymard, Maurice, 1995, 'L'Europa e i suoi contadini', in Aymard (ed.) 1995, pp. 529–64.

Aymard, Maurice and Henri Bresc, 1975, 'Nourritures et consommation en Sicile entre XIVe et XVIIIe siècle', in *Mélanges de l'École Française de Rome. Moyen Âge – Temps Modernes*, 87, pp. 535–81.

Aymard, Maurice, Claude Grignon and Françoise Sabban (eds), 1993, *Le Temps de manger. Alimentation, emploi du temps et rythmes sociaux*, Paris.

Baernstein, Renée, 1994, 'In widow's habit. Women between convent and family in sixteenth-century Milan', *Sixteenth Century Journal*, XXV, pp. 787–807.

Bailleux, Nathalie and Bruno Remaury, 1995, *Mode et vêtement*, Paris (Ital. trans. *La moda. Usi e costumi del vestire*, n.p., 1996).

Bairoch, Paul, 1987, 'Urbanizzazione e disurbanizzazione', in *Europa moderna. La disgregazione dell'Ancien Régime*, Enrico Castelnuovo and Valerio Castronovo (eds), Milan, pp. 249–59.

Bairoch, Paul, Jean Batou and Pierre Chèvre, 1988, *La Population des villes européennes. Banque de données et analyse sommaire des résultats, 800–1850*, Geneva.

Barbagli, Marzio (ed.), 1977, *Famiglia e mutamento sociale*, Bologna.

Barbagli, Marzio, 1987, 'Strutture e relazioni familiari', in Tranfaglia and Firpo (eds) 1987, pp. 23–43.

Barbagli, Marzio, 1990, 'Sistemi di formazione della famiglia in Italia', in *Società Italiana di Demografia Storica 1990*, pp. 3–43 (republished in Barbagli 1996 [1984 1st edn], pp. 483–526).

Barbagli, Marzio, 1996 (1984 1st edn), *Sotto lo stesso tetto. Mutamenti della famiglia in Italia dal XV al XX secolo*, Bologna.

Barbagli, Marzio and David I. Kertzer (eds), 1992, *Storia della famiglia italiana, 1750–1950*, Bologna (originally published as a special issue of the *Journal of Family History*, XV, 1990).

Barbagli, Marzio and David I. Kertzer (eds), 2001, *A History of the European Family*, I, *Family Life in Early Modern Times, 1500–1789*, New Haven and London.

Barbieri, Giuseppe and Lucio Gambi (ed.), 1970, *La casa rurale in Italia*, Florence.

Barley, Maurice Willmore, 1985, 'Rural building in England', in Thirsk (ed.) 1985, pp. 590–682.

Bassanini, Gisella, 1995 (1990 1st edn), *Tracce silenziose dell'abitare: la donna e la casa*, Milan.

Battaglia, Salvatore, 1961–, *Grande Dizionario della lingua italiana*, Turin.

Baudry, F., 1896, 'Familia', in *Dictionnaire des antiquités grecques et romaines d'après les textes et les monuments*, Charles Daremberg and Edmond Saglio (eds), Paris, 1877–1919, 10 vols, vol. II, part II, p. 972.

Baumgarten, Karl, 1965, 'Die Tischordnung im alten Mecklenburgischen Bauernhaus', *Deutsches Jahrbuch für Volkskunde*, 11, pp. 5–15.

Bellavitis, Anna, 1998, 'Patrimoni e matrimoni

a Venezia nel Cinquecento', in Calvi and Chabot (eds) 1998, pp. 149–60.

Belmont, Nicole, 1978, 'La Fonction symbolique du cortège dans les rituels populaires du mariage', *Annales. Économies, sociétés, civilisations*, 33, pp. 650–5.

Benedetto XIV, 1751, *Lettere, brevi, chirografi, bolle ed apostoliche determinazioni prese dalla Santità di Nostro Signore Papa Benedetto XIV nel suo Pontificato per la città di Bologna sua Patria*, Bologna, vol. II.

Benevolo, Leonardo, 1996 (1993 1st edn), *La città nella storia d'Europa*, Rome-Bari.

Benigno, Francesco, 1989, 'Famiglia mediterranea e modelli anglosassoni', *Meridiana*, 6, pp. 29–61.

Bennett, Judith, 1996, *Ale, Beer and Brewsters in England: Women's Work in a Changing World 1300–1600*, New York.

Bentini, Jadranka, Alessandra Chiappini, G.B. Panatta and Anna Maria Visser Travagli, 1988, *A tavola con il principe. Materiali per una mostra su alimentazione e cultura nella Ferrara degli Estensi*, Venice.

Benveniste, Émile, 1969, *Le Vocabulaire des institutions indoeuropéennes, I. Économie, parenté, société; II. Pouvoir, droit, religion*, Paris (Ital. trans. *Il vocabolario delle istituzioni indoeuropee, I. Economia, parentela, società; II Potere, diritto, religione*, Turin, 1976, 2 vols).

Benvenuti, Papi Anna, 1983, 'Frati mendicanti e pinzochere in Toscana: dalla marginalità sociale a modello di santità', in *Temi e problemi della mistica femminile trecentesca. Atti del XX convegno del Centro studi sulla spiritualità medievale*, Todi, pp. 109–35.

Berg, Maxine, 1996, 'Women's consumption and the Industrial classes of eighteenth-century England', *Journal of Social History*, 30, pp. 415–34.

Berg, Maxine, 1999, 'New commodities, luxuries and their consumers in eighteenth-century England', in Berg and Clifford (eds), 1999, pp. 63–85.

Berg, Maxine and Helen Clifford (eds), 1999, *Consumers and Luxury. Consumer Culture in Europe 1650–1850*, Manchester and New York.

Berkner, Lutz K., 1972, 'The stem family and the development cycle of the peasant household: an 18th century Austrian example', *American Historical Review*, 77, pp. 398–418 (Ital. trans. 'La famiglia ceppo e il ciclo

di sviluppo della famiglia contadina', in Barbagli (ed.) 1977, pp. 116–40).

Berkner, Lutz K. and F. Mendels Franklin, 1972, 'Inheritance systems: family structure and demographic patterns in Western Europe (1700–1900)', in *Historical Studies of Changing Fertility*, Charles Tilly (ed.) Princeton (Ital. trans. 'Sistemi di eredità, struttura familiare e modelli demografici in Europa (1700–1900)', in Barbagli (ed.) 1977, pp. 216–34).

Bermingham, Ann and John Brewer (eds) 1995, *The Consumption of Culture 1600–1800. Image, Object, Text*, London and New York.

Bertelli, Sergio and Giulia Calvi, 1985, 'Rituale, cerimoniale, etichetta nelle corti italiane', in Bertelli and Crifò (eds) 1985, pp. 11–27.

Bertelli, Sergio and Giuliano Crifò (eds), 1985, *Rituale cerimoniale etichetta*, Milan.

Bevilacqua, Piero (ed.), 1990, *Storia dell'agricoltura italiana in età contemporanea. II. Uomini e classi*, Venice.

Biagioli, Giuliana, 1986, La diffusione della mezzadria nell'Italia centrale: un modello di sviluppo demografico ed economico, in *Bollettino di Demografia Storica*, 3, pp. 59–66.

Bianchi, Adanella, 1997, 'La deresponsabilizzazione dei padri (Bologna secc. XVI–XVII)', in *Ricerche storiche*, XXVII, pp. 263–86.

Bianchini, Marco, Daniela Frigo and Cesare Mozzarelli, 1985, 'Governo della casa, governo della città', special issue of *Cheiron*, 2.

Bibliothèque Internationale de Gastronomie 1994, *Catalogo italiano e latino delle opere di Gastronomia*, Orazio Bagnasco (ed.), n.p., 3 vols.

Biet, Christian, 1994, 'Le cadet, point de départ des destins romanesques dans la littérature française du XVIIIe siècle', in Ravis-Giordani and Segalen (eds) 1994, pp. 289–302.

Biondi, Albano, 1981, 'Aspetti della cultura cattolica post-tridentina. Religione e controllo sociale', in *Storia d'Italia*, IV, *Intellettuali e potere*, Corrado Vivanti (ed.), Turin, pp. 253–302.

Bizzocchi, Roberto, 1982, 'La dissoluzione di un clan familiare: i Buondelmonti di Firenze nei secoli XV e XVI', *Archivio Storico Italiano*, 140, n. 511, pp. 3–46.

Bizzocchi, Roberto, 1997, 'Cicisbei. La morale italiana', in *Storica*, no. 9, pp. 63–90.

Bizzocchi, Roberto, 1999, 'Sentimenti e documenti', in *Studi storici*, 29, pp. 471–86.

Bizzocchi, Roberto, 2001, *In famiglia. Storie di interessi e affetti nell'Italia moderna*, Rome-Bari.

Bloch, Marc, 1970 (1954 1st edn), 'Les Aliments de l'ancienne France', in *Pour une Histoire de l'alimentation*, Jean-Jacques Hémardinquer (ed.), Paris, pp. 231–5.

Bloch, Oscar and Walther von Wartburg, 1960, *Dictionnaire étymologique de la langue française*, Paris.

Blok, Anton, 1995, 'Dietro le quinte: compare la sfera del privato', in Aymard (ed.) 1995, pp. 597–622.

Bock, Gisela, 2001, *Women in European History*, Oxford Ital. trans. *Le donnenella storin europen*, Rome-Bari.

Bonacchi, Gabriella and Angela Groppi (eds), 1993, *Il dilemma della cittadinanza. Diritti e doveri delle donne*, Rome-Bari.

Bonfield, Lloyd, 1995, 'La distribuzione dei beni tra gli eredi negli atti di successione matrimoniale inglesi dell'Età moderna', *Quaderni storici*, XXX, no. 88, pp. 63–83.

Bono, Salvatore, 1999, *Schiavi musulmani nell'Italia moderna. Galeotti, vu' cumprà, domestici*, Naples.

Borden, Arthur R., 1982, *A Comprehensive Old English Dictionary*, New York and London.

Borghero, Carlo (ed.), 1974, *La polemica sul lusso nel Settecento francese*, Turin.

Borghi, Giampaolo and Maurizio Pozzi, 1990, 'L'abitazione dell'uomo con animali, in montagna', in *Il sogno della casa. Modi dell'abitare a Bologna dal Medioevo ad oggi*, Renzo Renzi (ed.), Bologna, pp. 73–8.

Bossy, John, 1985, *Christianity in the West*, Oxford (Ital. trans. *L'Occidente cristiano*, Turin, 1990).

Bourdelais, Patrice and Vincent Gourdon, 2000, 'L'Histoire de la famille dans les revues françaises (1960–1995): la prégnance de l'anthropologie', in *Annales de démographie historique*, fasc. 2, pp. 5–48.

Bourdieu, Pierre, 1979, *La Distinction*, Paris (Ital. trans. *La distinzione. Critica sociale del gusto*, Bologna, 1983).

Bouvier, René and André Laffargue 1956, *La Vie napolitaine au XVIIIe siècle*, Paris (Ital. trans. *Vita napoletana nel XVIII secolo*, Bologna, 1960).

Božić-Bužančić, Danica, 1986, 'L'abbigliamento delle donne di Split dalla fine del XVII al primo decennio del XVIII secolo', in *La famiglia e la vita quotidiana*, 1986, pp. 503–15.

Braudel, Fernand, 1979 (1967 1st edn), *Civilisation matérielle, économie et capitalisme (XVe–XVIIIe siècle). Les Structures du quotidien: le possible et l'impossible*, Paris (Ital. trans. *Civiltà materiale, economia e capitalismo. Le strutture del quotidiano (secoli XV–XVIII)*, Turin, 1993 [1982 1st edn]).

Braudel, Fernand, 1982 (1949 1st edn), *La Méditerranée et le monde méditerranéen à l'époque de Philippe II*, Paris (Ital. trans. *Civiltà e imperi del Mediterraneo nell'età di Filippo II*, Turin, 1986 [1953 1st edn]).

Brewer, John and Roy Porter (eds), 1993, *Consumption and the World of Goods*, London and New York.

Brewer, John and Roy Porter, 1993, 'Introduction' to Brewer and Porter (eds) 1993, pp. 1–15.

Brizzi, Gian Paolo, 1976, *La formazione della classe dirigente nel Sei-Settecento. I seminaria nobilium nell'Italia centrosettentrionale*, Bologna.

Brown, Frank E., 1986, 'Continuity and change in the urban house: developments in domestic space organisation in seventeenth-century London', in *Comparative Studies in Society and History*, 28, pp. 558–90.

Brown, Judith C., 1986, 'A woman's place was in the home: women's work in Renaissance Tuscany', in Ferguson, Quilligan and Vickers (eds) 1986, pp. 191–224.

Brunner, Otto, 1950, 'Das "ganze Haus" und die alteuropäische "Ökonomik"', in *Zeitschrift für Nationalökonomie*, 13 (Ital. trans. 'La "casa come complesso" e l'antica "economica" europea', in Otto Brunner, *Per una nuova storia costituzionale e sociale*, ed. Pierangelo Schiera, Milan, 1970, pp. 133–64).

Bulst, Neithard, 1993, 'Kleidung als sozialer Konfliktstoff. Probleme kleidergesetzlicher Normierung im sozialen Gefüge', *Saeculum*, 44, pp. 32–46.

Burgelin, Olivier, 1977, 'Abbigliamento', in *Enciclopedia*, Turin, vol. I, pp. 79–104.

Burguière, André, 1978, 'Les Rituels de mariage en France: pratiques ecclésiastiques et pratiques populaires (XVIe–XVIIIe siècles)', in *Annales. Économies, sociétés, civilisations*, 33, pp. 637–49.

Burguière, André, 1986a (Ital. trans. 1988), 'Una geografia delle forme familiari', in

Burguière, Klapisch-Zuber, Segalen and Zonabend (series eds) 1986 (Ital. trans. 1988), pp. 26–60.

Burguière, André, 1986b (Ital. trans. 1988), 'Logica delle famiglie', in Burguière, Klapisch-Zuber, Segalen and Zonabend (series eds) 1986 (Ital. trans. 1988), pp. 61–94.

Burguière, André 1986c (Ital. trans. 1988), 'La formazione della coppia', in Burguière, Klapisch-Zuber, Segalen and Zonabend (series eds) 1986 (Ital. trans. 1988), pp. 113–44.

Burguière, André, 1991, 'La Révolution et la famille', *Annales. Économies, sociétés, civilisations*, 46, pp. 151–68.

Burguière, André, Christiane Klapisch-Zuber, Martine Segalen and Françoise Zonabend (series eds) 1986, *Histoire de la famille*, Paris (Ital. trans. *Storia universale della famiglia*, Albarosa Leone (ed.), Milan, 1988).

Burke, Peter, 1982, 'Conspicuous consumption in early modern Italy', in *Kwartalnik Historyczny Kultury Materialnej*, XXX, pp. 43–56 (Ital. trans. 'Il consumo di lusso nell'Italia del Seicento', in Peter Burke *Scene di vita quotidiana nell'Italia moderna*, Rome-Bari, 1988, pp. 169–89).

Burke, Peter, 1991, *New Perspectives on Historical Writing*, Cambridge (Ital. trans. *La storiografia contemporanea*, Rome-Bari, 1993).

Burke, Peter, 1993, 'Res et verba: conspicuous consumption in the early modern world', in Brewer and Porter (eds) 1993, pp. 148–61.

Buttafuoco, Annarita, 1988–89, 'Libertà, fraternità, uguaglianza: per chi? Donne nella Rivoluzione francese', in *Esperienza storica femminile nell'età moderna e contemporanea*, Anna Maria Crispino (ed.), Rome, 2 vols, vol. I, pp. 29–53.

Cabibbo, Sara and Marilena Modica, 1989, *La santa dei Tomasi. Storia di Suor Maria Crocifissa (1645–1699)*, Turin.

Callmann, Ellen, 1996, 'Cassone', in *The Dictionary of Art*, London and New York, vol. VI, 1996, pp. 1–6.

Calvi, Giulia, 1994a, *Il contratto morale. Madri e figli nella Toscana moderna*, Rome-Bari.

Calvi, Giulia, 1994b, 'Diritti e legami. Madri, figli, Stato in Toscana (XVI–XVIII secolo)', *Quaderni storici*, XXIX, no. 86, pp. 487–510.

Calvi, Giulia and Sergio Bertelli, 1983, 'La bocca del Signore . . . Commensalità e gerarchie sociali fra Cinquecento e Seicento', in *Metamorfosi*, 7: *Il linguaggio, il corpo, la festa. Per un ripensamento della tematica di Michail Bachtin.*

Calvi, Giulia and Isabelle Chabot (eds), 1998, *Le ricchezze delle donne. Diritti patrimoniali e poteri familiari in Italia (XII–XIX secc.)*, Turin.

Camporesi, Piero (ed.), 1973, *Il libro dei vagabondi*, Turin.

Camporesi, Piero, 1978, *Il paese della fame*, Bologna.

Camporesi, Piero, 1980, *Il pane selvaggio*, Bologna.

Camporesi, Piero, 1989, *La terra e la luna. Alimentazione folklore società*, Milan.

Capatti, Alberto, Alberto De Bernardi and Angelo Varni, 1998, *Storia d'Italia*, XIII, *L'alimentazione*, Turin.

Capatti, Alberto and Massimo Montanari, 1999, *La cucina italiana. Storia di una cultura*, Rome-Bari.

Caprettini, Gian Paolo, 1975, *La porta. Valenze mitiche e funzioni narrative (Saggio di analisi semiologica)*, Turin.

Carboni, Mauro, 1999, *Le doti della «povertà». Famiglie, risparmio, previdenza: il Monte del Matrimonio di Bologna (1583–1796)*, Bologna.

Cargnelutti, Liliana, 1994, 'Il «divorzio» in Friuli dopo il Concilio di Trento', in Corbellini (ed.) 1994, pp. 61–75.

Casali, Elide, 1979, '«Economica» e «creanza» cristiana', *Quaderni storici*, XIV, no. 41, pp. 555–83.

Casali, Elide, 1982, *Il villano dirozzato. Cultura società e potere nelle campagne romagnole della Controriforma*, Florence.

Casalini, Maria, 1997, *Servitù, nobili e borghesi nella Firenze dell'Ottocento*, Florence.

Casanova, Cesarina, 1997, *La famiglia italiana in Età moderna. Ricerche e modelli*, Rome-Bari.

Case contadine 1979, Milan.

Casey, John, 1989, *The History of the Family*, Oxford (Ital. trans. *La famiglia nella storia*, Rome, 1991).

Cataldi, Giancarlo (ed.), 1988, *Le ragioni dell'abitare*, Florence (special edition of *Studi e documenti di architettura*, n. 15).

Cavallo, Sandra, 1998, 'Proprietà o possesso? Composizione e controllo dei beni delle donne a Torino (1650–1710)', in Calvi and Chabot (eds) 1998, pp. 187–207.

Cavallo, Sandra, 2000, 'What did women transmit? Ownership and control of household goods and personal effects in early modern

Italy', in Donald and Hurcombe (eds) 2000, pp. 38–53.

Cazzola, Franco, 1988, 'La pluriattività nelle campagne italiane: alcuni problemi interpretative', extract from *Bollettino bibliografico 1985–1986*, Naples, pp. 79–90.

Cerman, Markus, 1997, 'Mitteleuropa und die "europäischen Muster". Heiratsverhalten und Familienstruktur in Mitteleuropa, 16.–19. Jahrhundert', in Ehmer, Hareven and Wall (eds) 1997, pp. 327–46.

Chabod, Federico, 1991 (1961 1st edn), *Storia dell'idea d'Europa*, ed. Ernesto Sestan and Armando Saitta, Rome-Bari.

Chabot, Isabelle, 1994, '«La sposa in nero». La ritualizzazione del lutto delle vedove fiorentine (secoli XIV–XV)', *Quaderni storici*, XXIX, no. 86, pp. 421–62.

Chabot, Isabelle and Massimo Fornasari, 1998, *L'economia della carità. Le doti del Monte di Pietà di Bologna*, Bologna.

Chartier, Roger, 1987, *Lectures et lecteurs dans la France d'Ancien Régime*, Paris (Ital. trans. *Letture e lettori nella Francia di Antico Regime*, Turin, 1988).

Chartier, Roger, 1986 (Ital. trans. 1987), *Le pratiche della scrittura*, in Ariès and Duby (series eds) 1986 (Ital. trans. 1987), pp. 76–117.

Cieraad, Irene, 1999, 'Dutch windows: female virtue and female vice', in *At Home. An Anthropology of Domestic Space*, Irene Cieraad (ed.), Syracuse, New York, pp. 31–52.

Clemente, Pietro, 1985, 'Espressioni linguistiche della scarsità alimentare: la carne nella dieta dei mezzadri toscani', *L'Uomo. Società Tradizione Sviluppo*, IX, pp. 215–46.

Clunas, Craig, 1999, 'Modernity global and local: consumption and the rise of the West', *American Historical Review*, 104, pp. 1497–1511.

Cole, John W. and Eric R. Wolf, 1974, *The Hidden Frontier. Ecology and Ethnicity in an Alpine Valley*, New York.

Collina-Girard, Jacques, 1994, *Le Feu avant les allumettes*, Paris.

Collomp, Alain, 1984, 'Tensions, dissensions, and ruptures inside the family in seventeenth- and eighteenth-century Haute Provence', in Medick and Sabean (eds) 1984, pp. 145–70.

Collomp, Alain, 1986 [Ital. trans. 1987], 'Famiglie. Abitazioni e coabitazioni', in Ariès and Duby (series eds) 1986 [Ital. trans. 1987], pp. 393–425.

Comaschi, Raffaella, 1983, 'Le Dimanche de Serra', *Annales. Économies, sociétés, civilisations*, 38, pp. 863–83.

Cooper, J.P., 1976, 'Patterns of inheritance and settlement by great landowners from the fifteenth to the eighteenth century', in Goody, Thirsk and Thompson (eds), 1976, pp. 192–327.

Coppola, Elisa, 1992, 'Le livree di Casa Savoia', in *Carrozze e livree. Il patrimonio artistico del Quirinale*, Elisabetta Carnelli and Elisa Coppola (eds), research coordinated by Kirsten Aschengreen Piacenti, Rome, 1992, pp. 113–32.

Corallo, Roberto, 1988, 'Tipologie primitive in Italia', in Cataldi (ed.) 1988, pp. 165–96.

Corbellini, Roberta (ed.), 1994, *Interni di famiglia. Patrimonio e sentimenti di figlie, mogli, vedove. Il Friuli tra Medioevo ed Età moderna*, Tavagnacco (Udine).

Corbin, Alain, 1982, *Le Miasme et la jonquille. L'Odorat et l'imaginaire social, XVIIIe–XIXe siecles*, Paris.

Cornaglia, Paolo, 2000, *L'Espace et ses règles. Distribution spatiale et vie sociale dans les demeures de la cour des rois de Sardaigne entre 1713 et 1831*, Hémpire de diplame de l'Éhess, Paris.

Corso, Raffaele, 1948, *Popoli dell'Europa. Usi e costumi*, Naples.

Cortelazzo, Mauro, and Paolo Zolli, 1979–88, *Dizionario etimologico della lingua italiana*, Bologna, 5 vols.

Cosandey, Fanny, 2000, *La Reine de France. Symbole et pouvoir*, Paris.

Cosenza, Luigi, 1974, *Storia dell'abitazione*, Milan.

Costa, Pietro, 1999, *Civitas. Storia della cittadinanza in Europa. I. Dalla civiltà comunale al settecento*, Rome-Bari.

Covarrubias, Sebastián de, 1987, *Tesoro de la lengua castellana o española, según la impresión de 1611, con las adiciones de Benito Remigio Noydens publicadas en la de 1674*, Barcelona.

Craveri, Benedetta, 2001, *La civiltà della conversazione*, Milan.

Cuisenier, Jean, 1991, *La Maison rustique: logique sociale et composition architecturale*, Paris.

Cunningham, Hugh, 1995, *Children and Childhood in Western Society since 1500*, New York (Ital. trans. *Storia dell'infanzia, XVI–XX secolo*, Bologna, 1997).

Cusatelli, Giorgio, 1994 (1983 1st edn), *Ucci, ucci. Piccolo manuale di gastronomia fiabesca*, Milan.

Czap Jr., Peter, 1983, ' "A large family: the peasant's greatest wealth": serf households in Mishino, Russia, 1814–1858' (Ital. trans. '«Una famiglia numerosa: la più grande ricchezza del contadino»: gli aggregati domestici dei servi della gleba di Mishino, Russia, 1814–1858'), in Wall, Robin and Laslett (eds) 1983 [Ital. trans. 1984], pp. 143–93.

Da Molin, Giovanna, 1990, 'Family forms and domestic service in southern Italy from the seventeenth to the nineteenth century', *Journal of Family History*, XV, pp. 503–27 (Ital. trans. 'Struttura della famiglia e personale di servizio nell'Italia meridionale', in Barbagli and Kertzer (eds) 1992, pp. 219–52).

Dal Pane, Luigi, 1958 (1944 1st edn), *Storia del lavoro in Italia dagli inizi del secolo XVIII al 1815*, Milan.

Dal Pane, Luigi, 1969, *Economia e società a Bologna nell'età del Risorgimento. Introduzione alla ricerca*, Bologna.

D'Ambrosio, Angelo and Mario Sperticato, 1998, *Cibo e clausura. Regimi alimentari e monastici nel Mezzogiorno moderno (secc. XVII–XIX)*, Bari.

D'Amelia, Marina (ed.), 1997, *Storia della maternità*, Rome-Bari.

D'Amelia, Marina, 1990, 'Economia familiare e sussidi dotali. La politica della Confraternita dell'Annunziata a Roma, secc. XVII–XVIII', in Istituto Internazionale di Storia Economica F. Datini, Prato 1990, pp. 195–215.

D'Amelia, Marina, 1993, ' «Una lettera a settimana». Geronima Veralli Malatesta al Signor Fratello 1575–1622', *Quaderni storici*, XXVIII, no. 83, pp. 381–413.

D'Amelia, Marina, 1997, 'La presenza delle madri nell'Italia medievale e moderna', in D'Amelia (ed.) 1997, pp. 3–52.

Darling Buck Carl, 1949, *A Dictionary of Selected Synonyms in the Principal Indo-European Languages*, Chicago, 2 vols.

Davico, Rosalba, 1987, 'Alimentazione e classi sociali', in Tranfaglia and Firpo (eds) 1987, pp. 45–61.

Davidoff, Leonore, 1991, 'Al di là della dicotomia pubblico/privato: pensando ad una storia femminista per gli anni Novanta', *Passato e Presente*, X, n. 27, pp. 133–52.

Davidoff, Leonore and Catherine Hall, 1987, *Family Fortunes. Men and Women of the English Middle Class*, London.

Davidson, Caroline, 1982, *A Women's Work is Never Done. A History of Housework in the British Isles 1650–1950*, London.

De Giorgio Michela 1996, 'Raccontare un matrimonio moderno', in De Giorgio and Klapisch-Zuber (eds) 1996, pp. 307–90.

De Giorgio, Michela and Christiane Klapisch-Zuber (eds) 1996, *Storia del matrimonio*, Rome-Bari.

De Grazia, Victoria and Ellen Furlough (eds), 1996, *The Sex of Things: Gender and Consumption in Historical Perspective*, Berkeley, CA.

De Gubernatis, Angelo, 1878, *Storia comparata degli usi nuziali in Italia e presso gli altri popoli indo-europei*, Milan.

de Vries, Jan, 1984, *European Urbanization 1500–1800*, London.

de Vries, Jan, 1993, 'Between purchasing power and the world of goods: understanding the household economy in early modern Europe', in Brewer and Porter (eds) 1993, pp. 85–132.

Dean, Trevor and Kate J.P. Lowe, 1998, *Marriage in Italy, 1300–1650*, Cambridge.

Deffontaines, Pierre, 1972, *L'Homme et sa maison*, Paris.

Delille, Gérard, 1985, *Famiglia e proprietà nel regno di Napoli, XV–XIX secolo*, Turin.

Delille, Gérard, 1986, Premessa a 'Aristo-crazie europee dell'Ottocento' *Quaderni storici*, XXI, no. 62, pp. 347–59.

Delille, Gérard, 1996a, 'Strategie di alleanza e demografia del matrimonio', in De Giorgio and Klapisch-Zuber 1996, pp. 283–303.

Delille, Gérard, 1996b, 'Matrimonio e doti delle donne in Italia (secoli XVI–XVII)', in *Donne e proprietà* 1996, pp. 67–89.

Delille, Gérard and Antonio Ciuffreda, 1993, 'Lo scambio dei ruoli: primogeniti-e, e cadetti-e tra Quattrocento e Settecento nel Mezzogiorno', *Quaderni storici*, XXVIII, no. 83, pp. 507–25.

Della Pina, Marco, 1990, 'Famiglia mezzadrile e celibato: le campagne di Prato nei secoli XVII e XVIII', in Società Italiana di Demografia Storica 1990, pp. 125–39.

Deonna, Waldemar and Marcel Renard, 1961, *Croyances et superstitions de table dans la Rome antique*, Brussels (Ital. trans. *A tavola con i Romani. Superstizioni e credenze conviviali*, Parma, 1994).

Derks, Hans, 1996, 'Über die Faszination des "Ganzen Hauses"', Geschichte und Gesellschaft, 22, pp. 221–42.

Derouet, Bernard, 1994, 'Transmettre la terre. Origines et inflexions récentes d'une problématique de la différence', Histoire et sociétés rurales, no. 2, pp. 33–67.

Dessureault, Christian, John A. Dickinson and Thomas Wien, 1994, 'Living standards of Norman and Canadian peasants, 1690–1835', in Schuurman and Walsh (eds) 1994, pp. 95–111.

Devance, Louis, 1977, 'Le Féminisme pendant la Revolution Française', Annales historiques de la Révolution Française, 229, pp. 341–76.

Devoto, Giacomo, 1967, Avviamento alla etimologia italiana. Dizionario etimologico, Florence.

Di Simplicio, Oscar, 1988, 'Le perpetue (Stato senese, 1600–1800)', Quaderni storici, XXIII, no. 68, pp. 381–412.

Di Simplicio, Oscar, 1994a, 'Il divorzio in Italia in antico regime. Problemi di ricerca', paper read to the international conference: Mutamenti della famiglia nei paesi occidentali, Bologna, 6–8 October (Session I: 'Fidanzamento, matrimonio e divorzio 1500–1800').

Di Simplicio, Oscar, 1994b, Peccato penitenza perdono. Siena 1575–1800. La formazione della coscienza nell'Italia moderna, Milan.

Dibbits, Hester, 'Between society and family values: the linen cupboard in early-modern households', in Schuurman and Spierenburg (eds) 1996, pp. 125–45.

Dinges, Martin, 1993, 'Von der "Lesbarkeit der Welt" zum universalisierten Wandel durch individuelle Strategien. Die soziale Funktion der Kleidung in der höfischen Gesellschaft', Saeculum, 44, pp. 90–112.

Donald, Moira, 2000, '"The greatest necessity for every rank of men": gender, clocks and watches', in Donald and Hurcombe (eds) 2000, pp. 54–75.

Donald, Moira and Linda Hurcombe (eds), 2000, Gender and Material Culture in Historical Perspective, London and New York.

Donati, Claudio, 1988, L'idea di nobiltà in Italia, secoli XIV–XVIII, Rome-Bari.

Donne e proprietà. Un'analisi comparata tra scienze storico-sociali, letterarie, linguistiche e figurative, Naples, 1996 (Donne e proprietà 1996).

Douglas, Mary, 1975, Implicit meanings. Essays in anthropology, London and Boston.

Douglas, Mary (ed.), 1984, Food in the Social Order. Studies of Food and Festivities in Three American Communities, New York.

Douglas, Mary and Baron Isherwood, 1979, The World of Goods: Toward an Anthropology of Consumption, New York (Ital. trans. Il mondo delle cose. Oggetti, valori, consumo, Bologna, 1984).

Douglass, William, 1993, 'The famille souche and its interpreters', Continuity and Change, 8, pp. 87–102.

Drummond, Jack Cecil and Anne Wilbraham, 1958 (1939 1st edn), The Englishman's Food. A History of Five Centuries of English Diet, London.

Dubert, García Isidro, 1992, Historia de la familia en Galicia durante la época moderna, 1550–1830 (Estructura, Modelos hereditarios y Conflictividad), A Coruña.

Dubert, Isidro, 2002, Del Campo a la Ciudad. Migraciones, familia y espacio urbano en la historia de Galicia, 1708–1924, Santiago.

Duby, Georges, 1974, 'Famiglia contadina e signoria domestica', in Famiglia e matrimonio nel capitalismo europeo, Agopik Manoukian (ed.), Bologna, pp. 43–56 (the extract is taken from Georges Duby, L'economia rurale nell'Europa medievale, Bari, 1966, pp. 7–10, 43–51 and 338–44).

Duby, Georges, 1985 (Ital. trans. 1987), 'Potere privato, potere pubblico. Partire dalle parole', in Ariès and Duby (series eds) 1985 (Ital. trans. 1987), pp. 5–33.

Duden. Das große Wörterbuch der deutschen Sprache 1976–81, Mannheim, Vienna and Zurich, 6 vols (Duden 1976–81).

Duerr, Hans Peter, 1988, Der Mythos vom Zivilisationsprozeß I. Nacktheit und Scham, Frankfurt (Ital. trans. Nudità e pudore. Il mito del processo di civilizzazione, Venice, 1991).

Duhet, Paule-Marie, 1971, Les Femmes et la Révolution, 1789–1794, Paris.

Dülmen, Richard van, 1990, Kultur und Alltag in der Frühen Neuzeit. 1. Das Haus und seine Menschen 16.–18. Jahrhundert, Munich.

Dupâquier, Jacques, 1987, 'Una società malthusiana: gli equilibri demografici', in Tranfaglia and Firpo (eds) 1987, pp. 1–22.

Duro, Aldo, 1986–94, Vocabolario della lingua italiana, Rome, 4 vols.

Ehmer, Josef, 1991, Heiratsverhalten, Sozialstruktur, ökonomischer Wandel, Göttingen.

Ehmer, Josef, 1992, '«Servi di donne». Matrimonio e costituzione di una propria famiglia da parte dei garzoni come campo di conflitto nel mondo artigiano mitteleuropeo', *Quaderni storici*, XXVII, no. 80, pp. 475–508.

Ehmer, Josef, 1998, 'House and the stem family in Austria', in Fauve-Chamoux and Ochiai (eds) 1998, pp. 59–81.

Ehmer, Josef, Tamara K. Hareven and Richard Wall (eds), 1997, *Historische Familien-forschung. Ergebnisse und Kontroversen*, Frankfurt and New York.

Elias, Norbert, 1969 (1939 1st edn), *Über den Prozess der Zivilisation. I. Wandlungen des Verhaltens in den weltlichen Oberschichten des Abendlandes*, Frankfurt (Ital. trans. *La civiltà delle buone maniere. Il processo di civilizzazione. I*, Bologna, 1982).

Elias, Norbert, 1969 and 1975, *Die höfische Gesellschaft*, Darmstadt and Neuwied (Ital. trans. *La società di corte*, Bologna, 1980).

Engelsing, Rolf, 1978 (1968 1st edn), 'Dienstbotenlektüre im 18. und 19. Jahrhundert', in Rolf Engelsing, *Zur Sozialgeschichte deutscher Mittel- und Unterschichten*, Göttingen, pp. 180–224.

Ernout, Alfred and Antoine Meillet, 1959–60 (4th edn), *Dictionnaire étymologique de la langue latine. Histoire des mots*, Paris, 2 vols.

Esquirou de Parieu, Marie-Louise-Pierre-Félix, n.d., *Traité des impôts: considérés sous le rapport historique, économique et politique en France et à l'étranger*, Paris (Ital. trans. *Trattato delle imposte considerato sotto l'aspetto storico, economico e politico in Francia ed all'-estero*, Biblioteca dell'Economista, Turin, 1865, series II, vol. IX).

Europa 1984, *Europa: fondamenti, formazione e realtà. Atti del Congresso internazionale, Rome, 3–7 May 1983*, Rome.

Evangelisti, Silvia, 1995, 'L'uso e la trasmissione delle celle nel monastero di Santa Giulia di Brescia (1597–1688)', *Quaderni storici*, XXX, no. 88, pp. 85–110.

Evangelisti, Silvia, 2000, 'Wives, widows, and brides of Christi: marriage and the convent in the historiography of early modern Italy', *Historical Journal*, 43, pp. 233–47.

Evans, Robin, 1978 (German trans. 1996), 'Menschen, Türen, Korridore', *Arch+*, December, pp. 85–97 (orig. pub. in *Architectural Design*, 4, pp. 267–77).

Faccioli, Emilio (ed.), 1992 (1987 1st edn), *L'arte della cucina in Italia*, Turin.

Faccioli, Emilio, 1973, 'La cucina', in *Storia d'-Italia*, V, *I documenti*, I, Turin, pp. 983–1030.

Fairchilds, Cissie, 1984, *Domestic Enemies. Servants and their Masters in Old Regime France*, Baltimore and London.

Fairchilds, Cissie, 1993a, 'The production and marketing of populuxe goods in eighteenth century Paris', in Brewer and Porter (eds) 1993, pp. 228–48.

Fairchilds, Cissie, 1993b, 'Consumption in early modern Europe. A review article', *Comparative Studies in Society and History*, 35, pp. 850–8.

Fantesca (La) composta pfr [sic] Bastiano di Francesco Linaiuolo Sanese. Sopra d'una Donna qual narrando le sue virtù, cerca di trovar padrone. Di nuovo stampata, n.p., n.d. [*La fantesca* n.d.].

Fantuzzi, Giovanni, 1781–94, *Notizie degli scrittori bolognesi*, Bologna, 9 vols.

Fara, Amelio, 1993, *La città da guerra nell'-Europa moderna*, Turin.

Faragó, Tamás 1998, 'Different household formation systems in Hungary at the end of the eighteenth century: variations on John Hajnal's thesis', *Historical Social Research*, 23, 83–111.

Farge, Arlette, 1979, *Vivre dans la rue à Paris au XVIIIe siècle*, Paris.

Fauve-Chamoux, Antoinette, 1981, 'La Femme seule. Présentation', *Annales de démographie historique*, pp. 207–13.

Fauve-Chamoux, Antoinette, 1987, 'Le fonctionnement de la famille-souche dans les Baronnies des Pyrénées avant 1914', *Annales de démographie historique*, pp. 241–62.

Fauve-Chamoux, Antoinette, 1993, '«Per la buona e la cattiva sorte». Convivenze nella Francia preindustriale', *Quaderni storici*, XXVIII, no. 83, pp. 471–506.

Fauve-Chamoux, Antoinette, 1994, 'Mariages sauvages contre mariages-souche: la guerre des cadets', in Ravis-Giordani and Segalen (eds) 1994, pp. 181–94.

Fauve-Chamoux, Antoinette, 2001, 'Marriage, widowhood and divorce', in Barbagli and Kertzer (eds) 2001, pp. 221–56.

Fauve-Chamoux, Antoinette and Emiko Ochiai (eds), 1998, *House and the stem family in Eurasian perspective/Maison et famille-souche: perspectives eurasiennes, Proceedings of the C18 Session, Twelfth International Economic History Congress*, Eurasian Project on Population and Family History. International Research Center for Japanese Studies, Kyoto.

Fauve-Chamoux, Antoinette and Emiko Ochiai, 1998, 'Introduction' to Fauve-Chamoux and Ochiai (eds) 1998, pp. 1–19.

Fazio, Ida, 1990 (but 1992), 'Trasmissione della proprietà, sussistenza e status femminile in Sicilia (Capizzi 1790–1900)', *Annali*, Istituto Alcide Cervi, 12, pp. 181–99.

Fazio, Ida, 1992, 'Valori economici e valori simbolici: il declino della dote nell'Italia dell'Ottocento', *Quaderni storici*, XXVII, no. 79, pp. 291–316.

Fazio, Ida, 1996, 'Percorsi coniugali nell'Italia moderna', in De Giorgio and Klapisch-Zuber (eds) 1996, pp. 151–214.

Fazio, Ida, 1999, 'La ricchezza delle donne: verso una ri-problematizzazione, Quaderni storici', XXXIV, no. 101, pp. 540–50.

Febvre, Lucien, 1930, 'Civilisation. Évolution d'un mot et d'un groupe d'idées', in *Civilisation, le mot, l'idée*, Ire Semaine Internationale de Synthèse, La Renaissance du Livre, Paris (Ital. trans. 'Civiltà: evoluzione di un termine e di un gruppo di idee', in Lucien Febvre, *Problemi di metodo storico*, Turin, 1992 [1966 1st edn], pp. 5–45).

Febvre, Lucien, 1970 (1922 1st edn), *La Terre et l'évolution humaine. Introduction géographique à l'histoire*, Paris (Ital. trans. *La terra e l'evoluzione umana. Introduzione geografica alla storia*, Turin, 1980).

Ferguson, Margaret W., Maureen Quilligan and Nancy J. Vickers (eds) 1986, *Rewriting the Renaissance. The Discourses of Sexual Difference in Early Modern Europe*, Chicago and London.

Fernández de Pinedo, Emiliano, 1995, 'Economia: la lenta e difficile affermazione della moneta e degli scambi commerciali', in Aymard (ed.) 1995, pp. 259–94.

Ferrante, Lucia, 1978, ' "Tumulto di più persone per causa del calo del pane . . ." Saccheggi e repressione a Bologna (1671, 1677)', *Rivista Storica Italiana*, XC, pp. 770–809.

Ferrante, Lucia, 1983, 'L'onore ritrovato. Donne della Casa del Soccorso di S. Paolo a Bologna (sec. XVI–XVII)', *Quaderni storici*, XXVIII, no. 53, 291–316.

Ferrante, Lucia, 1986, ' "Malmaritate" tra assistenza e punizione (Bologna, secc. XVI–XVII)', in *Forme e soggetti dell'intervento assistenziale in una città di antico regime. Atti del IV colloquio, Bologna 20–21 gennaio 1984*, Bologna, pp. 65–109.

Ferrante, Lucia, 1994a, 'Il matrimonio disciplinato: processi matrimoniali a Bologna nel Cinquecento' in Prodi (ed.) 1994, pp. 901–27.

Ferrante, Lucia, 1994b, 'Il matrimonio a Bologna prima del Concilio di Trento', paper read at the international conference *Mutamenti della famiglia nei paesi occidentali*, held in Bologna on 6–8 October (Session I, *Fidanzamento, matrimonio e divorzio 1500–1800*).

Ferrante, Lucia, 1996, 'Il valore del corpo ovvero la gestione economica della sessualità femminile', in Groppi (ed.), 1996, pp. 206–8.

Ferrante, Lucia, 1998, 'Legittima concubina, quasi moglie, anzi meretrice. Note sul concubinato tra Medioevo ed età moderna', in *Modernità. Definizioni ed esercizi*, Albano Biondi (ed.), Bologna, pp. 123–41.

Ferrante, Lucia, Palazzi Maura and Gianna Pomata (eds), 1988, *Ragnatele di rapporti. Patronage e reti di relazione nella storia delle donne*, Turin.

Ferrer i Alòs, Llorenç, 1993, 'Fratelli al celibato, sorelle al matrimonio. La parte dei cadetti nella riproduzione sociale dei gruppi agiati in Catalogna (sec. XVIII–XIX)', *Quaderni storici*, XXVIII, no. 83, pp. 527–54.

Fildes, Valerie, 1986, *Breasts, Bottles and Babies. A History of Infant Feeding*, Edinburgh.

Fildes, Valerie, 1988, *Wet nursing. A History from Antiquity to the Present*, Oxford (Ital. trans. *Madre di latte. Balie e baliatico dall'antichità al XX secolo*, Cinisello Balsamo, 1997).

Fine, Agnes, 1984, 'À propos du trousseau: une culture féminine?', in *Une Histoire des femmes est-elle possible?*, Michelle Perrot (ed.), Marseille, pp. 155–88.

Fine, Agnes, 1994, *Parrains, marraines: la parenté spirituelle en Europe*, Paris.

Finley, Moses I., 1973, *The Ancient Economy*, Berkeley, CA (Ital. trans. *Economia degli antichi e dei moderni*, Rome-Bari, 1977 [1974 1st edn]).

Finn, Margot, 2000, 'Men's things: masculine possession in the consumer revolution', *Social History*, 25, pp. 133–55.

Finzi, Ida and Francesco Cognasso, 1930a, 'Biancheria', in *Enciclopedia Italiana*, Rome, vol. VI, pp. 860–2.

Finzi, Ida and Francesco Cognasso, 1930b, 'Busto', in *Enciclopedia Italiana*, Rome, vol. VIII, pp. 174–6.

Finzi, Ida and Francesco Cognasso, 1930c,

'Calzoni', in *Enciclopedia Italiana*, Rome, vol. VIII, pp. 492–4.

Finzi, Roberto, 1976, *Un problema di storia sociale. L'alimentazione*, Bologna.

Finzi, Roberto, 1990 (but 1992), 'Differenze. La pellagra nella donna fertile', *Annali, Istituto Alcide Cervi*, 12, pp. 201–10.

Fiorino, Vinzia, 1993, 'Essere cittadine francesi: una riflessione sui principi dell'89', in Bonacchi and Groppi (eds) 1993, pp. 59–86.

Fiorino, Vinzia, 1999, 'Dai diritti civili ai diritti politici: la cittadinanza delle donne in Francia', *Passato e presente*, XVII, no. 47, pp. 67–91.

Fischler, Claude, 1985, 'Alimentation, cuisine et identité: l'identification des aliments et l'identité du mangeur', in *Identité alimentaire et altérité culturelle*, Recherches et travaux de l'Institut d'ethnologie Neuchâtel, no. 6, pp. 171–92.

Fiume, Giovanna (ed.), 1995, *Madri. Storia di un ruolo sociale*, Venice.

Fiume, Giovanna, 1997, 'Nuovi modelli e nuove codificazioni: madri e mogli tra Settecento e Ottocento', in D'Amelia (ed.) 1997, pp. 76–110.

Flandrin, Jean-Louis, 1975, *Les Amours paysannes (XVIᵉ–XIXᵉ siècle)*, Paris (Ital. trans. *Amori contadini. Amore e sessualità nelle campagne nella Francia dal 16. al 19. secolo*, Milan, 1980).

Flandrin, Jean-Louis, 1976, *Familles: parenté, maison, sexualité dans l'ancienne société*, Paris (Ital. trans. *La famiglia. Parentela, casa, sessualità nella società preindustriale*, Milan, 1979).

Flandrin, Jean-Louis, 1981, *Le Sexe et l'Occident. Évolution des attitudes et des comportements*, Paris.

Flandrin, Jean-Louis, 1983, 'Le Goût et la nécessité: réflexions sur l'usage des graisses dans les cuisines de l'Europe occidentale (XIVe–XVIIIe siècles)', *Annales. Économies, sociétés, civilisations*, 38, pp. 369–401.

Flandrin, Jean-Louis, 1986 (Ital. trans. 1987), 'La distinzione attraverso il gusto', in Ariès and Duby (series eds) 1986 (Ital. trans. 1987), pp. 205–40.

Flandrin, Jean-Louis, 1993, *Les Heures des repas en France avant le XIXe siècle*, in Aymard, Grignon and Sabban (eds) 1993, pp. 197–226.

Flandrin, Jean-Louis, 1996a, 'I tempi moderni', in Flandrin and Montanari (eds) 1996 (but 1997), pp. 427–48.

Flandrin, Jean-Louis, 1996b, 'L'alimentazione contadina in un'economia di sostentamento', in Flandrin and Montanari (eds) 1996 (but 1997), pp. 465–89.

Flandrin, Jean-Louis, 1996c, 'Scelte alimentari e arte culinaria (secoli XVI–XVIII)', in Flandrin and Montanari (eds) 1996 (but 1997), pp. 512–33.

Flandrin, Jean-Louis, 1996d, 'Cucina, condimenti e dietetica tra XIV e XVI secolo', in Flandrin and Montanari (eds) 1996 (but 1997), pp. 381–95.

Flandrin, Jean-Louis, 1997, 'Prix et statut gastronomique des viandes. Réflexions sur quelques examples des XVIe–XVIIe et XVIIIe siècles', in Istituto Internazionale di Storia Economica F. Datini, Prato 1997, pp. 591–610.

Flandrin, Jean-Louis, Montanari Massimo (eds) 1996 (but 1997), *Storia dell'alimentazione*, Rome-Bari.

Fontaine, Laurence, 1993, *Histoire du colportage en Europe, 15.–19. siècle*, Paris.

Fontana, Vincenzo, 1995, 'Venezia. Trasformazioni delle residenze signorili tra '600 e '700', in Simoncini (ed.) 1995, vol. I, pp. 141–79.

Foucault, Michel, 1975, *Surveiller et punir. Naissance de la prison*, Paris (Ital. trans. *Sorvegliare e punire. Nascita della prigione*, Turin, 1976).

Fragnito, Gigliola, 1988, ' "Parenti" e familiari" nelle corti cardinalizie del Rinascimento', in *«Familia» del principe e famiglia aristocratica*, Cesare Mozzarelli (ed.), Rome, 2 vols, vol. II, pp. 565–87.

Fragnito, Gigliola, 1991, 'La trattatistica cinque e seicentesca sulla corte cardinalizia. "Il vero ritratto di una bellissima e ben governata corte" ', *Annali dell'Istituto storico italo-germanico in Trento*, XVII, pp. 135–85.

Franceschi Ferrucci, Caterina, 1848 (1847 1st edn), *Della educazione morale della donna italiana libri tre*, Turin.

Frati, Luigi, 1923, *Il Settecento a Bologna*, n.p. (but Palermo).

Frigo, Daniela, 1985, *Il padre di famiglia. Governo della casa e governo civile nella tradizione dell'«economica» tra Cinque e Seicento*, Rome.

Frommel, Sabine, 1998, *Sebastiano Serlio architetto*, Milan.

Frugoni, Arsenio and Chiara, 1997, *Storia di un giorno in una città medievale*, Rome-Bari.

Fubini Leuzzi, Maria, 1994, '«Dell'allogare le fanciulle degli Innocenti»: un problema culturale ed economico, 1577–1652', in Prodi (ed,) 1994, pp. 863–99.

Gagliani, Dianella and Mariuccia Salvati (eds) 1995, *Donne e spazio nel processo di modernizzazione*, Bologna.

Galasso, Giuseppe, 1982, *L'altra Europa. Per un'antropologia storica del Mezzogiorno d'Italia*, Milan.

Gambi, Lucio, 1976, 'La casa contadina', in *Storia d'Italia*, VI, *Atlante*, Turin, pp. 479–504.

Garaud, Marcel and Romuald Sramkiewicz, 1978, *La Révolution Française et la famille*, Paris.

Garbero Zorzi, Elvira, 1985, 'Cerimoniale e spettacolarità. Il tovagliolo sulla tavola del principe', in Bertelli and Crifò (eds) 1985, pp. 67–83.

García González, Francisco (ed.), 1998, *Tierra y familia en la España meridional, siglos XIII–XIX. Formas de organización doméstica y reproducción social*, Murcia.

Garnot, Benoît, 1989, 'Le Logement populaire au XVIIIᵉ siècle: l'example de Chartres', *Revue d'Histoire moderne et contemporaine*, 36, pp. 185–210.

Garnot, Benoît, 1994, 'La Culture matérielle dans les villes françaises au XVIIIe siècle', in Schuurman and Walsh (eds) 1994, pp. 21–9.

Garrido Arce, Estrella, 1998, 'Tener o no tener en 1791. Estructuras familiares y tenencia de la tierra en la huerta de Valencia, siglo XVIII', in García González (ed.) 1998, pp. 193–224.

Gaudemet, Jean, 1987, *Le Mariage en Occident. Les Mœurs et le droit*, Paris (Ital. trans. *Il matrimonio in Occidente*, Turin, 1989).

Gaunt, David, 1983, 'The property and kin relationships of retired farmers in northern and central Europe', in Wall, Robin and Laslett (eds) 1983, pp. 249–79

Gaunt, David, 2001, 'Kinship: thin red lines or thick blue blood', in Barbagli and Kertzer (eds) 2001, pp. 257–87.

Geremek, Bronisław, 1974 (Ital. trans. 1992), 'Criminalità, vagabondaggio, pauperismo: la marginalità agli albori dell'Età moderna', in Geremek 1992, pp. 79–126 (orig. pub. in *Revue d'histoire moderne et contemporaine*, XXI, pp. 338–75).

Geremek, Bronisław, 1973, Il pauperismo nell'età preindustriale (secoli XIV–XVIII), in *Storia d'Italia*, V, *I documenti*, I, Turin, pp. 670–98.

Geremek, Bronisław, 1977, 'Les Hommes sans maître. La Marginalité sociale à l'époque préindustrielle', *Diogène*, 98, pp. 29–57 (Ital. trans. 'Uomini senza padrone. La marginalità sociale nell'epoca preindustriale', in Geremek 1992, pp. 127–50).

Geremek, Bronisław, 1982, 'L'arrivo degli zingari in Italia: dall'assistenza alla repressione', in *Timore e carità. I poveri nell'Italia moderna*, Giorgio Politi, Mario Rosa and Franco Della Peruta (eds), Cremona, 1982 (republished in Geremek 1992, pp. 151–80).

Geremek, Bronisław, 1988 (1986 1st edn), *La pietà e la forca. Storia della miseria e della carità in Europa*, Rome-Bari.

Geremek, Bronisław, 1992, *Uomini senza padrone. Poveri e marginali tra Medioevo e Età moderna*, Turin.

Gerola, Giuseppe, 1936, 'Stufa', in *Enciclopedia Italiana*, vol. XXXII, Rome, p. 394.

Gigli Marchetti, Ada, 1995, *Dalla crinolina alla minigonna. La donna, l'abito e la società dal XVIII al XX secolo*, Bologna.

Gillis, John R., 1974, *Youth and History*, New York (Ital. trans. *I giovani e la storia*, Milan, 1981).

Ginzburg, Carlo, 1994, 'Microstoria: due o tre cose che so di lei', *Quaderni storici*, XXIX, n. 86, pp. 511–38.

Giorgetti, Cristina, 1992, *Manuale di storia del costume e della moda*, Turin.

Giusberti, Fabio, 1982, 'Mobilité de la population et territoire urbain: un secteur de Bologne dans les années 1816 et 1820', *Annales de démographie historique*, pp. 183–90.

Giusberti, Fabio, 1990, 'Poveri in casa. Analisi familiare della povertà', in Società Italiana di Demografia Storica 1990, pp. 160–74.

Glennie, Paul, 1995, 'Consumption within historical studies', in *Acknowledging Consumption. A Review of New Studies*, Daniel Miller (ed.), London and New York, pp. 164–203.

Glossarium mediae et infimae latinitatis conditum a Carolo Du Fresne *Domino* Du Cange *auctum a monachis Ordinis S. Benedicti cum supplementis integris D. P.* Carpenterti Adelungii, *aliorum, suisque digessit* G. A. L. Henschel *sequuntur glossarium gallicum, tabulae, indices auctorum et rerum, dissertationes. Editio nova aucta pluribus verbis aliorum scriptorum a* Léopold Favre *Membre de la Société d'Histoire de France et correspondant de la Société des Antiquaires de France,*

Niort, 1883–87, 10 vols (Glossarium 1883–87).

Godefroy, Frédéric, 1881–1902, *Dictionnaire de l'Ancienne Langue Française et de tous ses dialectes du IXe au XVe siècle*, Paris, 10 vols.

Goldschmidt, Walter and Evalyn Jacobson Kunkel, 1971, 'Peasant family structure', *American Anthropologist*, 73, pp. 1058–76 (partial Ital. trans. *Sistemi di eredità e struttura della famiglia contadina*, in Barbagli (ed.) 1977, pp. 187–205).

Goldthwaite, Richard A., 1980, *The Building of Renaissance Florence. An Economic and Social History*, Baltimore and London (Ital. trans. *La costruzione della Firenze rinascimentale*, Bologna, 1984).

Goldthwaite, Richard A., 1987a, 'The economics of Renaissance Italy. The preconditions for luxury consumption', in *I Tatti Studies. Essays in the Renaissance*, 1987, vol. II, pp. 15–39.

Goldthwaite, Richard A., 1987b, 'The empire of things: consumer demand in Renaissance Italy', in *Patronage, Art and Society in Renaissance Italy*, Francis William Kent and Pateicia Simons (eds), Canberra and Oxford, pp. 153–75.

Goldthwaite, Richard A., 1989, 'The Economic and Social World of Italian Renaissance Maiolica', *Renaissance Quarterly*, XLII, pp. 1–32.

Goldthwaite, Richard A., 1993, *Wealth and the Demand for Art in Italy 1300–1600*, Baltimore and London (Ital. trans. *Ricchezza e domanda nel mercato dell'arte in Italia dal Trecento al Seicento. La cultura materiale e le origine del consumismo*, Milan, 1995).

Goody, Jack, 1972, 'The evolution of the family', in Laslett and Wall (eds) 1972, pp. 103–24 (Ital. trans. 'L'evoluzione della famiglia', in Barbagli (ed.) 1977, pp. 55–79).

Goody, Jack, 1983, *The Development of the Family and Marriage in Europe*, London (Ital. trans. *Famiglia e matrimonio in Europa. Origini e sviluppi dei modelli familiari dell'Occidente*, Milan, 1984).

Goody, Jack, 2000, *The European Family. An Historico-Anthropological Essay*, Oxford (Ital. trans. *La famiglia nella storia europea*, Rome-Bari, 2000).

Goody, Jack, Joan Thirsk and Edward P. Thompson (eds), 1976, *Family and Inheritance. Rural Society in Western Europe, 1200–1800*, Cambridge.

Goody, Jack, 1976, 'Introduction' to Goody, Thirsk and Thompson (eds) 1976, pp. 1–34.

Gottlieb, Beatrice, 1993, *The Family in the Western World from the Black Death to the Industrial Age*, New York.

Goubert, Jean-Pierre (ed.), 1988, *Du Luxe au confort*, Paris.

Goubert, Pierre, 1987 (1982 1st edn), *La Vie quotidienne des paysans français au XVIIe siècle*, Paris.

Gozze, Nicolò Vito di, 1589, *Governo della Famiglia*, Venice.

Grassi, Luigi, Mario Pepe and Giancarlo Sestieri, 1992 (1989 1st edn), *Dizionario di antiquariato. Dizionario storico-critico di Arte e Antiquariato dall'antichità all'inizio del Novecento*, Milan.

Green Carr, Louis, 1994, 'Emigration and the standard of living: the eighteenth-century Chesapeake', in Schuurman and Walsh (eds) 1994, pp. 83–94.

Grendi, Edoardo, 1994, 'Ripensare la microstoria?' *Quaderni storici*, XXIX, no. 86, pp. 539–49.

Grieco, Allen J., 1996, 'Alimentazione e classi sociali nel tardo Medioevo e nel Rinascimento in Italia', in Flandrin and Montanari (eds) 1996 (but 1997), pp. 479–90.

Grimm, Jacob and Wilhelm, 1854–1956, *Deutsches Wörterbuch*, Leipzig, 15 vols.

Groppi, Angela (ed.), 1996, *Il lavoro delle donne*, Rome-Bari.

Groppi, Angela, 1994, *I conservatori della virtù. Donne recluse nella Roma dei Papi*, Rome-Bari.

Groppi, Angela, 1996a, 'Lavoro e proprietà delle donne in Età moderna', in Groppi (ed.) 1996, pp. 119–63.

Groppi, Angela, 1996b, 'Il diritto del sangue. Le responsabilità familiari nei confronti delle vecchie e delle nuove generazioni (Roma, secoli XVIII–XIX)', *Quaderni storici*, XXXI, no. 92, pp. 305–33.

Groppi, Angela, 1999, 'Ebrei, donne, soldati e neofiti: l'esercizio del mestiere tra esclusioni e privilegi (Roma, XVII–XVIII secolo)', in Guenzi, Massa and Moioli (eds) 1999, pp. 533–57.

Groppi, Angela and Gabrielle Houbre (eds), 1998, 'Femmes, dots, patrimoines', *Clio, histoire, femmes et sociétés*, 7, pp. 5–198.

Grottanelli, Cristiano, 1985, 'Cibi, istinti, divieti', in Bertelli and Crifò (eds) 1985, pp. 31–52.

Guenzi, Alberto, 1982, *Pane e fornai a Bologna*, Venice.

Guenzi, Alberto, 1983, 'L'area protoindustriale del canale Reno in città nel secolo XVIII', in Istituto per la Storia di Bologna, *Problemi d'acque a Bologna. Atti del II colloquio, 10–11 ottobre 1981*, Bologna, pp. 173–210.

Guenzi, Alberto, 1984, 'I consumi alimentari: un problema da esplorare', in *Cheiron*, II, no. 3.

Guenzi, Alberto, 1986, 'La carne suina. Lavorazione, consumo e prezzi nella città di Bologna (secoli XVI–XVII)', in *Mercati e consumi. Organizzazione e qualificazione del commercio in Italia dal XII al XX secolo*, Bologna, pp. 879–903.

Guenzi, Alberto, 1990, 'La tessitura femminile tra città e campagna. Bologna, secoli XVII–XVIII', in Istituto Internazionale di Storia Economica F. Datini, Prato 1990, pp. 247–59.

Guenzi, Alberto, 1995, 'Le magistrature e le istituzioni alimentari', in *Archivi per la storia dell'alimentazione*, 1995, pp. 285–301.

Guenzi, Alberto, Paola Massa and Angelo Moioli (eds) 1999, *Corporazioni e Gruppi Professionali nell'Italia Moderna*, Milan.

Guenzi, Alberto and Carlo Poni, 1989, 'Un «network» plurisecolare, acqua e industria a Bologna', *Studi storici*, 30, pp. 359–77.

Guerci, Luciano, 1988a (1987 1st edn), *La discussione sulla donna nell'Italia del Settecento. Aspetti e problemi*, Turin.

Guerci, Luciano, 1988b, *La sposa obbediente. Donna e matrimonio nella discussione dell'Italia del Settecento*, Turin.

Guerreau-Jalabert, Anita, 1981, 'Sur les structures de parenté dans l'Europe médiévale', *Annales. Économies, sociétés, civilisations*, 36, pp. 1028–49.

Gullestad, Marianne and Martine Segalen (eds), 1997, *Family and Kinship in Europe*, London and Washington.

Hajnal, John, 1965, 'European marriage patterns in perspective', in *Population in History*, D.V. Glass and D.E.C. Eversley (eds), London, pp. 101–35 (Ital. trans. *Modelli europei di matrimonio in prospettiva*, in Barbagli (ed.) 1977, pp. 267–316).

Hajnal, John, 1983, 'Two kinds of preindustrial household formation system' (Ital. trans. *Due sistemi di formazione dell'aggregato domestico preindustriale*), in Wall, Robin and Laslett (eds) 1983 (Ital. trans. 1984), pp. 99–142.

Hall, Catherine, 1986, *Dolce casa*, in Ariès and Duby (series eds) 1986 (Ital. trans. 1988), pp. 38–72.

Hammel, Eugene A., 1972, 'The zadruga as process', in Laslett and Wall 1972, pp. 335–73.

Hammer, Carl I., 1983, 'Family and «familia» in early-medieval Bavaria', in Wall, Robin and Laslett (eds), 1983, pp. 217–48.

Hanawalt, Barbara A., 1994, 'La debolezza del lignaggio. Vedove, orfani e corporazioni nella Londra tardomedievale', *Quaderni storici*, XXIX, no. 86, pp. 463–85.

Hanley, Sarah, 1989, 'Engendering the state: family formation and state building in Early Modern France', *French Historical Studies*, 16, pp. 5–27.

Hareven, Tamara, 1991, 'The home and the family in historical perspective', *Social Research*, 58, pp. 254–85.

Hareven, Tamara, 1997, *Familie, Lebenslauf und Sozialgeschichte*, in Ehmer, Hareven and Wall (eds) 1997, pp. 17–37.

Harrington, Joel F., 1995, *Reordering Marriage in Reformation Germany*, Cambridge, New York and Melbourne.

Harris, Marvin, 1985, *Good to Eat. Riddles of Food and Culture*, New York (Ital. trans. *Buono da mangiare. Enigmi del gusto e consuetudini alimentari*, Turin, 1990 and 1992).

Hauser, Andrea, 1994, *Dinge des Alltags. Studien zur historischen Sachkultur eines schwäbischen Dorfes*, Tübingen.

Hayward, Helena, 1965 (Ital. trans. 1992), *Storia del mobile di tutti i paesi dall'antichità ai nostri giorni*, Reggio Emilia (orig. pub. London).

Head-König, Anne-Lise, 1993, 'Forced marriages and forbidden marriages in Switzerland: state control of the formation of marriage in catholic and protestant cantons in the eighteenth and nineteenth centuries', *Continuity and Change*, 8, pp. 441–65.

Hecht, Joseph Jean, 1980 (1956 1st edn), *The Domestic Servant in Eighteenth Century England*, London, Boston and Henley.

Henderson, John and Richard Wall (eds), 1994, *Poor Women and Children in the European Past*, New York.

Héritier, Françoise, 1979, 'Famiglia', in *Encidopedia*, Turin, vol. VI, pp. 3–16.

Herlihy, David, 1991, 'Family', *American Historical Review*, 96, pp. 1–16.

Herlihy, David and Christiane Klapisch-Zuber, 1978, *Les Toscans et leur familles: une étude du catasto florentin de 1427*, Paris (Ital. trans. *I Toscani e le loro famiglie. Uno studio sul catasto fiorentino del 1427*, Bologna, 1988).

Hochstrasser, Olivia, 1993, *Ein Haus und seine Menschen 1549–1989*, Tübingen.

Hoerder, Dirk and Leslie Page Moch (eds), 1996, *European Migrants. Global and Local Perspectives*, Boston.

Hoock, Jochen and Nicolas Jullien, 1998, 'Dots normandes (mi-XVIIe–XVIIIe siècle)', *Clio, histoire, femmes et sociétés*, 7, pp. 137–8.

Horn, James, 1994, 'Domestic standards of living in England and the Chesapeake, 1650–1700', in Schuurman and Walsh (eds) 1994, pp. 71–81.

Horn, Pamela, 1975, *The Rise and Fall of the Victorian Servant*, Dublin and New York, pp. 71–81.

Huetz de Lemps, Alain, 1996, 'Bevande coloniali e diffusione dello zucchero', in Flandrin and Montanari (eds), 1996 (but 1997), pp. 490–500.

Hufton, Olwen, 1971, 'Women in Revolution 1789–1796', *Past and Present*, 53, pp. 90–108.

Hufton, Olwen, 1974, *The Poor of Eighteenth-Century France, 1750–1789*, Oxford.

Hufton, Olwen, 1995, *A History of Women. I: The Prospect before Her*, London (Ital. trans. *Destini femminili*, Milan, 1996).

Hughes, Diane Owen, 1975 (Ital. trans. 1979), 'Ideali domestici e comportamento sociale: testimonianze dalla Genova medievale', in Rosenberg (ed.) 1975 (Ital. trans. 1979), pp. 147–83.

Hughes, Diane Owen, 1978, 'From brideprice to dowry in Mediterranean Europe', *Journal of Family History*, 3, pp. 262–96.

Hughes, Diane Owen, 1983, 'Sumptuary law and social relations in Renaissance Italy', in *Disputes and Settlements: Law and Human Relations in the West*, John Bossy (ed.), Cambridge, pp. 69–99 (Ital. trans. 'La moda proibita. La legislazione suntuaria nell'Italia rinascimentale', in *Memoria*, 11–12, 1984, pp. 82–105).

Hughes, Diane Owen, 1990, 'Le mode femminili e il loro controllo', in Georges Duby and Michelle Perrot (series eds), *Storia delle donne.*

Il Medioevo, Christiane Klapisch-Zuber (ed.), Rome-Bari, 1990, pp. 166–93.

Hughes, Diane Owen, 1996, 'Il matrimonio nell'Italia medievale', in De Giorgio and Klapisch-Zuber (eds) 1996, pp. 5–61.

Huguet, Edmond, 1925–73, *Dictionnaire de la Langue Française du Seizième Siécle*, Paris, 7 vols.

Hurwich, J. Judith, 1998, 'Marriage strategy among the German nobility, 1400–1699', *Journal of Interdisciplinary History*, XXIX, pp. 169–95.

Hyman, Philip and Mary Hyman, 1996, *La stampa in cucina: i libri di cucina in Francia tra il XV e il XIX secolo*, Flandrin and Montanari (eds) 1996 (but 1997), pp. 501–11.

Istituto Internazionale di Storia Economica F. Datini, Prato 1990, *La donna nell'economia, secc. XII–XVIII*, ed. Simonetta Cavaciocchi, Florence.

Istituto Internazionale di Storia Economica F. Datini, Prato 1997, *Alimentazione e nutrizione, secc. XIII–XVIII*, ed. Simonetta Cavaciocchi, Florence.

Istituto Internazionale di Storia Economica F. Datini, Prato 1998, *Prodotti e tecniche d'oltremare nelle economie europee, secc. XIII–XVIII*, ed. Simonetta Cavaciocchi, Florence.

Jardine, Lisa, 1996, *Worldly Goods. A New History of the Renaissance*, New York (Ital. trans. *Affari di genio. Una storia del Rinascimento europeo*, Rome, 2001).

Jaritz, Gerhard, 1993, 'Kleidung und Prestige-Konkurrenz. Unterschiedliche Identitäten in der stadtischen Gesellschaft unter Normierungszwängen', *Saeculum*, 44, pp. 8–31.

Jeanneret, Michel, 1994, 'Preface' to Deonna and Renard 1961 (Ital. trans. 1994), pp. 7–20.

Jestaz, Bertrand, 1995, *La Renaissance de l'architecture de Brunelleschi à Palladio*, Paris (Ital. trans. *Il Rinascimento dell'architettura da Brunelleschi a Palladio*, n.p., 1995).

Johnson, Susan M., 1992, 'Luther's Reformation and the (Un)holy Matrimony', *Journal of Family History*, 17, pp. 271–88.

Jones, Jennifer, 1996, '*Coquettes* and *Grisettes*: Women buying and selling in Ancien Régime Paris', in De Grazia and Furlough 1996, pp. 25–53.

Julia, Dominique, 1996, 'L'infanzia all'inizio dell'epoca moderna', in *Storia dell'infanzia in Occidente, 1. Dall'Antichità al XVII secolo*,

Egle Becchi and Dominique Julia (eds), Rome-Bari, pp. 286–373.

Jütte, Robert, 1993, 'Stigma-Symbole. Kleidung als identitätsstiftendes Merkmal bei spätmittelalterlichen und frühneuzeitlichen Randgruppen (Juden, Dirnen, Aussätzige, Bettler)', *Saeculum*, 44, pp. 65–89.

Jütte, Robert and Neithard Bulst (eds), 1993, 'Zwischen Sein und Schein. Kleidung und Identität in der ständischen Gesellschaft', *Saeculum*, 44, pp. 2–113.

Kaplan, Steven, 1996, *The Bakers of Paris and the Bread Question 1700–1775*, Durham (French trans. *Le Meilleur pain du monde. Les Boulangers de Paris au XVIIIe siécle*, Paris, 1996).

Karnoouh, Claude, 1979, 'Penser "maison" penser "famille": résidence domestique et parenté dans les sociétés rurales de l'Est de la France', *Études rurales*, 75, pp. 35–75.

Kaser, Karl, 1997, *Freier Bauer und Soldat. Die Militarizerung der agrarischen Gesellschaft in der Kroatisch-Slawonischen Militärgrenze (1535–1881)*, Vienna.

Kaser, Karl, 1998, 'The stem family in eastern Europe: Cross cultural and trans-temporal perspectives', in Fauve-Chamoux and Ochiai (eds) 1998, pp. 168–92.

Kaser, Karl, 2001, Serfdom in eastern Europe, in Barbagli and Kertzer (eds) 2001, pp. 63–84.

Kelly-Gadol, Joan, 1977, 'Did women have a Renaissance?', in *Becoming Visible. Women in European History*, Renate Bridenthal and Claudia Koonz (eds), Boston and Atlanta, pp. 137–64.

Kertzer, David I., 1981, *Famiglia contadina e urbanizzazione. Studio di una comunità alla periferia di Bologna*, Bologna.

Kertzer, David I., 1984, *Family Life in Central Italy 1880–1910*, New Brunswick, N.J.

Kertzer, David I., 1995, 'Toward a historical demography of aging', in *Aging in the Past: Demography, Society and Old Age*, David I. Kertzer and Peter Laslett (eds), Berkeley, CA, pp. 363–83.

Kirshner, Julius and Anthony Molho, 1978, 'The dowry fund and the marriage market in Early Quattrocento Florence', *Journal of Modern History*, 50, pp. 403–38.

Klapisch-Zuber, Christiane, 1979, 'Zacharie, ou le père evincé. Les rites nuptiaux toscans entre Giotto et le concile de Trente', *Annales. Économies, sociétés, civilisations*, 34, pp.

1216–43 (Ital. trans. 'Zaccaria, o il padre spodestato. I riti nuziali in Toscana tra Giotto e il Concilio di Trento', in Klapisch-Zuber 1988, pp. 109–51).

Klapisch-Zuber, Christiane, 1981, 'Une ethnologie du mariage au temps de l'Humanisme', *Annales. Économies, sociétés, civilisations*, 36, pp. 1016–27 (Ital. trans. 'Un'etnologia del matrimonio in età umanistica', in Klapisch-Zuber 1988, pp. 91–108).

Klapisch-Zuber, Christiane, 1982, 'Le complexe de Griselda. Dot et dons de mariage au Quattrocento', *Mélanges de l'École Française de Rome. Moyen Âge–Temps Modernes*, 94, n. 1, pp. 7–43 (Ital. trans. 'Il complesso di Grise N. Dotee doz dinizze nel Quettrocento' in Klapisch-Zuber 1988, pp. 153–91).

Klapisch-Zuber, Christiane, 1983a, 'Parents de sang, parents de lait. La Mise en nourrice à Florence 1300–1530', *Annales de démographie historique*, pp. 33–64 (Ital. trans. 'Genitori di sangue, «genitori» di latte. Andare a balia a Firenze', in Klapisch-Zuber 1988, pp. 213–52).

Klapisch-Zuber, Christiane, 1983b, 'La «Mère cruelle». Maternité veuvage et dot dans la Florence des XIVe–XVe siécles', *Annales. Économies, sociétés, civilisations*, 3, pp. 1097–109 (Ital. trans. 'La «madre crudele». Maternità, vedovanza e dote nella Firenze dei secoli XIV e XV', in Klapisch-Zuber 1988, pp. 287–303).

Klapisch-Zuber, Christiane, 1984, 'Le zane della sposa. La donna fiorentina e il suo corredo nel Rinascimento', *Memoria*, 11–12, pp. 12–23 (republished in Klapisch-Zuber 1988, pp. 93–211).

Klapisch-Zuber, Christiane, 1988, *La famiglia e le donne nel Rinascimento a Firenze*, Rome-Bari.

Klapisch-Zuber, Christiane, 1994, 'Les Coffres de mariage et les plateaux d'accouchée à Florence: archive, ethnologie, iconographie', in *À travers l'image. Lecture iconographique et sens de l'œuvre*, Sylvie Deswarte-Rosa (ed.), Paris, pp. 309–22.

Klapisch-Zuber, Christiane, 1998, 'La Bourse ou les boules de saint Nicolas. De quelques représentations des biens féminins en Italie (fin du Moyen Âge)', *Clio, histoire, femmes et sociétes*, 7, pp. 73–90.

Klapisch-Zuber, Christiane, 2000, *L'Ombre des ancê tres. Essai sur l'imaginaire médieval de la parenté*, Paris.

Klapisch-Zuber, Christiane and Michel Demonet, 1972, '«A uno pane e uno vino»: la famille rurale toscane au début du XVe siècle', *Annales. Économies, sociétés, civilisations*, 27, pp. 873–901 (Ital. trans. '«A uno pane a uno vino»: la famiglia rurale in Toscana all'inizio del XV secolo', in Manoukian (ed.) 1983, pp. III–35).

Kochanowicz, Jacek, 1983, 'The Polish peasant family as an economic unit', in Wall, Robin and Laslett (eds), 1983, pp. 153–66.

Komlos, John, 1998, 'Shrinking in a growing economy? The mystery of physical stature during the Industrial Revolution', *Journal of Economic History*, 58, pp. 773–802.

Kowaleski-Wallace, Elisabeth, 1997, *Consuming Subjects: Women, Shopping, and Business in the Eighteenth Century*, New York.

Kramer, Karl-S., 1985, 'Ländliche Wohnverhältnisse in holsteinischen Gutsbezirken', in Teuteberg (ed.) 1985, pp. 29–42.

Kriedte, Peter, Hans Medick and Jürgen Schlümbohn, 1977, *Industrialisierung vor der Industrialisierung. Gewerbliche Warenproduktion auf dem Land in der Formationsperiode des Kapitalismus*, Göttingen (Ital. trans. *L'industrializzazione prima dell'industrializzazione*, Bologna, 1984).

Kuchta, David, 1996 'The making of the self-made man: Class, clothing and English masculinity, 1688–1832', in De Grazia and Furlough (eds) 1996, pp. 54–78.

Kuklo, Cezary, 1998, *Kobieta samotna w spoleczenstwie miejskim u schylku Rzeczypospolitej szlcheckiej. Studium demograficznospoleczne* [*La Femme seule dans la societé urbaine à la fin de l'Ancienne Pologne. L'Étude sociale et démographique*], Bialystok.

Kula, Witold, 1972, 'La Famille paysanne en Pologne', *Annales. Économies, sociétés, civilisations*, 27, pp. 949–58.

La famiglia e la vita quotidiana in Europa dal '400 al '600, 1986, Rome.

Labatut, Jean-Pierre, 1978, *Les Noblesses européennes de la fin du XVe siècle à la fin du XVIIe siècle*, Paris (Ital. trans. *Le nobiltà europee*, Bologna, 1982).

Lanaro, Silvio, 1997, 'L'idea di contemporaneo', in *Storia contemporanea*, Rome, pp. 611–32.

Lanteri, Giacomo, 1560, *Della Economica Trattato*, Venice.

Lanziner, Margareth, 2001, '"Der Bittsteller hat vorerst einen Hausbesitz nachzuweisen . . .".

Heirat in lokalen und familien Kontexten, Innichen 1700–1900. Projeckt Bericht', *Geschichte und Region / Storia e Region*, 10, no. 1, pp. 85–107.

Laslett, Peter, 1971 (1965 1st edn), *The World we have lost*, London (Ital. trans. *Il mondo che abbiamo perduto. L'Inghilterra prima dell'era industriale*, Milan, 1979).

Laslett, Peter, 1972, 'Introduction: the history of the family', in Laslatt and Wall (eds) 1972, pp. 1–89.

Laslett, Peter, 1977a, 'Characteristics of the Western family considered over time', in Laslett 1977b, pp. 12–49 (Ital. trans. 'Caratteristiche della famiglia occidentale', in Barbagli (ed.) 1977, pp. 80–115).

Laslett, Peter, 1977b, *Family Life and Illicit Love in Earlier Generations*, Cambridge.

Laslett, Peter, 1983, 'Family and household as work and kin groups' (Ital. trans. 'La famiglia e l'aggregato domestico come gruppo di lavoro e come gruppo di parenti: aree dell'Europa tradizionale a confronto'), in Wall, Robin and Laslett (eds) 1983 (Ital. trans. 1984), pp. 253–323.

Laslett, Peter, 1988, 'Family, kinship and collectivity as systems of support in preindustrial Europe: a consideration of the 'nuclear hardship' hypothesis', *Continuity and Change*, 3 (2), pp. 153–75.

Laslett, Peter, Karla Oosterveen and Richard M. Smith (eds), 1980, *Bastardy and its Comparative History*, London.

Laslett, Peter and Richard Wall (eds), 1972, *Household and Family in Past Time*, London.

Laudani, Simona, 1996, 'Mestieri di donne, mestieri di uomini: le corporazioni in Età moderna', in Groppi (ed.) 1996, pp. 183–204.

Le Roy Ladurie, Emmanuel, 1967, *Histoire du climat depuis l'an mil*, Paris (Ital. trans. of enlarged English 1972 edn, *Tempo di festa, tempo di carestia. Storia del clima dall'anno mille*, Turin 1982).

Le Roy Ladurie, Emmanuel, 1976, 'Family structures and inheritance customs in sixteenth-century France', in Goody, Thirsk and Thompson (eds) 1976, pp. 37–70.

Le Roy Ladurie, Emmanuel and Pierre Couperie, 1970, 'Le Mouvement des loyers parisiens de la fin du Moyen Âge au XVIIIe siècle', *Annales. Économies, sociétés, civilisations*, 25, pp. 1002–23.

Lebrun, François, 1986a (Ital. trans. 1987), 'Le

Riforme: devozioni comunitarie e pietà personale', in Ariès and Duby (series eds) 1986 (Ital. trans. 1987), pp. 44–75.

Lebrun, François, 1986b, 'Il controllo esercitato sulla famiglia dalla chiesa e dallo stato', in Burguière, Klapisch-Zuber, Segalen and Zonabend (series eds) 1986 (Ital. trans. 1988), pp. 95–113.

Lemire, Beverly, 1991, 'Peddling fashion: salesmen, pawnbrokers, taylors, thieves, and second-hand clothes trade in England, c. 1700–1800', *Textile History*, 22, pp. 67–82.

Lepetit, Bernard, 1995, 'Gli spazi delle città', in Aymard (ed.) 1995, pp. 295–325.

Levi, Giovanni, 1976, 'Terre e strutture familiari in una comunità piemontese del '700', *Quaderni storici*, XI, no. 33, pp. 1095–121.

Levi, Giovanni, 1979, 'Innovazione tecnica e resistenza contadina: il mais nel Piemonte del '600', *Quaderni storici*, XIV, no. 42, pp. 1092–100.

Levi, Giovanni, 1985 (1973 1st edn), 'Famiglie contadine nella Liguria del Settecento', in Giovanni Levi, *Centro e periferia di uno stato assoluto. Tre saggi in Piemonte e Liguria in Età moderna*, Turin, 1985, pp. 71–149.

Levi, Giovanni, 1985, *L'eredità immateriale. Carriera di un esorcista nel Piemonte del Seicento*, Turin.

Levi, Giovanni, 1990, 'Family and kin – a few thoughts', *Journal of Family History*, 15, pp. 567–78 (Ital. trans. 'Famiglia e parentela: qualche tema di riflessione', in Barbagli and Kertzer (eds) 1992, pp. 307–21).

Levi, Giovanni, 1991a, 'A proposito di microstoria', in Burke (ed.) 1991 (Ital. trans. 1993), pp. 111–34.

Levi, Giovanni, 1991b, 'L'energia disponibile', in Romano (ed.) 1991, vol. II, pp. 141–68.

Levi, Giovanni, 1996, 'Comportements, ressources, procès: avant la «révolution» de la consommation', in *Jeux d'échelles. La Micro-analyse à l'expérience*, Jacques Revel (ed.), Paris, pp. 186–207.

Levi, Giovanni and Jean-Claude Schmitt, 1994, *Storia dei giovani*, Rome-Bari.

Levi Pisetzky, Rosita, 1973, 'Moda e costume', in *Storia d'Italia*, V, *I documenti*, I, Turin, pp. 983–1030.

Levi Pisetzky, Rosita, 1995 (1978 1st edn), *Il costume e la moda nella società italiana*, Turin.

Levin, Eve, 1989, *Sex and Society in the World of the Orthodox Slavs 900–1700*, Ithaca and London.

Lévi-Strauss, Claude, 1964, *Le Cru et le cuit* (Ital. trans. *Il crudo e il cotto. Dal rituale del fuoco all'analisi strutturale dei miti*, Milan, 1998, [1966 1st edn]).

Lexicon totius latinitatis ab Aegidio Forcellini *Seminarii patavini alumno lucubratum deinde a* Josepho Furlanetto *eiusdem Seminarii alumno emendatum et auctum nunc vero curantibus* Francisco Corradini et Iosepho Perin *Seminarii patavini item alumnis emendatius et auctius melioremque in formam redactum*, Arnaldus Forni excudebat Bononiae Gregoriana edente Patavii 1965 (2nd facsimile publication of 4th Paduan edn, 1864–1926, with appendices from 1940 1st facsimile edn), 6 vols (Lexicon 1864–1940).

Lieber, D. L. and Ben-Zion (Benno) Schereschewsky, 1971, 'Divorce', in *Encyclopaedia Judaica*, Jerusalem, vol. VI, cols 122–36.

Livi Bacci, Massimo, 1987, *Popolazione e alimentazione. Saggio sulla storia della demografia europea*, Bologna.

Livi Bacci, Massimo, 1989, *Storia minima della popolazione del mondo*, Turin.

Livi Bacci, Massimo, 1998, *La popolazione nella storia d'Europa*, Rome-Bari.

Lombardi, Daniela, 1988, *Povertà maschile, povertà femminile. L'ospedale dei mendicanti nella Firenze dei Medici*, Bologna.

Lombardi, Daniela, 1996, 'Fidanzamenti e matrimoni dal Concilio di Trento alle riforme settecentesche', in De Giorgio and Klapisch-Zuber (eds) 1996, pp. 215–50.

Lombardi, Daniela, 2001, *Matrimoni di antico regime*, Bologna.

Lombardi, Daniela and Flores Reggiani, 1990, 'Da assistita a serva. Circuiti di reclutamento delle serve attraverso le istituzioni assistenziali (Firenze-Milano, XVII–XVIII sec.)', in Istituto Internazionale di Storia Economica F. Datini, Prato 1990, pp. 301–19.

Loriga, Sabina, 1990, 'L'Identité militaire: expérience biographique et identité sociale en Piémont au XVIIIe siècle', doctoral thesis, Paris.

Loriga, Sabina, 1992, *Soldati: l'istituzione militare nel Piemonte del Settecento*, Venice.

Lovarini, Emilio (ed.), 1931, *La schiavitù del generale Marsigli sotto i tartari e i turchi da lui stesso narrata*, Bologna, 1931.

Lucassen, Jan and Leo Lucassen (eds), 1997, *Migration, Migration History, History. Old*

Paradigms and New Perspectives, Bern and Berlin.

Lucassen, Leo, 1997, 'Eternal vagrants? State formation, migration, and travelling groups in Western Europe 1350–1914', in Lucassen and Lucassen (eds) 1997, pp. 225–51.

Luttazzi-Gregori, Elsa, 1983, 'Cultura materiale, storia sociale: note sulla casa rurale nell'area dell'insediamento sparso mezzadrile', *Società e storia*, VI, pp. 137–64.

Luzio, Alessandro and Rodolfo Renier, 1891, 'Buffoni, nani e schiavi dei Gonzaga ai tempi di Isabella d'Este', in *Nuova Antologia di Scienze, Lettere ed Arti*, series III, vol. XXXIV, pp. 618–50 and vol. XXXV, pp. 112–46.

Mack, Arien (ed.), 1991, 'Home: a place in the world', *Social Research*, 58, pp. 5–307.

Madre Cristiana instruita nelle obbligazioni, che le corrono, e collo Sposo, per incontrarne il genio; e co' Figliuoli, per cristianamente, e civilmente formarne la educazione, Messina (*La Madre Cristiana* 1732).

Mafai, Giulia, 1998, *Storia della moda*, Rome.

Magnusson, Lars, 1995, 'Il settore economico: capitalismo mercantile, consumo di lusso, sviluppo della cultura di mercato', in Aymard (ed.) 1995, pp. 565–95.

Mainoni, Muzio, 1900, *Fedecommesso e sostituzione fedecommissaria*, in *Enciclopedia giuridica italiana*, Milan, vol. VI, part I, pp. 859–987.

Majorana, Bernadette, 1996, 'Finzioni, imitazioni, azioni. Donne e teatro', in Zarri (ed.) 1996, pp. 121–39.

Malanima, Paolo, 1990, *Il lusso dei contadini. Consumi e industrie nelle campagne toscane del Sei e Settecento*, Bologna.

Malanima, Paolo, 1994, 'Changing patterns in rural living conditions: Tuscany in the eighteenth century', in Schuurman and Walsh (eds) 1994, pp. 115–24.

Malanima, Paolo, 1997 (1995 1st edn), *Economia preindustriale. Mille anni: dal IX al XVIII secolo*, Milan.

Malettke, Klaus (ed.), 1998, *Imaginer l'Europe*, Paris (originally Berlin, 1998).

Manciulli, Andrea, 1996, 'Le arti della tavola', in *Et coquatur ponendo. Cultura della cucina e della tavola in Europa tra Medioevo ed Età moderna*, in Istituto Internazionale F. Datini, Prato 1997, pp. 325–45.

Manoukian, Agopik (ed.), 1983, *I vincoli familiari in Italia. Dal secolo XI al secolo XX*, Bologna.

Marchese, Pasquale, 1989, *L'invenzione della forchetta. Spillonii, schiodoncini lingule imbroccatoi pironi forcule forcine e forchette dai Greci ai nostri forchettoni*, Soveria Mannelli (CZ).

Marrone, Giovanni, 1972, *La sciavitù nella società siciliana dell' età moderna*, Caltanisetta.

Martin Casares, Aurelia, forthcoming, *Imigenes del sector doméstico: la servidumbre libre y esclava en la España moderna*.

Martini, Manuela, 1993, 'Una mobilità limitata. Prime ricerche su proprietari e famiglie contadine nelle campagne bolognesi (fine XVIII–inizio XIX secolo)', *Rivista di storia dell'agricoltura*, 33, pp. 65–90.

Martini, Manuela, 1996, 'Per una storia della dote in Italia e in Europa', in *Donne e proprietà* 1996, pp. 41–66.

Martini, Manuela, 1998a, 'Stratificazione sociale e prestigio nobiliare a Bologna alle soglie del XIX secolo', in *I «Giacobini» nelle Legazioni*, Angelo Varni (ed.), n.p., 3 vols, vol. II, pp. 59–85.

Martini, Manuela, 1998b, 'Rapports patrimoniaux et crédit dans les ménages nobles. Dot et apanage des femmes a Bologne au XIXe siècle', *Clio, histoire, femmes et sociétés*, 7, pp. 155–76.

Martini, Manuela, 1999, *Fedeli alla terra. Scelte economiche e attività politiche di una famiglia nobile bolognese nell'Ottocento*, Bologna.

Matthaiou, Anna, 1997, 'La Longue durée de l'alimentation: permanences rurales et différences urbaines en Grèce sous la domination ottomane', in Istituto Internazionale di Storia Economrica F. Datini, Prato 1997, pp. 313–24.

Matthews Grieco, Sara E., 1991a, 'Breastfeeding, wet nursing and infant mortality in Europe (1400–1800)', in Matthews Grieco and Corsini 1991, pp. 15–62.

Matthews Grieco, Sara E., 1991b, 'Corpo, aspetto, sessualità', in Georges Duby and Micheile Perrot (series eds), *Storia delle donne. Dal Rinascimento all'Età moderna*, Natalie Zemon Davis and Ariette Farge (eds), Rome-Bari, pp. 53–99.

Matthews Grieco, Sara E. and Carlo Corsini, 1991, *Historical Perspectives on Breastfeeding*, Florence.

Mattioda, Enrico, 1993, *Il dilettante «per mestiere». Francesco Albergati Capacelli commediografo*, Bologna.

Maza, Sarah, 1983, *Servants and Masters*

in Eighteenth Century France. The Uses of Loyalty, Princeton.

Mazzi, Maria Serena, 1991, *Prostitute e lenoni nella Firenze del Quattrocento*, Milan.

McKendrick, Neil, 1974, 'Home demand and economic growth: a new view of the role of women and children in the Industrial Revolution', in *Historical Perspectives. Studies in English Thought and Society in honour of J.H. Plumb*, Neil McKendrick (ed.), London, pp. 152–210.

McKendrick, Neil, John Brewer and J.H. Plumb, 1982, *The Birth of a Consumer Society: The Commercialization of Eighteenth-Century England*, London.

Medick, Hans, 1995, 'Una cultura delle apparenze. I vestiti e i loro colori a Laichingen (1750–1820)', *Quaderni storici*, XXX, no. 89, pp. 515–37 (also published in *Annales. Histoire, sciences sociales*, 50, pp. 753–74).

Medick, Hans and David Warren Sabean (eds), 1984, *Interest and Emotion: Essays on the Study of Family and Kinship*, Cambridge and Paris.

Medick, Hans and David Warren Sabean, 1984, 'Interest and emotion in family and kinship studies: a critique of social history and anthropology', in Medick and Sabean (eds) 1984, pp. 9–27.

Medick, Hans and David Warren Sabean, 1980, 'Note preliminari su famiglia e parentela: interessi materiali ed emozioni', *Quaderni storici*, XV, no. 45, pp. 1087–115.

Medioli, Francesca, 1990, *L'«Inferno monacale» di Arcangela Tarabotti*, Turin.

Medioli, Francesca, 1999, 'Lo spazio del chiostro: clausura protezione e costrizione nel XV'I secolo', in *Tempi e spazi della vita femminile nella prima Età moderna*, Silvana Seidel Menchi, Anne Jacobson Schutte and Thomas Kuehn (eds), Bologna, pp. 353–73.

Meldrum, Tim, 1999, 'Domestic service, privacy and the eighteenth-century metropolitan household', *Urban History*, 26, pp. 27–39.

Mendels, Franulin, 1972, 'Protoindustrialization: the first phase of the industrialization process', *Journal of Economic History*, 32, pp. 241–61.

Ménétra, Jacques-Louis (ed.), 1982, *Journal de ma vie. Jacques-Louis Ménétra Compagnon vitrier au 18e siècle*, ed. Daniel Roche, Paris (Ital. trans. *Così parlò Menetra. Diario di un vetraio del XVIII secolo*, Milan, 1992).

Mennell, Stephen, 1985, *All Manners of Food: Eating and Taste in England and France from the Middle Ages to the Present*, Oxford (French trans. *Français et Anglais à table du Moyen Âge à nos jours*, Paris, 1987).

Meriot, Christian, 1980, *Les Lapons et leur société: étude d'ethnologie historique*, Toulouse.

Merzario, Raul, 1981, *Il paese stretto. Strategie matrimoniali nella diocesi di Como, secoli XVI–XVIII*, Turin.

Merzario, Raul, 1989, *Il capitalismo nelle montagne. Strategie familiari nella prima fase di industrializzazione nel Comasco*, Bologna.

Merzario, Raul, 1996a, 'Donne sole nelle valli e nelle montagne', in Groppi (ed.) 1996, pp. 229–46.

Merzario, Raul, 1996b, 'Famiglie di emigranti ticinesi (secoli XVII–XVIII)', *Società e storia*, XIX, no. 71, pp. 39–55.

Metken, Sigrid, 1996, *Der Kampf um die Hose. Geschlechterstreit und die Macht im Haus. Die Geschichte eines Symbols*, Frankfurt, New York and Paris.

Mezzanotte, Gianni, 1995, 'Edilizia abitativa a Milano nell'età illuministica', in Simoncini (ed.) 1995, vol. I, pp. 25–65.

Michel, Dominique, 1999, *Vatel et la naissance de la gastronomie*, Paris.

Michelle, Perrot, 1998, 'Les Femmes et la citoyenneté en France. Histoire d'une exclusion', in Les Femmes ou les silence de l'histoire', Paris, 1998, pp. 267–80 (first published in Armelle Le Bras-Chopard and Janine Mossuz-Lavau (eds), *Les Femmes et la politique*, Paris, 1997, pp. 23–39).

Milillo, Aurora, 1994, 'Il sistema alimentare nelle fiabe popolari europee. Note di gastronomia fiabesca', *La ricerca folklorica*, 30, pp. 51–8.

Mintz, Sidney, 1985, *Sweetness and Power. The Place of Sugar in Modern History*, New York (Ital. trans. *Storia dello zucchero. Tra politica e cultura*, Turin, 1990).

Mira, Giuseppe, 1940, *Vicende economiche di una famiglia italiana dal XV al XVII secolo*, Milan.

Mitterauer, Michael, 1981, 'Marriage without co-residence: a special type of historic family form in rural Carinthia', *Journal of Family History*, 6, pp. 177–81.

Mitterauer, Michael, 1990, 'Servants and youth', *Continuity and Change*, 5, pp. 11–38.

Mitterauer, Michael and Reinhard Sieder, 1977

(1984 3rd edn), *Vom Patriarchat zur Partnerschaft. Zum Strukturwandel der Familie*, Munich (Eng. trans. *The European Family. Patriarchy to Partnership from Middle Ages to the Present*, Oxford, 1982).

Molho, Anthony, Roberto Barducci, Gabriella Battista and Francesco Donnini, 1994, 'Genealogia e parentado. Memorie del potere nella Firenze tardo medievale. Il caso di Giovanni Rucellai', *Quaderni storici*, XXIX, no. 86, pp. 365–403.

Montagu, Mary, 1718 (1763 1st edn), *Turkish Letters* (French trans. *L'Islam au péril des femmes. Une Anglaise en Turquie au XVIIIe siècle*, Anne-Marie Moulin and Pierre Chuvin (trans), Paris, 1981).

Montanari, Massimo, 1991, *Nuovo Convivio. Storia e cultura dei piaceri della tavola nell'Età moderna*, Rome-Bari.

Montanari, Massimo, 1994 (1993 1st edn), *La fame e l'abbondanza. Storia dell'alimentazione in Europa*, Rome-Bari.

Montanari, Massimo, 1997, 'Condimento, fondamento. Le materie grasse nella tradizione alimentare europea', in Istituto Internazionale di Storia Economica F. Datini, Prato 1997, pp. 27–51.

Montenegro, Riccardo, 1996, *Abitare nei secoli. Storia dell'arredamento dal Rinascimento ad oggi*, Milan.

Morineau, Michel, 1996, 'Crescere senza sapere perché: strutture di produzione, demografia e razioni alimentari', in Flandrinand Montanari (eds) 1996 (but 1997), pp. 449–64.

Moroni, Gaetano, 1840–61, *Dizionario di erudizione storico-ecclesiastica da S. Pietro sino ai nostri giorni*, Venice, 109 vols.

Motis Dolander, Miguel Angel, 1997, 'L'alimentazione degli ebrei nel Medioevo', in Flandrin and Montanari (eds) 1996 (but 1997), pp. 282–300.

Mozzarelli, Cesare (ed.), 1988, *«Familia» del principe e famiglia aristocratica*, Rome, 2 vols.

Mukerji, Chandra, 1983, *From Graven Images. Patterns of Modern Materialism*, New York.

Mukerji, Chandra, 1993, 'Reading and writing with nature: a materialist approach to French formal gardens', in Brewer and Porter (eds) 1993, pp. 439–61.

Müller, Heidi, 1985, *Dienstbare Geister. Leben und Arbeitswelt städtischer Dienstboten*, Staatliche Museen Preußischer Kulturbesitz.

Muzzarelli, Giuseppina, 1999, *Guardaroba medievale. Vesti e società dal XIII al XVI secolo*, Bologna.

Muzzarelli, Maria Giuseppina, 1996, *Gli inganni delle apparenze. Disciplina delle vesti e ornamenti alla fine del Medioevo*, Turin.

Nadi, Gasparo (ed.), 1886, *Diario bolognese di Gaspare Nadi*, ed. Corrado Ricci and A. Bacchi Della Lega, Bologna (republished, Bologna 1981).

Nava, Paola (ed.), 1992, *Operaie, serve, maestre, impiegate*, Turin.

Nazarov, Vladislav, 1997, 'L'Alimentation d'élite de l'État Russe (XVe–XVIIe siècles)', in Istituto Internazionale di Storia Economica F. Datini, Prato 1997, pp. 841–49.

Niccoli, Ottavia, 1981, 'Lotte per le brache. La donna indisciplinata nelle stampe popolari d'Ancien Régime', in *Memoria*, 2, pp. 49–63.

Niccoli, Ottavia, 1991, 'Introduction' to *Rinascimento al femminile*, Ottavia Niccoli (ed.), Rome-Bari, pp. v–xxvii.

Niccoli, Ottavia, 1995, 'Baci rubati. Gesti e riti nuziali in Italia prima e dopo il Concilio di Trento', in Sergio Bertelli and Monica Centanni (eds), *Il gesto nel rito e nel cerimoniale dal mondo antico ad oggi*, Florence, pp. 224–47.

Niccoli, Ottavia, 1995, *Il seme della violenza. Putti, fanciulli, mammoli nell'Italia tra Cinque e Seicento*, Rome-Bari.

Niccoli, Ottavia, 2000, *Storie di ogni giorno in una città del Seicento*, Rome-Bari.

Nicoloso Ciceri, Andreina, 1994, 'Dote e controdote negli usi locali', in Corbellini (ed.) 1994, pp. 33–59.

Nigro, Giampiero, 1997, 'Mangiare di grasso, mangiare di magro. Il consumo di carni e pesci tra Medioevo ed Età moderna', in Istituto Internazionale di Storia Economica F. Datini, Prato 1997, pp. 111–46.

Ogilvie, Sheilagh C. (ed.), 1993, special issue on 'proto-industrialization', *Continuity and Change*, 8, pp. 149ff.

Opitz, Claudia, 1994, 'Neue Wege der Sozialgeschichte? Ein kritischer Blick auf Otto Brunners Konzept des "ganzen Hauses"', *Geschichte und Gesellschaft*, 20, pp. 88–98.

Ortu, Gian Giacomo, 1988, 'Zerakkus e zerakkas sardi', *Quaderni storici*, XXIII, no. 68, pp. 413–35.

Osswald, Helena, 1990, 'Dowry, norms, and household formation: a case study from north Portugal', *Journal of Family History*, 15, pp. 201–24.

Outram, Dorinda, 1995, *The Enlightenment*, Cambridge (Ital. trans. *L'Illuminismo*, Bologna, 1997).

Oxford English Dictionary 1989 (2nd edn), Oxford, 20 vols (Oxford 1989).

Ozment, Steven, 1983, *When Fathers Ruled. Family Life in Reformation Europe*, Cambridge, Mass. and London.

Ozment, Steven, 2001, *Ancestors: The Loving Family in Old Europe*, Cambridge.

Palazzi, Fernando and Gianfranco Folena, 1992, *Dizionario della lingua italiana*, Turin.

Palazzi, Maura, 1985, 'Pigioni e inquilini nella Bologna del '700: le locazioni delle "case e botteghe di città"', in *Popolazione ed economia dei territori bolognesi durante il Settecento. Atti del 38 colloquio, Bologna, 15 gennaio 1983*, Bologna, pp. 337–434.

Palazzi, Maura, 1986, 'Abitare da sole. Donne capofamiglia alla fine del Settecento', *Memoria*, 18, pp. 37–57.

Palazzi, Maura, 1988, 'Vivere a compagnia e vivere a dozzina. Gruppi domestici non coniugali nella Bologna di fine Settecento', in *Ragnatele di rapporti. Patronage e reti di relazione nella storia delle donne*, Lucia Ferrante, Maura Palazzi and Gianna Pomata (eds), Turin, pp. 344–80.

Palazzi, Maura, 1990a, '«Tessitrici; serve, treccole». Donne, lavoro efamiglia a Bologna nel Settecento', in Istituto Internazionale di Storia Economica F. Datini, Prato 1990, pp. 359–76.

Palazzi, Maura, 1990b, 'Female solitude and patrilineage: unmarried women and widows during the eighteenth and nineteenth centuries', *Journal of Family History*, 15, pp. 443–59 (Ital. trans. *Solitudini femmmili e patrilignaggio. Nubili e vedove tra Sette e Ottocento*, in Barbagli and Kertzer (eds) 1992, pp. 130–58).

Palazzi, Maura, 1992, 'Donne povere tra lavoro, assistenza e «sigurtà». Tessitrici e filatrici della Casa d'industria e della Casa provinciale di lavoro (Bologna XVIII secolo)', in Nava (ed.) 1992, pp. 202–36.

Palazzi, Maura, 1992–93, 'Rotture di equilibri tradizionali nelle relazioni fra i sessi. I nuovi ruoli familiari e lavorativi delle donne contadine durante la crisi agraria', *Annali*, Istituto Alcide Cervi, 14–15, pp. 167–203.

Palazzi, Maura, 1997, *Donne sole. Storia dell'altra faccia dell'Italia tra antico regime e società contemporanea*, Milan.

Palumbo, Genoveffa, 1996, 'Per amore e per denaro', in *Donne e proprietà* 1996, pp. 105–68.

Palumbo-Fossati, Isabella, 1984, 'L'interno della casa dell'artigiano e dell'artista nella Venezia del Cinquecento', *Studi Veneziani*, VIII, pp. 109–53.

Palumbo Fossati, Isabella, 1995, 'Gli interni della casa veneziana nel Settecento: continuità e trasformazioni', in Simoncini (ed.) 1995, vol. I, pp. 165–79.

Paquet, Dominique, 1997, *Miroir, mon beau miroir. Une Histoire de la beauté*, Paris (Ital. trans. *Storia della bellezza. Canoni, rituali, belletti*, Milan, 1997).

Pardailhé-Galabrun, Annik, 1988, *La Naissance de l'intime. 3000 foyers parisiens XVIIe–XVIIIe siècles*, Paris.

Pasquali, Giorgio, 1939, '«Vin da famiglia»', *Lingua Nostra*, I, pp. 35–8.

Pastore, Alessandro, 2000, 'Il problema dei poveri agli inizi dell'età moderna. Linee generali', in Zamagni (ed.) 2000, pp. 185–205.

Pelaja, Margherita, 1994, *Matrimonio e sessualità a Roma nell'Ottocento*, Rome.

Pelaja, Margherita, 1996, 'La promessa', in De Giorgio and Klapisch-Zuber (eds) 1996, pp. 391–417.

Pellati, Francesco, 1929, 'Acquedotto. I. Storia', in *Enciclopedia Italiana*, Rome-Bari, vol. I, pp. 382–9.

Pepoli Sampieri, Anna, 1838, *La donna saggia e amabile*, Capolago.

Pescarolo, Alessandra, 1990 (but 1992), 'L'identità ambivalente: le trecciaiole toscane', *Annali*, Istituto Alcide Cervi, 12, pp. 147–64.

Pfister, Ulrich, 2001, 'Proto-Industrialization', in Barbagli and Kertzer (eds) 2001, pp. 63–84.

Phillips, Roderick, 1991, *Untying the Knot. A Short History of Divorce*, Cambridge and Melbourne.

Pianigiani, Ottorino, 1907, *Vocabolario etimologico della lingua italiana*, Rome and Milan, 2 vols.

Plakans, Andrej, 1975, 'Seigneural authority and peasant family life: the Baltic area in the eighteenth century', *Journal of Interdisciplinary History*, 5, pp. 629–54.

Plakans, Andrej, 1983, 'The familial context of early childhood in Baltic serf society', in Wall, Robin and Laslett 1983, pp. 167–206.

Plakans, Andrej and Charles Wetherell, 1997,

'Auf der Suche nach einer Verortnung. Die Geschichte der Familie in Osteuropa, 1800–2000', in Ehmer, Hareven and Wall (eds) 1997, pp. 301–25.

Pollock, Linda A., 1993, 'Living on the stage of the world: the concept of privacy among the elite of early modern England', in *Rethinking Social History. English Society 1570–1920 and its Interpretation*, Adrian Wilson (ed.), Manchester.

Pollock, Linda A., 2001, 'Parent–Child Relations', in Barbagli and Kertzer (eds) 2001, pp. 191–220.

Pomata, Gianna, 1980, 'Madri illegittime tra Ottocento e Novecento: storie cliniche e storie di vita', *Quaderni storici*, XV, no. 44, pp. 497–542.

Pomata, Gianna, 1983, 'La storia delle donne: una questione di confine', in *Il mondo contemporaneo*, Giovanni De Luna, Peppino Ortoleva, Marco Revelli and Nicola Tranfaglia (eds), *Gli strumenti della ricerca – 2 Questioni di metodo**, Florence, pp. 1434–69.

Pomata, Gianna, 1994a, *La promessa di guarigione. Malati e curatori in Antico Regime*, Rome-Bari.

Pomata, Gianna, 1994b, 'Legami di sangue, legami di seme. Consanguineità e agnazione nel diritto romano', *Quaderni storici*, XXIX, no. 86, pp. 299–334.

Pomata, Gianna, 1995, 'La «meravigliosa armonia». Il rapporto fra seni ed utero dall'anatomia vascolare all'endocrinologia', in Fiume (ed.) 1995, pp. 45–81.

Poni, Carlo, 1976, 'All'origine del sistema di fabbrica: tecnologia e organizzazione produttiva dei mulini da seta nell'Italia settentrionale (sec. XVII–XVIII)', *Rivista Storica Italiana*, 88, pp. 444–97.

Poni, Carlo, 1982, *La famiglia contadina e dpodere in Emilia Romagna*, in *Fossi e cavedagne benedicon le campagne. Studi di storia rurale*, Bologna, pp. 283–356.

Poni, Carlo, 1994, 'Tecnologie, organizzazione produttiva e divisione sessuale del lavoro: il caso dei mulini da seta', in Groppi (ed.) 1996, pp. 269–96.

Pounds, Norman J.G., 1979, *An Historical Geography of Europe 1500–1840*, Cambridge.

Pounds, Norman J.G., 1989, *Hearth & Home. A History of Material Culture*, Bloomington.

Povolo, Claudio, 1994, 'Eredità anticipata o esclusione per causa di dote?', in *Padre e figlia*, Luisa Accati, Marina Cattaruzza and Monica Verzar Bass (eds), Turin, pp. 41–73.

Praz, Mario, 1964 (ed. 1993), *La filosofia dell'arredamento*, Milan.

Priestley, Ursula, Penelope Corfield and H. Sutermeister, 1982, 'Rooms and room use in Norwich housing, 1580–1730', *Post-Medieval Archaeology*, 16, pp. 93–123.

Prodi, Paolo (ed.), 1994, *Disciplina dell'anima, disciplina del corpo e disciplina della società tra Medioevo ed Età moderna*, Bologna.

Prosperi, Adriano, 1981, 'Intellettuali e Chiesa all'inizio dell'Età moderna', in *Storia d'Italia*, IV, *Intellettuali e potere*, Corrado Vivanti (ed.), Turin, pp. 159–252.

Pullan, Brian, 1978, 'Poveri, mendicanti e vagabondi (secoli XIV–XVII)', in *Storia d'Italia*, I, *Dal feudalesimo al capitalismo*, Turin, pp. 981–1047.

Radin, Max, 1914, 'Gens, familia, stirps', *Classical Philology*, IX, pp. 235–47.

Raggio, Osvaldo, 1990, *Faide e parentele. Lo stato genovese visto dalla Fontanabuona*, Turin.

Raggio, Osvaldo, 1995, 'Visto dalla periferia. Formazioni politiche di antico regime e lo Stato moderno', in Aymard (ed.) 1995, pp. 483–527.

Raison, Jean-Pierre, 1977, 'Abitazione', in *Enciclopedia*, Turin, vol. I, pp. 115–45.

Ranum, Orest, 1986 (Ital. trans. 1987), 'I rifugi dell'intimità', in Ariès and Duby (series eds) 1986 (Ital. trans. 1987), pp. 161–204.

Rapoport, Amos, 1969, *House, Form and Culture*, Englewood Cliffs, N.J. (French trans. *Pour une anthropologie de la maison*, Paris, 1972).

Rassem, Mohammed, 1982 (but 1984), 'Riflessioni sul disciplinamento sociale nella prima Età moderna con esempi dalla storia della statistica', *Annali dell'Istituto storico italogermanico in Trento*, VIII, pp. 39–70.

Ravis-Giordani, Georges and Martine Segalen (eds), 1994, *Les Cadets*, Paris.

Razi, Zvi, 1993, 'The myth of the immutable English family', *Past and Present*, 140, pp. 3–45.

Real Academia Española 1992 (21st edn), *Diccionario de la lengua española*, Madrid.

Rebora, Giovanni, 1998, *La civiltà della forchetta. Storie di cibi e di cucina*, Rome-Bari.

Reher, David Sven, 1998, 'Family ties in western Europe: persistent contrasts', *Population and Development Review*, 24, pp. 203–35.

Revel, Jacques, 1975, 'Les Privilèges d'une

capitale: l'approvisionnement de Rome à l'époque moderne', *Mélanges de l'École Française de Rome. Moyen Âge–Temps Modernes*, 87, pp. 461–93.

Revel, Jacques, 1986 (Ital. trans. 1987), 'Gli «usi» delle buone maniere', in Ariès and Duby (series eds) 1986 (Ital. trans. 1987), pp. 125–60.

Revel, Jacques, 1994, 'Microanalisi e storia del sociale', *Quaderni storici*, XXIX, no. 86, pp. 549–75.

Ribeiro, Aileen, 1984, *Dress in Eighteenth Century Europe 1715–1789*, London.

Ricci, Corrado, 1891, *Una illustre avventuriera (Cristina di Nortumbria)*, Milan.

Ricci, Gianni, 1996, *Povertà, vergogna, superbia. I declassati fra Medioevo e Età moderna*, Bologna.

Ricci, Piero, 1994, '«Stare al segno». Ovvero la graziosa gestualità del trinciante', in *Nomi, pieghe, tracce. Studi di semiologia della cultura*, Urbino, 1994, pp. 105–21.

Riforma de' Capitoli, e Statuti della Congregazione di S. Vitale detta l'Università de' Servitori In Bologna Fatta l'Anno 1719, Bologna, 1719 (*Riforma* 1719).

Robert, Paul, 1953–64, *Dictionnaire alphabétique et analogique de la Langue Française*, Paris, 6 vols.

Roche, Daniel, 1981, *Le Peuple de Paris. Essai sur la culture populaire au XVIIIe siècle*, Paris.

Roche, Daniel, 1989, *La Culture des apparences. Une Histoire du vêtement (XVIIe–XVIIIe siècle)*, Paris (Ital. trans. *Il linguaggio della moda*, Turin, 1991).

Roche, Daniel, 1997, *Histoire des choses banales. Naissance de la consommation XVIIe–XIXe siècle*, Paris (Ital. trans. *Storia delle cose banali: La nascita del consumo in Occidente*, Rome, 1999).

Rogers, John, 1993, 'Nordic family history, themes and issues, old and new', *Journal of Family History*, 18, pp. 291–314.

Romani, Marzio Achille, 1975, *Nella spirale di una crisi: popolazione, mercato e prezzi a Parma tra Cinque e Seicento*, Milan.

Romani, Marzio Achille, 1997, 'Regalis coena: aspetti economici e sociali del pasto principesco (Italia settentrionale, secoli XVI–XIX)', in Istituto Internazionale di Storia Economica F. Datini, Prato 1997, pp. 719–40.

Romano, Ruggiero (ed.), 1991, *Storia dell'economia italiana*, II, *L'Età moderna: verso la crisi*, Turin.

Roper, Lyndal, 1985, '"Going to church and street": wedding in Reformation Augsburg', *Past and Present*, 106, pp. 62–101.

Roper, Lyndal, 1989, *The Holy Household. Religion, Morals and Order in Reformation Augsburg*, Oxford.

Rosanvallon, Pierre, 1992, *Le Sacre du citoyen. Du Suffrage universel en France*, Paris (Ital. trans. *La rivoluzione dell'uguaglianza. Storia del suffragio universale in Francia*, Milan, 1994).

Rosati, Claudio, 1995, 'Cuocere il cibo, cuocere la legna. Contaminazione tra pratiche di cottura della legna e pratiche di cottura alimentare', *La ricerca folklorica*, 30, pp. 33–7.

Rosenberg, Charles E. (ed.), 1975, *The Family in History*, Philadelphia (Ital. trans. *La famiglia nella storia. Comportamenti sociali e ideali domestici*, Turin, 1979).

Rösener, Werner, 1995, *I contadini nella storia d'Europa*, Rome-Bari.

Rosental, Paul-André, 1999, *Les Sentiers invisibles. Espaces, familles et migrations dans la France du 19e siècle*, Paris.

Rosental, Paul-André, 2000, 'Les Liens familiaux, forme historique?', in *Annales de démographie historique*, fasc. 2, pp. 49–81.

Rosselli, Donatella, 1996, '«Tamquam bruta animalia». L'immagine dei vagabondi a Roma tra Cinque e Seicento', *Quaderni storici*, XXXI, no. 92, pp. 363–404.

Roux, Simone, 1976, *La Maison dans l'histoire*, Paris (Ital. trans. *La casa nella storia*, Rome, 1982).

Rowland, Robert, 1987, 'Nupcialidade, familia, Mediterraneo', *Bollettino di Demografia Storica*, 5, pp. 128–43.

Rudolph, Richard L., 1992, 'The European family and economy: central themes and issues', *Journal of Family History*, 17, pp. 119–38.

Rybczynski, Witold, 1986 *Home. A Short History of an Idea*, New York.

Rykwert, Joseph, 1991, 'House and home', *Social Research*, 58, pp. 51–68.

Saavedra, Pegerto, 1994 (1992 1st edn), *La vida cotidiana en la Galicia del antiguo régimen*, Critica.

Sabean, David Warren, 1990, *Property, Production, and Family in Neckarhausen, 1700–1870*, Cambridge.

Sabean, David Warren, 1997, *Kinship in Neckarhausen 1700–1870*, New York.

Salaman, Roger N., 1985 (1948 1st edn), *The*

History and Social Influence of the Potato, Cambridge (Ital. trans. *Storia sociale della patata*, Milan, 1989).

Salvati, Mariuccia, 1995, 'A proposito di salotti', in Gagliani and Salvati (eds) 1995, pp. 43–659.

Salvatici, Silvia, 1995, 'Un mondo in affanno: famiglie agricole nell'Italia fascista', *Passato e Presente*, no. 36, pp. 93–115.

Sanga, Glauco, 1995, 'Il ritmo "paleolitico" dei marginali', *La ricerca folklorica*, 30, pp. 39–40.

Sarti, Raffaella, 1988, *Ricerche sulla servitù domestica a Bologna nell'Ottocento*, Tesi di laurea, Università degli studi di Bologna.

Sarti, Raffaella, 1991, 'Obbedienti e fedeli. Note sull'istruzione morale e religiosa di servi e serve tra Cinque e Settecento', *Annali dell'Istituto storico italo-germanico in Trento*, XVII, pp. 91–120.

Sarti, Raffaella, 1992, 'Servire al femminile, servire al maschile nella Bologna sette-ottocentesca', in Nava (ed.) 1992, pp. 237–64.

Sarti, Raffaella, 1994a, 'Per una storia del personale domestico in Italia. Il caso di Bologna (secc. XVIII–XIX)', doctoral thesis, in *Storia (Storia della società europea)*, Università degli Studi di Torino, examined on 28 September 1994.

Sarti, Raffaella, 1994b, 'Dalla famiglia servile alla famiglia coniugale. Prime considerazioni', paper read at the international conference *Mutamenti della famiglia nei paesi occidentali*, Bologna, 6–8 October (V Session: 'Serve e servi').

Sarti, Raffaella, 1994c, 'Donne e famiglia. A margine di un volume sul caso friulano', *Rassegna degli Archivi di Stato*, 3, pp. 675–88.

Sarti, Raffaella, 1994d, 'Zita, serva e santa. Un modello da imitare?', in *Modelli di santità e modelli di comportamento. Contrasti, intersezioni, complementarità*, Giulia Barone, Marina Caffiero and Francesco Scorza Barcellona (eds), Turin, pp. 307–59.

Sarti, Raffaella, 1995, 'Spazi domestici e identità di genere tra Età moderna e contemporanea', in Gagliani and Salvati (eds) 1995, pp. 13–41.

Sarti, Raffaella, 1997a, 'Notes on the feminization of domestic service. Bologna as a case study (18th–19th centuries)', in *Le Phénomène de la domesticité en Europe, XVIe–XXe siècles* (Acta Demographica, XIII), Antoinette Fauve-Chamoux and Ludmila Fialová (eds), Prague, pp. 125–63.

Sarti, Raffaella, 1997b, 'Il servizio domestico come problema storiografico', *Storia e Problemi Contemporanei*, 20, pp. 159–84.

Sarti, Raffaella, 1999a, 'L'Università dei Servitori di Bologna, secc. XVII–XIX, in *Corporazioni e gruppi professionali nell'Italia moderna*, Guenzi, Massa and Moioli (eds), 1999, pp. 717–54.

Sarti, Raffaella, 1999b, 'Viaggiatrici per forza. Schiave «turche» in Italia in Età moderna', in *Altrove. Viaggi di donne dall'antichità al Novecento*, Dinora Corsi (ed.), Rome, pp. 241–96.

Sarti, Raffaella, 1999c, 'Comparir con «equipaggio in scena». Servizio domestico e prestigio nobiliare (Bologna, fine XVII–inizio XIX secolo)', *Cheiron*, XVI, nos 31–2, pp. 133–69.

Sarti, Raffaella, 2001, 'Telling Zita's tale. Holy servants' stories and servants' history', in *Narratives of the Servant*, Regina Schulte and Pothiti Hantzaroula (eds), Florence, pp. 1–30.

Sarti, Raffaella, 2002 (forthcoming), 'Quali diritti per «la donna»?', in *Lavoratrici e cittadine*, Maura Palazzi and Simonetta Soldani (eds), Turin.

Saurer, Edith, 1997, 'Geschlechterbeziehungen, Ehe und Illegitimität in der Habsburgermonarchie. Venetien, Niederösterreich und Böhmen im frühen 19. Jahrhundert', in Ehmer, Hareven and Wall (eds) 1997, pp. 123–51.

Scarabello, Giovanni, 1987, 'Pauperismo, criminalità e istituzioni repressive', in Tranfaglia and Firpo (eds) 1987, pp. 113–32.

Scaraffia, Lucetta, 1993, *Rinnegati. Per una storia dell'identità occidentale*, Rome-Bari.

Scaraffia, Lucetta and Gabriella Zarri (eds), 1994, *Donne e fede. Santità e vita religiosa in Italia*, Rome-Bari.

Scardozzi, Mirella, 1998, 'Tra due codici: i contratti dotali nella Toscana preunitaria', in Calvi and Chabot (eds) 1998, pp. 95–120.

Schama, Simon, 1987, *The Embarrassment of Riches*, New York (Ital. trans. *La cultura olandese del secolo d'oro*, Milan, 1988).

Schama, Simon, 1993, 'Perishable commodities: Dutch still-life paintings and the "empire of things"', in Brewer and Porter (eds) 1993, pp. 478–88.

Schenda, Rudolf, 1986, *Folklore e letteratura popolare: Italia – Germania – Francia*, Rome.

Schenda, Rudolf, 1987, 'Leggere ad alta voce: tra analfabetismo e sapere libresco. Aspetti sociali e culturali di comunicazione semiletteraria', in *La ricerca folklorica*, 15, pp. 5–10.

Schereschewsky, Ben-Zion (Benno), 1972, 'Husband and wife', in *Encyclopaedia Judaica*, Jerusalem, vol. VIII, cols 1120–8.

Schereschewsky, Ben-Zion (Benno) and Editorial Staff, 1971, 'Dowry', in *Encyclopaedia Judaica*, Jerusalem, vol. VI, cols 186–9.

Schindler, Norbert, 1994, 'I tutori del disordine. Rituali della cultura giovanile agli inizi dell'età moderna', in Levi and Schmitt (eds) 1994, vol. I, pp. 303–74.

Schlumbohm, Jürgen, 1998, 'Strong myths and flexible practices: house and stem family in Germany', in Fauve-Chamoux and Ochiai (eds) 1998, pp. 44–57.

Schuller, Alexander and Anna Jutta Kleber (eds), 1994, *Verschlemmte Welt. Essen und Trinken historisch-anthropologisch*, Göttingen-Zurich.

Schuurman, Anton J. and Pieter Spierenburg (eds) 1996, *Private Domain, Public Inquiry. Families and Life-styles in the Netherlands and Europe 1550 to the Present*, Hilversum.

Schuurrnan, Anton J. and Lorena Walsh (eds), 1994, *Material Culture: Consumption, Lifestyle, Standard of Living, 1500–1900*, B4 Proceedings 11th International Economic History Congress, September 1994, Milan.

Schwab, Dieter, 1979 (1975 1st edn), 'Familie', in *Geschichtliche Grundbegriffe. Historisches Lexikon zur politisch-sozialen Sprache in Deutschland*, Otto Brunner, Werner Conze and Reinhardt Koselleck (eds), Stuttgart, 1972–1992, 7 vols, vol. II, pp. 253–301.

Schwarz, Gabriele, 1989 (4th edn), *Allgemeine Siedlungsgeographie*, Berlin and New York.

Schwarzenberg, Claudio, 1982, 'Patria potestà (diritto intermedio)', in *Encylopedia del diritto*, Milan, vol. XXXII, pp. 248–55.

Scott, Joan Wallach, 1989, 'French feminists and the rights of "Man": Olympe de Gouges's declarations', *History Workshop*, 28, pp. 1–21 (Ital. trans. in *Il primo femminismo (1791–1834)*, Anna Rossi-Doria (ed.), Milan 1993, pp. 93–118).

Scott, Joan Wallach and Louise A. Tilly, 1975 (Ital. trans. 1979), 'Lavoro femminile nell'Europa del XIX secolo', in Rosenberg (ed.) 1975 (Ital. trans. 1979), pp. 185–227.

Segalen, Martine, 1981 (in collaboration with Josselyne Charmat), *Amours et mariages de l'ancienne France*, Paris.

Segalen, Martine, 1991, *Jeux de familles*, Paris.

Seidel Menchi, Silvana and Diego Quaglioni (eds), 2000, *Coniugi nemici. La separazione in Italia dal XII al XVIII secolo*, Bologna.

Sereni, Emilio, 1981 (1958 1st edn), 'Note di storia dell'alimentazione nel Mezzogiorno: i Napoletani da "mangiafoglia" a "mangiamaccheroni"' in *Terra nuova e buoi rossi e altri saggi per una storia dell'agricoltura*, Turin, 1982, pp. 292–371.

Serlio, Sebastiano (ed.), 1994, *Architettura civile. Libri sesto settimo e ottavo nei manoscritti di Monaco e Vienna*, ed. Francesco Paolo Fiore, Milan.

Serventi, Silvano and Françoise Sabban, 2000, *La pasta: storia e cultura di un cibo universale*, Rome-Bari.

Sewell Jr., William H., 1980, *Work and Revolution in France. The Language of Labour from the Old Regime to 1848*, Cambridge (Ital. trans. *Lavoro e rivoluzione in Francia. Il linguaggio operaio dall'ancien régime al 1848*, Bologna, 1987).

Shammas, Carole, 1983, 'Food expenditure and economic well-being in early modern England', *Journal of Economic History*, 43, pp. 89–100.

Shammas, Carole, 1989, 'Explaining past changes in consumption and consumer behavior', *Historical Methods*, 22, pp. 61–7.

Shammas, Carole, 1993, 'Changes in English and Anglo-American consumption from 1550–1800', in Brewer and Porter (eds) 1993, pp. 177–205.

Shammas, Carole, 1994, 'The decline of textile prices in England and British America prior to industrialization', *Economic History Review*, 48, pp. 483–507.

Shilo, Shmuel, 1971, 'Succession', in *Encyclopaedia Judaica*, Jerusalem, vol. XV, cols 475–81.

Shorter, Edward, 1978, *The Making of the Modern Family*, New York (Ital. trans. *Famiglia e civiltà. L'evoluzione del matrimonio e il destino della famiglia nella storia occidentale*, Milan, 1978.

Sieder, Reinhardt and Michael Mitterauer, 1983, 'The reconstruction of the family life-course: theoretical problems and empirical results' (Ital. trans. 'La ricostruzione del corso di vita della famiglia: problemi teorici e risultati empirici'), in Wall, Robin and Laslett (eds) 1983 (Ital. trans. 1984), pp. 193–230.

Simoncini, Giorgio (ed.), 1995, *L'uso dello spazio domestico nell'età dell'Illuminismo*, Florence, 2 vols.

Simoncini, Giorgio, 1995, 'Residenze signorili, popolari e borghesi fra tardo Seicento e fine Settecento', in Simoncini (ed.) 1995, Vol. I, pp. 1–24.

Simon-Muscheid, Katharina, 1993, '"Und ob schon einen dienst finden, so sind sie nit bekleidet dernoch". Die Kleidung städtischer Unterschichten zwischen Projektionen und Realität im spätmittelalter und in der frühen Neuzeit', in *Saeculum*, 44, pp. 47–64.

Simon-Muscheid, Katharina, 1997, 'La Faim et l'aboundance. Les Repas dans la mémoire: les autobiographies des XVe et XVIe siècles', in Istituto Internazionale di Storia Economica F. Datini, Prato 1997, pp. 339–49.

Smith, Peter, 1985, 'Rural building in Wales', in Thirsk (ed.) 1985, pp. 686–810.

Società Italiana di Demografia Storica 1990, *Popolazione, società e ambiente. Temi di demografia storica italiana (secc. XVII-XIX). Relazioni e comunicazioni presentate da Autori italiani al I Congrés Hispano Luso Italià de Demografía Histórica, Barcellona, 22–25 aprile 1987*, Bologna.

Sogner, Sølvi and Hilde Sandvik, 1990, 'Minors in law, partners in work, equals in worth? Women in the Norwegian economy in the 16th to the 18th centuries', in Istituto Internazionale di Storia Economica F. Datini, Prato 1990, pp. 633–53.

Soldani, Simonetta (ed.), 2002, "Italiane! Appartenenza nazionale e cittadinanza negli scritti delle donne del Risorgimento", in *Genesis. Rivista della Società italiana delle Storiche*, 1, pp. 85–124.

Soler, Jean, 1997, 'Le ragioni della Bibbia: le norme alimentari ebraiche', in Flandrin and Montanari (eds) 1996 (but 1997), pp. 46–55.

Somogyi, Stefano, 1973, 'L'alimentazione nell'Italia unita', in *Storia d'Italia*, V, I, Turin, pp. 839–87.

Sorcinelli, Paolo, 1998, *Storia sociale dell'acqua. Riti e culture*, Milan.

Sori, Ercole, 2001, *La città e i rifiuti. Ecologia urbana dal medioevo al primo Novecento*, Bologna.

Spode, Hasso, 1991, *Alkohol und Zivilisation. Berauschung, Ernüchterung und Tischsitten in Deutschland bis zum Beginn des 20. Jahrhunderts*, Berlin.

Spode, Hasso, 1994, 'Von der Hand zum Gabel. Zur Geschichte der Eßwerkzeuge', in Schuller and Kleber (eds) 1994, pp. 20–46.

Spufford, Margaret, 1976, 'Peasant inheritance customs and land distribution in Cambridgeshire from the sixteenth to the eighteenth century', in Goody, Thirsk and Thompson (eds) 1976, pp. 156–76.

Spufford, Margaret, 1984, *The Great Reclothing of Rural England. Petty Chapmen and their Wares in the Seventeenth Century*, London.

Stearns, Peter N., 1997, 'Stages of consumerism: recent work on the issues of periodization', *Journal of Modern History*, 69, pp. 102–17.

Stols, Eddy, 1997, 'Habitudes et variations alimentaires au quotidien. Échanges et rejets culinaires du Nord au Sud et du Sud au Nord. XVIe–XVIIe', in Istituto Internazionale di Storia Economica F. Datini, Prato 1997, pp. 217–46.

Stone, Lawrence, 1977, *The Family, Sex and Marriage in England 1500–1800*, London (Ital. trans. *Famiglia, sesso e matrimonio in Inghilterra tra Cinque e Ottocento*, Turin, 1983).

Stone, Lawrence, 1990, *Road to Divorce. England 1530–1987*, Oxford, New York and Toronto.

Stone, Lawrence and Jeanne C. Fawtier Stone, 1984 and 1986, *An Open Elite? England 1540–1880*, Oxford (Ital. trans. *Una élite aperta? L'Inghilterra fra 1540 e 1880*, Bologna, 1989).

Styles, John, 1993, 'Manufacturing, consumption and design in eighteenth century England', in Brewer and Porter (eds) 1993, pp. 527–54.

Tadmor, Naomi, 1996, 'The concept of the household-family in eighteenth century England', *Past and Present*, 151, pp. 111–40.

Tamburini, Patrizia, 1988, 'Rilevamenti e campionature di tipologie primitive in Emilia Romagna', in Cataldi (ed.) 1988, pp. 197–226.

Tasso, Torquato, 1969 (1583 1st edn), *Dialoghi*, II, *Il padre di famiglia*, in Torquato Tasso, *Opere*, ed. Ettore Mazzali, Naples, vol. II, pp. 503–66.

Taylor, J.W., 1996, 'Bed', in *The Dictionary of Art*, London and New York, 1996, vol. III, pp. 482–85.

Teti, Vito, 1978 (1976 1st edn), *Il pane, la beffa e*

la festa. Cultura alimentare e ideologia dell'alimentazione nelle classi subalterne, Florence.

Teuteberg, Hans Jürgen (ed.), 1985, *Homo Habitans. Zur Sozialgeschichte des ländlichen und städtischen Wohnens in der Neuzeit,* Münster.

Thesaurus linguae latinae editus auctoritate et consilio academiarum quinque germanicarum berolinensis gottingensis lipsiensis monacensis vindoboniensis 1900–, in aedibus B.G. Teubneri, Lipsiae, vols. I–X/2 (Thesaurus 1900–).

Thirsk, Joan (ed.), 1985, *The Agrarian History of England and Wales,* 5, Cambridge.

Thirsk, Joan, 1997, 'The preparation of food in the kitchen, in Europe north of the Alps, 1500–1700', in Istituto Internazionale di Storia Economica F. Datini, Prato 1997, pp. 423–39.

Thomas, Yan, 1990, 'La divisione dei sessi nel diritto romano', in Georges Duby and Michelle Perrot (series eds), *Storia delle donne. L'antichità,* Pauline Schmitt Pantel (ed.), Rome-Bari, 1990, pp. 103–76.

Thompson, Edward P., 1977, 'Happy Families', in *New Society,* 8 September, pp. 499–501.

Thompson, Edward P. 1991, 'The sale of wives', in Id., *Customs in Common,* New York, pp. 404–66.

Thornton, Dora, 1997, *The Scholar in His Study: Ownership and Experience in Renaissance Italy,* New Haven and London.

Thornton, Peter, 1991, *The Italian Renaissance Interiors,* New York (Ital. trans. *Interni italiani del Rinascimento,* Milan, 1992).

Tilly, Louise and Joan Wallach Scott, 1978, *Women, Work and Family,* New York (Ital. trans. *Donne, lavoro e famiglia nell'evoluzione della società capitalistica,* Bari, 1981).

Tilly, Louise, Joan Wallach Scott and Miriam Cohen, 1976, 'Women's work and European fertility pattern', *Journal of Interdisciplinary History,* VI, pp. 447–76.

Toaff, Ariel, 1996, *La vita materiale,* in *Storia d'Italia,* XI, *Gli ebrei in Italia,* Corrado Vivanti (ed.), I. *Dall'alto Medioevo all'età dei ghetti,* Turin, pp. 237–63.

Toaff, Ariel, 2000, *Mangiare alla giudia. La cucina ebraica in Italia dal Rinascimento all'età moderna,* Bologna.

Tobler, Adolf and Erhard Lommatzsch, 1925–26, *Altfranzösisches Wörterbuch,* Wiesbaden.

Tocci, Giovanni, 1988, '"Forma urbis" e modi di vita nelle città', in *Vita civile degli italiani. Società, economia e cultura materiale. Mentalità, comportamenti e istituzioni tra Rinascimento e decadenza 1550–1700,* Giuseppe Galasso (ed.), Milan, pp. 118–39.

Tocci, Giovanni, 1997, 'Piccole e grandi città negli Stati italiani (secoli XV–XVII)', in *Giovanni Pico della Mirandola. Convegno internazionale di studi nel cinquecentesimo anniversario della morte (1494–1994), Mirandola, 4–8 ottobre 1994,* Gian Carlo Garfagnini (ed.), Florence, pp. 53–94.

Todd, Emmanuel, 1990, *L'Invention de l'Europe,* Paris.

Todorova, Maria, 1998, 'Zum erkenntnistheoretischen Wert von Familienmodellen. Der Balkan und die "europäische Familie"', in Ehmer, Hareven and Wall (eds) 1997, pp. 283–300.

Tommaseo, Niccolò, 1851–52, *Nuovo dizionario dei sinonimi della lingua italiana,* Milan (2nd Milanese edn), 2 vols.

Tommaseo, Niccolò and Bellini Bernardo, 1865–79, *Dizionario della lingua italiana,* L'Unione tipografico-editrice torinese, Rome and Naples, 4 vols, 7 tomes.

Tommasi, Francesco, 1580, *Reggimento del Padre di Famiglia,* Florence.

Torti, Cristiana, 1989, 'Economia di borghi e mestieri delle donne: la pluriattività femminile a Calcinaia e Santa Croce sull'Arno tra Settecento e Ottocento', *Annali,* Istituto Alcide Cervi, 11, pp. 113–22.

Tosh, John, 2000, 'Maschilità e genere nell'Inghilterra vittoriana', *Quaderni storici,* XXXXV, no. 105, pp. 803–22.

Tranfaglia, Nicola and Massimo Firpo (eds), 1987, *La storia. I grandi problemi dal Medioevo all'Età Contemporanea,* III, *L'Età moderna,* I, *I quadri generali,* Turin.

Trésor de la Langue Française. Dictionnaire de la langue du XIXe et du XXe siècle (1789–1960) 1980, Paris (Tresor 1980).

Trumbach, Randolph, 1978, *The Rise of Egalitarian Family. Aristocratic Kinship and Domestic Relations in Eighteenth-Century England,* New York, San Francisco and London (Ital. trans. *La nascita della famiglia egualitaria. Lignaggio e famiglia nell'aristocrazia del '700 inglese,* Bologna, 1982).

Turchi, Laura, 1998, 'L'eredità della madre. Un conflitto giuridico nello stato estense alla fine del Cinquecento', in Calvi and Chabot (eds), pp. 161–85.

Ungari, Paolo, 1974 (1970 1st edn), *Storia del diritto di famiglia in Italia (1796–1942)*, Bologna.

Valeri, Renée, 1977, 'Alimentazione', in *Enciclopedia*, Turin, vol. I, pp. 344–61.

Van Gennep, Arnold, 1909, *Les Rites de passage*, Paris (Ital. trans. *I riti di passaggio*, Turin, 1981).

Van Gennep, Arnold, 1980–82 (1943–46 1st edn), *Manuel de folklore français contemporain. Tome premier, I. Introduction générale et première partie: du berceau à la tombe: naissance – baptîme – enfance – adolescence – fiançailles*; II. *Du berceau à la tombe (fin): mariage – funérailles*, Paris.

Van Uytven, Raymond, 1997, 'Le Combat des boissons en Europe du moyen âge au XVIII siècle', in Istituto Internazionale di Storia Economica F. Datini, Prato 1997, pp. 53–89.

Vanneste, Dominique, 1986, 'Le Logement et la différenciation sociale et résidentielle dans la ville pré-industrielle en Europe occidentale (XVIᵉ–XVIIIᵉ)', *Espace Populations Sociétés*, I, pp. 125–36.

Vauchez, André, 1975, 1990, 'I cambiamenti del sistema assistenziale negli ultimi secoli del Medioevo', in *Ordini mendicanti e società italiana, XIII–XV secolo*, Milan, 1990, pp. 231ff.

Vauchez, André, 1981, *La Sainteté en Occident aux derniers siècles du Moyen Âge*, Rome (Ital. trans. *La santità nel Medioevo*, Bologna, 1989).

Veblen, Thornstein, 1899, *The `Theory of the Leisure Class*, New York and London (Ital. trans. 'La teoria della classe agiata' in Thornstein Veblen, *Opere*, ed. F. De Domenico, Turin, 1969. pp. 65–347).

Verdon, Michel, 1996, 'Rethinking complex households: the case of the Western Pyrenean "Houses"', *Continuity and Change*, 11, pp. 191–215.

Viazzo, Pier Paolo, 1989, *Upland Communities. Environment Population and Social Structure in the Alps since the Sixteenth Century*, Cambridge and New York (Ital. trans. *Comunita alpine*, Bologna, 1990).

Viazzo, Pier Paolo, 2001, 'Mortality, Fertility, and Family', in Barbagli and Kertzer (eds) 2001, pp. 157–87.

Vickery, Amanda, 1993a, 'Golden age to separate spheres? A review of the categories and chronology of English women's history', *Historical Journal*, 36, pp. 383–414.

Vickery, Amanda, 1993b, 'Women and the world of goods: a Lancashire consumer and her possessions', in Brewer and Porter (eds) 1993, pp. 274–301.

Vigarello, Georges, 1985, *Le Propre et le sale. L'Hygiène du corps depuis le Moyen Âge*, Paris (Ital. trans. *Lo sporco e il pulito. L'igiene del corpo dal Medio Evo ad oggi*, Venice, 1987).

Vigarello, Georges, 1993, *Le Sain et le malsain. Santé et mieux-être depuis le Moyen Âge*, Paris (Ital. trans. *Il sano e il malato. Storia della cura del corpo dal Medioevo a oggi*, Venice, 1996).

Visceglia, Maria Antonietta, 1988, *Il bisogno di eternità. Comportamenti nobiliari a Napoli in Età moderna*, Naples.

Visceglia, Maria Antonietta, 1991, 'I consumi in Italia in Età moderna', in Romano (ed.) 1991, XI, pp. 211–41.

Visceglia, Maria Antonietta (ed.), 1992, *Signori, patrizi, cavalieri nell'Italia centro-meridionale nell'Età moderna*, Rome-Bari.

Vizani, Pompeo, 1609, *Breve Trattato del Governo Famigliare Estratto dalle Institutioni Morali di Monsig. Alessandro Picolomini, Dalla Economica Christiana Del P. Chrisostomo Iavellio, et da altri buoni Autori*, Bologna.

Vocabolario degli Accademici della Crusca, Venice, 1612 1st edn (Vocabolario Crusca 1612); Venice, 1623 2nd edn (Vocabolario Crusca 1623); Florence, 1691 3rd edn, 4 vols; Florence, 1729–38 4th edn, 6 vols; Florence 1893–1923 5th edn, vols. I–XI (N–O) (Vocabolario Crusca 1893–1923).

Walde, Alois and Johann Baptist Hofmann, 1938–63, *Lateinisches etymologisches Wörterbuch*, Heidelberg, 3 vols.

Wall, Richard, 1981, 'Women alone in English society', *Annales de démographie historique*, pp. 303–17.

Wall, Richard, 1983, 'Introduction' to Wall, Robin and Laslett 1983 (Ital. trans. 1984), pp. 31–98.

Wall, Richard, 1997, 'Zum Wandel der Familienstrukturen im Europa der Neuzeit', in Ehmer, Hareven and Wall (eds) 1997, pp. 255–82.

Wall, Richard, Jean Robin and Peter Laslett (eds), 1983, *Family Forms in Historic Europe*, Cambridge (partial Ital. trans. *Forme di famiglia nella storia europea*, Bologna, 1984).

Waro-Desjardins, Françoise, 1993, 'Permanences et mutations de la vie domestique au

XVIIIᵉ siècle: un village du Vexin français', *Revue d'histoire moderne et contemporaine*, 40, pp. 3–29.

Watkin, David, 1986, *A History of Western Architecture*, London (Ital. trans. *Storia dell'architettura occidentale*, Bologna, 1990).

Watt, Jeffrey R., 2001, 'The impact of the Reformation and the Counter-Reformation', in Barbagli and Kertzer (eds) 2001, pp. 125–54.

Weatherill, Lorna, 1986, 'A possession of one's own: women and consumer behaviour in England, 1660–1740', *Journal of British Studies*, 23, pp. 131–6.

Weatherill, Lorna, 1988, *Consumer Behaviour & Material Culture in Britain 1660–1760*, London and New York.

Weatherill, Lorna, 1993, 'The meaning of consumer behaviour in late seventeenth- and early eighteenth-century England', in Brewer and Porter (eds) 1993, pp. 206–27.

Wendt, Reinhardt, 1998, 'Uberseeische Ernährungsprodukte im frühneuzeitlichen Zentraleuropa', in Istituto Internazionale di Storia Economica F. Datini, Prato 1998, pp. 143–74.

Wiesner, Merry E., 1986, 'Spinsters and seamstresses: women in cloth and clothing production', in Ferguson, Quilligan and Vickers (eds) 1986, pp. 191–203.

Wiesner, Merry E., 1987, 'Beyond women and the family: towards a gender analysis of the Reformation', *Sixteenth Century Journal*, XVIII, pp. 311–21.

Wiesner, Merry E., 1989, 'Corpi separati. Le associazioni dei lavoranti nella Germania moderna', *Memoria*, 27, pp. 44–67.

Wiesner, Merry E., 1998, *Gender, Church, and State in Early Modern Germany*, London and New York.

Wijsenbeek-Olthuis, Thera, 1994, 'A matter of taste. Lifestyle in Holland in the seventeenth and eighteenth centuries', in Schuurman and Walsh (eds) 1994, pp. 43–34.

Witthoft, Brucia, 1996, 'Riti nuziali e loro iconografia', in De Giorgio and Klapisch-Zuber (eds) 1996, pp. 119–48.

Woolf, Stuart J., 1988, *The Poor in Western Europe in the Eighteenth and Nineteenth Century*, London and New York (Ital. trans. *Porca miseria. Poveri e assistenza nell'Età moderna*, Rome-Bari, 1988).

Wrigley, Edward Anthony and Roger S. Schofield, 1981, *The Population History of England, 1541–1871. A Reconstruction*, London.

Wunder, Heide, 1992, *«Er ist die Sonn, sie ist der Mond». Frauen in der Frühen Neuzeit*, Munich.

Wyczanski, Andrzej, 1985, *La Consommation alimentaire en Pologne aux 16ᵉ et 17ᵉ siècles*, Paris.

Yun, Bartolomé, 1994, 'Peasant material culture in Castile (1750–1900)', in Schuurman and Walsh (eds) 1994, pp. 123–36.

Yver, Jean, 1966, *Egalité entre héritiers et exclusion des enfants dotés. Essai de géographie coutumière*, Paris.

Zamagni, Vera (ed.), 2000, *Povertà e innovazioni istituzionali in Italia dal medioevo ad oggi*, Bologna.

Zanetti, Dante E., 1972, *La demografia del patriziato milanese*, Pavia (partly republished in Manoukian (ed.) 1983, pp. 233–43).

Zanini, Piero, 1997, *Significati del confine. I limiti naturali, storici, mentali*, Milan.

Zarri, Gabriella, 1986, 'Monateri femminili e città (secoli XV–XVIII)', in *Storia d'Italia*, IX, *La Chiesa e il potere politico dal Medioevo all'età contemporanea*, Giorgio Chittolini and Giovanni Miccoli (eds), Turin, pp. 357–429.

Zarri, Gabriella, 1994, 'Dalla profezia alla disciplina', in Scaraffia and Zarri (eds) 1994, pp. 177–223.

Zarri, Gabriella (ed.), 1996, *Donna, disciplina, creanza cristiana dal XV al XVII secolo. Studi e testi a stampa*, Rome.

Zarri, Gabriella, 1996, 'Il matrimonio tridentino', in *Il Concilio di Trento e il moderno*, Paolo Prodi and Wolfgang Reinhard (eds), Bologna, pp. 437–83.

Zarri, Gabriella, 2000, *Recinti. Donne, clausura e matrimonio nella prima età moderna*, Bologna.

Zeller, Olivier, 1983, *Les Recensements lyonnais de 1597 et 1636. Démographie historique et geographie sociale*, Lyon.

Zemon Davis, Natalie, 1975, *Society and Culture in Early Modern France*, Stanford, CA (Ital. trans. *Le culture del popolo. Sapere, rituali e resistenze nella Francia del Cinquecento*, Turin, 1980).

Zemon Davis, Natalie, 1982, *Le Retour de Martin Guerre*, Paris (Ital. trans. *Il ritorno di Martin Guerre. Un caso di doppia identità nella Francia del Cinquecento*, Turin, 1984).

Zemon Davis, Natalie, 1986, 'Boundaries and the sense of self in sixteenth-century France', in *Reconstructing Individualism. Autonomy, Individuality, and the Self in Western Thought*, Thomas C. Heller, Morton Sosna and David E. Wellbery (eds), Stanford, pp. 53–63.

Zorzi, Alvise, 1990, *La vita quotidiana a Venezia nel secolo di Tiziano*, Milan.

Index